THE WAITE GROUP'S®

OBJECT-ORIENTED PROGRAMMING IN TURBO C++

ROBERT LAFORE

1999

Galgotia Publications pvt. ltd.

5, Ansari Road, Daryaganj New Delhi-110 002

Lafore, Robert (Robert W.)

The Waite Group's object-oriented programming in Turbo C++ / Robert Lafore - 1994

© 1991 by the Waite Group, Inc.

AUTHORIZED EDITION FOR SALE IN INDIA ONLY

Reprinted – 1998
Reprinted – 1999

Printed at Cambridge Printing Works, B-85, Naraina Industrial Area, Phase II, New Delhi-110 0

TABLE OF CONTENTS

Contents

CHAPTER 3: C++ PROGRAMMING BASICS   33

CHAPTER 6: FUNCTIONS   157

CHAPTER 8: ARRAYS   239

CHAPTER 9: OPERATOR OVERLOADING   281

CHAPTER 11: TURBO C++ GRAPHICS 369

CHAPTER 13: VIRTUAL FUNCTIONS AND OTHER SUBTLETIES   467

CHAPTER 17: JUST FOR FUN   629

CONTENTS

CHAPTER 19: THE VISUAL C++

INTRODUCTION

Object-oriented programming (OOP) is the most dramatic innovation in software development in the last decade. It ranks in importance with the development of the first higher-level languages at the dawn of the computer age. Sooner or later every programmer will be affected by the object-oriented approach to program design.

ADVANTAGES OF OOP

Why is everyone so excited about OOP? The chief problem with computer programs is complexity. Large programs are probably the most complicated entities ever created by humans. Because of this complexity, programs are prone to error, and software errors can be expensive and even life-threatening. Object-oriented programming offers a new and powerful way to cope with this complexity. Its goal is clearer, more reliable, more easily maintained programs.

LANGUAGES AND DEVELOPMENT PLATFORMS

Of the object-oriented programming languages, C++ is by far the most popular; and, if you want to learn C++, there are no better tools than Borland's Turbo C++ and its higher-priced cousin, Borland C++. These products provide a complete, easy-to-use development environment. They are also among the best platforms for professional software developers.

WHAT THIS BOOK DOES

This book teaches object-oriented programming with the C++ programming language, using either Turbo C++ or Borland C++. It is suitable for professional programmers, students, and kitchen-table enthusiasts.

New Concepts

OOP involves concepts that are new to programmers of traditional languages such as Pascal, Basic, and C. These ideas, such as data hiding, encapsulation, and polymorphism, lie at the heart of object-oriented programming. But it's easy to lose sight of these concepts when discussing the specifics of an object-oriented language. Many books tend to overwhelm the reader with the details of language features, while ignoring the reason these features exist. This book attempts to keep an eye on the big picture and relate the details to the larger concepts.

The Gradual Approach

We take a gradual approach in this book, starting with very simple programming examples and working up to full-fledged object-oriented applications. We will introduce new concepts slowly so that you will have time to digest one idea before going on to the next. We will use figures whenever possible to help clarify new ideas. Questions and programming exercises at the end of each chapter (with answers in the back of the book) enhance the book's usefulness in the classroom.

WHAT YOU NEED TO KNOW TO USE THIS BOOK

To use this book, you should have some experience with at least one computer language, such as Pascal, BASIC, or FORTRAN. Thus we will assume that you know what variables are, and that you are familiar with basic programming constructions such as loops and decisions.

You do *not* need to know the C language to use this book. Many books on C++ assume that you already know C, but this one does not. It teaches C++ from the ground up. If you *do* know C it, won't hurt, but you may be surprised at how little overlap there is between C and C++.

We assume you have some experience with MS-DOS (the operating system for IBM PCs and compatibles). You should know how to list, copy, and delete files, and how to move around in the directory structure and perform other DOS-related activities.

SOFTWARE AND HARDWARE

Here's the software and hardware you'll need for this book.

First, you should have either Borland's Turbo C++, or Borland C++. These are essentially similar products, but Borland C++ includes additional programs that professional software developers will find useful, such as an assembler, an enhanced debugger, and utilities to help develop Microsoft Windows programs. Either product allows you to develop C++ programs. If you plan to do serious development work in C++, you should know that the debugger in Borland C++ includes special features that support object-oriented programming. However, the less powerful debugger built into the regular Turbo C++ is adequate for smaller OOP projects.

A potentially confusing fact: Both Turbo C++ and Borland C++ can be used to develop programs in the C language as well as in C++. However, we will not be concerned with the C language in this book.

Turbo C++ and Borland C++ run on PC XTs, ATs, PS/2s, and compatibles. Turbo C++ requires MS-DOS 2.0 or higher, while Borland C++ requires MS-DOS 3.0 or higher. They both need at least 640K of memory, a hard disk, and a floppy disk drive. The hard disk should have somewhat more than 6M of free space. Both programs will run in a Microsoft Windows DOS box.

Both Turbo C++ and Borland C++ work with any 80-column monitor, either character-based (which usually means monochrome) or graphics-based (usually color). Most of the examples in this book need only a character display, but Chapter 11 requires a graphics display, as do a few other examples. These graphics examples aren't critical to learning C++, so a character display is adequate for this book.

Both Borland C++ products accommodate a mouse, in fact, a mouse is very convenient for interacting with these systems. However, it is not necessary; you can perform all operations from the keyboard.

Go For It!

You may have heard that C++ is difficult to learn. It's true that it might be a little more challenging than BASIC, but it's really quite similar to other languages, with two or three "grand ideas" thrown in. These new ideas are fascinating in themselves, and we think you'll have fun learning about them. They are also becoming part of the programming culture; they're something you should know a little bit about, like evolution and psychoanalysis. We hope this book will help you enjoy learning about these new ideas, at the same time it teaches you the details of programming in C++.

A NOTE TO TEACHERS

Teachers, and others who already know C, may be interested in some details of the approach we use in this book and how it's organized.

TREAT C++ AS A SEPARATE LANGUAGE

We should emphasize that C and C++ are entirely separate languages. It's true that their syntax is similar; C is actually a subset of C++. But the similarity is largely a historical accident. In fact, the basic approach in a C++ program is radically different from that in a C program.

We think that C++ is the language of the future—that it will become increasingly important in the years ahead and that it may soon surpass C as the most popular language for serious programmers. Thus we don't believe it is necessary or advantageous to teach C before teaching C++. Students who don't know C are saved the time and trouble of learning C and then learning C++; an inefficient approach. Students who already know C may be able to skim parts of some chapters, but they will find that a remarkable percentage of the material is new.

Optimize Organization for OOP

We could have begun the book by teaching the procedural concepts common to C and C++, and moved on to the new OOP concepts once the procedural approach had been digested. That seemed counterproductive, however, since one of our goals is to begin true object-oriented programming as quickly as possible. Accordingly we provide a minimum of procedural groundwork before getting to objects in Chapter 7. Even the initial chapters are heavily steeped in C++, as opposed to C, usage.

We introduce some concepts earlier than is traditional in books on C. For example, structures are a key feature for understanding C++, since classes are syntactically an extension of structures. For this reason, we introduce structures in Chapter 5 so that they will be familiar when we discuss classes.

Some concepts, such as pointers, are introduced later than in traditional C books. It's not necessary to understand pointers to follow the essentials of OOP, and pointers are usually a stumbling block for C and C++ students. Therefore, we defer a discussion of pointers until the main concepts of OOP have been thoroughly digested.

Substitute Superior C++ Features

Some features of C have been superseded by new approaches in C++. For instance, the `printf()` and `scanf()` functions, input/output workhorses in C, are seldom used in C++ because `cout` and `cin` do a better job. Consequently we leave out detailed descriptions of `printf()` and `scanf()`. Similarly, `#define` constants and macros in C have been largely superseded by the `const` qualifier and `inline` functions in C++, and need to be mentioned only briefly.

Minimize Irrelevant Capabilities

Since the focus in this book is on object-oriented programming, we can leave out some features of C that are seldom used and are not particularly relevant to OOP. For instance, it isn't necessary to understand the C bit-wise operators (used to operate on individual bits), to learn object-oriented programming. These and a few other features can be dropped from our discussion, or mentioned only briefly, with no loss in understanding of the major features of C++.

The result is a book that focuses on the fundamentals of OOP, moving the reader gently but briskly toward an understanding of new concepts and their application to real programming problems.

Dear Reader:

Thank you for considering the purchase of *The Waite Group's Object-Oriented Programming in Turbo C++*. Readers have come to know products from The Waite Group for the care and quality we put in them. Let me tell you a little about our group and how we make our books.

It started in 1976 when I could not find a computer book that really taught me anything. The books that were available talked down to people, lacked illustrations and examples, were poorly laid out, and were written as if you already understood all the terminology. So I set out to write a good book about microcomputers. This was to be a special book—very graphic, with a friendly and casual style, and filled with examples. The result was an instant best-seller.

Over the years, I developed this approach into a "formula" (nothing really secret here, just a lot of hard work—I am a crazy man about technical accuracy and high-quality illustrations). I began to find writers who wanted to write books in this way. This led to co-authoring and then to multiple-author books and many more titles (over seventy titles currently on the market). As The Waite Group author base grew, I trained a group of editors to manage our products. We now have a team devoted to putting together the best possible book package and maintaining the high standard of our existing books.

THE
WAITE
GROUP

We are most proud of this particular book, *Object-Oriented Programming in Turbo C++*. The author, Robert Lafore, also wrote *Turbo C Programming for the PC*, and *C Programming Using Turbo C++*, both known as clear, accessible C tutorials using Borland's low-end compilers. This new title on C++ specifically focuses on object-oriented programming and takes the approach that C++ is a stand-alone language, and therefore you don't have to know C to use this book. The examples and methodology also work on Borland's new high-end Borland C++. Lafore is one of the Waite Group's most popular authors; many of you have requested this particular title and we think you'll agree it was worth the wait.

We hope you enjoy this and all the other books upcoming from Waite Group Press. If you wish to be on our mailing list, or if you have any comments to tell us after you have purchased and read the book, please fill out and send in detachable postpaid card.

Mitchell Waite

Mitchell Waite
President

100 Shoreline Highway   Suite A-285   Mill Valley   California   94941   415-331-0575   Fax 415-331-1075

This book is dedicated to GGL and her indomitable spirit.

ACKNOWLEDGMENTS

My primary thanks go to Mitch Waite, who poured over every inch of the manuscript with painstaking attention to detail and made a semi-infinite number of helpful suggestions. Bill McCarty of Azusa Pacific University reviewed the content of the manuscript and its suitability for classroom use, suggested many excellent improvements, and attempted to correct my dyslexic spelling. George Leach ran all the programs, and, to our horror, found several that didn't perform correctly in certain circumstances. I trust these problems have all been fixed; if not, the fault is entirely mine. Scott Calamar of The Waite Group dealt with the myriad organizational aspects of writing and producing this book; his competence and unfailing good humor were an important ingredient in its completion. I would also like to thank Nan Borreson of Borland for supplying the latest releases of the software (among other useful tidbits), Harry Henderson for reviewing the exercises, Louise Orlando of The Waite Group for ably shepherding the book through production, Merrill Peterson of Matrix Productions for coordinating the most trouble-free production run I've ever been involved with, Juan Vargas for the innovative design, and Frances Hasegawa for her uncanny ability to decipher my sketches and produce beautiful and effective art.

ABOUT THE AUTHOR

Robert Lafore has been writing books about computer programming since 1982. His best-selling titles include *Assembly Language Programming for the IBM PC and XT*, *C Programming Using Turbo C++*, and *Microsoft C Programming for the PC*. Mr. Lafore holds degrees in mathematics and electrical engineering, and has been active in programming since the days of the PDP-5, when 4K of main memory was considered luxurious. His interests include hiking, windsurfing, and recreational mathematics.

THE BIG PICTURE

This book teaches you how to program in C++, a computer language that supports *object-oriented programming* (OOP). Why do we need OOP? What does it do that traditional languages like C, Pascal, and BASIC, don't? What are the principles behind OOP? Two key concepts in OOP are *objects* and *classes*. What do these terms mean? What is the relationship between C++ and the older C language?

This chapter explores these questions and provides an overview of the features to be dicussed in the balance of the book. What we say here will necessarily be rather general (although mercifully brief). If you find the discussion somewhat abstract, don't worry. The concepts we mention here will come into focus as we demonstrate them in detail in subsequent chapters.

WHY DO WE NEED OBJECT-ORIENTED PROGRAMMING?

Object-oriented programming was developed because limitations were discovered in earlier approaches to programming. To appreciate what OOP does, we need to understand what these limitations are and how they arose from traditional programming languages.

PROCEDURAL LANGUAGES

Pascal, C, BASIC, Fortran, and similar languages are *procedural* languages. That is, each statement in the language tells the computer to *do* something: Get some input, add these numbers, divide by 6, display that output. A program in a procedural language is a *list of instructions*.

For very small programs no other organizing principle (often called a *paradigm*) is needed. The programmer creates the list of instructions, and the computer carries them out.

Division into Functions

When programs become larger, a single list of instructions becomes unwieldy. Few programmers can comprehend a program of more than a few hundred statements unless it is broken down into smaller units. For this reason the *function* was adopted as a way to make programs more comprehensible to their human creators. (The term *function* is used in C++ and C. In other languages the same concept may be referred to as a *subroutine*, a *subprogram*, or a *procedure*.) A program is divided into functions, and (ideally, at least) each function has a clearly defined purpose and a clearly defined interface to the other functions in the program.

The idea of breaking a program into functions can be further extended by grouping a number of functions together into a larger entity called a *module*, but the principle is similar: a grouping of components that carry out specific tasks.

Dividing a program into functions and modules is one of the cornerstones of *structured programming*, the somewhat loosely defined discipline that has influenced programming organization for more than a decade.

Problems with Structured Programming

As programs grow ever larger and more complex, even the structured programming approach begins to show signs of strain. You may have heard about, or been involved in, horror stories of program development. The project is too complex, the schedule slips, more programmers are added, complexity increases, costs skyrocket, the schedule slips further, and disaster ensues. (See *The Mythical Man-Month*, by Frederick P. Brooks, Jr., Addison-Wesley, 1982, for a vivid description of this process.)

Analyzing the reasons for these failures reveals that there are weaknesses in the procedural paradigm itself. No matter how well the structured programming approach is implemented, large programs become excessively complex.

What are the reasons for this failure of procedural languages? One of the most crucial is the role played by data.

Data Undervalued

In a procedural language, the emphasis is on *doing* things—*read the keyboard*, *invert the vector*, *check for errors*, and so on. The subdivision of a program into functions continues this emphasis. Functions *do* things just as single program statements do. What they do may be more complex or abstract, but the emphasis is still on the action.

What happens to the data in this paradigm? Data is, after all, the reason for a program's existence. The important part of an inventory program isn't a function that displays the data, or a function that checks for correct input; it's the inventory data itself. Yet data is given second-class status in the organization of procedural languages.

For example, in an inventory program, the data that makes up the inventory is probably read from a disk file into memory, where it is treated as a global variable. By *global* we mean that the variables that constitute the data are declared outside of

4

any function, so they are accessible to all functions. These functions perform various operations on the data. They read it, analyze it, update it, rearrange it, display it, write it back to the disk, and so on.

We should note that most languages, such as Pascal and C, also support local variables, which are hidden within a single function. But local variables are not useful for important data that must be accessed by many different functions. Figure 1-1 shows the relationship between global and local variables.

Now suppose a new programmer is hired to write a function to analyze this inventory data in a certain way. Unfamiliar with the subtleties of the program, the programmer creates a function that accidentally corrupts the data. This is easy to do, because every function has complete access to the data. It's like leaving your personal papers in the lobby of your apartment building: Anyone can change or destroy them. In the same way, global data can be corrupted by functions that have no business changing it.

Another problem is that, since many functions access the same data, the way the data is stored becomes critical. The arrangement of the data can't be changed without modifying all the functions that access it. If you add new data items, for example, you'll need to modify all the functions that access the data so that they can also access these new items. It will be hard to find all such functions, and even harder to modify all of them correctly. It's similar to what happens when your local supermarket moves the bread from aisle 4 to aisle 12. Everyone who patronizes the supermarket must figure out where the bread has gone, and adjust their shopping habits accordingly. The relationship of functions and data in procedural programs is shown in Figure 1-2.

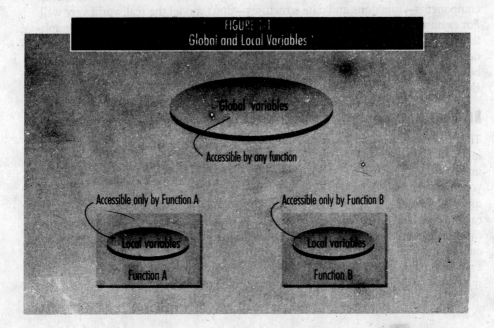

FIGURE 1-1
Global and Local Variables

Global Variables

Accessible by any function

Accessible only by Function A

Accessible only by Function B

Local variables

Local variables

Function A

Function B

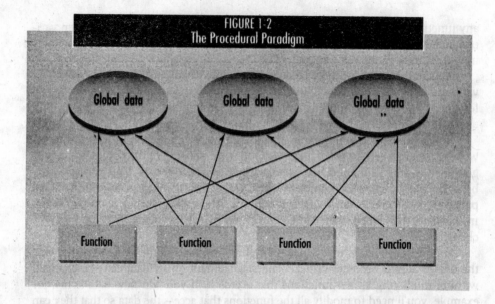

FIGURE 1-2
The Procedural Paradigm

What is needed is a way to restrict access to the data, to *hide* it from all but a few critical functions. This will protect the data, simplify maintenance, and offer other benefits as well (as we'll see).

Relationship to the Real World

Procedural programs are often difficult to design. The problem is that their chief components—functions and data structures—don't model the real world very well. For example, suppose you are writing a program to create the elements of a graphics user interface: menus, windows, and so on. Quick now, what functions will you need? What data structures? The answers are not obvious, to say the least. It would be better if windows and menus corresponded more closely to actual program elements.

New Data Types

There are other problems with traditional languages. One is the difficulty of creating new data types. Computer languages typically have several built-in data types: integers, floating-point numbers, characters, and so on. What if you want to invent your own data type? Perhaps you want to work with complex numbers, or two-dimensional coordinates, or dates—quantities the built-in data types don't handle easily. Being able to create your own types is called *extensibility*; you can extend the capabilities of the language. Traditional languages are not usually extensible. Without unnatural convolutions, you can't bundle together both X and Y coordinates into a single variable called *Point*, and then add and subtract values of this type. The result is that traditional programs are more complex to write and maintain.

THE OBJECT-ORIENTED APPROACH

The fundamental idea behind object-oriented languages is to combine into a single unit both *data* and *the functions that operate on that data*. Such a unit is called an *object*.

An object's functions, called *member functions* in C++, typically provide the only way to access its data. If you want to read a data item in an object, you call a member function in the object. It will read the item and return the value to you. You can't access the data directly. The data is *hidden*, so it is safe from accidental alteration. Data and its functions are said to be *encapsulated* into a single entity. *Data encapsulation* and *data hiding* are key terms in the description of object-oriented languages.

If you want to modify the data in an object, you know exactly what functions interact with it: the member functions in the object. No other functions can access the data. This simplifies writing, debugging, and maintaining the program.

A C++ program typically consists of a number of objects, which communicate with each other by calling one another's member functions. The organization of a C++ program is shown in Figure 1-3.

We should mention that what are called *member functions* in C++ are called *methods* in some other object-oriented (OO) languages (such as Smalltalk, one of the first OO languages). Also, data items are referred to as *instance variables*. Calling an object's member function is referred to as *sending a message* to the object. These terms are not usually used in C++.

An Analogy

You might want to think of objects as departments—such as sales, accounting, personnel, and so on—in a company. Departments provide an important approach to corporate organization. In most companies (except very small ones), people don't work on personnel problems one day, the payroll the next, and then go out in the field as salespeople the week after. Each department has its own personnel, with clearly assigned duties. It also has its own data: payroll, sales figures, personnel records, inventory, or whatever, depending on the department.

The people in each department control and operate on that department's data. Dividing the company into departments makes it easier to comprehend and control the company's activities, and helps maintain the integrity of the information used by the company. The payroll department, for instance, is responsible for the payroll data. If you are from the sales department, and you need to know the total of all the salaries paid in the southern region in July, you don't just walk into the payroll department and start rummaging through file cabinets. You send a memo to the appropriate person in the department, and then you wait for that person to access the data and send you a reply with the information you want. This ensures that the data is accessed accurately and that it is not corrupted by inept outsiders. (This view of

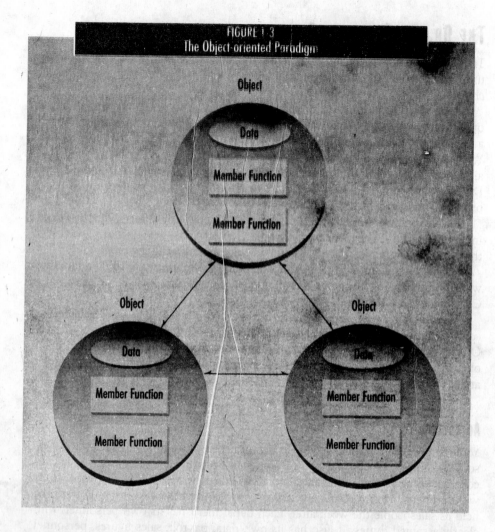

FIGURE 1-3
The Object-oriented Paradigm

corporate organization is shown in Figure 1-4.) In the same way, objects provide an approach to program organization, while helping to maintain the integrity of the program's data.

OOP: An Approach to Organization

Keep in mind that object-oriented programming is not primarily concerned with the details of program operation. Instead, it deals with the overall organization of the program. Most individual program statements in C++ are similar to statements in procedural languages, and many are identical to statements in C. Indeed, an entire member function in a C++ program may be very similar to a procedural function in C. It is only when you look at the larger context that you can determine whether a statement or a function is part of a procedural C program or an object-oriented C++ program.

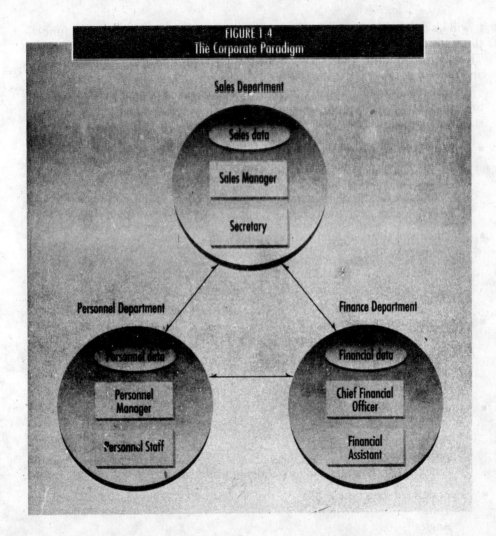

FIGURE 1.4
The Corporate Paradigm

CHARACTERISTICS OF OBJECT-ORIENTED LANGUAGES

Let's briefly examine a few of the major elements of object-oriented languages in general and C++ in particular.

OBJECTS

When you approach a programming problem in an object-oriented language, you no longer ask how the problem will be divided into functions, but how it will be divided into objects. Thinking in terms of objects, rather than functions, has a surprisingly helpful effect on how easily programs can be designed. This results from the close match between objects in the programming sense and objects in the real world.

What kinds of things become objects in object-oriented programs? The answer to this is limited only by your imagination, but here are some typical categories to start you thinking:

- **Physical objects**
  Automobiles in a traffic-flow simulation
  Electrical components in a circuit-design program
  Countries in an economics model
  Aircraft in an air-traffic-control system

- **Elements of the computer-user environment**
  Windows
  Menus
  Graphics objects (lines, rectangles, circles)
  The mouse and the keyboard

- **Programming Constructs**
  Customized arrays
  Stacks
  Linked lists
  Binary trees

- **Collections of data**
  An inventory
  A personnel file
  A dictionary
  A table of the latitudes and longitudes of world cities

- **User-defined data types**
  Time
  Angles
  Complex numbers
  Points on the plane

- **Components in computer games**
  Ghosts in a maze game
  Positions in a board game (chess, checkers)
  Animals in an ecological simulation
  Opponents and friends in adventure games

The match between programming objects and real-world objects is the happy result of combining data and functions: The resulting objects offer a revolution in program design. No such close match between programming constructs and the items being modeled exists in a procedural language.

CLASSES

In OOP we say that objects are *members of classes*. What does this mean? Let's look at an analogy. Almost all computer languages have built-in data types. For instance, a data type int, meaning *integer*, is predefined in C++ (as we'll see in Chapter 3). You can declare as many variables of type int as you need in your program:

```
int day;
int count;
int divisor;
int answer;
```

In a similar way, you can define many objects of the same *class*, as shown in Figure 1-5. A class serves as a plan, or template. It specifies what data and what

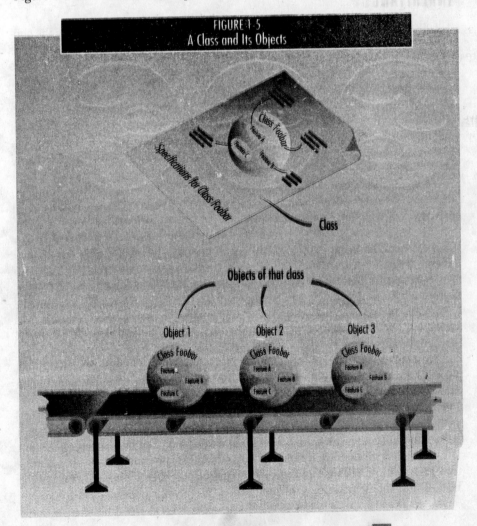

FIGURE 1-5
A Class and Its Objects

functions will be included in objects of that class. Defining the class doesn't create any objects, just as the mere existence of a type int doesn't create any variables.

A class is thus a collection of similar objects. This fits our nontechnical understanding of the word *class*. Prince, Sting, and Madonna are members of the class of rock musicians. There is no one person called "rock musician," but specific people with specific names are members of this class if they possess certain characteristics.

INHERITANCE

The idea of classes leads to the idea of *inheritance*. In our daily lives, we use the concept of classes being divided into subclasses. We know that the class of animals is divided into mammals, amphibians, insects, birds, and so on. The class of vehicles is divided into cars, trucks, buses, and motorcycles.

The principle in this sort of division is that each subclass shares common characteristics with the class from which it's derived. Cars, trucks, buses, and motorcycles all have wheels and a motor; these are the defining characteristics of vehicles. In addition to the characteristics shared with other members of the class, each subclass also has its own particular characteristics: buses, for instance, have seats for many people, while trucks have space for hauling heavy loads.

This idea is shown in Figure 1-6. Notice in the figure that features A and B, which are part of the base class, are common to all the derived classes, but that each derived class also has features of its own.

In a similar way, an OOP class can be divided into subclasses. In C++ the original class is called the *base class*; other classes can be defined that share its characteristics, but add their own as well. These are called *derived classes*.

Don't confuse the relation of objects to classes, on the one hand, with the relation of a base class to derived classes, on the other. Objects, which exist in the computer's memory, embody the exact characteristics of their class, which serves as a template. Derived classes inherit some characteristics from their base class, but add new ones of their own.

Inheritance is somewhat analogous to using functions to simplify a traditional procedural program. If we find that three different sections of a procedural program do almost exactly the same thing, we recognize an opportunity to extract the common elements of these three sections and put them into a single function. The three sections of the program can call the function to execute the common actions, and they can perform their own individual processing as well. Similarly, a base class contains elements common to a group of derived classes. As functions do in a procedural program, inheritance shortens an object-oriented program and clarifies the relationship among program elements.

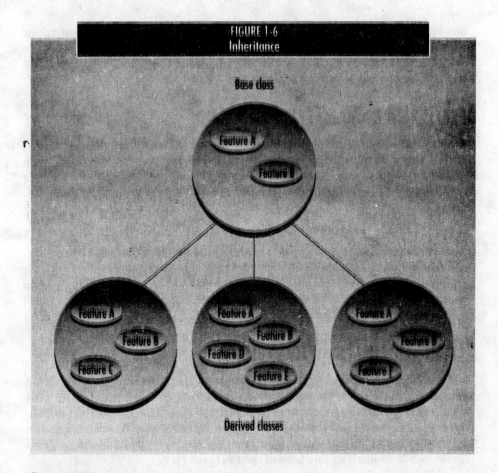

FIGURE 1-6
Inheritance

Base class

Feature A

Feature B

Feature A
Feature B
Feature C

Feature A
Feature D
Feature E

Feature A
Feature B
Feature F

Derived classes

REUSABILITY

Once a class has been written, created, and debugged, it can be distributed to other programmers for use in their own programs. This is called *reusability*. It is similar to the way a library of functions in a procedural language can be incorporated into different programs.

However, in OOP, the concept of inheritance provides an important extension to the idea of reusability. A programmer can take an existing class, and, without modifying it, add additional features and capabilities to it. This is done by deriving a new class from the existing one. The new class will inherit the capabilities of the old one, but is free to add new features of its own.

For example, you might have written (or purchased from someone else) a class that creates a menu system, such as that used in the Turbo C++ Integrated Development System (IDE). This class works fine, and you don't want to change it, but you want to add the capability to make some menu entries flash on and off. To do this, you simply create a new class that inherits all the capabilities of the existing one but adds flashing menu entries.

The ease with which existing software can be reused is a major benefit of OOP. We'll have more to say about this in Chapters 10 and 15.

CREATING NEW DATA TYPES

One of the benefits of objects is that they give the programmer a convenient way to construct new data types. Suppose you work with two-dimensional positions (such as X and Y coordinates, or latitude and longitude) in your program. You would like to express operations on these positional values with normal arithmetic operations, such as

```
position1 = position2 + origin;
```

where the variables position1, position2 and origin each represent a *pair* of independent numerical quantities. By creating a class that incorporates these two values, and declaring position1, position2 and origin to be objects of this class, we can, in effect, create a new data type. Many features of C++ are intended to facilitate the creation of new data types in this manner.

POLYMORPHISM AND OVERLOADING

Note that the = (equal) and + (plus) operators, used in the position arithmetic shown above, don't act the same way they do in operations on built-in types like int. The objects position1 and so on are not predefined in C++, but are programmer-defined objects of class Position. How do the = and + operators know how to operate on objects? The answer is that we can define new operations for these operators. These operators will be member functions of the Position class.

Using operators or functions in different ways, depending on what they are operating on, is called *polymorphism* (one thing with several distinct forms). When an existing operator, such as + or =, is given the capability to operate on a new data type, it is said to be *overloaded*. Overloading is a kind of polymorphism; it is also an important feature of OOP.

C++ AND C

C++ is derived from the C language. Strictly speaking, it is a superset of C: Almost every correct statement in C is also a correct statement in C++, although the reverse is not true. The most important elements added to C to create C++ are concerned with classes, objects, and object-oriented programming. (C++ was originally called "C with classes"). However, C++ has many other new features as well, including an improved approach to I/O and a new way to write comments. Figure 1-7 shows the relationship of C and C++.

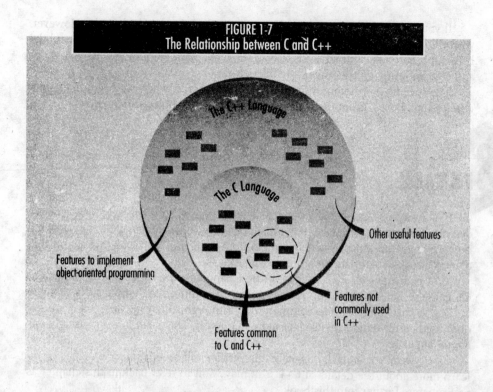

FIGURE 1-7
The Relationship between C and C++

The C++ Language

The C Language

Other useful features

Features to implement
object-oriented programming

Features not
commonly used
in C++

Features common
to C and C++

In fact, the practical differences between C and C++ are larger than you might think. Although you *can* write a program in C++ that looks like a program in C, hardly anyone does. C++ programmers not only make use of the new features of C++; they also emphasize the traditional C features in different proportions than do C programmers.

If you already know C, you will have a head start in learning C++ (although you may also have some bad habits to unlearn), but much of the material will be new.

LAYING THE GROUNDWORK

Our goal is to help you begin writing OOP programs as soon as possible. However, as we noted, much of C++ is inherited from C, so while the overall structure of a C++ program may be OOP, down in the trenches you need to know some old-fashioned procedural fundamentals. Chapters 3 through 6 of this book therefore deal with the "traditional" aspects of C++, many of which are also found in C. You will learn about variables and I/O, about control structures like loops and decisions, and about functions themselves. You will also learn about structures in general, since the same syntax that's used for structures is used for classes.

If you already know C, you might be tempted to skip these chapters. However, you will find that there are many differences, some obvious and some rather subtle, between C and C++. Our advice is to read these chapters, skimming what you know, and concentrating on the ways C++ differs from C.

The specific discussion of OOP starts in Chapter 7, when we begin to explore objects and classes. From then on the examples will be object-oriented.

SUMMARY

OOP is a way of organizing programs. The emphasis is on the way programs are designed, not on the details of individual operators. In particular, OOP programs are organized around objects, which contain both data and functions that act on that data. A class is a template for a number of objects.

C++ is a superset of C. It adds to the C language the capability to implement OOP. It also adds a variety of other features. In addition, the emphasis is changed in C++, so that some features common to C, although still available in C++, are seldom used, while others are used far more frequently. The result is a surprisingly different language.

The general concepts discussed in this chapter will become more concrete as you learn more about the details of C++. You may want to refer back to this chapter as you progress further into this book.

QUESTIONS

1. Pascal, BASIC, and C are p_____ languages, while C++ is an o_____ language.
2. A widget is to the blueprint for a widget as an object is to
   a. a member function
   b. a class
   c. an operator
   d. a data item
3. The two major components of an object are _____ and functions that _____.
4. In C++, a function contained within a class is called
   a. a member function
   b. an operator
   c. a class function
   d. a method

5. Protecting data from access by unauthorized functions is called
_____.

6. Which of the following are good reasons to use an object-oriented language?
   a. You can define your own data types.
   b. Program statements are simpler than in procedural languages.
   c. An OO program can be taught to correct its own errors.
   d. It's easier to conceptualize an OO program.

7. _____ model entities in the real world more closely than do functions.

8. True or false: A C++ program is similar to a C program except for the details of coding.

9. Bundling data and functions together is called _____.

10. When a language has the capability to produce new data types, it is said to be
    a. reprehensible
    b. encapsulated
    c. overloaded
    d. extensible

11. True or false: You can easily tell, from any two lines of code, whether a program is written in C or C++.

12. The ability of a function or operator to act in different ways on different data types is called _____.

13. A normal C++ operator that acts in special ways on newly defined data types is said to be
    a. glorified
    b. encapsulated
    c. classified
    d. overloaded

14. Memorizing the new terms used in C++ is
    a. critically important
    b. something you can return to later
    c. the key to wealth and success
    d. completely irrelevent

   c. An OO program can be lengthy when compared to its equivalent...

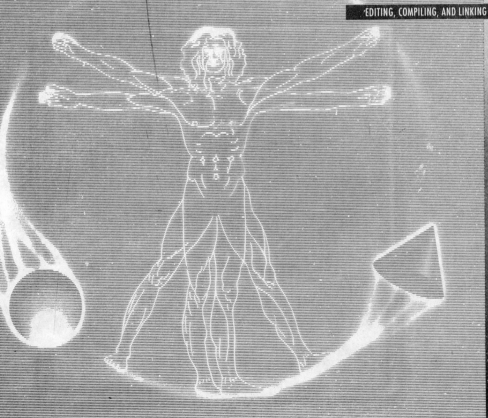

CHAPTER **2**

USING TURBO C++

SETTING UP TURBO C++ AND BORLAND C++

YOUR FIRST C++ PROGRAM

USING THE INTEGRATED DEVELOPMENT ENVIRONMENT

EDITING, COMPILING, AND LINKING

Turbo C++ and Borland C++ provide almost ideal platforms for learning C++. Their Integrated Development Environment (IDE) puts all the tools you need for C++ program development into a single, convenient screen display. In this chapter we describe how to use the IDE to develop C++ programs. As an example of this process you will develop your first short C++ program.

In general Turbo C++ and Borland C++ operate the same way. However, there are a few differences. In this chapter we will refer to Turbo C++, but—unless we indicate otherwise—what we say about Turbo C++ also applies to Borland C++.

SETTING UP TURBO C++

Turbo C++ provides a highly automated installation procedure. In general, you need only follow the prompts and answer the questions. However, you can help to optimize your system by answering a few of the questions in specific ways.

MEMORY MODELS

The installation program will ask you what memory models you want to use. If you don't know about memory models, this question may seem obscure.

C++ uses library routines to perform such tasks as I/O, graphics, and math operations. You'll need many of these routines for the examples in this book. Unfortunately, each routine comes in five different versions. Why is this? The segmented architecture of the 80x86 microprocessor is the culprit. A program consists of code (executable statements) and data. Code or data that fits within a segment, which can be up to 64K bytes long, executes quickly. When code or data exceeds the 64K limit, it must be accessed in a less efficient way, and the program executes more slowly. Depending on the size of the code and data in the program, the developer must select a memory model large enough to accommodate the program, but not unnecessarily large, lest execution speed be reduced.

Table 2-1 summarizes the memory models and the number of 64K segments available with each one.

TABLE 2-1 Memory Available with Different Memory Models			
Memory model	Code segments	Data segments	Segments for one data item
Tiny	(one for both code and data)		one
Small	one	one	one
Medium	many	one	one
Compact	one	many	one
Large	many	many	one
Huge	many	many	many

The Tiny model must squeeze both code and data into a single 64K segment. The Small, Medium, Compact, and Large models offer different combinations of segments. The Huge memory model is similar to the Large model, but allows a single data item (such as an array) to occupy several segments.

A set of library routines is available for each memory model (except for Tiny, which uses the same routines as the Small model). Which library routines you use depends on what memory model you decide to use for your program. For example, if your program requires more data than will fit in one 64K segment, but the code is less than a segment, you'll need to use the Compact memory model, so you'll need the library routines for this model.

When you install Turbo C++, you can specify which memory models you plan to use, and the installation program will create library files containing the appropriate routines. If you don't specify particular memory models, the routines for all the models will be installed on your hard disk. Since the files containing these routines take up considerable disk space, you may not want to choose the default.

All the example programs in this book, and probably all the programs you will write in the course of learning C++, can be compiled with the Small memory model. So unless you know you're going to need some other model, you should specify that only the Small memory model be used. The screen display in the installation procedure will show you how to do this. You won't need the other models until your programs grow many times larger than those we show here.

THE DEMONSTRATION TOUR

During the installation process in Turbo C++ (but not in Borland C++), you are also asked to choose whether you want to install the demonstration tour. This tour, which shows how to use the IDE, is important if this environment is new to you. If you've had experience with other Turbo products, such as Turbo Pascal, you may not need the tour.

BORLAND PROGRAM EXAMPLES

The examples provided with Turbo C++ include a number of C++ programs. Many of these are linked to a tutorial in the Turbo C++ documentation. You can profit from studying these examples, especially after you have absorbed some of the material in this book, so answer the question affirmatively about installing the examples.

BORLAND C++ OPTIONS

Borland C++ (unlike Turbo C++) has various additional programs: TD, a debugger; TASM, the Turbo assembler; and TPROF, a profiler. You don't need these optional programs to use this book, so, unless you have other reasons for using them, you can tell the installation program not to include them. You also don't need the examples that accompany these programs.

Borland C++ also includes a second compiler. This compiler does not use the IDE, but is operated by typing commands at the DOS prompt. This compiler is called *CMD*. It is useful in specialized situations, but since no such situations arise in this book, you can instruct the installation program not to include this program.

Once you have answered the preliminary questions, the installation process is almost completely automatic. All you need to do is put the requested disks in the drive when asked.

TAKE THE TOUR

When the installation process is complete (and if you're using Turbo C++, not Borland C++), you may want to take the guided tour that explains how to use the IDE. You should take the tour unless you're already familiar with the IDE on other Borland products. Go to the TOUR subdirectory in the TC directory, and enter **TCTOUR**. The program explains the essentials of the IDE's operation.

We'll assume that you've taken the tour or that you already know how to use the components of the IDE. You should be able to select menu items; close, move, and resize windows; and, in dialog boxes, enter text into fields and select items. All these operations can be carried out either with or without the mouse.

YOUR FIRST PROGRAM

In this section we'll show how to develop a C++ program, using the Turbo C++ Integrated Development Environment.

Invoking Turbo C++

To start Turbo C++, move to the directory in which you plan to do your C++ program development. It's best if you don't develop programs in the TC directory. You should create a separate directory for C++ development. From this directory, enter TC at the DOS prompt (or BC if you're using Borland C++):

```
C>tc
```

The IDE screen will appear. It will be mostly blank, with only the menu bar on top and the status line on the bottom.

Naming your Program

Select *New* from the File menu. An Edit window will appear, with the filename NONAME00.C. You need to change this name. You can use the *Save as. . .* selection from the File menu to do this. However, this selection does not show up initially on the File menu. Not all menu options are available when you first start up Turbo C++. To make all of them available, select *Full menus* from the Options menu.

Now you can select *Save as. . .* from the File menu. In the text field in the resulting dialog box, enter the name of your first program, FIRST.CPP (you can use upper- or lowercase letters). The new name will appear at the top of the Edit window.

Notice that you have changed not only the filename from NONAME00 to FIRST but the extension from .C to .CPP. Turbo C++ initially assumes that you want to write a program in C. To tell it otherwise, you must use the extension .CPP (C Plus Plus). This extension is the only way that Turbo C++ knows whether to use the C or the C++ compiler.

Using the Editor

The cursor should now be positioned in the upper-left corner of the Edit window. You can start typing your program. Here it is:

```
#include <iostream.h>

void main()
{
cout << "Every age has a language of its own";
}
```

We won't worry at this point about the details of the program. Instead, we'll concentrate on the steps needed to turn it into an executable file. However, you should make sure the program is typed in correctly. Note especially the use of lowercase letters for `main` and `cout`, the paired braces `{` and `}`, and the semicolon at the end of this line. Spell `void`, `main`, and `cout` correctly. Don't forget the quotation marks around the phrase "Every age has a language of its own" (a quote from the nineteenth-century English travel-writer Augustus Hare). When you have typed in your source file, the screen should be similar to that shown in Figure 2-1.

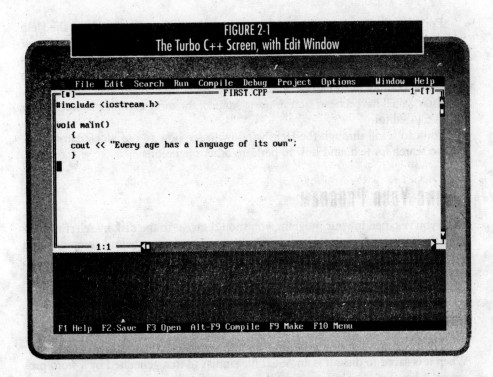

FIGURE 2-1
The Turbo C++ Screen, with Edit Window

You will find that operating the editor built into the IDE is quite intuitive. What you type will appear on the screen, and you can use the arrow keys to move the cursor. Pressing the (ENTER) key inserts a new line and drops the cursor to the start of the line. The (BACKSPACE) key deletes the character to the left of the cursor.

Here is a list of some of the more important cursor commands:

Keyboard key	Action
(↑)	Cursor up one line
(↓)	Cursor down one line
(←)	Cursor left one character
(→)	Cursor right one character
(CTRL)-(←)	Cursor left one word
(CTRL)-(→)	Cursor right one word
(HOME)	Cursor to start of line
(END)	Cursor to end of line
(PGUP)	Scroll one screen up
(PGDN)	Scroll one screen down
(ENTER)	Insert line, go to next line
(BACKSPACE)	Delete character to left of cursor
(DEL)	Delete character under cursor
(INS)	Toggle insert/write-over

For a handy list of information about the editor, select *Contents* from the Help menu (in Borland C++ follow this with *Editor Commands*), and then select *Cursor movement* in the resulting window. You will see a list of cursor commands. Most commands can be issued by using the old WordStar control commands, which are formed by holding the (CTRL) key and pressing one or more other keys. If you know Wordstar, you'll have a head start in using some of the more complex features of the Turbo C++ editor.

You can scroll through the Help window to see how to use block commands, how to search for text, and how to perform other operations.

SAVING YOUR PROGRAM

Once you've typed in your program, you should save it to the disk by selecting *Save* from the File menu, or by pressing (F2). It's good to do this before compiling and running your program, so that if a bug crashes the system you won't lose the changes to your source file.

COMPILING AND LINKING

The program that you type into the Edit window constitutes the *source file*. When it is saved to disk, it is an ASCII file similar to that generated by a word processor. It has the .CPP file extension. If you're not familiar with compiled languages, the process of transforming a source file into an executable program may seem rather mysterious.

Remember that a source file is not an executable program; it is only the instructions on how to create a program. Transforming your source file into an executable program requires two steps.

First, you must *compile* the source file into an object file. The object file, which has an .OBJ extension, contains machine-language instructions that can be executed by the computer. However, these instructions are not complete. A second step, called *linking*, is required.

The linking step is necessary because an executable program almost always consists of more than one object file. Linking combines the object files into a single executable program.

Why does a program consist of more than one object file? There are two major reasons. First, the programmer may have divided the program into several source files. Each of these source files is then compiled into a separate object file, and these object files must be linked together. We'll have more to say about multiple-file programs in Chapter 15. For now, our programs will consist of a single source file. Second, the library routines we mentioned earlier come in object-file form and must be combined with the user-written program.

Thus turning your source file into an executable file is a two-step process. First you compile your source file into an object file, and then you link it with the necessary library routines. Figure 2-2 shows the relationship between compiling and linking. Let's see how to use the IDE to compile and link your program.

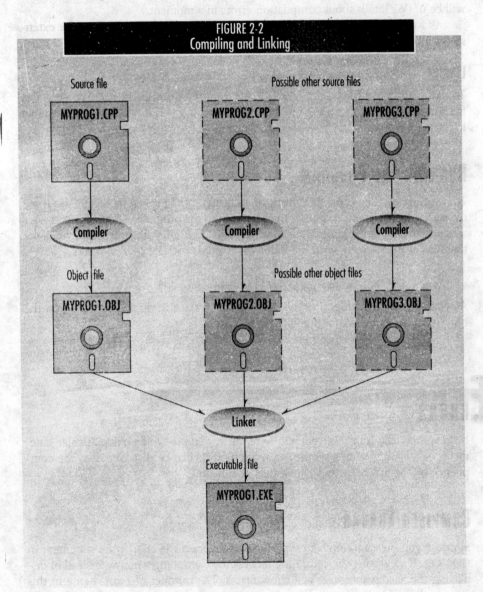

FIGURE 2-2
Compiling and Linking

Source file

Possible other source files

MYPROG1.CPP

MYPROG2.CPP

MYPROG3.CPP

Compiler

Compiler

Compiler

Object file

Possible other object files

MYPROG1.OBJ

MYPROG2.OBJ

MYPROG3.OBJ

Linker

Executable file

MYPROG1.EXE

Compiling

To compile the source file, select *Compile to OBJ* from the File menu. A window called *Compiling* will appear. An entry called *Lines compiled* will change as compiling progresses. When the process is finished, the window (if you're a careful typist) will display `Success: Press any key`. The entries for `Warnings` and `Errors` will be `0`. (We'll talk about compilation errors in a moment.)

As we noted, compilation creates an object file, which has the .OBJ file extension. The object file in our case is FIRST.OBJ.

Linking

To link your object file, select *Link EXE file* from the Compile menu. The FIRST.OBJ file will be combined with the one or more library files. The result is an executable file named FIRST.EXE.

RUNNING THE PROGRAM

To run the .EXE file, select *Run* from the Run menu (or press (CTRL)-(F9)). You'll see the screen flicker briefly. Where is the output from the program? To see it, select *User screen* from the Window menu, or type (ALT)-(F5). The IDE will vanish, and you'll see the normal DOS screen, with the following display:

```
C>tc
Every age has a language of its own
```

As you can see, the program has displayed the phrase in quotation marks on the output screen. To return to the IDE, press any key.

ERRORS

No one is perfect. It may be that you were unclear on the syntax of a particular statement, or that you made a typing error. Such errors can be discovered by the compiler or by the linker, or they can appear at run-time.

COMPILER ERRORS

Suppose you have forgotten to type the semicolon at the end of the statement in FIRST.CPP. If so, during the compiling process the Compiling window, instead of displaying the *Success* message, will show *Errors*. The number of errors—one in this case—will be listed.

Press any key, or click anywhere with the mouse. A Message window will appear at the bottom of the screen. It will contain the following line:

```
Error C:\FIRST.CPP 6: Statement missing ; in function main()
```

In the Edit window, the line with the closing brace is highlighted, and the brace itself is highlighted in a different color. This indicates the place where the compiler found the error. When it got to the brace, it realized that there should have been a semicolon earlier, so it signaled the error at that point. The screen will now resemble the one in Figure 2-3.

Press **F6** to move from the Message window to the Edit window. Correct the error. Your next compilation should complete correctly.

LINKER ERRORS

Errors can also appear during the linking process. For instance, suppose you spell the word `main` as `maid`. The program will compile correctly, but when you link it, the Linking window will display *Errors* instead of *Success*. Pressing a key will cause the Message window to display this message:

```
Linker Error: Undefined symbol _main in module CO.ASM
```

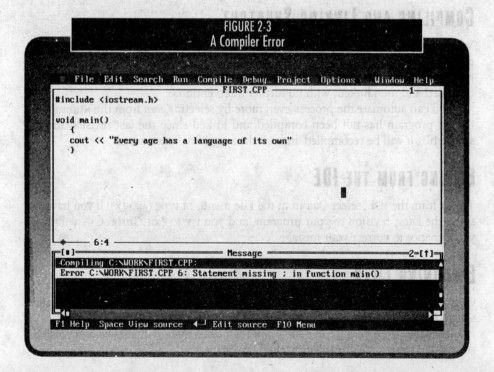

FIGURE 2-3
A Compiler Error

```
≡  File  Edit  Search  Run  Compile  Debug  Project  Options    Window  Help
┌──────────────────────────── FIRST.CPP ─────────────────────────1─┐
#include <iostream.h>

void main()
  {
  cout << "Every age has a language of its own"
  }



*── 6:4 ─
┌[■]──────────────────────── Message ───────────────────────2=[↑]─┐
 Compiling C:\WORK\FIRST.CPP:
 Error C:\WORK\FIRST.CPP 6: Statement missing ; in function main()


F1 Help  Space View source  ←┘ Edit source  F10 Menu
```

The linker must find a function called *main*; without this, it cannot create an executable file. The linker does not highlight the offending line in the source file, so you may sometimes have difficulty in tracking down such errors. Here the problem should be obvious:

RUN-TIME ERRORS

A comparatively small number of errors do not reveal themselves until the program executes. These errors include division by 0, stack overflow, and the dreaded *null pointer assignment*. We'll have more to say about run-time errors later on.

OTHER IDE FEATURES

The Turbo C++ IDE has many other features that make program development easier. We'll look at some of them here, but remember that the IDE is far richer than we can discuss. When you are comfortable with the basics, you should read through the Turbo C++ documentation and experiment at the keyboard to learn the ins and outs of this product.

COMPILING AND LINKING SHORTCUT

We've described a two-step process for compiling and linking. This approach emphasizes the underlying steps. However, you can compile and link with a single menu selection. Select *Make* EXE *file* from the Compile menu. Your program will be compiled and then linked, with no further intervention.

You can automate the process even more by selecting *Run* from the Run menu. If your program has not been compiled and linked since the last revision to the source file, it will be recompiled and relinked, and finally executed.

EXITING FROM THE IDE

To exit from the IDE, select *Quit* from the File menu, or type ALT-X. If you haven't saved the latest revision to your program, and you try to exit, Turbo C++ will give you a chance to correct your mistake.

EXAMINING FILES

Outside of the IDE, you can examine the files the system has created. You'll see the source file FIRST.CPP, the object file FIRST.OBJ, and the executable file FIRST.EXE.

If you've saved your source file more than once there will also be a file called FIRST.BAK. When a file already exists with the same name as the source file you are saving, Turbo C++ renames it with the .BAK extension before saving the current file. Sooner or later, a time will come when your .CPP file is mistakenly erased, and you will be glad this feature exists.

OPENING AN EXISTING FILE

Once a file has been written and saved to disk, you can open it from Turbo C++. You can do this in one of two ways.

If you're invoking Turbo C++ from the DOS prompt, you can simply add the name of the .CPP source file on the command line, as in

```
C>tc first.cpp
```

Use the complete name, including the .CPP extension. When Turbo C++ executes, it will open an Edit window containing this file.

If you have already started Turbo C++ and you want to open a file, select *Open* from the File menu. The resulting Load a File window contains a text entry field called *Name* and a list of files. Again, Turbo C++ assumes you are programming in C, so it shows you a list of files with the .C extension, used for C source files. Since you are programming in C++, type *.cpp in the Name field. The asterisk (*) acts as a wildcard, so this has the effect of showing only .CPP files. Select the file you want, and click on the Open button, or double-click on the name. You can also type the filename into the Name field. An Edit window containing this file will appear. Now you can edit the source file, and compile, link, and execute the program as before.

Note that several Edit windows can be open on the IDE screen at the same time. You can move them around and resize them so that you can see parts of two programs at the same time. You can also cut and paste text between two Edit windows. See the Turbo C++ documentation for details on these features.

To make an Edit window disappear from the screen, click on the square in the window's upper-left corner, choose *Close* from the Window menu, or press (ALT)-(F3). You will probably want to close any open Edit windows before quitting. Turbo C++ remembers which windows were open when you quit, and opens them when you restart it. If you don't close files before quitting, you may find an excessive number of open windows accumulating on the screen.

THE DOS SHELL

If you want to access a DOS function—such as listing, copying, or deleting files—without exiting from Turbo C++, you can select *DOS shell* from the File menu. The DOS command prompt will appear. You can carry out whatever DOS operation you want. When you have finished, enter exit at the DOS prompt to return to Turbo C++. This capability saves the time consumed in exiting and restarting Turbo C++.

SUMMARY

You've learned a few details about how to install your system. You've also learned how to start up Turbo C++, type in the text of your source file, compile the source file into an object file, and link the object file into an executable file. You now know how to execute your program, how to view the results on the output screen, and how to deal with errors detected by the compiler or linker.

In the next chapter we'll begin our exploration of C++ itself.

C++ PROGRAMMING BASICS

In any language there are some fundamentals you need to know before you can write even the most elementary programs. This chapter introduces three such fundamentals: basic program construction, variables, and input/output (I/O). It also touches on a variety of other language features, including comments, arithmetic operators, the increment operator, data conversion, and library functions.

Most of these topics are not conceptually difficult, but you may find that the style in C++ is a little austere compared with, say, BASIC and Pascal. Before you learn what it's all about, a C++ program may remind you more of a mathematics formula than of a computer program. Don't worry about this. You'll find that as you gain familiarity with C++ it starts to look less forbidding, while simultaneously other languages begin to seem unnecessarily fancy and verbose.

Basic Program Construction

Let's look more closely at the FIRST program introduced in Chapter 2. Here it is again:

```
#include <iostream.h>

void main()
{
cout << "Every age has a language of its own";
}
```

Despite its small size, this program demonstrates a great deal about the construction of C++ programs. Let's examine it in detail.

Functions

Functions are one of the fundamental building blocks of C++. The FIRST program consists almost entirely of a single function called `main()`. The only part of this program that is not part of the function is the first line—the one that starts with `#include`. (We'll see what this line does in a moment.)

We noted in Chapter 1 that a function can be part of a class, in which case it is called a *member* function. However, functions can also exist independent of classes. We are not yet ready to talk about classes, so we will show functions that are separate stand-alone entities, as `main()` is here.

Function Name

The parentheses following the word `main` are the distinguishing feature of a function. Without the parentheses the compiler would think that `main` referred to a variable or to some other program element. When we discuss functions in the text we'll follow the same convention that C++ uses: We'll put parentheses following the function name. Later on we'll see that the parentheses aren't always empty. They're used to hold function *arguments*: values passed from the calling program to the function.

The word `void` preceding the function name indicates that this particular function does not have a return value. Don't worry about this now; we'll learn about return values and type `void` in Chapter 6.

Braces and the Function Body

The *body* of a function is surrounded by braces (sometimes called *curly brackets*). These braces play the same role as the `BEGIN` and `END` keywords in Pascal and BASIC: They surround or *delimit* a block of program statements. Every function must use this pair of braces. In this example there is only one statement within the braces: the line starting with `cout`. However, a function body can consist of many statements.

Always Start with `main()`

When you run a C++ program, the first statement executed will be at the beginning of a function called `main()`. The program may consist of many functions, classes, and other program elements, but on startup control always goes to `main()`. If there is no function called `main()` in your program, the linker will signal an error.

In most C++ programs, as we'll see later, `main()` calls member functions in various objects to carry out the program's real work. The `main()` function may also contain calls to other stand-alone functions. This is shown in Figure 3-1.

PROGRAM STATEMENTS

The program statement is the fundamental unit of C++ programming. There's only one statement in the FIRST program: the line

```
cout << "Every age has a language of its own";
```

This statement tells the computer to display the quoted phrase. Most statements tell the computer to do something. In this respect, statements in C++ are similar to statements in other languages. In fact, as we've noted, the majority of statements in C++ are identical to statements in C.

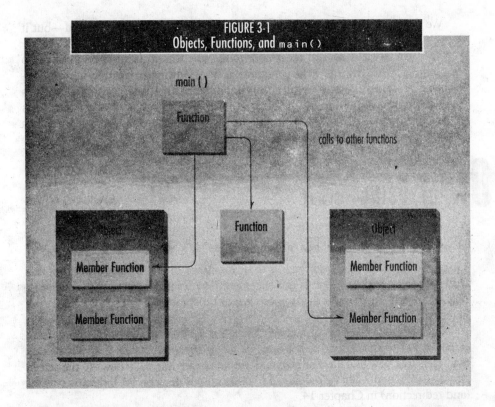

FIGURE 3-1
Objects, Functions, and main()

A semicolon signals the end of the statement. This is a crucial part of the syntax but easy to forget. In some languages (like BASIC), the end of a statement is signaled by the end of the line, but that's not true in C++. If you leave out the semicolon, the compiler will signal an error.

WHITE SPACE

Actually, the C++ compiler ignores white space almost completely. *White space* is defined as spaces, carriage returns, linefeeds, tabs, vertical tabs, and formfeeds. These characters are invisible to the compiler. You can put several statements on one line, separated by any number of spaces or tabs, or you can run a statement over two or more lines. It's all the same to the compiler. Thus the FIRST.CPP program could be written this way:

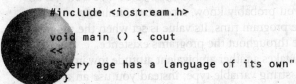

```
#include <iostream.h>

void main () { cout
<<
"Every age has a language of its own"
}
```

We don't recommend this syntax—it's nonstandard and hard to read—but it does compile correctly.

There are actually several exceptions to the rule that white space is invisible to the compiler. The first line of the program, starting with `#include`, is a *preprocessor directive*, which must be written on one line. Also, string constants, such as `"Every age has a language of its own"` cannot be broken into separate lines (although inserting a backslash \ at the break does permit multiline constructions in these circumstances).

OUTPUT USING cout

As you have seen, the statement

```
cout << "Every age has a language of its own";
```

causes the phrase in quotation marks to be displayed on the screen. How does this work? A complete description of this statement requires an understanding of objects, operator overloading, and other topics we won't discuss until later in the book, but here's a brief preview:

The identifier `cout` (pronounced "C out") is actually an *object*. It is predefined in Turbo C++ to correspond to the *standard output stream*. A *stream* is an abstraction that refers to a flow of data. The standard output stream normally flows to the screen display—although it can be redirected to other output devices. We'll discuss streams (and redirection) in Chapter 14.

The operator `<<` is called the *insertion* or *put to* operator. It directs the contents of the variable on its right to the object on its left. In FIRST it directs the string constant "Every age has a language of its own" to `cout`, which sends it to the display.

(If you know C, you'll recognize `<<` as the *left-shift* bit-wise operator and wonder how it can also be used to direct output. In C++, operators can be *overloaded*; That is, they can perform different activities, depending on the context. We'll learn about overloading in Chapter 9.)

Although the concepts behind the use of `cout` and `<<` may be obscure at this point, using them is easy. They'll appear in almost every example program. Figure 3-2 shows the result of using `cout` and the insertion operator `<<`.

STRING CONSTANTS

The phrase in quotation marks, `"Every age has a language of its own"`, is an example of a *string constant*. As you probably know, a constant, unlike a variable, cannot be given new values as the program runs. Its value is set when the program is written, and it retains this value throughout the program's existence.

As we'll see later, C++ (like C) takes a rather ambivalent attitude toward strings. On the one hand there is no real string variable type; instead you use an array of

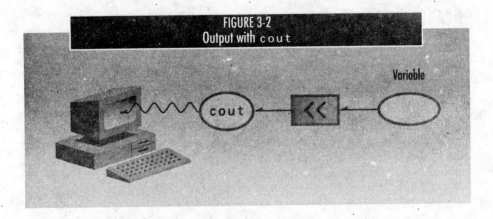

FIGURE 3-2
Output with cout

Variable

type **char** to hold string variables. On the other hand C++ recognizes string constants, surrounded by quotation marks as shown. We'll learn more about strings in Chapter 8.

PREPROCESSOR DIRECTIVES

The first line of the FIRST program,

```
#include <iostream.h>
```

might look like a program statement, but it's not. It isn't part of a function body and doesn't end with a semicolon, as program statements must. Instead, it starts with a number sign (#). It's called a *preprocessor directive*. Recall that program statements are instructions to the computer. A preprocessor directive, on the other hand, is an instruction to the compiler itself. A part of the compiler called the *preprocessor* deals with these directives before it begins the real compilation process.

THE #include DIRECTIVE

The preprocessor directive #include tells the compiler to insert another file into your source file. In effect, the #include directive is replaced by the contents of the file indicated. Using an #include directive to insert another file into your source file is similar to pasting a block of text into a document with your word processor.

HEADER FILES

In the FIRST example the preprocessor directive #include tells the compiler to add the source file IOSTREAM.H to the FIRST.CPP source file before compiling. Why do this? IOSTREAM.H is an example of a *header file* (sometimes called an *include file*). It contains declarations that are needed by the cout identifier and the << operator. Without these declarations, the compiler won't recognize cout and will think << is being used incorrectly. (In C, header files are often optional; in C++ they're always necessary.)

If you want to see what's in IOSTREAM.H, you can go to the TC\INCLUDE directory (\BORLANDC\INCLUDE in Borland C++) and use the DOS TYPE command (or the IDE editor) to examine the file. The contents won't make much sense at this point, but you will at least prove to yourself that IOSTREAM.H is a source file, written in normal ASCII characters.

We'll return to the topic of header files at the end of this chapter, when we introduce library functions.

#include is only one of many preprocessor directives, all of which can be identified by the initial # sign. The use of preprocessor directives is not as common in C++ as it is in C, but we'll look at a few additional examples as we go along.

COMMENTS

Comments are an important part of any program. They help the person writing a program, and anyone else who must read the source file, to understand what's going on. The compiler ignores comments, so they do not add to the file size or execution time of the executable program.

COMMENT SYNTAX

Let's rewrite our FIRST program, incorporating comments into our source file:

```
// comments.cpp
// demonstrates comments
#include <iostream.h>            // preprocessor directive

void main()                     // function name
    {                           // start function body
    cout << "Every age has a language of its own";  // statement
    }                           // end function body
```

Comments start with a double slash symbol (//) and terminate at the end of the line. (This is one of the exceptions to the rule that the compiler ignores white space.) A comment can start at the beginning of the line or on the same line following a program statement. Both possibilities are shown in the example.

WHEN TO USE COMMENTS

Comments are almost always a good thing. Most programmers don't use enough of them. If you're tempted to leave out comments, remember that not everyone is as smart as you; they may need more explanation than you do about what your program is doing. Also, you may not be as smart next month, when you've forgotten key details of your program's operation, as you are today.

Use comments to explain to the person looking at the listing what you're trying to do. The details are in the program statements themselves, so the comments should concentrate on the big picture, clarifying your reasons for using a certain statement.

ALTERNATIVE COMMENT SYNTAX

There's a second comment style available in C++:

```
/* this is an old-style comment */
```

This type of comment (the only comment available in C) begins with the /* character pair and ends with */ (*not* with the end of the line). These symbols are harder to type (since / is lowercase while * is uppercase) and take up more space on the line, so this style is not generally used in C++ However, it has advantages in special situations. You can write a multiline comment with only two comment symbols:

```
/* this
is a
potentially
very long
multiline
comment
*/
```

This is a good approach to making a comment out of a large text passage, since it saves inserting the // symbol on every line.

You can also insert a /* */ comment anywhere within the text of a program line:

```
func1()
    { /* empty function body */ }
```

If you attempt to use the // style comment in this case, the closing brace won't be visible to the compiler—since a // style comment runs to the end of the line—and the code won't compile correctly.

INTEGER VARIABLES

Variables are the most fundamental part of any language. A variable is a symbolic name that can be given a variety of values. Variables are stored in particular places in the computer's memory. When a variable is given a value, that value is actually placed in the memory space occupied by the variable. Most popular languages use the same general variable types, such as integers, floating-point numbers, and characters, so you are probably already familiar with the ideas behind them.

Integer variables represent integer numbers like 1; 30,000; and –27. Such numbers are used for counting discrete numbers of objects. Unlike floating-point numbers, integers have no fractional part; you can express the idea of *four* using integers, but not *four and one-half*.

DEFINING INTEGER VARIABLES

Integer variables exist in several sizes, but the most commonly used is type `int`. This type requires two bytes of storage (in MS-DOS computers) and holds numbers in the range –32,768 to 32,767. Figure 3-3 shows an integer variable in memory.

(While type `int` occupies two bytes in MS-DOS computers, it may occupy four bytes on some other computers, such as some mainframes.

Here's a program that defines and uses several variables of type `int`:

```
// intvars.cpp
// demonstrates integer variables
#include <iostream.h>

void main()
    {
    int var1;                    // define var1
    int var2;                    // define var2

    var1 = 20;                   // assign value to var1
    var2 = var1 + 10;            // assign value to var2
    cout << "var1+10 is ";       // output text
    cout << var2;                // output value of var2
    }
```

Type this program into the IDE, compile and link it, and then run it. Examine the output by pressing (ALT)-(F5).

The statements

```
int var1;
int var2;
```

define two integer variables, `var1` and `var2`. The keyword `int` signals the type of variable. These statements, which are called *definitions*, must terminate with a semicolon, like other program statements.

You must define a variable before using it. However, you can place variable definitions anywhere in a program. It's not necessary to define variables before the first executable statement (as you must do in C).

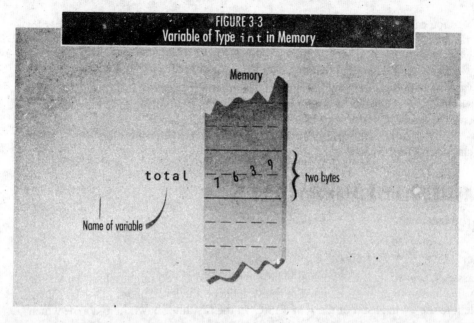

FIGURE 3-3
Variable of Type int in Memory

DECLARATIONS AND DEFINITIONS

Let's digress for a moment to note a subtle distinction between the terms *definition* and *declaration* as applied to variables.

A *declaration* introduces a variable's name (such as **var1**) into a program and specifies its type. If a declaration also sets aside memory for the variable, it is called a *definition*. The statements

```
int var1;
int var2;
```

in the INTVARS program are definitions because they set aside memory for **var1**. and **var2**. We'll be concerned mostly with declarations that are also definitions; but in Chapter 15, when we discuss multifile programs, we'll see examples of declarations that are not definitions.

VARIABLE NAMES

The program INTVARS uses variables named **var1** and **var2**. What are the rules for naming variables? You can use upper- and lowercase letters, and the digits from 1 to 9. You can also use the underscore (_). The first character must be a letter or underscore. Names can be as long as you like, but only the first 32 characters will be recognized. The compiler distinguishes between upper- and lowercase letters, so **Var** is not the same as **var** or **VAR**. (These same naming rules are used in C.)

You can't use a C++ *keyword* as a variable name. A keyword is the identifier for a language feature, like `int`, `class`, `if`, `while`, and so on. A complete list of keywords can be found in Appendix B and in Borland's documentation.

Many C++ programmers follow the convention of using all lowercase letters for variable names. Other programmers use a mixture of upper- and lowercase, as in `IntVar` or `dataCount`. Names in all uppercase are generally reserved for constants (see the discussion of `const` that follows).

These same conventions apply to naming other program elements such as classes and functions.

ASSIGNMENT STATEMENTS

The statements

```
var1 = 20;
var2 = var1 + 10;
```

assign values to the two variables. The equal sign =, as you might guess, causes the value on the right to be assigned to the variable on the left. The = in C++ is equivalent to the := in Pascal or the = in BASIC. In the first line shown here, `var1`, which previously had no value, is given the value 20.

INTEGER CONSTANTS

The number 20 is an *integer constant*. Constants don't change during the course of the program. An integer constant consists of numerical digits, as shown. There can be no decimal point in an integer constant, and it must lie within the range of integers.

In the second program line shown here, the plus sign + adds the value of `var1` and 10, in which 10 is another constant. The result of this addition is then assigned to `var2`.

OUTPUT VARIATIONS

The statement

```
cout << "var1+10 is ";
```

displays a string constant, as we've seen before. The next statement,

```
cout << var2;
```

displays the value of the variable `var2`. As you can see when you press (ALT)-(F5), the output of the program is

```
var1+10 is 30
```

Note that `cout` and the `<<` operator know how to treat an integer and a string differently. If we send them a string, they print it as text. If we send them an integer, they print it as a number. This may seem obvious, but it is another example of operator overloading, a key feature of C++. (C programmers will remember that such functions as `printf()` need to be told not only the *variable* to be displayed, but the *type* of the variable as well, which makes the syntax far less intuitive.)

As you can see, the output of the two `cout` statements appears on the same line on the output screen. In fact, if you run the program again, you'll see that the new output continues to appear on the same line:

```
var1+10 is 30var1+10 is 30
```

The moral is that no linefeed is inserted automatically. If you want to start on a new line, you must do it yourself. We'll see how in a moment.

CHARACTER VARIABLES

We've seen one kind of integer variable, type `int`. Another integer variable is type `char`. This type stores integers that range in value from –128 to 127. Variables of this type occupy only one byte of memory. Character variables are sometimes used to store numbers that confine themselves to this limited range, but they are more commonly used to store ASCII characters.

As you probably know, the ASCII character set is a way of representing characters such as 'a', 'B', '$', '3', and so on, as numbers. These numbers range from 0 to 127. (Most MS-DOS computers extend this range to 255 to accommodate various foreign-language and graphics characters.) Appendix A shows the ASCII character set.

CHARACTER CONSTANTS

Character constants use single quotation marks around a character, as shown in the previous paragraph. (Note that this differs from string constants, which use double quotation marks.) When the C++ compiler encounters such a character constant, it translates it into the corresponding ASCII code and stores that number in the program. The constant 'a' appearing in a program, for example, will be stored as 97, as shown in Figure 3-4.

Character variables can be assigned character constants as values. The following program shows some examples of character constants and variables:

```
// charvars.cpp
// demonstrates character variables

#include <iostream.h>        // for cout, etc.

void main()
   {
   char charvar1 = 'A';      // define char variable as character
   char charvar2 = '\t';     // define char variable as tab
```

```
cout << charvar1;          // display character
cout << charvar2;          // display character
charvar1 = 'B';            // set char variable to char constant
cout << charvar1;          // display character
cout << '\n';              // display newline character
}
```

INITIALIZATION

Variables can be initialized at the same time they are defined. In this program two variables of type char—charvar1 and charvar2—are initialized to the character constants 'A' and '\t'.

ESCAPE SEQUENCES

This second character constant, '\t', is an odd one. It is called an *escape sequence*, since the backslash causes an "escape" from the normal way characters are interpreted. In this case the t is interpreted not as the character 't' but as the tab character. (In Turbo C++ a tab causes printing to continue eight spaces to the right.)

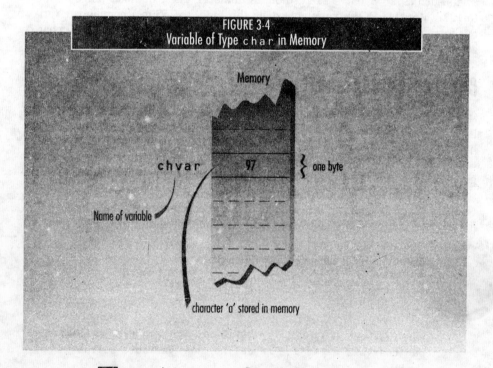

FIGURE 3-4
Variable of Type char in Memory

Another character constant, '\n', is sent directly to `cout` in the last line of the program. This is the escape sequence for the `newline` character. This character causes both a carriage return and linefeed, so that the next character to be printed appears at the beginning of the next line down. This is by far the most frequently used escape sequence.

Escape sequences can be used in both character and string constants. Table 3-1 shows a list of common escape sequences.

Since the backslash, the single quotation marks, and the double quotation marks all have specialized meanings when used in constants, they must be represented by escape sequences. Here's an example of a quoted phrase in a string constant:

```
cout << "\"Run, Spot, run,\" she said.";
```

Sometimes you need to represent a character constant that doesn't appear on the keyboard, such as the graphics characters above ASCII code 127. To do this, you can use the '\xdd' representation, where each d stands for a hexadecimal digit. If you want to print a solid rectangle, for example, you'll find such a character listed as decimal number 178, which is hexadecimal number B2 in the ASCII table. This character would be represented by the character constant '\xB2'. We'll see some examples of this later.

The CHARVARS program prints the value of `charvar1` ('A') and the value of `charvar2` (a tab). It then sets `charvar1` to a new value ('B'), prints that, and finally prints the newline. The output looks like this:

A   B

TABLE 3-1 Common Escape Sequences	
Escape Sequence	**Character**
\a	Bell (beep)
\b	Backspace
\f	Formfeed
\n	Newline
\r	Return
\t	Tab
\\	Backslash
\'	Single quotation mark
\"	Double quotation marks
\xdd	Hexadecimal representation

INPUT WITH cin

Now that we've seen some variable types in use, let's see how a program accomplishes input. The next example program asks the user for a temperature in degrees Fahrenheit, converts it to celsius, and displays the result.

```
// fahren.cpp
// demonstrates cin, newline
#include <iostream.h>

void main()
    {
    int ftemp;

    cout << "Enter temperature in fahrenheit: ";
    cin >> ftemp;
    int ctemp = (ftemp-32) * 5 / 9;
    cout << "Equivalent in Celsius is:  " << ctemp << '\n';
    }
```

The statement

```
cin >> ftemp;
```

causes the program to wait for the user to type in a number. The resulting number is placed in the variable ftemp. The keyword cin (pronounced "C in") is an object, predefined in C++ to correspond to the standard input stream. This stream represents data coming from the keyboard (unless it has been redirected). The >> is the *extraction* or *get from* operator. It takes the value from the stream object on its left and places it in the variable on its right.

Here's some sample interaction with the program:

```
Enter temperature in fahrenheit: 212
Equivalent in Celsius is: 100
```

Figure 3-5 shows input using cin and the extraction operator >>

VARIABLES DEFINED AT POINT OF USE

The FAHREN program has several new wrinkles besides its input capability. Look closely at the listing. Where is the variable ctemp defined? Not at the beginning of the program, but in the next-to-the-last line, where it's used to store the result of the arithmetic operation. As we noted earlier, you can define variables throughout a program, not just at the beginning. (Many languages, including C, require all variables to be defined before the first executable statement.)

Defining variables where they are used can make the listing easier to understand, since you don't need to refer repeatedly to the start of the listing to find the variable

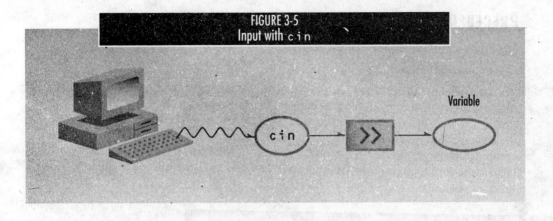

FIGURE 3-5
Input with c i n

Variable

c i n

>>

definitions. However, the practice should be used with discretion. Variables that are used in many places in a function are probably better defined at the start of the function.

CASCADING <<

The extraction operator **<<** is used repeatedly in the second **cout** statement in FAHREN. This is perfectly legal. The program first sends the phrase *Equivalent in centigrade is:* to **cout**, then it sends the value of **ctemp**, and finally the newline character '\n'.

The insertion operator **>>** can be cascaded with **cin** in the same way, allowing the user to enter a series of values. However, this capability is not used so often, since it eliminates the opportunity to prompt the user between inputs.

EXPRESSIONS

Any arrangement of variables and operators that specifies a computation is called an *expression*. Thus **alpha+12** and **(alpha-37)*beta/2** are expressions. When the computations specified in the expression are performed, the result is usually a value. Thus if **alpha** is 7, the first expression shown has the value 19.

Parts of expressions may also be expressions. In the second example, **alpha-37** and **beta/2** are expressions. Even single variables and constants, like **alpha** and 37, are considered to be expressions.

Note that expressions aren't the same as statements. Statements tell the compiler to do something and terminate with a semicolon, while expressions specify a computation. There can be several expressions in a statement.

PRECEDENCE

Note the parentheses in the expression

```
(ftemp-32) * 5 / 9
```

Without the parentheses, the multiplication would be carried out first, since * has higher priority than -. With the parentheses, the subtraction is done first, then the multiplication, since all operations inside parentheses are carried out first. Precedence and parentheses are normally applied this same way in algebra and in other computer languages, so their use probably seems quite natural. However, precedence is an important topic in C++. We'll return to it later when we introduce different kinds of operators.

TYPE float

We've talked about type `int` and type `char`, both of which represent numbers as integers—that is, numbers without a fractional part. Now let's examine a different way of storing numbers: as *floating point* variables.

Floating-point variables represent numbers with a decimal place—like 3.1415927, 0.0000625, and –10.2. They have both an integer part, to the left of the decimal point, and a fractional part, to the right. Floating-point variables represent *real numbers*, which are used for measurable quantities like distance, area, temperature, and so on, and typically have a fractional part.

There are three kinds of floating-point variables in C++: type `float`, type `double`, and type `long double`. Let's look at the smallest of these, type `float`.

Type `float` stores numbers in the range 3.4×10^{-38} to 3.4×10^{38}, with a precision of seven digits. It occupies four bytes in memory, as shown in Figure 3-6.

The following example program prompts the user to type in a floating-point number representing the radius of a circle. It then calculates and displays the circle's area.

```cpp
// circarea.cpp
// demonstrates floating point variables
#include <iostream.h>                  // for cout, etc.

void main()
  {
  float rad;                           // variable of type float
  const float PI = 3.14159;            // type const float

  cout << "Enter radius of circle: "; // prompt
  cin >> rad;                          // get radius
  float area = PI * rad * rad;         // find area
  cout << "Area is " << area << endl;  // display answer
  }
```

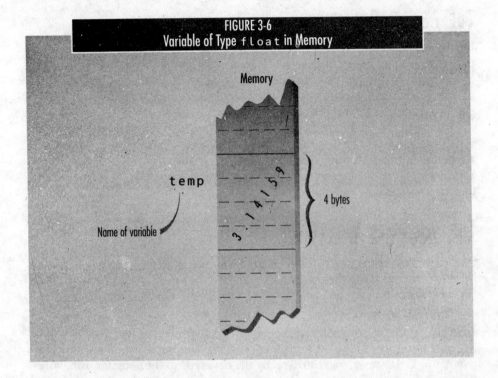

FIGURE 3-6
Variable of Type float in Memory

Memory

temp

3.14159

4 bytes

Name of variable

Here's a sample interaction with the program:

```
Enter radius of circle: 0.5
Area is 0.785398
```

This is the area in square feet of a 12-inch LP record (which has a radius of 0.5 feet). At one time this was an important quantity for manufacturers of vinyl.

FLOATING-POINT CONSTANTS

The number 3.14159 in CIRCAREA is an example of a *floating-point constant*. The decimal point signals that it is a floating-point constant, and not an integer. This number is written in normal decimal notation.

You can also write floating-point constants using exponential notation. For example, the number 1234.56 would be written 1.23456E3 in exponential notation. This is the same as 1.23456 times 10^3. The number following the E is called the *exponent*. It indicates how many places the decimal point must be moved to change the number to ordinary decimal notation.

The exponent can be positive or negative. The exponential number 6.35239E–5 is equivalent to 0.0000635239 in decimal notation. This is the same as 6.35239 times 10^{-5}

THE const QUALIFIER

Besides demonstrating variables of type `float`, the CIRCAREA example also introduces the qualifier `const`. The keyword `const` (for *constant*) precedes the data type of a variable. It specifies that the value of a variable *will not change* throughout the program. Any attempt to alter the value of a variable defined with this qualifier will elicit an error message from the compiler.

The qualifier `const` ensures that your program does not inadvertently alter a variable that you intended to be a constant, such as the value of PI in CIRCAREA. It also reminds anyone reading the listing that the variable is not intended to change. Variables with this qualifier are sometimes named in all uppercase, as a reminder that they are constants.

THE #define DIRECTIVE

Although the construction is not popular in C++, we should note that you can also specify constants using the preprocessor directive `#define`. This directive sets up an equivalence between an identifier and a text phrase. For example, the line

```
#define PI 3.14159
```

appearing at the beginning of your program specifies that the identifier PI will be replaced by the text 3.14159 throughout program. This construction has long been popular in C. However, you can't specify the data type of the constant using `#define`, which can lead to program bugs; so even in C `#define` is being superseded by `const` used with normal variables.

MANIPULATORS

Manipulators are operators used with the insertion operator `<<` to modify—or manipulate—the way data is displayed. We'll look at two of the most common here: `endl` and `setw`.

THE endl MANIPULATOR

The last `cout` statement in the CIRCAREA program ends with an unfamiliar word: `endl`. This is a manipulator that causes a linefeed to be inserted into the stream. It has the same effect as sending the single '\n' character, but is perhaps somewhat clearer.

THE setw MANIPULATOR

You can think of each value displayed by `cout` as occupying a *field*: an imaginary box with a certain width. The default field is just wide enough to hold the value.

That is, the integer 567 will occupy a field three characters wide, and the string **"pajamas"** will occupy a field seven characters wide. However, in certain situations this may not lead to optimal results. Here's an example. The WIDTH1 program prints the names of three cities in one column, and their populations in another.

```
// width1.cpp
// demonstrates need for setw manipulator
#include <iostream.h>

void main()
   {
   long pop1=2425785, pop2=47, pop3=9761;

   cout << "LOCATION " << "POP." << endl
        << "Portcity " << pop1 << endl
        << "Hightown " << pop2 << endl
        << "Lowville " << pop3 << endl;
   }
```

Here's the output from this program:

```
LOCATION POP.
Portcity 2425785
Hightown 47
Lowville 9761
```

Unfortunately, the output of WIDTH1 is not ideal. It's hard to compare the numbers; it would be better if they lined up to the right. Also, we had to insert spaces into the names of the cities to separate them from the numbers. This is an inconvenience.

Here's a variation of this program, WIDTH2, that uses the **setw** manipulator to eliminate these problems by specifying field widths for the names and the numbers:

```
// width2.cpp
// demonstrates setw manipulator
#include <iostream.h>
#include <iomanip.h>       // for setw

void main()
   {   ..
   long pop1=2425785, pop2=47, pop3=9761;

   cout << setw(8) << "LOCATION" << setw(12)
                                 << "POPULATION" << endl
        << setw(8) << "Portcity" << setw(12) << pop1 << endl
        << setw(8) << "Hightown" << setw(12) << pop2 << endl
        << setw(8) << "Lowville" << setw(12) << pop3 << endl;
   }
```

The **setw** manipulator causes the number (or string) that follows it in the stream to be printed within a field n characters wide, where n is the argument to **setw(n)**. The value is right-justified within the field. Figure 3-7 shows how this looks.

Here's the output of WIDTH2:

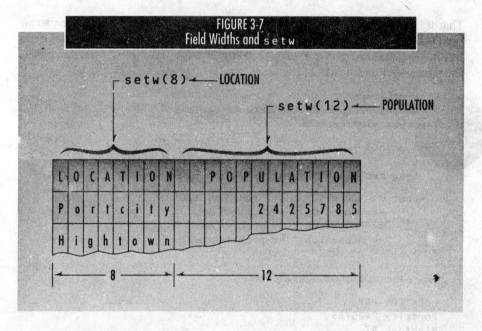

FIGURE 3-7
Field Widths and `setw`

```
LOCATION    POPULATION
Portcity      2425785
Hightown           47
Lowville         9761
```

TYPE Long

Besides the use of `setw`, there are several new aspects to the WIDTH1 and WIDTH2 programs. First, we've used a new data type: `long`. This is the third of the integer types, after `char` and `int`. Type `long` can also be written as `long int`; these mean the same thing. Type `long` can hold integers in the range –2,147,483,648 to 2,147,483,647. It's used when type `int` is too small for the values being stored. In WIDTH1 and WIDTH2 the population figures exceed the upper limit of type `int`—32,767—so type `long` must be used. Variables of type `long` occupy four bytes of memory (twice as much as type `int`), as shown in Figure 3-8.

If you want to create a constant of type `long`, use the letter L following the numerical value, as in

```
longvar = 7678L; // assigns long constant 7678 to longvar
```

If a constant's value is greater than 65,535, it is interpreted as type `long` whether you use the L or not.

CASCADING THE INSERTION OPERATOR

Note that there's only one `cout` statement in WIDTH1 and WIDTH2, although it's written on multiple lines. In doing this, we take advantage of the fact that the

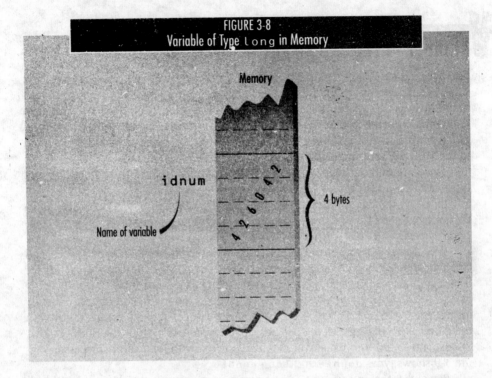

FIGURE 3-8
Variable of Type Long in Memory

compiler ignores white space, and that the insertion operator can be cascaded. The effect is the same as using four separate statements, each beginning with cout.

MULTIPLE DEFINITIONS

We've initialized the variables pop1, pop2, and pop3 to specific values at the same time we defined them. This is similar to the way we initialized char variables in the CHARVARS example. Here, however, we've defined and initialized all three variables on one line, using the same long keyword and separating the variable names with commas. This saves space where a number of variables are all the same type.

THE IOMANIP.H HEADER FILE

The declarations for the manipulators are not in the usual IOSTREAM.H header file, but in a separate header file called IOMANIP.H. When you use these manipulators you must #include this header file in your program, as we do in the WIDTH2 example.

VARIABLE TYPE SUMMARY

Our program examples so far have covered four data types—int, char, float, and long. There are two others we haven't seen yet: double and long double. Let's pause now to summarize these data types. Table 3-2 shows the keyword used to define the type, the numerical range the type can accommodate, the digits of precision (in the case of floating-point numbers), and the bytes of memory occupied in the MS-DOS environment.

There are three integer types: char, int, and long; and three floating-point types: float, double, and long double.

In theory there is another integer type not shown here: short. In the MS-DOS environment short is identical to int, so it is seldom used. However, on some computer systems short is smaller than int.

Type double occupies eight bytes, twice as much memory as type float, and stores floating-point numbers with much larger range and precision. It stands for *double precision floating point*. It's used when type float is too small or insufficiently precise. Floating-point type long double occupies ten bytes, and has only slightly greater range and precision than type double. However, it offers compatibility with the 80-bit numbers used in the optional math coprocessor chip (the 8087, 80287, 80387, and so on). It is usually used in conjunction with the math coprocessor. Figure 3-9 shows types double and long double.

Remember that integer type long extracts a performance penalty compared with type int. It is slower in arithmetic operations, and it occupies more memory, making your program larger. Similarly, the floating-point types double and long double

TABLE 3-2 Basic C++ Variable Types				
Keyword	Numerical range: low	high	Digits of precision	Bytes of memory
char	-128	127	n/a	1
int	$-32,768$	$32,767$	n/a	2
long	$-2,147,483,648$	$2,147,483,647$	n/a	4
float	3.4×10^{-38}	3.4×10^{38}	7	4
double	1.7×10^{-308}	1.7×10^{308}	15	8
long double	3.4×10^{-4932}	1.1×10^{4932}	19	10

are slower and larger than type `float`. You should use the smallest variable type that stores the values you're using in your program.

unsigned DATA TYPES

By eliminating the sign of the character and integer types, you can change their range to start at 0 and include only positive numbers. This allows them to represent numbers twice as big as the signed type. Table 3-3 shows the unsigned versions.

The `unsigned` types are used when the quantities represented are always positive—such as when representing a count of something—or when the positive range of the signed types is not quite long enough.

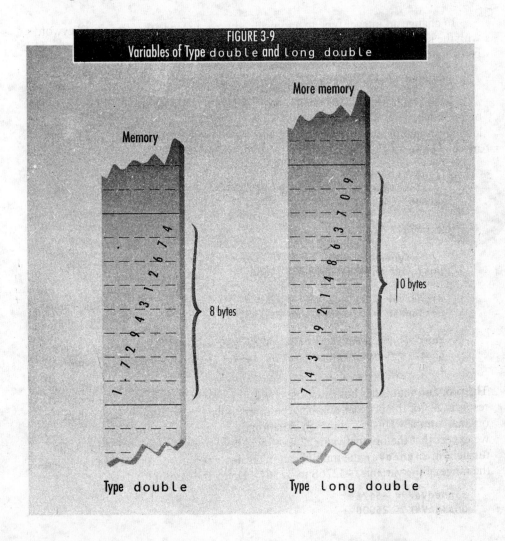

FIGURE 3-9
Variables of Type double and long double

TABLE 3-3			
Unsigned Integer Types			
Keyword	Numerical range: low	high	Bytes of memory
unsigned char	0	255	1
unsigned int	0	65,535	2
unsigned long	0	4,294,967,295	4

To change an integer type to an unsigned type, precede the data type keyword with the keyword `unsigned`. For example, an unsigned variable of type `char` would be defined as

```
unsigned char ucharvar;
```

Exceeding the range of signed types can lead to obscure program bugs. These bugs can sometimes be eliminated by using unsigned types. For example, the following program stores the constant 25000 both as an `int` in `signedVar`, and as an `unsigned int` in `unsignVar`.

```
// signtest.cpp
// tests signed and unsigned integers
#include <iostream.h>

void main()
    {
    int signedVar = 25000;              // signed: -32768 to 32767
    unsigned int unsignVar = 25000;     // unsigned: 0 to 65535

    signedVar = (signedVar * 2) / 3;    // calculation exceeds range
    unsignVar = (unsignVar * 2) / 3;    // calculation within range

    cout << "signedVar = " << signedVar << endl;   // wrong: -5178
    cout << "unsignVar = " << unsignVar << endl;   // ok: 16666
    }
```

The program multiplies both variables by 2, then divides them by 3. Although the result is 2/3 of the original number, the intermediate calculation is larger than the original number. This is a common situation, but it can lead to trouble. In SIGNTEST we expect that the original value, 25000, will be restored to both variables. Unfortunately, in `signedVar` the multiplication created a result—50,000—that exceeded the range of the variable (-32768 to 32767). Here's the output:

```
signedVar = -5178
unsignVar = 25000
```

The signed variable now displays an incorrect answer, while the unsigned variable, which is large enough to hold the intermediate result of the multiplication, records the result correctly. The moral is this: Be careful that all values generated in your program are within the range of the variables that hold them. (The results may be different on non-MS-DOS computers, which may use more bytes for type int.)

TYPE CONVERSION

C++, like C, is more forgiving than some languages in the way it treats expression involving several different data types. As an example, consider the MIXED program:

```
// mixed.cpp
// shows mixed expressions
#include <iostream.h>

void main()
    {
    int count = 7;
    float avgWeight = 155.5;

    double totalWeight = count * avgWeight;
    cout << "totalWeight=" << totalWeight << endl;
    }
```

Here a variable of type int is multiplied by a variable of type float to yield a result of type double. This program compiles without error, the compiler considers it normal that you want to multiply (or perform any other arithmetic operation on) numbers of different types.

Not all languages are this relaxed. Some don't permit mixed expressions, and would flag as an error the line that performs the arithmetic in MIXED. Such languages assume that when you mix types you're making a mistake, and they try to save you from yourself. C++ and C, however, assume that you must have a good reason for doing what you're doing, and they help to carry out your intentions. This is one reason for the popularity of C++ and C. They give you more freedom.

AUTOMATIC CONVERSIONS

Let's consider what happens when the compiler confronts such mixed-type expressions as that in MIXED. Types are considered "higher" or "lower," based roughly on the order shown in Table 3-4.

When two operands of different types are encountered in the same expression, the lower-type variable is converted to the type of the higher-type variable. Thus in

Data type	Order
TABLE 3-4 Order of Data Types.	
long double	(highest)
double	
float	
long	
int	
char	(lowest)

MIXED, the `int` value of `count` is converted to type `float` and stored in a temporary variable before being multiplied by the `float` variable `avgWeight`. The result (still of type `float`) is then converted to `double` so that it can be assigned to the `double` variable `totalWeight`. This process is shown in Figure 3-10.

These conversions take place invisibly, and ordinarily you don't need to think too much about them, C++ automatically does what you want. However, when we start to use objects, we will in effect be defining our own data types. We may want to use these new data types in mixed expressions, just as we use normal variables in mixed expressions. When this is the case, we must be careful to create our own conversion routines to change objects of one type into objects of another. The compiler won't do it for us, as it does here with the built-in data types.

CASTS

Casts sounds like something to do with classes in India, but in C++ the term applies to data conversions specified by the programmer, as opposed to the automatic data conversions we just described. What are casts for? Sometimes a programmer needs to convert a value from one type to another in a situation where the compiler will not do it automatically. Recall that in the SIGNTEST example an intermediate result exceeded the capacity of the variable type, resulting in an erroneous result. We fixed the problem by using `unsigned int` instead of `int`. This worked because the intermediate result—50,000—would fit in the range of the unsigned variable.

But suppose an intermediate result won't fit the unsigned type either. In such a case we might be able to solve the problem by using a *cast*. Here's an example:

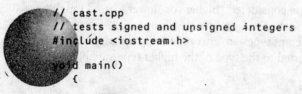

```
// cast.cpp
// tests signed and unsigned integers
#include <iostream.h>

void main()
{
```

```
    int intVar = 25000;                    // signed: -32768 to 32767
    intVar = (intVar * 10) / 10;           // result too large
    cout << "intVar = " << intVar << endl; // wrong answer


    intVar = 25000;
    intVar = ( long(intVar) * 10) / 10;    // cast to long
    cout << "intVar = " << intVar << endl; // right answer
    }
```

When we multiply the variable intVar by 10, the result—250,000—is far too large to fit in a variable of type int, or unsigned int. This leads to the wrong answer, as shown in the first part of the program.

We could redefine the data type of the variables to be long; this provides plenty of room, since this type holds numbers up to 2,147,483,647. But suppose that for some reason, such as keeping the program small, we don't want to change the variables to type long. In this case there's another solution: We can cast intVar

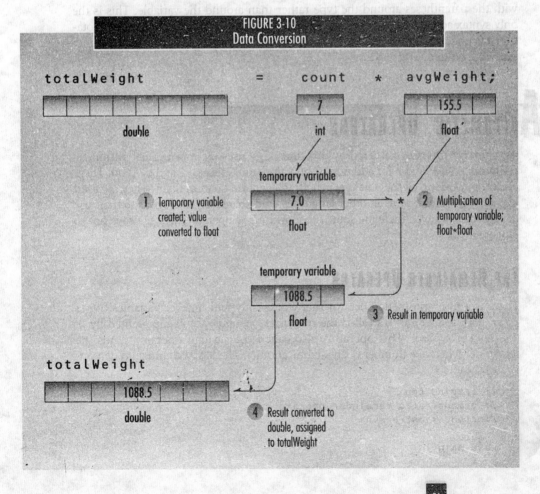

FIGURE 3-10
Data Conversion

totalWeight = count * avgWeight;

double   int   float

1 Temporary variable created; value converted to float

temporary variable

7.0

float

2 Multiplication of temporary variable; float*float

temporary variable

1088.5

float

3 Result in temporary variable

totalWeight

1088.5

double

4 Result converted to double, assigned to totalWeight

to type long before multiplying. This is sometimes called *coercion*; the data is *coerced* into becoming another type. The expression

```
long(intVar)
```

casts intVar to type long. It generates a temporary variable of type long with the same value as intVar. It is this temporary variable that is multiplied by 10. Since it is type long, the result fits. This result is then divided by 10 and assigned to the normal int variable intVar. Here's the program's output:

```
intVar = -1214
intVar = 25000
```

The first answer, without the cast, is wrong; but in the second answer, the cast produces the correct result.

You can use another syntax for casts. You can say

```
(long)intVar
```

with the parentheses around the type rather than around the variable. This is the only syntax acceptable in C, but in C++ the first approach (called "functional notation") is preferred, because it is similar to the way other parts of C++, such as functions, are written.

ARITHMETIC OPERATORS

As you have probably gathered by this time, C++ uses the four normal arithmetic operators +, -, *, and / for addition, subtraction, multiplication, and division. These operators work on all the data types, both integer and floating-point. They are used in much the same way as in other languages, and are closely analogous to their use in algebra. However, there are some other arithmetic operators whose use is not so obvious.

THE REMAINDER OPERATOR

There is a fifth arithmetic operator that works only with integer variables (types char, int and long). It's called the *remainder* operator, and is represented by %, the percent symbol. This operator (also called the *modulus* operator) finds the remainder when one number is divided by another. The REMAIND program demonstrates the effect.

```
// remaind.cpp
// demonstrates remainder operator
#include <iostream.h>

void main()
    {
```

```
cout <<   6 % 8 << endl      // 6
     <<   7 % 8 << endl      // 7
     <<   8 % 8 << endl      // 0
     <<   9 % 8 << endl      // 1
     <<  10 % 8 << endl;     // 2
}
```

Here the numbers 6 through 10 are divided by 8, using the remainder operator. The answers are 6, 7, 0, 1, and 2—the remainders of these divisions. The remainder operator is used in a wide variety of situations. We'll show examples as we go along.

A note about precedence: In the expression

```
cout << 6 % 8
```

the remainder operator is evaluated first because it has higher precedence than the << operator. If it did not, we would need to put parentheses around (6 % 8) to ensure it was evaluated before being acted on by <<.

ARITHMETIC ASSIGNMENT OPERATORS

C++ offers several ways to shorten and clarify your code. One of these is the *arithmetic assignment operator*. While not a key feature of the language, this operator is commonly used, and it helps to give C++ listings their distinctive appearance.

The following kind of statement is common in most languages:

```
total = total + item;  // adds "item" to "total"
```

In this situation you add something to an existing value (or you perform some other arithmetic operation on it). But the syntax of this statement offends those for whom brevity is important, because the name total appears twice. So C++ offers a condensed approach: the arithmetic assignment operator, which combines an arithmetic operator and an assignment operator, and eliminates the repeated operand. Here's a statement that has exactly the same effect as the one above:

```
total += item;   // adds "item" to "total"
```

Figure 3-11 emphasizes the equivalence of the two forms.

There are arithmetic assignment operators corresponding to all the arithmetic operations: +=, -=, *=, /=, and %= (and some other operators as well). The following example shows the arithmetic assignment operators in use:

```
// assign.cpp
// demonstrates arithmetic assignment operators
#include <iostream.h>

void main()
    {
    int ans = 27;
    ans += 10;                   // same as: ans = ans + 10;
```

```
cout << endl << ans;
ans -= 7;                      // same as: ans = ans - 7;
cout << endl << ans;
ans *= 2;                      // same as: ans = ans * 2;
cout << endl << ans;
ans /= 3;                      // same as: ans = ans / 3;
cout << endl << ans;
ans %= 3;                      // same as: ans = ans % 3;
cout << endl << ans;
}
```

Here's the output from this program:

```
37
30
60
20
2
```

You don't need to use arithmetic assignment operators in your code, but they are a common feature of the language; they'll appear in numerous examples in this book.

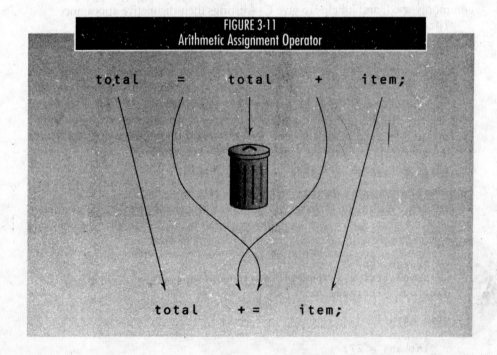

FIGURE 3-11
Arithmetic Assignment Operator

INCREMENT OPERATORS

Here's an even more specialized operator. You often need to add 1 to the value of an existing variable. You can do this the "normal" way:

```
count = count + 1;   // adds 1 to "count"
```

Or you can use an arithmetic assignment operator:

```
count += 1;   // adds 1 to "count"
```

But there's an even more condensed approach:

```
++count;   // adds 1 to "count"
```

The ++ operator *increments* (adds 1 to) its argument.

Prefix and Postfix

As if this weren't weird enough, the increment operator can be used in two ways: as a *prefix*, meaning that the operator precedes the variable; and as a *postfix*, meaning that the operator follows the variable. What's the difference? Often a variable is incremented within a statement that performs some other operation on it. For example,

```
totalWeight = avgWeight * ++count;
```

The question here is, Is the multiplication performed before or after count is incremented? In this case count is incremented first. How do we know that? Because *prefix* notation is used: ++count. If we had used postfix notation, count++, the multiplication would have been performed first, then count would have been incremented. This is shown in Figure 3-12.

Here's an example that shows both the prefix and postfix versions of the increment operator:

```
// increm.cpp
// demonstrates the increment operator
#include <iostream.h>

void main()
   {
   int count = 10;

   cout << "count=" << count << endl;     // displays 10
   cout << "count=" << ++count << endl;   // displays 11 (prefix)
   cout << "count=" << count << endl;     // displays 11
   cout << "count=" << count++ << endl;   // displays 11 (postfix)
   cout << "count=" << count << endl;     // displays 12
   }
```

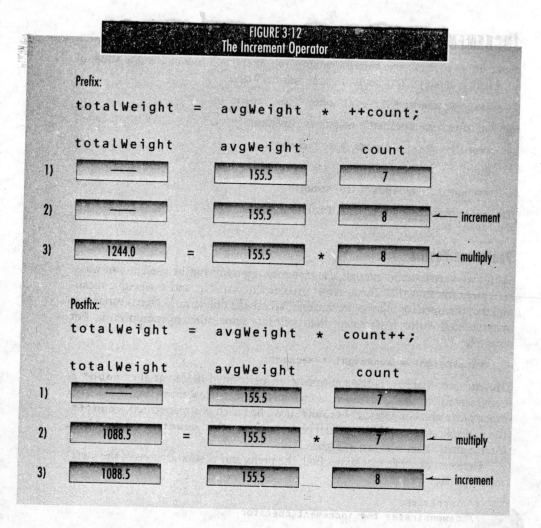

FIGURE 3-12
The Increment Operator

Prefix:

`totalWeight  =  avgWeight  *  ++count;`

	totalWeight	avgWeight	count	
1)	───	155.5	7	
2)	───	155.5	8	← increment
3)	1244.0 =	155.5 *	8	← multiply

Postfix:

`totalWeight  =  avgWeight  *  count++;`

	totalWeight	avgWeight	count	
1)	───	155.5	7	
2)	1088.5 =	155.5 *	7	← multiply
3)	1088.5	155.5	8	← increment

Here's the program's output:

```
count=10
count=11
count=11
count=11
count=12
```

The first time `count` is incremented, the prefix `++` operator is used. This causes the increment to happen at the beginning of the statement evaluation, before the output operation has been carried out. When the value of the expression `++count` is displayed, it has already been incremented, and `<<` sees the value 11. The second time `count` is incremented, the postfix `++` operator is used. When the expression `count++` is displayed, it retains its unincremented value of 11. Following the completion of this statement, the increment takes effect, so that in the last statement of the program we see that `count` has acquired the value 12.

The Decrement (−−) Operator

The decrement operator, `−−`, behaves very much like the increment operator, except that it subtracts 1 from its operand. It can also be used in both prefix and postfix forms.

LIBRARY FUNCTIONS

Many activities in C++ are carried out by *library functions*. These functions perform file access, mathematical computations, graphics, memory management, and data conversion, among other things. We don't want to dig too deeply into library functions before we explain how functions work (see Chapter 6), but you can use simple library functions without a thorough understanding of their operation. Here's a preview.

The next example, SQRT, uses the library function `sqrt()` to calculate the square root of a number entered by the user:

```
// sqrt.cpp
// demonstrates sqrt() library function
#include <iostream.h>          // for cout, etc.
#include <math.h>              // for sqrt()
void main()
    {
    double number, answer;     // sqrt() requires type double
    cout << "Enter a number: ";
    cin >> number;             // get the number
    answer = sqrt(number);     // find square root
    cout << "Square root is "
         << answer << endl;    // display it
    }
```

The program first obtains a number from the user. This number is then used as an *argument* to the `sqrt()` function, in the statement

```
answer = sqrt(number);
```

An argument is the input to the function; it is placed inside the parentheses following the function name. The function then processes the argument and *returns* a value; this is the output from the function. In this case the return value is the square root of the original number. *Returning a value* means that the function expression takes on this value, which can then be assigned to another variable—in this case `answer`. The program then displays this value. Here's some output from the program:

```
Enter a number: 1000
Square root is 31.622777
```

Multiplying 31.62777 by itself on your pocket calculator will verify that this answer is pretty close.

The arguments to a function, and their return values, must be the correct data type. You can find what these data types are by looking at the description of the library function in the Borland library documentation, which describes each of the hundreds of library functions. For `sqrt()` the description specifies both an argument and a return value of type `double`, so we use variables of this type in the program.

HEADER FILES

As with `cout` and other such objects, you must `#include` a header file that contains various declarations describing any library functions you use. In the documentation for the `sqrt()` function, you'll see that the specified header file is MATH.H. In SQRT the preprocessor directive

```
#include <math.h>
```

takes care of incorporating this header file into our source file.

If you don't include the appropriate header file when you use a library function, you'll get an error message like this from the compiler:

```
Function 'sqrt' should have a prototype in function main()
```

LIBRARY FILES

We mentioned earlier that a file containing library functions and objects will usually be linked to your program to create an executable file. This is true for all the programs in this chapter, since they use `cout` and other objects. If you're using the Small memory model, this library file is called CS.LIB (where the S indicates *Small*). The `sqrt()` function is also found in this file. It is extracted from the file automatically by the linker, and the proper connections are made so that it can be called (that is, invoked or accessed) from the SQRT program.

HEADER FILES AND LIBRARY FILES

The relationship between library files and header files can be confusing, so let's review it. To use a library function like `sqrt()`, you must link the library file CS.LIB to your program. The appropriate functions from the library file are then connected to your program by the linker.

However, that's not the end of the story. The functions in your source file need to know the names and types of the functions and other elements in the library file. They are given this information in a header file. Each header file contains information for a particular group of functions. The functions themselves are in CS.LIB, but the information about them is scattered throughout a number of header files. The IOSTREAM.H header file contains information for various I/O functions and objects, including cout, while the MATH.H header file contains information for mathematics functions like sqrt(). If you were using memory management functions, you would include MEMORY:H, while string functions would require STRING.H, and so on.

Figure 3-13 shows the relationship of header files and library files to the other files used in program development.

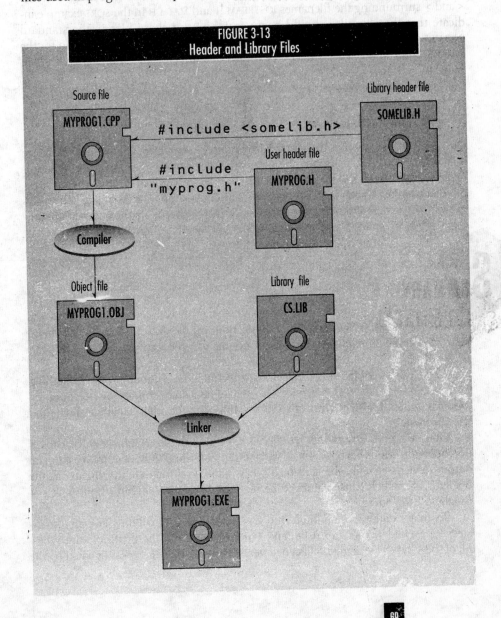

FIGURE 3-13
Header and Library Files

Source file
MYPROG1.CPP

`#include <somelib.h>`

Library header file
SOMELIB.H

User header file
MYPROG.H

`#include "myprog.h"`

Compiler

Object file
MYPROG1.OBJ

Library file
CS.LIB

Linker

MYPROG1.EXE

The use of header files is common in C++. Whenever you use a library function or a predefined object or operator, you will need to use a header file that contains appropriate declarations.

TWO WAYS TO USE #include

We should mention that you can use #include in two ways. The angle brackets < and > surrounding the filenames IOSTREAM.H and MATH.H in the SQRT example indicate that the compiler should begin searching for these files in the standard INCLUDE directory. This directory holds the header files supplied by Borland for the system. You can see what Turbo C++ thinks this directory is (and change it if you want) by selecting *Directory* from the Options menu.

Instead of angle brackets around the filename, you can also use quotation marks, as in

```
#include "myheader.h"
```

Quotation marks instruct the compiler to begin its search for the header file in the *current* directory; this is usually the directory that contains the source file. You normally use quotation marks for header files you write yourself (a situation we'll explore in Chapter 15, on larger programs). Either quotation marks or angle brackets work in any case, but making the appropriate choice speeds up the compilation process slightly by giving the compiler a hint about where to find the file.

SUMMARY

In this chapter we've learned that a major building block of C++ programs is the *function*. A function named main() is always the first one executed when a program is executed.

A function is composed of *statements*, which tell the computer to do something. Each statement ends with a semicolon. A statement may contain one or more *expressions*, which are sequences of variables and operators that usually evaluate to a specific value.

Output is most commonly handled in C++ with the cout object and << insertion operator, which together cause variables or constants to be sent to the standard output device—usually the screen. Input is handled with cin and the extraction operator >>, which cause values to be received from the standard input device—usually the keyboard.

Six major data types are built into C++: char, int, and long int are the integer types; and float, double, and long double are the floating-point types. All of these types are signed. Unsigned versions of the integer types, signaled by the keyword `unsigned`, hold numbers twice as large. The `const` keyword stipulates that a variable's value will not change in the course of a program.

A variable is converted from one type to another in mixed expressions (those involving different data types) and by casting, which allows the programmer to specify a conversion.

C++ employs the usual arithmetic operators `+`, `-`, `*`, and `/`. In addition, the remainder operator, `%`, returns the remainder of integer division.

The arithmetic assignment operators `+=`, `+-`, and so on, perform an arithmetic operation and an assignment simultaneously. The increment and decrement operators `++` and `--` increase or decrease a variable by 1.

Preprocessor directives consist of instructions to the compiler, rather than to the computer. The `#include` directive tells the compiler to insert another file into the present source file, and the `#define` directive tells it to substitute one thing for another.

If you use a library function in your program, the code for the function is in a library file, which is automatically linked to your program. A header file containing the function's declaration must be inserted into your source file with an `#include` statement.

QUESTIONS

1. Dividing a program into functions
   a. is the key to object-oriented programming
   b. makes the program easier to conceptualize
   c. may reduce the size of the program
   d. makes the program run faster

2. A function name must be followed by _____.

3. A function body is delimited by _____.

4. Why is the `main()` function special?

5. A C++ instruction that tells the computer to do something is called a

_____.

6. Write an example of a normal C++ comment and an example of an old-fashioned `/*` comment.

7. An expression
   a. usually evaluates to a numerical value
   b. indicates the emotional state of the program
   c. always occurs outside a function
   d. may be part of a statement

8. Specify how many bytes are occupied by the following data types in Turbo C++ and Borland C++:
   a. Type `int`
   b. Type `long double`
   c. Type `float`
   d. Type `long`

9. True or false: A variable of type `char` can hold the value 301.

10 What kind of program elements are the following?
   a. `12`
   b. `'a'`
   c. `4.28915`
   d. `JungleJim`
   e. `JungleJim()`

11. Write statements that display on the screen
   a. the character 'x'
   b. the name *Jim*
   c. the number 509

12. True or false: In an assignment statement, the value on the left of the equals sign is always equal to the value on the right.

13. Write a statement that displays the variable `george` in a field 10 characters wide.

14. What header file must you `#include` with your source file to use `cout` and `cin`?

15. Write a statement that gets a numer l value from the keyboard and places it in the variable `temp`.

16. What header file must you `#incl ` with your program to use `setw` and `endl`?

17. Three exceptions to the rule that he compiler ignores white space are _____, _____, and _____.

18. True or false: It's perfectly all right to se variables of different data types in the same arithmetic expression.

19. The expression `11%3` evaluates to _____.

20. An arithmetic assignment operator co ines the effect of what two operators?

21. Write a statement that uses an arithm c assignment operator to increase the value of the variable `temp` by 23. Writ the same statement without the arithmetic assignment operator.

22. The increment operator increases the v e of a variable by how much?

23. Assuming `var1` starts with the value 20, what will the following code fragment print out?

```
cout << var1--;
cout << ++var1;
```

24. In the examples we've seen so far, header files have been used for what purpose?
25. If you use the Small memory model, what library file must be linked to your program to provide standard library functions?

EXERCISES

1. Assuming there are 7.481 gallons in a cubic foot, write a program that asks the user to enter a number of gallons, and then displays the equivalent in cubic feet.
2. Write a program that generates the following table:

```
1990        135
1991       7290
1992      11300
1993      16200
```

Use a single **cout** statement for all output.

3. Write a program that generates the following output:

```
10
20
19
```

Use an integer constant for the 10, an arithmetic assignment operator to generate the 20, and a decrement operator to generate the 19.

LOOPS AND DECISIONS

Not many programs execute all their statements in strict order from beginning to end. Most programs (like many humans) decide what to do in response to changing circumstances. The flow of control jumps from one part of the program to another, depending on calculations performed in the program. Program statements that cause such jumps are called *control statements*. There are two major categories: loops and decisions.

How many times a loop is executed, or whether a decision results in the execution of a section of code, depends on whether certain expressions are true or false. These expressions typically involve a kind of operator called a *relational operator*, which compares two values. Since the operation of loops and decisions is so closely involved with these operators, we'll examine them first.

RELATIONAL OPERATORS

A relational operator compares two values. The values can be any built-in C++ data type, such as **char**, **int**, and **float**, or—as we'll see later—they can be user-defined classes. The comparison involves such relationships as *equal to, less than, greater than*, and so on. The result of the comparison is true or false; for example, either two values are equal (true), or they're not (false).

Our first program, RELAT, demonstrates relational operators in a comparison of integer variables and constants.

```
// relat.cpp
// demonstrates relational operators
#include <iostream.h>

void main()
    {
    int numb;

    cout << "Enter a number: ";
    cin >> numb;
```

```
    cout << "numb<10  is " << (numb < 10)  << endl;
    cout << "numb>10  is " << (numb > 10)  << endl;
    cout << "numb==10 is " << (numb == 10) << endl;
    }
```

This program performs three kinds of comparisons between 10 and a number entered by the user. Here's the output when the user enters 20:

```
Enter a number: 20
numb<10  is 0
numb>10  is 1
numb==10 is 0
```

The first expression is true if numb is less than 10. The second expression is true if numb is greater than 10, and the third is true if numb is equal to 10. As you can see from the output, the C++ compiler considers that a true expression has the value 1, while a false expression has the value 0. Some languages have special Boolean variables to represent true and false values, but C++ does not. It uses the integer values 0 and 1 instead.

Here's the complete list of C++ relational operators:

Operator	Meaning
>	Greater than
<	Less than
==	Equal to
!=	Not equal to
>=	Greater than or equal to
<=	Less than or equal to

Now let's look at some expressions that use relational operators, and also look at the value of each expression. The first two lines are assignment statements that set the values of the variables harry and jane. You might want to hide the comments with your old Jose Canseco baseball card and see if you can predict which expressions evaluate to true and which to false.

```
jane = 44;          // assignment statement
harry = 12;         // assignment statement
(jane == harry)     // false
(harry <= 12)       // true
(jane > harry)      // true
(jane >= 44)        // true
(harry != 12)       // false
(7 < harry)         // true
(0)                 // false (by definition)
(44)                // true (since it's not 0)
```

Note that the equals operator, ==, uses two equals signs. A common mistake is to use a single equals sign—the assignment operator—as a relational operator. This is a nasty bug, since the compiler won't notice anything wrong. However, your program won't do what you want.

Although C++ generates a 1 to indicate true, it assumes that any value other than 0 (such as –7 or 44) is true; only 0 is false. Thus the last expression in the list is true.

Now let's see how these operators are used in typical situations. We'll examine loops first, then decisions.

LOOPS

Loops cause a section of your program to be repeated a certain number of times. The repetition continues while a condition is true. When the condition becomes false, the loop ends and control passes to the statements following the loop.

There are three kinds of loops in C++: the for loop, the while loop, and the do loop.

THE for LOOP

The for loop is (for many people, anyway) the easiest to understand of the C++ loops. All its loop-control elements are gathered in one place, while in the other loop constructions they are scattered about the program, which can make it harder to unravel how these loops work. Also, the for loop is a key concept in other languages; for a long time it was the *only* loop construction available in BASIC, for example.

The for loop executes a section of code a fixed number of times. It's usually (although not always) used when you know, before entering the loop, how many times you want to execute the code.

Here's an example, FORDEMO, that displays the squares of the numbers from 0 to 14:

```
// fordemo.cpp
// demonstrates simple FOR loop
#include <iostream.h>

void main()
   {
   int j;                      // define a loop variable

   for(j=0; j<15; ++j)         // loop from 0 to 14,
      cout << j * j << "  ";    // displaying the square of j
   }
```

Here's the output:

```
0  1  4  9  16  25  36  49  64  81  100  121  144  169  196
```

How does this work? The for statement controls the loop. It consists of the keyword for, followed by parentheses that contain three expressions separated by semicolons:

```
for(j=0; j<15; j++)
```

These three expressions are the *initialization expression*, the *test expression*, and the *increment expression*, as shown in Figure 4-1.

These three expressions usually (but not always) involve the same variable, which we can call the *loop variable*. In the FORDEMO example the loop variable is j. It's defined before the loop begins.

The *body* of the loop is the code to be executed each time through the loop. Repeating this code is the *raison-d'être* for the loop. In this example the loop body consists of a single statement:

```
cout << j * j << "  ";
```

This statement prints out the square of j, followed by two spaces. The square is found by multiplying j by itself. As the loop executes, j goes through the sequence 0, 1, 2, 3, and so on up to 14; so the squares of these numbers are displayed—0, 1, 4, 9, up to 196.

Note that the for statement is not followed by a semicolon. That's because the for statement and the loop body are *together* considered to be a program statement.

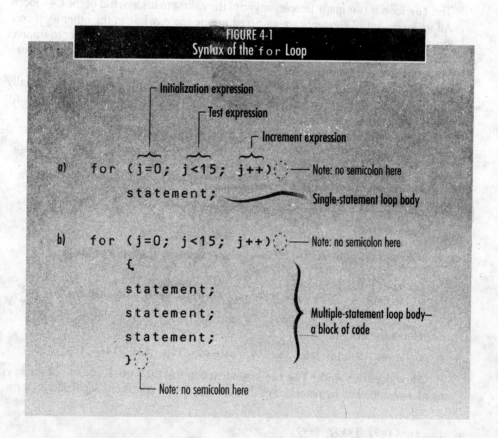

FIGURE 4-1
Syntax of the for Loop

This is an important detail. If you put a semicolon after the `for` statement, the compiler will think there is no loop body, and the program will do things you don't expect.

Let's see how the three expressions in the `for` statement control the loop.

The Initialization Expression

The initialization expression is executed only once, when the loop first starts. It gives the loop variable an initial value. In the FORDEMO example it sets `j` to 0.

The Test Expression

The test expression usually involves a relational operator. It is evaluated each time through the loop, just before the body of the loop is executed. It determines whether the loop will be executed again. If the test expression is true, the loop is executed one more time. If it's false, the loop ends, and control passes to the statements following the loop. In the FORDEMO example there are no statements following the loop, so the program ends when the test expression becomes false.

The Increment Expression

The increment expression changes the value of the loop variable, often by incrementing it. It is always executed at the end of the loop, after the loop body has been executed. Here the increment operator `++` adds 1 to `j` each time through the loop. Figure 4-2 shows a flowchart of a `for` loop's operation.

How Many Times?

The loop in the FOR example executes exactly 15 times. The first time, `j` is 0. This is ensured in the initialization expression. The last time through the loop, `j` is 14. This is determined by the test expression `j<15`. When `j` becomes 15, the loop terminates; the loop body is not executed when `j` has this value. The arrangement shown is commonly used to do something a fixed number of times: start at 0, use a test expression with the less-than operator and a value equal to the desired number of iterations, and increment the loop variable after each iteration.

Here's another `for` loop example:

```
for(count=0; count<100; count++)
    // loop body
```

How many times will the loop body be repeated here? Exactly 100 times, with `count` going from 0 to 99.

Multiple Statements in Loop Body

Of course you may want to execute more than one statement in the loop body. Multiple statements are delimited by braces, just as functions are. Note that there is no semicolon following the final brace of the loop body, although there are semicolons

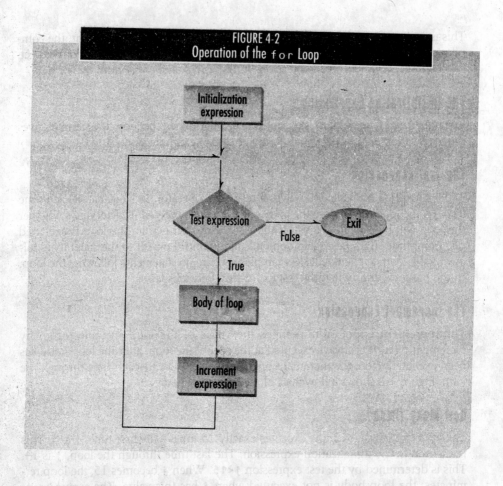

FIGURE 4-2
Operation of the for Loop

following the individual statements in the loop body. See Figure 4-1-b for the syntax of a multistatement for loop.

The next example, CUBELIST, uses three statements in the loop body. It prints out the cubes of the numbers from 1 to 10, using a two-column format.

```
// cubelist.cpp
// lists cubes from 1 to 10
#include <iostream.h>
#include <iomanip.h>                          // for setw

void main()
    {
    int numb;                                 // define loop variable

    for(numb=1; numb<=10; numb++)             // loop from 1 to 10
        {
```

```
cout << setw(4) << numb;            // display 1st column
int cube = numb*numb*numb;          // calculate cube
cout << setw(6) << cube << endl;    // display 2nd column
}
}
```

Here's the output from the program:

```
 1     1
 2     8
 3    27
 4    64
 5   125
 6   216
 7   343
 8   512
 9   729
10  1000
```

We've made another change in the program, to show there's nothing immutable about the format used in the last example. The loop variable is initialized to 1, not to 0. It also ends at 10, not at 9, by virtue of <=, the less-than-or-equal-to operator. The effect is that the loop body is executed 10 times, with the loop variable running from 1 to 10 (not from 0 to 9).

Blocks and Variable Visibility

The loop body, which consists of braces delimiting several statements, is called a **block** of code. One important aspect of a block is that a variable defined inside the block is not visible outside it. In CUBELIST we define the variable **cube** inside the block, in the statement

```
int cube = numb*numb*numb;
```

You can't access this variable outside the block; it's only visible within the braces. Thus if you placed the statement

```
cube = 10;
```

after the loop body, the compiler would signal an error because the variable **cube** would be undefined outside the loop.

One advantage of restricting the visibility of variables is that the same variable name can be used within different blocks in the same program. We'll see examples later. (Defining variables inside a block, as we did in CUBELIST, is common in C++ but is not popular in C.)

Indentation and Loop Style

Good programming style dictates that the loop body be indented—that is, shifted right, relative to the loop statement (and to the rest of the program). In the FOR example one line is indented, and in CUBELIST the entire block, including the braces, is indented. This indentation is an important visual aid to the programmer: It makes it easy to see where the loop body begins and ends. The compiler doesn't care whether you indent or not (at least there's no way to tell if it cares).

There is a common variation on the style we use for loops in this book. We show the braces aligned vertically, but some programmers prefer to place the opening brace just after the loop statement, like this:

```
for(numb=1; numb<=10; numb++)  {
    cout << setw(4) << numb;
    int cube = numb*numb*numb;
    cout << setw(6) << cube << endl;
    }
```

This saves a line in the listing but makes it more difficult to read, since the opening brace is harder to see and harder to match with the corresponding closing brace

USING TURBO C++ DEBUGGING FEATURES

You can use the debugging features built into Turbo C++ (or Borland C++)to create a dramatic animated display of loop operation. The key feature is *single-stepping*. The Turbo C++ IDE makes this easy. With your program displayed in an Edit window, simply press the (F8) function key. If necessary, the program will be recompiled. Then the first line of the program will be highlighted. The highlighted line is the line about to be executed. Each time you press (F8), the highlight moves to the next line.

Single-Stepping in CUBELIST

Try this with CUBELIST. Open an Edit window on CUBELIST.CPP, make sure the window is active, and press (F8). The first executable line will be highlighted. (Preprocessor directions and variable declarations are not considered executable.) Continue to press (F8). When you enter the for loop, you can watch the highlight cycle through the statements in the loop body.

The Watch Window

As you're single-stepping, you'll often find it useful to see how the values of certain variables change. To do this you can open a *Watch window*. Select *Watches* from the Debug menu, and from the submenu select *Add watch*. In the resulting dialog box, enter the name of the variable to be watched; in this case, enter numb. A window called *Watch* will appear on the bottom of the screen; it will display the value of numb. As you step through the loop, the value of numb will change, and these changes will be reflected in the Watch window. You can add as many variables as you like to the Watch window; they will all be displayed.

Single-stepping and the Watch window are powerful debugging tools. If your loop doesn't behave as you think it should, you can use these features to monitor the values of key variables as you step through the loop. Usually the source of the problem will become clear.

for LOOP VARIATIONS

The increment expression doesn't need to increment the loop variable; it can perform any operation it likes. In the next example it *decrements* the loop variable. This program, FACTOR, asks the user to type in a number, and then calculates the factorial of this number. (The factorial is calculated by multiplying the original number by all the positive integers smaller than itself. Thus the factorial of 5 is 5*4*3*2*1, or 120.)

```
// factor.cpp
// calculates factorials, demonstrates FOR loop
#include <iostream.h>

void main()
    {
    unsigned int numb;
    unsigned long fact=1;             // long for larger numbers

    cout << "\nEnter a number: ";
    cin >> numb;                      // get number

    for(int j=numb; j>0; j--)         // multiply 1 by
        fact *= j;                    // numb, numb-1, ..., 2, 1
    cout << "Factorial is " << fact;  // result is factorial
    }
```

In this example the initialization expression sets j to the value entered by the user. The test expression causes the loop to execute as long as j is greater than 0. The increment expression decrements j after each iteration.

We've used type unsigned long for the factorial, since the factorials even of small numbers are very large, as can be seen in the following output:

```
Enter a number: 10
Factorial is 3628800
```

Even using type unsigned long, the largest number you can use for input is 12.

Variables Defined in for Statements

There's another wrinkle in this program: The loop variable j is defined inside the for statement:

```
for(int j=numb; j>0; j--)
```

This is a common construction in C++. It defines the variable as close as possible to its point of use in the listing. Variables defined in the loop statement this way are visible from the point of definition onward in the listing (unlike variables defined within a block, which are visible only within the block).

Multiple Initialization and Test Expressions

You can put more than one expression in the initialization part of the `for` statement, separating the different expressions by commas. You can also have more than one increment expression, although you can have only one test expression. Here's an example:

```
for( j=0, alpha=100; j<50; j++, beta-- )
   {
   // body of loop
   }
```

This example has a normal loop variable `j`, but it also initializes another variable, `alpha`, and increments a third, `beta`. The variables `alpha` and `beta` don't need to have anything to do with each other, or with `j`. Multiple initialization expressions and multiple increment expressions are separated by commas.

We'll avoid using such multiple expressions. While this approach can make the listing more concise, it also tends to decrease its readability. It's always possible to use stand-alone statements to achieve the same effect.

THE while LOOP

The `for` loop does something a fixed number of times. What happens if you don't know how many times you want to do something before you start the loop? In this case a different kind of loop may be used: the `while` loop.

In the next example, ENDON0, we ask the user to enter a series of numbers. When the number entered is 0, the loop terminates. Notice that there's no way for the program to know in advance how many numbers will be typed before the 0 appears; that's up to the user.

```
// endon0.cpp
// demonstrates WHILE loop
#include <iostream.h>

void main()
   {
   int n = 99;          // make sure n isn't initialized to 0

   while( n != 0 )      // loop until n is 0
      cin >> n;         // read a number into n
   }
```

Here's some sample output. The user enters numbers, and the loop continues until 0 is entered, at which point the program terminates.

```
1
27
33
144
9
0
```

The `while` loop looks like a simplified version of the `for` loop. It contains a test expression but no initialization or increment expressions. Figure 4-3 shows the syntax of the `while` loop.

As long as the test expression is true, the loop continues to be executed. In ENDON0, the text expression

```
n != 0
```

is true until the user enters 0.

Figure 4-4 shows the operation of a `while` loop. The simplicity of the `while` loop is a bit illusory. Although there is no initialization expression, the loop variable (`n` in ENDON0) must be initialized before the loop begins. The loop body must also contain some statement that changes the value of the loop variable; otherwise the loop would never end. In ENDON0 it's `cin>>j;`.

Multiple Statements in `while` Loop

The next example, WHILE4, uses multiple statements in a `while` loop. It's a variation of the CUBELIST program shown earlier with a `for` loop, but it calculates the fourth power, instead of the cube, of a series of integers. Let's assume that in this

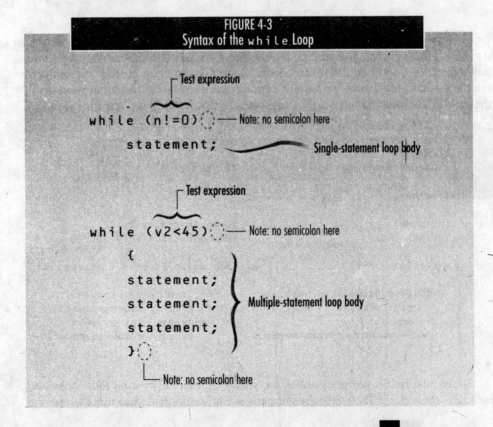

FIGURE 4-3
Syntax of the `while` Loop

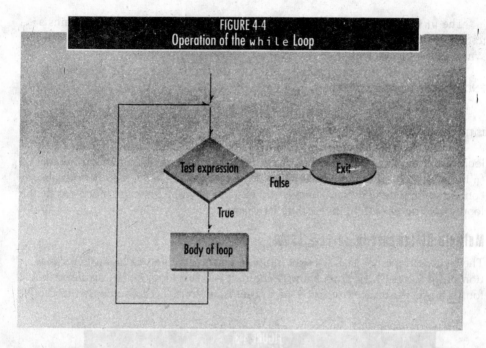

FIGURE 4-4
Operation of the while Loop

program it's important to put the results in a column 4 digits wide. To ensure that the results fit this column width, we must stop the loop before the results become larger than 9999. Without prior calculation we don't know what number will generate a result of this size, so we let the program figure it out. The test expression in the while statement terminates the program before the powers become too large.

```
// while4.cpp
// prints numbers raised to fourth power
#include <iostream.h>
#include <iomanip.h>                // for setw

void main()
    {
    int pow=1;                      // power initially 1
    int numb=1;                     // numb goes from 1 to ???

    while( pow<9999 )               // loop while power < 4 digits
        {
        cout << setw(2) << numb;    // display number
        cout << setw(5) << pow << endl;  // display fourth power
        ++numb;                     // get ready for next power
        pow = numb*numb*numb*numb;  // calculate fourth power
        } .
    }
```

To find the fourth power of numb, we simply multiply it by itself four times. Each time through the loop we increment numb. But we don't use numb in the test expression in `while`; instead, the resulting value of `pow` determines when to terminate the loop. Here's the output:

```
1    1
2   16
3   81
4  256
5  625
6 1296
7 2401
8 4096
9 6561
```

The next number would be 10,000—too wide for our four-digit column; but by this time the loop has terminated.

Precedence: Arithmetic and Relational Operators

The next program touches on the question of operator precedence. It generates the famous sequence of numbers called *the Fibonacci series*. Here are the first few terms of the series:

```
1   1   2   3   5   8   13   21   34   55
```

Each term is found by adding the two previous ones: 1+1 is 2, 1+2 is 3, 2+3 is 5, 3+5 is 8, and so on. The Fibonacci series has applications in amazingly diverse fields, from sorting methods in computer science to the number of spirals in sunflowers.

One of the most interesting aspects of the Fibonacci series is its relation to the *golden ratio*. The golden ratio is supposed to be the ideal proportion in architecture and art, and was used in the design of ancient Greek temples. As the Fibonacci series is carried out further and further, the ratio of the last two terms approaches closer and closer to the golden ratio. Here's the listing for FIBO.CPP:

```cpp
// fibo.cpp
// demonstrates WHILE loops using fibonacci series
#include <iostream.h>

void main()
    {                                       // largest unsigned long
    const unsigned long limit = 4294967295;
    unsigned long next=0;                   // next-to-last term
    unsigned long last=1;                   // last term

    while( next < limit / 2 )   // don't let results get too big
        {
        cout << last << "  ";   // display last term
        long sum = next + last; // add last two terms
        next = last;            // variables move forward
        last = sum;             //    in the series
        }
    }
```

Here's the output:

```
 1   1   2   3   5   8   13   21   34   55   89   144   233   377   610   987
1597   2584   4181   6765   10946   17711   28657   46368   75025   121393
196418   317811   514229   832040   1346269   2178309   3524578
5702887   9227465   14930352   24157817   39088169   63245986
102334155   165580141   267914296   433494437   701408733   1134903170
1836311903   2971215073
```

For you temple builders, the ratio of the last two terms gives an approximation of the golden ratio as 0.618033988—close enough for government work.

The FIBO program uses type **unsigned long**, the type that holds the largest positive integers. The test expression in the **while** statement terminates the loop before the numbers exceed the limit of this type. We define this limit as a **const** type, since it doesn't change. We must stop when **next** becomes larger than half the limit, otherwise **sum** would exceed the limit.

The test expression uses two operators:

```
(next < limit / 2)
```

Our intention is to compare **next** with the result of **limit/2**. That is, we want the division to be performed before the comparison. We could put parentheses around the division, to ensure that it's performed first:

```
(next < (limit/2) )
```

But we don't need the parentheses. Why not? Because arithmetic operators have a higher precedence than relational operators. This guarantees that **limit/2** will be evaluated before the comparison is made, even without the parentheses. We'll summarize the precedence situation later in this chapter, when we look at logical operators.

THE do LOOP

In a **while** loop, the test expression is evaluated at the *beginning* of the loop. If the test expression is false when the loop is entered, the loop body won't be executed at all. In some situations this is what you want. But sometimes you want to guarantee that the loop body is executed at least once, no matter what the initial state of the test expression. When this is the case you should use the **do** loop, which places the test expression at the *end* of the loop.

Our example, DIVDO, invites the user to enter two numbers: a dividend (the top number in a division) and a divisor (the bottom number). It then calculates the quotient (the answer) and the remainder, using the / and % operators, and prints out the result.

```
// divdo.cpp
// demonstrates DO loop
#include <iostream.h>

void main()
    {
```

```
long dividend, divisor;
char ch;

do                                          // start of do loop
    {                                       // do some processing
    cout << "Enter dividend: "; cin >> dividend;
    cout << "Enter divisor: ";  cin >> divisor;
    cout << "Quotient is " << dividend / divisor;
    cout << ", remainder is " << dividend % divisor;

    cout << "\nDo another? (y/n): ";  // do it again?
    cin >> ch;
    }
while( ch != 'n' );                         // loop condition
}
```

Most of this program resides within the **do** loop. First, the keyword **do** marks the beginning of the loop. Then, as with the other loops, braces delimit the body of the loop. Finally a **while** statement provides the test expression and terminates the loop. This **while** statement looks much like the one in a **while** loop, except for its position at the end of the loop, and the fact that it ends with a semicolon (which is easy to forget!). The syntax of the **do** loop is shown in Figure 4-5.

Following each computation, DIVDO asks if the user wants to do another. If so, the user enters a 'y' character, and the test expression

```
ch != 'n'
```

remains true. If the user enters **'n'**, the test expression becomes false and the loop terminates. Figure 4-6 flowcharts the **do** loop. Here's an example of **divdo**'s output:

```
Enter dividend: 11
Enter divisor: 3
Quotient is 3, remainder is 2
Do another? (y/n): y
Enter dividend: 222
Enter divisor: 17
Quotient is 13, remainder is 1
Do another? (y/n): n
```

WHEN TO USE WHICH LOOP

We've made some general statements about how loops are used. The **for** loop is appropriate when you know in advance how many times the loop will be executed. The **while** and **do** loops are used when you don't know in advance when the loop will terminate; the **while** when you may not want to execute the loop body even once, and the **do** loop when you're sure you want to execute the loop body at least once.

FIGURE 4-5
Syntax of the do Loop

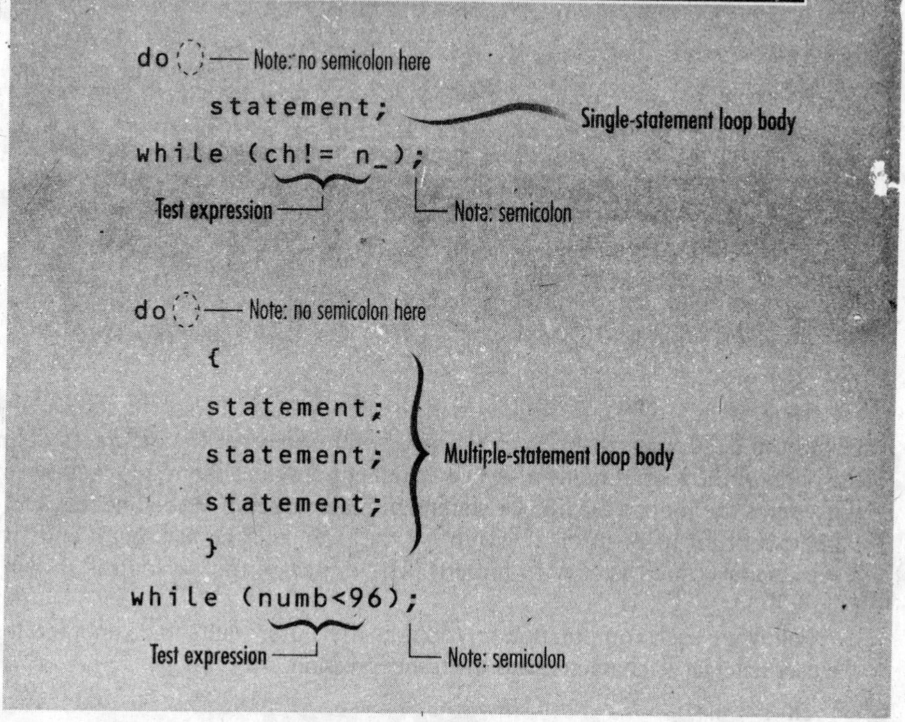

```
do ( )  — Note: no semicolon here

    statement;  ————————  Single-statement loop body

while (ch!= n_);

Test expression ——       └— Nota: semicolon


do ( )  — Note: no semicolon here

    {

    statement;

    statement;  }  Multiple-statement loop body

    statement;

    }

while (numb<96);

Test expression ——       └— Note: semicolon
```

These criteria are somewhat arbitrary. Which loop type to use is more a matter of style than of hard-and-fast rules. You can actually make any of the loop types work in almost any situation. You should choose the type that makes your program the clearest and easiest to follow.

DECISIONS

The decisions in a loop always relate to the same question: Should we do this (the loop body) again? As humans we would find it boring to be so limited in our decision-making processes. We need to decide, not only whether to go to work again today (continuing the loop), but also whether to buy a red shirt or a green one (or no shirt at all), whether to take a vacation, and if so, in the mountains or by the sea.

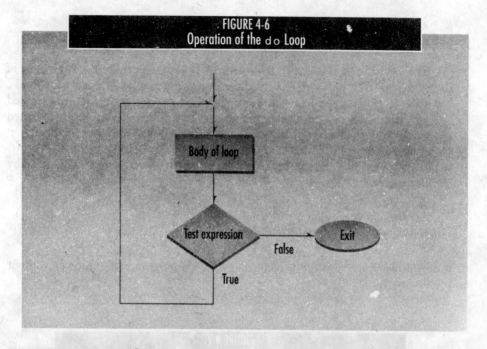

FIGURE 4-6
Operation of the do Loop

Programs also need to make these one-time decisions. In a program a decision causes a one-time jump to a different part of the program, depending on the value of an expression. Decisions can be made in C++ in several ways. The most important is with the **if...else** statement, which chooses between two alternatives. This statement can be used without the **else**, as a simple **if** statement. Another decision statement, **switch**, creates branches for multiple alternative sections of code, depending on the value of a single variable. Finally the *conditional operator* is used in specialized situations. We'll examine each of these constructions.

THE if STATEMENT

The **if** statement is the simplest of the decision statements. Our next program, IFDEMO, provides an example.

```
// ifdemo.cpp
// demonstrates IF statement
#include <iostream.h>

void main()
   {
   int x;

   cout << "Enter a number: ";
   cin >> x;
```

```
if( x > 100 )
    cout << "That number is greater than 100\n";
}
```

The if keyword is followed by a test expression in parentheses. The syntax of the if is shown in Figure 4-7. As you can see, the syntax of if is very much like that of while. The difference is that the statements following the if are executed only once if the test expression is true; the statements following while are executed repeatedly until the test expression becomes false. Figure 4-8 shows the operation of the if statement.

Here's an example of the IFDEMO program's output when the number entered by the user is greater than 100:

```
C>if
Enter a number: 2000
That number is greater than 100
C>
```

If the number entered is not greater than 100, the program will terminate without printing anything.

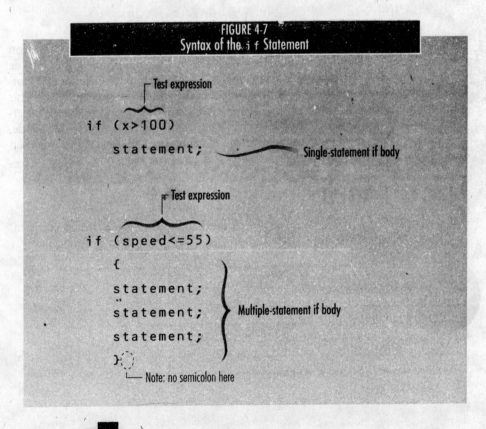

FIGURE 4-7
Syntax of the if Statement

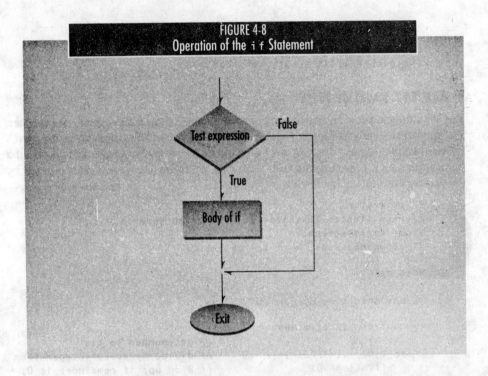

FIGURE 4-8
Operation of the if Statement

Multiple Statements in the if Body

As in loops, the code in an if body can consist of a single statement—as shown in the IFDEMO example—or of a block of statements delimited by braces. This variation on IFDEMO, called IF2, shows how that looks:

```
// if2.cpp
// demonstrates IF with multiline body
#include <iostream.h>

void main()
    {
    int x;

    cout << "Enter a number: ";
    cin >> x;
    if( x > 100 )
        {
        cout << "The number " << x;
        cout << " is greater than 100\n";
        }
    }
```

Here's some output from IF2:

```
Enter a number: 12345
The number 12345 is greater than 100
```

Nesting ifs Inside Loops

The loop and decision structures we've seen so far can be nested inside one another. You can nest ifs inside loops, loops inside ifs, ifs inside ifs, and so on. Here's an example, PRIME, that nests an if within a for loop. This example tells you if a number you enter is a prime number. (Prime numbers are integers divisible only by themselves and 1. The first few primes are 1, 3, 5, 7, 11, 13, 17, and so on.)

```
// prime.cpp
// demonstrates IF statement with prime numbers
#include <iostream.h>
#include <process.h>      // for exit()

void main()
    {
    unsigned long n, j;

    cout << "Enter a number: ";
    cin >> n;                           // get number to test
    for(j=2; j < n/2; j++)              // divide by every integer from
        if(n%j == 0)                    // 2 on up; if remainder is 0,
            {                           // it's divisible by j
            cout << "It's not prime; divisible by " << j << endl;
            exit(0);                    // exit from the program
            }
    cout << "It's prime\n";
    }
```

In this example the user enters a number that is assigned to n. The program then uses a for loop to divide n by all the numbers from 2 up to n/2. The divisor is j, the loop variable. If any value of j divides evenly into n, then n is not prime. When a number divides evenly into another, the remainder is 0; so we use the remainder operator % in the if statement to test for this condition with each value of j. If the number is not prime, we tell the user and we exit from the program.

Here's some output:

```
C>prime
Enter a number: 13
It's prime
C>prime
Enter a number: 22229
It's prime
C>prime
Enter a number: 22231
It's not prime; divisible by 11
```

(Beware: If you enter a number that is substantially larger than those shown, and it happens to be prime, the program will take a long time to execute.)

Notice that there are no braces around the loop body. This is because the **if** statement and the statements in *its* body, are considered to be a single statement.

Library Function exit()

When PRIME discovers that a number is not prime, it exits immediately, since there's no use proving more than once that a number isn't prime. This is accomplished with the library function **exit()**. This function causes the program to terminate, no matter where it is in the listing. It has no return value. Its single argument, 0 in our example, is returned to the operating system when the program exits. (This value is useful in batch files, where you can use the ERRORLEVEL value to query the return value provided by **exit()**. The value 0 is normally used for a successful termination; other numbers indicate errors.)

THE if...else STATEMENT

The **if** statement lets you do something if a condition is true. If it isn't true, nothing happens. But suppose we want to do one thing if a condition is true, and do something else if it's false. That's where the **if...else** statement comes in. It consists of an **if** statement, followed by a statement or block of statements, followed by the keyword **else**, followed by *another* statement or block of statements. The syntax is shown in Figure 4-9.

Here's a variation of our IF example, with an **else** added to the **if**:

```
// ifelse.cpp
// demonstrates IF...ELSE statememt
#include <iostream.h>

void main()
    {
    int x;

    cout << "\nEnter a number: ";
    cin >> x;
    if( x > 100 )
        cout << "That number is greater than 100\n";
    else
        cout << "That number is not greater than 100\n";
    }
```

If the test expression in the **if** statement is true, the program prints one message; if it isn't, it prints the other.

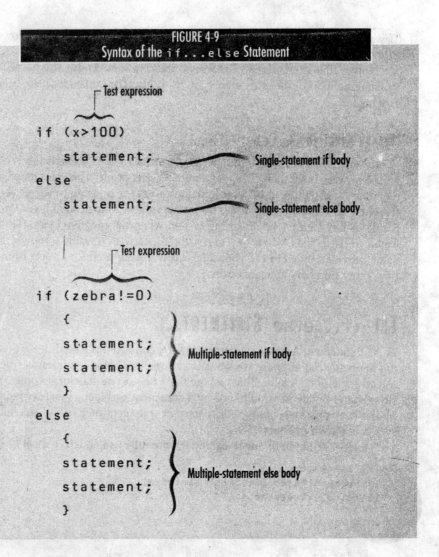

FIGURE 4-9
Syntax of the if...else Statement

Test expression

```
if (x>100)

    statement;          Single-statement if body

else

    statement;          Single-statement else body



                Test expression

if (zebra!=0)

    {

    statement;
                        Multiple-statement if body
    statement;

    }

else

    {

    statement;
                        Multiple-statement else body
    statement;

    }
```

Here's some output:

```
C>ifelse
Enter a number: 300
That number is greater than 100
C>ifelse
Enter a number: 3
That number is not greater than 100
C>
```

The operation of the if...else statement is shown in Figure 4-10.

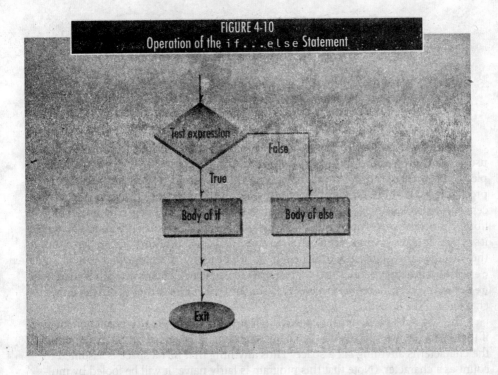

FIGURE 4-10
Operation of the if...else Statement

The getche() Library Function

Our next example shows an if...else statement embedded in a while loop. It also introduces a new library function: getche(). This program, CHCOUNT, counts the number of words and the number of characters in a phrase typed in by the user.

```
// chcount.cpp
// counts characters and words typed in
#include <iostream.h>
#include <conio.h>                    // for getche()

void main()
    {
    int chcount=0;                   // counts non-space characters
    int wdcount=1;                   // counts spaces between words
    char ch = 'a';                   // ensure it isn't '\r'

    while( ch != '\r' )              // loop until Enter typed
        {
        ch = getche();               // read one character
```

```
        if( ch==' ' )              // if it's a space
            wdcount++;             // count a word
        else                       // otherwise,
            chcount++;             // count a character
        }                          // display results
    cout << "\nWords=" << wdcount << endl
         << "Letters=" << chcount-1 << endl;
    }
```

So far we've used only `cin` and `>>` for input. That approach requires that the user always presses the (ENTER) key to inform the program that the input is complete. This is true even for single characters: The user must type the character, then press (ENTER). However, as in the present example, a program often needs to process each character typed by the user without waiting for an Enter. The `getche()` library function performs this service. It returns each character typed, as soon as it's typed. It takes no arguments, and requires the CONIO.H header file. In CHCOUNT the value of the character returned from `getche()` is assigned to `ch`. (The `getche()` function echoes the character to the screen. That's why there's an `e` in `getche`. Another function, `getch()`, is similar to `getche()` but doesn't echo the character to the screen.)

The `if...else` statement causes the word count `wdcount` to be incremented if the character is a space, and the character count `chcount` to be incremented if the character is anything *but* a space. Thus anything that *isn't* a space is assumed to count as a character. (Note that this program is fairly naïve; it will be fooled by multiple spaces between words.)

Here's some sample interaction with CHCOUNT:

```
For while and do
Words=4
Letters=13
```

The test expression in the `while` statement checks to see if `ch` is the '\r' character, which is the character received from the keyboard when the (ENTER) key is pressed. If so, the loop and the program terminate.

Assignment Expressions

The CHCOUNT.CPP program can be rewritten to save a line of code and demonstrate some important points about assignment expressions and precedence. The result is a construction that looks rather peculiar but is commonly used in C++ (and in C).

Here's the rewritten version, called CHCNT2:

```
// chcnt2.cpp
// counts characters and words typed in
#include <iostream.h>
#include <conio.h>              // for getche()

void main()
    {
```

```
    int chcount=0;
    int wdcount=1;               // space between two words
    char ch;

    while( (ch=getche()) != '\r' )   // loop until Enter typed
        {
        if( ch==' ' )            // if it's a space
            wdcount++;           // count a word
        else                     // otherwise,
            chcount++;           // count a character
        }                        // display results
    cout << "\nWords=" << wdcount << endl
         << "Letters=" << chcount-1 << endl;

    }
```

The value returned by getche() is assigned to ch as before, but this entire assignment expression has been moved inside the test expression for while. The assignment expression is compared with '\r' to see if the loop should terminate. This works because the entire assignment expression takes on the value used in the assignment. That is, if getche() returns 'a', then not only does ch take on the value 'a', but the expression

```
    (ch=getche())
```

also takes on the value 'a'. This is then compared with '\r'.

The fact that assignment expressions have a value is also used in statements such as

```
    x = y = z = 0;
```

This is perfectly legal in C++. First, z takes on the value 0, then z = 0 takes on the value 0, which is assigned to y. Then the expression y = z = 0 likewise takes on the value 0, which is assigned to x.

The parentheses around the assignment expression in

```
    (ch=getche())
```

are necessary because the assignment operator = has a lower precedence than the relational operator !=. Without the parentheses the expression would be evaluated as

```
    while( ch = (getche() != '\r') )   // not what we want
```

which would assign a true or false value to ch; not what we want.

The while statement in CHCNT2 provides a lot of power in a small space. It is not only a test expression (checking ch to see if it's '\r'); it also gets a character from the keyboard and assigns it to ch. It's also not easy to unravel the first time you see it.

Nested if...else Statements

Remember adventure games? You move your "character" around an imaginary landscape, and discover castles, sorcerers, treasure, and so on. This program, ADIFELSE, models a small part of an adventure game.

```
// adifelse.cpp
// demonstrates IF...ELSE with adventure program
#include <iostream.h>
#include <conio.h>        // for getche()

void main()
   {
   char dir='a';
   int x=10, y=10;

   cout << "Type Enter to quit\n";
   while( dir != '\r' )          // until Enter is typed
      {
      cout << "\nYour location is " << x << ", " << y;
      cout << "\nPress direction key (n, s, e, w): ";
      dir = getche();            // get character
      if( dir=='n')              // go north
         y--;
      else
         if( dir=='s' )          // go south
            y++;
         else
            if( dir=='e' )       // go east
               x++;
            else
               if( dir=='w' )    // go west
                  x--;
      } // end while
   } // end main
```

When the game starts, you find yourself on a barren moor. You can go one "unit" north, south, east, or west, while the program keeps track of where you are, and reports your position, which starts at coordinates 10,10. Unfortunately, nothing exciting happens to your character, no matter where you go; the moor stretches on almost limitlessly in all directions, as shown in Figure 4-11. We'll try to provide a little more excitement to this game later on.

Here's some sample interaction with ADIFELSE:

```
Your location is 10, 10
Press direction key (n, s, e, w): n
Your location is 10, 9
Press direction key (n, s, e, w): e
Your location is 11, 9
Press direction key (n, s, e, w):
```

You can press the (ENTER) key to exit from the program.

This program may not cause a sensation in the video arcades, but it does demonstrate one way to handle multiple branches. It uses an **if** statement nested inside an **if...else** statement, which is nested inside another **if...else** statement,

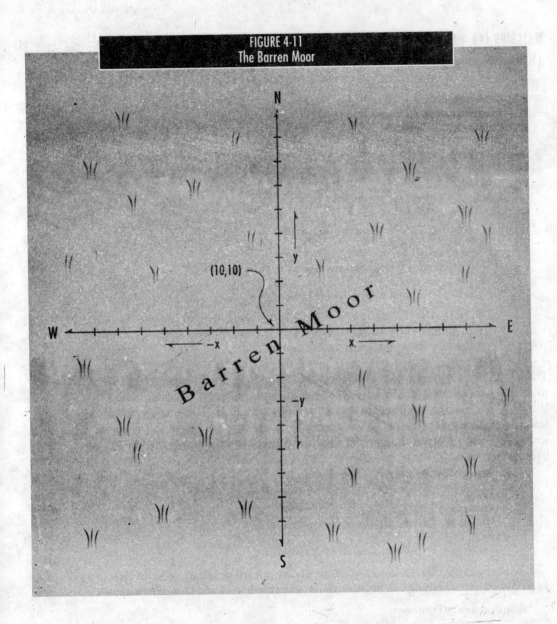

FIGURE 4-11
The Barren Moor

which is nested inside yet another **if...else** statement. If the first test condition is false, the second one is examined, and so on until all four have been checked. If any one proves true, the appropriate action is taken—changing the **x** or **y** coordinate—and the program exits from all the nested decisions. Such a nested group of **if...else** statements is called a *decision tree*.

Matching the else

There's a potential problem in nested if...else statements: You can inadvertently match an else with the wrong if. BADELSE provides an example:

```
// badelse.cpp
// demonstrates ELSE matched with wrong IF
#include <iostream.h>

void main()
    {
    int a, b, c;
    cout << "Enter a, b, and c:\n";
    cin >> a >> b >> c;

    if( a==b )
        if( b==c )
            cout << "a, b, and c are the same";
    else
        cout << "a and b are different";
    }
```

We've used multiple values with a single cin. Press (ENTER) following each value you type in; the three values will be assigned to a, b, and c.

What happens if you enter 2, then 3, and then 3? Variable a is 2, and b is 3. They're different, so the first test expression is false, and you would expect the else to be invoked, printing a and b are different. But in fact nothing is printed. Why not? Because the else is matched with the wrong if. The indentation would lead you to believe that the else is matched with the first if, but in fact it goes with the second if. Here's the rule: An else is matched with the last if that doesn't have its own else.

Here's a corrected version:

```
if(a==b)
    if(b==c)
        cout << "a, b, and c are the same";
    else
        cout << "b and c are different";
```

We changed the indentation and also the phrase printed by the else body. Now if you enter 2, 3, 3, nothing will be printed. But entering 2, 2, 3 will cause the output

```
b and c are different
```

If you really want to pair an else with an earlier if, you can use braces around the inner if:

```
if(a==b)
    {
    if(b==c)
        cout << "a, b, and c are the same";
```

```
        }
    else
        cout << "a and b are different";
```

Here the `else` is paired with the first `if`, as the indentation indicates. The braces make the material within them invisible to the following `else`.

THE else...if CONSTRUCTION

The nested `if...else` statements in the ADIFELSE program look clumsy and can be hard—for humans—to interpret, especially if they are nested more deeply than shown. However there's another approach to writing the same statements. We need only reformat the program, obtaining the next example, ADELSEIF.

```
// adelseif.cpp
// demonstrates ELSE...IF with adventure program
#include <iostream.h>
#include <conio.h>        // for getche()

void main()
    {
    char dir='a';
    int x=10, y=10;

    cout << "Type Enter to quit\n";
    while( dir != '\r' )            // until Enter is typed
        {
        cout << "\nYour location is " << x << ", " << y;
        cout << "\nPress direction key (n, s, e, w): ";
        dir = getche();            // get character
        if( dir=='n' )             // go north
            y--;
        else if( dir=='s' )        // go south
            y++;
        else if( dir=='e' )        // go east
            x++;
        else if( dir=='w' )        // go west
            x--;
        }  // end while
    }  // end main
```

The compiler sees this as identical to ADIFELSE, but we've rearranged the `if`'s so that they directly follow the `else`'s. The result looks almost like a new keyword: `else if`. The program goes down the ladder of `else...if`'s until one of the test expressions is true. It then executes the following statement and exits from the ladder. This format is clearer and easier to follow than the `if...else` approach.

THE switch STATEMENT

If you have a large decision tree, and all the decisions depend on the value of the same variable, you will probably want to consider a **switch** statement instead of a series of **if...else** or **else if** constructions. Here's a simple example called PLAT-TERS that will appeal to nostalgia buffs:

```
// platters.cpp
// demonstrates SWITCH statement
#include <iostream.h>

void main()
    {
    int speed;                          // turntable speed

    cout << "\nEnter 33, 45, or 78: ";
    cin >> speed;                       // user enters speed
    switch(speed)                       // selection based on speed
        {
        case 33:                        // user entered 33
            cout << "LP album\n";
            break;
        case 45:                        // user entered 45
            cout << "Single selection\n";
            break;
        case 78:                        // user entered 78
            cout << "Obsolete format\n";
            break;
        }
    }
```

This program prints one of three possible messages, depending on whether the user inputs the number **33**, **45**, or **78**. The keyword **switch** is followed by a *switch variable* in parentheses:

```
switch(speed)
```

Braces then delimit a number of **case** statements. Each **case** keyword is followed by a constant, which is not in parentheses but is followed by a colon:

```
case 33:
```

The data type of the case constants should match that of the switch variable. Figure 4-12 shows the syntax of the **switch** statement.

Before entering the switch, the program should assign a value to the switch variable. This value will usually match a constant in one of the **case** statements. When this is the case (pun intended!), the statements immediately following the keyword **case** will be executed, until a **break** is reached.

Here's an example of **platter**'s output:

```
Enter 33, 45, or 78: 45
Single selection
```

The break Statement

PLATTERS has a **break** statement at the end of each **case** section. The **break** keyword causes the entire **switch** statement to exit. Control goes to the first statement following the end of the **switch** construction, which in PLATTERS is the end of the program. Don't forget the **break**; without it, control passes down (or "falls through") to the statements for the next **case**, which is usually not what you want (although sometimes it's useful).

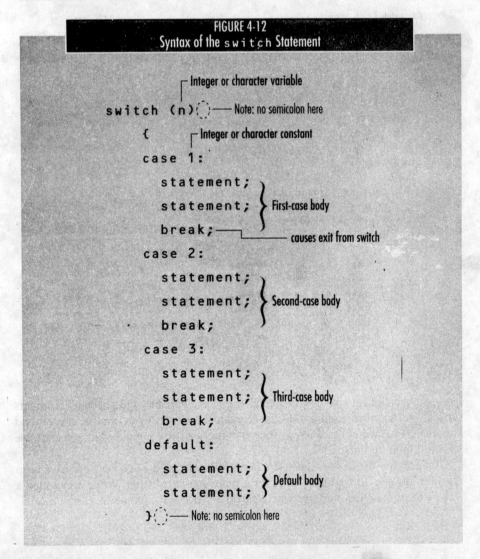

FIGURE 4-12
Syntax of the switch Statement

If the value of the switch variable doesn't match any of the `case` constants, then control passes to the end of the switch without doing anything. The operation of the `switch` statement is shown in Figure 4-13. The `break` keyword is also used to escape from loops; we'll discuss this soon.

switch Statement with Character Variables

The PLATTERS example showed a `switch` statement based on a variable of type `int`. You can also use type `char`. Here's our ADELSEIF program rewritten as ADSWITCH:

```
// adswitch.cpp
// demonstrates SWITCH with adventure program
#include <iostream.h>
#include <conio.h>        // for getche()

void main()
   {
   char dir='a';
   int x=10, y=10;

   while( dir != '\r' )
      {
      cout << "\nYour location is " << x << ", " << y;
      cout << "\nEnter direction (n, s, e, w): ";
      dir = getche();                       // get character
      switch(dir)                           // switch on it
         {
         case 'n': y--; break;              // go north
         case 's': y++; break;              // go south
         case 'e': x++; break;              // go east
         case 'w': x--; break;              // go west
         case '\r': cout << "Exiting\n"; break; // Enter key
         default:  cout << "Try again\n";   // unknown char
         } // end switch
      } // end while
   } // end main
```

A character variable `dir` is used as the switch variable, and character constants 'n', 's', and so on are used as the case constants. (Note that you can use integers and characters as switch variables, as shown in the last two examples, but you can't use floating-point numbers.)

Since they are so short, the statements following each `case` keyword have been written on one line, which makes for a more compact listing. We've also added a `case` to print an exit message when (ENTER) is typed.

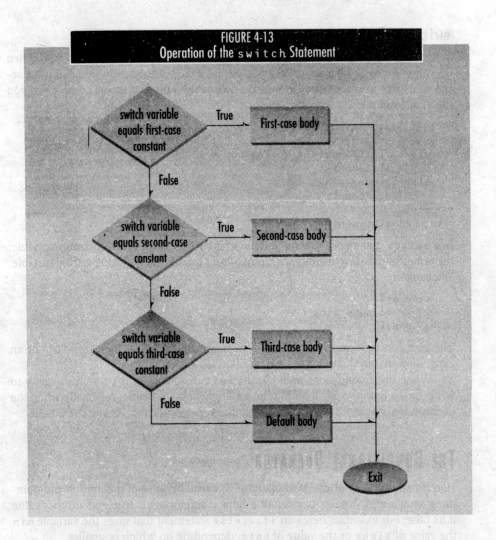

FIGURE 4-13
Operation of the switch Statement

The default Keyword

In the ADSWITCH program, where you expect to see the last **case** at the bottom of the **switch** construction, you'll instead see the keyword **default**. This keyword gives the **switch** construction a way to take an action if the value of the loop variable doesn't match any of the **case** constants. Here we use it to print *Try again* if the user types an unknown character. No **break** is necessary after **default**, since we're at the end of the **switch** anyway.

A **switch** statement is a common approach to *parsing* (figuring out) input entered by the user. Each of the possible characters is represented by a **case**.

switch versus if...else

When do you use a series of `if...else` (or `else...if`) statements, and when do you use a `switch` statement? In an `if...else` construction you can use a series of expressions that involve unrelated variables and that are as complex as you like. For example:

```
if( SteamPressure*Factor > 56 )
    // statements
else if( VoltageIn + VoltageOut < 23000)
    // statements
else if( day==Thursday )
    // statements
else
    // statements
```

In a `switch` statement, however, all the branches are selected by the same variable; the only thing distinguishing one branch from another is the value of this variable. You can't say

```
case a<3:
    // do something
break;
```

The case constant must be an integer or character constant, like `3` or `'a'`, or an expression that evaluates to a constant, like `'a'+32`.

When these conditions are met, the `switch` statement is very clean—easy to write and to understand. It should be used whenever possible, especially when the decision tree has more than a few possibilities.

THE CONDITIONAL OPERATOR

Here's a strange sort of decision operator. It exists because of a common programming situation: A variable is given one value if something is true and another value if it's false. For example, here's an `if...else` statement that gives the variable `min` the value of `alpha` or the value of `beta`, depending on which is smaller.

```
if( alpha < beta )
    min = alpha;
else
    min = beta;
```

This sort of construction is so common that the designers of C++ (actually the designers of C, long ago) invented a compressed way to express it: the *conditional operator*. This operator consists of two symbols, which operate on three operands. It's the only such operator in C++; other operators operate on one or two operands. Here's the equivalent of the same program fragment, using a conditional operator:

```
min = (alpha<beta) ? alpha : beta;
```

The part of this statement to the right of the equals sign is called the *conditional expression*:

```
(alpha<beta) ? alpha : beta    // conditional expression
```

The question mark and the colon make up the conditional operator. The expression before the question mark,

```
(alpha<beta)
```

is the test expression. It and `alpha` and `beta` are the three operands.

If the test expression is true, then the entire conditional expression takes on the value of the operand following the question mark: `alpha` in this example. If the test expression is false, the conditional expression takes on the value of the operand following the colon: `beta`. The parentheses around the test expression aren't needed for the compiler, but they're customary; they make the statement easier to read (and it needs all the help it can get). Figure 4-14 shows the syntax of the conditional statement, and Figure 4-15 shows its operation.

The conditional expression can be assigned to another variable, or used anywhere a value can be. In this example it's assigned to the variable `min`.

Here's another example: a statement that uses a conditional operator to find the absolute value of a variable n. (The absolute value of a number is the number with any negative sign removed, so it's always positive.)

```
absvalue = n<0 ? -n : n;
```

If n is less than 0, the expression becomes -n, a positive number. If n is not less than 0, the expression remains n. The result is the absolute value of n, which is assigned to `absvalue`.

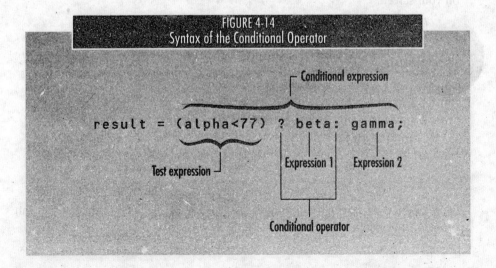

FIGURE 4-14
Syntax of the Conditional Operator

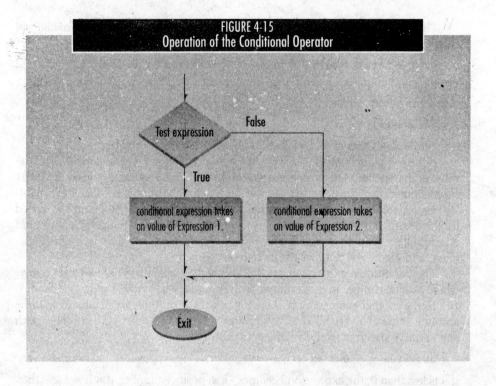

FIGURE 4-15
Operation of the Conditional Operator

Here's a program, CONDI.CPP, that uses the conditional operator to print an **x** every eight spaces in a line of text. You might use this to see where the tab stops are on your screen.

```
// condi.cpp
// prints 'x' every 8 columns
// demonstrates conditional operator
#include <iostream.h>

void main()
    {
    for(int j=0; j<80; j++)              // for every column,
        {                                // ch is 'x' if column is
        char ch = (j%8) ? ' ' : 'x';     // multiple of 8, and
        cout << ch;                      // ' ' (space) otherwise
        }
    }
```

Some of the right side of the output is lost because of the page width, but you can probably imagine it:

```
x       x       x       x       x       x       x       x
```

As j cycles through the numbers from 0 to 7, the remainder operator causes the expression (j % 8) to become false—that is, 0—only when j is a multiple of 8. So the conditional expression

```
(j%8) ? ' ' : 'x'
```

has the value ' ' when j is not a multiple of 8, and the value 'x' when it is.

You may think this is terse, but we could have combined the two statements in the loop body into one, eliminating the ch variable:

```
cout << ( (j%8) ? ' ' : 'x' );
```

Hotshot C++ (and C) programmers love this sort of thing—getting a lot of bang from very little code. But you don't need to strive for concise code if you don't want to. Sometimes it becomes so obscure it's not worth the effort. Even using the conditional operator is optional: An if...else statement and a few extra program lines will accomplish the same thing.

LOGICAL OPERATORS

So far we've seen two families of operators (besides the oddball conditional operator). First are the arithmetic operators +, -, *, /, and %. Second are the relational operators <, >, <=, >=, ==, and !=.

Let's examine a third family of operators, called *logical operators*. These operators allow you to logically combine Boolean (true/false) values. For example, *today is a weekday* has a Boolean value, since it's either true or false. Another Boolean expression is *Maria took the car*. We can connect these expressions logically: *If today is a weekday, and Maria took the car, then I'll have to take the bus*. The logical connection here is the word *and*, which provides a true or false value to the combination of the two phrases. Only if they are both true will I have to take the bus.

LOGICAL AND OPERATOR

Let's see how logical operators combine Boolean expressions in C++. Here's an example, ADVENAND.CPP, that uses a logical operator to spruce up the adventure game from the ADSWITCH example. We'll bury some treasure at coordinates (7,11) and see if the player can find it.

```
// advenand.cpp
// demonstrates AND logical operator
#include <iostream.h>
#include <process.h>              // for exit()
#include <conio.h>               // for getche()
void main()
    {
```

```
char dir='a';
int x=10, y=10;

while( dir != '\r' )
   {
   cout << "\nYour location is " << x << ", " << y;
   cout << "\nEnter direction (n, s, e, w): ";
   dir = getche();            // get direction
   switch(dir)
      {
      case 'n': y--; break;    // update coordinates
      case 's': y++; break;
      case 'e': x++; break;
      case 'w': x--; break;
      }
   if( x==7 && y==11 )         // if x is 7 and y is 11
      {
      cout << "\nYou found the treasure!\n";
      exit(0);                 // exit from program
      }
   } // end switch
} // end main
```

The key to this program is the **if** statement

```
if( x==7 && y==11 )
```

The test expression will be true only if *both* x is 7 *and* y is 11. The logical AND operator **&&** joins the two relational expressions to achieve this result.

Notice that parentheses are not necessary around the relational expressions:

```
( (x==7) && (y==11) )    // inner parentheses not necessary
```

This is because the relational operators have higher precedence than the logical operators.

Here's some interaction as the user arrives at these coordinates:

```
Your location is 7, 10
Enter direction (n, s, e, w): s
You found the treasure!
```

There are three logical operators in C++:

Operator	Effect
&&	Logical AND
||	Logical OR
!	Logical NOT

Let's look at examples of the | | and ! operators.

THE LOGICAL OR OPERATOR

Suppose in the adventure game you decide there will be dragons if the user goes too far east or too far west. Here's an example, ADVENOR, that uses the logical OR operator to implement this frightening impediment to free adventuring. It's a variation on the ADVENAND program.

```
// advenor.cpp
// demonstrates OR logical operator
#include <iostream.h>
#include <process.h>              // for exit()
#include <conio.h>               // for getche()
void main()
    {
    char dir='a';
    int x=10, y=10;

    while( dir != '\r' )          // quit on Enter key
        {
        cout << "\n\nYour location is " << x << ", " << y;

        if( x<5 || x>15 )          // if x west of 5 OR east of 15
            cout << "\nBeware: dragons lurk here";

        cout << "\nEnter direction (n, s, e, w): ";
        dir = getche();           // get direction
        switch(dir)
            {
            case 'n': y--; break;   // update coordinates
            case 's': y++; break;
            case 'e': x++; break;
            case 'w': x--; break;
            }
        }
    }
```

The expression

```
x<5 || x>15
```

is true whenever *either* x is less than 5 (the player is too far west), or x is greater than 15 (the player is too far east). Again, the || operator has lower precedence than the relational operators < and >, so no parentheses are needed in this expression.

THE LOGICAL NOT OPERATOR

The logical NOT operator ! is a unary operator—that is, it takes only one operand. (Almost all the operators we've seen thus far are binary operands; they take two operands. The conditional operator is the only ternary operator in C++.) The effect of the ! is that the logical value of its operand is reversed: If something is true, ! makes it false; if it is false, ! makes it true.

For example, (x==7) is true if x is equal to 7; but !(x==7) is true if x is *not* equal to 7. (In this situation you could use the relational *not equals* operator, x != 7, to achieve the same effect.)

A True/False Value for Every Integer Variable

We may have given you the impression that for an expression to have a true/false value, it must involve a relational operator. But in fact, every integer expression has a true/false value, even if it is only a single variable. The expression x is true whenever x is not 0, and false when x is 0. Applying the ! operator to this situation, we can see that the !x is true whenever x *is* 0, since it reverses the truth value of x.

Let's put these ideas to work. Imagine in your adventure game that you wanted to place a mushroom on all the locations where both x and y are a multiple of 7. (As you probably know, mushrooms, when consumed by the player, confer magical powers.) The remainder when x is divided by 7, which can be calculated by x%7, is 0 only when x is a multiple of 7. So to specify the mushroom locations, we can write

```
if( x%7==0 && y%7==0 )
    cout << "There's a mushroom here.\n";
```

However, remembering that expressions are true or false even if they don't involve relational operators, you can use the ! operator to provide a more concise format:

```
if( !(x%7) && !(y%7) )   // if not x%7 and not y%7
```

This has exactly the same effect.

We've said that the logical operators && and || have lower precedence than the relational operators. Why then do we need parentheses around x%7 and y%7? Because, even though it is a logical operator, ! is a unary operator, which has higher precedence than relational operators.

PRECEDENCE SUMMARY

Lets summarize the precedence situation for the operators we've seen so far. The operators higher on the list have higher precedence than those lower down. Operators with higher precedence are evaluated before those with lower precedence. Operators on the same row have equal precedence. You can force an expression to be evaluated first by placing parentheses around it.

Operator type	Operators
Unary	!, ++, --, -
Arithmetic	
Multiplicative	*, /, %
Additive	+, -
Relational	
inequality	<, >, <=, >=
equality	==, !=
Logical	
and	&&
or	||
Conditional	?:
Assignment	=, +=, -=, *=, /=, %=

OTHER CONTROL STATEMENTS

There are several other control statements in C++. We've already seen one, break, used in switch statements, but it can be used other places as well. Another statement, continue, is used only in loops, and a third, goto, should be avoided. Let's look at these statements in turn.

THE break STATEMENT

The break statement causes an exit from a loop, just as it does from a switch statement. The next statement after the break is executed is the statement following the loop. Figure 4-16 shows the operation of the break statement.

To demonstrate break, here's a program, SHOWPRIM, that displays the distribution of prime numbers in graphical form:

```
// showprim.cpp
// displays prime number distribution
#include <iostream.h>
#include <conio.h>                    // for getche()

void main()
   {
   const unsigned char WHITE = 219;   // solid color (primes)
   const unsigned char GRAY  = 176;   // gray (non primes)
   unsigned char ch;
                                      // for each screen position
   for(int count=0; count<80*25-1; count++)
      {
```

```
ch = WHITE;                    // assume it's prime
for(int j=2; j<count; j++)     // divide by every integer from
   if(count%j == 0)            // 2 on up; if remainder is 0,
      {
      ch = GRAY;               // it's not prime
      break;                   // break out of inner loop
      }
   cout << ch;                 // display the character
   }
getche();                      // freeze screen until keypress
}
```

In effect every position on the screen is numbered, from 0 to 1999 (which is 80*25–1). If the number at a particular position is prime, the position is colored white (or whatever color your monitor displays); if it's not prime, it's colored gray.

Figure 4-17 shows the display. Strictly speaking, 0 is not considered a prime, but it's shown as white to avoid complicating the program. Think of the columns across the top as being numbered from 0 to 79. Notice that no primes appear in even-numbered columns, since they're all divisible by 2. Is there a pattern to the other numbers? The mathematics world will be very excited if you find a pattern that allows you to predict whether any given number is prime.

When the inner for loop determines that a number is not prime, it sets the character ch to GRAY, and then executes break to escape from the inner loop. (We

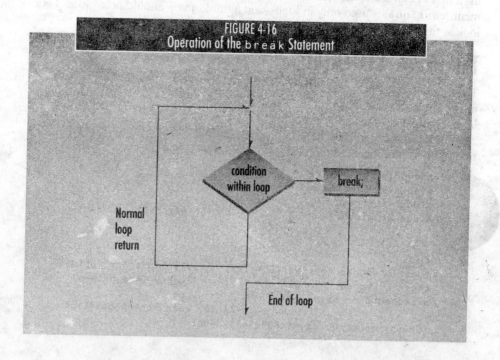

FIGURE 4-16
Operation of the break Statement

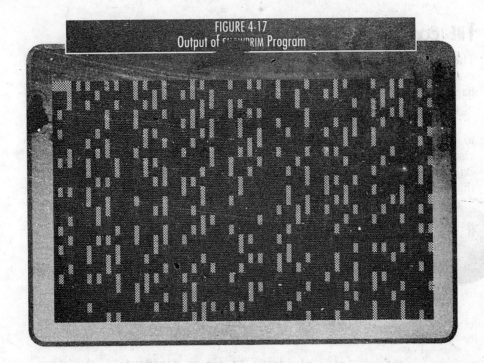

FIGURE 4-17
Output of SHOWPRIM Program

don't want to exit from the entire program, as in the PRIME example, since we have a whole series of numbers to work on.)

Notice that **break** only takes you out of the *innermost* loop. This is true no matter what constructions are nested inside each other: **break** only takes you out of the construction in which it's embedded. If there were a **switch** within a loop, a **break** in the **switch** would only take you out of the **switch**, not out of the loop.

The last **cout** statement prints the character, and then the loop continues, testing the next number for primeness.

IBM Extended Character Set

This program uses two characters from the *extended IBM character set*, the characters represented by the numbers from 128 to 255, as shown in Appendix A. The value 219 represents a solid-colored block (white on a black-and-white monitor), while 176 represents a gray block.

The SHOWPRIM example uses **getche()** in the last line, to keep the DOS prompt from scrolling the screen up when the program terminates. It freezes the screen until you press a key.

We use type **unsigned char** for the character variables in SHOWPRIM, since it goes up to 255. Type **char** only goes up to **127**.

THE continue STATEMENT

The **break** statement takes you out of the bottom of a loop. Sometimes, however, you want to go back to the top of the loop when something unexpected happens. Executing **continue** has this effect. Figure 4-18 shows the operation of **continue**.

Here's a variation on the DIVDO example. This program, which we saw earlier in this chapter, does division, but it has a fatal flaw: If the user inputs 0 as the divisor, the program undergoes catastrophic failure and terminates with the run-time error message *Divide error*. The revised version of the program, DIVDO2, deals with this situation more gracefully.

```
// divdo2.cpp
// demonstrates CONTINUE statement
#include <iostream.h>

void main()
    {
    long dividend, divisor;
    char ch;

    do
        {
        cout << "Enter dividend: "; cin >> dividend;
        cout << "Enter divisor: ";  cin >> divisor;
        if( divisor == 0 )                // if attempt to
            {                             // divide by 0,
            cout << "Illegal divisor\n";  // display message
            continue;                     // go to top of loop
            }
        cout << "Quotient is " << dividend / divisor;
        cout << ", remainder is " << dividend % divisor;

        cout << "\nDo another? (y/n): ";
        cin >> ch;
        }
    while( ch != 'n' );
    }
```

If the user inputs 0 for the divisor, the program prints an error message and, using **continue**, returns to the top of the loop to issue the prompts again. Here's some sample output:

```
Enter dividend: 10
Enter divisor: 0
Illegal divisor
Enter dividend:
```

A **break** statement in this situation would cause an exit from the **do** loop and the program, an unnecessarily harsh response.

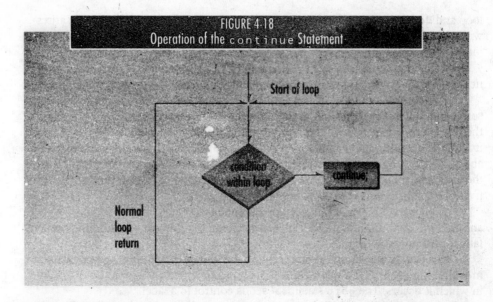

FIGURE 4-18
Operation of the continue Statement

THE goto STATEMENT

We'll mention the goto statement here for the sake of completeness—not because it's a good idea to use it. If you've had any exposure to structured programming principles, you know that goto's can quickly lead to "spaghetti" code that is difficult to understand and debug. There is almost never any need to use goto, as is demonstrated by its absence in the program examples in this book.

With that lecture out of the way, here's the syntax. You insert a *label* in your code at the desired destination for the goto. The label is always terminated by a colon. The keyword goto, followed by this label name, then takes you to the label. The following code fragment demonstrates this approach:

```
goto SystemCrash;
// other statements
SystemCrash:
// control will begin here following goto
```

SUMMARY

Relational operators compare two values to see if they're equal, if one is larger than the other, and so on. The result is a logical or Boolean value, which is true or false. False is indicated by 0, and true by any other number.

There are three kinds of loops in C++. The for loop is most often used when you know in advance how many times you want to execute the loop. The while loop and do loops are used when the condition causing the loop to terminate arises within the loop, with the while loop not necessarily executing at all, and the do loop always executing at least once.

A loop body can be a single statement, or a block of multiple statements delimited by braces. A variable defined within a block is visible only within that block.

There are four kinds of decision-making statements. The if statement does something if a test expression is true. The if...else statement does one thing if the test expression is true, and another thing if it isn't. The else if construction is a way of rewriting a ladder of nested if...else statements to make it more readable. The switch statement branches to multiple sections of code, depending on the value of a single variable. The conditional operater simplifies returning one value if a test expression is true, and another if it's false.

The logical AND and OR operators combine two Boolean expressions to yield another one, and the logical NOT operator changes a Boolean value from true to false, or from false to true.

The break statement sends control to the end of the innermost loop or switch in which it occurs. The continue statement sends control to the top of the loop in which it occurs. The goto statement sends control to a label.

Precedence specifies which kinds of operations will be carried out first. The order is unary, arithmetic, relational, logical, conditional, assignment.

QUESTIONS

1. A relational operator
   a. assigns one operand to another
   b. yields a Boolean result
   c. compares two operands
   d. logically combines two operands

2. Write an expression that uses a relational operator to return true if the variable george is not equal to sally.

3. Is −1 true or false?

4. Name and describe the usual purpose of three expressions in a for statement.

5. In a for loop with a multistatement loop body, semicolons should appear following
   a. the for statement itself
   b. the closing brace in a multistatement loop body
   c. each statement within the loop body
   d. the test expression

6. True or false: The increment expression in a for loop can decrement the loop variable.

7. Write a `for` loop that displays the numbers from 100 to 110. Thank you.

8. A block of code is delimited by _____.

9. A variable defined within a block is visible
   a. from the point of definition onward in the program
   b. from the point of definition onward in the function
   c. from the point of definition onward in the block
   d. throughout the function

10. Write a `while` loop that displays the numbers from 100 to 110.

11. True or false: Relational operators have a higher precedence than arithmetic operators.

12. How many times is the loop body executed in a `do` loop?

13. Write a `do` loop that displays the numbers from 100 to 110.

14. Write an `if` statement that prints `Yes` if a variable `age` is greater than 21.

15. The library function `exit()` causes an exit from
   a. the loop in which it occurs
   b. the block in which it occurs
   c. the function in which it occurs
   d. the program in which it occurs

16. Write an `if...else` statement that displays *Yes* if a variable `age` is greater than 21, and displays *No* otherwise.

17. The `getche()` library function
   a. returns a character when any key is pressed
   b. returns a character when (ENTER) is pressed
   c. displays a character on the screen when any key is pressed
   d. does not display a character on the screen

18. What is the character obtained from `cin` when the user presses the (ENTER) key?

19. An `else` always matches the _____ `if`, unless the `if` is

_____.

20. The `else` `if` construction is obtained from `if...else` by

_____.

21. Write a `switch` statement that prints `Yes` if a variable `ch` is 'y', prints `No` if `ch` is 'n', and prints `Unknown response` otherwise.

22. Write a statement that uses a conditional operator to set `ticket` to 1 if `speed` is greater than 55, and to 0 otherwise.

23. The `&&` and `||` operators
   a. compare two numeric values
   b. combine two numeric values
   c. compare two Boolean values
   d. combine two Boolean values

24. Write an expression involving a logical operator that is true if `limit` is 55 and `speed` is greater than 55.

25. Arrange in order of precedence (highest first) the following kinds of operators: logical, unary, arithmetic, assignment, relational, conditional.
26. The **break** statement causes an exit
    a. only from the innermost loop
    b. only from the innermost switch
    c. from all loops and switches
    d. from the innermost loop or switch
27. Executing the **continue** operator from within a loop causes control to go to
    _____
28. The **goto** statement causes control to go to
    a. an operator
    b. a label
    c. a variable
    d. a function

EXERCISES

1. Assume you want to generate a table of multiples of any given number. Write a program that allows the user to enter the number, and then generates the table, formatting it into ten columns and 20 lines. Interaction with the program should look like this (only the first three lines are shown):

```
Enter a number: 7
    7    14    21    28    35    42    49    56    63    70
   77    84    91    98   105   112   119   126   133   140
  147   154   161   168   175   182   189   196   203   210
```

2. Write a temperature-conversion program that gives the user the option of converting Fahrenheit to Celsius or Celsius to Fahrenheit. Then carry out the conversion. Use floating-point numbers. Interaction with the program might look like this:

```
Type 1 to convert Fahrenheit to Celsius,
     2 to convert Celsius to Fahrenheit: 1
Enter temperature in Fahrenheit: 70
In Celsius that's 21.111111
```

3. Operators such as **>>**, which read input from the keyboard, must be able to convert a series of digits into a number. Write a program that does the same thing. It should allow the user to type up to six digits, and then display the resulting number as a type **long** integer. The digits should be read individually, as characters, using **getche()**. Constructing the number involves multiplying the existing value by 10 and then adding the new digit. (Hint: Subtract 48 or '0' to go from ASCII to a numerical digit.)

Here's some sample interaction:

```
Enter a number: 123456
Number is: 123456
```

4. Create the equivalent of a four-function calculator. The program should request the user to enter a number, an operator, and another number. It should then carry out the specified arithmetical operation: adding, subtracting, multiplying, or dividing the two numbers. (It should use a `switch` statement to select the operation.) Finally it should display the result.

When it finishes the calculation, the program should ask if the user wants to do another calculation. The response can be 'y' or 'n'. Some sample interaction with the program might look like this:

```
Enter first number, operator, second number: 10 / 3
Answer = 3.333333
Do another (y/n)? y
Enter first number, operator, second number: 12 + 100
Answer = 112
Do another (y/n)? n
```

STRUCTURES

We've seen variables of simple data types, such as `float`, `char`, and `int`. Variables of such types represent one item of information: a height, an amount, a count, and so on. But just as eggs are organized into cartons, employees into departments, and soldiers into platoons and regiments, it's often convenient to organize simple variables into more complex entities. The C++ construction called the *structure* is one way to do this.

The first part of this chapter is devoted to structures. In the second part we'll look at a related topic: the enumerated data type.

STRUCTURES

A structure is a collection of simple variables. The variables in a structure can be of different types: Some can be `int`, some can be `float`, and so on. (This is unlike the array, which we'll meet later, in which all the variables must be the same type.) The data items in a structure are called the *members* of the structure.

In books on C programming, structures are often considered an advanced feature and are introduced toward the end of the book. However, for C++ programmers, structures are one of the two important building blocks in the understanding of objects and classes. In fact, the syntax of a structure is almost identical to that of a class. A structure (as typically used) is a collection of data, while a class is a collection of both data and functions. So by learning about structures we'll be paving the way for an understanding of classes and objects. Structures in C++ (and C) serve a similar purpose to *records* in BASIC and Pascal.

A SIMPLE STRUCTURE

Let's start off with a structure that contains three variables: two integers and a floating-point number. This structure represents an item in a widget company's parts inventory. It is a template for information about a single widget part. The company makes several kinds of widgets, so the widget model number is the first member of the structure. The number of the part itself is the next member, and the final member is the part's cost. (Those of you who consider part numbers unexciting need to open your eyes to the romance of commerce.)

The program PARTS specifies the structure `part`, defines a structure variable of that type called `part1`, assigns values to its members, and then displays these values.

```
// parts.cpp
// uses parts inventory to demonstrate structures
#include <iostream.h>

struct part            // specify a structure
   {
   int modelnumber;    // ID number of widget
   int partnumber;     // ID number of widget part
   float cost;         // cost of part
   };

void main()
   {
   part part1;                     // define a structure variable

   part1.modelnumber = 6244;  // give values to structure members
   part1.partnumber = 373;
   part1.cost = 217.55;
                                   // display structure members
   cout << "\nModel "  << part1.modelnumber;
   cout << ", part "   << part1.partnumber;
   cout << ", costs $" << part1.cost;
   }
```

The program's output looks like this:

```
Model 6244, part 373, costs $217.55
```

The PARTS program has three main aspects: specifying the structure, defining a structure variable, and accessing the members of the structure. Let's look at each of these.

SPECIFYING THE STRUCTURE

The structure *specifier* tells how the structure is organized: It specifies what members the structure will have. Here it is:

```
struct part
   {
   int modelnumber;
   int partnumber;
   float cost;
   };
```

This construction is often called a structure *declaration*. However, the word *declaration* is also used in another sense—as we'll see later—so for clarity we'll use the word *specifier*.

Syntax of the Structure Specifier

The keyword `struct` introduces the specifier. Next comes the *structure name* or *tag*, which is `part`. The declarations of the structure members—`modelnumber`, `partnumber`, and `cost`—are enclosed in braces. A semicolon follows the closing brace, terminating the entire structure. Note that this use of the semicolon for structures is unlike the usage for a block of code. As we've seen, blocks of code, which are used in loops, decisions, and functions, are also delimited by braces. However, they don't use a semicolon following the final brace. Figure 5-1 shows the syntax of the structure specifier.

Use of the Structure Specifier

The specifier serves as a blueprint for the creation of variables of type `part`. The specifier does not itself define any variables; that is, it does not set aside any space in memory. It's merely a specification for how such structure variables will look when they are defined. This is shown in Figure 5-2.

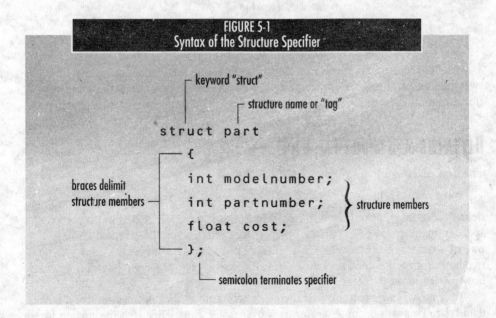

FIGURE 5-1
Syntax of the Structure Specifier

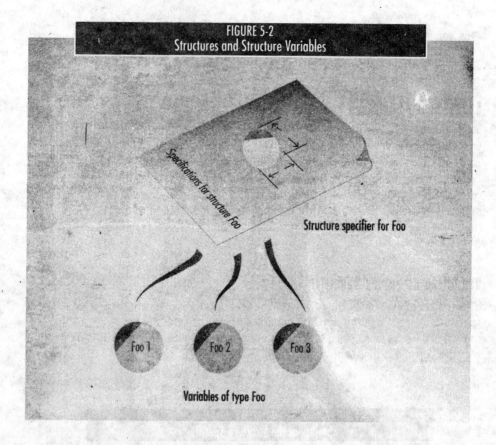

FIGURE 5-2
Structures and Structure Variables

Structure specifier for Foo

Foo 1   Foo 2   Foo 3

Variables of type Foo

It's not accidental that this description sounds like the distinction we noted between classes and objects, in Chapter 1. As we'll see, an object has the same relationship to its class that a variable of a structure type has to the structure specifier.

DEFINING A STRUCTURE VARIABLE

The first statement in `main()`,

```
part part1;
```

defines a variable, called `part1`, of type structure `part`. This definition reserves space in memory for `part1`. How much space? Enough to hold all the members of `part1`—namely `modelnumber`, `partnumber`, and `cost`. In this case there will be two bytes for each of the two `int`s, and four bytes for the `float`. Figure 5-3 shows how `part1` looks in memory.

In some ways we can think of the `part` structure as the specification for a new data type. This will become clearer as we go along, but notice that the format for

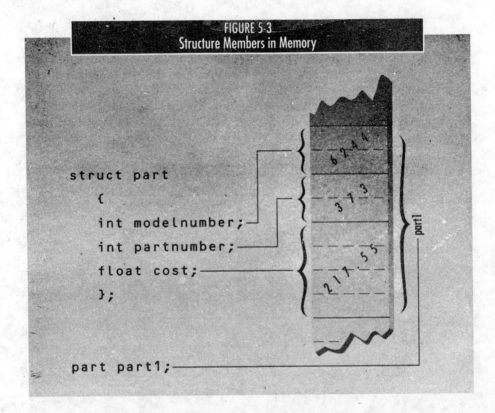

FIGURE 5-3
Structure Members in Memory

defining a structure variable is the same as that for defining a built-in data type such as int:

```
part part1;
int var1;
```

This similarity is not accidental. One of the aims of C++ is to make the syntax and the operation of user-defined data types as similar as possible to that of built-in data types. (In C you need to include the keyword **struct** in structure definitions, as in **struct part part1;**. In C++ the keyword is not necessary.)

ACCESSING STRUCTURE MEMBERS

Once a structure variable has been defined, its members can be accessed using something called the *dot operator*. Here's how the first member is given a value:

```
part1.modelnumber = 6244;
```

The structure member is written in three parts: the name of the structure variable (**part1**); the dot operator, which consists of a period (**.**); and the member name (**modelnumber**). This means "the **modelnumber** member *of* **part1**."

Remember that the first component of an expression involving the dot operator is the name of the specific structure variable (`part1` in this case), not the name of the structure specifier (`part`). The variable name must be used to distinguish one variable from another when there is more than one, such as `part1`, `part2`, and so on, as shown in Figure 5-4.

Structure members are treated just like other variables. In the statement `part1.modelnumber = 6244;`, the member is given the value 6244 using a normal

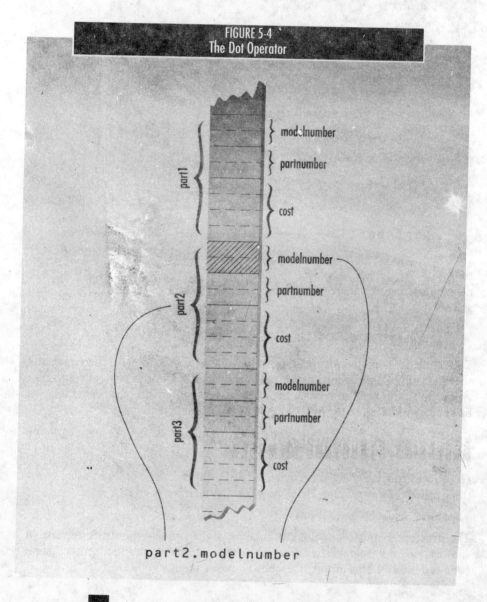

FIGURE 5-4
The Dot Operator

part2.modelnumber

assignment operator. The program also shows members used in `cout` statements such as:

```
cout << "\nModel " << part1.modelnumber;
```

These statements output the values of the structure members.

OTHER STRUCTURE FEATURES

Structures are surprisingly versatile. Let's look at some additional features of structure syntax and usage.

Combining Specifier and Definition

In the PARTS example we showed the structure specifier and the definition as two separate statements. These two statements can also be combined into a single statement, as shown in the next example, PARTSCOM:

```
// partscom.cpp
// uses parts inventory to demonstrate structures
#include <iostream.h>

struct                 // no tag needed
    {
    int modelnumber;   // ID number of widget
    int partnumber;    // ID number of widget part
    float cost;        // cost of part
    } part1;           // definition goes here

void main()
    {
    part1.modelnumber = 6244;  // give values to structure members
    part1.partnumber = 373;
    part1.cost = 217.55;
                               // display structure members
    cout << "\nModel "  << part1.modelnumber;
    cout << ", part "   << part1.partnumber;
    cout << ", costs $" << part1.cost;
    }
```

In this program there is no separate statement for the structure definition:

```
part part1;
```

Instead, the variable name `part1` is placed at the end of the specifier:

```
struct
    {
    int modelnumber;
    int partnumber;
    float cost;
    } part1;
```

Notice that the tag name in the structure specifier can be removed, as we show here, if no more variables of this structure type will be defined.

Merging the structure specification and definition this way is a shorthand approach that can save a few program lines. Generally it is less clear and less flexible than using separate specifiers and definitions.

Initializing Structure Members

The next example shows how structure members can be initialized when the structure is defined. It also demonstrates that you can have more than one variable of a given structure type (we hope you suspected this all along).

Here's the listing for PARTINIT:

```
// partinit.cpp
// shows initialization of structure variables
#include <iostream.h>

struct part              // specify a structure
   {
   int modelnumber;      // ID number of widget
   int partnumber;       // ID number of widget part
   float cost;           // cost of part
   };

void main()
   {
   part part1 = { 6244, 373, 217.55 };  // initialize variable
   part part2;                          // define variable
                         // display first variable
   cout << "\nModel "  << part1.modelnumber;
   cout << ", part "   << part1.partnumber;
   cout << ", costs $" << part1.cost;

   part2 = part1;              // assign first variable to second
                               // display second variable
   cout << "\nModel "  << part2.modelnumber;
   cout << ", part "   << part2.partnumber;
   cout << ", costs $" << part2.cost;
   }
```

This program defines two variables of type part: part1 and part2. It initializes part1, prints out the values of its members, assigns part1 to part2, and prints out its members.

Here's the output:

```
Model 6244, part 373, costs $217.55
Model 6244, part 373, costs $217.55
```

Not surprisingly the same output is repeated, since one variable is made equal to the other.

Initializing Structure Variables

The `part1` structure variable's members are initialized when the variable is defined:

```
part part1 = { 6244, 373, 217.55 };
```

The values to be assigned to the structure members are surrounded by braces and separated by commas. The first value in the list is assigned to the first member, the second to the second member, and so on.

Structure Variables in Assignment Statements

As can be seen in PARTINIT, one structure variable can be assigned to another:

```
part2 = part1;
```

The value of each member of `part1` is assigned to the corresponding member of `part2`. Since a large structure can have dozens of members, such an assignment statement can require the computer to do a considerable amount of work.

Note that one structure variable can be assigned to another only when they are of the same structure type. If you try to assign a variable of one structure type to a variable of another type, the compiler will complain.

A MEASUREMENT EXAMPLE

Let's see how a structure can be used to group a different kind of information. If you've ever looked at an architectural drawing, you know that (at least in the United States) distances are measured in feet and inches. The length of a living room, for example, might be given as 12'-8", meaning 12 feet 8 inches. The hyphen isn't a negative sign; it merely separates the feet from the inches. This is part of the English system of measurement. (We'll make no judgment here on the merits of English versus metric.) Figure 5-5 shows typical length measurements in the English system.

Suppose you want to create a drawing or architectural program that uses the English system. It will be convenient to store distances as two numbers, representing feet and inches. The next example, ENGLSTRC, gives an idea how this could be done using a structure. This program will show how two measurements of type **Distance** can be added together.

```
// englstrc.cpp
// demonstrates structures using English measurements
#include <iostream.h>

struct Distance                    // English distance
    {
    int feet;
    float inches;
    };

void main()
    {
```

```
Distance d1, d3;               // define two lengths
Distance d2 = { 11, 6.25 }; // define & initialize one length

                            // get length d1 from user
cout << "\nEnter feet: ";  cin >> d1.feet;
cout << "Enter inches: ";  cin >> d1.inches;

                            // add lengths d1 and d2 to get d3
d3.inches = d1.inches + d2.inches;  // add the inches
d3.feet = 0;                         // (for possible carry)
if(d3.inches >= 12.0)                // if total exceeds 12.0,
   {                                 // then decrease inches
   d3.inches -= 12.0;                // by 12.0 and
   d3.feet++;                        // increase feet
   }                                 // by 1
d3.feet += d1.feet + d2.feet;       // add the feet

                            // display all lengths
cout << d1.feet << "\'-" << d1.inches << "\" + ";
cout << d2.feet << "\'-" << d2.inches << "\" = ";
cout << d3.feet << "\'-" << d3.inches << "\"\n";
}
```

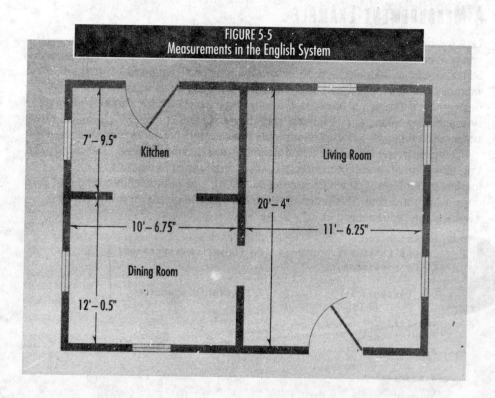

FIGURE 5-5
Measurements in the English System

Kitchen

Living Room

7'– 9.5"

20'– 4"

10'– 6.75"

11'– 6.25"

Dining Room

12'– 0.5"

Here the structure `Distance` has two members: `feet` and `inches`. The `.inches` variable may have a fractional part, so we'll use type `float` for it. Feet are always integers, so we'll use type `int` for them.

We define two such distances, `d1` and `d3`, without initializing them, while we initialize another, `d2`, to 11'–6.25". The program asks the user to enter a distance in feet and inches, and assigns this distance to `d1`. (The inches value should be smaller than 12.0.) It then adds the distance `d1` to `d2`, obtaining the total distance `d3`. Finally the program displays the two initial distances and the newly calculated total distance. Here's some output:

```
Enter feet: 10
Enter inches: 6.75
10'-6.75" + 11'-6.25" = 22'-1"
```

Notice that we can't add the two distances with a program statement like

```
d3 = d1 + d2;   // can't do this in ENGLSTRC
```

Why not? Because there is no routine built into C++ that knows how to add variables of type `Distance`. The `+` operator works with built-in types like `float`, but not with types we define ourselves, like `Distance`. (However, one of the benefits of using classes, as we'll see, is the ability to add and perform other operations on user-defined data types.)

STRUCTURES WITHIN STRUCTURES

You can nest structures within other structures. Here's a variation on the ENGLSTRC program that shows how this looks. In this program we want to create a data structure that stores the dimensions of a typical room: its length and width. Since we're working with English distances, we'll use two variables of type `Distance` as the length and width variables, like this:

```
struct Room
   {
   Distance length;
   Distance width;
   }
```

Here's a program, ENGLAREA, that uses the `Room` structure to represent a room.

```
// englarea.cpp
// demonstrates nested structures
#include <iostream.h>

struct Distance               // English distance
   {
   int feet;
   float inches;
   };
```

```
struct Room                     // rectangular area
    {
    Distance length;            // length of rectangle
    Distance width;             // width of rectangle
    };

void main()
    {
    Room dining;                        // define a room

    dining.length.feet = 13;        // assign values to room
    dining.length.inches = 6.5;
    dining.width.feet = 10;
    dining.width.inches = 0.0;

                                // convert length & width
    float l = dining.length.feet + dining.length.inches/12;
    float w = dining.width.feet  + dining.width.inches/12;
                                // find area and display it
    cout << "\nDining room area is " << l * w
         << " square feet" ;
    }
```

This program defines a single variable—dining—of type Room, in the line

```
    Room dining;  // variable dining of type Room
```

It then assigns values to the various members of this structure.

Accessing Nested Structure Members

Because one structure is nested inside another, we must apply the dot operator twice to access the structure members:

```
    dining.length.feet = 13;
```

In this statement dining is the name of the structure variable, as before; length is the name of a member in the outer structure (Room); and feet is the name of a member of the inner structure (Distance). The statement means "take the feet member of the length member of the variable dining and assign it the value 13." Figure 5-6 shows how this works.

Once values have been assigned to members of dining, the program calculates the floor area of the room, as shown in Figure 5-7.

To find the area, the program converts the length and width from variables of type Distance to variables of type float, l, and w, representing distances in feet. The values of l and w are found by adding the feet member of Distance to the inches member divided by 12. The feet member is converted to type float automatically before the addition is performed, and the result is type float. The l and w variables are then multiplied together to obtain the area.

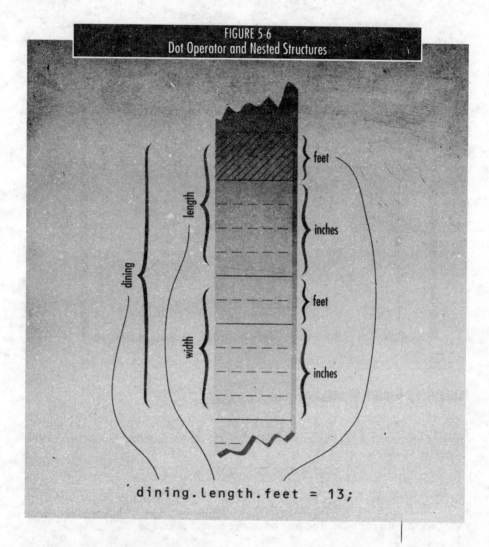

FIGURE 5-6
Dot Operator and Nested Structures

```
dining.length.feet = 13;
```

User-Defined Type Conversions

Note that the program converts two distances of type Distance to two distances of type float: the variables L and w. In effect it also converts the room's area, which is stored as four separate variables in a structure of type Room, to a single floating-point number representing the area in square feet. Here's the output:

```
Dining room area is 135.416672 square feet
```

Converting a value of one type to a value of another is an important aspect of programs that employ user-defined data types.

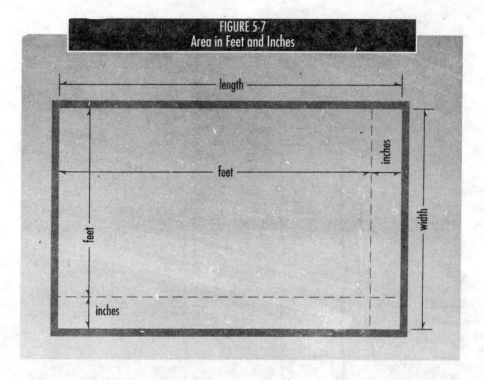

FIGURE 5-7
Area in Feet and Inches

Initializing Nested Structures

How do you initialize a structure variable that itself contains structures? The following statement initializes the variable `dining` to the same values it is given in the ENGLAREA program:

```
Room dining = { {13, 6.5}, {10, 0.0} };
```

Each structure of type `Distance`, which is embedded in `Room`, is initialized separately. Remember that this involves surrounding the values with braces and separating them with commas. The first `Distance` is initialized to

```
{13, 6.5}
```

and the second to

```
{10, 0.0}
```

These two `Distance` values are then used to initialize the `Room` variable, again surrounding them with braces and separating them by commas.

Depth of Nesting

In theory, structures can be nested to any depth. In a program that designs apartment buildings, you might find yourself with statements like

```
apartment1.laundry_room.washing_machine.width.feet
```

A CARD-GAME EXAMPLE

Let's examine a different kind of example. This one uses a structure to model a playing card. The program imitates a game played by cardsharps (professional gamblers) at carnivals. The cardsharp shows you three cards, then places them face down on the table and interchanges their positions several times. If you can guess correctly where a particular card is, you win. Everything is in plain sight, yet the cardsharp switches the cards so rapidly and confusingly that the player (the "mark") almost always loses track of the card and loses the game (which is, of course, played for money).

Here's the structure the program uses to represent a playing card:

```
struct card
   {
   int number;
   int suit;
   }
```

This structure uses separate members to hold the number of the card and the suit. The number runs from 2 to 14, where 11, 12, 13, and 14 represent the jack, queen, king, and ace, respectively (this is the order used in poker). The suit runs from 0 to 3, where these four numbers represent clubs, diamonds, hearts, and spades.

Here's the listing for CARDS:

```
// cards.cpp
// demonstrates structures using playing cards
#include <iostream.h>

const int clubs = 0;
const int diamonds = 1;
const int hearts = 2;
const int spades = 3;

const int jack = 11;
const int queen = 12;
const int king = 13;
const int ace = 14;

struct card
   {
   int number;    // 2 to 10, jack, queen, king, ace
   int suit;      // clubs, diamonds, hearts, spades
   };

void main()
   {
   card temp, chosen, prize;                    // define cards
   int position;
```

```
card card1 = { 7, clubs };                  // initialize card1
cout << "Card 1 is the 7 of clubs\n";

card card2 = { jack, hearts };              // initialize card2
cout << "Card 2 is the jack of hearts\n";

card card3 = { ace, spades };               // initialize card3
cout << "Card 3 is the ace of spades\n";

prize = card3;                   // copy this card, to remember it

cout << "I'm swapping card 1 and card 3\n";
temp = card3; card3 = card1; card1 = temp;

cout << "I'm swapping card 2 and card 3\n";
temp = card3; card3 = card2; card2 = temp;

cout << "I'm swapping card 1 and card 2\n";
temp = card2; card2 = card1; card1 = temp;

cout << "Now, where (1, 2, or 3) is the ace of spades? ";
cin >> position;

switch (position)
    {
    case 1: chosen = card1; break;
    case 2: chosen = card2; break;
    case 3: chosen = card3; break;
    }
if(chosen.number == prize.number &&          // compare cards
                    chosen.suit == prize.suit)
    cout << "That's right!  You win!\n";
else
    cout << "Sorry. You lose.\n";
}
```

Here's some sample interaction with the program:

```
Card 1 is the 7 of clubs
Card 2 is the jack of hearts
Card 3 is the ace of spades
I'm swapping card 1 and card 3
I'm swapping card 2 and card 3
I'm swapping card 1 and card 2
Now, where (1, 2, or 3) is the ace of spades? 3
Sorry. You lose.
```

In this case the hapless mark chose the wrong card (the right answer is 2).

The program begins by defining a number of variables of type const for the face card and suit values. (Not all these variables are used in the program; they're included for completeness.) Next the card structure is specified. The program then defines three uninitialized variables of type card: temp, chosen, and prize. It also defines three cards—card1, card2, and card3—which it initializes to three arbitrary card values. It prints out the values of these cards for the user's information. It then sets a card variable, prize, to one of these card values as a way of remembering it. This card is the one whose location the player will be asked to guess at the end of the game.

Next the program rearranges the cards. It swaps the first and third cards, the second and third cards, and the first and second cards. Each time it tells the user what it's doing. (If you find the program too easy, you can add more such statements to further shuffle the cards. Flashing the statements on the screen for a limited time would also increase the challenge.)

Finally the program asks the player what position a particular card is in. It sets a card variable, chosen, to the card in this position, and then compares chosen with the prize card. If they match, it's a win for the player; if not, it's a loss.

Notice how easy swapping cards is:

```
temp = card3;  card3 = card1;  card1 = temp;
```

Although the cards represent structures, they can be moved around very naturally, thanks to the ability of the assignment operator = to work with structures.

Unfortunately, just as structures can't be added, they also can't be compared. You can't say

```
if( chosen == prize )                          // not legal yet
```

because there's no routine built into the == operator that knows about the card structure. But, as with addition, this problem can be solved with operator overloading, as we'll see later.

STRUCTURES AND CLASSES

We must confess to having misled you slightly on the capabilities of structures. It's true that structures are usually used to hold data only, and classes are used to hold both data and functions. However, in C++, structures can in fact hold both data and functions. (In C they can hold only data.) The syntactical distinction between structures and classes in C++ is minimal, so they can in theory be used interchangeably. But most C++ programmers use structures as we have in this chapter, exclusively for data. Classes are usually used to hold both data and functions, as we'll see in Chapter 7.

ENUMERATED DATA TYPES

As we've seen, structures can be looked at as a way to provide user-defined data types. Another approach to defining your own data type is the *enumerated data type*. This feature of C++ is somewhat less crucial than structures. You can write perfectly good object-oriented programs in C++ without knowing anything about enumerated data types. However, they are very much in the spirit of C++, in that, by allowing you to define your own data types, they can simplify and clarify your programming. C++ programmers use enumerated types frequently. (C programmers use them less often.) Enumerated types exist in Pascal.

DAYS OF THE WEEK

Enumerated types work when you know in advance a finite (usually short) list of values that a data type can take on. Here's an example program, DAYENUM, that uses an enumerated data type for the days of the week:

```
// dayenum.cpp
// demonstrates enum types
#include <iostream.h>
                                    // specify enum type
enum days_of_week { Sun, Mon, Tue, Wed, Thu, Fri, Sat };

void main()
   {
   days_of_week day1, day2;    // define variables
                               // of type days_of_week
   day1 = Mon;                 // give values to
   day2 = Thu;                 // variables

   int diff = day2 - day1;     // can do integer arithmetic
   cout << "Days between = " << diff << endl;

   if(day1 < day2)             // can do comparisons
      cout << "day1 comes before day2\n";
   }
```

An **enum** specifier defines the set of all names that will be permissible values of the type. These permissible values are called *members*. The **enum** type **days_of_week** has seven members: **Sun**, **Mon**, **Tue**, and so on, up to **Sat**. Figure 5-8 shows the syntax of an **enum** specifier.

Enumerated means that all the values are listed. This is unlike the specification of an **int**, for example, which is given in terms of a range of possible values. In an **enum** you must give a specific name to every possible value. Figure 5-9 shows the difference between an **int** and an **enum**.

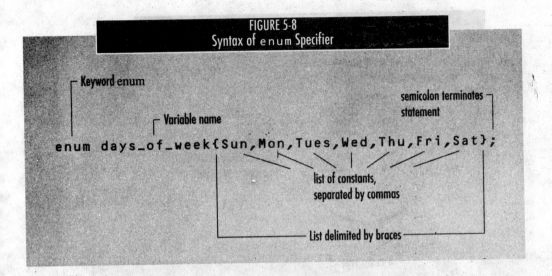

FIGURE 5-8
Syntax of enum Specifier

Keyword enum

Variable name

semicolon terminates statement

`enum days_of_week{Sun,Mon,Tues,Wed,Thu,Fri,Sat};`

list of constants,
separated by commas

List delimited by braces

Once you've specified the data type `days_of_week` as shown, you can define variables of this type. DAYENUM has two such variables, `day1` and `day2`, defined in the statement

```
days_of_week  day1, day2;
```

(In C you must use the keyword `enum` before the type name, as in

```
enum days_of_week day1, day2;
```

In C++ this isn't necessary.)

Variables of an enumerated type, like `day1` and `day2`, can be given any of the values listed in the `enum` specifier. In the example we give them the values `Mon` and `Thu`. You can't use values that weren't listed in the specifier. Such statements as

```
day1 = halloween;
```

are illegal.

You can use the standard arithmetic operators on `enum` types. In the program we subtract two values. You can also use the comparison operators, as we show. Here's the program's output:

```
Days between = 3
day1 comes before day2
```

The use of arithmetic and relational operators doesn't make much sense with some `enum` types. For example, if you have the specifier

```
enum pets { cat, dog, hamster, canary, ocelot };
```

then it may not be clear what expressions like `dog + canary` or `(cat < hamster)` mean.

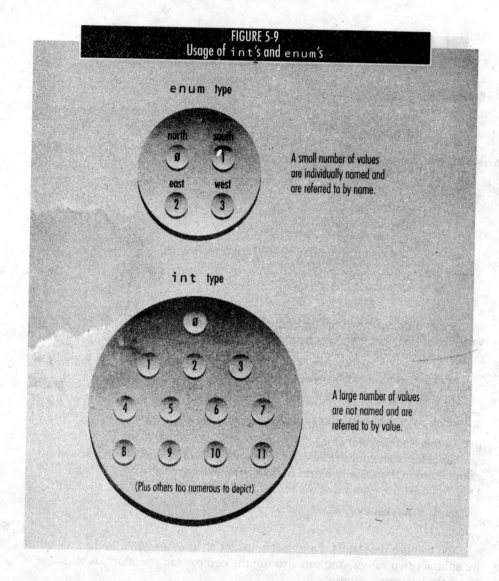

FIGURE 5-9
Usage of int's and enum's

enum type

A small number of values
are individually named and
are referred to by name.

int type

A large number of values
are not named and are
referred to by value.

(Plus others too numerous to depict)

Enumerated data types are treated internally as integers. (This explains why you can perform arithmetic and relational opertions on them.) Ordinarily the first name in the list is given the value 0, the next name is given the value 1, and so on. In the DAYENUM example the values Sun through Sat are stored as the integer values 0 through 6.

Arithmetic operations on **enum** types take place on the integer values. However, although the compiler knows that your **enum** variables are really integers, you must be careful of trying to take advantage of this fact. If you say

```
day1 = 5;
```

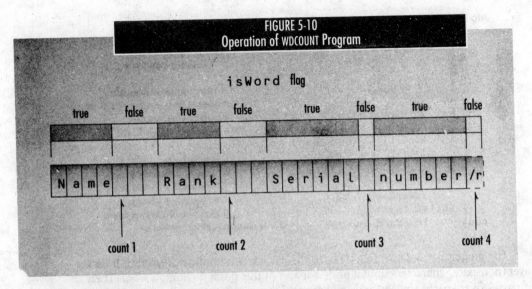

FIGURE 5-10
Operation of WDCOUNT Program

the compiler will issue a warning (although it will compile). It's better to forget—whenever possible—that enum's are really integers.

INVENTING A BOOLEAN TYPE

We noted in the last chapter that there is no Boolean (false or true) data type in C++; the integer values 0 and 1 are used instead. However, it is easy to invent your own Boolean type using enum.

Our next example counts the words in a phrase typed in by the user. Unlike the earlier CHCOUNT example, however, it doesn't simply count spaces to determine the number of words. Instead it counts the places where a string of nonspace characters changes to a space, as shown in Figure 5-10.

This way you don't get a false count if you type multiple spaces between words. (It still doesn't handle tabs and other whitespace characters.) Here's the listing for WDCOUNT:

```
// wdcount.cpp
// demonstrates enums, counts words in phrase
#include <iostream.h>
#include <conio.h>                    // for getche()

enum boolean { false, true };      // false=0, true=1

void main()
    {
    boolean isWord = false;        // true when in a word,
                                   // false when in whitespace
    char ch = 'a';                 // character read from keyboard
    int wordcount = 0;             // number of words read
```

```
do
   {
   ch = getche();                       // get character
   if(ch==' ' || ch=='\r')              // if white space,
      {
      if( isWord )                      // and doing a word,
         {                              // then it's end of word
         wordcount++;                   // count the word
         isWord = false;                // reset flag
         }
      }                                 // otherwise, it's
   else                                 // normal character
      if( !isWord )                     // if start of word,
         isWord = true;                 // then set flag
   } while( ch != '\r' );               // quit on Enter key
cout << "\n--Word count is " << wordcount << "--\n";
}
```

The program cycles in a **do** loop, reading characters from the keyboard. It passes over (nonspace) characters until it finds a space. At this point it counts a word. Then it passes over spaces until it finds a character, and again counts characters until it finds a space. Doing this requires the program to remember whether it's in the middle of a word, or in the middle of a string of spaces. It remembers this with the variable isWord. This variable is defined to be of type **boolean**. This type is specified in the statement

```
enum boolean { false, true };
```

Variables of type **boolean** have only two possible values: *false* and *true*. Notice that the list starts with *false*, so this value will be given the value 0—the value of false used in comparisons.

The isWord variable is set to **false** when the program starts. When the program encounters the first nonspace character, it sets isWord to **true** to indicate that it's in the middle of a word. It keeps this value until the next space is found, at which point it's set back to **false**. Notice that, since isWord is either true or false, we can use the expression

```
if( isWord )
```

This will be true if isWord is true (1), and false if isWord is false (0).

Note also that we need an extra set of braces around the second **if** statement in the program, so that the **else** will match with the first **if**.

This specification of a Boolean data type is commonly used in C++ programming when flags and similar variables must be defined.

ORGANIZING THE CARDS

Here's another example of **enum** types. Remember that in the CARDS program earlier in this chapter we defined a group of constants of type **const int** to represent a card's suits:

```
const int clubs = 0;
const int diamonds = 1;
const int hearts = 2;
const int spades = 3;
```

This sort of list is somewhat clumsy. Let's revise the CARDS program to use enumerated data types instead. Here's the listing for CARDENUM:

```
// cardenum.cpp
// demonstrates the enumerated data type
#include <iostream.h>

const int jack = 11;    // 2 through 10 are unnamed integers
const int queen = 12;
const int king = 13;
const int ace = 14;

enum Suit { clubs, diamonds, hearts, spades };

struct card
   {
   int number;        // 2 to 10, jack, queen, king, ace
   Suit suit;         // clubs, diamonds, hearts, spades
   };

void main()
   {
   card temp, chosen, prize;            // define cards
   int position;

   card card1 = { 7, clubs };           // initialize card1
   cout << "Card 1 is the seven of clubs\n";

   card card2 = { jack, hearts };       // initialize card2
   cout << "Card 2 is the jack of hearts\n";

   card card3 = { ace, spades };        // initialize card3
   cout << "Card 3 is the ace of spades\n";

   prize = card3;              // copy this card, to remember it

   cout << "I'm swapping card 1 and card 3\n";
   temp = card3; card3 = card1; card1 = temp;

   cout << "I'm swapping card 2 and card 3\n";
   temp = card3; card3 = card2; card2 = temp;

   cout << "I'm swapping card 1 and card 2\n";
   temp = card2; card2 = card1; card1 = temp;

   cout << "Now, where (1, 2, or 3) is the ace of spades? ";
   cin >> position;
```

```
switch (position)
    {
    case 1: chosen = card1; break;
    case 2: chosen = card2; break;
    case 3: chosen = card3; break;
    }
if(chosen.number == prize.number &&            // compare cards
                    chosen.suit == prize.suit)
    cout << "That's right!  You win!\n";
else
    cout << "Sorry. You lose.\n";
}
```

Here the set of definitions for suits used in CARDS has been replaced by an **enum** specifier:

```
enum Suit { clubs, diamonds, hearts, spades };
```

This is a cleaner approach than using `const` variables. We know exactly what the possible values of the suit are; attempts to use other values, as in

```
card1.suit = 5;
```

result in warnings from the compiler.

SPECIFYING INTEGER VALUES

We said that in an **enum** specifier the first name was given the integer value 0, the second the value 1, and so on. This ordering can be altered by using an equals sign to specify a starting point other than 0. For example, if you want the suits to start with 1 instead of 0, you can say

```
enum Suit { clubs=1, diamonds, hearts, spades };
```

Subsequent names are given values starting at this point, so `diamonds` is 2, `hearts` is 3, and `spades` is 4.

NOT PERFECT

One annoying aspect of **enum** types is that they are not recognized by C++ Input/Output statements. As an example, what do you think the following code fragment will cause to be displayed?

```
enum direction { north, south, east, west };
direction dir1 = south;
cout << dir1;
```

Would you guess the output will be `south`? That would be nice, but C++ I/O treats variables of `enum` types as integers, so the output will be `1`.

OTHER EXAMPLES

Here are some other examples of enumerated data specifiers, to give you a feeling for possible uses of this feature:

```
enum months { Jan, Feb, Mar, Apr, May, Jun,
              Jul, Aug, Sep, Oct, Nov, Dec };

enum switch { off, on };

enum meridian { am, pm };

enum chess { pawn, knight, bishop, rook, queen, king };

enum coins { penny, nickel, dime, quarter, half-dollar, dollar }
```

We'll see other examples in future programs.

SUMMARY

We've covered two topics in this chapter: structures and the enumerated data type. Structures are an important component of C++, since their syntax is the same as that used in classes. In fact, classes are nothing more than structures that include functions. Structures are typically used to group several data items together to form a single entity. A structure specifier lists the variables that make up the structure. Definitions then set aside memory for structure variables. Structure variables are treated as indivisible units in some situations (such as setting one structure variable equal to another), but in other situations their members are accessed individually (often using the dot operator).

The enumerated data type is a programmer-defined type that is limited to a fixed list of values. A specifier gives the type a name and specifies the permissible values. Definitions then create variables of this type. Internally the compiler treats enumerated variables as integers.

Structures should not be confused with enumerated data types. Structures are a powerful and flexible way of grouping a diverse collection of data into a single entity. An enumerated data type allows the definition of variables that can take on a fixed set of values that are listed (enumerated) in the type's specifier.

QUESTIONS

1. A structure brings together a group of
   a. items of the same data type
   b. related data items
   c. integers with user-defined names
   d. variables

2. True or false: A structure and a class use similar syntax.

3. The closing brace of a structure is followed by a _____.

4. Write a structure specification that includes three variables—all of type `int`—called `hrs`, `mins`, and `secs`. Call this structure `time`

5. True or false: A structure specifier creates space in memory for a variable.

6. When accessing a structure member, the identifier to the left of the dot operator is the name of
   a. a structure member
   b. a structure tag
   c. a structure variable
   d. the keyword `struct`

7. Write a statement that sets the `hrs` member of the `time2` structure variable equal to 11.

8. If you have three variables defined to be of type `struct time`, and this structure contains three `int` members, how many bytes of memory do the variables use together?

9. Write a definition that initializes the members of `time1`—which is a variable of type `struct time`, as defined in question 4—to `hrs = 11`, `mins = 10`, `secs = 59`.

10. True or false: You can assign one structure variable to another, provided they are of the same type.

11. Write a statement that sets the variable `temp` equal to the `paw` member of the `dogs` member of the `fido` variable.

12. An enumerated data type brings together a group of
    a. items of different data types
    b. related data variables
    c. integers with user-defined names
    d. constant values

13. Write a statement that declares an enumerated data type called `players` with the values B1, B2, SS, B3, RF, CF, LF, P, and C.

14. Assuming the **enum** type **team** as declared in Question 13, define two variables **joe** and **tom**, and assign them the values LF and P, respectively.

15. Assuming the statements of questions 13 and 14, state whether each of the following statements is legal:
    a. `joe = QB;`
    b. `tom = SS;`
    c. `LF = tom;`
    d. `difference = joe - tom;`

16. The first three members of an **enum** type are normally represented by the values _____, _____, and _____.

17. Write a statement that declares an enumerated data type called **speeds** with the values **obsolete**, **single**, and **album**. Give these three names the integer values 78, 45, and 33.

18. State the reason why

    `enum boolean{ false, true };`

    is better than

    `enum boolean{ true, false };`

EXERCISES

1. A phone number, such as (212) 767-8900, can be thought of as having three parts: the area code (212), the exchange (767), and the number (8900). Write a program that uses a structure to store these three parts of a phone number separately. Call the structure **phone**. Create two structure variables of type **phone**. Initialize one, and have the user input a number for the other one. Then display both numbers. The interchange might look like this:

```
Enter your area code, exchange, and number: 415 555 1212
My number is (212) 767-8900
Your number is (415) 555-1212
```

2. A point on the two-dimensional plane can be represented by two numbers: an X coordinate and a Y coordinate. For example, (4,5) represents a point 4 units to the right of the origin along the X axis, and 5 units up the Y axis. The sum of two points can be defined as a new point whose X coordinate is the sum of the X coordinates of the two points, and whose Y coordinate is the sum of their Y coordinates.

    Write a program that uses a structure called **point** to model a point. Define three points, and have the user input values to two of them. Then set the third point equal to the sum of the other two, and display the value of the new point. Interaction with the program might look like this:

```
Enter coordinates for p1: 3 4
Enter coordinates for p2: 5 7
Coordinates of p1+p2 are: 8, 11
```

3. Create a structure called Volume that uses three variables of type Distance (from the ENGLSTRC example) to model the volume of a room. Initialize a variable of type Volume to specific dimensions, then calculate the volume it represents, and print out the result. To calculate the volume, convert each dimension from a Distance variable to a variable of type float representing feet and fractions of a foot, and then multiply the resulting three numbers.

CHAPTER **6**

FUNCTIONS

A function groups a number of program statements into a unit and gives it a name. This unit can then be invoked from other parts of the program.

The most important reason to use functions is to aid in the conceptual organization of a program. Dividing a program into functions is, as we discussed in Chapter 1, one of the major principles of structured programming. (However, as we also noted, object-oriented programming provides other, more powerful ways to organize programs.)

Another reason to use functions (and the reason they were invented, long ago) is to reduce program size. Any sequence of instructions that appears in a program more than once is a candidate for being made into a function. The function's code is stored in only one place in memory, even though the function is executed many times in the course of the program. Figure 6-1 shows how a function is invoked from different sections of a program.

Functions in C++ (and C) serve the same purpose as subprograms and procedures in BASIC, and procedures and functions in Pascal.

SIMPLE FUNCTIONS

Our first example demonstrates a simple function whose purpose is to print a line of 45 asterisks. The example program generates a table, and lines of asterisks are used to make the table more readable. Here's the listing for TABLE:

```
// table.cpp
// demonstrates simple function
#include <iostream.h>

void starline();                    // function declaration
                                    //    (prototype)

void main()
    {
    starline();                     // call to function
```

```
   cout << "Data type    Range" << endl;
   starline();                            // call to function
   cout << "char        -128 to 127" << endl
        << "int         -32,768 to 32,767" << endl
        << "double      -2,147,483,648 to 2,147,483,647" << endl;
   starline();                            // call to function
   }


// starline()
// function definition
void starline()                          // function declarator
   {
   for(int j=0; j<45; j++)                // function body
       cout << '*';
   cout << endl;
   }
```

The output from the program looks like this:

```
*********************************************
Data type    Range
*********************************************
char        -128 to 127
int         -32,768 to 32,767
double      -2,147,483,648 to 2,147,483,647
*********************************************
```

The program consists of two functions: `main()` and `starline()`. You've already seen many programs that use `main()` alone. What other components are necessary to add a function to the program? There are three: the function declaration, the calls to the function, and the function definition.

THE FUNCTION DECLARATION

Just as you can't use a variable without first telling the compiler what it is, you also can't use a function without telling the compiler about it. The most common approach is to *declare* the function at the beginning of the program. In the TABLE program the function `starline()` is declared in the line

```
   void starline();
```

The declaration tells the compiler that at some later point we plan to present a function called *starline*. The keyword `void` specifies that the function has no return value, and the empty parentheses indicate that it takes no arguments. (You can also use the keyword `void` in parentheses to indicate that the function takes no arguments, as is often done in C, but leaving them empty is the more common practice in C++.) We'll have more to say about arguments and return values soon.

Notice that the function declaration is terminated with a semicolon. It is a complete statement in itself.

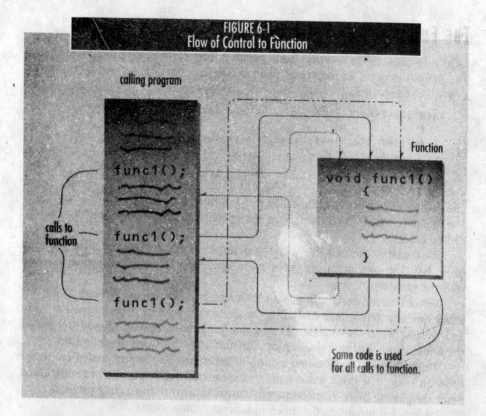

FIGURE 6-1
Flow of Control to Function

Function declarations are also called *prototypes*, since they provide a model or blueprint for the function. They tell the compiler, "a function that looks like this is coming up later in the program, so it's all right if you see references to it before you see the function itself."

CALLING THE FUNCTION

The function is *called* (or invoked, or executed) three times from main(). Each of the three calls looks like this:

```
starline();
```

This is all we need to call the function: the function name, followed by parentheses. The syntax of the call is very similar to that of the declaration, except that the return type is not used. The call is terminated by a semicolon. Executing the call statement causes the function to execute; that is, control is transferred to the function, the statements in the function definition (which we'll examine in a moment) are executed, and then control returns to the statement following the function call.

The Function Definition

Finally we come to the function itself, which is referred to as the function *definition*. The definition contains the actual code for the function. Here's the definition for `starline()`:

```
void starline()                    // declarator
   {
   for(int j=0; j<45; j++)         // function body
      cout << '*';
   cout << endl;
   }
```

The definition consists of a line called the *declarator*, followed by the function body. The function body is composed of the statements that make up the function, delimited by braces.

The declarator must agree with the declaration: It must use the same function name, have the same argument types in the same order (if there are arguments), and have the same return type.

Notice that the declarator is *not* terminated by a semicolon. As with loops, the entire function definition—including the declarator, opening brace, function body, and closing brace—is considered to be one program statement. Figure 6-2 shows the syntax of the function declaration, function call, and function definition.

When the function is called, control is transferred to the first statement in the function body. The other statements in the function body are then executed, and when the closing brace is encountered, control returns to the calling program.

Table 6-1 summarizes the different function components.

Comparison with Library Functions

We've already seen some library functions in use. We have embedded calls to library functions, such as

```
   ch = getche();
```

in our program code. Where are the declaration and definition for this library function? The declaration is in the header file specified at the beginning of the program (CONIO.H, for `getche()`). The definition (compiled into executable code) is in the library file CS.LIB (or a similar file). When we use a library function we don't need to write the declaration or definition.

But when we write our own functions, the declaration and definition are part of our source file, as we've shown in the TABLE example. (Things get more complicated in multifile programs, as we'll discuss in Chapter 15.)

Eliminating the Declaration

We should note that you can eliminate the function declaration if the function definition (the function itself) appears in the listing before the first call to the function.

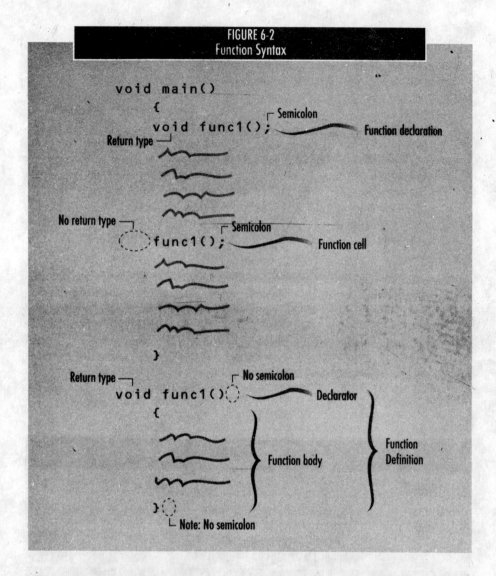

FIGURE 6-2
Function Syntax

For example, we could rewrite TABLE to produce TABLE2, in which the function definition appears first:

```
// table2.cpp
// demonstrates function definition preceding function calls
#include <iostream.h>
                                        // no function declaration

// starline()                          // function definition
void starline()
    {
```

```
   for(int j=0; j<45; j++)
      cout << '*';
   cout << endl;
   }

void main()                              // main follows function
   {
   starline();                           // call to function
   cout << "Data type   Range" << endl;
   starline();                           // call to function
   cout << "char         -128 to 127" << endl
        << "int          -32,768 to 32,767" << endl
        << "double       -2,147,483,648 to 2,147,483,647" << endl;
   starline();                           // call to function
   }
```

This approach is simpler for short programs, in that it removes the declaration, but it is less flexible. To use this technique when there are more than a few functions, the programmer must give considerable thought to arranging the functions so that each one appears before it is called by any other. Sometimes this is impossible. Also, many programmers prefer to place `main()` first in the listing, since it is where execution begins. In general we'll stick with the first approach, using declarations and starting the listing with `main()`.

	TABLE 6-1 Function Components	
Component	Purpose	Example
Declaration (prototype)	Specifies function name, argument types, and return value. Alerts compiler (and programmer) that function is coming up later.	`void func();`
Call	Causes the function to be executed.	`func();`

Definition	The function itself. Contains the lines of code that constitute the function.	`void func()`
		`{`
		`// lines of code`
		`}`

Declarator	First line of definition.	`void func()`

PASSING ARGUMENTS TO FUNCTIONS

An argument is a piece of data (an `int` value, for example) passed from a program to the function. Arguments allow a function to operate with different values, or even to do different things, depending on the requirements of the program calling it.

PASSING CONSTANTS

As an example, let's suppose we decide that the `starline()` function in the last example is too rigid. Instead of a function that always prints 45 asterisks, we want a function that will print any character any number of times.

Here's a program, TABLEARG, that incorporates just such a function. We use arguments to pass the character to be printed and the number of times to print it.

```
// tablearg.cpp
// demonstrates function arguments
#include <iostream.h>

void repchar(char, int);                    // function declaration

void main()
    {
    repchar('-', 43);                       // call to function
    cout << "Data type    Range" << endl;
    repchar('=', 23);                       // call to function
    cout << "char         -128 to 127" << endl
         << "int          -32,768 to 32,767" << endl
         << "double       -2,147,483,648 to 2,147,483,647" << endl;
    repchar('-', 43);                       // call to function
    }

// repchar()
// function definition
void repchar(char ch, int n)                // function declarator
    {
    for(int j=0; j<n; j++)                  // function body
        cout << ch;
    cout << endl;
    }
```

The new function is called `repchar()`. Its declaration looks like this:

```
void repchar(char, int);    // declaration specifies data types
```

The items in the parentheses are the data types of the arguments that will be sent to `repchar()`: `char` and `int`.

In the function call, specific values—constants in this case—are inserted in the appropriate place in the parentheses:

```
repchar('-', 43);    // function call specifies actual values
```

This statement instructs `repchar()` to print a line of 43 dashes. The values supplied in the call must be of the types specified in the declaration: the first argument, the '–' character, must be of type `char`; and the second argument, the number 43, must be of type `int`. The types in the declaration and the definition must also agree..

The next call to `repchar()`,

```
repchar('=', 23);
```

tells it to print a line of 23 equal signs. The third call again prints 43 dashes. Here's the output from TABLEARG:

```
--------------------------------------------
Data type     Range
==========================
char          -128 to 127
int           -32,768 to 32,767
double        -2,147,483,648 to 2,147,483,647
--------------------------------------------
```

The calling program supplies arguments, such as '–' and 43, to the function. The variables used within the function to hold the argument values are called *parameters*; in `repchar()` they are `ch` and `n`. (We should note that many programmers use the terms *argument* and *parameter* interchangeably.) The declarator in the function definition specifies both the data types and the names of the parameters:

```
void repchar(char ch, int n)  // declarator specifies parameter
                              // names and data types
```

These parameter names, `ch` and `n`, are used in the function as if they were normal variables. Placing them in the declarator is equivalent to defining them with statements like

```
char ch;
int n;
```

When the function is called, its parameters are automatically initialized to the values passed by the calling program.

PASSING VARIABLES

In the TABLEARG example the arguments were constants: '–', 43, and so on. Let's look at an example where variables, instead of constants, are passed as arguments. This program, VARARG, incorporates the same `repchar()` function as did TABLEARG, but lets the user specify the character and the number of times it should be repeated.

```
// vararg.cpp
// demonstrates variable arguments
#include <iostream.h>

void repchar(char, int);                          // function declaration

void main()
   {
   char chin;
   int nin;

   cout << "Enter a character: ";
   cin >> chin;
   cout << "Enter number of times to repeat it: ";
   cin >> nin;
   repchar(chin, nin);
   }

// repchar()
// function definition
void repchar(char ch, int n)                      // function declarator
   {
   for(int j=0; j<n; j++)                          // function body
      cout << ch;
   cout << endl;
   }
```

Here's some sample interaction with VARARG:

```
Enter a character: +
Enter number of times to repeat it: 20
++++++++++++++++++++
```

Here chin and nin in main() are used as arguments to repchar():

```
repchar(chin, nin);    // function call
```

The data types of variables used as arguments must match those specified in the function declaration and definition, just as they must for constants. That is, chin must be a char, and nin must be an int.

PASSING BY VALUE

In VARARG the particular values possessed by chin and nin when the function call is executed will be passed to the function. As it did when constants were passed to it, the function creates new variables to hold the values of these variable arguments. The function gives these new variables the names and data types of the parameters specified in the declarator: ch of type char and n of type int. It initializes these parameters to the values passed. They are then accessed like other variables by statements in the function body.

Passing arguments in this way, where the function creates copies of the arguments passed to it, is called *passing by value*. We'll explore another approach, passing by reference, later in this chapter. Figure 6-3 shows how new variables are created in the function when arguments are passed by value.

PASSING STRUCTURE VARIABLES

Entire structures can be passed as arguments to functions. The next example features a function that uses an argument of type `Distance`, the same structure type we saw in several programs in Chapter 5. Here's the listing for ENGLDISP:

```
// engldisp.cpp
// demonstrates passing structure as argument
#include <iostream.h>

struct Distance                    // English distance
   {
   int feet;
   float inches;
   };

void engldisp( Distance );         // declaration

void main()
   {
   Distance d1, d2;                // define two lengths

                                   // get length d1 from user
   cout << "\nEnter feet: ";  cin >> d1.feet;
   cout << "Enter inches: ";  cin >> d1.inches;

                                   // get length d2 from user
   cout << "\nEnter feet: ";  cin >> d2.feet;
   cout << "Enter inches: ";  cin >> d2.inches;

   cout << "\nd1 = ";
   engldisp(d1);                   // display length 1
   cout << "\nd2 = ";
   engldisp(d2);                   // display length 2
   }

// engldisp()
// display structure of type Distance in feet and inches
void engldisp( Distance dd )    // parameter dd of type Distance
   {
   cout << dd.feet << "\'-" << dd.inches << "\"";
   }
```

The `main()` part of this program accepts two distances in feet-and-inches format from the user, and places these values in two structures, `d1` and `d2`. It

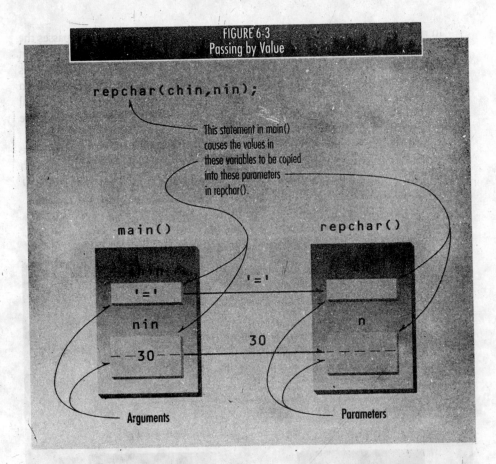

FIGURE 6-3
Passing by Value

then calls a function, engldisp, that takes a `Distance` structure variable as an argument. The purpose of the function is to display the distance passed to it in the standard format, such as 10'–2.25". Here's some sample interaction with the program:

```
Enter feet: 6
Enter inches: 4

Enter feet: 5
Enter inches: 4.25

d1 = 6'-4"
d2 = 5'-4.25"
```

The function declaration and the function calls in `main()`, and the declarator in the function body, treat the structure variables just as they would any other variable used as an argument; this one just happens to be type `Distance`, rather than a basic type like `char` or `int`.

In `main()` there are two calls to the function `engldisp()`. The first passes the structure `d1`; the second passes `d2`. The function `engldisp()` uses a parameter that is a structure of type `Distance`, which it names `dd`. As with simple variables, this structure variable is automatically initialized to the value of the structure passed from `main()`. Statements in `engldisp()` can then access the members of `dd` in the usual way, with the expressions `dd.feet` and `dd.inches`. Figure 6-4 shows a structure being passed as an argument to a function.

As with simple variables, the structure parameter `dd` in `engldisp()` is not the same as the arguments passed to it (`d1` and `d2`). Thus `engldisp()` could (although it doesn't do so here) modify `dd` without affecting `d1` and `d2`. That is, if `engldisp()` contained statments like

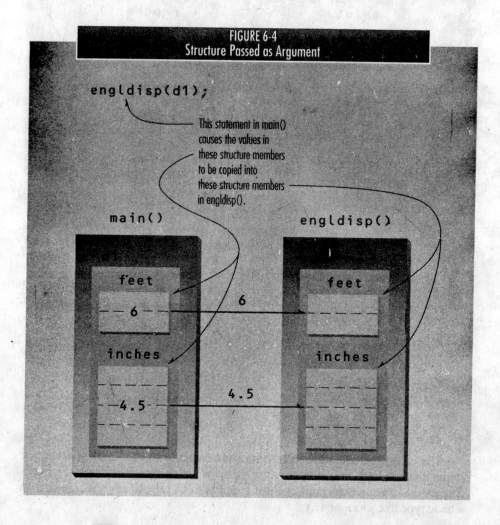

FIGURE 6-4
Structure Passed as Argument

`engldisp(d1);`

This statement in main() causes the values in these structure members to be copied into these structure members in engldisp().

main()   engldisp()

feet   feet
6   6
inches   inches
4.5   4.5

```
dd.feet = 2;
dd.inches = 3.25;
```

this would have no effect on d1 or d2 in main().

NAMES IN THE DECLARATION

Here's a way to increase the clarity of your function declarations. The idea is to insert meaningful names in the declaration, along with the data types. For example, suppose you were using a function that displayed a point on the screen. You could use a declaration with only data types:

```
void display_point(int, int);   // declaration
```

but a better approach is

```
void display_point(int horiz, int vert);   // declaration
```

These two declarations mean exactly the same thing to the compiler. However, the first approach, with (int, int), doesn't contain any hint about which argument is for the vertical and which is for the horizontal coordinate. The advantage of the second approach is clarity for the programmer: Anyone seeing this declaration is more likely to use the correct arguments when calling the function.

Note that the names in the declaration have no effect on the names you use when calling the function. You are perfectly free to use any argument names you want:

```
display_point(x, y);   // function call
```

We'll use this name-plus-datatype approach when it seems to make the listing clearer.

RETURNING VALUES FROM FUNCTIONS

When a function completes its execution it can return a single value to the calling program. Usually this return value consists of an answer to the problem the function has solved. The next example demonstrates a function that returns a weight in kilograms, after being given a weight in pounds. Here's the listing for CONVERT:

```
// convert.cpp
// demonstrates return values, converts pounds to kg
#include <iostream.h>

float lbstokg(float);

void main()
    {
    float lbs, kgs;
```

```
cout << "\nEnter your weight in pounds: ";
cin >> lbs;
kgs = lbstokg(lbs);
cout << "Your weight in kilograms is " << kgs;
}

// lbstokg()
// converts pounds to kilograms
float lbstokg(float pounds)
    {
    float kilograms = 0.453592 * pounds;
    return kilograms;
    }
```

Here's some sample interaction with this program:

```
Enter your weight in pounds: 182
Your weight in kilograms is 82.553741
```

When a function returns a value, the data type of this value must be specified. The function declaration does this by placing the data type, **float** in this case, before the function name in the declaration and the definition. Functions in earlier program examples returned no value, so the return type was **void**. In the CONVERT program the function **lbstokg()** (*pounds to kilograms*, where **lbs** means pounds) returns type **float**, so the declaration is

```
float lbstokg(float);
```

The first **float** specifies the return type. The **float** in parentheses specifies that an argument to be passed to **lbstokg()** is also of type **float**.

When a function returns a value, the call to the function

```
lbstokg(lbs)
```

is considered to be an expression that takes on the value returned by the function. We can treat this expression like any other variable; in this case we use it in an assignment statement:

```
kgs = lbstokg(lbs);
```

This causes the variable **kgs** to be assigned the value returned by **lbstokg()**.

THE return STATEMENT

The function **lbstokg()** is passed an argument representing a weight in pounds, which it stores in the parameter **pounds**. It calculates the corresponding weight in kilograms by multiplying this pounds value by a constant; the result is stored in the variable **kilograms**. The value of this variable is then returned to the calling program using a **return** statement:

```
return kilograms;
```

Notice that both `main()` and `lbstokg()` have a place to store the kilogram variable: `kgs` in `main()`, and `kilograms` in `lbstokg()`. When the function returns, the value in kilograms is copied into `kgs`. The calling program does not access the `kilograms` variable in the function; only the value is returned. This process is shown in Figure 6-5.

While many arguments may be sent to a function, only one argument may be returned from it. This is a limitation when you need to return more information. However, there are other approaches to returning multiple variables from functions. One is to pass arguments by reference, which we'll look at later in this chapter.

You should always include a function's return type in the function declaration. If the function doesn't return anything, use the keyword `void` to indicate this fact. If you don't use a return type in the declaration, the compiler will assume that the function returns an `int` value. For example, the declaration

```
somefunc();   // declaration -- assumes return type is int
```

tells the compiler that `somefunc()` has a return type of `int`.

The reason for this is historical, based on usage in early versions of C. In practice you shouldn't take advantage of this default type. Always specify the return type explicitly, even if it's `int`. This keeps the listing consistent and readable.

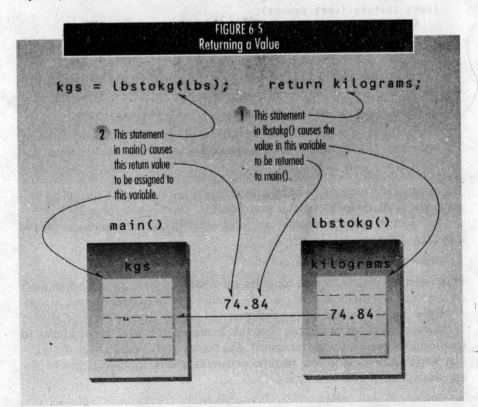

FIGURE 6-5
Returning a Value

Eliminating Unnecessary Variables

The CONVERT program contains several variables that were used in the interest of clarity but are not really necessary. A variation of this program, CONVERT2, shows how expressions can often be used in place of variables:

```
// convert2.cpp
// eliminates unnecessary variables
#include <iostream.h>

float lbstokg(float);

void main()
    {
    float lbs;

    cout << "\nEnter your weight in pounds: ";
    cin >> lbs;
    cout << "Your weight in kilograms is " << lbstokg(lbs);
    }

// lbstokg()
// converts pounds to kilograms
float lbstokg(float pounds)
    {
    return 0.453592 * pounds;
    }
```

In main() the variable kgs from the CONVERT program has been eliminated. Instead the expression lbstokg(lbs) is inserted directly into the cout statement:

```
cout << "Your weight in kilograms is " << lbstokg(lbs);
```

Also in the lbstokg() function the variable kilograms is no longer with us. The expression 0.453592*pounds is inserted directly into the return statement:

```
return 0.453592 * pounds;
```

The calculation is carried out, and the resulting value is returned to the calling program, just as the value of a variable would be.

For clarity, programmers often put parentheses around the expression used in a return statement:

```
return (0.453592 * pounds);
```

Even when not required by the compiler, extra parentheses in an expression don't do any harm, and they may help make the listing easier for us poor humans to read.

Experienced C++ (and C) programmers will probably prefer the concise form of CONVERT2 to the more verbose CONVERT. However, CONVERT2 is not so easy to understand, especially for the nonexpert. The brevity-versus-clarity issue is a question of style, depending on your personal preference, and on the expectations of others who will be reading your listing.

RETURNING STRUCTURE VARIABLES

We've seen that structures can be used as arguments to functions. You can also use them as return values. Here's a program, RETSTRC, that incorporates a function that adds variables of type structure **Distance** and returns a value of this same type.

```
// retstrc.cpp
// demonstrates returning a structure
#include <iostream.h>

struct Distance                      // English distance
   {
   int feet;
   float inches;
   };

Distance addengl(Distance, Distance);  // declarations
void engldisp(Distance);

void main()
   {
   Distance d1, d2, d3;              // define three lengths
                                     // get length d1 from user
   cout << "\nEnter feet: ";  cin >> d1.feet;
   cout << "Enter inches: ";  cin >> d1.inches;
                                     // get length d2 from user
   cout << "\nEnter feet: ";  cin >> d2.feet;
   cout << "Enter inches: ";  cin >> d2.inches;

   d3 = addengl(d1, d2);            // d3 is sum of d1 and d2

   engldisp(d1); cout << " + ";  // display all lengths
   engldisp(d2); cout << " = ";
   engldisp(d3); cout << "\n";
   }

// addengl()
// adds two structures of type Distance, returns sum
Distance addengl( Distance dd1, Distance dd2 )
   {
   Distance dd3;       // define a new structure for sum

   dd3.inches = dd1.inches + dd2.inches; // add the inches
   dd3.feet = 0;                         // (for possible carry)
   if(dd3.inches >= 12.0)                // if inches >= 12.0,
      {                                  // then decrease inches
      dd3.inches -= 12.0;                // by 12.0 and
      dd3.feet++;                        // increase feet
      }                                  // by 1
```

```
dd3.feet += dd1.feet + dd2.feet;       // add the feet
return dd3;                             // return structure
}

// engldisp()
// display structure of type Distance in feet and inches
void engldisp( Distance dd )
   {
   cout << dd.feet << "\'-" << dd.inches << "\"";
   }
```

The program asks the user for two lengths, in feet-and-inches format, adds them together by calling the function `addengl()`, and displays the results using the `engldisp()` function introduced in the ENGLDISP program. Here's some output from the program:

```
Enter feet: 4
Enter inches: 5.5

Enter feet: 5
Enter inches: 6.5

4'-5.5" + 5'-6.5" = 10'-0"
```

The `main()` part of the program adds the two lengths, each represented by a structure of type `Distance`, by calling the function `addEngl`:

```
d3 = addengl(d1, d2);
```

This function returns the sum of **d1** and **d2**, and the result is assigned to the structure **d3**.

Internally the `addengl()` function must create a new variable of type `Distance` to hold the results of its calculation. It can't simply return an expression, as in

```
return dd1+dd2;    // doesn't make sense
```

because the process of adding the two structures actually takes several steps: The inches are added separately from the feet. Instead the values of the individual members of **d3** are calculated, and then **d3** is returned to the calling program with the statement

```
return d3;
```

Besides showing how structures are used as return values, this program also shows two functions (three if you count `main()`) used in the same program. You can arrange the functions in any order. The only rule is that the function declarations must appear in the listing before any calls are made to the functions.

REFERENCE ARGUMENTS

A reference provides an alias—a different name—for a variable. By far the most important use for references is in passing arguments to functions.

We've seen examples of function arguments passed by value. When arguments are passed by value, the called function creates a new variable of the same type as the argument and copies the argument's value into it. As we noted, the function does not have access to the original variable in the calling program, only to the copy it created. Passing arguments by value is useful when the function does not need to modify the original variable in the calling program. In fact, it offers insurance that the function cannot harm the original variable.

Passing arguments by reference uses a different mechanism. Instead of a value being passed to the function, a reference to the original variable, in the calling program, is passed.

The primary advantage of passing by reference is that the function can access the actual variables in the calling program. Among other benefits this provides a mechanism for returning more than one value from the function back to the calling program

PASSING SIMPLE DATA TYPES BY REFERENCE

The next example, REF, shows a simple variable passed by reference:

```
// ref.cpp
// demonstrates passing by reference
#include <iostream.h>

void main()
   {
   void intfrac(float, float&, float&);        // prototype
   float number, intpart, fracpart;            // float variables
   do
      {
      cout << "\nEnter a real number: ";        // number from user
      cin >> number;
      intfrac(number, intpart, fracpart);       // find int and frac
      cout << "Integer part is " << intpart     // print them
           << ", fraction part is " << fracpart;
      } while( number != 0 );                   // exit loop on 0
   }

// intfrac()
// finds integer and fractional parts of real number
void intfrac(float n, float& intp, float& fracp)
   {
   intp = float( long(n) );   // convert to int, back to float
   fracp = n - intp;          // subtract integer part
   }
```

The main() part of this program asks the user to enter a number of type float. The program will separate this number into an integer and a fractional part. That is, if the user's number is 12.456, the program should report that the integer part is 12.0 and the fractional part is 0.456. To find these values, main() calls the function intfrac(). Here's some sample interaction:

```
Enter a real number: 99.44
Integer part is 99, fractional part is 0.44
```

The `intfrac()` function finds the integer part by converting the number (which was passed to the parameter n) into a variable of type `long int` with a cast, using the expression

```
long(n)
```

This effectively chops off the fractional part of the number, since integers (of course) store only the integer part. The result is then converted back to type `float` with another cast:

```
float( long(n) )
```

The fractional part is simply the original number less the integer part. (We should note that a library function, `fmod()`, performs a similar function for type `double`.)

The `intfrac()` function can find the integer and fractional parts, but how does it pass them back to `main()`? It could use a `return` statement to return one value but not both. The problem is solved using reference arguments. Here's the declarator for the function:

```
void intfrac(float n, float& intp, float& fracp)
```

Reference arguments are indicated by the ampersand (`&`) following the data type of the argument:

```
float& intp
```

The `&` indicates that `intp` is an alias—another name—for whatever variable is passed as an argument. In other words, when you use the name `intp` in the `intfrac()` function, you are really referring to `intpart` in `main()`. The `&` can be taken to mean *reference to*, so

```
float& intp
```

means `intp` is *a reference to the* `float` *variable passed to it*. Similarly, `fracp` is an alias for—or a reference to—`fracpart`.

The function declaration echoes the usage of the ampersand in the definition:

```
void intfrac(float, float&, float&);    // ampersands
```

As in the definition, the ampersand follows those arguments that are passed by reference.

The ampersand is *not* used in the function call:

```
intfrac(number, intpart, fracpart);    // no ampersands
```

From the function call alone there's no way to tell whether an argument will be passed by reference or by value.

While `intpart` and `fracpart` are passed by reference, the variable `number` is passed by value. `intp` and `intpart` are different names for the same place in memory, as are `fracp` and `fracpart`. On the other hand, since it is passed by value, the parameter n in intfrac() is a separate variable into which the value of **number** is copied. It can be passed by value because the intfrac() function doesn't need to modify **number**. Figure 6-6 shows how reference arguments work.

(C programmers should not confuse the ampersand that is used to mean *reference to* with the same symbol used to mean *address of*. These are different usages. We'll discuss the *address of* meaning of **&** when we talk about pointers in Chapter 12.)

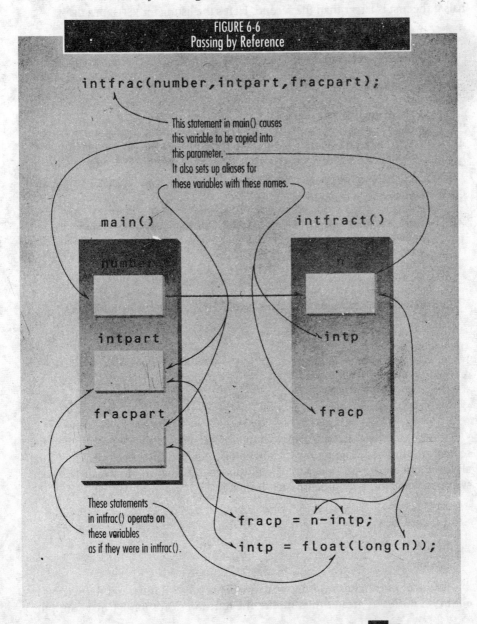

FIGURE 6-6
Passing by Reference

A MORE COMPLEX PASS BY REFERENCE

Here's a somewhat more complex example of passing simple arguments by reference. Suppose you have pairs of numbers in your program, and you want to be sure that the smaller one always precedes the larger one. To do this you call a function, order(), which checks two numbers passed to it by reference and swaps the originals if the first is larger than the second. Here's the listing for REFORDER.CPP:

```
// reforder.cpp
// orders two arguments passed by reference
#include <iostream.h>

void main()
    {
    void order(int&, int&);          // prototype

    int n1=99, n2=11;                // this pair not ordered
    int n3=22, n4=88;                // this pair ordered

    order(n1, n2);                   // order each pair of numbers
    order(n3, n4);

    cout << endl << "n1=" << n1;     // print out all numbers
    cout << endl << "n2=" << n2;
    cout << endl << "n3=" << n3;
    cout << endl << "n4=" << n4;
    }

void order(int& numb1, int& numb2)   // orders two numbers
    {
    if(numb1 > numb2)                // if 1st larger than 2nd,
        {
        int temp = numb1;            // swap them
        numb1 = numb2;
        numb2 = temp;
        }
    }
```

In main() there are two pairs of numbers—the first pair not ordered and the second pair ordered. The order() function is called once for each pair, and then all the numbers are printed out. The output reveals that the first pair has been swapped while the second pair hasn't. Here it is:

```
n1=11

n2=99

n3=22

n4=88
```

In the order() function the first variable is called numb1 and the second is numb2. If numb1 is greater than numb2 the function stores numb1 in temp, puts numb2 in numb1, and finally puts temp back in numb2. Remember that numb1 and numb2 are simply different names for whatever arguments were passed: in this case n1 and n2 on the first call to the function, and n2 and n3 on the second call. The effect is to check the ordering of the original arguments in the calling program and swap them if necessary.

Using reference arguments in this way is a sort of remote-control operation. The calling program tells the function what variables in the calling program to operate on, and the function modifies these variables without ever knowing their real names. It's as if you called the housepainters and then sat back and watched as your dining room walls mysteriously changed color.

PASSING STRUCTURES BY REFERENCE

You can pass structures by reference just as you can simple data types. Here's a program, REFERST, that performs scale conversions on values of type Distance. A scale conversion involves multiplying a group of distances by a factor. If a distance is 6'–8", and a scale factor is 0.5, the new distance is 3'–4". Such a conversion might be applied to all the dimensions of a building to make the building shrink but remain in proportion.

```
// referst.cpp
// demonstrates passing structure by reference
#include <iostream.h>

struct Distance                         // English distance
    {
    int feet;
    float inches;
    };

void scale( Distance&, float );         // function
void engldisp( Distance );              // declarations

void main()
    {
    Distance d1 = { 12, 6.5 };          // initialize d1 and d2
    Distance d2 = { 10, 5.5 };

    cout << "\nd1 = "; engldisp(d1);     // display old d1 and d2
    cout << "\nd2 = "; engldisp(d2);

    scale(d1, 0.5);                      // scale d1 and d2
    scale(d2, 0.25);

    cout << "\nd1 = "; engldisp(d1);     // display new d1 and d2
    cout << "\nd2 = "; engldisp(d2);
    }
```

```
// scale()
// scales value of type Distance by factor
void scale( Distance& dd, float factor)
    {
    float inches = (dd.feet*12 + dd.inches) * factor;
    dd.feet = inches / 12;
    dd.inches = inches - dd.feet * 12;
    }
```

```
// engldisp()
// display structure of type Distance in feet and inches
void engldisp( Distance dd )   // parameter dd of type Distance
    {
    cout << dd.feet << "\'-" << dd.inches << "\"";
    }
```

REFERST intializes two Distance variables—d1 and d2—to specific values, and displays them. Then it calls the scale() function to multipy d1 by 0.5 and d2 by 0.25. Finally it displays the resulting values of the distances. Here's the program's output:

```
d1 = 12'-6.5"
d2 = 10'-5.5"
d1 = 6'-3.25"
d2 = 2'-7.375"
```

Here are the two calls to the function scale():

```
scale(d1, 0.5);
scale(d2, 0.25);
```

The first call causes d1 to be multiplied by 0.5, the second causes d2 to be multiplied by 0.25. Notice that these changes take place directly to d1 and d2. The function doesn't return anything; the operation is performed directly on the Distance argument, which is passed by reference to scale. (Since only one value is changed in the calling program, you could rewrite the function to pass the argument by value and return the scaled value. Calling the function would look like this:

```
d1 = scale(d1, 0.5);
```

However, this is inelegant and unnecessarily verbose.)

NOTES ON PASSING BY REFERENCE

Passing arguments by reference is also possible in Pascal and BASIC. References don't exist in C, where pointers serve a somewhat similar purpose, although often less conveniently. Reference arguments were introduced into C++ to provide flexibility in a variety of situations involving objects as well as simple variables.

The third way to pass arguments to functions, besides by value and by reference, is to use pointers. We'll explore this when we discuss pointers in Chapter 12.

OVERLOADED FUNCTIONS

An overloaded function appears to perform different activities depending on the kind of data sent to it. Overloading is like the joke about the famous scientist who insisted that the thermos bottle was the greatest invention of all time. Why? "It's a miracle device," he said. "It keeps hot things hot, but cold things it keeps cold. How does it know?"

It may seem equally mysterious how an overloaded function knows what to do. It performs one operation on one kind of data but another operation on a different kind. Let's clarify matters with some examples.

DIFFERENT NUMBERS OF ARGUMENTS

Recall the `starline()` function in the TABLE example, and the `repchar()` function from the TABLEARG example, both shown earlier in this chapter. The `starline()` function printed a line using 45 asterisks, while `repchar()` used a character and a line length that were both specified when the function was called. We might imagine a third function, `charline()`, that always prints 45 characters but that allows the calling program to specify the character to be printed. These three functions—`starline()`, `repchar()`, and `charline()`—perform similar activities but have different names. For programmers using these functions, that means three names to remember and three places to look them up if they are listed alphabetically in an application's *Function Reference* documentation.

It would be far more convenient to use the same name for all three functions, even though they each have different arguments. Here's a program, OVERLOAD, that makes this possible:

```
// overload.cpp
// demonstrates function overloading
#include <iostream.h>

void repchar();
void repchar(char);
void repchar(char, int);

void main()
    {
    repchar();
    repchar('=');
    repchar('+', 30);
    }

// repchar()
// displays 45 asterisks
```

```
void repchar()
   {
   for(int j=0; j<45; j++)   // always loops 45 times
      cout << '*';           // always prints asterisk
   cout << endl;
   }

// repchar()
// displays 45 copies of specified character
void repchar(char ch)
   {
   for(int j=0; j<45; j++)   // always loops 45 times
      cout << ch;            // prints specified character
   cout << endl;
   }

// repchar()
// displays specified number of copies of specified character
void repchar(char ch, int n)
   {
   for(int j=0; j<n; j++)    // loops n times
      cout << ch;            // prints specified character
   cout << endl;
   }
```

This program prints out three lines of characters. Here's the output:

```
*********************************************
=============================================
++++++++++++++++++++++++++++++
```

The first two lines are 45 characters long, and the third is 30.

The program contains three functions with the same name. There are three declarations, three function calls, and three function definitions. What keeps the compiler from becoming hopelessly confused? It uses the number of arguments, and their data types, to distinguish one function from another. In other words, the declaration

```
void repchar();
```

which takes no arguments, describes an entirely different function than does the declaration

```
void repchar(char);
```

which takes one argument of type char, or the declaration

```
void repchar(char, int);
```

which takes one argument of type char and another of type int.

The compiler, seeing several functions with the same name but different numbers of arguments, could decide the programmer had made a mistake (which is what it would do in C). Instead, it very tolerantly sets up a separate function for every such

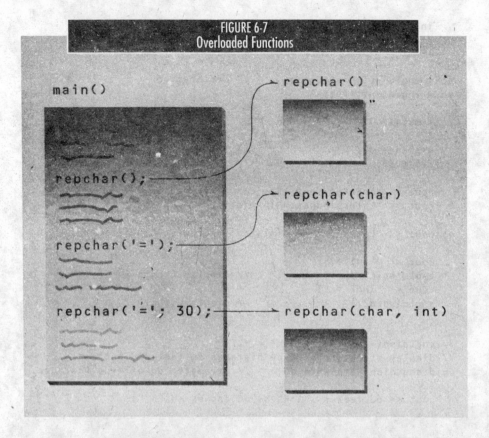

FIGURE 6-7
Overloaded Functions

definition. Which one of these functions will be called depends on the number of arguments supplied in the call. Figure 6-7 shows this process.

DIFFERENT KINDS OF ARGUMENTS

In the OVERLOAD example we created several functions with the same name but different numbers of arguments. The compiler can also distinguish between overloaded functions with the same number of arguments, provided their type is different. Here's a program, OVERENGL, that uses an overloaded function to display a quantity in feet-and-inches format. The single argument to the function can be either a structure of type `Distance` (as used in the ENGLDISP example) or a simple variable of type `float`. Different functions are used depending on the type of argument.

```
// overengl.cpp
// demonstrates overloaded functions
#include <iostream.h>

struct Distance                    // English distance
    {
```

```
    int feet;
    float inches;
    };

void engldisp( Distance );        // declarations
void engldisp( float );

void main()
    {
    Distance d1;                   // distance of type Distance
    float d2;                      // distance of type float
                                   // get length d1 from user
    cout << "\nEnter feet: ";  cin >> d1.feet;
    cout << "Enter inches: ";  cin >> d1.inches;
                                   // get length d2 from user
    cout << "Enter entire distance in inches: "; cin >> d2;

    cout << "\nd1 = ";
    engldisp(d1);                  // display length 1
    cout << "\nd2 = ";
    engldisp(d2);                  // display length 2
}

// engldisp()
// display structure of type Distance in feet and inches
void engldisp( Distance dd )   // parameter dd of type Distance
    {
    cout << dd.feet << "\'-" << dd.inches << "\"";
    }

// engldisp()
// display variable of type float in feet and inches
void engldisp( float dd )   // parameter dd of type float
    {
    int feet = dd / 12;
    float inches = dd - feet*12;
    cout << feet << "\'-" << inches << "\"";
    }
```

The user is invited to enter two distances, the first with separate feet and inches inputs, the second with a single large number for inches (109.5 inches, for example, instead of 9'–1.5"). The program calls the overloaded function engldisp() to display a value of type Distance for the first distance and of type float for the second. Here's a sample interaction with the program:

```
Enter feet: 5
Enter inches: 10.5
Enter entire distance in inches: 76.5
d1 = 5'-10.5"
d2 = 6'-4.5"
```

Notice that, while the different versions of `engldisp()` do similar things, the code is quite different. The version that accepts the all-inches input has to convert to feet and inches before displaying the result.

Overloaded functions can simplify the programmer's life by reducing the number of function names to be remembered. As an example of the complexity that arises when overloading is not used, consider the Turbo C++ library routines for finding the absolute value of a number. Because these routines must work with C (which does not allow overloading) as well as with C++, there must be separate versions of the absolute value routine for each data type. There are four of them: `abs()` for type `int`, `cabs()` for complex numbers, `fabs()` for type double, and `labs()` for type `long int`. In C++ a single name, `abs()`, would suffice for all these data types.

As we'll see later, overloaded functions are also useful for handling different types of objects.

INLINE FUNCTIONS

We mentioned that functions save memory space because all the calls to the function cause the same code to be executed; the function body need not be duplicated in memory. When the compiler sees a function call, it normally generates a jump to the function. At the end of the function it jumps back to the instruction following the call, as we showed in Figure 6-1.

While this sequence of events may save memory space, it takes some extra time. There must be an instruction for the jump to the function (actually the assembly-language instruction CALL), instructions for saving registers, instructions for pushing arguments onto the stack in the calling program and removing them from the stack in the function (if there are arguments), instructions for restoring registers, and an instruction to return to the calling program. The return value (if any) must also be dealt with. All these instructions slow down the program.

To save execution time in short functions you may elect to put the code in the function body directly in line with the code in the calling program. That is, each time there's a function call in the source file, the actual code from the function is inserted, instead of a jump to the function. The difference between a function and inline code is shown in Figure 6-8.

Long sections of repeated code are generally better off as normal functions: The saving in memory space is worth the comparatively small sacrifice in execution speed. But making a short section of code into a function may result in little saving in memory space, while imposing just as much time penalty as a larger function. In fact, if a function is very short, the instructions necessary to call it may even take up as much space as the instructions within the function body, so that there is not only a time penalty but a space penalty as well.

In such cases you could simply repeat the necessary code in your program, inserting the same group of statements wherever it was needed. The trouble with

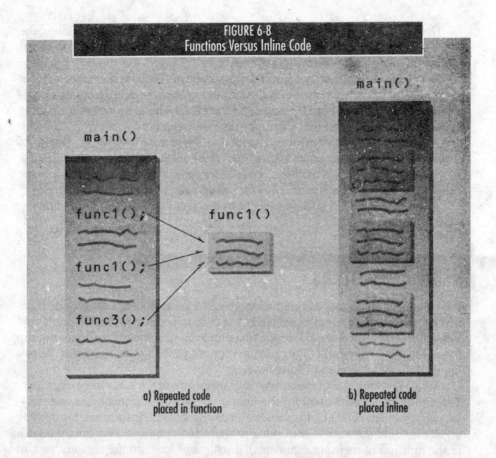

FIGURE 6-8
Functions Versus Inline Code

main()

main()

func1();

func1()

func1();

func3();

a) Repeated code
placed in function

b) Repeated code
placed inline

repeatedly inserting the same code is that you lose the benefits of program organization and clarity that come with using functions. The program may run faster and take less space, but the listing is longer and more complex.

The solution to this quandary is the *inline function*. This kind of function is written like a normal function in the source file but compiles into inline code instead of into a function. The source file remains well organized and easy to read, since the function is shown as a separate entity. However, when the program is compiled, the function body is actually inserted into the program wherever a function call occurs.

Functions that are very short, say one or two statements, are candidates to be inlined. Here's INLINE, a variation on the CONVERT2 program. It inlines the `lbstokg()` function.

```
// inline.cpp
// demonstrates inline functions
#include <iostream.h>

// lbstokg()                              // definition of
// converts pounds to kilograms          // inline function
```

```
inline float lbstokg(float pounds)   // (must precede calls
   {                                  // to it)
   return 0.453592 * pounds;
   }

void main()                          // main() must follow any
   {                                 // inline definitions
   float lbs;

   cout << "\nEnter your weight in pounds: ";
   cin >> lbs;
   cout << "Your weight in kilograms is " << lbstokg(lbs);
   }
```

It's easy to make a function inline: All you need is the keyword `inline` in the function definition:

```
inline float lgstokg(float pounds)
```

However, there are some subtleties to using inline functions. The compiler must have seen the function definition (not just the declaration) before it gets to the first function call. This is because it must insert the actual code into the program, not just instructions to call the function. In INLINE we must place the definition of `lbstokg()` before `main()`. When you do this the function declaration is unnecessary and can be eliminated.

You should be aware that the `inline` keyword is actually just a *request* to the compiler. Sometimes the compiler will ignore the request and compile the function as a normal function. It might decide the function is too long to be inline, for instance.

(C programmers should note that inline functions largely take the place of `#define` macros in C. They serve the same purpose but provide better type checking and do not need special care with parentheses as macros do.)

DEFAULT ARGUMENTS

Surprisingly, a function can be called without specifying all its arguments. This won't work on just any function: The function declaration must provide default values for those arguments that are not specified.

Here's an example, a variation on the OVERLOAD program, that demonstrates this effect. In OVERLOAD we used three different functions with the same name to handle different numbers of arguments. The present example, MISSARG, achieves the same effect in a different way.

```
// missarg.cpp
// demonstrates missing and default arguments
#include <iostream.h>

void repchar(char='*', int=45);   // prototype with
                                   // default arguments
```

```
void main()
   {
   repchar();          // prints 45 asterisks
   repchar('=');       // prints 45 equal signs
   repchar('+', 30);   // prints 30 plus signs
   }

// repchar()
// displays line of characters
void repchar(char ch, int n)  // defaults supplied if necessary
   {
   for(int j=0; j<n; j++)   // loops n times
      cout << ch;           // prints ch
   cout << endl;
   }
```

In this program the function repchar() takes two arguments. It's called three times from main(). The first time it's called with no arguments, the second time with one, and the third time with two. Why do the first two calls work? Because the called function provides *default arguments*, which will be used if the calling program doesn't supply them. The default arguments are specified in the prototype to repchar():

```
void repchar(char='*', int=45);  // prototype (declaration)
```

The default argument follows an equals sign, which is placed directly after the type name. You can also use variable names, as in

```
void repchar(char reptChar='*', int numberReps=45);
```

If one argument is missing when the function is called, it is assumed to be the last argument. The repchar() function assigns the value of the single argument to the ch parameter and uses the default value 45 for the n parameter.

If both arguments are missing, the function assigns the default value '*' to ch and the default value 45 to n. Thus the three calls to the function all work, even though each has a different number of arguments.

Remember that missing arguments must be the trailing arguments—those at the end of the argument list. You can leave out the last three arguments, but you can't leave out the next-to-last and then put in the last. This is reasonable; how would the compiler know which arguments you meant, if you left out some in the middle? (Missing arguments could have been indicated with commas, but commas are notoriously subject to misprints, so the designers of C++ ignored this possibility.) Not surprisingly, the compiler will flag an error if you leave out arguments for which the function you're calling does not provide default values.

Default arguments are useful if you just don't want to go to the trouble of writing arguments that, for example, almost always have the same value. They are also useful in cases where, after a program is written, the programmer decides to increase the capability of a function by adding another argument. Using default arguments means that the existing function calls can continue to use the old number of arguments, while new function calls can use more.

VARIABLES AND STORAGE CLASSES

Now that we know about functions, we can explore a feature of C++ that's related to the interaction of variables and functions: the `storage class`. The storage class of a variable determines which parts of the program can access it and how long it stays in existence. We'll look at variables with three storage classes—automatic, external, and static.

AUTOMATIC VARIABLES

So far all the variables we've used in example programs have been defined inside the function in which they are used. That is, the definition occurs inside the braces that delimit the function body:

```
void somefunc()
    {
    int somevar;        // variables defined within
    float othervar;     // the function body
    // other statements
    }
```

Variables may be defined inside `main()` or inside other functions; the effect is the same, since `main()` is a function. Variables defined within a function body are called *automatic variables*. Actually, a keyword, `auto`, can be used to specify an automatic variable. You would say

```
void somefunc()
    {
    auto int somevar;       // same as int somevar
    auto float othervar;    // same as float othervar
    // other statements
    }
```

However, since this is the default, there is seldom any need to use the `auto` keyword. Variables defined within a function are automatic anyway.

Let's look at the two important characteristics of automatic variables—lifetime and visibility.

Lifetime

An automatic variable is not created until the function in which it is defined is called. (More accurately, we can say that variables defined within any block of code are not created until the block is executed.) In the program fragment just given, the variables

VARIABLES AND STORAGE CLASSES

somevar and othervar don't exist until the somefunc() function is called. That is, there is no place in memory where their values are stored; they are undefined. When control is transferred to somefunc(), the variables are created and memory space is set aside for them. Later, when somefunc() exits and control is returned to the calling program, the variables are destroyed and their values are lost. The name *automatic* is used because the variables are automatically created when a function is called and automatically destroyed when it returns.

The time period between the creation and destruction of a variable is called its *lifetime* (or sometimes its *duration*). The lifetime of an automatic variable coincides with the time when the function in which it is defined is executing.

The idea behind limiting the lifetime of variables is to save memory space. If a function is not executing, the variables it uses during execution are presumably not needed. Removing them frees up memory that can then be used by other functions.

Visibility

A variable's *visibility* describes where within a program it can be accessed. It can be referred to in statements in some parts of the program; in others, attempts to access it lead to an *unknown variable* error message. The word *scope* is also used to describe visibility. The scope of a variable is that part of the program where the variable is visible.

Automatic variables are only **visible**, meaning they can only be accessed, within the function in which they are defined. Suppose you have two functions in a program:

```
void somefunc()
   {
   int somevar;      // automatic variables
   float othervar;

   somevar = 10;     // ok
   othervar = 11;    // ok
   nextvar = 12;     // illegal: not visible in somefunc()
   }

void otherfunc()
   {
   int nextvar;      // automatic variable

   somevar = 20;     // illegal: not visible in otherfunc()
   othervar = 21;    // illegal: not visible in otherfunc()
   nextvar = 22;     // ok
   }
```

The variable nextvar is invisible in function somefunc(), and the variables somevar and othervar are invisible in otherfunc().

Limiting the visibility of variables helps to organize and modularize the program. You can be confident that the variables in one function are safe from accidental alteration by other functions, because the other functions can't see them. This is an important part of structured programming, the methodology for organizing old-fashioned procedural programs. Limiting visibility is also an important part of object-oriented programming.

In the case of automatic variables, lifetime and visibility coincide: These variables exist only while the function in which they are defined is executing, and are only visible within this function. For some storage classes, however, lifetime and visibility are not the same.

Initialization

When an automatic variable is created, the compiler does not try to initialize it. Thus it will start off with an arbitrary value, which may be 0 but probably will be something else. If you want it initialized, you must do it explicitly, as in

```
int n = 33;
```

then it will start off with this value.

Automatic variables are sometimes called *local* variables, since they are visible only locally, in the function where they are defined.

EXTERNAL VARIABLES

The next major storage class is *external*. While automatic variables are defined within functions, external variables are defined outside of any function. External variables are also called *global* variables, since they are known by all the functions in a program.

Here's a program, EXTERN, in which three functions all access an external variable.

```
// extern.cpp
// demonstrates external variables
#include <iostream.h>
#include <conio.h>              // for getch()

char ch = 'a';                  // exteral variable ch

void getachar();                // function declarations
void putachar();

void main()
    {
    while( ch != '\r' )        // main() accesses ch
        {
        getachar();
        putachar();
        }
    }

void getachar()                 // getachar() accesses ch
    {
```

```
    ch = getch();
    }

void putachar()              // putachar() accesses ch
    {
    cout << ch;
    }
```

One function in EXTERN, `getachar()`, reads characters from the keyboard. It uses the library function `getch()`, which is like `getche()` except that it doesn't echo the character typed to the screen (hence the absence of the `e` in the name). A second EXTERN function, `putachar()`, displays each character on the screen. The effect is that what you type is displayed in the normal way:

```
I'm typing in this line of text
```

The significant thing about this program is that the variable `ch` is not defined in any of the functions. Instead it is defined at the beginning of the file, before the first function. It is an external variable. Any function that follows the definition of `ch` in the listing can access it—in this case all the functions in EXTERN: `main()`, `getachar()`, and `putachar()`. Thus the visibility of `ch` is the entire source file.

Role of External Variables

The external storage class is used when a variable must be accessible to more than one function in a program. In procedural programs external variables are often the most important variables in the program. However, as we noted in Chapter 1, external variables create organizational problems for the very reason that they can be accessed by any function. The wrong functions may access them, or functions may access them incorrectly. In an object-oriented program there is less necessity for external variables.

Initialization

If an external variable is initialized by the program, as in

```
int exvar = 199;
```

this initialization takes place when the file is first loaded but not thereafter. If an external variable is not initialized explicitly by the program—for example, if it is defined as

```
int exvar;
```

—then it is initialized automatically to 0 when it is created. (This is unlike automatic variables, which are not initialized and probably contain random or "garbage" values when they are created.)

Lifetime and Visibility

External variables exist for the life of the program. That is, memory space is set aside for them when the program begins, and continues in existence until the program ends.

External variables are visible in the file in which they are defined, starting at the point where they are defined. If `ch` were defined following `main()` but before `getachar()`, it would be visible in `getachar()` and `putachar()`, but not in `main()`.

STATIC VARIABLES

We'll touch on another storage class: *static*. Here we'll be concerned with static automatic variables. There are static external variables, but they are meaningful only in multifile programs, which we don't examine until Chapter 15.

A static automatic variable has the visibility of a local variable but the lifetime of an external variable. Thus it is visible only inside the function in which it is defined, but it remains in existence for the life of the program.

Static automatic variables are used when it's necessary for a function to remember a value when it is not being executed; that is, between calls to the function. In the next example, a function, `getavg()`, calculates a running average. It remembers the total of the numbers it has averaged before, and how many there were. Each time it receives a new number, sent as an argument from the calling program, it adds this number to the total, adds 1 to a count, and returns the new average by dividing the total by the count. Here's the listing for STATIC:

```
// static.cpp
// demonstrates static variables
#include <iostream.h>

float getavg(float);                    // prototype

void main()
   {
   float data=1, avg;

   while( data != 0 )
      {
      cout << "Enter a number: ";
      cin >> data;
      avg = getavg(data);
      cout << "New average is " << avg << endl;
      }
   }

// getavg()
// finds average of old plus new data
float getavg(float newdata)
   {
```

```
static float total = 0;    // static variables are initialized
static int count = 0;      // only once per program

count++;                   // increment count
total += newdata;          // add new data to total
return total / count;      // return the new average
}
```

Here's some sample interaction:

```
Enter a number: 10
New average is 10          ←——— total is 10, count is 1
Enter a number: 20
New average is 15          ←——— total is 30, count is 2
Enter a number: 30
New average is 20          ←——— total is 60, count is 3
```

The static variables `total` and `count` in `getavg()` retain their values after `getavg()` returns, so they're available the next time it's called.

Initialization

When static variables are initialized, as `total` and `count` are in `getavg()`, the initialization takes place only once—at the beginning of the program. They are not reinitialized each time the function is called, as ordinary automatic variables are.

STORAGE

If you're familiar with the architecture of MS-DOS computers, you might be interested to know that automatic variables are stored in the stack segment, while external and static variables are stored in the data segment.

Table 6-2 summarizes the lifetime, visibility, and some other aspects of automatic, external, and automatic static variables:

TABLE 6-2 Storage Types			
Storage type	automatic	static auto	external
Visibility	function	function	file
Lifetime	function	program	program
Initialized value	not initialized	0	0
Storage	stack segment	data segment	data segment
Purpose	variables used by a single function	same as auto, but must retain value when function terminates	variables used by several functions

RETURNING BY REFERENCE

Now that we know about external variables, we can examine a rather odd-looking C++ feature. It turns out that, besides passing values by reference, you can also return a value by reference. Why you would want to do this may seem obscure. The primary reason is to allow you to use a function call *on the left side of the equal sign.* This is a somewhat bizarre concept, so let's look at an example. The RETREF program shows the mechanism:

```
// retref.cpp
// returning reference values
#include <iostream.h>

int x;                       // global variable
int& setx();                 // function declarations

void main()
    {                        // set x to a value, using
    setx() = 92;             // function call on left side
    cout << "\nx=" << x;     // display new value in x
    }

int& setx()
    {
    return x;                // returns the value to be modified
    }
```

In this program the function `setx()` is declared with a reference type, `int&`, as the return type:

```
int& setx();
```

This function contains the statement

```
return x;
```

where x has been defined as an external variable. Now—and this is what looks so strange—you can put a call to this function on the left side of the equals sign:

```
setx() = 92;
```

The result is that the variable returned by the function is assigned the value on the right side of the equals sign. That is, x is given the value 92. The output from the program,

```
x=92
```

verifies that this assignment has taken place.

197

Of course, the question remains why such an activity is necessary. In procedural programming there probably isn't too much use for it. As in the present example, there are easier ways to achieve the same result. However, when we cover overloaded operators in Chapter 9, we'll find that returning by reference is an indispensable technique. Until then, keep it in the back of your mind.

Summary

Functions provide a way to help organize programs, and to reduce program size, by giving a block of code a name and allowing it to be executed from other parts of the program. Function declarations specify what the function looks like, function calls transfer control to the function, and function definitions contain the statements that make up the function. The function declarator is the first line of the definition.

Arguments can be sent to functions either by value, where the function works with a copy of the argument; or by reference, where the function works with the original argument in the calling program.

Functions can return only one value. Functions can return a reference, which allows the function call to be used on the left side of an assignment statement. Arguments and return values can be either simple data types or structures.

An overloaded function is actually a group of functions with the same name. Which of them is executed when the function is called depends on the type and number of arguments supplied in the call.

An inline function looks like a normal function in the source file but inserts the function's code directly into the calling program. Inline functions execute faster but may require more memory than normal functions unless they are very small.

If a function uses default arguments, calls to it need not include all the arguments shown in the declaration. Default values supplied by the function are used for the missing arguments.

Variables possess a characteristic called the storage class. The most common storage class is automatic. Variables of this class exist only while the function in which they are defined is executing, and are visible only within that function. External variables exist for the life of a program and can be visible throughout an entire file. Static automatic variables exist for the life of a program but are visible only in their own function.

In the last chapter we examined one of the two major parts of objects: structures, which are collections of data. In this chapter we explored the second part: functions. Now we're ready to put these two components together to create objects, the subject of the next chapter.

QUESTIONS

1. A function's single most important role is to
   a. give a name to a block of code
   b. reduce program size
   c. accept arguments and provide a return value
   d. help organize a program into conceptual units

2. A function itself is called the function d_____

3. Write a function called **foo()** that displays the word *foo*.

4. A one-statement description of a function is referred to as a function d_____ or a p_____.

5. The statements that carry out the work of the function constitute the function _____.

6. A program statement that invokes a function is a function _____.

7. The first line of a function definition is referred to as the _____.

8. A function argument is
   a. a variable in the function that receives a value from the calling program.
   b. a way that functions resist accepting the calling program's values
   c. a value sent to the function by the calling program
   d. a value returned by the function to the calling program

9. True or false: When arguments are passed by value, the function works with the original arguments in the calling program.

10. What is the purpose of using argument names in a function declaration?

11. Which of the following can legitimately be passed to a function:
    a. a constant
    b. a variable
    c. a structure
    d. a header file

12. What is the significance of empty parentheses in a function declaration?

13. How many values can be returned from a function?

14. True or false: When a function returns a value, the entire function call can appear on the right side of the equals sign and be assigned to another variable.

15. Where is a function's return type specified?

16. A function that doesn't return anything has return type _____.

17. Here's a function:

```
int times2(int a)
    {
    return (a*2);
    }
```

    Write a `main()` program that includes everything necessary to call this function.

18. When an argument is passed by reference,
    a. a variable is created in the function to hold the argument's value
    b. the function cannot access the argument's value
    c. a temporary variable is created in the calling program to hold the argument's value
    d. the function accesses the argument's original value in the calling program

19. What is the principle reason for passing arguments by reference?

20. Overloaded functions
    a. are a group of functions with the same name
    b. all have the same number and types of arguments
    c. make life simpler for programmers
    d. may fail unexpectedly due to stress

21. Write declarations for two overloaded functions named `bar()`. They both return type `int`. The first takes one argument of type `char`, and the second takes two arguments of type `char`. If this is impossible, say why.

22. In general, an inline function executes _____ than a normal function, but requires _____ memory.

23. Write the declarator for an inline function named `foobar()` that takes one argument of type `float` and returns type `float`.

24. A default argument has a value that
    a. may be supplied by the calling program
    b. may be supplied by the function
    c. must have a constant value
    d. must have a variable value

25. Write a declaration for a function called `blyth()` that takes two arguments and returns type `char`. The first argument is type `int`, and the second is type `float` with a default value of 3.14159.

26. Storage class is concerned with the _____ and _____ of a variable.

27. What functions can access an external variable that appears in the same file with them?

28. What functions can access an automatic variable?
29. A static automatic variable is used to
    a. make a variable visible to several functions
    b. make a variable visible to only one function
    c. conserve memory when a function is not executing
    d. retain a value when a function is not executing
30. In what unusual place can you use a function call when a function returns a value by reference?

EXERCISES

1. Refer to the CIRCAREA program of Chapter 3. Write a function called `circarea()` that finds the area of a circle in a similar way. It should take an argument of type `float` and return an argument of the same type. Write a `main()` function that gets a radius value from the user, calls `circarea()`, and displays the result.

2. Raising a number n to a power p is the same as multiplying n by itself p times. Write a function called `power()` that takes a `double` value for n and an `int` value for p, and returns the result as `double` value. Use a default argument of 2 for p, so that if this argument is omitted, the number will be squared. Write a `main()` function that gets values from the user to test this function.

3. Write a function called `zeroSmaller()` that is passed two `int` arguments by reference and then sets the smaller of the two numbers to 0. Write a `main()` program to exercise this function.

4. Write a function that takes two `Distance` values as arguments and returns the larger one. Include a `main()` program that accepts two `Distance` figures from the user, compares them, and displays the larger. (See the RETSTRC program for hints.)

And now, the topics you've all been waiting for: objects and classes. The preliminaries are out of the way. We've learned about structures, which provide a way to group data elements. We've examined functions, which organize program actions into named entities. In this chapter we'll put these ideas together. We'll introduce several classes, starting with simple ones and working up toward more complicated examples. We'll focus first on the details of classes and objects. At the end of the chapter we'll take a wider view, discussing what is to be gained by using the OOP approach.

As you read this chapter you may want to refer back to the concepts introduced in Chapter 1.

A SIMPLE CLASS

Our first program contains a class and two objects of that class. Although it's simple, the program demonstrates the syntax and general features of classes in C++. Here's the listing for the SMALLOBJ program:

```
// smallobj.cpp
// demonstrates a small, simple object
#include <iostream.h>

class smallobj                  // specify a class
   {
   private:
      int somedata;             // class data
   public:
      void setdata(int d)       // member function to set data
         { somedata = d; }
      void showdata()           // member function to display data
         { cout << "\nData is " << somedata; }
   };

void main()
   {
   smallobj s1, s2;     // define two objects of class smallobj
```

```
s1.setdata(1066);   // call member function to set data
s2.setdata(1776);

s1.showdata();      // call member function to display data
s2.showdata();
}
```

The class smallobj specified in this program contains one data item and two member functions. These functions provide the only access to the data item from outside the class. The first member function sets the data item to a value, and the second displays the value. (This may sound like Greek, but we'll see what these terms mean as we go along.)

Placing data and functions together into a single entity is the central idea of object-oriented programming. This is shown in Figure 7-1.

CLASSES AND OBJECTS

Recall from Chapter 1 that an object has the same relationship to a class that a variable has to a data type. An object is said to be an *instance* of a class, in the same way my 1954 Chevrolet is an instance of a vehicle. In SMALLOBJ, the class—whose name is smallobj—is specified in the first part of the program. Later, in main(), we define two objects—s1 and s2—that are instances of that class.

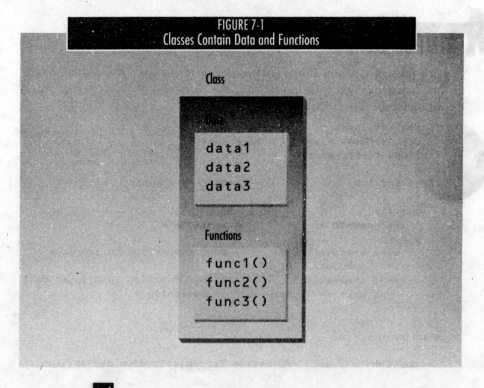

FIGURE 7-1
Classes Contain Data and Functions

Class

Data

data1
data2
data3

Functions

func1()
func2()
func3()

Each of the two objects is given a value, and each displays its value. Here's the output of the program:

```
Data is 1066        ←——— object s1 displayed this
Data is 1776        ←——— object s2 displayed this
```

We'll begin by looking in detail at the first part of the program—the specification for the class smallobj. Later we'll focus on what main() does with objects of this class.

SPECIFYING THE CLASS

Here's the specifier for the class smallobj, copied from the SMALLOBJ listing:

```
class smallobj                    // specify a class
   {
   private:
      int somedata;               // class data
   public:
      void setdata(int d)         // member function to set data
         { somedata = d; }
      void showdata()             // member function to display data
         { cout << "\nData is " << somedata; }
   };
```

The specifier starts with the keyword class, followed by the class name—smallobj in this example. Like a structure, the body of the class is delimited by braces and terminated by a semicolon. (Don't forget the semicolon. Remember, data constructs like structures and classes end with the semicolon, while control constructs like functions and loops do not.)

private and public

The body of the class contains two unfamiliar keywords: private and public. What is their purpose?

A key feature of object-oriented programming is *data hiding*. This term does not refer to the activities of particularly paranoid programmers; rather it means that data is concealed within a class, so that it cannot be accessed mistakenly by functions outside the class. The primary mechanism for hiding data is to put it in a class and make it *private*. Private data or functions can only be accessed from within the class. Public data or functions, on the other hand, are accessible from outside the class. This is shown in Figure 7-2.

Hidden from Whom?

Don't confuse data hiding with the security techniques used to protect computer databases. To provide a security measure you might, for example, require a user to supply a password before granting access to a database. The password is meant to keep unauthorized or malevolent users from altering (or often even reading) the data.

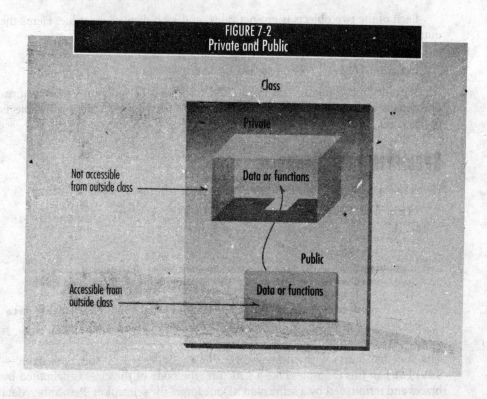

FIGURE 7-2
Private and Public

Data hiding, on the other hand, is designed to protect well-intentioned programmers from honest mistakes. Programmers who really want to can figure out a way to access `private` data, but they will find it hard to do so by accident.

Class Data

The `smallobj` class contains one data item: `somedata`, which is of type `int`. There can be any number of data items in a class, just as there can be any number of data items in a structure. The data item `somedata` follows the keyword `private`, so it can be accessed from within the class, but not from outside.

Member Functions

Member functions are functions that are included within a class. (In some object-oriented languages, such as Smalltalk, member functions are called *methods*; some writers use this term in C++ as well.) There are two member functions in `smallobj`: `setdata()` and `showdata()`. The function bodies of these functions have been written on the same line as the braces that delimit them. You could also use the more traditional format for these function definitions:

```
    void setdata(int d)
        {
        somedata = d;
        }
```

and

```
    void showdata(int d)
        {
        cout << "\nData is " << somedata;
        }
```

However, when member functions are small, it is common to compress their definitions this way to save space.

Figure 7-3 shows the syntax of a class specifier. Because `setdata()` and `showdata()` follow the keyword `public`, they can be accessed from outside the class. We'll see how this is done in a moment.

Public and Private

Usually the data within a class is private and the functions are public. This is a result of how classes are used. The data is hidden so it will be safe from accidental manipulation, while the functions that operate on the data are public so they can be accessed from outside the class. However, there is no rule that data must be

FIGURE 7-3
Syntax of a Class Specifier

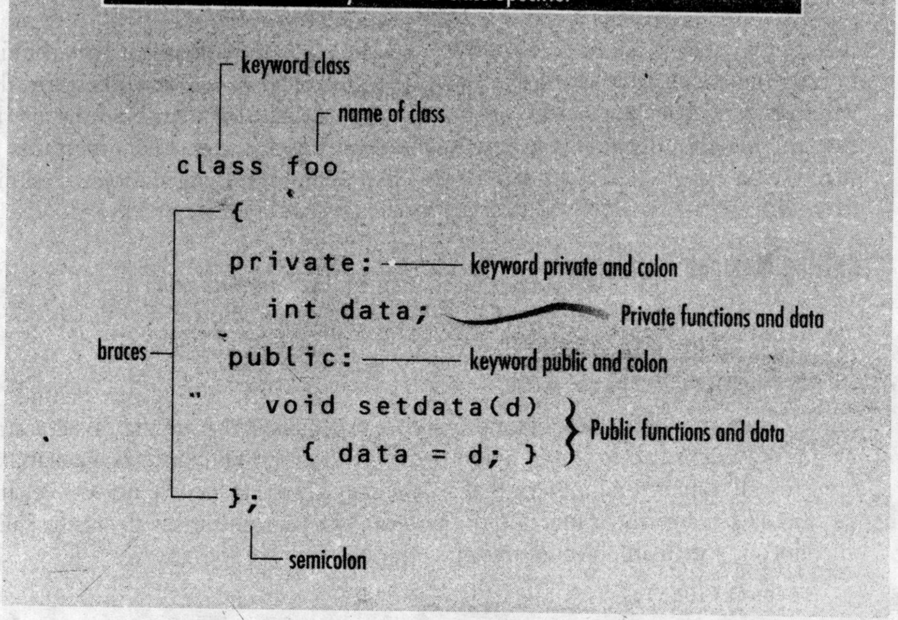

private and functions public; in some circumstances you may find you'll need to use private functions and public data.

Member Functions within Class Specifier

The member functions in the `smallobj` class perform operations that are quite common in classes: setting and retrieving the data stored in the class. The `setdata()` function accepts a value as a parameter and sets the `somedata` variable to this value. The `showdata()` function displays the value stored in `somedata`.

Note that the member functions `setdata()` and `showdata()` are *definitions*: The actual code for the function is contained within the class specification. Member functions defined inside a class this way are created as *inline* functions by default. (Inline functions were discussed in the last chapter.) We'll see later that it is also possible to *declare* a function within a class but *define* it elsewhere. Functions defined outside the class are not normally inline.

USING THE CLASS

Now that the class is specified, let's see how `main()` makes use of it. We'll see how objects are defined, and, once defined, how their member functions are accessed.

Defining Objects

The first statement in `main()`,

```
smallobj s1, s2;
```

defines two objects, `s1` and `s2`, of class `smallobj`. Remember that the specification for the class `smallobj` does not create any objects. It only describes how they will look when they are created, just as a structure specifier describes how a structure will look but doesn't create any structure variables. It is the definition that actually creates objects that can be used by the program. Defining an object is similar to defining a variable of any data type: Space is set aside for it in memory.

Calling Member Functions

The next two statements in `main()` call the member function `setdata()`:

```
s1.setdata(1066);
s2.setdata(1776);
```

These statements don't look like normal function calls. Why are the object names `s1` and `s2` connected to the function names with a period? This strange syntax is used to call a member function that is associated with a specific object. Because `setdata()` is a member function of the `smallobj` class, it must always be called in connection with an object of this class. It doesn't make sense to say

```
setdata(1066);
```

by itself, because a member function is always called to act on a specific object, not on the class in general. Attempting to access the class this way would be like trying to drive the blueprint of a car. Not only does this statement not make sense, but the compiler will issue an error message if you attempt it. Member functions of a class can be accessed only by an object of that class.

To use a member function, the dot operator (the period) connects the object name and the member function. The syntax is similar to the way we refer to structure members, but the parentheses signal that we're executing a member function rather than referring to a data item. The dot operator is also called the *class member access operator*.

The first call to `setdata()`,

```
s1.setdata(1066);
```

executes the `setdata()` member function of the `s1` object. This function sets the variable `somedata` in object `s1` to the value 1066. The second call,

```
s2.setdata(1776);
```

causes the variable `somedata` in `s2` to be set to 1776. Now we have two objects whose `somedata` variables have different values, as shown in Figure 7-4.

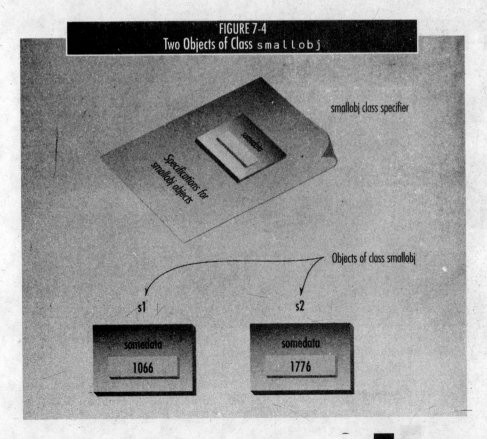

FIGURE 7-4
Two Objects of Class `smallobj`

smallobj class specifier

Specifications for smallobj objects

Objects of class smallobj

s1

s2

somedata

1066

somedata

1776

Similarly, the following two calls to the `showdata()` function will cause the two objects to display their values:

```
s1.showdata();
s2.showdata();
```

Messages

Some object-oriented languages, such as Smalltalk, refer to calls to member functions as *messages*. Thus the call

```
s1.showdata();
```

can be thought of as sending a message to `s1` telling it to display itself. The term *message* is not a formal part of C++, but it is a useful idea to keep in mind as we discuss member functions. Talking about messages emphasizes that objects are discrete entities and that we communicate with them by calling their member functions. Referring to the analogy with company organization in Chapter 1, it's like sending a message to the secretary in the sales department to get a list of products sold in the southwest distribution area.

C++ Objects as Physical Objects

The `smallobj` class in the last example had only one data item. Let's examine an example of a somewhat more ambitious class. (These are not the same ambitious classes dicussed in political science courses.) We'll create a class based on the structure for the widget parts inventory, last seen in such examples as PARTS in Chapter 5. Here's the listing for OBJPART:

```
// objpart.cpp
// widget part as an object
#include <iostream.h>

class part                   // specify an object
    {
    private:
        int modelnumber;      // ID number of widget
        int partnumber;       // ID number of widget part
        float cost;           // cost of part
    public:
        void setpart(int mn, int pn, float c)  // set data
            {
            modelnumber = mn;
            partnumber = pn;
            cost = c;
            }
        void showpart()                         // display data
            {
```

```
        cout << "\nModel "  << modelnumber;
        cout << ", part "   << partnumber;
        cout << ", costs $" << cost;
        }
    };

void main()
    {
    part part1;                              // define object
                                             //    of class part
    part1.setpart(6244, 373, 217.55);  // call member function
    part1.showpart();                  // call member function
    }
```

This program features the class part. Instead of one data item, as smallobj had, this class has three: modelnumber, partnumber, and cost. A single member function, setpart(), serves to supply values to all three data items at once. Another function, showpart(), displays the values stored in all three items.

In this example only one object of type part is created: part1. The member function setpart() sets the three data items in this part to the values 6244, 373, and 217.55. The member function showpart() then displays these values. Here's the output:

```
Model 6244, part 373, costs $217.55
```

This is a somewhat more realistic example than SMALLOBJ. If you were designing an inventory program you might actually want to create a class something like part. It's an example of a C++ object representing a physical object in the real world—a widget part.

C++ OBJECTS AS DATA TYPES

Here's another kind of entity C++ objects can represent: variables of a user-defined data type. We'll use objects to represent distances measured in the English system, as discussed in Chapter 5. Here's the listing for ENGLOBJ:

```
// englobj.cpp
// objects using English measurements
#include <iostream.h>

class Distance                          // English Distance class
    {
    private:
        int feet;
        float inches;
    public:
        void setdist(int ft, float in)    // set distance to args
            { feet = ft; inches = in; }
```

```
    void getdist()                  // get length from user
      {
      cout << "\nEnter feet: ";  cin >> feet;
      cout << "Enter inches: ";  cin >> inches;
      }

    void showdist()                 // display distance
      { cout << feet << "\'-" << inches << '\"'; }
   };

void main()
   {
   Distance dist1, dist2;           // define two lengths

   dist1.setdist(11, 6.25);         // set dist1

   dist2.getdist();                 // get dist2 from user

                                    // display lengths
   cout << "\ndist1 = ";  dist1.showdist();
   cout << "\ndist2 = ";  dist2.showdist();
   }
```

In this program the class **Distance** contains two data items, **feet** and **inches**. This is similar to the **Distance** structure seen in examples in Chapter 5, but here the class **Distance** also has three member functions: **setdist()**, which uses arguments to set **feet** and **inches**; **getdist()**, which gets values for **feet** and **inches** from the user at the keyboard; and **showdist()**, which displays the distance in feet-and-inches format.

The value of an object of class **Distance** can thus be set in either of two ways. In **main()** we define two objects of class **Distance**: **dist1** and **dist2**. One is given a value using the **setdist()** member function with the arguments 11 and 6.25, and the other is given a value that is supplied by the user. Here's a sample interaction with the program:

```
Enter feet: 10
Enter inches: 4.75

dist1 = 11'-6.25"          ←——— provided by arguments
dist2 = 10'-4.75"          ←——— input by the user
```

CONSTRUCTORS

The ENGLOBJ example shows two ways to give values to the data items in an object. Sometimes, however, it's convenient if an object can initialize itself when it's first created, without the need to make a separate call to a member function. Automatic initialization is carried out using a special member function called a *constructor*. A constructor is a member function that is executed automatically whenever an object is created.

A Counter Example

As an example, we'll create a class of objects that might be useful as a general-purpose programming element. A *counter* is a variable that counts things. Maybe it counts file accesses, or the number of times the user presses the (ENTER) key, or the number of customers entering a bank. Each time such an event takes place, the counter is incremented (1 is added to it). The counter can also be accessed to find the current count.

Let's assume that this counter is important in the program and must be accessed by many different functions. In procedural languages such as C a counter would probably be implemented as an external variable. However, as we noted in Chapter 1, external variables may be modified accidentally. This example, COUNTER, provides a counter variable that can be modified only through its member functions.

```cpp
// counter.cpp
// object represents a counter variable
#include <iostream.h>

class Counter
   {
   private:
      unsigned int count;                        // count
   public:
      Counter()            { count = 0; }        // constructor
      void inc_count()     { count++; }          // increment count
      int get_count()      { return count; }     // return count
   };

void main()
   {
   Counter c1, c2;                               // define and initialize

   cout << "\nc1=" << c1.get_count();            // display
   cout << "\nc2=" << c2.get_count();

   c1.inc_count();                               // increment c1
   c2.inc_count();                               // increment c2
   c2.inc_count();                               // increment c2

   cout << "\nc1=" << c1.get_count();            // display again
   cout << "\nc2=" << c2.get_count();
   }
```

The Counter class has one data item: count, of type unsigned int (since the count is always positive). It has three member functions: Counter(), which we'll look at in a moment; `inc_count`, which adds 1 to `count`; and `get_count()`, which returns the current value of `count`.

Automatic Initialization

When an object of type `Counter` is first created, we want its `count` to be initialized to 0. After all, most counts start at 0. We could provide a `set_count()` function to do this, and call it with an argument of 0, or we could provide a `zero_count()` function, which would always set `count` to 0. However, such functions would need to be executed every time we created a `Counter` object:

```
Counter c1;          // every time we do this,
c1.zero_count();     // we must do this too
```

It's more convenient, especially when there are a great many objects of a given class, to cause each object to initialize itself. In the `Counter` class the constructor `Counter()` does this. This function is called automatically whenever a new object of type `Counter` is created. Thus in `main()` the statement

```
Counter c1, c2;
```

creates two objects of type `Counter`. As each is created, its constructor, `Counter()`, is executed. This function sets the `count` variable to 0. So the effect of this single statement is to not only create two objects but to initialize their `count` variables to 0.

Same Name as the Class

There are some unusual aspects to constructor functions. First, it is no accident that they have exactly the same name (`Counter` in this example), as the class of which they are members. This is how the compiler knows they are constructors.

Second, no return type is used for constructors. Why not? Since the constructor is called automatically by the system, there's no program for it to return anything to; a return value wouldn't make sense.

Messing with the Format

Note that, in writing the functions in this example, we've compressed them so they occupy only one line each:

```
Counter()  { count = 0; }
```

This is just the same (as far as the compiler is concerned) as the normal function syntax

```
Counter()
   {
   count = 0;
   }
```

The `main()` part of this program exercises the `Counter` class by creating two counters, `c1` and `c2`. It causes the counters to display their initial values, which—

216

as arranged by the constructor—are 0. It then increments c1 once and c2 twice, and again causes the counters to display themselves (noncriminal behavior in this context). Here's the output:

```
c1=0
c2=0
c1=1
c2=2
```

If this isn't enough proof that the constructor is operating as advertised, we can rewrite the constructor to print a message when it executes:

```
Counter() { count = 0; cout << "I'm the constructor\n"; }
```

Now the program's output looks like this:

```
I'm the constructor
I'm the constructor
c1=0
c2=0
c1=1
c2=2
```

As you can see, the constructor is executed twice—once for c1 and once for c2—when the statement

```
Counter c1, c2;
```

is executed in main().

Do-It-Yourself Data

Constructors are pretty amazing when you think about it. Whoever writes language compilers (for C or BASIC or even for C++) must execute the equivalent of a constructor when the user defines a variable. If you define an int, for example, somewhere there's a constructor allocating two bytes of memory for it. If we can write our own constructors we can start to take over some of the tasks of a compiler writer. This is one step on the path to creating our own data types, as we'll see later.

DESTRUCTORS

We've seen that a special member function—the constructor—is called automatically when an object is first created. You might guess that another function is called automatically when an object is destroyed. This is indeed the case. Such a function is called a *destructor*. A destructor has the same name as the constructor (which is the same as the class name) but preceded by a tilde:

```
class Foo
    {
    private:
        int data;
```

```
public:
    Foo() { data = 0; }   // constructor (same name as class)
    ~Foo() { }            // destructor (same name with tilde)
}
```

Like constructors, destructors do not have a return value. They also take no arguments (the assumption being that there's only one way to destroy an object).

The most common use of destructors is to de-allocate memory that was allocated for the object by the constructor. We'll investigate these activities in Chapter 12. Until then we won't have much use for destructors.

OBJECTS AS FUNCTION ARGUMENTS

Our next program adds some embellishments to the earlier ENGLOBJ example. It also demonstrates some new aspects of classes: constructor overloading, defining member functions outside the class, and—perhaps most importantly—objects as function arguments. Here's the listing for ENGLCON.CPP:

```
// englcon.cpp
// constructors, adds objects using member function
#include <iostream.h>

class Distance                          // English Distance class
    {
    private:
        int feet;
        float inches;
    public:
        Distance()                      // constructor (no args)
            { }
        Distance(int ft, float in)      // constructor (two args)
            { feet = ft; inches = in; }

        void getdist()                  // get length from user
            {
            cout << "\nEnter feet: ";   cin >> feet;
            cout << "Enter inches: ";   cin >> inches;
            }

        void showdist()                 // display distance
            { cout << feet << "\'-" << inches << '\"'; }

        void add_dist( Distance, Distance );   // declaration
    };
                                        // add lengths d2 and d3
void Distance::add_dist(Distance d2, Distance d3)
    {
```

```
        inches = d2.inches + d3.inches;  // add the inches
        feet = 0;                        // (for possible carry)
        if(inches >= 12.0)               // if total exceeds 12.0,
            {                            // then decrease inches
            inches -= 12.0;              // by 12.0 and
            feet++;                      // increase feet
            }                            // by 1
        feet += d2.feet + d3.feet;       // add the feet
        }

void main()
    {
    Distance dist1, dist3;               // define two lengths
    Distance dist2(11, 6.25);            // define and initialize dist2

    dist1.getdist();                     // get dist1 from user
    dist3.add_dist(dist1, dist2);        // dist3 = dist1 + dist2

                                         // display all lengths
    cout << "\ndist1 = ";  dist1.showdist();
    cout << "\ndist2 = ";  dist2.showdist();
    cout << "\ndist3 = ";  dist3.showdist();
    }
```

This program starts with a distance set to an initial value, and adds to it a distance supplied by the user, to obtain the sum of the distances. It then displays all three distances:

```
Enter feet: 17
Enter inches: 5.75

dist1 = 17'-5.75"
dist2 = 11'-6.25"
dist3 = 29'-0"
```

Let's see how the new features in this program are implemented.

OVERLOADED CONSTRUCTORS

It would be nice to be able to give variables of type **Distance** a value when they are first created. That is, we would like to use definitions like

```
Distance width(5, 6.25);
```

which defines an object, **width**, and simultaneously initializes it to a value of 5 for **feet** and 6.25 for **inches**.

To do this we write a constructor like this:

```
Distance(int ft, float in)
    { feet = ft; inches = in; }
```

219

This sets the class data **feet** and **inches** to whatever values are passed as arguments to the constructor. So far so good.

However, we also want to define variables of type **Distance** without initializing them, as we did in ENGLOBJ:

```
Distance dist1, dist2;
```

In that program there was no constructor, but our definitions worked just fine. How could they work without a constructor? Because an implicit constructor was built into the program automatically by the compiler, and it created the objects, even though we didn't define it in the class.

Unfortunately, once we define one constructor, we must also define the implicit constructor. So we need the definition

```
Distance()
   { }            // no function body, doesn't do anything
```

in class **Distance**. The empty braces mean that the function doesn't do anything; it's just there to satisfy the compiler.

Since there are now two constructors with the same name, **Distance()**, we say the constructor is overloaded. Which of the two constructors is exectuted when an object is created depends on how many arguments are used in the definition:

```
Distance length;          // calls first constructor
Distance width(11, 6.0);  // calls second constructor
```

Member Functions Defined Outside the Class

So far we've seen member functions that were defined inside the class specifier. This need not always be the case. ENGLCON shows a member function, **add_dist()**, that is not defined within the **Distance** class specifier. It is only declared inside the class, with the statement

```
void add_dist(Distance, Distance);
```

This tells the compiler that this function is a member of the class but that it will be defined outside the class specifier, someplace else in the listing.

In ENGLCON the function is defined immediately after the class specifier. It is adapted from the ENGLSTRC program of Chapter 5:

```
                         // add lengths d2 and d3
void Distance::add_dist(Distance d2, Distance d3)
   {
   inches = d2.inches + d3.inches;  // add the inches
   feet = 0;                        // (for possible carry)
   if(inches >= 12.0)               // if total exceeds 12.0,
      {                             // then decrease inches
      inches -= 12.0;              // by 12.0 and
```

```
      feet++;                    // increase feet
      }                          // by 1
   feet += d2.feet + d3.feet;    // add the feet
   }
```

The declarator in this definition contains some unfamiliar syntax. The function name, `add_dist()`, is preceded by the class name, `Distance`, and a new symbol— the double colon (`::`). This symbol is called the *scope resolution operator*. It is a way of specifying what class something is associated with. In this situation it means *the `add_dist()` member function of the `Distance` class*. Figure 7-5 shows its usage.

OBJECTS AS ARGUMENTS

Now we can see how ENGLCON works. The distances `dist1` and `dist3` are created using the constructor that takes no arguments; this constructor does not do any initialization. The distance `dist2` is created with the constructor that takes two arguments, and is initialized to the values passed in these arguments. A value is obtained for `dist1` by calling the member function `getdist()`, which obtains values from the user.

Now we want to add `dist1` and `dist2` to obtain `dist3`. The function call in `main()`,

```
   dist3.add_dist(dist1, dist2);
```

does this. The two distances to be added, `dist1` and `dist2`, are supplied as arguments to `add_dist()`. The syntax for arguments that are objects is the same as that for arguments that are simple data types like `int`: The object name is supplied as

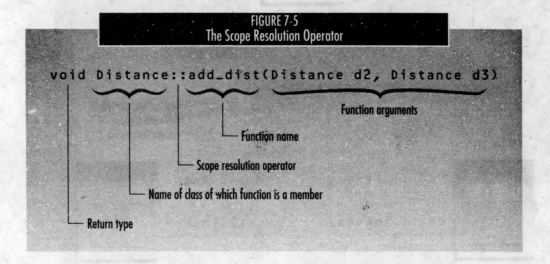

FIGURE 7-5
The Scope Resolution Operator

void Distance::add_dist(Distance d2, Distance d3)

Function arguments

Function name

Scope resolution operator

Name of class of which function is a member

Return type

the argument. Since `add_dist()` is a member function of the `Distance` class, it can access the private data in any object of class `Distance` supplied to it as an argument, using names like `dist1.inches` and `dist2.feet`.

Close examination of `add_dist()` emphasizes some important truths about member functions. When a member function is called, it is given access to only one object: *the object of which the function is a member*. In the following statement in ENGLCON, what objects can `add_dist()` access?

```
dist3.add_dist(dist1, dist2);
```

It can access `dist1` and `dist2`, because they are supplied as arguments. It can also access `dist3`, because it is a member function of `dist3`. You might think of `dist3` as a sort of phantom argument; the member function always has access to it, even though it is not supplied as an argument. That's what this statement means: "Execute the `add_dist()` member function of `dist3`." When the variables `feet` and `inches`

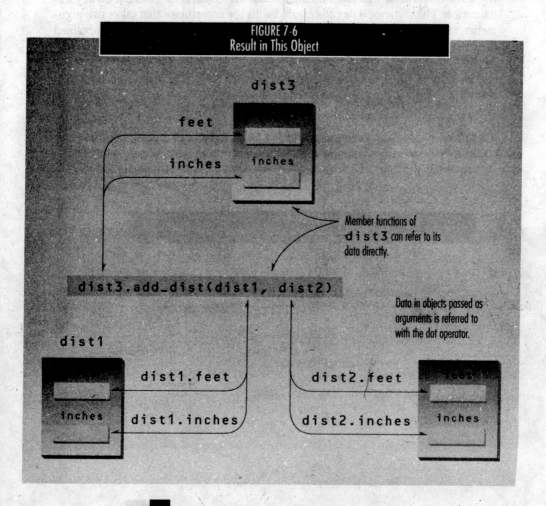

FIGURE 7-6
Result in This Object

are referred to within this function, they refer to `dist3.feet` and `dist3.inches`. Later in this book we'll see that a member function can refer to the entire object of which it is a member with the keyword `this`. The term `this` emphasizes the close relationship between a function and the object of which it is a member.

Notice that the result is not returned by the function. The return type of `add_dist()` is `void`. The result is stored automatically in the `dist3` object. Figure 7-6 shows the two distances `dist1` and `dist2` being added together, with the result stored in `dist3`.

Returning Objects from Functions

In the ENGLCON example we saw objects being passed as arguments to functions. Now we'll see an example of a function that returns an object. We'll modify the ENGLCON program to produce ENGLRET:

```
// englret.cpp
// function returns value of type Distance
#include <iostream.h>

class Distance                      //English Distance class
    {
private:
    int feet;
    float inches;
public:
    Distance()                      // constructor (no args)
        { feet = 0; inches = 0.0; }
    Distance(int ft, float in)  // constructor (two args)
        { feet = ft; inches = in; }

    void getdist()                  // get length from user
        {
        cout << "\nEnter feet: ";  cin >> feet;
        cout << "Enter inches: ";  cin>> inches;
        }

    void showdist()                 // display distance
        { cout << feet << "\'-" << inches << '\"'; }

    Distance add_dist( Distance );  // add
    };
                                    // add this distance to d2
Distance Distance::add_dist(Distance d2)   // return the sum
    {
    Distance temp;                          // temporary variable
    temp.inches = inches + d2.inches;  // add the inches
```

```
    if(temp.inches >= 12.0)              // if total exceeds 12.0,
        {                                // then decrease inches
        temp.inches -= 12.0;             // by 12.0 and
        temp.feet = 1;                   // increase feet
        }                                // by 1
    temp.feet += feet + d2.feet;         // add the feet
    return temp;
    }

void main()
    {
    Distance dist1, dist3;               // define two lengths
    Distance dist2(11, 6.25);            // define, initialize dist2

    dist1.getdist();                     // get dist1 from user
    dist3 = dist1.add_dist(dist2);       // dist3 = dist1 + dist2

                                         // display all lengths
    cout << "\ndist1 = ";  dist1.showdist();
    cout << "\ndist2 = ";  dist2.showdist();
    cout << "\ndist3 = ";  dist3.showdist();
    }
```

From the user's viewpoint the ENGLRET operates just the same as ENGLCON. In fact, the program is very similar to ENGLCON, but the differences reveal how functions work with objects. In ENGLCON two distances were passed to **add_dist()** as arguments, and the result was stored in the object of which **add_dist()** was a member, namely **dist3**. In ENGLRET one distance, **dist2**, is passed to **add_dist()** as an argument. It is added to the object, **dist1**, of which **add_dist()** is a member, and the result is returned from the function. In **main()** the result is assigned to **dist3**, in the statement

```
dist3 = dist1.add_dist(dist2);
```

The effect is the same as the corresponding statement in ENGLCON, but it is more natural-looking, since the assignment operator, =, is used in a natural way. In Chapter 9 we'll see how to use the arithmetic + operator to achieve the even more obvious expression

```
dist3 = dist1 + dist2;
```

ENGLCON and ENGLRET perform the same operation, but they do it differently. Here's the **add_dist()** function from ENGLRET:

```
                                            // add this distance to d2
Distance Distance::add_dist(Distance d2)    // return the sum
    {
    Distance temp;                          // temporary variable
    temp.inches = inches + d2.inches;       // add the inches
```

```
        if(temp.inches >= 12.0)          // if total exceeds 12.0,
        {                                // then decrease inches
            temp.inches -= 12.0;         // by 12.0 and
            temp.feet = 1;               // increase feet
        }                                // by 1
        temp.feet += feet + d2.feet;     // add the feet
        return temp;
    }
```

Compare this with the same function in ENGLCON. As you can see, there are some subtle differences. In this ENGLRET version, a temporary object of class **Dis-tance** is created. This object holds the sum until it can be returned to the calling program. The sum is calculated by adding two distances. The first is the object of

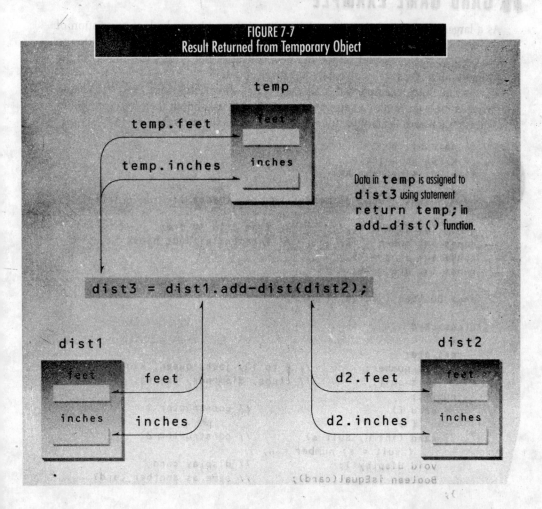

FIGURE 7-7
Result Returned from Temporary Object

temp

temp.feet → feet

temp.inches → inches

Data in **temp** is assigned to **dist3** using statement **return temp;** in **add_dist()** function.

dist3 = dist1.add-dist(dist2);

dist1

feet ← feet

inches ← inches

dist2

d2.feet → feet

d2.inches → inches

which `add_dist()` is a member, `dist1`. Its member data is accessed as `feet` and `inches`. The second is the object passed as an argument, `dist2`. Its member data is accessed as `d2.feet` and `d2.inches`. The result is stored in `temp` and accessed as `temp.feet` and `temp.inches`. The `temp` object is then returned by the function using the statement

```
return temp;
```

and the statement in `main()` assigns it to `dist3`. Notice that `dist1` is not modified; it simply supplies data to `add_dist()`. Figure 7-7 shows how this looks.

A CARD GAME EXAMPLE

As a larger example of objects modeling the real world, let's look at a variation of the CARDS program from Chapter 5. This program, CARDOBJ, has been rewritten to use objects. It does not introduce any new concepts, but it does use almost all the programming ideas we've discussed up to this point.

As the CARDS example did, CARDOBJ creates three cards with fixed values and switches them around in an attempt to confuse the user about their location. But in CARDOBJ each card is an object of class `card`. Here's the listing:

```
// cardobj.cpp
// cards as objects
#include <iostream.h>

enum Suit { clubs, diamonds, hearts, spades };

const int jack = 11;        // from 2 to 10 are
const int queen = 12;       // integers without names
const int king = 13;
const int ace = 14;

enum Boolean { false, true };

class card
   {
   private:
      int number;           // 2 to 10, jack, queen, king, ace
      Suit suit;            // clubs, diamonds, hearts, spades
   public:
      card ()               // constructor 1
         { }
      card (int n, Suit s)  // constructor 2
         { suit = s; number = n; }
      void display();       // display card
      Boolean isEqual(card); // same as another card?
   };
```

```
void card::display()                // display the card
  {
  if( number >= 2 && number <= 10 )
     cout << number << " of ";
  else
    switch(number)
       {
       case jack:  cout << "jack of ";  break;
       case queen: cout << "queen of "; break;
       case king:  cout << "king of ";  break;
       case ace:   cout << "ace of ";   break;
       }
    switch(suit)
       {
       case clubs:    cout << "clubs"; break;
       case diamonds: cout << "diamonds"; break;
       case hearts:   cout << "hearts"; break;
       case spades:   cout << "spades"; break;
       }
  }

Boolean card::isEqual(card c2)    // return true if cards equal
  {
  return ( number==c2.number && suit==c2.suit ) ? true : false;
  }

void main()
  {
  card temp, chosen, prize;        // define various cards
  int position;

  card card1( 7, clubs );          // define & initialize card1
  cout << "\nCard 1 is the ";
  card1.display();                 // display card1

  card card2( jack, hearts );      // define & initialize card2
  cout << "\nCard 2 is the ";
  card2.display();                 // display card2

  card card3( ace, spades );       // define & initialize card3
  cout << "\nCard 3 is the ";
  card3.display();                 // display card3

  prize = card3;                   // prize is the card to guess

  cout << "\nI'm swapping card 1 and card 3";
  temp = card3; card3 = card1; card1 = temp;

  cout << "\nI'm swapping card 2 and card 3";
  temp = card3; card3 = card2; card2 = temp;
```

```
   )ut << "\nI'm swapping card 1 and card 2";
   temp = card2; card2 = card1; card1 = temp;

   cout << "\nNow, where (1, 2, or 3) is the ";
   prize.display();              // display prize card
   cout << "? ";
   cin >> position;             // get user's guess of positior

   switch (position)
      {                          // set chosen to user's choice
      case 1: chosen = card1; break;
      case 2: chosen = card2; break;
      case 3: chosen = card3; break;
      }
   if( chosen.isEqual(prize) )   // is chosen card the prize?
      cout << "That's right!  You win!";
   else
      cout << "Sorry. You lose.";
   cout << "  You chose the ";
   chosen.display();            // display chosen card
   cout << endl;
   }
```

There are two constructors in class **card**. The first, which takes no arguments, is used in **main()** to create the cards **temp**, **chosen**, and **prize**, which are not initialized. The second constructor, which takes two arguments, is used to create **card1**, **card2**, and **card3** and to initialize them to specific values. Besides the constructors, **card** has two other member functions, both defined outside the class. The **display()** function takes no arguments; it simply displays the card object of which it is a member, using the **number** and **suit** data items in the card. The **isEqual()** function checks whether the card is equal to a card supplied as an argument. The statement in **main()**

```
   chosen.display();
```
displays the card chosen by the user.

The **isEqual()** member function uses the conditional operator to compare the card of which it is a member with a card supplied as an argument. This function could also have been written with an **if...else** statement:

```
   if( number==c2.number && suit==c2.suit )
      return true;
   else
      return false;
```
but the conditional operator is more compact.

In **isEqual()** the argument is called **c2** as a reminder that there are two cards in the comparison: The first card is the object of which **isEqual()** is a member. The expression

```
if( chosen.isEqual(prize) )
```

in `main()` compares the card `chosen` with the card `prize`.

Here's the output when the user guesses an incorrect card:

```
Card 1 is the 7 of clubs
Card 2 is the jack of hearts
Card 3 is the ace of spades
I'm swapping card 1 and card 3
I'm swapping card 2 and card 3
I'm swapping card 1 and card 2
Now, where (1, 2, or 3) is the ace of spaces? 1
Sorry, you lose. You chose the 7 of clubs.
```

STRUCTURES AND CLASSES

The examples so far in this book have portrayed structures as a way to group data, and classes as a way to group both data and functions. In fact, you can use structures in almost exactly the same way that you use classes. The only formal difference between `class` and `struct` is that in a class the members are private by default, while in a structure they are public by default.

Here's the format we've been using for classes:

```
class foo
    {
    private:
        int data1;
    public:
        void func();
    };
```

Since in classes `private` is the default, this keyword is unnecessary. You can just as well write

```
class foo
    {
        int data1;
    public:
        void func();
    };
```

and the `data1` will still be private. Many programmers prefer this style. We like to include the `private` keyword because it offers a small increase in clarity.

If you want to use a structure to accomplish the same thing as this class, you can dispense with the keyword `public`, provided you put the public members before the private ones:

```
struct foo
    {
    void func();
private:
    int data1;
    };
```

since public is the default. However, in most situations programmers use structures to group data, and classes to group data and functions.

CLASSES, OBJECTS, AND MEMORY

We've probably given you the impression that each object created from a class contains separate copies of that class's data and member functions. This is a good first approximation, since it emphasizes that objects are complete, self-contained entities, designed using the class specifier. The mental image here is of cars (objects) rolling off an assembly line, each one made according to a blueprint (the class specifier).

However, things are not quite so simple. It's true that each object has its own separate data items. (In some object-oriented languages, such as Smalltalk, a data item that is part of a class is called an *instance variable*, since there is an instance of it for each object created.)

On the other hand, contrary to what you may have been led to believe, all the objects in a given class use the same member functions. The member functions are created and placed in memory only once—when they are defined in the class specifier. This makes sense; there's really no point in duplicating all the member functions in a class every time you create another object of that class, since the functions for each object are identical. The data items, however, will hold different values, so there must be a separate instance of each data item in each object. Data is therefore placed in memory when each object is defined, so there is a set for each object. Figure 7-8 shows how this looks.

In the SMALLOBJ example there are two objects of type smallobj, so there are two instances of somedata in memory. However, there is only one instance of the functions setdata() and showdata(). These functions are shared by all the objects of the class. There is no conflict because (at least in a single-tasking system) only one function is executed at a time.

In most situations you don't need to know that there is only one member function for an entire class. It's simpler to visualize each object as containing both its own data and its own member functions. But in some situations, such as in estimating the size of an executing program, it's helpful to know what's happening behind the scenes.

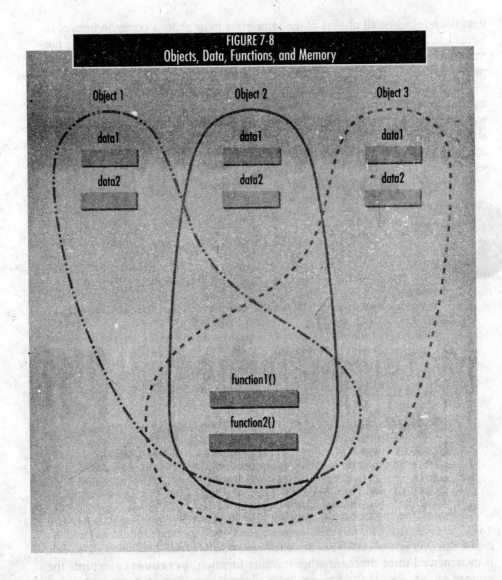

FIGURE 7-8
Objects, Data, Functions, and Memory

STATIC CLASS DATA

Having said that each object contains its own separate data, we must now amend that slightly. If a data item in a class is defined as `static`, then only one such item is created for the entire class, no matter how many objects there are. A static data item is useful when all objects of the same class must share a common item of information. A member variable defined as **static** has similar characteristics to a normal static variable: It is visible only within the class, but its lifetime is the entire program. (See Chapter 6 for a discussion of static variables.)

As an example, suppose an object needed to know how many other objects of its class were in the program. In a road-racing game, for example, a race car might want to know how many other cars were still in the race. In this case a static variable **count** could be included as a member of the class. All the objects would have access to this variable; it would be the same variable for all of them; they would all see the same count.

Here's an example, STATDATA, that demonstrates the effect:

```
// statdata.cpp
// static class data
#include <iostream.h>

class foo
   {
   private:
      static int count;    // only one data item for all objects
   public:
      foo() { count++; }  // increments count when object created
      int getcount()  { return count; }     // returns count
   };

void main()
   {
   foo f1, f2, f3;        // create three objects

   cout << "\ncount is " << f1.getcount();  // each object
   cout << "\ncount is " << f2.getcount();  // sees the same
   cout << "\ncount is " << f3.getcount();  // value of count
   }
```

The class **foo** in this example has one data item, **count**, which is type **static int**. The constructor for this class causes **count** to be incremented. In **main()** we define three objects of class **foo**. Since the constructor is called three times, **count** is incremented three times. Another member function, **getcount()**, returns the value in **count**. We call this function from all three objects, and—as we expected—each prints the same value. Here's the output:

```
count is 3        ←——— static data
count is 3
count is 3
```

If we had used an ordinary automatic variable—as opposed to a static variable—for **count**, each constructor would have incremented its own private copy of **count** once, and the output would have been

```
count is 1
count is 1          ←———— automatic data
count is 1
```

Static class variables are not used often, but they are important in special situations, and knowing about them helps to clarify how the more common automatic variables work. Figure 7-9 shows how static variables compare with automatic variables.

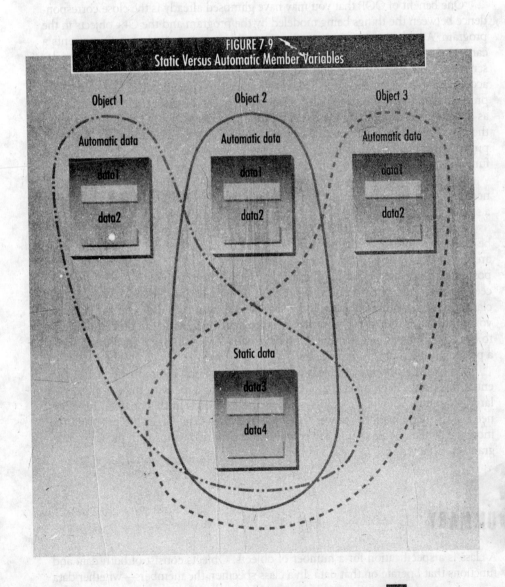

FIGURE 7-9
Static Versus Automatic Member Variables

WHAT DOES IT ALL MEAN?

Now that you've been introduced to classes and objects, you may wonder what benefit they really offer. After all, as you can see by comparing several of the programs in this chapter with those in Chapter 5, it's possible to do the same sorts of things with a procedural approach as it is with objects.

One benefit of OOP that you may have glimpsed already is the close correspondence between the things being modeled by the program and the C++ objects in the program. A widget part object represents a widget part, a card object represents a card, and so on. In C++ everything about a widget part is included in its class description—the part number and other data items, and the functions necessary to access and operate on this data. This makes it easy to conceptualize a programming problem. You figure out what parts of the problem can be most usefully represented as objects, and then put all the data and functions connected with that object into the class specification. If you're using a C++ class to represent a playing card, you put into this class the data items that represent the value of the card, and also the functions to set value, retrieve it, display it, compare it, and so on.

In a procedural program, by contrast, the external variables and functions connected with a real-world object are distributed all over the listing; they don't form a single, easily grasped unit.

In some situations it may not be obvious what parts of a real-life situation should be made into objects. If you're writing a program that plays chess, for instance, what are the objects? The chessmen, the squares on the board, or possibly entire board positions? There are no hard and fast rules for this sort of analysis. Often you proceed by trial and error. You break a problem into objects in one way and write trial class specifiers for these objects. If the classes seem to match reality in a useful way, you continue. If they don't, you may need to start over, selecting different entities to be classes. The more experience you have with OOP, the easier it will be to break a programming problem into classes.

Some of the benefits of object-oriented programming are probably not apparent at this point. Remember that OOP was devised to cope with the complexity of large programs. Smaller programs, such as the examples in this chapter, have less need of the organizational power that OOP provides. The larger the program, the more the benefit. Some of this power will become more obvious with the larger programs in Chapter 15.

SUMMARY

A class is a specification for a number of objects. Objects consist of both data and functions that operate on that data. In a class specifier, the members—whether data or functions—can be **private**, meaning they can be accessed only by member functions of that class, or **public**, meaning they can be accessed by any function in the program.

A member function is a function that is a member of a class. Member functions have access to an object's private data, while nonmember functions do not.

A constructor is a member function, with the same name as its class, that is executed every time an object of the class is created. A constructor has no return type but can take arguments. It is often used to give initial values to object data members. Constructors can be overloaded, so an object can be initialized in different ways.

A destructor is a member function with the same name as its class but preceded by a tilde (~). It is called when an object is destroyed. A destructor takes no arguments and has no return value.

There is a separate copy of the data members for each object that is created from a class, but only one copy of a class's member functions. A data item can be restricted to a single instance for all objects of a class by making it **static**.

One reason to use OOP is the close correspondence between real-world objects and OOP classes. There are no rules on how to break a programming problem into classes. Often trial and error is necessary.

QUESTIONS

1. What is the purpose of a class specifier (declaration)?
2. A _____ has the same relation to an _____ that a basic data type has to a variable of that type.
3. In a class specifier, data or functions designated **private** are accessible
   a. to any function in the program
   b. only if you know the password
   c. to member functions of that class
   d. only to public members of the class
4. Write a class specifier that creates a class called **leverage** with one private data member, **crowbar**, of type **int** and one public function whose declaration is **void pry()**.
5. True or false: Data items in a class must be private.
6. Write a statement that defines an object called **lever1** of the **leverage** class described in question 4.
7. The dot operator (or class member access operator) connects the following two entities (reading from left to right):
   a. a class member and a class object
   b. a class object and a class
   c. a class and a member of that class
   d. a class object and a member of that class

8. Write a statement that executes the **pry()** function in the **lever1** object, as described in questions 4 and 6.

9. Member functions defined inside a class specifier are _____ by default.

10. Write a member function called **getcrow()** for the **leverage** class described in question 4. This function should return the value of the **crowbar** data. Assume the function is defined within the class specifier.

11. A constructor is executed automatically when an object is _____.

12. A constructor's name is the same as _____.

13. Write a constructor that initializes to 0 the **crowbar** data, a member of the **leverage** class described in question 4. Assume the constructor is defined within the class specifier.

14. True or false: In a class you can have more than one constructor with the same name.

15. A member function can always access the data
    a. in the object of which it is a member
    b. in the class of which it is a member
    c. in any object of the class of which it is a member
    d. in the public part of its class

16. Assume the member function **getcrow()** described in question 10 is defined outside the class specifier. Write the declaration that goes inside the class specifier.

17. Write a revised version of the **getcrow()** member function from question 10 that is defined outside the class specifier.

18. The only technical difference between structures and classes in C++ is that _____

19. If three objects of a class are defined, how many copies of that class's data items are stored in memory? How many copies of its member functions?

20. *Sending a message* to an object is the same as _____.

21. Classes are useful because they
    a. are removed from memory when not in use
    b. permit data to be hidden from other classes
    c. bring together all aspects of an entity in one place
    d. can closely model objects in the real world

22. True or false: There is a precise methodology for dividing a real-world programming problem into classes.

EXERCISES

1. Create a class that imitates part of the functionality of the basic data type int. Call the class Int (note different spelling). The only data in this class is an int varible. Include member functions to initialize an Int to 0, to initialize it to an int value, to display it (it looks just like an int), and to add two Int values.

   Write a program that exercises this class by creating two initialized and one uninitialized Int values, adding these two initialized values and placing the response in the uninitialized value, and then displaying this result.

2. Imagine a tollbooth at a bridge. Cars passing by the booth are expected to pay a fifty-cent toll. Mostly they do, but sometimes a car goes by without paying. The tollbooth keeps track of the number of cars that have gone by, and of the total amount of money collected.

   Model this tollbooth with a class called tollBooth. The two data items are a type unsigned int to hold the total number of cars, and a type double to hold the total amount of money collected. A constructor initializes both these to 0. A member function called payingCar() increments the car total and adds 0.50 to the cash total. Another function, called nopayCar(), increments the car total but adds nothing to the cash total. Finally, a member function called display() displays the two totals.

   Include a program to test this class. This program should allow the user to push one key to count a paying car, and another to count a nonpaying car. Pushing the (ESC) key should cause the program to print out the total cars and total cash and then exit.

3. Create a class called time that has separate int member data for hours, minutes, and seconds. One constructor should initialize this data to 0, and another should initialize it to fixed values. A member function should display it, in 11:59:59 format. The final member function should add two objects of type time passed as arguments.

   A main() program should create two initialized time objects, and one that isn't initialized. Then it should add the two initialized values together, leaving the result in the third time variable. Finally it should display the value of this third variable.

ARRAYS

In everyday life we commonly group similar objects into units. We buy peas by the can and eggs by the carton. In computer languages we also need to group together data items of the same type. The mechanism that accomplishes this in C++ is the *array*. Arrays can hold a few data items, or tens of thousands. The data items grouped in an array can be simple types like `int` or `float`, or they can be user-defined types like structures and objects.

Arrays are like structures in that they both group a number of items into a larger unit. But while a structure usually groups items of different types, an array groups items of the same type. More importantly, the items in a structure are accessed by name, while those in an array are accessed by an index number. Using an index number to specify an item allows easy access to a large number of items.

Arrays exist in almost every computer language, including Pascal and BASIC. Arrays in C++ are similar to those in other languages, and identical to those in C.

In this chapter we'll look first at arrays of basic data types like `int` and `char`. Then we'll examine arrays used as data members in classes, and arrays used to hold objects. Thus this chapter is intended not only to introduce arrays but to increase your understanding of object-oriented programming. We'll finish the chapter with an introduction to *strings*, which are arrays of type `char`.

ARRAY FUNDAMENTALS

A simple example program will serve to introduce arrays. This program, REPLAY, creates an array of four integers, representing the ages of four people. It then asks the user to enter four values, which it places in the array. Finally, it displays all four values.

```
// replay.cpp
// gets four ages from user, displays them
#include <iostream.h>

void main()
    {
```

```
int age[4];                              // array 'age' of 4 ints

cout << endl;
for(int j=0; j<4; j++)                   // get 4 ages
   {
   cout << "Enter an age: ";
   cin >> age[j];                        // access array element
   }
for(j=0; j<4; j++)                       // display 4 ages
   cout << "\nYou entered " << age[j];
}
```

Here's a sample interaction with the program:

```
Enter an age: 44
Enter an age: 16
Enter an age: 23
Enter an age: 68

You entered 44
You entered 16
You entered 23
You entered 68
```

The first for loop gets the ages from the user and places them in the array, while the second reads them from the array and displays them.

DEFINING ARRAYS

Like other variables in C++, an array must be defined before it can be used to store information. And, like other definitions, an array definition specifies a variable type and a name. But it includes another feature: a size. The size specifies how many data items the array will contain. It immediately follows the the name, and is surrounded by square brackets. Figure 8-1 shows the syntax of an array definition.

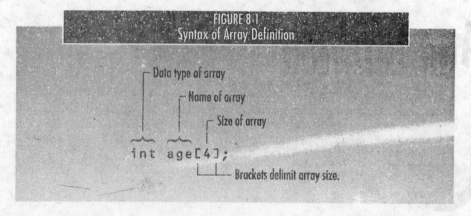

FIGURE 8-1
Syntax of Array Definition

In the REPLAY example the array is type `int`. The name of the array comes next, followed immediately by an opening bracket, the array size, and a closing bracket. The number in brackets must be a constant or an expression that evaluates to a constant, and should also be an integer. In the example we use the value 4.

ARRAY ELEMENTS

The items in an array are called *elements* (in contrast to the items in a structure, which are called *members*). As we noted, all the elements in an array are of the same type; only the values vary. Figure 8-2 shows the elements of the array `age`.

Following the conventional (although in some ways backward) approach, memory grows downward in the figure. That is, the first array elements are on the top of the page; later elements extend downward.

Since each element in `age` is an integer, it occupies two bytes. As specified in the definition, the array has exactly four elements.

Notice that the first array element has the value 0. Thus, since there are four elements, the last one is number 3. This is a potentially confusing situation; you might think the last element in a four-element array would be number 4, but it's not.

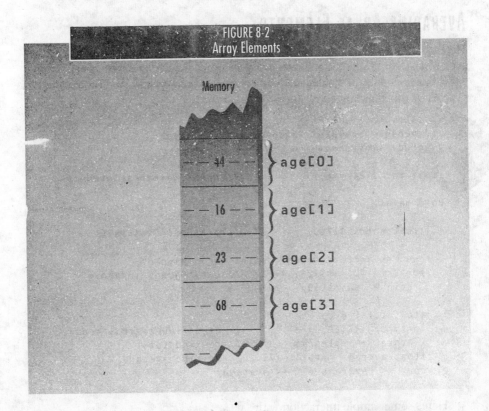

FIGURE 8-2
Array Elements

Memory

44 — age[0]

16 — age[1]

23 — age[2]

68 — age[3]

ACCESSING ARRAY ELEMENTS

In the REPLAY example we access each array element twice. The first time, we insert a value into the array, with the line

```
cin >> age[j];
```

and the second time, we read it out with the line

```
cout << "\nYou entered " << age[j];
```

In both cases the expression for the array element is

```
age[j]
```

This consists of the name of the array, followed by brackets delimiting a variable j. Which of the four array elements is specfied by this expression depends on the value of j; age[0] refers to the first element, age[1] to the second, age[2] to the third, and age[3] to the fourth. The variable (or constant) in the brackets is called the array *index*.

Since j is the loop variable in both for loops, it starts at 0 and is incremented until it reaches 3, thereby accessing each of the array elements in turn.

AVERAGING ARRAY ELEMENTS

Here's another example of an array at work. This one, SALES, invites the user to enter a series of six values, representing widget sales for each day of the week (including Saturday), and then calculates the average of these values. We use an array of type float so that monetary values can be entered.

```
// sales.cpp
// averages a weeks's widget sales (6 days)
#include <iostream.h>

const int SIZE = 6;               // number of array elements

void main()
   {
   float sales[SIZE];             // array of 6 variables

   cout << "\nEnter widget sales for 6 days\n";
   for(int j=0; j<SIZE; j++)      // put figures in array
      cin >> sales[j];

   float total = 0;
   for(j=0; j<SIZE; j++)          // read figures from array
      total += sales[j];          // to find total
   float average = total / SIZE;  // find average
   cout << "Average = " << average;
   }
```

Here's some sample interaction with SALES:

```
Enter widget sales for 6 days
352.64
867.70
781.32
867.35
746.21
189.45
Average = 634.11
```

A new detail in this program is the use of a `const` variable for the array size and loop limits. This variable is defined at the start of the listing:

```
const int SIZE = 6;
```

Using a variable (instead of a constant, such as the 4 used in the last example) makes it easier to change the array size: Only one program line needs to be changed to change the array size, loop limits, and anywhere else the array size appears. The all-uppercase name reminds us that the variable is a constant and cannot be modified in the program.

INITIALIZING ARRAYS

You can give values to each array element when the array is first defined. Here's an example, DAYS, that sets 12 array elements in the array `days_per_month` to the number of days in each month.

```
// days.cpp
// shows days from start of year to date specified
#include <iostream.h>

void main()
    {
    int month, day, total_days;
    int days_per_month[12] = { 31, 28, 31, 30, 31, 30,
                               31, 31, 30, 31, 30, 31 };

    cout << "\nEnter month (1 to 12): ";   // get date
    cin >> month;
    cout << "Enter day (1 to 31): ";
    cin >> day;
    total_days = day;                      // separate days
    for(int j=0; j<month-1; j++)           // add days each month
        total_days += days_per_month[j];
    cout << "Total days from start of year is: " << total_days;
    }
```

The program calculates the number of days from the beginning of the year to a date specified by the user. (Beware: It doesn't work for leap years.) Here's some sample interaction:

```
Enter month (1 to 12): 3
Enter day (1 to 31): 11
Total days from start of year is: 70
```

Once it gets the month and day values, the program adds the number of days to the total. Then it cycles through a loop, where it adds values from the `days_per_month` array to the `total_days` variable. The number of such values to add is one less than the number of months. For instance, if the user entered month 5, the values of the first four array elements (31, 28, 31, and 30) are added to the total.

The values to which `days_per_month` is initialized are surrounded by braces and separated by commas. They are connected to the array expression by an equals sign. Figure 8-3 shows the syntax.

Actually, we don't need to use the array size when we initialize all the array elements, since the compiler can figure it out by counting the initializing variables. Thus we can write

```
int days_per_month[] = { 31, 28, 31, 30, 31, 30,
                         31, 31, 30, 31, 30, 31 };
```

What happens if you do use an explicit array size, but it doesn't agree with the number of initializers? If there are too few initializers, the missing elements will be set to 0. If there are too many, an error is signaled.

MULTIDIMENSIONAL ARRAYS

So far we've looked at arrays of one dimension: A single variable specifies each array element. But arrays can have higher dimensions. Here's a program, SALEMON, that uses a two-dimensional array to store sales figures for several districts and several months.

```
// salemon.cpp
// displays sales chart using 2-d array
#include <iostream.h>
#include <iomanip.h>                      // for setprecision, etc.

const int DISTRICTS = 4;                  // array dimensions
const int MONTHS = 3;

void main()
   {
   int d, m;
   float sales[DISTRICTS][MONTHS];    // two-dimensional array
                                      // definition
   cout << endl;
   for(d=0; d<DISTRICTS; d++)             // get array values
      for(m=0; m<MONTHS; m++)
         {
         cout << "Enter sales for district " << d+1;
         cout << ", month " << m+1 << ": ";
         cin >> sales[d][m];            // put number in array
         }

   cout << "\n\n";
   cout << "                    Month\n";
   cout << "                1       2       3";
```

```
   for(d=0; d<DISTRICTS; d++)
     {
     cout <<"\nDistrict " << d+1;
     for(m=0; m<MONTHS; m++)          // display array values
        cout << setiosflags(ios::fixed)       // not exponential
             << setiosflags(ios::showpoint)   // always use point
             << setprecision(2)               // digits to right
             << setw(10)                       // field width
             << sales[d][m];          // get number from array
     } // end for(d)
   } // end main
```

This program accepts the sales figures from the user and then displays them in a table:

```
Enter sales for district 1, month 1: 3964.23
Enter sales for district 1, month 2: 4135.87
Enter sales for district 1, month 3: 4397.98
Enter sales for district 2, month 1: 867.75
Enter sales for district 2, month 2: 923.59
Enter sales for district 2, month 3: 1037.01
Enter sales for district 3, month 1: 12.77
Enter sales for district 3, month 2: 378.32
Enter sales for district 3, month 3: 798.22
Enter sales for district 4, month 1: 2983.53
Enter sales for district 4, month 2: 3983.73
Enter sales for district 4, month 3: 9494.98
```

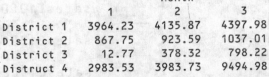

```
                      Month
                1         2         3
District 1   3964.23   4135.87   4397.98
District 2    867.75    923.59   1037.01
District 3     12.77    378.32    798.22
Distruct 4   2983.53   3983.73   9494.98
```

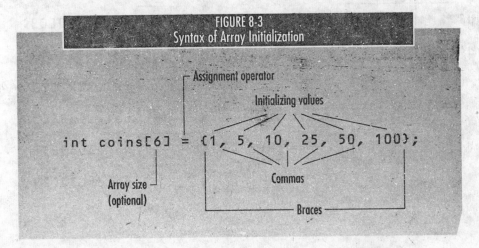

FIGURE 8-3
Syntax of Array Initialization

Assignment operator

Initializing values

`int coins[6] = {1, 5, 10, 25, 50, 100};`

Array size
(optional)

Commas

Braces

Defining Multidimensional Arrays

The array is defined with two size specifiers, each enclosed in brackets:

```
float sales[DISTRICTS][MONTHS];
```

One way to think about this statement is that `sales` is an array of arrays. It is an array of `DISTRICTS` elements, each of which is an array of `MONTHS` elements. Figure 8-4 shows how this looks.

(Of course there can be arrays of dimensions higher than two. A three-dimensional array is an array of arrays of arrays. It is accessed with three indexes:

```
elem = dimen3[i][j][k];
```

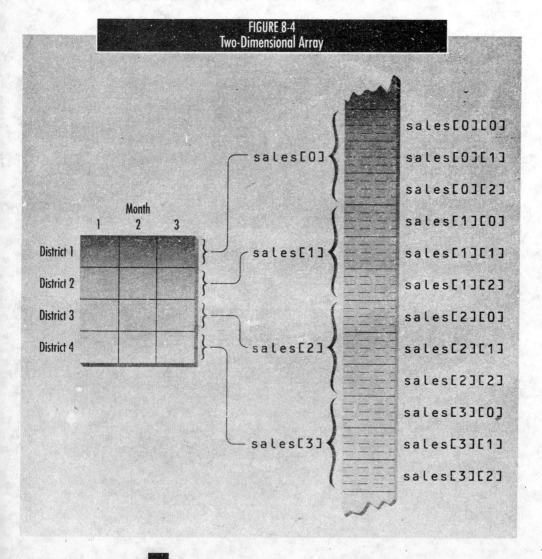

FIGURE 8-4
Two-Dimensional Array

This is entirely analogous to one- and two-dimensional arrays; it is an array of arrays of arrays.)

Accessing Multidimensional Array Elements

Array elements in two-dimensional arrays require two indexes:

```
sales[d][m]
```

Notice that each index has its own set of brackets. Don't write `sales[d,m]`; this works in some languages, but not in C++.

Formatting Numbers

The SALEMON program displays a table of dollar values. It's important that such values be formatted properly, so let's digress long enough to see how this is done in C++. With dollar values you normally want to have exactly two digits to the right of the decimal point, and you want the decimal points of all the numbers in a column to line up. It's also nice if trailing zeros are displayed; you want 79.50, not 79.5.

Convincing the C++ I/O streams to do all this requires a little work. You've already seen the manipulator `setw()`, used to set the output field width. Formatting decimal numbers requires several additional manipulators.

Here's a statement that prints a floating point number called `fpn` in a field 10 characters wide, with two digits to the right of the decimal point:

```
cout << setiosflags(ios::fixed)        // fixed (not exponential)
     << setiosflags(ios::showpoint)    // always show decimal point
     << setprecision(2)                // two decimal places
     << setw(10)                       // field width 10
     << fpn;                           // finally, the number
```

A group of one-bit flags in a `long int` in the `ios` class determines how formatting will be carried out. At this point we don't need to know what the `ios` class is, or the reasons for the exact syntax used with this class, to make the manipulators work.

We're concerned with two of the `ios` flags: `fixed` and `showpoint`. To set the flags you use the manipulator `setiosflags`, with the name of the flag as an argument. The name must be preceded by the class name, `ios`, and the scope resolution operator (`::`).

The first two lines of the `cout` statement set the `ios` flags. (If you need to unset—that is, clear—the flags at some later point in your program, you can use the `resetiosflags` manipulator.) The `fixed` flag prevents numbers from being printed in exponential format, such as 3.45e3. The `showpoint` flag specifies that there will always be a decimal point, even if the number has no fractional part: 123.00, instead of 123.

To set the precision to two digits to the right of the decimal place, you use the `setprecision` manipulator, with the number of digits as an argument. We've already seen how to set the field width by using the `setw` manipulator. Once all these manipulators have been sent to `cout`, you can send the number itself; it will be displayed in the desired format.

Initializing Multidimensional Arrays

As you might expect, you can initialize multidimensional arrays. The only prerequisite is a willingness to type a lot of braces and commas. Here's a variation of the SALEMON program that uses an initialized array instead of asking for input from the user. This program is called SALEINIT.

```
// saleinit.cpp
// displays sales chart, initializes 2-d array
#include <iostream.h>
#include <iomanip.h>                   // for setprecision, etc.

const int DISTRICTS = 4;               // array dimensions
const int MONTHS = 3;

void main()
    {
    int d, m;
                                       // initialize array elements
    float sales[DISTRICTS][MONTHS]
                   = { { 1432.07,    234.50,    654.01 },
                       {  322.00, 13838.32, 17589.88 },
                       { 9328.34,    934.00,  4492.30 },
                       { 12838.29,  2332.63,    32.93 }  };
    cout << "\n\n";
    cout << "                        Month\n";
    cout << "              1         2         3";
    for(d=0; d<DISTRICTS; d++)
        {
        cout <<"\nDistrict " << d+1;
        for(m=0; m<MONTHS; m++)
            cout << setw(10) << setiosflags(ios::fixed)
                 << setiosflags(ios::showpoint) << setprecision(2)
                 << sales[d][m];  // access array element
        }
    }
```

Remember that a two-dimensional array is really an array of arrays. The format for initializing such an array is based on this fact. The initializing values for each subarray are enclosed in braces and separated by commas:

```
{ 1432.07, 234.50, 654.01 }
```

and then all four of these subarrays, each of which is an element in the main array, is likewise enclosed by braces and separated by commas, as can be seen in the listing.

PASSING ARRAYS TO FUNCTIONS

Arrays can be used as arguments to functions. Here's an example, a variation of the SALEINIT program, that passes the array of sales figures to a function whose purpose is to display the data as a table. Here's the listing for SALEFUNC:

```cpp
// salefunc.cpp
// passes array as argument
#include <iostream.h>
#include <iomanip.h>              // for setprecision, etc.

const int DISTRICTS = 4;     // array dimensions
const int MONTHS = 3;

void display( float[DISTRICTS][MONTHS] );  // prototype

void main()
   {                          // initialize two-dimensional array
   float sales[DISTRICTS][MONTHS]
           = { {  1432.07,    234.50,    654.01 },
               {   322.00, 13838.32, 17589.88 },
               {  9328.34,    934.00,  4492.30 },
               { 12838.29,  2332.63,     32.93 }  };

   display(sales);            // call function, array as argument
   } // end main

// display()
// function to display 2-d array passed as argument
void display( float funsales[DISTPICTS][MONTHS] )
   {
   int d, m;

   cout << "\n\n";
   cout << "                        Month\n";
   cout << "                1         2         3";

   for(d=0; d<DISTRICTS; d++)
      {
             ...District " << d+1;
      for(m=0; m<MONTHS; m++)
         cout << setiosflags(ios::fixed) << setw(10)
              << setiosflags(ios::showpoint) << setprecision(2)
              << funsales[d][m];    // array element
      } // end for(d)
   } // end display
```

Function Declaration with Array Argument

In a function declaration, array arguments are represented by the data type and sizes of the array. Here's the declaration of the `display()` function:

```
void display( float[DISPLAY][MONTHS] );   // declaration
```

Actually, there is one unnecessary piece of information here. The following statement works just as well:

```
void display( float[][MONTHS] );   // declaration
```

Why doesn't the function need the size of the first dimension? Again, remember that a two-dimensional array is an array of arrays. The function first thinks of the argument as an array of districts. It doesn't need to know how many districts there are, but it does need to know how big each district element is, so it can calculate where a particular element is (by multiplying the bytes per element times the index). So we must tell it the size of each element, which is MONTHS, but not how many there are, which is DISTRICTS.

It follows that if we were declaring a function that used a one-dimensional array as an argument, we would not need to use the array size:

```
void somefunc( int elem[] );   // declaration
```

Function Call with Array Argument

When the function is called, only the name of the array is used as an argument:

```
display(sales);   // function call
```

This name (`sales` in this case) actually represents the memory *address* of the array. We aren't going to explore addresses in detail until Chapter 12 on pointers, but here are a few preliminary points about them.

Using an address for an array argument is similar to using a reference argument, in that the values of the array elements are not duplicated (copied) into the function. (See the discussion of reference arguments in Chapter 6.) Instead, the function works with the original array, although it refers to it by a different name. This system is used for arrays because they can be very large; duplicating an entire array in every function that called it would be both time-consuming and wasteful of memory.

However, an address is not the same as a reference. No ampersand (&) is used with the array name in the function declaration. Until we discuss pointers, take it on faith that arrays are passed using their name alone, and that the function accesses the original array, not a duplicate.

Function Definition with Array Argument

In the function definition the declarator looks like this:

```
void display( float funsales[DISTRICTS][MONTHS] )   // declarator
```

The array argument uses the data type, a name, and the sizes of the dimensions. The array name used by the function (`funsales` in this example) can be different from the name that defines the array (sales), but they both refer to the same array. All the array dimensions must be specified; the function needs them to properly access the array elements.

References to array elements in the function use the function's name for the array:

```
funsales[d][m]
```

But in all other ways the function can access array elements as if the array had been defined in the function.

ARRAYS OF STRUCTURES

Arrays can contain structures as well as simple data types. Here's an example based on the part structure from Chapter 5.

```
// partaray.cpp
// structure variables as array elements
#include <iostream.h>

const int SIZE = 4;                  // number of parts in array

struct part                          // specify a structure
    {
    int modelnumber;                 // ID number of widget
    int partnumber;                  // ID number of widget part
    float cost;                      // cost of part
    };

void main()
    {
    int n;
    part apart[SIZE];                // define array of structures

    for(n=0; n<SIZE; n++)            // get values for all members
        {
        cout << endl;
        cout << "Enter model number: ";
        cin >> apart[n].modelnumber;     // get model number
        cout << "Enter part number: ";
        cin >> apart[n].partnumber;      // get part number
        cout << "Enter cost: ";
        cin >> apart[n].cost;            // get cost
        }
    for(n=0; n<SIZE; n++)            // show values for all members
        {
        cout << "\nModel " << apart[n].modelnumber;
        cout << "  Part " << apart[n].partnumber;
        cout << "  Cost " << apart[n].cost;
        }
    }
```

The user types in the model number, part number, and cost of a part. The program records this data in a structure. However, this structure is only one element in an array of structures. The program asks for the data for four different parts, and stores it in the four elements of the `apart` array. It then displays the information. Here's some sample input:

```
Enter model number: 44
Enter part number: 4954
Enter cost: 133.45

Enter model number: 44
Enter part number: 8431
Enter cost: 97.59

Enter model number: 77
Enter part number: 9343
Enter cost: 109.99

Enter model number: 77
Enter part number: 4297
Enter cost: 3456.55

Model 44   Part 4954   Cost 133.45
Model 44   Part 8431   Cost 97.59
Model 77   Part 9343   Cost 109.99
Model 77   Part 4297   Cost 3456.55
```

The array of structures is defined in the statement

```
part apart[SIZE];
```

This has the same syntax as that of arrays of simple data types. Only the type name, `part`, shows that this is an array of a more complex type.

Accessing a data item that is a member of a structure that is itself an element of an array involves a new syntax. For example,

```
apart[n].modelnumber
```

refers to the `modelnumber` member of the structure that is element n of the `apart` array. Figure 8-5 shows how this looks.

Arrays of structures are a useful data type in a variety of situations. We've shown an array of car parts, but we could also store an array of personnel data (name, age, salary), an array of geographical data about cities (name, population, elevation, and many other types of data.

ARRAYS AS CLASS MEMBER DATA

Arrays can be used as data items in classes. Let's look at an example that models a common computer data structure: the stack.

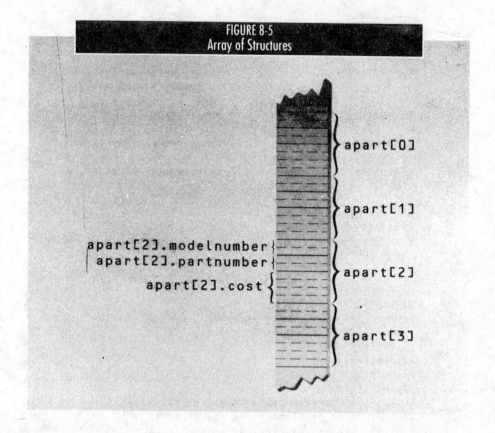

FIGURE 8-5
Array of Structures

A stack works like the spring-loaded devices that hold trays in cafeterias. When you put a tray on top, the stack sinks down a little; when you take a tray off, it pops up. The last tray placed on the stack is always the first tray removed.

Stacks are one of the cornerstones of the architecture of the 80x86 microprocessor used in MS-DOS computers. As we've mentioned earlier, functions pass their arguments and store their return address on the stack. This kind of stack is implemented partly in hardware and is most conveniently accessed in assembly language. However, stacks can also be created completely in software. Software stacks offer a useful storage device in certain programming situations, such as in parsing (analyzing) algebraic expressions.

Our example program, STAKARAY, creates a simple stack class:

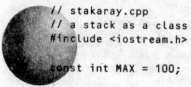

```
// stakaray.cpp
// a stack as a class
#include <iostream.h>

const int MAX = 100;
```

```cpp
class Stack
   {
   private:
      int st[MAX];              // stack: array of integers
      int top;                  // number of top, of stack
   public:
      Stack()                   // constructor
         { top = 0; }
      void push(int var)        // put number on stack
         { st[++top] = var; }
      int pop()                 // take number off stack
         { return st[top--]; }
   };

void main()
   {
   Stack s1;

   s1.push(11);
   s1.push(22);
   cout << "1: " << s1.pop() << endl;   // 22
   cout << "2: " << s1.pop() << endl;   // 11
   s1.push(33);
   s1.push(44);
   s1.push(55);
   s1.push(66);
   cout << "3: " << s1.pop() << endl;   // 66
   cout << "4: " << s1.pop() << endl;   // 55
   cout << "5: " << s1.pop() << endl;   // 44
   cout << "6: " << s1.pop() << endl;   // 33
   }
```

The stack itself consists of the array st. An int variable, top, indicates the index of the last item placed on the stack; the location of this item is the top of the stack. Figure 8-6 shows the stack.

Since memory grows downward in the figure, the top of the stack is at the bottom in the figure. When an item is added to the stack, the address in top is incremented to point to the new top of the stack. When an item is removed, the value in top is decremented. (We don't need to erase the old value left in memory when an item is popped; it just becomes irrelevent.)

To place an item on the stack—a process called *pushing* the item—you call the push() member function with the value to be stored as an argument. To retrieve (or *pop*) an item from the stack, you use the pop() member function, which returns the value of the item.

The main() program in STAKARAY exercises the stack class by creating an object, s1, of the class. It pushes two items onto the stack, and pops them off and displays them. Then it pushes four more items onto the stack, and pops them off and displays them. Here's the output:

```
1: 22
2: 11
3: 66
4: 55
5: 44
6: 33
```

As you can see, items are popped off the stack in reverse order; the last thing pushed is the first thing popped.

Notice the subtle use of prefix and postfix notation in the increment and decrement operators. The statement

```
st[++top] = var;
```

in the push() member function first increments top so that it points to the next available array element—one past the last element. It then assigns var to this location, which becomes the new top of the stack. The statement

```
return st[top--];
```

first returns the value it finds at the top of the stack, and then decrements top so that it points to the preceding element.

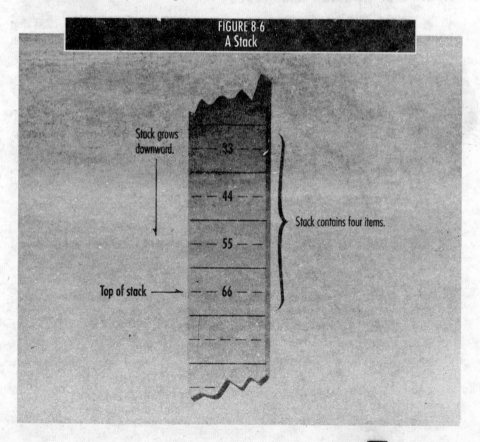

FIGURE 8-6
A Stack

Stack grows downward.

Stack contains four items.

Top of stack

The stack class is an example of an important feature of object-oriented programming: using a class to implement a certain kind of data-storage mechanism. In Chapter 16, when we discuss the Borland container class library, we'll see that a stack is only one of a number of ways to store data. There are also queues, sets, linked lists, and so on. A data-storage scheme is chosen that matches the specific requirements of the program. Using a preexisting class to provide data-storage means that the programmer does not need to waste time duplicating the details of a data-storage mechanism.

ARRAYS OF OBJECTS

We've seen how an object can contain an array. We can also reverse that situation and create an array of objects. We'll look at two situations: an array of English distances and a deck of cards.

ARRAYS OF ENGLISH DISTANCES

In the last chapter we showed several examples of an English Distance class that incorporated feet and inches into an object representing a new data type. The next program, ENGLARAY, demonstrates an array of such objects.

```
// englaray.cpp
// objects using English measurements
#include <iostream.h>

const int MAX = 100;                // maximum number of elements

class Distance                      // English Distance class
   {
   private:
      int feet;
      float inches;
   public:
      void getdist()                // get length from user
         {
         cout << "\n   Enter feet: ";  cin >> feet;
         cout << "   Enter inches: ";  cin >> inches;
         }
      void showdist()               // display distance
         { cout << feet << "\'-" << inches << '\"'; }
   };

void main()
   {
   Distance dist[MAX];              // array of distances
   int n=0;                         // count the entries
   char ans;                        // user response ('y' or 'n')
```

```
        cout << endl;
        do                              // get distances from user
           {
           cout << "Enter distance number " << n+1;
           dist[n++].getdist();         // store distance in array
           cout << "Enter another (y/n)?: ";
           cin >> ans;
           }                            // quit if user types 'n'
        while( ans != 'n' );

        for(int j=0; j<n; j++)          // display all distances
           {
           cout << "\nDistance number " << j+1 << " is ";
           dist[j].showdist();
           }
        }
```

In this program the user types in as many distances as desired. After each distance is entered, the program asks if the user desires to enter another. If not, it terminates, and displays all the distances entered so far. Here's a sample interaction when the user enters three distances:

```
Enter distance number 1
    Enter feet: 5
    Enter inches: 4
Enter another (y/n)? y
Enter distance number 2
    Enter feet: 6
    Enter inches: 2.5
Enter another (y/n)? y
Enter distance number 3
    Enter feet: 5
    Enter inches: 10.75
Enter another (y/n)? n

Distance number 1 is 5'-4"
Distance number 2 is 6'-2.5"
Distance number 3 is 5'-10.75"
```

Of course, instead of simply displaying the distances already entered, the program could have averaged them, written them to disk, or operated on them in other ways. For simplicity we avoid these embellishments.

Array Bounds

This program uses a do loop to get input from the user. This way the user can input data for as many structures of type part as seems desirable, up to MAX, the size of the array (which is set to 100).

Although it's hard to imagine anyone having the patience, what would happen if the user entered more than 100 distances? The answer is, something unpredictable but almost certainly bad. There is no bounds-checking in C++ arrays. If the program inserts something beyond the end of the array, neither the compiler nor the run-time system will object. However, the renegade data will probably be written on top of other data or the program code itself. This may cause bizarre effects or crash the system completely.

The moral is that it is up to the programmer to deal with the array bounds checking. If it seems possible that the user will insert too much data for an array to hold, then the array should be made larger, or some means of warning the user should be devised. For example, you could insert the following code at the beginning of the do loop in ENGLARAY:

```
if( n >= MAX )
   {
   cout << "\nThe array is full!!!";
   break;
   }
```

This causes a break out of the loop and prevents the array from overflowing.

Accessing Objects in an Array

The specification of the Distance class in this program is similar to that used in previous programs. However, in the main() program we define an array of such objects:

```
Distance dist[MAX];
```

Here the data type of the dist array is Distance, and it has MAX elements. Figure 8-7 shows what this looks like.

A class member function that is an array element is accessed similarly to a structure member that is an array element, as in the PARTARAY example. Here's how the showdist() member function of the jth element of the array dist is invoked:

```
dist[j].showdist();
```

As you can see, a member function of an object that is an array element is accessed using the dot operator: The array name followed by the index in brackets is joined, using the dot operator, to the member function name followed by parentheses. This is similar to accessing a structure (or class) data member, except that the function name and parentheses are used instead of the data name.

Notice that when we call the getdist() member function to put a distance into the array, we take the opportunity to increment the array index n:

```
dist[n++].getdist();
```

This way the next group of data obtained from the user will be placed in the structure in the next array element in dist. The n variable must be incremented manually like this because we use a do loop instead of a for loop. In the for loop, the loop variable—which is incremented automatically—can serve as the array index.

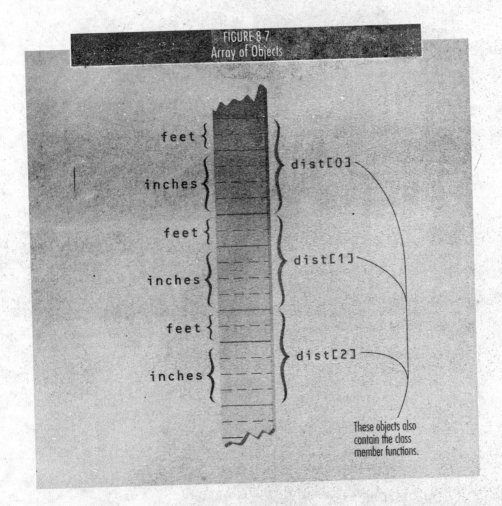

FIGURE 8-7
Array of Objects

feet
inches
} dist[0]

feet
inches
} dist[1]

feet
inches
} dist[2]

These objects also
contain the class
member functions.

ARRAYS OF CARDS

Here's another, somewhat longer, example of an array of objects. You will no doubt remember the CARDOBJ example from the last chapter. We'll borrow the `card` class from that example, and group an array of 52 such objects together in an array, thus creating a deck of cards. Here's the listing for CARDARAY.CPP:

```
// cardaray.cpp
// cards as objects
#include <iostream.h>
#include <stdlib.h>          // for randomize(), rand
#include <time.h>            // for randomize()
```

```
enum Suit { clubs, diamonds, hearts, spades };

const int jack = 11;         // from 2 to 10 are
const int queen = 12;        // integers without names
const int king = 13;
const int ace = 14;

enum Boolean { false, true };

class card
   {
   private:
      int number;            // 2 to 10, jack, queen, king, ace
      Suit suit;             // clubs, diamonds, hearts, spades
   public:
      card()                           // constructor
         { }
      void init(int n, Suit s)    // initialize card
         { suit = s; number = n; }
      void display();               // display card
      Boolean isEqual(card);        // same as another card?
   };

void card::display()                  // display the card
   {
   if( number >= 2 && number <= 10 )
      cout << number;
   else
      switch(number)
         {
         case jack:  cout << "J"; break;
         case queen: cout << "Q"; break;
         case king:  cout << "K"; break;
         case ace:   cout << "A"; break;
         }
   switch(suit)
      {
      case clubs:    cout << char(5); break;
      case diamonds: cout << char(4); break;
      case hearts:   cout << char(3); break;
      case spades:   cout << char(6); break;
      }
   }

void main()
   {
   card deck[52];
   int  num;
   Suit su;
```

```
cout << endl;
for(int j=0; j<52; j++)
   {
   int num = (j % 13) + 2;   // cycles through 2 to 14, 4 times
   Suit su = Suit(j / 13);   // cycles through 0 to 3, 13 times
   deck[j].init(num, su);    // set card
   }

cout << "\nOrdered deck:\n";
for(j=0; j<52; j++)          // display ordered deck
   {
   deck[j].display();
   cout << "  ";
   if( !( (j+1) % 13) )      // newline every 13 cards
      cout << endl;
   }

randomize();                 // seed random number generator
for(j=0; j<52; j++)          // for each card in the deck,
   {
   int k = random(52);       // pick another card at random
   card temp = deck[j];      // and swap them
   deck[j] = deck[k];
   deck[k] = temp;
   }

cout << "\nShuffled deck:\n";
for(j=0; j<52; j++)          // display shuffled deck
   {
   deck[j].display();
   cout << ", ";
   if( !( (j+1) % 13) )      // newline every 13 cards
      cout << endl;
   }
} // end main
```

Once we've created a deck, it's hard to resist the temptation to shuffle it. We display the cards in the deck, shuffle it, and then display it again. To conserve space we use the IBM graphics characters for the club, diamond, heart, and spade. Figure 8-8 shows the output from the program. This program incorporates several new ideas, so let's look at them in turn.

IBM Graphics Characters

There are several special characters in the range below ASCII code 32. (See Appendix A for a list of ASCII codes.) In the `display()` member function of `card` we use

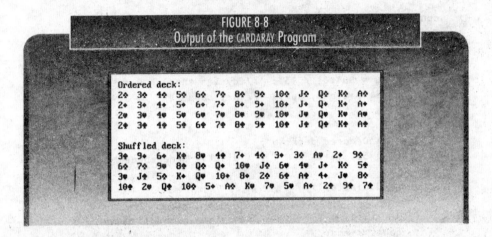

FIGURE 8-8
Output of the CARDARAY Program

```
Ordered deck:
2♣  3♣  4♣  5♣  6♣  7♣  8♣  9♣  10♣  J♣  Q♣  K♣  A♣
2♦  3♦  4♦  5♦  6♦  7♦  8♦  9♦  10♦  J♦  Q♦  K♦  A♦
2♥  3♥  4♥  5♥  6♥  7♥  8♥  9♥  10♥  J♥  Q♥  K♥  A♥
2♠  3♠  4♠  5♠  6♠  7♠  8♠  9♠  10♠  J♠  Q♠  K♠  A♠

Shuffled deck:
3♣  9♣  6♦  K♥  8♥  4♠  7♦  4♦  3♦  3♥  A♥  2♦  9♠
6♣  7♣  9♥  8♦  Q♥  Q♠  10♥  J♦  6♥  4♥  J♠  K♦  5♠
3♥  J♠  5♣  K♦  Q♥  10♦  8♦  2♠  6♣  A♠  4♦  J♥  8♣
10♠  2♥  Q♠  10♦  5♦  A♣  K♥  7♥  5♥  A♦  2♣  9♠  7♠
```

codes 5, 4, 3, and 6 to create the characters for a club, a diamond, a heart, and a spade, respectively. Casting these numbers to type `char`, as in

```
char(5)
```

causes the `<<` operator to print them as characters rather than as numbers.

The Card Deck

The array of structures that constitutes the deck of cards is defined in the statement

```
card deck[52];
```

which creates an array called `deck`, consisting of 52 objects of type `card`. To display the `j`th card in the deck we call the `display()` member function:

```
deck[j].display();
```

Random Numbers

It's always fun and sometimes even useful to generate random numbers. In this program we use them to shuffle the deck. Two steps are necessary to obtain random numbers in Turbo C++. First the random-number generator must be *seeded* or initialized. To do this we call the `randomize()` library function. This function uses the system time as the seed, so it requires two header files, STDLIB.H and TIME.H.

To actually generate a random number we call the `random()` library function. This function takes a single integer argument: the highest number, plus one, in the desired range. Thus if this argument is `max`, the function returns a random number in the range from 0 to max-1. To obtain a number in the range 0 to 51, we use the expression

```
random(52);
```

The resulting random number is then used as an index to swap two cards. We go through the `for` loop, swapping one card, whose index points to each card in

0-to-51 order, with another card, whose index is the random number. When all 52 cards have been exchanged with a random card, the deck is considered to be shuffled. This program could form the basis for a card-playing program, but we'll leave these details for the reader.

Arrays of objects are widely used in C++ programming. We'll see other examples as we go along.

STRINGS

Now that we have some familiarity with arrays, we can examine strings, which are a specialized way to use arrays of type **char**. As with other data types, strings can be variables or constants. We'll look at these two entities before going on to examine more complex string operations.

STRING VARIABLES

Here's an example that defines a single string variable. It asks the user to enter a string, and places this string in the string variable. Then it displays the string. Here's the listing for STRINGIN:

```
// stringin.cpp
// simple string variable
#include <iostream.h>
const int MAX = 80;                    // max characters in string

void main()
    {
    char str[MAX];                     // string variable str

    cout << "\nEnter a string: ";
    cin >> str;                        // put string in str
    cout << "You entered: " << str;    // display string from str
    }
```

The definition of the string variable **str** looks like (and is) the definition of any array of type **char**:

```
char str[MAX];
```

We use the insertion operator **>>** to read a string from the keyboard and place it in the string variable **str**. This operator knows how to deal with strings; it understands that they are arrays of characters. If the user enters the string **"Amanuensis"** (one employed to copy manuscripts) in this program, the array **str** will look something like Figure 8-9.

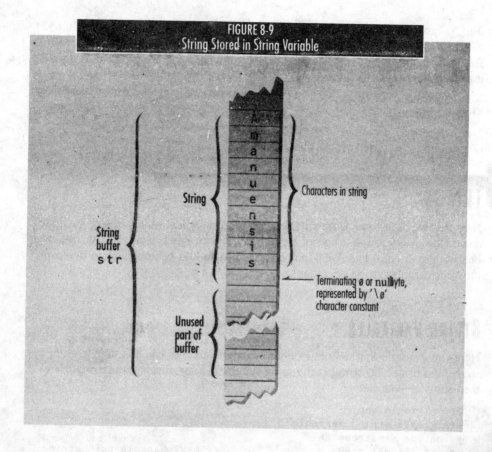

FIGURE 8-9
String Stored in String Variable

String buffer **str**

String

Characters in string

Terminating ø or null byte, represented by '\ø' character constant

Unused part of buffer

Each character occupies one byte of memory. An important aspect of strings in C++ is that they must terminate with a byte containing 0. This is often represented by the character constant '\0', which is a character with an ASCII value of 0. This terminating zero is called the *null* character. When the << operator displays the string, it displays characters until it encounters the null character.

AVOIDING BUFFER OVERFLOW

The STRINGIN program invites the user to type in a string. What happens if the user enters a string that is longer than the array used to hold it? As we mentioned earlier, there is no built-in mechanism in C++ to keep a program from inserting array elements outside an array. So an overly enthusiastic typist could end up crashing the system.

However, it is possible to tell the **>>** operator to limit the number of characters it places in an array. The SAFETYIN program demonstrates the approach:

```
// safetyin.cpp
// avoids buffer overflow with cin.width
#include <iostream.h>
#include <iomanip.h>                  // for setw
const int MAX = 20;                   // max characters in string

void main()
   {
   char str[MAX];                     // string variable str

   cout << "\nEnter a string: ";
   cin >> setw(MAX) >> str;           // put string in str,
                                      // no more than MAX chars
   cout << "You entered: " << str;    // display string from str
   }
```

This program uses the **setw** manipulator to specify the maximum number of characters the input buffer can accept. The user may type more characters, but the **>>** operator won't insert them into the array. Actually, one character fewer than the number specified is inserted, so there is room in the buffer for the terminating null character. Thus in SAFETYIN, a maximum of 19 characters are inserted.

STRING CONSTANTS

You can initialize a string to a constant value when you define it. Here's an example, STRINIT, that does just that (with the first line of a Shakespearean sonnet):

```
// strinit.cpp
// initialized string
#include <iostream.h>

void main()
   {
   char str[] = "Farewell! thou art too dear for my possessing";

   cout << str;
   }
```

Here the string constant is written as a normal English phrase, delimited by quotes. This may seem surprising, since a string is an array of type **char**. In past examples you've seen arrays initialized to a series of values delimited by braces and separated by commas. Why isn't **str** intialized the same way? In fact you could use such a sequence of character constants:

```
char str[] = { 'F', 'a', 'r', 'w', 'e', 'l', 'l', ' ', 't', 'h',
```

and so on. Fortunately, the designers of C++ (and C) took pity on us and provided the shortcut approach shown in STRINIT. The effect is the same: The characters are placed one after the other in the array. As with all strings, the last character is a null (zero).

READING EMBEDDED BLANKS

If you tried the STRINGIN program with strings that contained more than one word, you may have had an unpleasant surprise. Here's an example:

```
Enter a string: Law is a bottomless pit.
You entered: Law
```

Where did the rest of the phrase (a quotation from the Scottish writer John Arbuthnot, 1667–1735) go? It turns out that the insertion operator >> considers a space to be a terminating character. Thus it will read strings consisting of a single word, but anything typed after a space is thrown away.

To read text containing blanks we use another function, `cin::get()`. This syntax means a member function `get()` of the `cin` stream class. The following example, BLANKSIN, shows how it's used:

```
// blanksin.cpp
// reads string with embedded blanks
#include <iostream.h>
const int MAX = 80;              // max characters in string

void main()
    {
    char str[MAX];               // string variable str

    cout << "\nEnter a string: ";
    cin.get(str, MAX);           // put string in str
    cout << "You entered: " << str;  // display string from str
    }
```

The first argument to `cin::get()` is the array address where the string being input will be placed. The second argument specifies the maximum size of the array, thus automatically avoiding buffer overrun.

Using this function, the input string is now stored in its entirety:

```
Enter a string: Law is a bottomless pit.
You entered: Law is a bottomless pit.
```

READING MULTIPLE LINES

We may have solved the problem of reading strings with embedded blanks, but what about strings with multiple lines? It turns out that the `cin::get()` function can take a third argument to help out in this situation. This argument specifies the character that tells the function to stop reading. The default value for this argument is the newline ('\n') character, but if you call the function with some other character for this argument, the default will be overridden by the specified character.

In the next example, LINESIN, we call the function with a dollar sign ('$') as the third argument:

```
// linesin.cpp
// reads multiple lines, terminates on '$' character
#include <iostream.h>
const int MAX = 80;                    // max characters in string

void main()
   {
   char str[MAX];                      // string variable str

   cout << "\nEnter a string:\n";
   cin.get(str, MAX, '$');             // terminate with $
   cout << "You entered:\n" << str;    // display string from str
   }
```

Now you can type as many lines of input as you want. The function will continue to accept characters until you enter the terminating character (or until you exceed the size of the array). Remember, you must still press ⏎ENTER⏎ after typing the '$' character. Here's a sample interaction with a poem from Thomas Carew, 1595–1639:

```
Enter a string:
Ask me no more where Jove bestows
When June is past, the fading rose;
For in your beauty's orient deep
These flowers, as in their causes, sleep.
$
You entered:
Ask me no more where Jove bestows
When June is past, the fading rose;
For in your beauty's orient deep
These flowers, as in their causes, sleep.
```

We terminate each line with ⏎ENTER⏎, but the program continues to accept input until we enter '$'.

COPYING A STRING THE HARD WAY

The best way to understand the true nature of strings is to deal with them character by character. The following program does this.

```
// strcopy1.cpp
// copies a string using a for loop
#include <iostream.h>
#include <string.h>            // for strlen()
const int MAX = 80;           // size of str2 buffer
void main()
```

```
{                                         // initialized string
char str1[] = "Oh, Captain, my Captain! "
              "our fearful trip is done";

char str2[MAX];                           // empty string

for(int j=0; j<strlen(str1); j++)   // copy strlen characters
   str2[j] = str1[j];                //    from str1 to str2
str2[j] = '\0';                      // insert null character
cout << endl;
cout << str2;                             // display str2

}
```

This program creates a string constant, str1, and a string variable, str2. It then uses a for loop to copy the string constant to the string variable. The copying is done one character at a time, in the statement

```
str2[j] = str1[j];
```

This program also introduces string library functions. Because there are no string operators built into C++, strings must usually be manipulated using library functions. Fortunately there are many such functions. The one we use in this program, strlen(), finds the length of a string (that is, how many characters are in it). We use this length as the limit in the for loop so that the right number of characters will be copied. When string functions are used, the header file STRING.H must be #included in the program.

The copied version of the string must be terminated with a null. However, the string length returned by strlen() does not include the null. We could copy one additional character, but it's safer to insert the null overtly. We do this with the line

```
str2[j] = '\0';
```

If you don't insert this character, you'll find that the string printed by the program includes all sorts of weird characters following the string you want. The << just keeps on printing characters, whatever they are, until by chance it encounters a '\0'

COPYING A STRING THE EASY WAY

Of course you don't need to use a for loop to copy a string. As you might have guessed, a library function will do it for you. Here's a revised version of the program, STRCOPY2, that uses the strcpy() function.

```
// strcopy2.cpp
// copies a string using strcpy() function
#include <iostream.h>
#include <string.h>            // for strcpy()
const int MAX = 80;           // size of str2 buffer
void main()
   {
```

```
        static char str1[] = "Tiger, tiger, burning bright\n"
                             "In the forests of the night";

        char str2[MAX];                     // empty string

        strcpy(str2, str1);                 // copy str1 to str2
        cout << endl;
        cout << str2;                       // display str2

        }
```

Note that you call this function like this:

```
    strcpy(destination, source)
```

with the destination first. The right-to-left order is reminiscent of the format of normal assignment statements: The variable on the right is copied to the variable on the left.

ARRAYS OF STRINGS

If there are arrays of arrays, of course there can be arrays of strings. This is actually quite a useful construction. Here's an example, STRARAY, that puts the names of the days of the week in an array:

```
// straray.cpp
// array of strings
#include <iostream.h>
const int DAYS = 7;              // number of strings in array
const int MAX = 10;              // maximum size of each string

void main()
    {                            // array of strings
    char star[DAYS][MAX] = { "Sunday", "Monday", "Tuesday",
                             "Wednesday", "Thursday",
                             "Friday", "Saturday" };
    for(int j=0; j<DAYS; j++)    // display every string
        cout << star[j] << endl;
    }
```

The program prints out each string from the array:

```
Sunday
Monday
Tuesday
Wednesday
Thursday
Friday
Saturday
```

Since a string is an array, it must be that **star**—an array of strings—is really a two-dimensional array. The first dimension of this array, **DAYS**, tells how many strings are in the array. The second dimension, MAX, specifies the maximum length of the strings (9 characters for "Wednesday" plus the terminating null makes 10). Figure 8-10 shows how this looks.

Notice that some bytes are wasted following strings that are less than the maximum length. We'll learn how to remove this inefficiency when we talk about pointers.

The syntax for accessing a particular string may look surprising:

```
star[j];
```

If we're dealing with a two-dimensional array, where's the second index? Since a two-dimensional array is an array of arrays, we can access elements of the "outer" array, each of which is an array (in this case a string), individually. To do this we don't need the second index. So star[j] is string number j in the array of strings.

STRINGS AS CLASS MEMBERS

Strings frequently appear as members of classes. The next example, a variation of the OBJPART program of Chapter 7, uses a string to hold the name of the widget part.

```
// strpart.cpp
// string used in widget part object
#include <iostream.h>
#include <string.h>         // for strcpy()

class part
    {
    private:
        char partname[30];    // name of widget part
        int partnumber;       // ID number of widget part
        float cost;           // cost of part
    public:
        void setpart(char pname[], int pn, float c)
            {
            strcpy(partname, pname);
            partnumber = pn;
            cost = c;
            }
        void showpart()                          // display data
            {
            cout << "\nName=" << partname;
            cout << ", number=" << partnumber;
            cout << ", cost=$" << cost;
            }
    };

void main()
    {
    part part1, part2;
```

```
part1.setpart("handle bolt", 4473, 217.55);
part2.setpart("start lever", 9924, 419.25);
cout << "\nFirst part: "; part1.showpart();
cout << "\nSecond part: "; part2.showpart();
}
```

This program defines two objects of class `part`, and gives them values with the `setpart()` member function. Then it displays them with the `showpart()` member function. Here's the output:

```
First part:
Name=handle bolt, number=4473, cost=$217.55
Second part:
Name=start lever, number=9924, cost=$419.25
```

To reduce the size of the program we've dropped the model number from the class members.

In the `setpart()` member function we use the `strcpy()` string library function to copy the string from the argument `pname` to the class data member `partname`. Thus this function serves the same purpose with string variables that an assignment statement does with simple variables.

Besides those we've seen, there are library functions to add a string to another, compare strings, search for specific characters in strings, and perform many other actions. Descriptions of these functions can be found in the Turbo C++ documentation. (See the bibliography for other books that contain descriptions of library functions.)

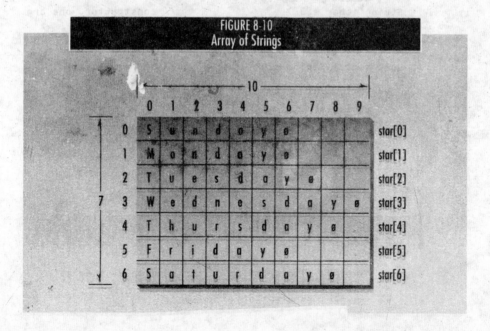

FIGURE 8-10
Array of Strings

A USER-DEFINED STRING TYPE

There are some problems with strings as normally used in C++. For one thing, you can't use the perfectly reasonable expression

```
strDest = strSrc;
```

to set one string equal to another. (In some languages, like BASIC, this is perfectly all right.) But if we define our own string type, using a C++ class, we can use just such assignment statements. (Many other string operations can be simplified as well, but we'll have to wait until we've learned about overloaded operators in the next chapter to see how this is done.)

The STROBJ program creates a class **String**. Here's the listing:

```cpp
// strobj.cpp
// a string as a class
#include <iostream.h>
#include <string.h>          // for strcpy(), strcat()

const int SZ = 80;           // size of all Strings

class String
   {
   private:
      char str[SZ];
   public:
      String()                         // constructor, no args
         { str[0] = '\0'; }
      String( char s[] )               // constructor, one arg
         { strcpy(str, s); }
      void display()                   // display string
         { cout << str; }
      void concat(String s2)           // add arg string to
         {                             // this string
         if( strlen(str)+strlen(s2.str) < SZ )
            strcat(str, s2.str);
         else
            cout << "\nString too long";
         }
   };

void main()
   {
   String s1("Merry Christmas!  ");    // uses constructor 2
   String s2 = "Season's Greetings!";  // alternate form of 2
   String s3;                          // uses constructor 1

   cout << "\ns1="; s1.display();      // display them all
   cout << "\ns2="; s2.display();
   cout << "\ns3="; s3.display();
```

```
    s3 = s1;                                  // assignment
    cout << "\ns3="; s3.display();            // display s3

    s3.concat(s2);                            // concatenation
    cout << "\ns3="; s3.display();            // display s3
    }
```

The `String` class contains a single data item: an array of type `char`. It may seem that our newly defined class is just the same as the original definition of a string: an array of type `char`. But, by making it a class, we have achieved some interesting benefits. Since an object can be assigned the value of another object of the same class, we can use statements like

```
    s3 = s1;
```

as we do in `main()`, to set one string equal to another. We can also define our own member functions to deal with Strings (objects of class `string`).

In the STROBJ program all Strings have the same length: `SZ` characters (which we set to 80). There are two constructors. The first creates a string object and sets the first character to the null character, '\0', so the string has a length of 0. This constructor is called with statements like

```
    String s3;
```

The second constructor sets the String object to a "normal" (that is, not a String) string constant. It uses the `strcpy()` library function to copy the string constant into the object's data. It's called with statements like

```
    String s1("Merry Christmas! ");
```

An alternative format for calling this constructor, which works with any one-argument constructor, is

```
    String s1 = "Merry Christmas! ");
```

Whichever format is used, this constructor effectively converts a string to a String—that is, a normal string constant to an object of class `string`. A member function, `display()`, displays the String.

Another member function, `concat()`, concatenates (adds) one String to another. The original String is the object of which `concat()` is a member. To this String will be added the String passed as an argument. Thus the statement in `main()`,

```
    s3.concat(s2);
```

causes `s2` to be added to the existing `s3`. Since `s2` has been initialized to "Season's Greetings!" and `s3` has been assigned the value of `s1`, which was "Merry Christmas ," the resulting value of `s3` is "Merry Christmas, Season's Greetings!"

The `concat()` function uses the `strcat()` C++ library function to do the concatenation. This library function adds the string specified in the second argument to the string specified in the first argument. The output from the program is

```
    s1=Merry Christmas!
```

```
s2=Season's Greetings!
s3=                                    ←————nothing here yet
s3=Merry Christmas!                    ←————set equal to s1
s3=Merry Christmas! Season's Greetings! ←————s2 concatenated
```

If the two Strings given to the `concat()` function together exceed the maximum String length, then the concatenation is not carried out, and a message is sent to the user.

SUMMARY

Arrays contain a number of data items of the same type. This type can be a simple data type, a structure, or a class. The items in an array are called elements. Elements are accessed by number; this number is called an index. Elements can be initialized to specific values when the array is defined. Arrays can have multiple dimensions. A two-dimensional array is an array of arrays. The address of an array can be used as an argument to a function; the array itself is not copied. Arrays can be used as member data in classes. Care must be taken to prevent data from being placed in memory outside an array.

Strings are arrays of type `char`. The last character in a string must be the null character, '\0'. String constants take a special form so that they can be written conveniently. A variety of string library functions are used to manipulate strings. An array of strings is an array of arrays of type `char`. Strings are frequently used as class members.

QUESTIONS

1. An array element is accessed using
   a. a first-in–first-out approach
   b. the dot operator
   c. a member name
   d. an index number
2. All the elements in an array must be the _____ data type.
3. Write a statement that defines a one-dimensional array called `doubleArray` of type `double` that holds 100 elements.
4. The elements of a ten-element array are numbered from _____ to _____.
5. Write a statement that takes element `j` of array `doubleArray` and writes it to `cout` with the insertion operator.

6. Element `doubleArray[7]` is which element of the array?
    a. the sixth
    b. the seventh
    c. the eighth
    d. impossible to tell

7. Write a statement that defines an array `coins` of type `int` and initializes it to the values of the penny, nickel, dime, quarter, half-dollar, and dollar.

8. When a multidimensional array is accessed, each array index is
    a. separated by commas
    b. surrounded by brackets and separated by commas
    c. separated by commas and surrounded by brackets
    d. surrounded by brackets

9. Write an expression that accesses element 4 in subarray 2 in a two-dimensional array called `twoD`.

10. True or false: In C++ there can be an array of four dimensions.

11. For a two-dimensional array of type `float`, called `flarr`, write a statement that declares the array and initializes the first subarray to 52, 27, 83; the second to 94, 73, 49; and the third to 3, 6, 1.

12. An array name, used in the source file, represents the _____ of the array.

13. When an array name is passed to a function, the function
    a. accesses exactly the same array as the calling program
    b. accesses a copy of the array passed by the program
    c. refers to the array using the same name as that used by the calling program
    d. refers to the array using a different name from that used by the calling program

14. Tell what this statement defines:

    `employee emplist[1000];`

15. Write an expression that accesses a structure member called `salary` in a structure variable that is the 17th element in an array called `emplist`.

16. In a stack, the data item placed on the stack first is
    a. not given an index number
    b. given the index number 0
    c. the first data item to be removed
    d. the last data item to be removed

17. Write a statement that defines an array called `manybirds` that holds 50 objects of type `bird`.

18. True or false: The compiler will complain if you try to access array element 14 in a ten-element array.

19. Write a statement that executes the member function `cheep()` in an object of class `bird` that is the 27th element in the array `manybirds`.

20. A string in C++ is an _____ of type _____.

21. Write a statement that defines a string variable called `city` that can hold a string of up to 20 characters (this is slightly tricky).

22. Write a statement that defines a string constant, called `dextrose`, that has the value "C6H12O6-H2O".

23. True or false: The `<<` insertion operator stops reading a string when it encounters a space.

24. You can read input that consists of multiple lines of text using
    a. the normal `cout <<` combination
    b. the `cin.get()` function with one argument
    c. the `cin.get()` function with two arguments
    d. the `cin.get()` function with three arguments

25. Write a statement that uses a string library function to copy the string `name` to the string `blank`.

26. Write the specification for a class called `dog` that contains two data members: a string called `breed` and an `int` called `age`. (Don't include any member functions.)

EXERCISES

1. Write a function called `reversit()` that reverses a string (an array of `char`). Use a `for` loop that swaps the first and last characters, then the second and next-to-last characters, and so on. The string should be passed to `reversit()` as an argument.

   Write a program to exercise `reversit()`. The program should get a string from the user, call `reversit()`, and print out the result. Use an input method that allows embedded blanks. Test the program with Napoleon's famous phrase, "Able was I ere I saw Elba."

2. Create a class called `employee` that contains a name (an array of `char`) and an employee number (type `long`). Include a member function called `getdata()` to get data from the user for insertion into the object, and another function called `putdata()` to display the data. Assume the name has no embedded blanks.

   Write a `main()` program to exercise this class. It should create an array of type `employee`, and then invite the user to input data for up to 100 employees. Finally, it should print out the data for all the employees.

3. Write a program that calculates the average of up to 100 English distances input by the user. Create an array of objects of the `Distance` class, as in the ENGLARAY example in this chapter. To calculate the average, you can borrow the

dist_add() member function from the ENGLCON example in Chapter 7. You'll also need a member function that divides a **Distance** value by an integer. Here's one possibility:

```
void Distance::div_dist(Distance d2, int divisor)
   {
   float fltfeet = d2.feet + d2.inches/12.0;
   fltfeet /= divisor;
   feet = int(fltfeet);
   inches = (fltfeet-feet) * 12.0,
   }
```

OPERATOR OVERLOADING

Operator overloading is one of the most exciting features of object-oriented programming. It can transform complex, obscure program listings into intuitively obvious ones. For example, a statement like

```
d3.addobjects(d1, d2);
```

can be changed to the much more readable

```
d3 = d1 + d2;
```

The rather forbidding term *operator overloading* refers to giving the normal C++ operators, such as +, *, <=, and +=, additional meanings when they are applied to user-defined data types. Normally

```
a = b + c;
```

works only with basic types like **int** and **float**, and attempting to apply it when **a**, **b**, and **c** are objects of a user-defined class will cause complaints from the compiler. However, using overloading, you can make this statement legal even when **a**, **b**, and **c** are user-defined types.

In effect, operator overloading gives you the opportunity to redefine the C++ language. If you find yourself limited by the way the C++ operators work, you can change them to do whatever you want. By using classes to create new kinds of variables, and operator overloading to create new definitions for operators, you can extend C++ to be, in many ways, a new langue of your own design.

Another kind of operation, *data type conversion*, is closely connected with operator overloading. C++ handles the conversion of simple types, like **int** and **float**, automatically; but conversions involving user-defined types require some work on the programmer's part. We'll look at data conversions in the second part of this chapter.

Overloaded operators are not all beer and skittles. We'll discuss some of the dangers in their use at the end of the chapter.

Overloading Unary Operators

Let's start off by overloading a *unary operator*. As you may recall from Chapter 2, unary operators act on only one operand. (An operand is simply a variable acted on by an operator). Examples of unary operators are the increment and decrement operators ++ and --, and the unary minus, as in –33.

In the COUNTER example in Chapter 7 we created a class `Counter` to keep track of a count. Objects of that class were incremented by calling a member function:

```
c1.inc_count();
```

That did the job, but the listing would have been more readable if we could have used the increment operator ++ instead:

```
++c1;
```

All dyed-in-the-wool C++ (and C) programmers would guess immediately that this expression increments `c1`.

Let's rewrite COUNTER to make this possible. Here's the listing for COUNTPP1:

```
// countpp1.cpp
// increment counter variable with ++ operator
#include <iostream.h>

class Counter
    {
    private:
        unsigned int count;                    // count
    public:
        Counter()        { count = 0; }        // constructor
        int get_count()  { return count; }     // return count
        void operator ++ ()     { count++; }   // increment count
    };

void main()
    {
    Counter c1, c2;                            // define and initialize

    cout << "\nc1=" << c1.get_count();         // display
    cout << "\nc2=" << c2.get_count();

    c1++;                                       // increment c1
    c2++;                                       // increment c2 (postfix)
    ++c2;                                       // increment c2 (prefix)

    cout << "\nc1=" << c1.get_count();          // display again
    cout << "\nc2=" << c2.get_count();
    }
```

In this program we create two objects of class `Counter`: `c1` and `c2`. The counts in the objects are displayed; they are initially 0. Then, using the overloaded ++

operator, we increment c1 once and c2 twice, and display the resulting values. Here's the program's output:

```
c1=0            ←——————— counts are initially 0
c2=0
c1=1            ←——————— incremented once
c2=2            ←——————— incremented twice
```

The statements responsible for these operations are

```
c1++;
c2++;
++c2;
```

The ++ operator is applied once to c1 and twice to c2. Both prefix and postfix notation are used on c2.

THE operator KEYWORD

How do we teach a normal C++ operator to act on a user-defined operand? The keyword operator is used to overload the ++ operator in this declarator:

```
void operator ++ ()
```

The return type (void in this case) comes first, followed by the keyword opera-tor, followed by the operator itself (++), and finally the argument list enclosed in parentheses (which are empty here). This declarator syntax tells the compiler to call this member function whenever the ++ operator is encountered, provided the operand (the variable operated on by the ++) is of type Counter.

We've already seen in Chapter 6 that the only way the compiler can distinguish between overloaded functions is by looking at the data type of their arguments. In the same way, the only way it can distinguish between overloaded operators is by looking at the data type of their operands. If the operand is a basic type like an int, as in

```
intvar++;
```

then the compiler will use its built-in routine to increment an int. But if the operand is a Counter variable, then the compiler will know to use our user-written operator++() instead.

OPERATOR ARGUMENTS

In main() the ++ operator is applied to a specific object, as in the expression c1++;. Yet operator++() takes no arguments. What does this operator increment? It increments the count data in the object of which it is a member function. Since member functions can always access the particular object for which they've been called, this operator requires no arguments. This is shown in Figure 9-1.

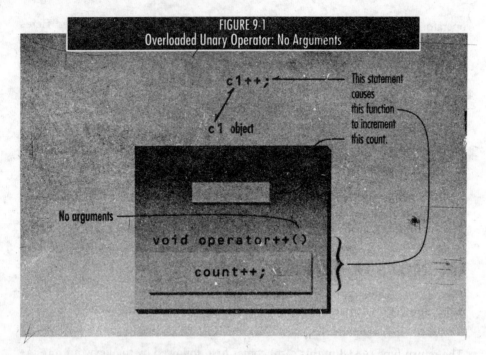

FIGURE 9-1
Overloaded Unary Operator: No Arguments

c1++;

This statement causes this function to increment this count.

c1 object

No arguments

```
void operator++()

count++;
```

OPERATOR RETURN VALUES

The `operator++()` function in the COUNTPP1.CPP program has a subtle defect. You will discover it if you use a statement like this in `main()`:

```
c1 = c2++;
```

The compiler will complain. Why? Because we have defined the `++` operator to have a return type of `void` in the `operator++()` function, while in the assignment statement it is being asked to return a variable of type `Counter`. That is, the compiler is being asked to return whatever value `c2` has after being operated on by the `++` operator, and assign this value to `c1`. So as defined in COUNTPP1 we can't use `++` to increment `Counter` objects in expressions; it must always stand alone with its operand. (Of course the normal `++` operator, applied to basic data types like `int`, would not have this problem.)

To make it possible to use our homemade `operator++()` in expressions, we must provide a way for it to return a value. The next program, COUNTPP2, does just that.

```
// countpp2.cpp
// increment counter variable with ++ operator, return value
#include <iostream.h>

class Counter
    {
    private:
        unsigned int count;                // count
```

```
    public:
        Counter()            { count = 0; }      // constructor
        int get_count()  { return count; } // return count
        Counter operator ++ ()                   // increment count
        {
        count++;             // increment count
        Counter temp;        // make a temporary Counter
        temp.count = count;  // give it same value as this obj
        return temp;         // return the copy
        }
    };

void main()
    {
    Counter c1, c2;                              // c1=0, c2=0

    cout << "\nc1=" << c1.get_count();    // display
    cout << "\nc2=" << c2.get_count();

    c1++;                                        // c1=1
    c2 = c1++;                                   // c1=2, c2=2

    cout << "\nc1=" << c1.get_count();    // display again
    cout << "\nc2=" << c2++.get_count();  // c2=3
    }
```

In this program the `operator++()` function creates a new object of type `Counter`, called `temp`, to use as a return value. It increments the `count` data in its own object as before, then creates the new `temp` object and assigns `count` in the new object the same value as in its own object. Finally it returns the `temp` object. This has the desired effect: Expressions like

```
    c1++
```

now return a value, so they can be used in other expressions, such as:

```
    c2 = c1++;
```

and

```
    c2++.get_count()
```

as shown in COUNTPP2. In the first of these statements the value returned from `c1++` will be assigned to `c2`, and in the second it will be used to display itself using the `get_count()` member function.

NAMELESS TEMPORARY OBJECTS

In COUNTPP2 we created a temporary object of type `Counter`, named `temp`, whose sole purpose was to provide a return value for the `++` operator. This required three statements:

```
Counter temp;              // make a temporary Counter object
temp.count = count;        // give it same value as this object
return temp;               // return it
```

There are more convenient ways to return objects from functions and overloaded operators. Let's examine another approach, as shown in the program COUNTPP3:

```
// countpp3.cpp
// increment counter variable with ++ operator
// uses unnamed temporary object
#include <iostream.h>

class Counter
   {
   private:
      unsigned int count;                // count
   public:
      Counter()        { count = 0; }    // constructor  no args
      Counter(int c)   { count = c; }    // constructor, one arg
      int get_count()  { return count; } // return count
      Counter operator ++ ()             // increment count
         {
         count++;                 // increment count, return
         return Counter(count);   // an unnamed temporary object
         }                        // initialized to this count
   };

void main()
   {
   Counter c1, c2;                              // c1=0, c2=0

   cout << "\nc1=" << c1.get_count();           // display
   cout << "\nc2=" << c2.get_count();

   c1++;                                        // c1=1
   c2 = c1++;                                   // c1=2, c2=2

   cout << "\nc1=" << c1.get_count();           // display again
   cout << "\nc2=" << c2++.get_count();         // c2=3
   }
```

In this program a single statement,

```
return Counter(count);
```

does what all three statements did in COUNTPP2. This statement creates an object of type Counter. This object has no name; it won't be around long enough to need one. This unnamed object is initialized to the value provided by the argument count.

But wait: Doesn't this require a constructor that takes one argument? It does, and to make this statement work we sneakily inserted just such a constructor into the member function list in COUNTPP3:

```
Counter(int c)  { count = c; }  // constructor, one arg
```

Once the unnamed object is initialized to the value of `count` it can then be returned.

The approaches in both COUNTPP2 and COUNTPP3 involved making a copy of the original object (the object of which the function is a member), and returning the copy. Another approach is to return the value of the original object, using the `this` pointer, as we'll see in Chapter 11.

LIMITATION OF INCREMENT OPERATORS

In the COUNTPP1 example we showed both prefix and postfix notation: `c2++` and `++c2`. When applied to basic variable types, prefix notation causes a variable to be incremented *before* its value is used in an expression, while postfix causes it to be incremented after its value is used. Unfortunately, when `++` and `--` are overloaded, there is no distinction between prefix and postfix notation. The expression

```
c2 = c1++;
```

has exactly the same effect as

```
c2 = ++c1;
```

In both cases `c1` is incremented before being assigned to `c2`. If these were basic types the first expression would cause assignment *before* incrementing. In this regard the use of the `++` operator with objects is not completely equivalent to its use with normal data types.

As you know, there is a decrement operator `--` as well as an increment operator. Can it be overloaded as well? Yes, in a completely analogous way. The other unary operators can be overloaded as well.

We should note parenthetically that this description of the overloaded increment and decrement operators applies only to the current version of Turbo C++ and Borland C++. Ellis and Stroustrup (see the bibliography) describe a different implementation that requires two overloaded operators, one for prefix and one for postfix:

```
operator ++();      // does prefix (++var)
operator ++(int);   // does postfix (var++)
```

The second declaration uses a dummy `int` argument which is set to 0 automatically by the postfix `++` operator. This extra argument allows the compiler to distinguish the two forms.

If this new approach is implemented in future releases of Turbo C++ and Borland C++, then the overloaded increment and deccrement operators will work in the same way they do for basic types.

OVERLOADING BINARY OPERATORS

Binary operators can be overloaded just as easily as unary operators. We'll look at examples that overload arithmetic operators, comparison operators, and arithmetic assignment operators.

ARITHMETIC OPERATORS

In the ENGLCON program in Chapter 7 we showed how two English Distance objects could be added using a member function add_dist():

```
dist3.add_dist(dist1, dist2);
```

By overloading the + operator we can reduce this dense-looking expression to

```
dist3 = dist1 + dist2;
```

Here's the listing for ENGLPLUS, which does just this:

```
// englplus.cpp
// overloaded '+' operator adds two Distances
#include <iostream.h>

class Distance                     // English Distance class
   {
   private:
      int feet;
      float inches;
   public:
      Distance()                   // constructor (no args)
         { feet = 0; inches = 0.0; }
      Distance(int ft, float in)  // constructor (two args)
         { feet = ft; inches = in; }

      void getdist()               // get length from user
         {
         cout << "\nEnter feet: ";  cin >> feet;
         cout << "Enter inches: ";  cin >> inches;
         }

      void showdist()              // display distance
         { cout << feet << "\'-" << inches << '\"'; }

      Distance operator + ( Distance );  // add two distances
   };
                                   // add this distance to d2
Distance Distance::operator + (Distance d2)   // return the sum
   {
   int f = feet + d2.feet;         // add the feet
   float i = inches + d2.inches;   // add the inches
   if(i >= 12.0)                   // if total exceeds 12.0,
      {                            // then decrease inches
      i -= 12.0;                   // by 12.0 and
      f++;                         // increase feet by 1
      }                            // return a temporary Distance
   return Distance(f,i);           // initialized to sum
   }
```

```
void main()
    {
    Distance dist1, dist3, dist4;     // define distances
    dist1.getdist();                   // get dist1 from user

    Distance dist2(11, 6.25);          // define, initialize dist2

    dist3 = dist1 + dist2;             // single '+' operator

    dist4 = dist1 + dist2 + dist3;     // multiple '+' operators

                                       // display all lengths
    cout << "\ndist1 = ";  dist1.showdist();
    cout << "\ndist2 = ";  dist2.showdist();
    cout << "\ndist3 = ";  dist3.showdist();
    cout << "\ndist4 = ";  dist4.showdist();
    }
```

To show that the result of an addition can be used in another addition as well as in an assignment, another addition is performed in `main()`. We add `dist1`, `dist2`, and `dist3` to obtain `dist4` (which should be double the value of `dist3`), in the statement

```
dist4 = dist1 + dist2 + dist3;
```

Here's the output from the program:

```
Enter feet: 10
Enter inches: 6.5

dist1 = 10'-6.5"          ◄──────── from user
dist2 = 11'-6.25"         ◄──────── initialized in program
dist3 = 22'-0.75"         ◄──────── dist1+dist2
dist4 = 44'-1.5"          ◄──────── dist1+dist2+dist3
```

In class `Distance` the declaration for the `operator+()` function looks like this:

```
Distance operator + ( Distance );
```

This function has a return type of `Distance`, and takes one argument of type `Distance`.

In expressions like

```
dist3 = dist1 + dist2;
```

it's important to understand how the return value and arguments of the operator relate to the objects. When the compiler sees this expression it looks at the argument types, and finding only type `Distance`, it realizes it must use the `Distance` member function `operator+()`. But what does this function use as its argument— `dist1`, or `dist2`? And doesn't it need two arguments, since there are two numbers to be added?

Here's the key: The argument on the *left side* of the operator (**dist1** in this case) is the object of which the operator is a member function. The object on the *right* side of the operator (**dist2**) must be furnished as an argument to the operator. The operator returns a value, which can be assigned or used in other ways; in this case it is assigned to **dist3**. Figure 9-2 shows how this looks.

In the **operator+()** function, the left operand is accessed directly—since this is the object of which the function is a member—using **feet** and **inches**. The right operand is accessed as function's argument, as **d2.feet** and **d2.inches**.

We can generalize and say that an overloaded operator always requires one less argument than its number of operands, since one operand is the object of which the operator is a member function. That's why unary operators require no arguments. (This rule does not apply to **friend** functions and operators, a C++ feature we'll discuss in Chapter 13.)

To calculate the return value of **operator+()** in ENGLPLUS, we first add the feet and inches from the two operands (adjusting for a carry if necessary). The resulting values, **f** and **i**, are then used to initialize a nameless **Distance** object, which is returned in the statement

```
return Distance(f, i);
```

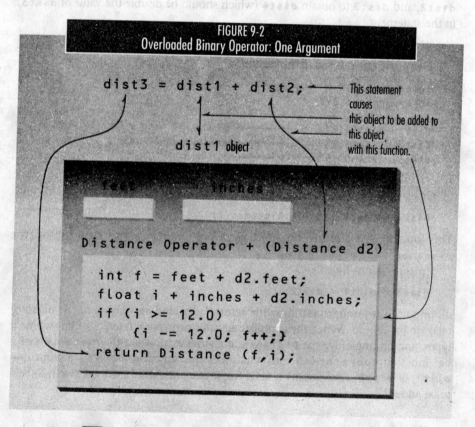

FIGURE 9-2
Overloaded Binary Operator: One Argument

```
dist3 = dist1 + dist2;        This statement
                              causes
                              this object to be added to
                              this object,
        dist1 object          with this function.



    feet            inches




Distance Operator + (Distance d2)

   int f = feet + d2.feet;
   float i + inches + d2.inches;
   if (i >= 12.0)
       {i -= 12.0; f++;}
   return Distance (f,i);
```

This is similar to the construction used in COUNTPP3, except that the constructor takes two arguments instead of one. The statement

```
dist3 = dist1 + dist2;
```

in main() then assigns the value of the nameless Distance object to dist3. Compare this intuitively obvious statement with the use of a function call to perform the same task, as in the ENGLCON example in Chapter 7.

Similar functions could be created to overload other operators in the Distance class, so you could subtract, multiply, and divide objects of this class in natural-looking ways.

Adding Polar Coordinates

Here's another example of operator overloading. Points on a plane are commonly specified with a pair of rectangular coordinates (x, y). Thus a point (4, 3) is located where x is 4 and y is 3, as shown in Figure 9-3.

There's another way to describe a point on the plane: using polar coordinates of the form (radius, angle). In this system a line called the radius, drawn from the origin to the point, and the angle this line makes with the positive X axis, specify the point, as shown in Figure 9-4.

Polar coordinates are handy for describing certain curves, such as spirals. They are commonly found on scientific calculators; pushing buttons performs conversions between polar and rectangular coordinates.

Our example program will show a class, Polar, that models polar coordinates. We'll use the overloaded + operator to add two objects of type Polar.

What does it mean to add two points on the two-dimensional plane? If the points are considered to be the end points of directed lines, they can show a distance and

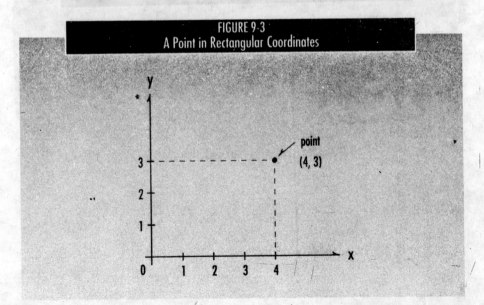

FIGURE 9-3
A Point in Rectangular Coordinates

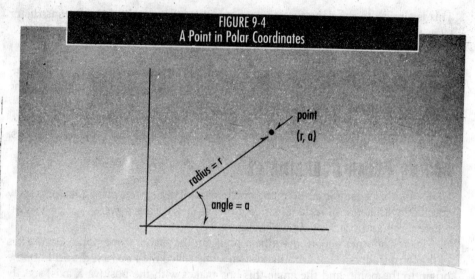

FIGURE 9-4
A Point in Polar Coordinates

direction traveled, say by an airplane. If you fly north from Toledo 100 miles, and then fly east 50 miles, how far from Toledo are you, and in which direction? Adding two variables of type **Polar** solves this kind of problem, as shown in Figure 9-5.

Adding points expressed in polar coordinates requires several steps. It turns out it's easier to add points when they are expressed in rectangular coordinates. This

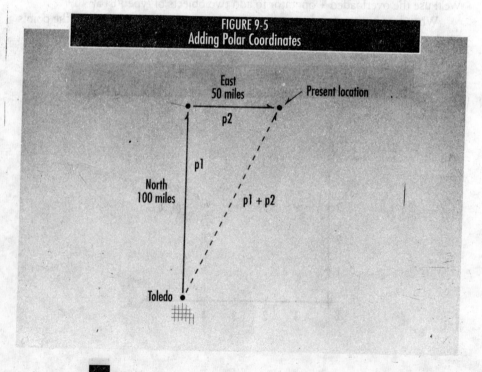

FIGURE 9-5
Adding Polar Coordinates

FIGURE 9-6
Adding Points in Rectangular Coordinates

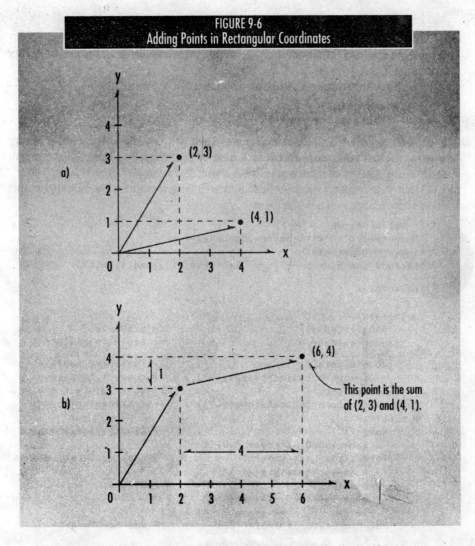

is done by adding the X and Y coordinates separately. Say you have two points expressed in rectangular coordinates—(4,1) and (2,3)—as shown in Figure 9-6-a. To add the points, we first add their X coordinates: 4+2=6. Then we add their Y co-ordinates: 1+3=4. The resulting point is (6, 4), as shown in Figure 9-6-b.

Adding points in polar coordinates requires a three-step approach. First we con-vert the points to rectangular coordinates, then we add the points as described above, and finally we convert the result back into polar coordinates.

How do we convert between polar and rectangular coordinates? These conver-sions involve several trigonometric formulas. It doesn't matter if you've forgotten your trig; you need only plug values into the formulas to make them work.

To convert from polar to rectangular, use these formulas (expressed in C++ form):

```
x = radius * cos(angle);
y = radius * sin(angle);
```

The cos() and sin() (cosine and sine) functions are available as Turbo C++ library functions.

To convert back from rectangular to polar, use the formulas

```
angle = atan(x/y);
radius = sqrt(x*x + y*y);
```

The functions atan() (for *arctangent*) and sqrt() (for *square root*) are also library functions. The Pythagorean theorem is used to find the radius, and the arctangent of the X and Y sides of the triangle is the angle, as shown in Figure 9-7.

The POLAPLUS program makes use of this three-step approach to add two points in polar coordinates. Here's the listing:

```cpp
// polaplus.cpp
// operator '+' with polar coordinates
#include <iostream.h>
#include <math.h>                   // for sin(), cos(), etc.

class Polar
    {
    private:
        double radius;                    // distance
        double angle;                     // angle in radians

        double getx()                     // these two functions
            { return radius*cos(angle); } // convert this Polar
        double gety()                     // object into x and y
            { return radius*sin(angle); } // rectangular coords
    public:
        Polar()                           // constructor, no args
            { radius=0.0; angle=0.0; }
        Polar(float r, float a)           // constructor, two args
            { radius=r; angle=a; }
        void display()                    // display
            { cout << "(" << radius
                   << ", " << angle << ")"; }
        Polar operator + (Polar p2)       // add two Polars
            {
            double x = getx() + p2.getx(); // add x and y coords
            double y = gety() + p2.gety(); // for this and p2
            double r = sqrt(x*x + y*y);    // convert new x and y
            double a = atan(y/x);          // to Polar
            return Polar(r, a);            // return temp Polar
            }
    };

void main()
    {
    Polar p1(10.0, 0.0);          // line to the right
    Polar p2(10.0, 1.570796325);  // line straight up
    Polar p3;                     // uninitialized Polar
```

```
p3 = p1 + p2;                          // add two Polars
cout << "\np1="; p1.display();   // display all Polars
cout << "\np2="; p2.display();
cout << "\np3="; p3.display();
}
```

The `Polar` class contains two data items: `radius` and `angle`. Since we'll be using Turbo C++ math library functions to operate on this data, and since these functions mostly use type `double`, we'll define `radius` and `angle` to be of this type. Angles are measured in radians. (There are 2*pi, or about 6.28, radians in a circle, so a radian is about 57 degrees.)

Constructors in `Polar` initialize a variable to 0 or initialize it to specified values. Another member function displays these values.

Two other member functions, `getx()` and `gety()`, convert polar coordinates to rectangular coordinates. These functions are needed because, as we noted, adding two points in polar coordinates involves converting to rectangular coordinates before adding. The `getx()` and `gety()` functions are made private because they don't need to be accessed from outside the class; they're only used internally.

The `operator+()` function adds two `Polar` variables. It does this by converting the `Polar` operands to rectangular coordinates, and adding the x coordinates to obtain `x` and the y coordinates to obtain `y`. The `x` and `y` variables are then used to find the `radius` and `angle` of the sum, which is returned.

In the `main()` part of POLAPLUS, one `Polar` variable is initialized to (10.0, 0.0). This represents a point located 10 units horizontally along the X axis. Another variable is initialized to (10.0, 1.570796325). Since these angles are measured in radians, this represents a point 10 units straight up on the Y axis. (1.570796325 radians is 90 degrees.)

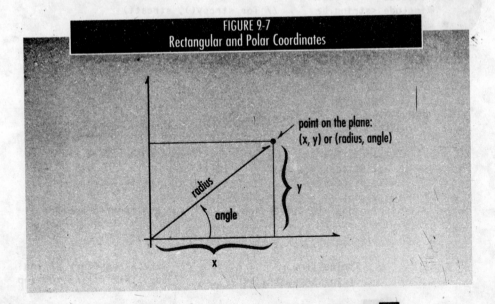

FIGURE 9-7
Rectangular and Polar Coordinates

These two variables are then added, in the statement

```
p3 = p1 + p2;
```

The result should be a point at 45 degrees (half of 90), as shown in Figure 9-8. Here's the actual output:

```
p1=(10, 0)              ←──────── point on X axis (0 degrees)
p2=(10, 1.570796325)    ←──────── point on Y axis (90 degrees)
p3=(14.142136, 0.785398) ←─────── point at 45 degree angle
```

The point (14.142136, 0.785398) is indeed at 45 degrees.

This example has shown how to overload only one operator: +. We could also overload the other arithmetic operators for the **Polar** type, so such coordinates could be subtracted, multiplied, divided, and so on.

CONCATENATING STRINGS

In C++ the + operator cannot normally be used to concatenate strings, as it can in some languages such as BASIC. That is, you can't say

```
str3 = str1 + str2;
```

where **str1**, **str2**, and **str3** are string variables (arrays of type **char**), as in "cat" plus "bird" equals "catbird". However, if we use our own **String** class, as shown in the STROBJ program of Chapter 7, then we can overload the + operator to do such concatenation. This is another example of redefining the C++ language. Here's the listing for STRPLUS:

```cpp
// strplus.cpp
// overloaded '+' operator concatenates strings
#include <iostream.h>
#include <string.h>        // for strcpy(), strcat()

const int SZ = 80;         // size of all String objects

class String              // user-defined string type
   {
   private:
      char str[SZ];                   // holds a string
   public:
      String()                        // constructor, no args
         { strcpy(str, ""); }
      String( char s[] )              // constructor, one arg
         { strcpy(str, s); }
      void display()                  // display the String
         { cout << str; }
      String operator + (String ss)   // add a String to another
         {
         if( strlen(str) + strlen(ss.str) < SZ )
            {
            String temp;                 // make a temporary String
            strcpy(temp.str, str);       // copy this string to temp
```

```
        strcat(temp.str, ss.str);   // add the argument string
        return temp;                // return temp String
        }
    else
        cout << "\nString overflow";
    }
};

void main()
    {
    String s1 = "\nMerry Christmas!  ";   // uses constructor 2
    String s2 = "Happy new year!";        // uses constructor 2
    String s3;                            // uses constructor 1

    s1.display();          // display strings
    s2.display();
    s3.display();

    s3 = s1 + s2;          // add s2 to s1, assign to s3

    s3.display();          // display s3
    }
```

The program first displays three strings separately. (The third is empty at this point, so nothing is printed when it displays itself.) Then the first two strings are concatenated and placed in the third, and the third string is displayed again. Here's the output:

```
Merry Christmas!  Happy new year!     ←——————— s1, s2, and s3 (empty)
Merry Christmas!  Happy new year!     ←——————— s3 after concatenation
```

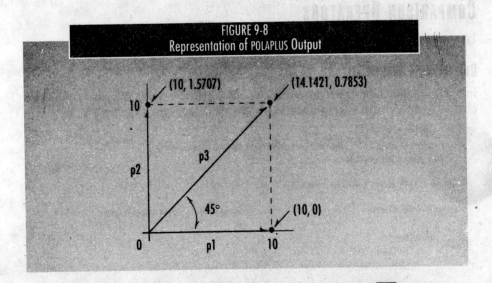

FIGURE 9-8
Representation of POLAPLUS Output

By now the basics of overloading the + operator should be somewhat familiar. The declarator

```
String operator + (String ss)
```

shows that the + operator takes one argument of type **String** and returns an object of the same type. The concatenation process in **operator+()** involves creating a temporary object of type **String**, copying the string from our own **String** object into it, concatenating the argument string using the library function **strcat()**, and returning the resulting temporary string. Note that we can't use the

```
return String(string);
```

approach, where a nameless temporary **String** is created, because we need access to the temporary **String** not only to initialize it but to concatenate the argument string to it.

We must be careful that we don't overflow the fixed-length strings used in the **String** class. To prevent such accidents in the **operator+()** function, we check that the combined length of the two strings to be concatenated will not exceed the maximum string length. If they do, we print an error message instead of carrying out the concatenation operation. (We could handle errors in other ways, like returning a 0 if an error occurred.)

MULTIPLE OVERLOADING

We've seen three different uses of the + operator: to add English distances, to add polar coordinates, and to concatenate strings. You could put all these classes together in the same program, and C++ would still know how to interpret the + operator: It selects the correct function to carry out the "addition" based on the type of operand.

COMPARISON OPERATORS

Let's see how to overload a different kind of C++ operator: comparison operators.

Comparing Distances

In our first example we'll overload the *less than* operator < in the English **Distance** class, so that we can compare two distances. Here's the listing for ENGLESS:

```
// engless.cpp
// overloaded '<' operator compares two Distances
#include <iostream.h>

enum boolean { false, true };

class Distance                          // English Distance class
    {
    private:
        int feet;
        float inches;
```

```
public:
    Distance()                      // constructor (no args)
        { feet = 0; inches = 0.0; }
    Distance(int ft, float in)  // constructor (two args)
        { feet = ft; inches = in; }
    void getdist()                  // get length from user
        {
        cout << "\nEnter feet: ";  cin >> feet;
        cout << "Enter inches: ";  cin >> inches;
        }
    void showdist()                 // display distance
        { cout << feet << "\'-" << inches << '\"'; }
    boolean operator < (Distance);  // compare distances
    };
                                    // compare this distance with d2
boolean Distance::operator < (Distance d2)   // return true or false
    {
    float bf1 = feet + inches/12;
    float bf2 = d2.feet + d2.inches/12;
    return (bf1 < bf2) ? true : false;
    }

void main()
    {
    Distance dist1;                     // define Distance dist1
    dist1.getdist();                    // get dist1 from user

    Distance dist2(6, 2.5);             // define and initialize dist2
                                        // display distances
    cout << "\ndist1 = ";  dist1.showdist();
    cout << "\ndist2 = ";  dist2.showdist();

    if( dist1 < dist2 )                 // overloaded '<' operator
        cout << "\ndist1 is less than dist2";
    else
        cout << "\ndist1 is greater than dist2";
    }
```

This program compares a distance entered by the user with a distance, 6'-2.5",
initialized by the program. Depending on the result, it then prints one of two possible sentences. Here's some typical output:

```
Enter feet: 5
Enter inches: 11.5
dist1 = 5'-11.5"
dist2 = 6'-2.5"
dist1 is less than dist2
```

The approach used in the operator<() function in ENGLESS is similar to overloading the + operator in the ENGLPLUS program, except that here the operator<()
function has a return type of boolean (defined in the enum statement at the

beginning of the program). The return value is `false` or `true`, depending on the comparison of the two distances. The comparison is made by converting both distances to floating-point feet, and comparing them using the normal `<` operator. Remember that the statement

```
return (bf1 < bf2) ? true : false;
```

is the same as

```
if(bf1 < bf2)
    return true;
else
    return false;
```

Comparing Strings

Here's another example of overloading a comparison operator, this time the *equals* (`==`) operator. We'll use it to compare two strings, returning `true` if the strings are the same and `false` if they're different. Here's the listing for STREQUAL:

```
// strequal.cpp
// overloaded '==' operator compares strings
#include <iostream.h>
#include <string.h>        // for strcmp()

const int SZ = 80;         // size of all String objects
enum boolean { false, true };

class String               // user-defined string type
    {
    private:
        char str[SZ];                          // holds a string
    public:
        String()                               // constructor, no args
            { strcpy(str, ""); }
        String( char s[] )                     // constructor, one arg
            { strcpy(str, s); }
        void display()                         // display a String
            { cout << str; }
        void getstr()                          // read a string
            { cin.get(str, SZ); }
        boolean operator == (String ss)  // check for equality
            {
            return ( strcmp(str, ss.str)==0 ) ? true : false;
            }
    };

void main()
    {
    String s1 = "yes";
    String s2 = "r.o";
    String s3;
```

```
cout << "\nEnter 'yes' or 'no': ";
s3.getstr();                              // get String from user

if(s3==s1)                                // compare with "yes"
   cout << "You typed yes\n";
else if(s3==s2)                           // compare with "no"
   cout << "You typed no\n";
else
   cout << "You didn't follow instructions\n";
}
```

The `main()` part of this program uses the `==` operator twice, once to see if a string input by the user is "yes" and once to see if it's "no". Here's the output when the user types "yes":

```
Enter 'yes or 'no': yes
You typed yes
```

The `operator==()` function uses the library function `strcmp()` to compare the two strings. This function returns 0 if the strings are equal, a negative number if the first is less than the second, and a positive number if the first is greater than the second. Here *less than* and *greater than* are used in their lexicographical sense to indicate whether the first string appears before or after the second in an alphabetized listing.

Other comparison operators, such as `<` and `>`, could also be used to compare the lexicographical value of strings. Or, alternatively, these comparison operators could be redefined to compare string lengths. Since you're the one defining how the operators are used, you can use any definition that seems appropriate to your situation.

ARITHMETIC ASSIGNMENT OPERATORS

Let's finish up our exploration of overloaded binary operators with an arithmetic assignment operator: the `+=` operator. Recall that this operator combines assignment and addition into one step. We'll use this operator to add one English distance to a second, leaving the result in the first. This is similar to the ENGLPLUS example shown earlier, but there is a subtle difference. Here's the listing for ENGLPLEQ:

```
// englpleq.cpp
// overloaded '+=' assignment operator
#include <iostream.h>

class Distance                            // English Distance class
   {
   private:
      int feet;
      float inches;
   public:
      Distance()                          // constructor (no args)
         { feet = 0; inches = 0.0; }
```

```
      Distance(int ft, float in)    // constructor (two args)
         { feet = ft; inches = in; }
      void getdist()                 // get length from user
         {
         cout << "\nEnter feet: ";  cin >> feet;
         cout << "Enter inches: ";  cin >> inches;
         }
      void showdist()                // display distance
         { cout << feet << "\'-" << inches << '\"'; }
      void operator += ( Distance );
   };
                                     // add distance to this one
   void Distance::operator += (Distance d2)
      {
      feet += d2.feet;               // add the feet
      inches += d2.inches;           // add the inches
      if(inches >= 12.0)             // if total exceeds 12.0,
         {                           // then decrease inches
         inches -= 12.0;             // by 12.0 and
         feet++;                     // increase feet
         }                           // by 1
      }

   void main()
      {
      Distance dist1;                // define dist1
      dist1.getdist();               // get dist1 from user
      cout << "\ndist1 = ";  dist1.showdist();

      Distance dist2(11, 6.25);      // define, initialize dist2
      cout << "\ndist2 = ";  dist2.showdist();

      dist1 += dist2;                // dist1 = dist1 + dist2
      cout << "\nAfter addition,";
      cout << "\ndist1 = ";  dist1.showdist();
      }
```

In this program we obtain a distance from the user, and add to it a second distance, initialized to 11'-6.25" by the program. Here's a sample of interaction with the program:

```
Enter feet: 3
Enter inches: 5.75
dist1 = 3'-5.75"
dist2 = 11'-6.25"
After addition,
dist1 = 15'-0"
```

In this program the addition is carried out in main() with the statement

```
dist1 += dist2;
```

This causes the sum of dist1 and dist2 to be placed in dist1.

Notice the difference between the function used here, `operator+=()`, and that used in ENGLPLUS, `operator+()`. In the earlier `operator+()` function, a new object of type `Distance` had to be created and returned by the function, so it could be assigned to a third `Distance` object, as in

```
dist3 = dist1 + dist2;
```

In the `operator+=()` function in ENGLPLEQ, the object that takes on the value of the sum is the object of which the function is a member. Thus it is `feet` and `inches` that are given values, not temporary variables used only to return an object. The `operator+=()` function has no return value; it returns type `void`. A return value is not usually needed with arithmetic assignment operators like +=, because the result of the assignment operator is not assigned to anything. The operator is used alone, in expressions like the one in the program:

```
dist1 += dist2;
```

If you wanted to use this operator in more complex expressions, like

```
dist3 = dist1 += dist2;
```

then you would need to provide a return value. This can be done by ending the `operator+=()` function with a statement like

```
return Distance(feet, inches);
```

in which a nameless object is initialized to the same values as this object, and returned.

DATA CONVERSION

We've discussed how several kinds of operators can be overloaded, but we haven't looked at the assignment operator =. This is a rather special operator, with complex properties.

You already know that the = operator will assign a value from one variable to another, in statements like

```
intvar1 = intvar2;
```

where `intvar1` and `intvar2` are integer variables. You may also have noticed that = assigns the value of one user-defined object to another, provided they are of the same type, in statements like

```
dist3 = dist1 + dist2;
```

where the result of the addition, which is type `Distance`, is assigned to another object of type `Distance`, `dist3`. Normally, when the value of one object is assigned to another of the same type, the values of all the member data items are simply copied into the new object. The compiler doesn't need any special instructions to use = for the assignment of user-defined objects such as `Distance` objects.

Thus assignments between types, whether they are basic types or user-defined types, are handled by the compiler with no effort on our part, provided that the same data type is used on both sides of the equals sign. But what happens when the variables on different sides of the = are of different types? This is a more thorny question, one which we will devote the balance of this chapter to exploring. We'll first review how the compiler handles the conversion of basic types, which it does automatically. Then we'll explore several situations where the compiler doesn't handle things automatically and we need to tell it what to do. These include conversions between basic types and user-defined types, and conversions between different user-defined types.

You might think it represents poor programming practice to routinely convert from one type to another. After all, languages such as Pascal go to considerable trouble to keep you from doing such conversions. However, the philosophy in C++ (and in C) is that the flexibility provided by allowing conversions outweighs the dangers of making mistakes by allowing type mixing.

CONVERSIONS BETWEEN BASIC TYPES

When we write a statement like

```
intvar = floatvar;
```

where `intvar` is of type `int` and `floatvar` is of type `float`, we are assuming that the compiler will call a special routine to convert the value of `floatvar`, which is expressed in floating-point format, to an integer format so that it can be assigned to `intvar`. There are of course many such conversions: from `float` to `double`, `char` to `float`, and so on. Each such conversion has its own routine, built into the compiler and called up when the data types on different sides of the = sign so dictate. We say such conversions are *implicit*, because they aren't apparent in the listing.

Sometimes we want to force the compiler to convert one type to another. To do this we use the cast operator. For instance, to convert `float` to `int` we could say

```
intvar = int(floatvar);
```

Casting provides *explicit* conversion: It's obvious in the listing that the `int()` conversion function will convert from `float` to `int`. However, such explicit conversions use the same built-in routines as implicit conversions.

CONVERSIONS BETWEEN OBJECTS AND BASIC TYPES

When we want to convert between user-defined data types and basic types, we can't rely on built-in conversion routines, since the compiler doesn't know anything about user-defined types besides what we tell it. Instead, we must write these routines ourselves.

Our next example shows how to convert between a basic type and a user-defined type. In this example the user-defined type is (surprise!) the English `Dis-tance` class from previous examples, and the basic type is `float`, which we use to represent meters, a unit of length in the metric measurement system.

The example shows conversion both from Distance to float, and from float to Distance. Here's the listing for ENGLCONV:

```
// englconv.cpp
// conversions: Distance to meters, meters to Distance
#include <iostream.h>

const float MTF = 3.280833;              // meters to feet

class Distance                           // English Distance class
    {
    private:
        int feet;
        float inches;
    public:
        Distance()                       // constructor (no args)
            { feet = 0; inches = 0.0; }
        Distance( float meters )         // constructor (one arg)
            {                            // convert meters to Distance
            float fltfeet = MTF * meters;  // convert to float feet
            feet = int(fltfeet);           // feet is integer part
            inches = 12*(fltfeet-feet);    // inches is what's left
            }
        Distance(int ft, float in)       // constructor (two args)
            { feet = ft; inches = in; }
        void getdist()                   // get length from user
            {
            cout << "\nEnter feet: ";  cin >> feet;
            cout << "Enter inches: ";  cin >> inches;
            }
        void showdist()                  // display distance
            { cout << feet << "\'-" << inches << '\"'; }

        operator float()                 // conversion function
            {                            // converts Distance to meters
            float fracfeet = inches/12;  // convert the inches
            fracfeet += float(feet);     // add the feet
            return fracfeet/MTF;         // convert to meters
            }
    };

void main()
    {
    Distance dist1 = 2.35;               // uses 1-arg constructor to
                                         // convert meters to Distance
    cout << "\ndist1 = "; dist1.showdist();

    dist1 = 1.00;                        // this form also uses
                                         // 1-arg constructor
    cout << "\ndist1 = ";  dist1.showdist();
```

```
Distance dist2(5, 10.25);        // uses 2-arg constructor

float mtrs = float(dist2);       // uses conversion function to
                                 // convert Distance to meters
cout << "\ndist2 = " << mtrs << " meters";

mtrs = dist1;                    // this form also uses
                                 // conversion function
cout << "\ndist1 = " << mtrs << " meters";
}
```

In `main()` the program first converts a fixed `float` quantity—2.35, representing meters—to feet and inches, using the one-argument constructor:

```
Distance dist1 = 2.35;
```

It converts a second quantity in meters to feet and inches in the statement

```
dist1 = 1.00;
```

Going in the other direction, it converts a `Distance` to meters in the statements

```
float mtrs =float(dist2);
```

and

```
mtrs = dist1;
```

Here's the output:

```
dist1 = 7'-8.519485"      ←————— this is 2.35 meters
dist1 = 3'-3.369996"      ←————— this is 1.0 meters
dist2 = 1.784354 meters   ←————— this is 5'-10.25"
dist1 = 1 meters          ←————— this is 3'-3.369996"
```

We've seen how conversions are performed using simple assignment statements in `main()`. Now let's see what goes on behind the scenes, in the `Distance` member functions.

Converting a user-defined type to a basic type requires a different approach thán converting a basic type to a user-defined type. We'll see how both types of conversions are carried out in ENGLCONV.

From Basic to User-Defined

To go from a basic type—`float` in this case—to a user-defined type such as `Distance`, we use a constructor with one argument. Here's how it looks in ENGLCONV:

```
Distance(float meters)
    {
    float fltfeet = MTF * meters;
    feet = int(fltfeet);
    inches = 12 * (fltfeet-feet);
    }
```

This function is called when an object of type **Distance** is created with a single argument. The function assumes this argument represents meters. It converts the argument to feet and inches, and assigns the resulting values to the object. Thus the conversion from meters to **Distance** is carried out along with the creation of an object, in the statement

```
Distance dist1 = 2.35;
```

But there is another way to perform the same conversion. In the program, after defining dist1 and displaying its value, we then say

```
dist1 = 1.0;
```

What is the compiler to make of this? We're converting **float** to **Distance**, but we're not creating a new object. Surprisingly, the one-argument constructor will be called in this situation as well. Confronted with a statement that calls for a particular conversion, the compiler looks for any tool that might do the job. In this case it finds a constructor that converts **float** to **Distance**, so it applies it to the assignment situation, creating an unnamed temporary object with feet-and-inches values corresponding to 1.0 meters. It assigns this object to **dist1**, and voilà, **dist1** has been assigned the correct values, converted from meters.

Thus the compiler blurs the distinction between definition and assignment. If no overloaded = operator is available, it will look for a constructor to do the same job.

From User-Defined to Basic

What about going the other way, from a user-defined type to a basic type? The trick here is to overload the cast operator, creating something called a *conversion function.* Here's where we do that in ENGLCONV:

```
operator float()
   {
   float fracfeet = inches/12;
   fracfeet += float(feet);
   return fracfeet/MTF;
   }
```

This operator takes the value of the **Distance** object of which it is a member, converts this value to a **float** value representing meters, and returns this value.

This operator can be called like this:

```
mtrs = float(dist2);
```

This converts the **Distance** object **dist2** to its equivalent **float** value in meters.

Again the compiler uses the same conversion in assignment statements. You can say

```
mtrs = dist2;
```

This has exactly the same effect. When the compiler finds that you want to convert a user-defined type to a basic type, it looks for the appropriate conversion function.

Here the compiler starts by looking for an overloaded = operator. But when it doesn't find one, it doesn't give up. It finds the conversion function and uses that instead.

Conversion between Strings and String Objects

Here's another example that uses a one-argument constructor and a conversion function. It operates on the **String** class that we saw in such examples as STRPLUS earlier in this chapter.

```
// strconv.cpp
// convert between ordinary strings and class String
#include <iostream.h>
#include <string.h>        // for strcpy(), etc.

const int SZ = 80;         // size of all String objects

class String               // user-defined string type
   {
   private:
      char str[SZ];        // holds a string
   public:
      String()             // constructor 0, no args
         { str[0] = '\0'; }

      String( char s[] )   // constructor 1, one arg
         { strcpy(str, s); }  // convert string to String

      void display()       // display the String
         { cout << str; }

      operator char*()     // conversion function
         { return str; }   // convert String to string
   };

void main()
   {
   String s1;              // use constructor 0
   char xstr[] =           // create and initialize string
            "\nJoyeux Noel! ";
   s1 = xstr;              // use constructor 1
                           // to convert string to String
   s1.display();           // display String

   String s2 = "Bonne Annee!";  // uses constructor 1
                                // to initialize String

   cout << s2;             // use conversion function
                           // to convert String to string
                           // before sending to << op
   }
```

The one-argument constructor converts a normal string (an array of `char`) to an object of class `String`:

```
String(char s[])
   { strcpy(str, s); }
```

The string `s` is passed as an argument, and copied into the `str` data member in a newly created `String` object.

This conversion will be applied when a string is created, as in

```
String s2 = "Bonne Annee!";
```

or it will be applied in assignment statements, as in

```
s1 = xstr;
```

where `s1` is type `String` and `xstr` is a normal string.

A conversion function is used to convert from a `String` type to a normal string:

```
operator char*()
   { return str; }
```

The use of the asterisk in this expression means *pointer to*. We won't explore pointers until Chapter 12, but its use here is not hard to figure out. It means *pointer to* `char`, which is very similar to *array of type* `char`. Thus `char*` is similar to `char[]`. It's another way of specifying a string data type.

The conversion function is used by the compiler in the statement

```
cout << s2;
```

Here the `s2` variable is an argument supplied to the overloaded operator `<<`. Since the `<<` operator doesn't know anything about our user-defined `String` type, the compiler looks for a way to convert `s2` to a type that `<<` does know about. It finds our conversion function and uses it to generate a normal string, which is then sent on to `<<` to be displayed. (The effect is similar to calling the `String::display()` function, but given the ease and intuitive clarity of displaying with `<<`, the `display()` function is redundant and could be removed.)

Here's the output from STRCONV:

```
Joyeux Noel! Bonne Annee!
```

The STRCONV example demonstrates that conversions take place automatically not only in assignment statements but in other appropriate places, such as in arguments sent to operators (like `<<`) or functions. If you supply an operator or a function with arguments of the wrong type, they will be converted to arguments of an acceptable type, provided you have defined such a conversion.

CONVERSIONS BETWEEN OBJECTS OF DIFFERENT CLASSES

What about converting between objects of different user-defined classes? The same two methods just shown for conversion between basic types and user-defined types also apply to conversions between two user-defined types. That is, you can use a one-argument constructor, or you can use a conversion function. The choice depends on whether you want to put the conversion routine in the class specifier of the source object or of the destination object. For example, suppose you say

```
objecta = objectb;
```

where **objecta** is a member of class **A** and **objectb** is a member of class **B**. Is the conversion routine located in **A** (the destination class, since **objecta** receives the value) or **B** (the source class)? We'll look at both cases.

Routine in Source Object

The next example program shows a conversion routine located in the source class. When the conversion routine is in the source class, it is commonly implemented as a conversion function.

The two classes used in the next program are **Rec** and **Polar**. We've already seen an example of the **Polar** class, in the POLAPLUS program earlier in this chapter. The **Rec** class is similar in that its objects are points in a two-dimensional plane. However, it uses a rectangular coordinate system, where the location of each point is specified by X and Y coordinates. Its member functions are similar to those for **Polar** but are adapted to rectangular coordinates. Here's the listing for POLAREC1.CPP:

```cpp
// polarec1.cpp
// converts from Polar to Rec using routines in Polar (source)
#include <iostream.h>
#include <math.h>                 // for sin(), cos(), etc.

class Rec
   {
   private:
      double xco;                 // x coordinate
      double yco;                 // y coordinate
   public:
      Rec()                       // constructor 0, no args
         { xco = 0.0; yco = 0.0; }
      Rec(double x, double y)     // constructor 2, two args
         { xco = x; yco = y; }
      void display()              // display
         { cout << "(" << xco
                << ", " << yco << ")"; }
   };

class Polar
   {
   private:
      double radius;
      double angle;
   public:
      Polar()                     // constructor 0, no args
```

```
                    { radius=0.0; angle=0.0; }
         Polar(double r, double a)          // constructor 2, two args
                    { radius=r; angle=a; }
         void display()                     // display
                    { cout << "(" << radius
                           << ", " << angle << ")"; }
         operator Rec()                     // conversion function
                    {                       // Polar to Rect
                    double x = radius * cos(angle);   // find x and y to
                    double y = radius * sin(angle);   // initialize nameless
                    return Rec(x, y);       // Rec for return
                    }
         };

void main()
     {
     Rec rec;                          // Rec using constructor 0
     Polar pol(10.0, 0.785398);        // Polar using constructor 2

     rec = pol;                        // convert Polar to Rec
                                       // using conversion function
                                       // (or use  rec = Rect(pol);

     cout << "\npol="; pol.display();  // display original Polar
     cout << "\nrec="; rec.display();  // display equivalent Rect
     }
```

In the `main()` part of POLAREC1 we define an object of type `Rec`, called `rec`, which is not initialized. We also define an object of type `Polar`, called `pol`, which is initialized to a radius of 10.0 and an angle of 0.785398 radians (45 degrees).

Now we want to be able to assign the value of the `pol` object to `rec`, with the statement

```
rec = pol;
```

Since these objects are from different classes, the assignment involves a conversion, and—as we specified—in this program the conversion function is a member of the `Polar` class:

```
operator Rec()
    {
    double x = radius * cos(angle);
    double y = radius * sin(angle);
    return Rec(x, y);
    }
```

This function transforms the object of which it is a member to a `Rec` object, and returns this object, which `main()` then assigns to `rec`. Here's the output from POLAREC1:

```
pol=(10, 0.785398)
rec=(7.071069, 7.071067)
```

Routine in Destination Object

Let's see how the same conversion is carried out when the conversion routine is in the destination class. In this situation it's common to use a one-argument constructor. However, things are complicated by the fact that the constructor in the destination class must be able to access the data in the source class to perform the conversion. The data in `Polar`—the radius and angle—is private, so we must provide special functions to allow direct access to it.

Here's the listing for POLAREC2.CPP:

```cpp
// polarec2.cpp
// converts Polar to Rec using routine in Rec (destination)
#include <iostream.h>
#include <math.h>                     // for sin(), cos(), etc.

class Polar                          // point, polar coordinates
   {
   private:
      double radius;                 // radius coord
      double angle;                  // angle coord (radians)
   public:
      Polar()                        // constructor, no args
         { radius=0.0; angle=0.0; }
      Polar(double r, double a)      // constructor, two args
         { radius=r; angle=a; }
      void display()                 // display
         { cout << "("  << radius
                << ", " << angle << ")"; }
      double getr()                  // these routines allow
         { return radius; }          // radius and angle to be
      double geta()                  // accessed from outside
         { return angle; }           // the class
   };

class Rec                            // point, rectangular coords
   {
   private:
      double xco;                    // x coordinate
      double yco;                    // y coordinate
   public:
      Rec()                          // constructor 0, no args
         { xco = 0.0; yco = 0.0; }
      Rec(double x, double y)        // constructor 2, two args
         { xco = x; yco = y; }
      Rec(Polar p)                   // constructor 1, one arg
         {                           //     Polar to Rec
         float r = p.getr();
         float a = p.geta();         // get r and a from Polar
         xco = r * cos(a);           // using getr() and geta()
         yco = r * sin(a);           // change to our xco and yco
         }
```

```
        void display()                    // display
           { cout << "(" << xco
                  << ", " << yco << ")"; }
        };

    void main()
        {
        Rec rec;                          // Rec using constructor 1
        Polar pol(10.0, 0.785398);        // Polar using constructor 2

        rec = pol;                        // convert Polar to Rec

        cout << "\npol="; pol.display();  // display original Polar
        cout << "\nrec="; rec.display();  // display converted Rec
        }
```

Here's the conversion routine, a one-argument constructor, from the `Rec` class:

```
Rec(Polar p)
    {
    float r = p.getr();
    float a = p.geta();
    xco = r * cos(a);
    yco = r * sin(a);
    }
```

This function sets the object of which it is a member to the rectangular coordinates that correspond to the polar coordinates of the object received as an argument.

To perform the conversion, this constructor must be able to access the data values of the `Polar` object sent as an argument. The `Polar` class contains the following two routines to allow this:

```
double getr()
    { return radius; }
double geta()
    { return angle; }
```

The `main()` part of POLAREC2 is the same as that in POLAREC1. The one-argument constructor again allows the `Polar` to `Rec` conversion to take place in the statement

```
rec = pol;
```

CONVERSIONS: WHEN TO USE WHAT

When should you use the one-argument constructor in the destination class, as opposed to the conversion function in the source class? Sometimes the choice is made for you. If you have purchased a library of classes, you may not have access to their source code. If you use an object of such a class as the source in a conversion, then you'll have access only to the destination class, and you'll need to use a one-argument constructor. Or, if the library class object is the destination, then you must use a conversion function in the source.

PITFALLS OF OPERATOR OVERLOADING AND CONVERSION

Operator overloading and type conversions give you the opportunity to create what amounts to an entirely new language. When **a**, **b**, and **c** are objects from user-defined classes, and **+** is overloaded, the statement

```
a = b + c;
```

means something quite different than it does when **a**, **b**, and **c** are variables of basic data types. The ability to redefine the building blocks of the language can be a blessing in that it can make your listing more intuitive and readable. It can also have the opposite effect, making it more obscure and hard to understand. Here are some guidelines.

USE SIMILAR MEANINGS

Use overloaded operators to perform operations that are as similar as possible to those performed on basic data types. You could overload the + sign to perform subtraction, for example, but that would hardly make your listings more comprehensible.

Overloading an operator assumes that it makes sense to perform a particular operation on objects of a certain class. If we're going to overload the + operator in class X, then the result of adding two objects of class X should have a meaning at least somewhat similar to addition. For example, in this chapter we showed how to overload the + operator for the English **Distance** class. Adding two distances is clearly meaningful. We also overloaded + for the **String** class. Here we interpret the addition of two strings to mean placing one string after another to form a third. This also has an intuitively satisfying interpretation. But for many classes it may not be reasonable to talk about "adding" their objects. You probably wouldn't want to add two objects of a class called **employee** that held personal data, for example.

USE SIMILAR SYNTAX

Use overloaded operators in the same way they are used for basic types. For example, if **alpha** and **beta** are basic types, the assignment operator in the statement

```
alpha.+= beta;
```

sets **alpha** to the sum of **alpha** and **beta**. Any overloaded version of this operator should do something analogous. It should probably do the same thing as

```
alpha = alpha + beta;
```

where the + is overloaded.

Some syntactical characteristics of operators can't be changed even if you want to. As you may have discovered, you can't overload a binary operator to be a unary operator, or vice versa.

SHOW RESTRAINT

Remember that if you have overloaded the + operator, anyone unfamiliar with your listing will need to do considerable research to find out what a statement like

```
a = b + c;
```

really means. If the number of overloaded operators grows too large, and if they are used in nonintuitive ways, then the whole point of using them is lost, and the listing becomes less readable instead of more. Use overloaded operators sparingly, and only when the usage is obvious. When in doubt, use a function instead of an overloaded operator, since a function name can state its own purpose. If you write a function to find the left side of a string, for example, you're better off calling it getleft() than trying to overload some operator like && to do the same thing.

AVOID AMBIGUITY

Suppose you use both a one-argument constructor and a conversion function to perform the same conversion (Polar to Rec, for example). How will the compiler know which conversion to use? The answer is that it won't. The compiler does not like to be placed in a situation where it doesn't know what to do, and it will signal an error. So avoid doing the same conversion in more than one way.

NOT ALL OPERATORS CAN BE OVERLOADED

The following operators cannot be overloaded: the member access or dot operator (.), the scope resolution operator (::), and the conditional operator (?:). Also, the pointer-to-member operator (.*), which we have not yet encountered, cannot be overloaded.

SUMMARY

In this chapter we've seen how the normal C++ operators can be given new meanings when applied to user-defined data types. The keyword operator is used to overload an operator, and the resulting operator will adopt the meaning supplied by the programmer.

Closely related to operator overloading is the issue of type conversion. Some conversions take place between user-defined types and basic types. Two approaches are used in such conversions: A one-argument constructor changes a basic type to a user-

	TABLE 9.1 Type Conversions	
	Routine in Destination	Routine in Source
Basic to basic	(Built-in conversion functions)	
Basic to class	Constructor	NA
Class to basic	NA	Conversion function
Class to class	Constructor	Conversion function

defined type, and a conversion operator converts a user-defined type to a basic type. When one user-defined type is converted to another, either approach can be used.

Table 9.1 summarizes these conversions.

QUESTIONS

1. Operator overloading is
   a. making C++ operators work with objects
   b. giving C++ operators more than they can handle
   c. giving new meanings to existing C++ operators
   d. making new C++ operators

2. Assuming that class X does not use any overloaded operators, write a statement that subtracts an object of class X, x1, from another such object, x2, and places the result in x3.

3. Assuming that class X includes a routine to overload the – operator, write a statement that would perform the same task as that specified in Question 2.

4. True or false: The >= operator can be overloaded.

5. Write a complete definition for an overloaded operator for the Counter class of the COUNTPP1 example that, instead of incrementing the count, decrements it.

6. How many arguments are required in the definition of an overloaded unary operator?

7. Assume a class C with objects obj1, obj2, and obj3. For the statement obj3 = obj1 – obj2 to work correctly, the overloaded – operator must
   a. take two arguments
   b. return a value
   c. create a named temporary object
   d. use the object of which it is a member as an operand

8. Write a complete definition for an overloaded ++ operator for the Distance class from the ENGLPLUS example. It should add 1 to the feet member data, and make possible statements like:

```
dist1++;
```

9. Repeat Question 7, except statements like the following should be allowed:

```
dist2 = dist1++;
```

10. When used in prefix form, what does the overloaded **++** operator do differently from what it does in postfix form?

11. Here are two declarators that describe ways to add two String objects:

```
void add(String s1, String s2)
String operator + (String s)
```

Match the following from the first declarator with the appropriate selection from the second:

function name (**add**) matches _____

return value (type **void**) matches _____

first argument (**s1**) matches _____

second argument (**s2**) matches _____

object of which function is a member matches _____

a. argument (**s**)
b. object of which operator is a member
c. operator (**+**)
d. return value (type **String**)
e. no match for this item

12. When an object of type **Polar** is added to itself, the result is a radius _____ as long at the _____ angle.

13. When you overload an arithmetic assignment operator, the result
a. goes in the object to the right of the operator
b. goes in the object to the left of the operator
c. goes in the object of which the operator is a member
d. must be returned

14. Write the complete definition of an overloaded **++** operator that works with the **String** class from the STRPLUS example and has the effect of changing its operand to uppercase. You can use the the library function **toupper()** (header file CTYPE.H), which takes as its only argument the character to be changed, and returns the changed character (or the same character if no change is necessary).

15. To convert from a user-defined class to a basic type, you would most likely use
a. a built-in conversion function
b. a one-argument constructor
c. an overloaded = operator
d. a conversion function that's a member of the class

16. True or false: The statement **objA=objB;** will cause a compiler error if the objects are of different classes.

.17. To convert from a basic type to a user-defined class, you would most likely use
   a. a built-in conversion function
   b. a one-argument constructor
   c. an overloaded = operator
   d. a conversion function that's a member of the class

18. True or false: If you've defined a constructor to handle definitions like `aclass obj = intvar;` you can also make statements like `obj = intvar;`.

19. If `objA` is in class A, and `objb` is in class B, and you want to say `objA = objB;`, and you want the conversion routine to go in class A, what type of conversion routine might you use?

20. True or false: The compiler won't object if you overload the `*` operator to perform division.

EXERCISES

1. To the `Distance` class in the ENGLPLUS program in this chapter, add an overloaded `-` operator for the `Distance` class that subtracts two distances. It should allow statements like `dist3=dist1-dist2;`. Assume the operator will never be used to subtract a larger number from a smaller one (that is, negative distances are not allowed).

2. Write a program that substitutes an overloaded `+=` operator for the overloaded `+` operator in the STRPLUS program in this chapter. This operator should allow statements like

   ```
   s1 += s2;
   ```

   where `s2` is added (concatenated) to `s1` and the result left in `s1`. The operator should also permit the results of the operation to be used in other calculations, as in

   ```
   s3 = s1 += s2.
   ```

3. Modify the `time` class from Exercise 3 in Chapter 7 so that instead of a function `add_time()` it uses the overloaded `+` operator to add two times. Write a program to test this class.

4. Create a class `Int` based on Exercise 1 in Chapter 7. Overload all five integer arithmetic operators (`+`, `-`, `*`, `/`, and `%`) so that they operate on objects of type `Int`. If the result of any such arithmetic operation exceeds the normal range of `int`'s—from –32,768 to 32,767—have the operator print a warning and terminate the program. Such a data type might be useful where mistakes caused by arithmetic overflow are unacceptable. Hint: To facilitate checking for overflow, perform the calculations using type `long`. Write a program to test this class.

INHERITANCE

Inheritance is probably the most powerful feature of object-oriented programming, after classes themselves. Inheritance is the process of creating new classes, called *derived classes*, from existing or *base classes*. The derived class inherits all the capabilities of the base class but can add embellishments and refinements of its own. The base class is unchanged by this process. The inheritance relationship is shown in Figure 10-1.

The arrow in this figure goes in the opposite direction to what you might expect. If it pointed downward we would label it *inheritance*. However, the more common approach is to point the arrow up, from the derived class to the base class, and think of it as a "derived from" arrow.

Inheritance has important advantages. Most importantly, it permits code *reusability*. Once a base class is written and debugged, it need not be touched again but can nevertheless be adapted to work in different situations. Reusing existing code saves time and money and increases a program's reliability. Inheritance can also help in the original conceptualization of a programming problem, and in the overall design of the program.

One result of reusability is the ease of distributing class libraries. A programmer can use a class created by another person or company, and, without modifying it, derive other classes from it that are suited to particular situations.

We'll examine these features of inheritance in more detail after we've seen some specific instances of inheritance at work.

DERIVED CLASS AND BASE CLASS

Remember the COUNTPP3 example from Chapter 9? This program used a class **Counter** as a general-purpose counter variable. A count could be initialized to 0 or to a specified number with constructors, incremented with the **++** operator, and read with the **get_count()** operator.

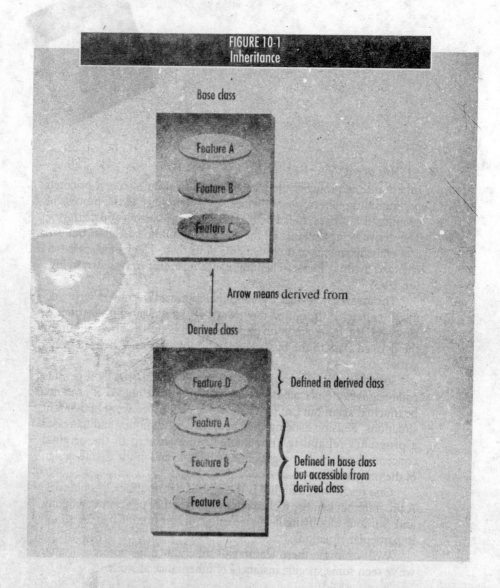

FIGURE 10-1
Inheritance

Base class

Feature A

Feature B

Feature C

↑ Arrow means derived from

Derived class

Feature D } Defined in derived class

Feature A

Feature B } Defined in base class but accessible from derived class

Feature C

Let's suppose that we worked long and hard to make the Counter class operate just the way we want, and we're pleased with the results, except for one thing. We really need a way to decrement the count. Perhaps we're counting people entering a bank, and we want to increment the count when they come in and decrement it when they go out, so that the count represents the number of people in the bank at any moment.

We could insert a decrement routine directly into the source code of the Counter class. However, there are several reasons why we might not want to do this. First, the Counter class works very well and has undergone many hours of testing and debugging. (Of course that's an exaggeration in this case, but it would be true in a larger and more complex class.) If we start fooling around with the source code for Counter, the testing process will need to be carried out again, and of course we may foul something up and spend hours debugging code that worked fine before we modified it.

In some situations there might be another reason for not modifying the Counter class: We might not have access to its source code, especially if it had been distributed as part of a class library. (We'll discuss this issue further in Chapter 15.)

To avoid these problems we can use inheritance to create a new class based on Counter, without modifying Counter itself. Here's the listing for COUNTEN, which includes a new class, CountDn, that adds a decrement operator to the Counter class:

```
// counten.cpp
// inheritance with Counter class
#include <iostream.h>

class Counter                         // base class
    {
    protected:                                // NOTE: not private
        unsigned int count;                   // count
    public:
        Counter()        { count = 0; }       // constructor, no args
        Counter(int c)   { count = c; }       // constructor, one arg
        int get_count()  { return count; }    // return count
        Counter operator ++ ()                // increment count
            {
            count++;                          // increment count, return
            return Counter(count);            // an unnamed temporary object
            }                                 // initialized to this count
    };

class CountDn : public Counter    // derived class
    {
    public:
        Counter operator -- ()        // decrement count
            {
            count--;                          // decrement count, return
            return Counter(count);            // an unnamed temporary object
            }                                 // initialized to this count
    };

void main()
    {
    CountDn c1;                               // c1 of class CountDn

    cout << "\nc1=" << c1.get_count();        // display c1

    c1++; c1++; c1++;                         // increment c1
    cout << "\nc1=" << c1.get_count();        // display it
```

```
c1--; c1--;                              // decrement c1
cout << "\nc1=" << c1.get_count();       // display it
```

The listing starts off with the `Counter` class, which (with one small exception, which we'll look at later) has not changed since its appearance in COUNTPP3.

SPECIFYING THE DERIVED CLASS

Following the `Counter` class in the listing is the specification for a new class, `CountDn`. This class incorporates a new function, `operator--()`, which decrements the count. However—and here's the key point—the new `CountDn` class inherits all the features of the `Counter` class. `CountDn` doesn't need a constructor or the `get_count()` or `operator++()` functions, because these already exist in `Counter`.

The first line of `CountDn` specifies that it is derived from `Counter`:

```
class CountDn : public Counter
```

Here we use a single colon (not the double colon used for the scope resolution operator), followed by the keyword `public` and the name of the base class `Counter`. This sets up the relationship between the classes. This line says `CountDn` *is derived from the base class* `Counter`. (We'll explore the effect of the keyword `public` later.) The relationship is shown in Figure 10-2.

Remember that the arrow in diagrams like this means *derived from*. The arrows point this way to emphasize that the derived class *refers to* functions and data in the base class, while the base class has no access to the derived class. Mathematicians call this kind of diagram a *directed acyclic graph*, or DAG (as in "DAGonnit, I drew the arrow the wrong way"). They are also called *inheritance trees*.

ACCESSING BASE CLASS MEMBERS

An important topic in inheritance is knowing when a member function in the base class can be used by objects of the derived class. This is called *accessibility*. Let's see how the compiler handles the accessibility issue in the COUNTEN example.

Substituting Base Class Constructors

In the `main()` part of COUNTEN we create an object of class `CountDn`:

```
CountDn c1;
```

This causes `c1` to be created as an object of class `CountDn` and initialized to 0. But wait—how is this possible? There is no constructor in the `CountDn` class specifier, so what entity carries out the initialization? It turns out that—at least under certain circumstances—if you don't specify a constructor, the derived class will use an appropriate constructor from the base class. In COUNTEN there's no constructor in `CountDn`, so the compiler uses the no-argument constructor from `Count`.

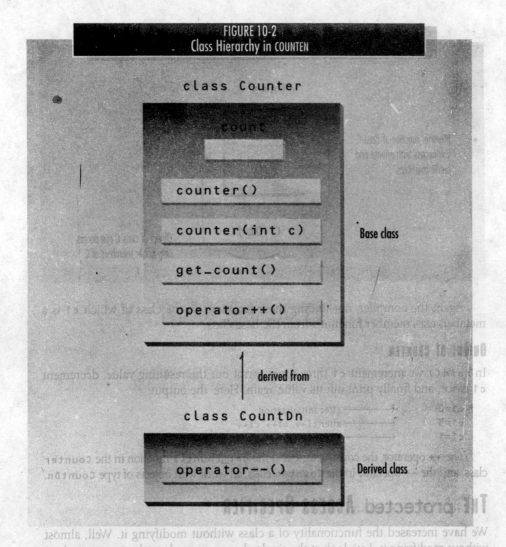

FIGURE 10-2
Class Hierarchy in COUNTEN

This flexibility on the part of the compiler—using one function because another isn't available—appears regularly in inheritance situations. Generally the substitution is what you want, but sometimes it can be unnerving.

Substituting Base Class Member Functions

The object c1 of the CountDn class also uses the operator++() and get_count() functions from the Counter class. The first is used to increment c1:

```
c1++;
```

and the second is used to display the count in c1:

```
cout << "\nc1=" << c1.get_count();
```

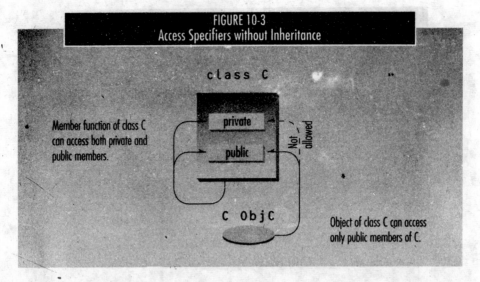

FIGURE 10-3
Access Specifiers without Inheritance

class C

private

public

Not allowed

Member function of class C can access both private and public members.

C ObjC

Object of class C can access only public members of C.

Again the compiler, not finding these functions in the class of which c1 is a member, uses member functions from the base class.

Output of COUNTEN

In main() we increment c1 three times, print out the resulting value, decrement c1 twice, and finally print out its value again. Here' the output:

```
c1=0        ←————— after initialization
c1=3        ←————— after cl++, cl++, cl++
c1=1        ←————— after cl--, cl--
```

The ++ operator, the constructors, and the get_count() function in the Counter class, and the -- operator in the CountDn class, all work with objects of type CountDn.

THE protected ACCESS SPECIFIER

We have increased the functionality of a class without modifying it. Well, almost without modifying it. Let's look at the single change we made to the Counter class.

The data in the classes we've looked at so far, including count in the Counter class in the earlier COUNTPP3 program, have used the private access specifier.

In the Counter class in COUNTEN, count is given a new specifier: protected. What does this do?

Let's first review what we know about the access specifiers private and public. Class members (which can be data or functions) can always be accessed by functions *within their own class*, whether the members are private or public. But objects of a class defined *outside the class* can access class members only if the members are public. For instance, suppose an object objA is an instance of class A, and function funcA() is a member function of A. Then in main() (or any other function that is not a member of A) the statement

```
objA.funcA();
```

will not be legal unless `func()` is public. The object `objA` cannot access private members of class A. Private members are, well, *private*. This is shown in Figure 10-3.

This is all we need to know if we don't use inheritance. With inheritance, however, there is a whole raft of additional possibilities. The question that concerns us at the moment is, can member functions of the derived class access members of the base class? In other words, can `operator--()` in `CountDn` access `count` in `Counter`? The answer is that member functions can access members of the base class if the members are `public`, or if they are `protected`. They can't access `private` members.

We don't want to make `count public`, since that would allow it to be accessed by any function anywhere in the program, and eliminate the advantages of data-hiding. A `protected` member, on the other hand, can be accessed by member functions in its own class or—and here's the key—in any class derived from its own class. It can't be accessed from functions outside these classes, such as `main()`. This is just what we want. The situation is shown in Figure 10-4.

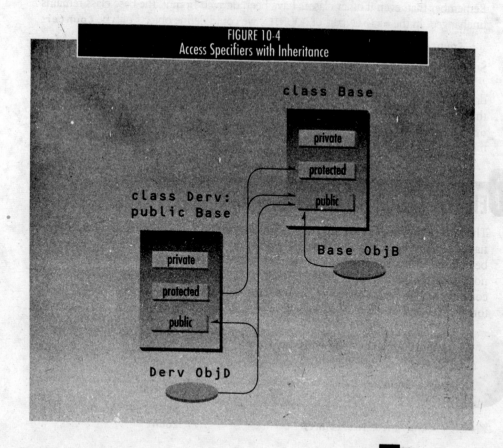

FIGURE 10-4
Access Specifiers with Inheritance

The following table summarizes the situation in a different way:

Access Specifier	Accessible from own class	Accessible from derived class	Accessible from objects outside class
public	yes	yes	yes
protected	yes	yes	no
private	yes	no	no

The moral is that if you are writing a class that you suspect might be used, at any point in the future, as a base class for other classes, then any data or functions that the derived classes might need to access should be made `protected` rather than `private`. This ensures that the class is "inheritance ready" (to adapt a phrase from TV set advertising).

Base Class Unchanged

Remember that, even if other classes have been derived from it, the base class remains unchanged. In the `main()` part of COUNTEN we could define objects of type `Counter`:

```
Counter c2;          ←————————— object of base class
```

Such objects would behave just as they would if `CountDn` didn't exist.

Note also that inheritance doesn't work in reverse. The base class and its objects don't know anything about any classes derived from the base class. In this example that means that objects of class `Counter`, such as `c2` defined here, can't use the `operator--()` function in `CountDn`. If you want a counter that you can decrement, it must be of class `CountDn`, not `Counter`.

DERIVED CLASS CONSTRUCTORS

There's a potential glitch in the COUNTEN program. What happens if we want to initialize a `CountDn` object to a value? Can the one-argument constructor in `Counter` be used? The answer is no. As we saw in COUNTEN, the compiler will substitute a no-argument constructor from the base class, but it draws the line at more complex constructors. To make such a definition work we must write a new set of constructors for the derived class. This is shown in the COUNTEN2 program:

```
// counten2.cpp
// constructors in derived class
#include <iostream.h>

class Counter
   {
   protected:                          // NOTE: not private
      unsigned int count;              // count
```

```
public:
    Counter()            { count = 0; }  // constructor, no args
    Counter(int c)       { count = c; }  // constructor, one arg
    int get_count()      { return count; } // return count
    Counter operator ++ ()               // increment count
    {
    count++;                             // increment count, return
    return Counter(count);               // an unnamed temporary object
    }                                    // initialized to this count
};

class CountDn : public Counter
    {
public:
    CountDn() : Counter()                // constructor, no args
        { }
    CountDn(int c) : Counter(c)          // constructor, 1 arg
        { }
    CountDn operator -- ()               // decrement count
        {
        count--;                         // decrement count, return
        return CountDn(count);           // an unnamed temporary object
        }                                // initialized to this count
    };

void main()
    {
    CountDn c1;                          // class CountDn
    CountDn c2(100);

    cout << "\nc1=" << c1.get_count();   // display
    cout << "\nc2=" << c2.get_count();   // display

    c1++; c1++; c1++;                    // increment c1
    cout << "\nc1=" << c1.get_count();   // display it

    c2--; c2--;                          // decrement c2
    cout << "\nc2=" << c2.get_count();   // display it

    CountDn c3 = c2--;                   // create c3 from c2
    cout << "\nc3=" << c3.get_count();   // display c3
    }
```

This program uses two new constructors in the CountDn class. Here is the one-argument constructor:

```
CountDn() : Counter()
    { }
```

This constructor has an unfamiliar feature: the colon followed by a function name. This construction causes the `CountDn()` constructor to call the `Counter()` constructor in the base class. In `main()`, when we say

```
CountDn c1;
```

the compiler will create an object of type `CountDn` and then call the `CountDn` constructor to initialize it. This constructor will in turn call the `Counter` constructor, which carries out the work. The `CountDn()` constructor could add additional statements of its own, but in this case it doesn't need to, so the function body between the braces is empty.

The statement

```
CountDn c2(100);
```

in `main()` uses the one-argument constructor in `CountDn`. This constructor also calls the corresponding constructor in the base class:

```
CountDn(int c) : Counter(c)      ←——————— argument c is passed to Counter
   { }
```

This construction causes the argument `c` to be passed from `CountDn()` to `Counter()`, where it is used to initialize the object.

In `main()`, after initializing the `c1` and `c2` objects, we increment one and decrement the other and then print the results. The one-argument constructor is also used in an assignment statement:

```
CountDn c3 = c2--;
```

OVERRIDING MEMBER FUNCTIONS

You can use member functions in a derived class that have the same name as those in the base class. You might want to do this so that calls in your program work the same way for objects of both base and derived classes.

Here's an example based on the STAKARAY program from Chapter 8. That program modeled a stack, a simple data storage device. It allowed you to push integers onto the stack and pop them off. However, STAKARAY had a potential flaw. If you tried to push too many items onto the stack, the program might bomb, since data would be placed in memory beyond the end of the `st[]` array. Or if you tried to pop too many items, the results would be meaningless, since you would be reading data from memory locations outside the array.

To cure these defects we've created a new class, `Stack2`, derived from `Stack`. Objects of `Stack2` behave in exactly the same way as those of `Stack`, except that you will be warned if you attempt to push too many items on the stack, or if you try to pop an item from an empty stack. Here's the listing for STAKEN.CPP:

```
// staken.cpp
// overloading functions in base and derived classes
#include <iostream.h>
#include <process.h>                     // for exit()

const int MAX = 100;                     // maximum size of stack

class Stack
   {
   protected:                            // NOTE: can't be private
      int st[MAX];                       // stack: array of integers
      int top;                           // index to top of stack
   public:
      Stack()                            // constructor
         { top = 0; }
      void push(int var)                 // put number on stack
         { st[++top] = var; }
      int pop()                          // take number off stack
         { return st[top--]; }
   };

class Stack2 : public Stack
   {
   public:
      void push(int var)                 // put number on stack
         {
         if(top < MAX)                   // if stack not full,
            Stack::push(var);            // call push() in Stack class
         else
            { cout << "\nError: stack is full"; exit(1); }
         }
      int pop()                          // take number off stack
         {
         if(top > 0)                     // if stack not empty,
            return Stack::pop();         // call pop() in Stack class
         else
            { cout << "\nError: stack is empty"; exit(1); }
         }
   };

void main()
   {
   Stack2 s1;

   s1.push(11);                          // push some values onto stack
   s1.push(22);
   s1.push(33);

   cout << endl << s1.pop();             // pop some values from stack
   cout << endl << s1.pop();
```

```
cout << endl << s1.pop();
cout << endl << s1.pop();        // woops, pops one too many...
}
```

In this program the `Stack` class is just the same as it was in the STAKARAY program, except that the data members have been made `protected`.

WHICH FUNCTION IS USED?

The `Stack2` class contains two functions, `push()` and `pop`. These functions have the same names, and the same argument and return types, as the functions in `Stack`. When we call these functions from main, in statements like

```
s1.push(11);
```

how does the compiler know which of the two `push()` functions to use? Here's the rule: When the same function exists in both the base class and the derived class, the function in the derived class will be executed. (This is true of objects of the derived class. Objects of the base class don't know anything about the derived class and will always use the base class functions.) We say that the derived class function *overrides* the base class function. So in the statement above, since `s1` is an object of class `Stack2`, the `push()` function in `Stack2` will be executed, not the one in `Stack`.

The `push()` function in `Stack2` checks to see if the stack is full. If it is, it displays an error message and causes the program to exit. If it isn't, it calls the `push()` function in `Stack`. Similarly, the `pop()` function in `Stack2` checks to see if the stack is empty. If it is, it prints an error message and exits; otherwise, it calls the `pop()` function in `Stack`.

In `main()` we push three items onto the stack, but we pop four. The last pop elicits an error message:

```
33
22
11
Error: stack is empty
```

and terminates the program.

SCOPE RESOLUTION WITH OVERRIDDEN FUNCTIONS

How do `push()` and `pop()` in `Stack2` access `push()` and `pop()` in `Stack`? They use the scope resolution operator, `::`, in the statements:

```
Stack::push(var);
```

and

```
return Stack::pop();
```

These statements specify that the `push()` and `pop()` functions in `Stack` are to be called. Without the scope resolution operator, the compiler would think the `push()`

and `pop()` functions in `Stack2` were calling themselves, which—in this case—would lead to program failure. Using the scope resolution operator allows you to specify exactly what class the function is a member of.

INHERITANCE IN THE ENGLISH DISTANCE CLASS

Here's a somewhat more complex example of inheritance. So far in this book the various programs that used the English `Distance` class assumed that the distances to be represented would always be positive. This is usually the case in architectural drawings. However, if we were measuring, say, the water level of the Pacific Ocean as the tides varied, we might want to be able to represent negative feet-and-inches quantities. (Tide levels below mean-lower-low-water are called *minus tides*; they prompt clam diggers to take advantage of the larger area of exposed beach.)

Let's derive a new class from `Distance`. This class will add a single data item to our feet-and-inches measurements: a sign, which can be positive or negative. When we add the sign, we'll also need to modify the member functions so they can work with signed distances. Here's the listing for ENGLEN:

```
// englen.cpp
// inheritance using English Distances
#include <iostream.h>

class Distance                    // English Distance class
    {
    protected:                    // NOTE: can't be private
        int feet;
        float inches;
    public:
        Distance()                // constructor (no args)
            { feet = 0; inches = 0.0; }
        Distance(int ft, float in)  // constructor (two args)
            { feet = ft; inches = in; }
        void getdist()            // get length from user
            {
            cout << "\nEnter feet: ";  cin >> feet;
            cout << "Enter inches: ";  cin >> inches;
            }
        void showdist()           // display distance
            { cout << feet << "\'-" << inches << '\"'; }
    };

enum posneg { pos, neg };  // for sign in DistSign

class DistSign : public Distance  // adds sign to Distance
    {
    private:
        posneg sign;              // sign is pos or neg
```

```
    public:
                                    // constructor  (no args)
        DistSign() : Distance()     // call base constructor
            { sign = pos; }         // set the sign to +

                                    // constructor (2 or 3 args)
        DistSign(int ft, float in, posneg sg=pos) :
                Distance(ft, in)    // call base constructor
            { sign = sg; }          // set the sign

        void getdist()              // get length from user
            {
            Distance::getdist();    // call base getdist()
            char ch;                // get sign from user
            cout << "Enter sign (+ or -): ";  cin >> ch;
            sign = (ch=='+') ? pos : neg;
            }

        void showdist()             // display distance
            {
            cout << ( (sign==pos) ? "(+)" : "(-)" );  // show sign
            Distance::showdist();                     // ft and in
            }
    };

void main()
    {
    DistSign alpha;                     // no-arg constructor
    alpha.getdist();                    // get alpha from user

    DistSign beta(11, 6.25);            // 2-arg constructor

    DistSign gamma(100, 5.5, neg);      // 3-arg constructor

                                        // display all distances
    cout << "\nalpha = ";  alpha.showdist();
    cout << "\nbeta = ";  beta.showdist();
    cout << "\ngamma = ";  gamma.showdist();
    }
```

The `Distance` class in this program is just the same as in previous programs, except that, as usual, the data is `protected`. The `DistSign` class adds the functionality to deal with signed numbers.

Operation of ENGLEN

The `main()` program declares three different signed distances. It gets a value for `alpha` from the user, initializes `beta` to (+)11'-6.25" and `gamma` to (–)100'-5.5".

We use parentheses around the sign to avoid confusion with the hyphen separating feet and inches. Here's some sample output:

```
Enter feet: 6
Enter inches: 2.5
Enter sign (+ or -): -

alpha = (-)6'-2.5"
beta = (+)11'-6.25"
gamma = (-)100'-5.5"
```

The `DistSign` class is derived from `Distance`. It adds a single variable, `sign`, which is of type `posneg`. The `sign` variable will hold the sign of the distance. The `posneg` type is defined in an `enum` statement to have two possible values: `pos` and `neg`.

CONSTRUCTORS IN DistSign

`DistSign` has two constructors, mirroring those in `Distance`. The first takes no arguments, the second takes either two or three arguments. The third, optional, argument in the second constructor is a sign, either `pos` or `neg`. Its default value is `pos`. These constructors allow us to define variables (objects) of type `DistSign` in several ways.

Both constructors in `DistSign` call the corresponding constructors in `Distance` to set the feet-and-inches values. They then set the `sign` variable. The no-argument constructor always sets it to `pos`. The second constructor sets it to `pos` if no third-argument value has been provided, or to a value (`pos` or `neg`) if the argument is specified.

The arguments `ft` and `in`, passed from `main()` to the second constructor in `DistSign`, are simply forwarded to the constructor in `Distance`.

MEMBER FUNCTIONS IN DistSign

Adding a sign to `Distance` has consequences for both its member functions. The `getdist()` function in the `DistSign` class must ask the user for the sign as well as for feet-and-inches values, and the `showdist()` function must display the sign along with the feet and inches. These functions call the corresponding functions in `Distance`, in the lines

```
Distance::getdist();
```

and

```
Distance::showdist();
```

These calls get and display the feet and inches values. The body of `getdist()` and `showdist()` in `DistSign` then go on to deal with the sign.

ABETTING INHERITANCE

C++ is designed to make it efficient to create a derived class. Where we want to use parts of the base class, it's easy to do so, whether these parts are data, constructors, or member functions. Then we add the functionality we need to create the new improved class. Notice that in ENGLEN we didn't need to duplicate any code; instead we make use of the appropriate functions in the base class.

CLASS HIERARCHIES

In the examples so far in this chapter, inheritance has been used to add functionality to an existing class. Now let's look at an example where inheritance is used for a different purpose: as part of the original design of a program.

Our example models a database of employees of a widget company. We've simplified the situation so that only three kinds of employees are represented. Managers manage, scientists perform research to develop better widgets, and laborers operate the dangerous widget-stamping presses.

The database stores a name and an employee identification number for all employees, no matter what category they are. However, for managers, it also stores their

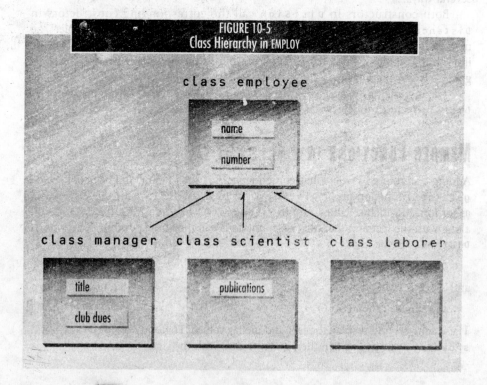

FIGURE 10-5
Class Hierarchy in EMPLOY

class employee

name

number

class manager   class scientist   class laborer

title

club dues

publications

titles and golf club dues. For scientists it stores the number of scholarly articles they have published. Laborers need no additional data beyond their names and numbers.

Our example program starts with a base class `employee`. This class handles the employee's last name and employee number. From this class three other classes are derived: `manager`, `scientist`, and `laborer`. The `manager` and `scientist` classes contain additional information about these categories of employee, and member functions to handle this information, as shown in Figure 10-5.

Here's the listing for EMPLOY:

```
// employ.cpp
// models employee database using inheritance
#include <iostream.h>

const int LEN = 80;               // maximum length of names

class employee                    // employee class
   {
   private:
      char name[LEN];             // employee name
      unsigned long number;       // employee number
   public:
      void getdata()
         {
         cout << "\n   Enter last name: "; cin >> name;
         cout << "   Enter number: ";      cin >> number;
         }
      void putdata()
         {
         cout << "\n   Name: " << name;
         cout << "\n   Number: " << number;
         }
   };

class manager : public employee        // management class
   {
   private:
      char title[LEN];   // "vice-president" etc.
      double dues;       // golf club dues
   public:
      void getdata()
         {
         employee::getdata();
         cout << "   Enter title: ";          cin >> title;
         cout << "   Enter golf club dues: "; cin >> dues;
         }
      void putdata()
         {
         employee::putdata();
         cout << "\n   Title: " << title;
         cout << "\n   Golf club dues: " << dues;
```

```
        }
    };
class scientist : public employee          // scientist class
    {
    private:
        int pubs;          // number of publications
    public:
        void getdata()
            {
            employee::getdata();
            cout << "   Enter number of pubs:'"; cin >> pubs;
            }
        void putdata()
            {
            employee::putdata();
            cout << "\n   Number of publications: " << pubs;
            }
    };


class laborer : public employee          // laborer class
    {
    };

void main()
    {
    manager m1, m2;
    scientist s1;
    laborer l1;

    cout << endl;
    cout << "\nEnter data for manager 1";       // get data for
    m1.getdata();                                // several employees

    cout << "\nEnter data for manager 2";
    m2.getdata();

    cout << "\nEnter data for scientist 1";
    s1.getdata();

    cout << "\nEnter data for laborer 1";
    l1.getdata();

    cout << "\nData on manager 1";               // display data for
    m1.putdata();                                // several employees

    cout << "\nData on manager 2";
    m2.putdata();
```

```
cout << "\nData on scientist 1";
s1.putdata();

cout << "\nData on laborer 1";
l1.putdata();
}
```

The `main()` part of the program declares four objects of different classes: two managers, a scientist, and a laborer. (Of course many more employees of each type could be defined, but the output would become rather large.) It then calls the `getdata()` member functions to obtain information about each employee, and the `putdata()` function to display this information. Here's a sample interaction with EMPLOY. First the user supplies the data:

```
Enter data for manager 1
   Enter last name: Wainsworth
   Enter number: 10
   Enter title: President
   Enter golf club dues: 1000000
Enter data on manager 2
   Enter last name: Bradley
   Enter number: 124
   Enter title: Vice-President
   Enter golf club dues: 500000
Enter data for scientist 1
   Enter last name: Hauptman-Frenglish
   Enter number: 234234
   Enter number of pubs: 999
Enter data for laborer 1
   Enter last name: Jones
   Enter number: 6546544
```

The program then plays it back:

```
Data on manager 1
   Name: Wainsworth
   Number: 10
   Title: President
   Golf club dues: 1000000
Data on manager 2
   Name: Bradley
   Number: 124
   Title: Vice-President
   Golf club dues: 500000
Data on scientist 1
   Name: Hauptman-Frenglish
   Number: 234234
   Number of publications: 999
```

```
Data on laborer 1
    Name: Jones
    Number: 6546544
```

A more sophisticated program would use an array or some other more complex way to arrange the data, so that a large number of employee objects could be accommodated.

"ABSTRACT" BASE CLASS

Notice that we don't define any objects of the base class `employee`. We use this as a general class whose sole purpose is to act as a base from which other classes are derived.

The `laborer` class operates identically to the `employee` class, since it contains no additional data or functions. It may seem that the `laborer` class is unnecessary, but by making it a separate class we emphasize that all classes are descended from the same source, `employee`. Also, if in the future we decided to modify the `laborer` class, we would not need to change the specifier for `employee`.

Classes used only for deriving other classes, as `employee` is in EMPLOY, are sometimes loosely called *abstract* classes, meaning that no actual instances (objects) of this class are created. However, the term *abstract* has a more precise definition, connected with virtual functions, which we'll look at in Chapter 13.

CONSTRUCTORS AND MEMBER FUNCTIONS

There are no constructors in either the base or derived classes, so the compiler creates objects of the various classes automatically when it encounters definitions like

```
manager m1, m2;
```

The `getdata()` and `putdata()` functions in `employee` accept a name and number from the user, and display a name and number. Functions also called `getdata()` and `putdata()` in the `manager` and `scientist` classes use the functions in `employee`, and also do their own work. In `manager` the `getdata()` function asks the user for a title and the amount of golf club dues, and `putdata()` displays these values. In `scientist` these functions handle the number of publications.

PUBLIC AND PRIVATE INHERITANCE

C++ provides a wealth of ways to fine-tune access to class members. One such access-control mechanism is the way derived classes are declared. Our examples so far have used publicly declared classes, with specifiers like

```
class manager : public employee
```

which appeared in the EMPLOY example.

What is the effect of the **public** keyword in this statement, and what are the alternatives? Listen up: The keyword **public** specifies that objects of the derived class are able to access public member functions of the base class. The alternative is the keyword **private**. When this keyword is used, objects of the derived class cannot access public member functions of the base class. Since objects can never access **private** or **protected** members of a class, the result is that no member of the base class is accessible to objects of the derived class.

ACCESS COMBINATIONS

There are so many possibilities for access that it's instructive to look at an example program that shows what works and what doesn't. Here's the listing for PUBPRIV:

```
// pubpriv.cpp
// tests publicly- and privately-derived classes
#include <iostream.h>

class A                    // base class
    {
    private:
        int privdataA;      // (functions have the same access
    protected:              // rules as the data shown here)
        int protdataA;
    public:
        int pubdataA;
    };

class B : public A         // publicly-derived class
    {
    public:
        void funct()
            {
            int a;
            a = privdataA;   // error: not accessible
            a = protdataA;   // ok
            a = pubdataA;    // ok
            }
    };

class C : private A        // privately-derived class
    {
    public:
        void funct()
            {
            int a;
            a = privdataA;   // error: not accessible
            a = protdataA;   // ok
            a = pubdataA;    // ok
            }
    };
```

```
void main()              // main()
   int a;

   B objB;
   a = objB.privdataA;   // error: not accessible
   a = objB.protdataA;   // error: not accessible
   a = objB.pubdataA;    // ok                    (B is public)

   C objC;
   a = objC.privdataA;   // error: not accessible
   a = objC.protdataA;   // error: not accessible
   a = objC.pubdataA;    // error: not accessible (C is private)
   }
```

The program specifies a base class, A, with private, protected, and public data items. Two classes, B and C, are derived from A. B is publicly derived, and C is privately derived.

As we've seen before, functions in the derived classes can access protected and public data in the base class. Also, objects of the derived classes cannot access private or protected members of the base class.

What's new is the difference between publicly derived and privately derived classes. Objects of the publicly derived class B can access public members of the base class A, while objects of the privately derived class C cannot. This is shown in Figure 10-6.

If you don't supply any access specifier when creating a class, private is assumed.

CLASSES AND STRUCTURES

Remember that access specifiers are the only way to distinguish structures and classes. In structures the default is public; for classes it's private.

```
class X : A        // private is assumed
   { };
struct X : A       // public is assumed
   { };  ..
```

ACCESS SPECIFIERS: WHEN TO USE WHAT

When would you use private as opposed to public class derivation? Suppose you used a function in the base class that worked fine with objects of the base class but gave erroneous results with objects of derived classes. Further suppose that there was no function of the same name in the derived class to override the base class. How do you make sure that the function can be called only by objects of the base class? One way to handle this is to make a dummy function with the same name for the derived class and have it print an error message if called by an object of the

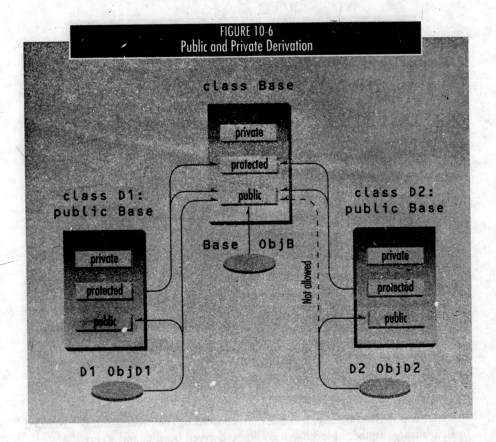

FIGURE 10-6
Public and Private Derivation

derived class. However, a more elegant approach is to make the derived class **private**. Now the function will simply not be accessible to objects of the derived class, although it is still accessible to objects of the base class.

LEVELS OF INHERITANCE

Classes can be derived from classes that are themselves derived. Here's a mini-program that shows the idea:

```
class A
    { };
class B : public A
    { };
class C : public B
    { };
```

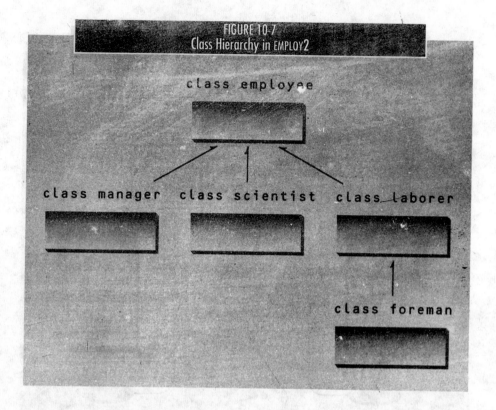

FIGURE 10-7
Class Hierarchy in EMPLOY2

Here **B** is derived from **A**, and **C** is derived from **B**. The process can be extended to an arbitrary number of levels—**D** could be derived from **C**, and so on.

As a more concrete example, suppose that we decided to add a special kind of laborer called a *foreman* to the EMPLOY program. We'll create a new program, EMPLOY2, that incorporates objects of class **foreman**.

Since foremen are a kind of laborer, the **foreman** class is derived from the **laborer** class, as shown in Figure 10-7.

Foremen oversee the widget-stamping operation, supervising groups of laborers. They are responsible for the widget production quota for their group. A foreman's ability is measured by the percentage of production quotas successfully met. The **quotas** data item in the **foreman** class represents this percentage. Here's the listing for EMPLOY2:

```
// employ2.cpp
// multiple levels of inheritance
#include <iostream.h>

const int LEN = 80;                 // maximum length of names

class employee
   {
```

```
   private:
      char name[LEN];          // employee name
      unsigned long number;    // employee number
   public:
      void getdata()
         {
         cout << "\n   Enter last name: "; cin >> name;
         cout << "    Enter number: ";       cin >> number;
         }
      void putdata()
         {
         cout << "\n   Name: " << name;
         cout << "\n   Number: " << number;
         }
   };

class manager : public employee      // management class
   {
   private:
      char title[LEN];   // "vice-president" etc.
      double dues;        // golf club dues
   public:
      void getdata()
         {
         employee::getdata();
         cout << "   Enter title: ";          cin >> title;
         cout << "   Enter golf club dues: "; cin >> dues;
         }
      void putdata()
         {
         employee::putdata();
         cout << "\n   Title: " << title;
         cout << "\n   Golf club dues: " << dues;
         }
   };
class scientist : public employee      // scientist class
   {
   private:
      int pubs;   // number of publications
   public:
      void getdata()
         {
         employee::getdata();
         cout << "   Enter number of pubs: "; cin >> pubs;
         }
      void putdata()
         {
         employee::putdata();
         cout << "\n   Number of publications: " << pubs;
         }
   };
```

```
    class laborer : public employee          // laborer class
       {
       };

    class foreman : public laborer           // foreman class
       {
    private:
       float quotas;       // percent of quotas met successfully
    public:
       void getdata()
          {
          laborer::getdata();
          cout << "   Enter quotas: "; cin >> quotas;
          }
       void putdata()
          {
          laborer::putdata();
          cout << "\n   Quotas: " << quotas;
          }
       };

    void main()
       {
       laborer l1;
       foreman f1;

       cout << endl;
       cout << "\nEnter data for laborer 1";
       l1.getdata();
       cout << "\nEnter data for foreman 1";
       f1.getdata();

       cout << endl;
       cout << "\nData on laborer 1";
       l1.putdata();
       cout << "\nData on foreman 1";
       f1.putdata();
       }
```

Notice that a class hierarchy is not the same as an organization chart. An organization chart shows lines of command. A class hierarchy results from generalizing common characteristics. The more general the class, the higher it is on the chart. Thus a laborer is more general than a foreman, who is a specialized kind of laborer, so laborer is shown above foreman in the class hierarchy.

MULTIPLE INHERITANCE

A class can be derived from more than one base class. This is called *multiple inheritance*. Figure 10-8 shows how this looks when a class C is derived from base classes A and B.

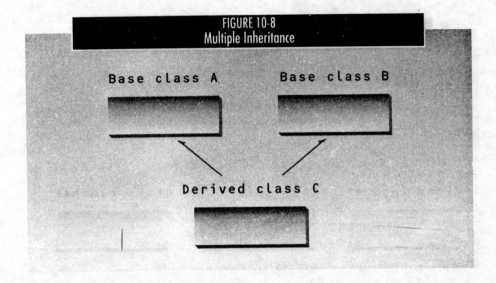

FIGURE 10-8
Multiple Inheritance

The syntax for multiple inheritance is similar to that for single inheritance. In the situation shown in the figure, the relationship is expressed like this:

```
class A                              // base class A
   {
   };
class B                              // base class B
   {
   };
class C : public A, public B         // C is derived from A and B
   {
   };
```

The base classes from which C is derived are listed following the colon in C's specification; they are separated by commas.

MEMBER FUNCTIONS IN MULTIPLE INHERITANCE

As an example of multiple inheritance, suppose that we needed to record the educational experience of some of the employees in the EMPLOY program. Let's also suppose that, perhaps in a different project, we had already developed a class called student that models students with different educational backgrounds. We decide that instead of modifying the employee class to incorporate educational data, we will add this data by multiple inheritance from the student class.

The student class stores the name of the school or university last attended, and the highest degree received. Both these data items are stored as strings. Two member functions, getedu() and putedu(), ask the user for this information and display it.

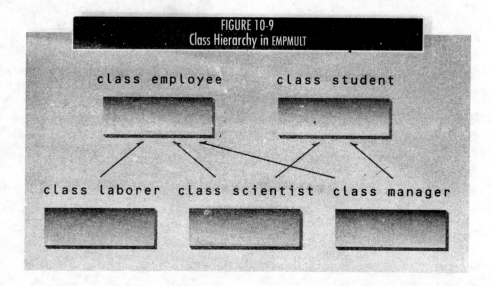

FIGURE 10-9
Class Hierarchy in EMPMULT

Educational information is not relevant to every class of employee. Let's suppose, somewhat undemocratically, that we don't need to record the educational experience of laborers; it's only relevant for managers and scientists. We therefore modify **manager** and **scientist** so that they inherit from both the **employee** and **student** classes, as shown in Figure 10-9.

Here's a mini-program that shows these relationships (but leaves out everything else):

```
class student
    { };
class employee
    { };
class manager : private employee, private student
    { };
class scientist : private employee, private student
    { };
class laborer : public employee
    { };
```

And here, featuring considerably more detail, is the listing for EMPMULT:

```
// empmult.cpp
// multiple inheritance with employees and education
#include <iostream.h>

const int LEN = 80;                // maximum length of names

class student                      // educational background
    {
```

```
   private:
      char school[LEN];   // name of school or university
      char degree[LEN];   // highest degree earned
   public:
      void getedu()
         {
         cout << "   Enter name of school or university: ";
         cin >> school;
         cout << "   Enter highest degree earned \n";
         cout << "   (Highschool, Bachelor's, Master's, PhD): ";
         cin >> degree;
         }
      void putedu()
         {
         cout << "\n   School or university: " << school;
         cout << "\n   Highest degree earned: " << degree;
         }
   };

class employee
   {
   private:
      char name[LEN];         // employee name
      unsigned long number;   // employee number
   public:
      void getdata()
         {
         cout << "\n   Enter last name: "; cin >> name;
         cout << "   Enter number: ";      cin >> number;
         }
      void putdata()
         {
         cout << "\n   Name: " << name;
         cout << "\n   Number: " << number;
         }
   };

class manager : private employee, private student  // management
   {
   private:
      char title[LEN];   // "vice-president" etc.
      double dues;       // golf club dues
   public:
      void getdata()
         {
         employee::getdata();
         cout << "   Enter title: ";           cin >> title;
         cout << "   Enter golf club dues: "; cin >> dues;
         student::getedu();
         }
```

```cpp
      void putdata()
         {
         employee::putdata();
         cout << "\n   Title: " << title;
         cout << "\n   Golf club dues: " << dues;
         student::putedu();
         }
   };

class scientist : private employee, private student   // scientist
   {
   private:
      int pubs;       // number of publications
   public:
      void getdata()
         {
         employee::getdata();
         cout << "   Enter number of pubs: "; cin >> pubs;
         student::getedu();
         }
      void putdata()
         {
         employee::putdata();
         cout << "\n   Number of publications: " << pubs;
         student::putedu();
         }
   };


class laborer : public  employee         // laborer
   {
   };


void main()
   {
   manager m1;
   scientist s1, s2;
   laborer l1;

   cout << endl;
   cout << "\nEnter data for manager 1";       // get data for
   m1.getdata();                               // several employees

   cout << "\nEnter data for scientist 1";
   s1.getdata();

   cout << "\nEnter data for scientist 2";
   s2.getdata();

   cout << "\nEnter data for laborer 1";
   l1.getdata();
```

```
        cout << "\nData on manager 1";          // display data for
        m1.putdata();                           // several employees

        cout << "\nData on scientist 1";
        s1.putdata();

        cout << "\nData on scientist 2";
        s2.putdata();

        cout << "\nData on laborer 1";
        l1.putdata();
        }
```

The `getdata()` and `putdata()` functions in the `manager` and `scientist` classes incorporate calls to functions in the `student` class, such as

```
        student::getedu();
```

and

```
        student::putedu();
```

These routines are accessible in `manager` and `scientist` because these classes are descended from `student`.

Here's some sample interaction with EMPMULT:

```
Enter data for manager 1
   Enter last name: Bradley
   Enter number: 12
   Enter title: Vice-President
   Enter golf club dues: 100000
   Enter name of school or university: Yale
   Enter highest degree earned
   (Highschool, Bachelor's, Master's, PhD): Bachelor's

Enter data for scientist 1
   Enter last name: Twilling
   Enter number: 764
   Enter number of pubs: 99
   Enter name of school or university: MIT
   Enter highest degree earned
   (Highschool, Bachelor's, Master's, PhD): PhD

Enter data for scientist 2
   Enter last name: Yang
   Enter number: 845
   Enter number of pubs: 101
   Enter name of school or university: Stanford
   Enter highest degree earned
   (Highschool, Bachelor's, Master's, PhD): Master's
```

```
Enter data for laborer 1
   Enter last name: Jones
   Enter number: 48323
```

As we saw in the EMPLOY and EMPLOY2 examples, the program then displays this information in roughly the same form.

private Derivation in EMPMULT

The manager and scientist classes in EMPMULT are privately derived from the employee and student classes. There is no need to use public derivation because objects of manager and scientist never call routines in the employee and student base classes. However, the laborer class must be publicly derived from employer, since it has no member functions of its own and relies on those in employee.

CONSTRUCTORS IN MULTIPLE INHERITANCE

EMPMULT has no constructors. Let's look at an example that does use constructors, and see how they're handled in multiple inheritance.

Imagine that we're writing a program for building contractors, and that this program models lumber-supply items. It uses a class that represents a quantity of lumber of a certain type: 100 eight-foot-long construction grade 2x4s, for example.

The class should store various kinds of data about each such lumber item. We need to know the length (3'-6" long or whatever) and we need to store the number of such pieces of lumber and their unit cost.

We also need to store a description of the lumber we're talking about. This has two parts. The first is the nominal dimensions of the cross-section of the lumber. This is given in inches. For instance, lumber two inches by four inches (for you metrickers, about 5 cm by 10 cm) is called a *two-by-four*. This is usually written 2x4. (The actual dimensions are smaller than these nominal dimensions, but that doesn't matter here.) We also need to know the grade of lumber—rough-cut, construction grade, surfaced-four-sides, and so on. We find it convenient to create a Type class to hold this data about the lumber. This class incorporates member data for the nominal dimensions and the grade of the lumber, both expressed as strings, such as 2x6 and *construction*. Member functions get this information from the user and display it.

We'll use the Distance class from previous examples to store the length. Finally we create a Lumber class that inherits both the Type and Distance classes. Here's the listing for ENGLMULT:

```
// englmult.cpp
// multiple inheritance with English Distances
#include <iostream.h>
#include <string.h>          // for strcpy()

const int LEN = 40;          // maximum length of strings
```

```cpp
class Type                          // type of lumber
   {
   private:
      char dimensions[LEN];
      char grade[LEN];
   public:
      Type()                        // constructor (no args)
         { strcpy(dimensions, "N/A"); strcpy(grade, "N/A"); }

      Type(char di[], char gr[])    // constructor (two args)
         { strcpy(dimensions, di); strcpy(grade, gr); }

      void gettype()                // get type from user
         {
         cout << "   Enter nominal dimensions (2x4 etc.): ";
         cin >> dimensions;
         cout << "   Enter grade (rough, const, etc.): ";
         cin >> grade;
         }
      void showtype()               // display type
         {
         cout << "\n   Dimensions: " << dimensions;
         cout << "\n   Grade: " << grade;
         }
   };

class Distance                      // English Distance class
   {
   private:
      int feet;
      float inches;
   public:
      Distance()                    // constructor (no args)
         { feet = 0; inches = 0.0; }
      Distance(int ft, float in)    // constructor (two args)
         { feet = ft; inches = in; }
      void getdist()                // get length from user
         {
         cout << "   Enter feet: ";  cin >> feet;
         cout << "   Enter inches: ";  cin >> inches;
         }
      void showdist()               // display distance
         { cout  << feet << "\'-" << inches << '\"'; }
   };

class Lumber : public Type, public Distance
   {
   private:
      int quantity;                          // number of pieces
      float price;                           // price of each piece
```

```
public:
    Lumber() : Type(), Distance()       // constructor (no args)
        { quantity = 0; price = 0.0; }

                                        // constructor (6 args)
    Lumber( char di[], char gr[],       // args for Type
            int ft, float in,           // args for Distance
            int qu, float prc ) :       // our own args
            Type(di, gr),               // call Type constructor
            Distance(ft, in)            // call Distance constr
        {
        quantity = qu; price = prc;     // use our own args
        }
    void getlumber()
        {
        Type::gettype();
        Distance::getdist();
        cout << "   Enter quantity: "; cin >> quantity;
        cout << "   Enter price per piece: "; cin >> price;
        }
    void showlumber()
        {
        Type::showtype();
        cout << "\n   Length: ";
        Distance::showdist();
        cout << "\n   Price for " << quantity
             << " pieces: $" << price * quantity;
        }
    };

void main()
    {
    Lumber siding;                      // constructor (no args)

    cout << "\nSiding data:\n";
    siding.getlumber();                 // get siding from user

                                        // constructor (6 args)
    Lumber studs( "2x4", "const", 8, 0.0, 200, 4.45 );

                                        // display lumber data
    cout << "\nSiding"; siding.showlumber();
    cout << "\nStuds";    studs.showlumber();
    }
```

The major new feature in this program is the use of constructors in the derived class Lumber. These constructors call the appropriate constructors in Type and Distance.

No-Argument Constructor

The no-argument constructor in `Type` looks like this:

```
Type()
    { strcpy(dimensions, "N/A"); strcpy(grade, "N/A"); }
```

This constructor fills in "N/A" (not available) for the `dimensions` and `grade` variables, so the user will be made aware if an attempt is made to display data for an uninitialized lumber object.

You're already familiar with the no-argument constructor in the `Distance` class:

```
Distance()
    { feet = 0; inches = 0.0; }
```

The no-argument constructor in `Lumber` calls both these constructors:

```
Lumber() : Type(), Distance()
```

The names of the base-class constructors follow the colon and are separated by commas. These base-class constructors will be called in order when the `Lumber()` constructor is invoked.

Multi-Argument Constructor

The situation is more complex when constructors with arguments are used. Here is the two-argument constructor for `Type`:

```
Type(char di[], char gr[])
    { strcpy(dimensions, di); strcpy(grade, gr); }
```

This constructor copies string arguments to the `dimensions` and `grade` member data items.

Here's the constructor for `Distance`, which is again familiar from previous programs:

```
Distance(int ft, float in)
    { feet = ft; inches = in; }
```

The constructor for `Lumber` calls both these constructors, so it must supply values for their arguments. In addition it has two arguments of its own: the quantity of lumber and the unit price. So this constructor has six arguments. It then makes two calls to the two constructors, each of which takes two arguments. Here's what it looks like:

```
Lumber( char di[], char gr[],         ←————— args for Type class
        int ft, float in,             ←————— args for Distance class
        int qu, float prc ) :         ←————— args for this class
        Type(di, gr),                 ←————— call Type constructor
        Distance(ft, in);             ←————— call Distance constructor
```

```
{
    quantity = qu; price = prc;        ←————————set our own data
}
```

As before, a colon signals the start of the list of constructors to be called, with the members of the list being separated by commas. The first four arguments passed to **Lumber** are passed on to **Type()** and **Distance()**. The last two arguments are used to initialize the **quantity** and **price** members of **Lumber**, in the body of the function.

AMBIGUITY IN MULTIPLE INHERITANCE

Odd sorts of problems may surface in certain situations involving multiple inheritance. Here's a common one. Two base classes have functions with the same name, while a class derived from both base classes has no function with this name. How do objects of the derived class access the correct base class function? The name of the function alone is insufficient, since the compiler can't figure out which of the two functions is meant.

Here's an example, AMBIGU, that demonstrates the situation:

```
// ambigu.cpp
// demonstrates ambiguity in multiple inheritance
#include <iostream.h>

class A
    {
    public:
        void show()  { cout << "\nClass A"; }
    };
class B
    {
    public:
        void show()  { cout << "\nClass B"; }
    };
class C : public A, public B
    {
    };

void main()
    {
    C objC;            // object of class C
    objC.show();       // ambiguous--will not compile
    objC.A::show();    // ok
    objC.B::show();    // ok
    }
```

The problem is resolved using the scope-resolution operator to specify the class in which the function lies. Thus

```
objC.A::show();
```

refers to the version of `show()` that's in the `A` class, while

```
objC.B::show();
```

refers to the function in the `B` class.

The scope-resolution operator resolves the ambiguity and keeps the compiler happy.

CONTAINERSHIP: CLASSES WITHIN CLASSES

In inheritance, if a class B is derived from a class A, we can say that "B is a kind of A." This is because B has all the characteristics of A, and in addition some of its own. It's like saying that a starling is a kind of bird: A starling has the characteristics shared by all birds (wings, feathers, and so on) but has some distinctive characteristics of its own (such as dark iridescent plumage). For this reason inheritance is sometimes called a "kind of" relationship.

There's another kind of relationship, called a "has a" relationship, or *containership*. We say that a starling has a tail, meaning that each starling includes an instance of a tail. In object-oriented programming the "has a" relationship occurs

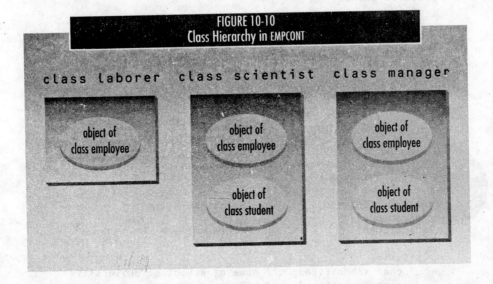

FIGURE 10-10
Class Hierarchy in EMPCONT

class laborer   class scientist   class manager

object of
class employee

object of
class employee

object of
class employee

object of
class student

object of
class student

when one object is contained in another. Here's a case where an object of class B is contained in a class A:

```
class A
   {
   B b;    // b is an object of class B
   };
class B
   {
   };
```

In some situations inheritance and containership relationships can serve similar purposes. For example, we can rewrite the EMPMULT program to use containership instead of inheritance. In EMPMULT the manager and scientist classes are derived from the employee and student classes using the inheritance relationship. In our new program, EMPCONT, the manager and scientist classes contain instances of the employee and student classes, as shown in Figure 10-10.

The following mini-program shows these relationships in a different way:

```
class student
   {};
class employee
   {};
class manager
   {
   student stu;     // stu is an object of class student
   employee emp;    // emp is an object of class employee
   };
class scientist
   {
   student stu;     // stu is an object of class student
   employee emp;    // emp is an object of class employee
   };
class laborer
   {
   employee emp;    // emp is an object of class employee
   };
```

Here's the full-scale listing for EMPCONT:

```
// empcont.cpp
// containership with employees and education
#include <iostream.h>

const int LEN = 80;                // maximum length of names

class student                      // educational background
   {
   private:
      char school[LEN];  // name of school or university
      char degree[LEN];  // highest degree earned
```

```
    public:
       void getedu()
          {
          cout << "   Enter name of school or university: ";
          cin >> school;
          cout << "   Enter highest degree earned \n";
          cout << "   (Highschool, Bachelor's, Master's, PhD): ";
          cin >> degree;
          }
       void putedu()
          {
          cout << "\n   School or university: " << school;
          cout << "\n   Highest degree earned: " << degree;
          }
    };


class employee
    {
    private:
       char name[LEN];            // employee name
       unsigned long number;      // employee number
    public:
       void getdata()
          {
          cout << "\n   Enter last name: "; cin >> name;
          cout << "   Enter number: ";        cin >> number;
          }
       void putdata()
          {
          cout << "\n   Name: " << name;
          cout << "\n   Number: " << number;
          }
    };


class manager                // management
    {
    private:
       char title[LEN];     // "vice-president" etc.
       double dues;         // golf club dues
       employee emp;        // object of class employee
       student stu;         // object of class student
    public:
       void getdata()
          {
          emp.getdata();
          cout << "   Enter title: ";            cin >> title;
          cout << "   Enter golf club dues: "; cin >> dues;
          stu.getedu();
          }
```

```
        void putdata()
            {
            emp.putdata();
            cout << "\n    Title: " << title;
            cout << "\n    Golf club dues: " << dues;
            stu.putedu();
            }
    };
class scientist            // scientist
    {
    private:
        int pubs;            // number of publications
        employee emp;        // object of class employee
        student stu;         // object of class student
    public:
        void getdata()
            {
            emp.getdata();
            cout << "    Enter number of pubs: "; cin >> pubs;
            stu.getedu();
            }
        void putdata()
            {
            emp.putdata();
            cout << "\n    Number of publications: " << pubs;
            stu.putedu();
            }
    };

class laborer            // laborer
    {
    private:
        employee emp;  // object of class employee
    public:
        void getdata()
            { emp.getdata(); }
        void putdata()
            { emp.putdata(); }
    };

void main()
    {
    manager m1;
    scientist s1, s2;
    laborer l1;

    cout << endl;
    cout << "\nEnter data for manager 1";     // get data for
    m1.getdata();                             // several employees
```

```
        cout << "\nEnter data for scientist 1";
        s1.getdata();

        cout << "\nEnter data for scientist 2";
        s2.getdata();

        cout << "\nEnter data for laborer 1";
        l1.getdata();

        cout << "\nData on manager 1";          // display data for
        m1.putdata();                           // several employees

        cout << "\nData on scientist 1";
        s1.putdata();

        cout << "\nData on scientist 2";
        s2.putdata();

        cout << "\nData on laborer 1";
        l1.putdata();
        }
```

The **student** and **employee** classes are the same in EMPCONT as they were in EMPMULT, but they are used in a different way by the **manager** and **scientist** classes.

Containership is clearly useful with classes that act like a data type, as does the **Distance** class, for example. Then an object of that type can be used in a class in almost the same way a variable would be. In other situations you will need to examine the problem carefully and perhaps try different approaches to see what makes sense. Often the inheritance relationship is simpler to implement and offers a clearer conceptual framework.

INHERITANCE AND PROGRAM DEVELOPMENT

The program-development process, as practiced for decades by programmers everywhere, is being fundamentally altered by object-oriented programming. This is due not only to the use of classes in OOP but to inheritance as well. Let's see how this comes about.

Programmer A creates a class. Perhaps it's something like the **Distance** class, with a complete set of member functions for arithmetic operations on a user-defined data type.

Programmer B likes the **Distance** class but thinks it could be improved by using signed distances. The solution is to create a new class, like **DistSign** in the

ENGLEN example, that is derived from **Distance** but incorporates the extensions necessary to implement signed distances.

Programmers C and D then write applications that use the **DistSign** class.

It may be that programmer B does not have access to the source code for the **Distance** member functions, and that programmers C and D don't have access to the source code for **DistSign**. Yet, because of the software reusability feature of C++, B can modify and extend the work of A; and C and D can make use of the work of B (and A).

Notice that the distinction between software tool developers and application writers is becoming blurred. Programmer A creates a general-purpose programming tool, the **Distance** class. Programmer B creates a specialized version of this class, the **DistSign** class. Programmers C and D create applications. A is a tool developer, and C and D are applications developers. B is somewhere in between. In any case OOP is making the programming scene more flexible and at the same time more complex.

In Chapter 15, on larger programs, we'll see how a class can be divided into a client-accessible part and a part that is distributed only in object form, so it can be used by other programmers without the distribution of source code.

SUMMARY

A class, called the derived class, can inherit the features of another class, called the base class. The derived class can add other features of its own, so it becomes a specialized version of the base class. Inheritance provides a powerful way to extend the capabilities of existing classes, and to design programs using hierarachical relationships.

Accessibility of base class members from derived classes and from objects of derived classes is an important issue. Data or functions in the base class that are prefaced by the keyword **protected** can be accessed from derived classes but not by objects of derived classes. Classes may be publicly or privately derived from base classes. Objects of a publicly derived class can access public members of the base class, while objects of a privately derived class cannot.

A class can be derived from more than one base class. This is called multiple inheritance. A class can also be contained within another class.

Inheritance permits the reusability of software: Derived classes can extend the capabilities of base classes with no need to modify—or even access the source code of—the base class. This leads to new flexibility in the software development process, and to a wider range of roles for software developers.

QUESTIONS

1. Inheritance is a way to
   a. make general classes into more specific classes
   b. pass arguments to objects of classes
   c. add features to existing classes without rewriting them
   d. improve data-hiding and encapsulation

2. A "child" class is said to be _____ from a base class.

3. Advantages of inheritance include
   a. providing class growth through natural selection
   b. facilitating class libraries
   c. avoiding the rewriting of code
   d. providing a useful conceptual framework

4. Write the first line of the specifier for a class Bosworth that is publicly derived from a class Alphonso.

5. True or false: Adding a derived class to a base class requires fundamental changes to the base class.

6. To be accessed from a member function of the derived class, data or functions in the base class must be public or _____.

7. If a base class contains a member function basefunc(), and a derived class does not contain a function with this name, can an object of the derived class access basefunc()?

8. Assume the classes mentioned in Question 4, and that class Alphonso contains a member function called alfunc(). Write a statement that allows object BosworthObj of class Bosworth to access alfunc().

9. True or false: If no constructors are specified for a derived class, objects of the derived class will use the constructors in the base class.

10. If a base class and a derived class each include a member function with the same name, which member function will be called by an object of the derived class, assuming the scope-resolution operator is not used?

11. Write a declarator for a no-argument constructor of the derived class Bosworth of Question 4 that calls a no-argument constructor in the base class Alphonso.

12. The scope-resolution operator usually
    a. limits the visibility of variables to a certain function
    b. tells what base class a class is derived from
    c. specifies a particular class
    d. resolves ambiguities

13. True or false: It is sometimes useful to specify a class from which no objects will ever be created.

14. Assume there is a class **Derv** that is derived from a base class **Base**. Write the declarator for a derived-class constructor that takes one argument and passes this argument along to the constructor in the base class.

15. Assume a class **Derv** that is privately derived from class **Base**. An object of class **Derv** located in **main()** can access
    a. public members of **Derv**
    b. protected members of **Derv**
    c. private members of **Derv**
    d. public members of **Base**
    e. protected members of **Base**
    f. private members of **Base**

16. True or false: A class **D** can be derived from a class **C**, which is derived from a class **B**, which is derived from a class **A**.

17. A class hierarchy
    a. shows the same relationships as an organization chart
    b. describes "has a" relationships
    c. describes "is a kind of" relationships
    d. shows the same relationships as a family tree

18. Write the first line of a specifier for a class **Tire** that is derived from class **Wheel** and from class **Rubber**

19. Assume a class **Derv** derived from a base class **Base**. Both classes contain a member function **func()** that takes no arguments. Write a statement to go in a member function of **Derv** that calls **func()** in the base class.

20. True or false: It is illegal to make objects of one class members of another class.

EXERCISES

1. Imagine a publishing company that markets both book and audio-cassette versions of its works. Create a class **publication** that stores the title (a string) and price (type **float**) of a publication. From this class derive two classes: **book**, which adds a page count (type **int**); and **tape**, which adds a playing time in minutes (type **float**). Each of these three classes should have a **getdata()** function to get its data from the user at the keyboard, and a **putdata()** function to display its data.

   Write a **main()** program to test the **book** and **tape** classes by creating instances of them, asking the user to fill in their data with **getdata()**, and then displaying the data with **putdata()**.

2. Recall the STRCONV example from Chapter 9. The `String` class in this example has a flaw: It does not protect itself if its objects are initialized to have too many characters. (The SZ constant has the value 80.) For example, the definition

```
String s = "This string will surely exceed the width of the \
screen, which is what the SZ constant represents.";
```

will cause the `str` array in `s` to overflow, with unpredictable consequences, such as crashing the system. (The '\' character in this statement permits a long string to wrap over two lines in the source file, while the compiler sees an unbroken string.)

With `String` as a base class, derive a class `Pstring` (for "protected String") that prevents buffer overflow when too long a string constant is used in a definition. A new constructor in the derived class should copy only SZ-1 characters into `str` if the string constant is longer, but copy the entire constant if it's shorter. Write a `main()` program to test different lengths of strings

3. Start with the `publication`, `book`, and `tape` classes of Exercise 1. Add a base class `sales` that holds an array of three `floats` so that it can record the dollar sales of a particular publication for the last three months. Include a `getdata()` function to get three sales amounts from the user, and a `putdata()` function to display the sales figures. Alter the `book` and `tape` classes so they are derived from both `publication` and `sales`. An object of class `book` or `tape` should input and output sales data along with its other data. Write a `main()` function to create a `book` object and a `tape` object and exercise their input/output capabilities.

CHAPTER 11

TURBO C++ GRAPHICS

- TEXT-MODE GRAPHICS
- SETTING UP FOR GRAPHICS MODE
- SHAPES, LINES, COLOR, AND PATTTERN
- GRAPHICS SHAPES AS C++ OBJECTS
- TEXT IN GRAPHICS MODE

Turbo C++ and Borland C++ include an extensive collection of graphics-oriented library functions. These functions open up an exciting new world: With them you can place almost any sort of image on the screen. Graphics and object-oriented programming work together particularly well because specific images, such as balls or text boxes, can be represented by objects. Graphics provides a visual way to see objects in action.

Turbo C++ graphics functions fall into two categories: those that work in text mode and those that work in graphics mode. The text mode functions, which we'll look at first, are concerned with placing text in certain areas of the screen. They work with any graphics monitor and adapter, so you can use them even if you have only a monochrome system. (Of course you can also use any of the graphics characters, as shown in Appendix A, in text mode; so you can do simple graphics operations like drawing boxes around text.)

The graphics mode functions, which we look at in the second part of the chapter, require a graphics monitor and adapter card, such as CGA, EGA, or VGA. (See the description of the `initgraph()` function in the the Turbo C++ documentation for a complete list of supported graphics adapters.) Graphics-mode functions allow you to draw dots, lines, and shapes (like circles and rectangles), add color to lines and areas, and perform many other graphics-related activities.

The emphasis in this chapter is on how graphics images can be implemented as C++ objects. No new object-oriented topics are introduced, so this chapter gives you a chance to reinforce the concepts you've learned already, including objects, classes, and inheritance. Even if your computer does not have a graphics display, you should read this chapter, as graphics provide an intuitive, visual demonstration of object-oriented programming.

We do not cover all the Turbo C++ graphics functions. Our aim is to show the most important functions and how they work in the object-oriented environment. However, we show the general approach to a variety of situations, so you can probably figure out the remaining graphics functions on your own. (The books *C Programming Using Turbo C++* and *Turbo C++ Bible*, listed in the bibliography, contain more details on Turbo C++ graphics functions.)

Text-Mode Graphics Functions

When you first boot up your computer, it's probably in text mode. In this mode the screen is divided into character positions, typically 80 columns by 25 rows (although there are also 40x25, 80x43, and other arrangements). The video output functions we've seen so far, such as `cout` and `<<`, are text-mode functions. However, Turbo C++ adds additional text-mode functions to facilitate writing text to *windows*. A window in this context is a rectangular area on the screen that confines the text written to it.

Windows are useful in programs that use a Graphical User Interface (GUI) display in text mode. The Turbo C++ environment itself is an example of this kind of display. It uses windows in character mode.

We should note that, unlike most of the Turbo C++ library functions mentioned in this book, the graphics-oriented library functions described in this chapter work only in the MS-DOS environment. They are not portable to other platforms such as Unix, or even to other compilers besides Turbo C++ and Borland C++.

The window() Function

The key library function for text mode is `window()`. This function (which requires the CONIO.H header file) takes four integer arguments that determine the left, top, right, and bottom coordinates of the window. On an 80x25 display, the columns run from 1 to 80, and the rows from 1 to 25. Text written by certain functions will appear inside the window, starting at the upper-left corner. Text too long for the width of the window is automatically wrapped at the right edge. Text that goes beyond the bottom of the window causes the contents of the window to scroll upward. Note that `window()` doesn't draw a border or outline around the window; it only confines text to a rectangular area. Thus you can't see where the window is until you start writing text in it.

Actually the text window is always in effect in text mode, but since its default coordinates are the entire screen, you don't notice its existence unless you've changed its coordinates with `window()`.

Using Text-Mode Functions

Unlike graphics mode, which requires special functions to initialize the graphics system, text mode needs no preparation before use, since you're already in it when you're at the DOS prompt. You can start right in using `window()` and other functions.

Here's an example that makes use of the `window()` library function. This program, WINDOW, creates a class called `box`. This class represents a window and the text contained in it. Here's the listing for WINDOW:

```
// window.cpp
// text window as a class
#include <string.h>        // for strcpy()
#include <conio.h>         // for window(), gotoxy(), etc.

const int LEN = 500;       // maximum length of string

class box                  // text box class
   {
   private:
      int left, top, right, bottom;      // window dimensions
      char str[LEN];                     // window text
   public:
                                         // constructor (5 args)
      box(int l, int t, int r, int b, char s[])
         {
         left=l; top=t; right=r; bottom=b;
         strcpy(str, s);
         window(left, top, right, bottom);   // set window
         cputs(str);                         // display text
         }
      void erase()         // erase the window
         {
         window(left, top, right, bottom);   // set window
         clrscr();                           // clear window
         }
   };

void main()
   {
   clrscr();                      // clear entire screen

   char s1[] = "The disk drive is jammed\n\r\
or on fire, or the CPU\n\r\
is flooded.  Correct the\n\r\
situation and try again.\n\r\
Press Enter to continue: ";

   char s2[] = "This is a string that will wrap at the right \
edge of the window, probably breaking words inappropriately \
in the process.";

   box a(25, 6, 55, 18, s1);       // string 1, middle of screen
   getch();                        // wait for keypress
   a.erase();                      // erase box a

   box b(1, 1, 25, 10, s2);        // string 2, upper left corner
   getch();                        // wait for keypress
   }
```

The constructor for the **box** class takes five arguments. The first four establish the coordinates of the box (left, top, right, bottom). The fifth specifies the string that will be displayed in the box. The constructor sets a text window using the **window()** function, and writes the text into it with the **cputs()** library function.

THE cputs() FUNCTION

The usual approach to text output, using **cout** and the **<<** operator, does not work within a text window. Most C++ functions don't recognize the existence of text windows; they assume they have the entire screen to work with. To work within a text window you must use library functions specifically created for that purpose. One of the most useful is the function **cputs()**, which writes a string of text to a window. We use this function to display the text from the **box** class on the screen.

A peculiarity of **cputs()** is that it does not translate a newline character ('\n') into the carriage-return-plus-linefeed combination. We must do this manually, by inserting both a linefeed (represented by the '\n' character) and a separate carriage return (represented by '\r') wherever we want to start a new line. This combination is used to terminate each line in **s1** and **s2**.

Note: In this chapter we'll be talking about two kinds of functions: Turbo C++ library functions like **window()**, **initgraph()**, and **cputs** on the one hand; and member functions of classes we create ourselves on the other. We will try to clarify which kind of function we mean by describing it as either a *library function* or a *member function* when it is introduced, but you should be aware of the possibility of confusion.

THE clrscr() FUNCTION

The **clrscr()** library function erases the text window. It is used twice in WINDOW. The first time is in **main()**, where—since the **window()** function has not yet been invoked to change the text window from its default setting—**clrscr()** erases the entire screen. It's also used in the **box::erase()** member function to erase the contents of the window.

The **main()** part of WINDOW defines two strings and then creates two windows. The first window, in the middle of the screen, displays the first string. Then, after the user presses a key, the second window displays the second string. Figures 11-1 and 11-2 show the display at these two points.

A FANCIER box CLASS

Let's rewrite the **box** class from WINDOW so that, in addition to displaying text, it also outlines itself with a rectangle. This will give it a more "window-like" appearance. We'll do this with graphics characters that represent vertical and horizontal line segments and corners. We'll also make the **box** class more flexible by giving it more

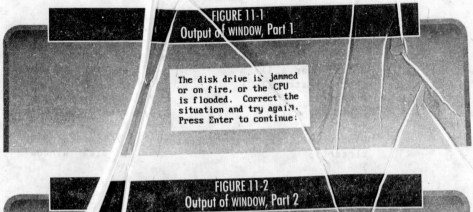

FIGURE 11-1
Output of WINDOW, Part 1

The disk drive is jammed
or on fire, or the CPU
is flooded. Correct the
situation and try again.
Press Enter to continue:

FIGURE 11-2
Output of WINDOW, Part 2

This i s a string that wil
l wra p at the right edge
of t e window, probably b
real king words: inappropria
te y in the process.

member functions. Since the window created by this class is enclosed by lines, we'll refer to it as a text box. Here's the listing for BOXES:

```
// boxes.cpp
// dialog boxes as objects
#include <string.h>      // for strcpy()
#include <conio.h>       // for window(), gotoxy(), etc.

const int LEFT = 25;       // default window dimensions
const int TOP = 6;
const int RIGHT = 55;
const int BOTTOM = 18;
const int LEN = 500;       // maximum length of text strings

class box                  // text box
    {
    private:
        int left, top, right, bottom;   // window dimensions
        char str[LEN];                  // window text
        int color;                      // text color
    public:
        box()                           // no-arg constructor
            {
            left=LEFT; top=TOP;         // set to default
            right=RIGHT; bottom=BOTTOM; // dimensions
```

```
           color = WHITE;                         // and color
           }                                       // 5-arg constructor
        box(int l, int t, int r, int b, int c=WHITE)
           { left=l; top=t; right=r; bottom=b; color=c; }
        void text(char s[])                        // put text in window
           { strcpy(str, s); }
        void draw();                               // display the window
        void erase()                               // erase the window
           {
           window(left, top, right, bottom);       // frame window
           clrscr();                               // clear window
           }
        };

void box::draw()
   {
   erase();                                    // erase area under window
   window(left, top, right, bottom+1);  // frame window
   int width = right - left + 1;
   int height = bottom - top + 1;
   textcolor(color);                           // set text color

   for(int j=1; j<=width; j++)                  // draw horiz lines
      {
      gotoxy(j, 1);          putch(char(205));  // top
      gotoxy(j, height);     putch(char(205));  // bottom
      }
   for(j=1; j<=height; j++)                      // draw vertical lines
      {
      gotoxy(1, j);          putch(char(186));  // left
      gotoxy(width, j);      putch(char(186));  // right
      }
                                                 // draw corners
   gotoxy(1, 1);             putch(char(201));  // upper left
   gotoxy(width, 1);         putch(char(187));  // upper right
   gotoxy(1, height);        putch(char(200));  // lower left
   gotoxy(width, height);    putch(char(188));  // lower right

   window(left+2, top+1, right-2, bottom-3);  // text window
   cputs(str);                                // display text

   window(left, top, right, bottom+1);        // frame window
   gotoxy(3, height-1);                       // go to last line
   cputs("Press any key to continue: ");      // display prompt
   textcolor(WHITE);                          // restore color
   }

void main()
   {
   clrscr();                                  // clear screen
```

```
    box a;                          // create box, 1-arg constructor
    box b(1, 1, 31, 8, YELLOW);     // create box, 4-arg constructor

                                    // text for box a
    a.text("\"The time,\" said the\n\r\
Duchess, \"is surely ripe;\n\r\
make haste, lest seconds\n\r\
spoil.\"");
                                    // text for box b
    b.text("Should you continue\n\r\
along the present path you\n\r\
risk investigation\n\r\
for felonious chicanery.");

    a.draw();                       // draw box a
    getch();                        // wait for keypress
    a.erase();                      // erase box a
    b.draw();                       // draw box b
    getch();                        // wait for keypress
    b.erase();                      // erase box b
    b.text("Thank you");            // new text for box b
    b.draw();                       // draw box b
    getch();                        // wait for keypress
    }
```

The **box** class in this program has two constructors. One uses no arguments and creates a text box with standard dimensions in the middle of the screen. The other sets the text box to dimensions chosen by the user. The text is added to the text box by a separate member function: **text()**. This permits changing the text inside an existing box. The **draw()** member function displays the text box, and the **erase()** member function erases it.

The **draw()** member function uses two new Turbo C++ graphics functions to draw the box, and a third to set its color. Let's see what they are.

The gotoxy() Function

The **gotoxy()** library function positions the cursor within a text window. Since text is usually written starting at the cursor position, this allows us to position text where we want it. The **gotoxy()** function takes two integer parameters: the X and Y coordinates where the cursor should go. The coordinate system is that of the window, not the screen, so 1,1 is the upper-left corner of the window.

The putch() Function

The **putch()** library function displays a single character at the cursor position. Its parameter is the character to be displayed. We use it to display graphics characters (see Appendix A) to draw the box around the window.

377

The textcolor() Function

The fifth argument of the five-argument constructor specifies the color to be used for the box outline and for the text within the box. This color value is stored as a private member of the box class. Our member function draw() supplies this value to the library function textcolor(), which it executes before displaying the characters. The possible values for the argument to textcolor() are shown in Table 11-1.

Other functions, which we don't use in the program, can be used to change the appearance of text written to the screen. For instance, you can set the background color for each character with the textbackground() library function. This function

TABLE 11-1
Text-mode colors

Color number	Color constant
0	BLACK
1	BLUE
2	GREEN
3	CYAN
4	RED
5	MAGENTA
6	BROWN
7	LIGHTGRAY
8	DARKGRAY
9	LIGHTBLUE
10	LIGHTGREEN
11	LIGHTCYAN
12	LIGHTRED
13	LIGHTMAGENTA
14	YELLOW
15	WHITE
128	BLINK

accepts only the first eight of the colors in Table 11-1. The function `highvideo()` turns on high-intensity text, and `normvideo()` restores the orginal intensity.

Figures 11-3, 11-4 and 11-5 show three stages in the output of BOXES. Each new screen display is elicited when the user presses a key.

The first figure shows box **a**, the second shows box **b** with its first string, and the third shows the same box with its second string. Box **a** is displayed in white, while box **b** is yellow.

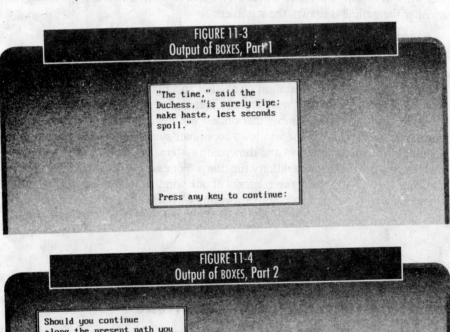

FIGURE 11-3
Output of BOXES, Part 1

```
"The time," said the
Duchess, "is surely ripe;
make haste, lest seconds
spoil."


Press any key to continue:
```

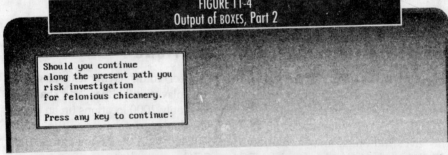

FIGURE 11-4
Output of BOXES, Part 2

```
Should you continue
along the present path you
risk investigation
for felonious chicanery.

Press any key to continue:
```

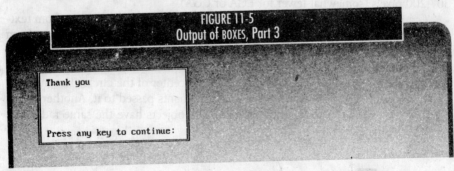

FIGURE 11-5
Output of BOXES, Part 3

```
Thank you


Press any key to continue:
```

Windows within Windows

The `draw()` member function in BOXES uses the `window()` function in several different ways. Early in `draw()` the statement

```
window(left, top, right, bottom+1);
```

sets up what we call the *frame* window: the rectangle where the outline of the window will be drawn. The bottom of this outline is one line lower than the dimensions specified in `box` because we want to be able to display the lower-right-corner character without causing the entire window contents to scroll upward.

After the outline is drawn, the statement

```
window(left+2, top+1, right-2, bottom-3);
```

specifies the rectangle where the text will actually be drawn. The dimensions are smaller than those in the `box` object because we want to keep the text inside the outline, with a one-space separation on the left and right edges. The bottom spacing allows room for the line *Press Enter to Continue:*, which is always placed at the bottom of the window. Remember that once a window is in effect, the `gotoxy()` library function works with the window's coordinate system. Figure 11-6 shows the relation of the various windows and dimension systems.

There are other text-mode library functions. For example, you can erase, insert and delete lines of text, copy the contents of one window to another, and read the contents of a window back into your program. We'll leave the exploration of such functions as an exercise for the reader.

GRAPHICS-MODE GRAPHICS FUNCTIONS

In text mode you are restricted (as you might expect) to displaying text (or graphics characters), but in graphics mode you can display points, lines, and shapes of arbitrary complexity. In text mode you can address only 2000 locations (in an 80x25 display), but in graphics mode you address individual *pixels*, or dots on the screen. This gives you much finer resolution: In a 640x480 VGA mode you can address 307,200 pixels (somewhat fewer for EGA or CGA).

Graphics-mode programs use a completely different set of functions from text-mode programs to put images on the screen. A graphics program must also perform some preliminary work to set the appropriate graphics mode. Let's look at a simple program that uses a class `ball` to model circles displayed on the screen.

The `ball` class stores the coordinates of the center of the circle. The member function `set()` sets these coordinates from arguments passed to it. Another member function, `draw()`, draws the ball. All `ball` objects have the same radius, as specified by the external variable RAD.

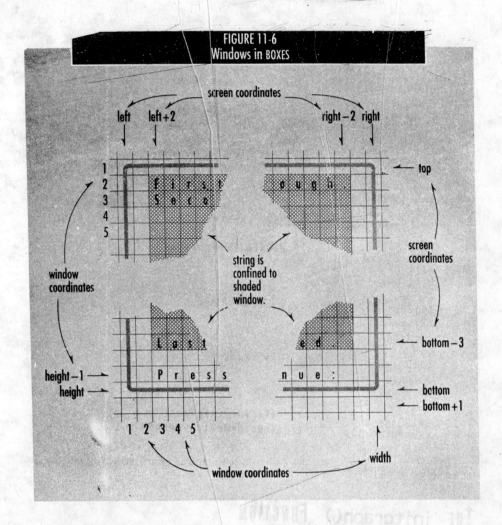

FIGURE 11-6
Windows in BOXES

Here's the listing for EZBALL:

```
// ezball.cpp
// stationary ball class
#include <graphics.h>          // for graphics functions
#include <conio.h>             // for getch()

const int RAD = 75;

class ball                     // ball class
    {
    private:
        int xCo, yCo;          // coordinates of center
```

```
   public:
      ball()                          // no-argument constructor
         { xCo=0; yCo=0; }
      void set(int x, int y)  // set position
         { xCo=x; yCo=y; }
      void draw()                     // draw the ball
         { circle(xCo, yCo, RAD); }
   };

void main()
   {
   int driver, mode;
   driver = DETECT;                   // set to best graphics mode
   initgraph(&driver, &mode, "\\tc\\bgi");

   ball b1;                           // create three balls
   ball b2;
   ball b3;

   b1.set(320, 150);    // position them
   b2.set(255, 150);
   b3.set(385, 150);

   b1.draw();                         // draw them
   b2.draw();
   b3.draw();

   getch();            // wait for keypress
   closegraph();       // close graphics system
   }
```

There are several new graphics functions in this program, so we'll describe the role each one plays.

THE initgraph() FUNCTION

The initgraph() library function must be executed before any other graphics-mode functions can be used. It switches your computer's display system into the appropriate graphics mode. This function—like all the graphics mode functions—requires the GRAPHICS.H header file.

There are two ways to handle the choice of display mode. You can specify it yourself, or you can let the system select it. In the examples in this chapter we'll let the system select the best mode. This is the most versatile approach, since programs written this way will run on systems with different graphics displays. However, we'll first explain how to specify a particular mode.

The Graphics Driver

To specify the mode, you need to choose appropriate values for the parameters to initgraph(). The first argument to initgraph() specifies the graphics *driver* to be used. This is the software routine that interfaces with the display adapter. The most common choices are shown in Table 11-2.

The constants in Table 11-2 represent numerical values and are defined in the GRAPHICS.H file. (Other possibilities are shown in the description of `initgraph()` in the Turbo C++ or Borland C++ documentation.) Ordinarily you choose the constant for the system you're using: `EGA` if you have an EGA display, and so on. However, because the PC's display adapters are backward compatible, you can also select a less powerful mode; if you have a VGA display you can select EGA or CGA mode, for example. This is useful if you want to test a program with other display modes.

The Graphics Mode

The second parameter to `initgraph()` specifies the particular mode. Each adapter can use several possible modes. Table 11-3 shows the choices for CGA, EGA, and VGA:

A *palette* is a set of colors. CGA has four palettes, each representing a different set of four colors. EGA and VGA don't use palettes. The normal mode choice for EGA is EGAHI, which gives the highest resolution. In VGA the normal choice is VGAHI.

As an example, here are the statements you would use to intialize EGAHI mode:

```
int driver = EGA;                              // EGA driver
int mode = EGAHI;                              // EGA hi-res mode
initgraph(&driver, &mode, "\\TC\\BGI");
```

Let the System Decide

If you let the system decide what graphics mode to use, it will check your adapter and choose the driver and mode that give the highest resolution. This is called *auto-detect*. To do this, set the driver argument to the constant `DETECT`. You don't need to specify a mode argument. The example programs show how this is done.

TABLE 11-2 Common display adapters	
Display adapter	Constant for `initgraph()`
CGA	CGA
EGA	EGA
VGA	VGA

TABLE 11-3
Display modes for common adapters

Driver selected	Mode constant	Display mode
CGA	CGAC0	320x200, 4 color, palette 0
	CGAC1	320x200, 4 color, palette 1
	CGAC2	320x200, 4 color, palette 2
	CGAC3	320x200, 4 color, palette 3
	CGAHI	640x200, 2 color
EGA	EGALO	640x200, 16 color
	EGAHI	640x350, 16 color
VGA	VGALO	640x200, 16 color
	VGAMED	640x350, 16 color
	VGAHI	640x480, 16 color

The *Address of* Operator: &

You may have noticed that instead of placing the constants like EGA and EGAHI directly into the function call, we place them in the variables driver and mode, and then use the names of these variables in initgraph(), preceded by a & symbol, as in &driver. What does this do?

It turns out that in C++ the & symbol means *address of*, so we are actually telling initgraph() the addresses where the constants are stored, rather than telling it the constants themselves. This is similar to (but by no means the same as) passing arguments by reference. Understanding addresses is one of the keys to understanding pointers, which we'll cover in Chapter 12. For the moment, don't worry about this syntax. Just set up the constants as shown in the examples, and everything should work properly.

The Path

The third argument to initgraph() is the path to the graphics driver. This argument must be specified whether you use auto-detect or specify a mode yourself. The drivers are supplied as part of Turbo C++ or Borland C++, and are installed in a specific directory. In Turbo C++ this is usually the \TC\BGI directory; in Borland C++ it's \BORLANDC\BGI. The drivers all have the .BGI extension (for Borland Graphics Interface). For CGA the driver is called CGA.BGI, and for EGA and VGA it's EGAVGA.BGI.

You need the path to the driver but not the driver name. Here's how to specify this argument in Turbo C++:

```
"\\tc\\bgi"
```

Either upper- or lowercase can be used. If you have installed the drivers elsewhere, then you'll need to modify the path accordingly.

The pathname is a string, and must be surrounded by quotes in `initgraph()`. Notice that, since the backslash \ is an escape character in C++ strings, you must double it to give it its normal value: \\. Forgetting to do this leads to particularly hard-to-diagnose program bugs.

CREATING STAND-ALONE PROGRAMS

The approach described here, using `initgraph()` to specify the path to the directory that contains the .BGI files, requires the existence of such a directory in the system. Thus programs written with this approach won't run in a system that doesn't already have Turbo C++ installed in it. To create a stand-alone program you need a different approach. This is described in Appendix C.

THE circle() FUNCTION

In `main()` we use `initgraph()` to initialize the graphics system. Then we create three objects of class `ball`, set their locations with the `set()` member function, and display the objects with `draw()`. The `draw()` member function uses the Turbo C++ library function `circle()` to actually draw a circle.

The `circle()` library function takes three integer parameters: the X and Y coordinates of the center of the circle, and the radius of the circle. We use a fixed radius, `RAD`, for all objects of class `ball`. The X and Y coordinates are taken from the private data in `ball`, so the call to `circle()` looks like this:

```
circle(xCo, yCo, RAD);
```

The three invocations of the `ball` constructor in `main()` establish three overlapping balls with centers on the same horizontal line. Figure 11-7 shows the output of EZBALL.

THE closegraph() FUNCTION

When you exit from a graphics program you should restore the system to the video mode that was previously in use—probably a text mode. If you don't, you may experience undesirable effects, such as the loss of the cursor, or off-size characters, as the operating system tries to write text in a graphics mode.

To restore the previous mode, and to release whatever memory the graphics system was using, execute the `closegraph()` library function just before exiting your program.

FIGURE 11-7
Output of EZBALL

COLORS

If you have a color display you can draw lines, circles, and so on in different colors. You can also fill enclosed areas with color. Our next program, COLORBAL, is a variation of the EZBALL program that demonstrates the use of color. Here's the listing:

```
// colorbal.cpp
// adds colors to ball class
#include <graphics.h>          // for graphics functions
#include <conio.h>             // for getch()

const int RAD = 75;

class ball                     // ball class
   {
   private:
      int xCo, yCo;            // coordinates of center
      int linecolor;          // color of outline
      int fillcolor;          // color of interior
   public:
      ball()                   // no-arg constructor
         { xCo=0; yCo=0; linecolor=WHITE; fillcolor=WHITE; }
      void set(int x, int y, int lc, int fc)   // set data
         { xCo=x; yCo=y; linecolor=lc; fillcolor=fc; }
      void draw()              // draw the ball
         {
         setcolor(linecolor);                             // line color
         setlinestyle(SOLID_LINE, 0, THICK_WIDTH); // line width
                                                          // draw circle
         circle(xCo, yCo, RAD);
         setfillstyle(SOLID_FILL, fillcolor);    // set fill color
         floodfill(xCo, yCo, linecolor);         // fill circle
         }
   };
```

```
void main()
    {
    int driver, mode;
    driver = DETECT;                        // set to best graphics mode
    initgraph(&driver, &mode, "\\tc\\bgi");

    ball b1;                                // create three balls
    ball b2;
    ball b3;

    b1.set(100, 150, YELLOW, RED);   // set position and colors
    b2.set(200, 150, YELLOW, GREEN);
    b3.set(300, 150, YELLOW, BLUE);

    b1.draw();                              // draw them
    b2.draw();
    b3.draw();

    getch();                                // wait for keypress
    closegraph();                           // close graphics system
    }
```

The `ball` class in this program now features a four-argument `set()` function. The first two arguments are the center of the circle as before. The third argument specifies the color of the circle's outline, and the fourth specifies the color used to fill the interior of the circle. Figure 11-8 shows the effect. Unfortunately, we can't show the figure in color; instead different kinds of shading are used to indicate the colors.

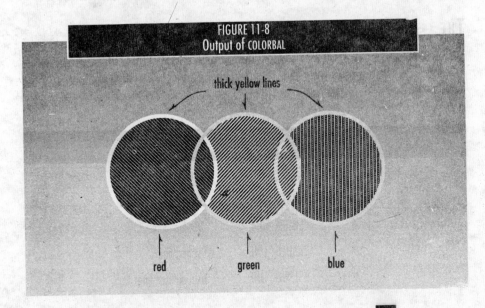

FIGURE 11-8
Output of COLORBAL

thick yellow lines

red   green   blue

The changes to this program lie mostly in the **draw()** member function. Here it is:

```
void draw()
   {
   setcolor(linecolor);
   setlinestyle(SOLID_LINE, 0, THICK_WIDTH);
   circle(xCo, yCo, RAD);
   setfillstyle(SOLID_FILL, fillcolor);
   floodfill(xCo, yCo, linecolor);
   }
```

Let's examine the new Turbo C++ graphics functions used in the **draw()** member function, and see how they generate colors. Note that this program is written for EGA and VGA displays. If you're using CGA or another display adapter you may need to make some adjustments to achieve an equivalent output. See the Turbo or Borland C++ documentation for detailed descriptions of the individual library functions.

THE setcolor() FUNCTION

The **setcolor()** library function sets the color used for drawing lines. The word *lines* here means not only straight lines but also the *outlines* of shapes such as circles and rectangles. The interior of shapes is not affected by **setcolor()**.

In EGA and VGA modes there are 16 colors available to **setcolor()**. These are the same colors that are available for the **textcolor()** library function and are listed in Table 11-1. In the **draw()** member function the **setcolor()** library function uses the **linecolor** member data as its single argument. In **main()** all three balls have their outlines set to YELLOW by the **set()** member function.

THE setlinestyle() FUNCTION

We use the **setlinestyle()** library function to specify thick lines for the circle outlines. The first argument to this function specifies a *style*. This can be one of the constants shown in Table 11-4.

		TABLE 11-4 Line styles
0	SOLID_LINE	Solid line
1	DOTTED_LINE	Dotted line
2	CENTER_LINE	Dot-dash line
3	DASHED_LINE	Dashed line
4	USERBIT_LINE	User-defined line

Unfortunately these styles apply only to straight lines, not to circles, so in our program it doesn't matter what we put as the first argument. The second argument specifies a user-defined style if the first argument is set to `USERBIT_LINE`. We'll ignore this possibility, so we set this argument to 0. The third argument has two possible values, as shown in Table 11-5.

By using THICK_WIDTH we cause wider lines to be drawn for our circle outlines.

THE setfillstyle() Function

Now let's see how to fill the interior of a shape with a specific color. There are two parts to this. First we set the color to be filled, using the `setfillstyle()` library function. This function takes two arguments. The first argument is a pattern, shown in Table 11-6.

	TABLE 11-5 Line widths	
0	NORM_WIDTH	Line 1 pixel wide (default)
3	THICK_WIDTH	Line 3 pixels wide

	TABLE 11-6 Patterns	
0	EMPTY_FILL1	Background color
1	SOLID_FILL	Solid color
2	LINE_FILL	Horizontal lines
3	LTSLASH_FILL	SW-NE light lines
4	SLASH_FILL	SW-NE heavy lines
5	BKSLASH_FILL	NW-SE heavy lines
6	LTBKSLASH_FILL	NW-SE light lines
7	HATCH_FILL	Light cross hatch
8	XHATCH_FILL	Heavy cross hatch
9	INTERLEAVE_FILL	Interleave
10	WIDE_DOT_FILL	Wide-spaced dots
11	CLOSE_DOT_FILL	Close-spaced dots
12	USER_FILL	User-defined

The second argument to `setfillstyle()` is the color. This can be one of the same color constants used for the `setcolor()` library function shown in Table 11-1. We use SOLID_FILL for the pattern, and the color from the `fillcolor` member data in `ball`. In `main()` we choose three different colors for the three balls: RED, GREEN, and BLUE.

THE floodfill() FUNCTION

The `floodfill()` library function fills in the color in the interior of the circle. This function starts the fill at a particular X,Y location inside the object. This location is specified by the first two arguments. The fill, in the color and pattern specified by `setfillstyle()`, expands outward from this point until it reaches a boundary. The color of this boundary is specified in the third parameter to `floodfill()`. Remember that this argument is the boundary color, not the fill color.

Notice in the figure that, since the red ball is drawn and filled first, it is the only one completely filled with a color. The fill for the other two balls stops at the edge of the previously drawn circle. The fill will always stop at the specified boundary color.

You may find that with a CGA display the `floodfill()` library function does not work perfectly. The colors tend to escape from their boundaries and engulf the entire screen. This appears to be a bug in the function.

RECTANGLES AND LINES

The next program is very similar to COLORBAL, except that it models rectangles rather than circles. Each rectangle represented by the `rect` class is filled with color, with a diagonal line across it. Here's the listing for RECTLINE:

```
// rectline.cpp
// rectangle and line
#include <graphics.h>          // for graphics functions
#include <conio.h>             // for getch()

const int W = 75;              // 1/2 width of rectangle

class rect                     // rect class
   {
   private:
      int xCo, yCo;            // coordinates of center
      int linecolor;           // color of outline
      int fillcolor;           // color of interior
   public:
      rect()                   // no-arg constructor
         { xCo=0; yCo=0; linecolor=WHITE; fillcolor=WHITE; }
      void set(int x, int y, int lc, int fc)  // set data
         { xCo=x; yCo=y; linecolor=lc; fillcolor=fc; }
```

```
        void draw()              // draw the rectangle
            {
            setcolor(linecolor);                  // line color
            setlinestyle(SOLID_LINE, 0, THICK_WIDTH); // line width
            rectangle(xCo-W, yCo-W, xCo+W, yCo+W); // draw rectangle
            setfillstyle(SOLID_FILL, fillcolor);  // set fill color
            floodfill(xCo, yCo, linecolor);       // fill rectangle
            line(xCo-W, yCo+W, xCo+W, yCo-W);     // draw diagonal
            }
    };

void main()
    {
    int driver, mode;
    driver = DETECT;            // set to best graphics mode
    initgraph(&driver, &mode, "\\tc\\bgi");

    rect r1;                    // create three rects
    rect r2;
    rect r3;

    r1.set(80, 150, YELLOW, RED);  // set position and colors
    r2.set(250, 150, YELLOW, GREEN);
    r3.set(420, 150, YELLOW, BLUE);

    r1.draw();                  // draw them
    r2.draw();
    r3.draw();

    getch();                    // wait for keypress
    closegraph();               // close graphics system
    }
```

Figure 11-9 shows the output of this program. The new library functions used in RECTLINE are `rectangle()` and `line`.

THE rectangle() FUNCTION

The `rectangle()` library function draws the outline of a rectangle. You specify the edges of the rectangle with four integers, like this:

```
rectangle(left, top, right, bottom);
```

THE line() FUNCTION

The `line()` library function draws a line from one point to another. The first two arguments to the function specify the X and Y coordinates of the line's starting point, and the last two arguments specify the end point:

```
line(x1, y1, x2, y2);
```

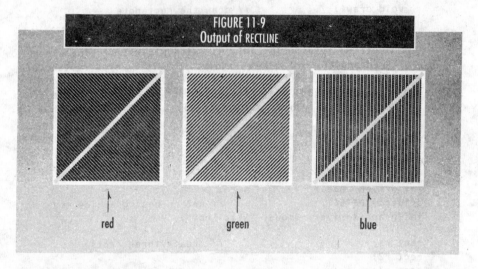

FIGURE 11-9
Output of RECTLINE

red   green   blue

The line can be given a style and thickness with the `setlinestyle()` function described previously.

POLYGONS AND INHERITANCE

The next example uses inheritance to tie together the circular and rectangular shapes generated in the COLORBAL and RECTLINE examples, and a new triangle shape. This program also introduces a new graphics library function, `fillpoly()`, which it uses to create the triangle. Here's the listing for MULTSHAP:

```cpp
// multshap.cpp
// balls, rects, and polygons
#include <graphics.h>          // for graphics functions
#include <conio.h>             // for getch()

const int W = 75;              // size of images

class shape                    // base class
   {
   protected:
      int xCo, yCo;            // coordinates of center
      int linecolor;           // color of outline
      int fillcolor;           // color of interior
   public:
      shape()                  // no-arg constructor
         { xCo=0; yCo=0; linecolor=WHITE; fillcolor=WHITE; }
   void set(int x, int y, int lc, int fc)  // set data
         { xCo=x; yCo=y; linecolor=lc; fillcolor=fc; }
      void draw()
         {
```

```
            setcolor(linecolor);                    // line color
            setlinestyle(SOLID_LINE, 0, THICK_WIDTH); // line width
            setfillstyle(SOLID_FILL, fillcolor);    // set fill color
            }
    };


class ball : public shape
    {
    public:
        ball() : shape()          // no-arg constr
            { }
        void set(int x, int y, int lc, int fc)    // set data
            { shape::set(x, y, lc, fc); }
        void draw()               // draw the ball
            {
            shape::draw();                          // set colors
            circle(xCo, yCo, W);                    // draw circle
            floodfill(xCo, yCo, linecolor);         // fill circle
            }
    };


class rect : public shape
    {
    public:
        rect() : shape()          // no-arg constr
            { }
        void set(int x, int y, int lc, int fc)    // set data
            { shape::set(x, y, lc, fc); }
        void draw()               // draw the rectangle
            {
            shape::draw();                          // set colors
            rectangle(xCo-W, yCo-W, xCo+W, yCo+W); // draw rectangle
            floodfill(xCo, yCo, linecolor);         // fill rectangle
            moveto(xCo-W, yCo+W);                   // draw diagonal
            lineto(xCo+W, yCo-W);                   //     line
            }
    };


class tria : public shape
    {
    public:
        tria() : shape()          // no-arg constr
            { }
        void set(int x, int y, int lc, int fc)    // set data
            { shape::set(x, y, lc, fc); }
        void draw()               // draw the triangle
            {
            int triarray[] = { xCo,   yCo-W,        // top
                               xCo+W, yCo+W,        // bottom right
                               xCo-W, yCo+W };      // bottom left
```

```
            shape::draw();                      // set colors
            fillpoly(3, triarray);              // draw triangle
            }
    };

    void main()
        {
        int driver, mode;
        driver = DETECT;                    // set to best graphics mode
        initgraph(&driver, &mode, "\\tc\\bgi");

        ball b1;                            // create ball
        rect r2;                            // create rectangle
        tria t3;                            // create triangle

        b1.set(80, 150, YELLOW, RED);       // set position and colors
        r2.set(250, 150, YELLOW, GREEN);
        t3.set(420, 150, YELLOW, BLUE);

        b1.draw();                          // draw them
        r2.draw();
        t3.draw();

        getch();                            // wait for keypress
        closegraph();                       // close graphics system
        }
```

THE shape CLASS

If you look at the **ball** class in the COLORBAL example, and at the **rect** class from
RECTLINE, you will see that they have many similarities. They both store the coordinates of the center of the shape and the colors of the shape's outline and interior.
They both have a **set()** member function that supplies values for these data members, and a **draw()** function that draws the shape, although of course the draw functions do different things.

In designing a C++ program we look for common elements of classes. Such
common elements are candidates for a base class, from which the other classes will
be derived. In MULTSHAP we create a base class **shape**, from which revised **ball** and
rect classes are descended. The **shape** class contains the common elements of
ball and **rect**, which we saw in previous examples.

POLYGONS

We've added another class to MULTSHAP, the **tria** class, which models a triangle.
This new class is also derived from **shape**. A triangle is the simplest example of a
polygon—a number of straight-line segments that outline a closed shape. The triangle polygon in MULTSHAP is created using a library function called **fillpoly()**.

This is a somewhat more complex graphics function than those we've seen before. Before it can be used, an array must be created that contains the points that define the polygon. For a polygon with four points, such an array might look like this:

```
int polyarray[] = { x1, y1,  x2, y2,  x3, y3,  x4, y4 };
```

This array could represent the corners of a square, parallelogram, or any other closed figure made of four line segments. This is shown in Figure 11-10.

The `fillpoly()` library function takes two arguments. The first is the number of points specified in the array (not the number of integers!). The second is the address of the array. (Remember that the name of an array, with no brackets, is its address.) Here's a call that uses the array just shown:

```
fillpoly(4, polyarray);
```

The function draws a line from the first point specified to the second point, from the second point to the third, and from the third to the fourth. This creates three of the four line segments for our four-sided figure. Very cleverly, `fillpoly()` then completes the figure by drawing the fourth line segment from the fourth point back to the first. You don't need to specify the first point again at the end of the sequence to make it do this; it's automatic. After that the function fills the figure using the color and pattern set with the `setfillstyle()` library function.

Another Turbo C++ library function, `drawpoly()`, can be used to draw a polygon without filling it.

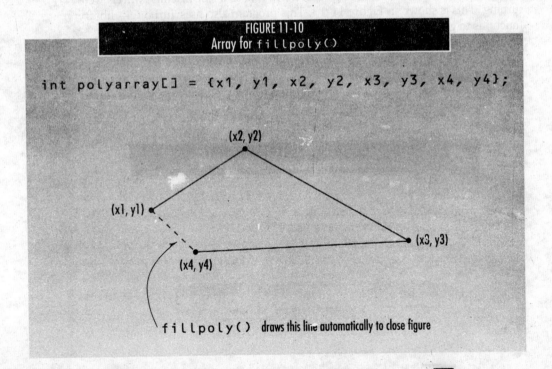

FIGURE 11-10
Array for `fillpoly()`

```
int polyarray[] = {x1, y1, x2, y2, x3, y3, x4, y4};
```

(x2, y2)

(x1, y1)

(x3, y3)

(x4, y4)

`fillpoly()` draws this line automatically to close figure

PROGRAM DESIGN

We created the shape class by extracting the common parts of the ball, rect, and tria classes. However, shape can also be understood as a generalization of balls, rectangles, and triangles. One of the important mental processes engaged in by humans is that of creating a general category from specific cases. We do this naturally; any six-year-old could tell you that circles, squares, and triangles are all shapes. The C++ inheritance mechanism gives us a way to model this kind of abstraction in a computer language.

The shape class concentrates all the features of shapes into one place. As a result, the ball, rect, and tria classes are simpler than before. When we look at them we can see immediately what is unique about them, since the only code and data in them are what is needed to make them different from the generic shape. Figure 11-11 shows the class hierarchy in MULTSHAP.

The main() part of MULTSHAP creates and displays three objects—a red ball, a green rectangle, and a blue triangle. The result is shown in Figure 11-12.

SOUND AND MOTION

Here's a program that uses the approach shown in previous examples to model a slot machine, where colored shapes appear in a window, as if slot-machine wheels were turning. This is shown in Figure 11-13. This program also uses Turbo C++ library functions to generate sound.

When you first start the program, three square windows appear on the screen. One of four different shapes appears randomly in each window: a red circle (representing a cherry), a blue circle (representing a grape), a square, and a pyramid. Each time the shapes appear, a clicking sound is heard. Gradually the shapes appear

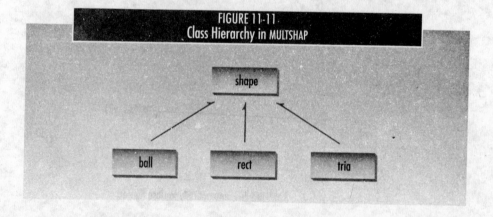

FIGURE 11-11
Class Hierarchy in MULTSHAP

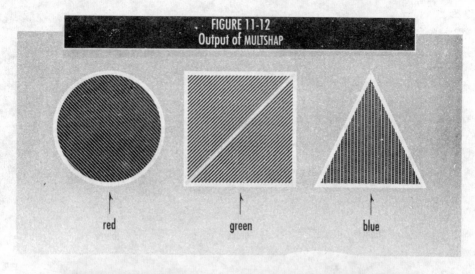

FIGURE 11-12
Output of MULTSHAP

red   green   blue

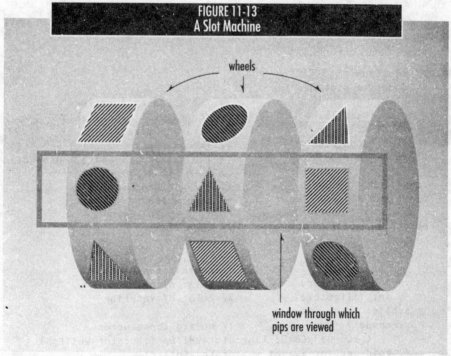

FIGURE 11-13
A Slot Machine

wheels

window through which
pips are viewed

more and more slowly, as if the slot-machine wheels were slowing down. Finally they stop, and the program sounds a two-tone signal. If three cherries are displayed, you win. Figure 11-14 shows a typical display.

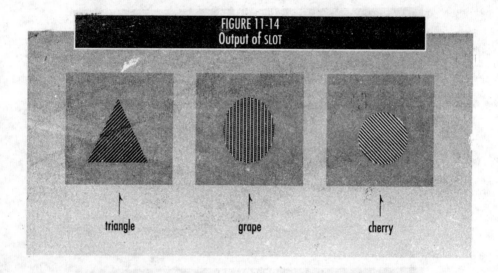

FIGURE 11-14
Output of SLOT

triangle   grape   cherry

Here's the listing for SLOT:

```
// slot.cpp
// models a slot machine
#include <graphics.h>          // for graphics functions
#include <stdlib.h>            // for rand(), randomize()
#include <time.h>              // for randomize()
#include <conio.h>             // for getche()
#include <dos.h>               // for delay(), sound('), nosound()

const int W = 15;              // 1/2 width of images
const int MAR = 10;            // margin around images

class shape                    // base class
   {
   protected:
      int xCo, yCo;            // coordinates of center
      int linecolor;           // color of outline
      int fillcolor;           // color of interior
   public:
      shape()                  // no-arg constructor
         { xCo=0; yCo=0; linecolor=WHITE; fillcolor=WHITE; }
      void set(int x, int y, int lc, int fc)
         { xCo=x; yCo=y; linecolor=lc; fillcolor=fc; }
      void draw()
         {
         setcolor(linecolor);                    // set line color
         setfillstyle(SOLID_FILL, fillcolor);  // set fill color
         }
   };
```

```
class ball : public shape
    {
    public:
        ball() : shape()            // no-arg constructor
        { }
        void set(int x, int y, int lc, int fc)    // set data
        { shape::set(x, y, lc, fc); }
        void draw()                 // draw the ball
        {
        shape::draw();                          // set colors
        circle(xCo, yCo, W);                    // draw circle
        floodfill(xCo, yCo, linecolor);         // fill circle
        }
    };

class rect : public shape
    {
    public:
        rect() : shape()            // no-arg constructor
        { }
        void set(int x, int y, int lc, int fc)    // set data
        { shape::set(x, y, lc, fc); }
        void draw()                 // draw the rectangle
        {
        shape::draw();                          // set colors
        rectangle(xCo-W, yCo-W, xCo+W, yCo+W); // draw rectangle
        floodfill(xCo, yCo, linecolor);         // fill rectangle
        moveto(xCo-W, yCo+W);                   // draw diagonal
        lineto(xCo+W, yCo-W);                   //      line
        }
    };

class tria : public shape
    {
    public:
        tria() : shape()            // no-arg constructor
        { }
        void set(int x, int y, int lc, int fc)    // set data
        { shape::set(x, y, lc, fc); }
        void draw()                 // draw the triangle
        {
        int triarray[] = { xCo,    yCo-W,       // top
                           xCo+W, yCo+W,         // bottom right
                           xCo-W, yCo+W };       // bottom left
        shape::draw();                          // set colors
        fillpoly(3, triarray);                  // draw triangle
        }

    };
class noshape : public shape
    {
```

399

```
public:
    void erase()                    // erase old shape
        {
        int border[] =                      // rectangle to erase
                { xCo-W-MAR, yCo-W-MAR,    // upper-left
                  xCo+W+MAR, yCo-W-MAR,    // upper-right
                  xCo+W+MAR, yCo+W+MAR,    // bottom-right
                  xCo-W-MAR, yCo+W+MAR };  // bottom-left
        setfillstyle(SOLID_FILL, DARKGRAY); // background color
        fillpoly(4, border);              // fill it
        }
    };

class Cherry : public ball, public noshape
    {
    public:
        Cherry() : ball()                // no-arg constructor
            { }
        void set(int x, int y)           // set data
            {
            ball::set(x, y, WHITE, RED);
            noshape::set(x, y, WHITE, RED);
            }
        void draw()                      // draw a cherry
            { erase(); ball::draw(); }
    };

class Grape : public ball, public noshape
    {
    public:
        Grape() : ball()                 // no-arg constructor
            { }
        void set(int x, int y)           // set data
            {
            ball::set(x, y, WHITE, BLUE);
            noshape::set(x, y, WHITE, BLUE);
            }
        void draw()                      // draw a grape
            { erase(); ball::draw(); }
    };

class Square : public rect, public noshape
    {
    public:
        Square() : rect()                // no-arg constructor
            { }
        void set(int x, int y)           // set data
            {
            rect::set(x, y, WHITE, CYAN);
            noshape::set(x, y, WHITE, CYAN);
            }
```

```
        void draw()                              // draw a square
            { erase(); rect::draw(); }
    };


class Pyramid : public tria, public noshape
    {
    public:
        Pyramid() : tria()                       // no-arg constructor
            { }
        void set(int x, int y)                   // set data
            {
            tria::set(x, y, WHITE, GREEN);
            noshape::set(x, y, WHITE, GREEN);
            }
        void draw()                              // draw a pyramid
            { erase(); tria::draw(); }
    };


class Wheel : public shape
    {
    private:
        Cherry ch;    // make one pip of each kind
        Grape gr;
        Square sq;
        Pyramid py;
    public:
        Wheel()                      // no-arg constructor
            { xCo=0; yCo=0; }
        void set(int x, int y)
            {
            xCo=x; yCo=y;                 // set our position
            ch.set(xCo, yCo);             // set four pips to
            gr.set(xCo, yCo);             //     our position
            sq.set(xCo, yCo);
            py.set(xCo, yCo);
            }
        void draw();                      // draw a random pip
    };


void Wheel::draw()                        // draw a random pip
    {
    setcolor(WHITE);                      // draw border
    rectangle(xCo-W-MAR, yCo-W-MAR, xCo+W+MAR, yCo+W+MAR);
    switch( random(4) )                   // random number from 0 to 3
        {
        case 0 : ch.draw(); break;   // draw one of the pips
        case 1 : gr.draw(); break;   // selected randomly
        case 2 : sq.draw(); break;
        case 3 : py.draw(); break;
        }
    }
```

```
void main()
   {
   const int NUMBER = 60;        // number of times to cycle
   int driver, mode;
   driver = DETECT;              // set to best graphics mode
   initgraph(&driver, &mode, "\\tc\\bgi");
   randomize();                  // seed random number generator

   Wheel w1;                     // make three wheels
   Wheel w2;
   Wheel w3;

   w1.set(100, 100);             // position in horizontal row
   w2.set(160, 100);
   w3.set(220, 100);

   for(int j=0; j<NUMBER; j++)   // spin the wheels
      {
      w1.draw();                 // draw each wheel
      w2.draw();
      w3.draw();
      sound(100); delay(20); nosound();  // click
      delay( j*j/20 );           // delay gets longer and longer
      }
   sound(400); delay(400);       // two tones to signal done
   sound(500); delay(800); nosound();
   getche();                     // wait for keypress
   closegraph();                 // close graphics system
   }
```

This is a more complicated program, so we'll examine the overall organization first and then discuss some new functions.

CLASS HIERARCHY IN SLOT

The SLOT program uses the classes from previous programs in this chapter: shape, ball, rect, and tria Our goal is to use these classes with as little modification as possible. This reflects the situation where you have purchased a library of commercial classes, or where you simply want to make use of existing code with a minimum of effort.

SLOT creates four new classes that are shapes with particular colors: Cherry, derived from ball and colored red; Grape, derived from ball and colored blue; Square, derived from rect and colored cyan (greenish blue); and Pyramid, derived from tria and colored green. The set() member functions in these new derived classes simply call the set() functions in their base classes but with these specific colors (the line color is always white).

In addition, the class noshape is introduced to erase shapes. We need to erase each shape before drawing a new one on top of it. Otherwise, the corners of the triangle would still be sticking out when you draw a circle over it. The noshape class contains a single member function, erase(), which erases the area on the screen occupied by the shape.

The classes Cherry, Grape, Square, and Pyramid are derived not only from ball and similar classes but also, through multiple inheritance, from noshape. This gives them the capability to erase themselves. Because noshape needs a place to store coordinates, just as the other shapes do, it is derived from the shape class, although it is not exactly a shape in the same sense the other classes are.

Finally a class Wheel represents one wheel of a slot machine. Since Wheel also needs to know where it is, it is descended from shape so it can make use of its xCo and yCo data members.

Figure 11-15 shows the relationship of the different classes in SLOT.

OPERATION OF SLOT

The main() function creates three objects of type Wheel. Using the set() member function, it positions them in a row in the upper left of the screen. Then, in a for loop, it repeatedly draws and redraws the wheels.

The Wheel class contains one each of the four different kinds of pips: Cherry, Grape, Square, and Pyramid. Wheel creates these four pips as data elements in its private section; they're called ch, gr, sq, and py. (Notice that although Wheel

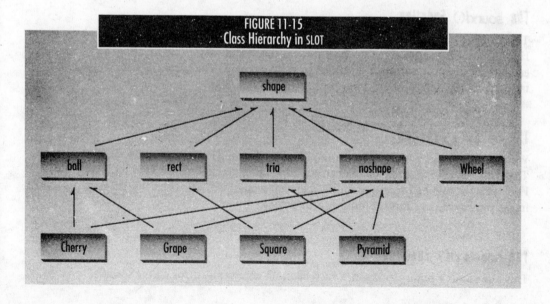

FIGURE 11-15
Class Hierarchy in SLOT

contains instances of these other classes, this relationship is not shown in the hier-archy diagram, which deals with inheritance, not containership.) The `set()` member function in `Wheel` specifies the wheel's position and sets all the pips to the same position. A `draw()` member function draws a border around the pip's location and then draws one of the pips, selecting which pip to draw based on a random num-ber. Thus the image drawn by each wheel changes randomly from one pip to an-other each time that wheel's `draw()` function is called.

Each time all three wheels are redrawn, the program generates a clicking sound and then delays for a fixed amount of time. The delay grows longer each time through the loop. This gives the illusion that the wheels are rotating—rapidly at first, and then slower and slower, until they stop.

THE SOUND GENERATION FUNCTIONS

Sound generation in C++ requires three steps: (1) turning the sound on, (2) delay-ing for an appropriate amount of time, and (3) turning the sound off again. To make the click after redrawing the wheels, the following line is used:

```
sound(100); delay(20); nosound();
```

All three of the Turbo C++ library functions in this line require the DOS.H header file.

The sound() Function

The `sound()` library function sets the sound generator to a specific frequency in Hertz, supplied as an argument, and turns on the sound. Once this function is ex-ecuted, the sound remains on until specifically stopped. The value 100 shown is fairly low; you can use values from about 15 to about 3000.

The delay() Function

We use the `delay()` library function to control how long the sound will continue. This function takes a single parameter: the time in milliseconds the sound will last. For a delay of one-half second, for example, you would use 500. The value 20 used in the program is so short it produces only a click.

The nosound() Function

This `nosound()` library function, which takes no arguments, turns off the sound.

THINKING ABOUT CLASSES

The SLOT program starts to show some of the organizational power of object-oriented programming. Starting with simple classes, we use inheritance to create more complex classes. Multiple inheritance gives even more flexibility.

The relationships among the different parts of the program are—once you get used to them, anyway—more intuitive than those in a traditional procedural program. In C++ these relationships are among classes, while in a procedural program they are among functions. Classes are often better than functions at modeling objects in the real world (or on the screen), and inheritance corresponds, more closely than functions, to something we do every day: create a more general concept from a number of specific instances.

TEXT IN GRAPHICS MODE

Creating text is far more flexibile in graphics mode than it is in character mode. You can use different fonts (character designs), change the size and proportions of the characters, print vertically as well as horizontally, and in general exercise far more control over the appearance of the finished text.

Our example program demonstrates these capabilities, and also uses objects to represent graphics strings. These strings are somewhat similar to the string objects seen in previous examples, except that they include a variety of graphics characteristics.

A GRAPHICS STRING CLASS

The example, GRAST (GRAphics STring), uses a single class of type `Gstring`. This class contains private data that specifies the graphical characteristics of the string. This includes the contents of the string, its starting point, the font in which it's displayed, its direction (vertical or horizontal), the character size and color, how the text is justified (positioned relative to its starting point), and the proportions of the characters (tall and thin, short and wide, and so on).

All these characteristics have default values, set by a no-argument constructor when an object of class `Gstring` is defined. The values can be modified using member functions. You modify only as many values as you need to. The simplest is to use all the defaults and specify only the string itself.

Here's the listing for GRAST:

```
// grast.cpp
// string class for graphics modes
#include <graphics.h>          // for graphics functions
#include <conio.h>             // for getch()
#include <string.h>            // for strcpy()

class Gstring                  // graphics string class
   {
   protected:
      char str[80];            // string to store text
      int xCo, yCo;            // coordinates of text
      int font;                // DEFAULT_FONT, TRIPLEX_FONT, etc.
      int direction;           // HORIZ_DIR or VERT_DIR
      int size;                // 1, 2, 3, etc.
      int color;               // BLUE, RED, etc.
      int horzjustify;         // LEFT_TEXT, etc.
      int vertjustify;         // BOTTOM_TEXT, etc.
      int multx, divx;         // horizontal scale factors
      int multy, divy;         // vertical scale factors
   public:
      Gstring()                // no-arg constructor
         {                     // set to default values
         str[0] = '\0';        // empty string
         xCo = 0; yCo = 0;     // position
         font = DEFAULT_FONT;  // font
         direction = HORIZ_DIR;   // horizontal or vertical
         size = 4;             // character size
         color = WHITE;        // character color
         horzjustify = LEFT_TEXT; // horizontal positioning
         vertjustify = TOP_TEXT;  // vertical positioning
         multx = 1; divx = 1;  // horizontal scale factors
         multy = 1; divy = 1;  // vertical scale factors
         }
      void DrawText()          // draw the text
         {
         moveto(xCo, yCo);
         settextstyle(font, direction, size);
         setcolor(color);
         settextjustify(horzjustify, vertjustify);
         setusercharsize(multx, divx, multy, divy);
         outtext(str);
         }
      void SetText(char s[])   // set text string
         { strcpy(str, s); }
      void SetPosition(int x, int y)  // set position
         { xCo=x; yCo=y; }
      void SetFont(int f)      // set font
```

```
          { font = f; }
      void SetDirection(int d)  // set direction
          { direction = d; }
      void SetSize(int s)       // set size
          { size = s; }
      void SetColor(int c)      // set color
          { color = c; }
      void SetHJust(int hj)     // set horizontal justification
          { horzjustify = hj; }
      void SetVJust(int vj)     // set vertical justification
          { vertjustify = vj; }
      void SetHorzSize(int m, int d)  // set horiz proportions
          { size=0; multx=m; divx=d; };
      void SetVertSize(int m, int d)  // set vertical proportions
          { size=0; multy=m; divy=d; };
   };

void main()
   {
   int driver, mode;
   driver = DETECT;                         // use best graphics mode
   initgraph(&driver, &mode, "\\tc\\bgi");

   Gstring s1, s2, s3, s4, s5, s6;    // make some strings

   s1.SetText("Default everything");   // all defaults

   s2.SetText("Gothic Font");          // gothic font
   s2.SetFont(GOTHIC_FONT);
   s2.SetPosition(0, 75);

   s3.SetText("Vertical Sans Serif");  // vertical
   s3.SetFont(SANS_SERIF_FONT);
   s3.SetPosition(600, 0);
   s3.SetDirection(VERT_DIR);

   s4.SetText("Centered Triplex");        // centered
   s4.SetFont(TRIPLEX_FONT);
   s4.SetPosition(300, 150);
   s4.SetHJust(CENTER_TEXT);

   s5.SetText("Centered Sans Serif");  // centered
   s5.SetFont(SANS_SERIF_FONT);
   s5.SetSize(6);
   s5.SetPosition(300, 225);
   s5.SetHJust(CENTER_TEXT);

   s6.SetText("Tall and narrow Triplex");  // change proportions
   s6.SetFont(TRIPLEX_FONT);
```

```
        s6.SetPosition(0, 300);
        s6.SetHorzSize(2, 3);          // two-thirds as wide
        s6.SetVertSize(4, 1);          // four times as high

        s1.DrawText();                 // display all
        s2.DrawText();                 // the Gstrings
        s3.DrawText();
        s4.DrawText();
        s5.DrawText();
        s6.DrawText();

        getch();                       // wait for keypress
        closegraph();                  // close graphics system
        }
```

In the **main()** function we create six objects of class **Gstring** (for Graphics string). The first string is printed with all the defaults set. The second uses a Gothic font instead of the default font. The third is displayed vertically, and the fourth and fifth are centered about their starting points. In the sixth the proportions of the characters are changed.

When the characteristics of the six graphics strings have been specified, they are all displayed. Figure 11-16 shows the result.

TURBO C++ GRAPHICS TEXT FUNCTIONS

The **DrawText()** member function in **Gstring** displays the text. This function uses a variety of Turbo C++ library functions to change the characteristics of the text to be displayed. Let's examine these library functions.

The moveto() Function

Turbo C++ uses an imaginary point on the screen called the *current position*, or CP, to act as the starting point for text display. The library function **moveto()** sets the location of the CP, using two **int** arguments to indicate the X and Y coordinates. Text is normally displayed with the CP in the upper-left corner (although this can be modified, as we'll see in a moment).

The settextstyle() Function

The **settextstyle()** library function modifies three different characteristics of the text: the font, the direction, and the character size. These are specified as three integer arguments.

The current versions of Turbo C++ and Borland C++ have five possible fonts, which can be specified by constants defined in GRAPHICS.H. These constants are shown in Table 11-7.

To use these fonts you must ensure that appropriate font files are available in the directory specified in the path argument to **initgraph()**. This path is normally \TC\BGI in Turbo C++ and \BORLANDC\BGI in Borland C++. The files all have the .CHR

FIGURE 11-16
Output of GRAST

TABLE 11-7 Fonts	
Constant	**Type of font**
DEFAULT_FONT	Bitmapped font, "computer look"
TRIPLEX_FONT	Serif font, like Times Roman
SMALL_FONT	Best for small text
SANS_SERIF_FONT	Sans serif font, like Helvetica
GOTHIC_FONT	Gothic font, old English style

(for *character*) extension. TRIP.CHR contains descriptions of the Triplex font, SANS.CHR describes the Sans Serif font, and so on.

We noted earlier that the .BGI files you use must be in your system, in a directory specified in the `initigraph()` function. The same is true of the .CHR files needed to use text in graphics. To create a stand-alone program that will run without these external directories, see Appendix C.

409

The second argument to `settextstyle` has one of two values: HORIZ_DIR or VERT_DIR. Vertically oriented text runs from the bottom of the screen up, rather than from left to right.

The third argument specifies the character size. A value of 1 gives the smallest characters. Size 2 gives characters twice as big, 3 makes them three times as big, and so on.

The settextjustify() Function

The `settextjustify()` library function specifies where the text will be displayed relative to the CP. There are two arguments—one specifying the horizontal position and the other the vertical position, as shown in Tables 11-8 and 11-9.

As we noted, the default is for the CP to be in the upper-left corner. Figure 11-17 shows the possibilities.

The setusercharsize() Function

The `setusercharsize()` library function changes the proportions of the characters by independently changing their width and height. For this function to be effective, the size argument to `settextstyle()` must be set to 0. This automatically gives the fonts a size of 4. The `setusercharsize()` library function then modifies this size.

This function takes four arguments. The first two represent the numerator and denominator of a fraction that modifies the width. The normal width of the character is multiplied by the fraction. Thus if the first two arguments are 5 and 2, the new character width will be 5/2 times 4, or 10. The third and fourth arguments operate similarly on the character height.

TABLE 11-8 Horizontal justification (first argument)	
LEFT_TEXT	CP on left end of text (default)
CENTER_TEXT	CP in horizontal center of text
RIGHT_TEXT	CP on right end of text

TABLE 11-9 Vertical justification (second argument)	
TOP_TEXT	CP on top of text (default)
CENTER_TEXT	CP in vertical center of text
BOTTOM_TEXT	CP on bottom of text

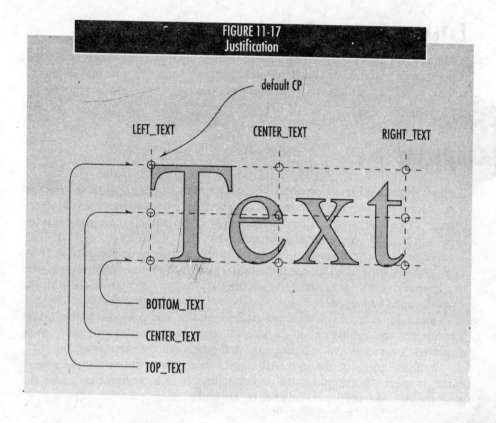

FIGURE 11-17
Justification

The outtext() Function

Graphics text is displayed with the `outtext()` library function. This function takes as its single argument the string to be displayed. Other text-output library functions, such as `cout` and `<<`, don't work in graphics modes.

REDEFINING A FUNCTION SET

Notice that the effect of using the `Gstring` class is to redefine the set of functions used to specify the text characteristics. For instance, Turbo C++ uses a single library function, `settextstyle()`, to specify the font, direction, and size, while the `Gstring` class uses three separate member functions—`SetFont()`, `SetDirection()`, and `SetSize()`. Which approach you use is a matter of taste, but it's nice to know you can redefine an existing set of functions if you don't like their syntax.

EXTENDING THE Gstring CLASS

The Gstring class could be extended to include such features as overloading the + operator to perform concatenation (described in Chapter 9). This and similar additions could provide a powerful and versatile class for use in graphics programs.

SUMMARY

Turbo C++ has two kinds of functions loosely called graphics functions. The first kind works only with text displays and is concerned with displaying text in a rectangular area of the screen called a window. The key function in this mode is window(), which defines the rectangular area.

The second kind of graphics function requires a graphics display such as CGA, EGA, or VGA. Programs that use these functions must initialize the display system to a graphics mode using the initgraph() function, and terminate with the closegraph() function.

Library functions can write lines, circles, squares, and polygons to the screen, use different line widths, and fill shapes with color. Text in a variety of fonts can be displayed, and its size, color, positioning, and aspect ratio can be manipulated.

Graphics objects on the screen can have a close relationship with C++ objects in the program. This simplifies the conceptualization of a program and allows the generalization of common characteristics into a base class.

QUESTIONS

1. Using Turbo C++ library functions you can
   a. color any closed figure
   b. draw lines and circles
   c. write text in a variety of fonts and sizes
   d. make sounds of different pitches
2. The key function that confines character-mode text inside a window on the screen is _____.
3. True or false: A program that uses text-mode functions like cputs() must start with the initgraph() function.
4. Write the code to initialize the graphics system to a VGA adapter in VGAHI mode.
5. With a VGA adapter, in text mode, you can display up to _____ colors.

6. True or false: A graphics program must ordinarily run in the Turbo C++ (or Borland C++) development environment.

7. The pathname supplied to `initgraph()` must
   a. be used unless autodetect is specified
   b. be surrounded by quotes
   c. specify the desired .BGI file
   d. use double backslashes to separate directories

8. Write a statement that draws a circle centered at (99,44), with a radius of 13.

9. True or false: The `setcolor()` function determines what color will be displayed by the `rect()` function.

10. Write the code necessary to draw a line from (2,7) to (5,11).

11. The `setfillstyle` function is used to specify
    a. the width of a line
    b. the color of a polygon
    c. the pattern of a square
    d. the position of a circle

12. Write a statement that will cause all straight lines to be written in dot-dash, dot-dash style with normal width.

13. In graphics programs, C++ objects correspond nicely to
    a. relationships
    b. shapes
    c. functions
    d. programs

14. Write the code to draw a triangle with points (0,10), (5,0), (10,10).

15. A base class will often
    a. model more specific objects than its derived classes
    b. correspond to something in the real world
    c. behave badly when the chips are down
    d. be a generalized version of its derived classes

16. Write the code to create a two-second beep at 1000 Hertz.

17. The random-number generator should be seeded so that it doesn't always _____.

18. In the SLOT program, multiple inheritance is used to add to an object the ability to _____ itself.

19. To display text in the gothic font, you would use
    a. `drawtext()`
    b. `cputs()`
    c. `outtext()`
    d. `cout`

20. The point on a graphics screen where the next pixel will be drawn is called the _____.

EXERCISES

1. Modify the **ball** class in the EZBALL program in this chapter so that the size of the ball is an instance variable rather than a constant. You can call this data member **rad**. Change the **set()** member function to accept a value for the radius, and the **draw()** function so that it uses **rad** to draw a circle with any radius. Change the **main()** program so that each ball object is set to a different radius as well as to a different position.

2. Modify the **shape** class from the MULTSHAP program in this chapter so that the size of an object is variable rather than constant. Use both **width** and **height** as member data items so that the shape as well as the size of the shape can be specified.

    Change the **set()** function to accept the width and height as arguments, along with the position. Modify the **set()** member function in the **ball** and **rect** classes so that it passes the width and height values along to **shape::set()**. (You can delete the **tria** class.) Modify the **draw()** member functions in **ball** and **rect** so that they use the width and height data (one or the other is enough for **ball**).

    Modify the **main()** program to draw a car, using a rectangle for the lower part of the car, another rectangle for the windows area, and two **ball** objects for the wheels.

3. To the program in Exercise 2, add a class called **car** that models the car image that was created from four separate objects in **main()** in Exercise 2. The **car** class should make cars the same size and color but allow different positions. In **main()** create three **car** objects, set them to different positions with **set()**, and display them with **draw()**.

POINTERS

Pointers are the hobgoblin of C++ (and C) programming; seldom has such a simple idea inspired so much perplexity for so many. But fear not. In this chapter we will try to demystify pointers and show practical uses for them in C++ programming.

What are pointers for? Here are some common uses:

- Accessing array elements
- Passing arguments to a function when the function needs to modify the original argument
- Passing arrays and strings to functions
- Obtaining memory from the system
- Creating data structures such as linked lists

Pointers are much more commonly used in C++ (and C) than in many other languages (such as BASIC and Pascal). Is this emphasis on pointers really necessary? You can do a lot without them, as their absence from the preceding chapters demonstrates. Some operations that use pointers in C++ can be carried out in other ways. For example, array elements can be accessed with array notation rather than pointer notation (we'll see the difference soon), and a function can modify arguments passed by reference, as well as those passed by pointer.

However, in some situations pointers provide an essential tool for increasing the power of C++. A notable example is the creation of data structures such as linked lists and binary trees. In fact, several key features of C++, such as virtual functions and the this pointer (to be discussed in the next chapter), require the use of pointers. So, although you can do a lot of programming in C++ without using pointers, you will find them essential to obtaining the most from the language.

In this chapter we'll introduce pointers gradually, starting with fundamental concepts and working up to complex pointer applications.

If you already know C, you can probably skim over the first half of the chapter. However, you should read the sections in the second half on the new and delete operators, accessing member functions using pointers, arrays of pointers to objects, and linked-list objects.

Addresses and Pointers

The ideas behind pointers are not complicated. Here's the first key concept: Every byte in the computer's memory has an *address*. Addresses are numbers, just as they are for houses on a street. The numbers start at 0 and go up from there—1, 2, 3, and so on. If you have 640K of memory, the highest address is 655,359; for 1 MB of memory, it is 1,048,575.

Your program, when it is loaded into memory, occupies a certain range of these addresses. That means that every variable and every function in your program starts at a particular address. Figure 12-1 shows how this looks.

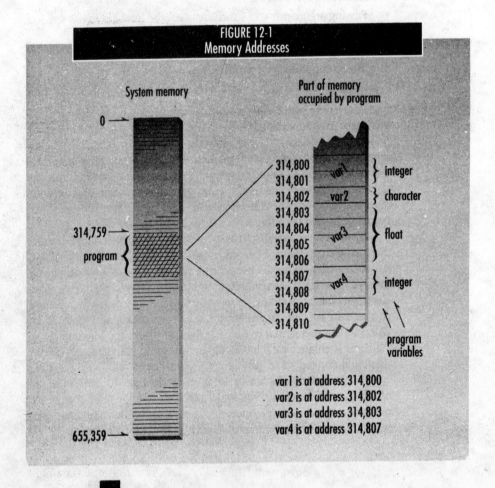

FIGURE 12-1
Memory Addresses

var1 is at address 314,800
var2 is at address 314,802
var3 is at address 314,803
var4 is at address 314,807

THE ADDRESS OF OPERATOR &

You can find out the address occupied by a variable by using the *address of* operator &. Here's a short program, VARADDR, that demonstrates how to do this:

```
// varaddr.cpp
// addresses of variables
#include <iostream.h>

void main()
    {
    int var1 = 11;              // define and initialize
    int var2 = 22;              // three variables
    int var3 = 33·

    cout << endl << &var1       // print out the addresses
         << endl << &var2       // of these variables
         << endl << &var3;
    }
```

This simple program defines three integer variables and initializes them to the values 11, 22, and 33. It then prints out the addresses of these variables.

The actual addresses occupied by the variables in a program depend on many factors, such as the computer the program is running on, the size of the operating system, and whether any other programs are currently in memory. For these reasons you probably won't get the same addresses we did when you run this program. Here's the output on our machine:

```
0x8f4ffff4        ←————————address of var1
0x8f4ffff2        ←————————address of var2
0x8f4ffff0        ←————————address of var3
```

Remember that the *address* of a variable is not at all the same as its *contents*. The contents of the three variables are 11, 22, and 33. Figure 12-2 shows the three variables in memory.

The << insertion operator interprets the addresses in hexadecimal arithmetic, as indicated by the prefix 0x before each number. This is the usual way to show memory addresses. If you aren't familiar with the hexadecimal number system, don't worry. All you really need to know is that each variable starts at a unique address. However, you might note in the output above that each address differs from the next by exactly two bytes. That's because integers occupy two bytes of memory. If we had used variables of type **char** they would have adjacent addresses, since **char**s occupy one byte; and if we had used type **double** the addresses would have differed by eight bytes.

The addresses appear in descending order because automatic variables are stored on the stack, which grows downward in memory. If we had used external variables they would have ascending addresses, since external variables are stored on the heap, which grows upward. Again, you don't need to worry too much about these considerations, since the compiler keeps track of the details for you.

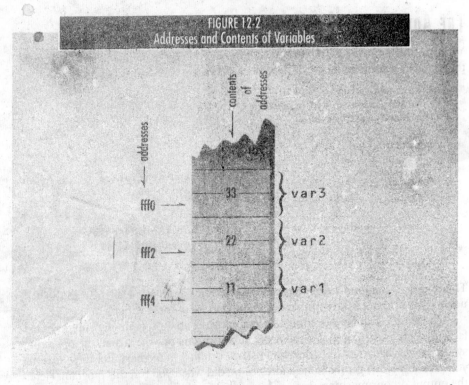

FIGURE 12-2
Addresses and Contents of Variables

Don't confuse the address of operator &, which precedes a variable name, with the reference operator &, which follows the variable name. (References were discussed in Chapter 6.)

POINTER VARIABLES

Addresses by themselves are rather limited. It's nice to know that we can find out where things are in memory, as we did in VARADDR, but printing out address values is not all that useful. The potential for increasing our programming power requires an additional idea: *variables that hold address values*. We've seen variable types that store characters, integers, floating-point numbers, and so on: Addresses are stored similarly. A variable that holds an address value is called a *pointer variable*, or simply a *pointer*.

What is the data type of pointer variables? It's not the same as the variable whose address is being stored; a pointer to int is not type int. You might think a pointer data type would be called something like pointer or ptr. However, things are slightly more complicated. The next program, PTRVAR, shows the syntax for pointer variables:

```
// ptrvar.cpp
// pointers (address variables)
#include <iostream.h>

void main()
{
```

```
int var1 = 11;              / two integer variables
int var2 = 22;

cout << endl << &var1       // print addresses of variables
     << endl << &var2;

int* ptr;                   // pointer to integers

ptr = &var1;                // pointer points to var1
cout << endl << ptr;        // print pointer value

ptr = &var2;                // pointer points to var2
cout << endl << ptr;        // print pointer value
}
```

This program defines two integer variables, var1 and var2, and initializes them to the values 11 and 22. It then prints out their addresses.

The program next defines a *pointer variable* in the line

```
int* ptr;
```

To the uninitiated this is a rather bizarre syntax. The asterisk means *pointer to*. Thus the statement defines the variable ptr as a *pointer to* int. This is another way of saying that this variable can hold the addresses of integer variables.

What's wrong with the idea of a general-purpose pointer type that holds pointers to any data type? If we called it type pointer we could write declarations like

```
pointer ptr;
```

The problem is that the compiler needs to know what kind of variable the pointer points to. (We'll see why when we talk about pointers and arrays.) The syntax used in C++ allows pointers to any type to be declared

```
char* cptr;         // pointer to char
int* iptr;          // pointer to int
float* fptr;        // pointer to float
Distance* distptr;  // pointer to user-defined Distance class
```

and so on.

Syntax Quibbles

We should note that it is common to write pointer definitions with the asterisk closer to the variable name than to the type:

```
char *charptr;
```

It doesn't matter to the compiler, but placing the asterisk next to the type helps to emphasize that the asterisk is part of the variable type (pointer to char), not part of the name itself.

If you define more than one pointer of the same type on one line, you need only insert the type-pointed-to once, but you need to place an asterisk before each variable name:

```
char* ptr1, * ptr2, * ptr3;   // three variables of type char*
```

Or you can use the asterisk-next-to-the-name approach:

```
char *ptr1, *ptr2, *ptr3;   // three variables of type char*
```

Pointers Must Have a Value

An address like 0x8f4ffff4 can be thought of as a *pointer constant*. A pointer like ptr can be thought of as a *pointer variable*. Just as the integer variable var1 can be assigned the constant value 11, so can the pointer variable ptr be assigned the constant value 0x8f4ffff4.

When we first define a variable, it holds no value (unless we initialize it at the same time). It may hold a garbage value, but this has no meaning. In the case of pointers, a garbage value is the address of something in memory, but probably not of something that we want. So before a pointer is used, a specific address must be placed in it. In the PTRVAR program ptr is first assigned the address of var1 in the line

```
ptr = &var1;          ←——————— put address of var1 in ptr
```

Following this the program prints out the value contained in ptr, which should be the same address printed for &var1. The same pointer variable ptr is then assigned the address of var2, and this value is printed out. Figure 12-3 shows the operation of the PTRVAR program. Here's the output of PTRVAR:

```
0x8f51fff4          ←——————— address of var1
0x8f51fff2          ←——————— address of var2
0x8f51fff4          ←——————— ptr set to address of var1
0x8f51fff2          ←——————— ptr set to address of var2
```

To summarize: A pointer can hold the address of any variable of the correct type; it's a receptacle awaiting an address. However, it must be given *some* value, otherwise it will point to an address we don't want it to point to, such as into our program code or the operating system. Rogue pointer values can result in system crashes and are difficult to debug, since the compiler gives no warning. The moral: Make sure you give every pointer variable a valid address value before using it.

ACCESSING THE VARIABLE POINTED TO

Suppose that we don't know the name of a variable but we do know its address. Can we access the contents of the variable? (It may seem like mismanagement to lose track of variable names, but we'll soon see that there are many variables whose names we don't know.)

The answer is that there is a special syntax to access the value of a variable using its address instead of its name. Here's an example program, PTRACC, that shows how it's done:

```
// ptracc.cpp
// accessing the variable pointed to
#include <iostream.h>

void main()
    {
```

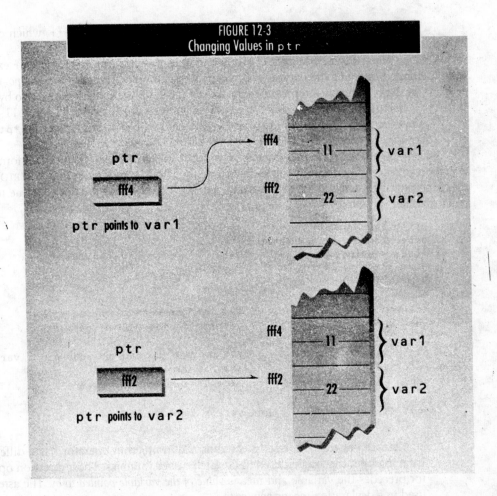

FIGURE 12-3
Changing Values in ptr

```
int var1 = 11;              // two integer variables
int var2 = 22;

int* ptr;                  // pointer to integers

ptr = &var1;               // pointer points to var1
cout << endl << *ptr;      // print contents of pointer (11)

ptr = &var2;               // pointer points to var2
cout << endl << *ptr;      // print contents of pointer (22)
}
```

This program is very similar to PTRVAR, except that instead of printing the address values in **ptr**, we print the integer value stored at the address that's stored in **ptr**. Here's the output:

```
11
22
```

The expression that accesses the variables `var1` and `var2` is `*ptr`, which occurs in each of the two `cout` statements.

When an asterisk is used in front of a variable name, as it is in the `*ptr` expression, it is called the *indirection operator*. It means *the value of the variable pointed to by*. Thus the expression `*ptr` represents the value of the variable pointed to by `ptr`. When `ptr` is set to the address of `var1`, the expression `*ptr` has the value 11, since `var1` is 11. When `ptr` is changed to the address of `var2`, the expression `*ptr` acquires the value 22, since `var1` is 22. Figure 12-4 shows how this looks.

You can use a pointer not only to display a variable's value but to perform any operation you would perform on the variable directly. Here's a program, PTRTO, that uses a pointer to assign a value to a variable, and then to assign that value to another variable:

```
// ptrto.cpp
// other access using pointers
#include <iostream.h>

void main()
    {
    int var1, var2;          // two integer variables
    int* ptr;                // pointer to integers

    ptr = &var1;             // set pointer to address of var1
    *ptr = 37;               // same as var1=37
    var2 = *ptr;             // same as var2=var1

    cout << endl << var2;    // verify var2 is 37
    }
```

Remember that the asterisk used as the indirection operator has a different meaning from the asterisk used to declare pointer variables. The indirection operator precedes the variable and means *value of the variable pointed to by*. The asterisk used in a declaration means *pointer to*.

```
int* ptr;     // declaration:
*ptr = 37;    // indirection:
```

Using the indirection operator to access the value stored in an address is called *indirect addressing*, or sometimes *dereferencing*, the pointer.

Here's a capsule summary of what we've learned so far:

```
int v;        // defines variable v of type int
int* p;       // defines p as a pointer to int
p = &v;       // assigns address of variable v to pointer p
v = 3;        // assigns 3 to v
*p = 3;       // also assigns 3 to v
```

The last two statements show the difference between normal or direct addressing, where we refer to a variable by name, and pointer or indirect addressing, where we refer to the same variable using its address.

424

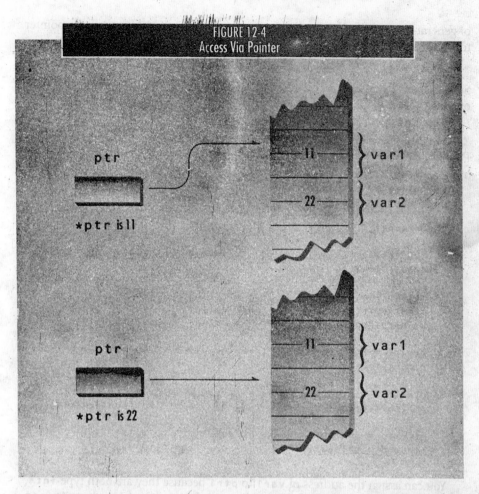

FIGURE 12-4
Access Via Pointer

These two approaches are vaguely analogous to delivering a letter to a friend. If you drive to the friend's house and stick the letter in the mailslot, that's direct addressing. You can also write the address on the envelope and put the letter in a public mailbox. The mail personnel will read the address and see that the letter gets to the right place. That's indirect addressing.

In the example programs we've shown so far in this chapter, there's really no advantage to using the pointer expression to access variables, since we can access them directly. Pointers come into their own when you can't access a variable directly, as we'll see.

POINTER TO void

Before we go on to see pointers at work, we should note one peculiarity of pointer data types. Ordinarily, the address that you put in a pointer must be the same type as the pointer. You can't assign the address of a float variable to a pointer to int, for example. However, there is an exception to this. There is a sort of general-purpose pointer that can point to any data type. This is called a pointer to void, and is defined like this:

```
void* ptr;    // ptr can point to any data type
```

Such pointers have certain specialized uses, such as passing pointers to functions that operate independently of the data type pointed to.

The next example uses a pointer to void and also shows that, if you don't use void, you must be careful to assign pointers an address of the same type as the pointer. Here's the listing for PTRVOID:

```
// ptrvoid.cpp
// pointers to type void
#include <iostream.h>

void main()
   {
   int intvar;                // integer variable
   float flovar;              // float variable

   int* ptrint;               // define pointer to int
   float* ptrflo;             // define pointer to float
   void* ptrvoid;             // define pointer to void

   ptrint = &intvar;          // ok, int* to int*
// ptrint = &flovar;          // error, float* to int*

// ptrflo = &intvar;          // error, int* to float*
   ptrflo = &flovar;          // ok, float* to float*

   ptrvoid = &intvar;         // ok, int* to void*
   ptrvoid = &flovar;         // ok, float* to void*
   }
```

You can assign the address of var1 to ptr1 because they are both type int*, but you can't assign the address of var2 to ptr1 because the first is type float* and the second is type int*. However, ptr3 can be given any pointer value, such as int*, because it is a pointer to void.

POINTERS AND ARRAYS

There is a close association between pointers and arrays. We saw in Chapter 8 how array elements are accessed. The following program, ARRNOTE, provides a review:

```
// arrnote.cpp
// array accessed with array notation
#include <iostream.h>

void main()
   {
```

```
int intarray[5] = { 31, 54, 77, 52, 93 };  // array

for(int j=0; j<5; j++)                      // for each element
    cout << endl << intarray[j];            // print value
}
```

The `cout` statement prints each array element in turn. For instance, when j is 3, the expression `intarray[j]` takes on the value `intarray[3]` and accesses the fourth array element, the integer 52. Here's the output of ARRNOTE:

```
31
54
77
52
93
```

Surprisingly, array elements can be accessed using pointer notation as well as array notation. The next example, PTRNOTE, is similar to ARRNOTE except that it uses pointer notation:

```
// ptrnote.cpp
// array accessed with pointer notation
#include <iostream.h>

void main()
{
    int intarray[5] = { 31, 54, 77, 52, 93 };  // array

    for(int j=0; j<5; j++)                      // for each element,
        cout << endl << *(intarray+j);          // print value
}
```

The expression `*(intarray+j)` in PTRNOTE has exactly the same effect as `intarray[j]` in ARRNOTE, and the output of the programs is identical. But how do we interpret the expression `*(intarray+j)`? Suppose j is 3, so the expression is equivalent to `*(intarray+3)` We want this to represent the contents of the fourth element of the array (52). Remember that the name of an array is its address. The expression `intarray+j` is thus an address with something added to it. You might expect that `interray+3` would cause three bytes to be added to `intarray`. But that doesn't produce the result we want: `intarray` is an array of integers, and 3 bytes into this array is the middle of the second element, which is not very useful. We want to obtain the fourth *integer* in the array, not the fourth byte, as shown in Figure 12-5.

The C++ compiler is smart enough to take the size of the data into account when it performs arithmetic on data addresses. It knows that `intarray` is an array of type `int` because it was declared that way. So when it sees the expression `intarray+3` it interprets it as the address of the fourth *integer* in `intarray`, not the fourth byte.

But we want the *value* of this fourth array element, not the *address*. To take the value, we use the indirection operator `*`. The resulting expression, when j is 3, is `*(intarray+3)`, which is the contents of the fourth array element, or 52.

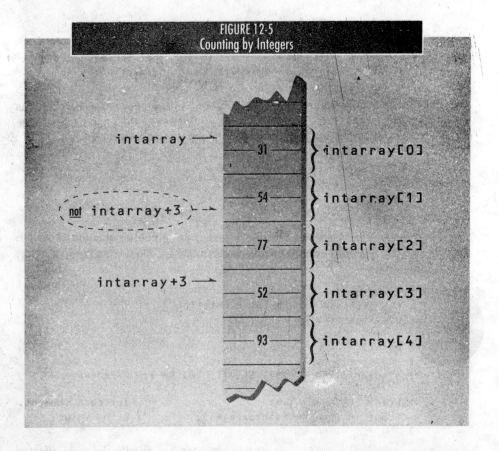

FIGURE 12-5
Counting by Integers

Now we see why a pointer declaration must include the type of the variable pointed to. The compiler needs to know whether a pointer is a pointer to `int` or a pointer to `double` so that it can perform the correct arithmetic to access elements of the array. It multiplies the index value by 2 in the case of type `int`, but by 8 in the case of `double`.

POINTER CONSTANTS AND POINTER VARIABLES

Suppose that, instead of adding `j` to `intarray` to step through the array addresses, you wanted to use the increment operator. Could you write `*(intarray++)`?

The answer is no, and the reason is that you can't increment a constant (or indeed change it in any way). The expression `intarray` is the address where the system has chosen to place your array, and it will stay at this address until the program terminates. `intarray` is a constant. You can't say `intarray++` any more than you can say `7++`. (In a multitasking system, variable addresses may change during program execution. An active program may be swapped out to disk and then reloaded at a different memory location. However, this process is invisible to your program.)

While you can't increment an address, you can increment a pointer that holds an address. The next example, PTRINC, shows how:

```
// ptrinc.cpp
// array accessed with pointer
#include <iostream.h>

void main()
{
    int intarray[] = { 31, 54, 77, 52, 93 }; // array
    int* ptrint;                             // pointer to int
    ptrint = intarray;                       // points to intarray

    for(int j=0; j<5; j++)                   // for each element,
        cout << endl << *(ptrint++);         // print value
}
```

Here we define a pointer to int—ptrint—and give it the value intarray, the address of the array. Now we can access the contents of the array elements with the expression

```
*(ptrint++)
```

The variable ptrint starts off with the same address value as intarray, thus allowing the first array element, intarray[0], which has the value 31, to be accessed as before. But, because ptrint is a variable and not a constant, it can be incremented. After it is incremented, it points to the second array element, intarray[1]. The expression *(ptrint++) then represents the contents of the second array element, or 54. The loop causes the expression to access each array element in turn. The output of PTRINC is the same as that for PTRNOTE.

POINTERS AND FUNCTIONS

In Chapter 6 we noted that there are three ways to pass arguments to a function: by value, by reference, and by pointer. If the function is intended to modify variables in the calling program, then these variables cannot be passed by value, since the function obtains only a copy of the variable. However, either a reference argument or a pointer can be used in this situation.

PASSING SIMPLE VARIABLES

We'll first review how arguments are passed by reference, and then compare this to passing pointer arguments. The PASSREF program shows passing by reference:

```
// passref.cpp
// arguments passed by reference
#include <iostream.h>

void main()
{
```

```
    void centimize(double&);      // prototype

    double var = 10.0;            // var has value of 10 inches
    cout << endl << "var=" << var << " inches";

    centimize(var);               // change var to centimeters
    cout << endl << "var=" << var << " centimeters";
    }

void centimize(double& v)
    {
    v *= 2.54;                    // v is the same as var
    }
```

Here we want to convert a variable var in main() from inches to centimeters. We pass the variable by reference to the function centimize(). (Remember that the & following the data type double in the prototype for this function indicates that the argument is passed by reference.) The centimize() function multiplies the original variable by 2.54. Notice how the function refers to the variable. It simply uses the argument name v; v and var are different names for the same thing.

Once it has converted var to centimeters, main() displays the result. Here's the output of PASSREF:

```
var=25.4 centimeters
```

The next example, PASSPTR, shows an equivalent situation when pointers are used:

```
// passptr.cpp
// arguments passed by pointer
#include <iostream.h>

void main()
    {
    void centimize(double*);      // prototype

    double var = 10.0;            // var has value of 10 inches
    cout << endl << "var=" << var << " inches";

    centimize(&var);              // change var to centimeters
    cout << endl << "var=" << var << " centimeters";
    }

void centimize(double* ptrd)
    {
    *ptrd *= 2.54;                // *ptrd is the same as var
    }
```

The output of PASSPTR is the same as that of PASSREF.

The function centimize() is declared as taking an argument that is a pointer to double:

```
void centimize(double*)    // argument is pointer to double
```

When main() calls the function it supplies the address of the variable as the argument:

```
centimize(&var);
```

Remember that this is not the variable itself, as it is in passing by reference, but the variable's address.

Because the `centimize()` function is passed an address, it must use the indirection operator, `*ptrd`, to access the value stored at this address:

```
*ptrd *= 2.54;  // multiply the contents of ptrd by 2.54
```

Of course this is the same as

```
*ptrd = *ptrd * 2.54;  // multiply the contents of ptrd by 2.54
```

where the stand-alone asterisk means multiplication. (This operator really gets around.)

Since `ptrd` contains the address of `var`, anything done to `*ptrd` is actually done to `var`. Figure 12-6 shows how changing `*ptrd` in the function changes `var` in the calling program.

Passing a pointer as an argument to a function is in some ways similar to passing a reference. They both permit the variable in the calling program to be modified by the function. However, the mechanism is different. A reference is an alias for the original variable, while a pointer is the address of the variable.

PASSING ARRAYS

We've seen numerous examples, starting in Chapter 8, of arrays passed as arguments to functions, and their elements being accessed by the function. Until this chapter, since we had not yet learned about pointers, this was done using array notation.

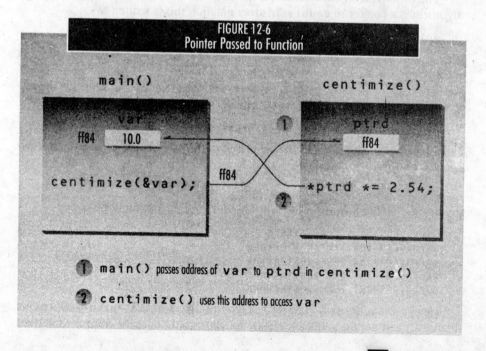

FIGURE 12-6
Pointer Passed to Function

1 main() passes address of var to ptrd in centimize()

2 centimize() uses this address to access var

However, it's more common to use pointer notation instead of array notation when arrays are passed to functions. The PASSARR program shows how this looks:

```
// passarr.cpp
// array passed by pointer
#include <iostream.h>

const int MAX = 5;                  // number of array elements

void main()
    {
    void centimize(double*);   // prototype

    double varray[MAX] = { 10.0, 43.1, 95.9, 59.7, 87.3,};

    centimize(varray);              // change elements of varray to cm

    for(int j=0; j<MAX; j++)   // display new array values
        cout << endl << "varray[" << j << "]="
             << varray[j] << " centimeters";
    }
void centimize(double* ptrd)
    {
    for(int j=0; j<MAX; j++)
        *ptrd++ *= 2.54;            // ptrd points to elements of varray
    }
```

The prototype for the function is the same as in PASSPTR; the function's single argument is a pointer to `double`. In array notation this is written as

```
void centimize(double[]);
```

That is, `double*` is equivalent here to `double[]`, although the pointer syntax is more commonly used.

Since the name of an array is the array's address, there is no need for the address operator `&` when the function is called:

```
centimize(varray);   // pass array address
```

In `centimize()` this array address is placed in the variable `ptrd`. To point to each element of the array in turn, we need only increment `ptrd`:

```
*ptrd++ *= 2.54;
```

Figure 12-7 shows how the array is accessed. Here's the output of PASSARR:

```
varray[0]=25.4 centimeters
varray[1]=109.474 centimeters
varray[2]=243.586 centimeters
varray[3]=151.638 centimeters
varray[4]=221.742 centimeters
```

Here's a syntax question: How do we know that the expression `*ptrd++` increments the pointer and not the pointer contents? In other words, does the compiler interpret

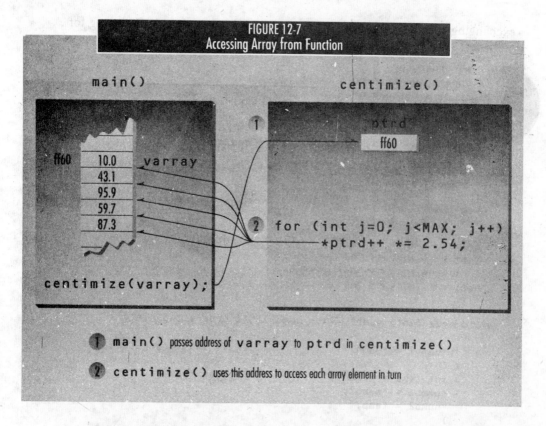

FIGURE 12-7
Accessing Array from Function

main()

centimize()

ff60

10.0   varray
43.1
95.9
59.7
87.3

centimize(varray);

①   ptrd
     ff60

②   for (int j=0; j<MAX; j++)
     *ptrd++ *= 2.54;

① **main()** *passes address of* **varray** *to* **ptrd** *in* **centimize()**

② **centimize()** *uses this address to access each array element in turn*

it as `*(ptrd++)`, which is what we want, or as `(*ptrd)++`? It turns out that `*` (when used as the indirection operator) and `++` have the same precedence. However, operators of the same precedence are distinguished in a second way: by **associativity**. Associativity is concerned with whether the compiler performs operations starting with an operator on the right or an operator on the left. If a group of operators have right associativity, the compiler performs the operation on the right side of the expression first, then works its way to the left. The unary operators like `*` and `++` do have right associativity, so the expression is interpreted as `*(ptrd++)`, with the pointer being incremented first and the indirection operator applied to the result.

SORTING ARRAY ELEMENTS

As a further example of using pointers to access array elements, let's see how to sort the contents of an array. We'll use two program examples—the first to lay the groundwork, and the second, an expansion of the first, to demonstrate the sorting process.

Ordering with Pointers

The first program is similar to the REFORDER program in Chapter 6, except that it uses pointers instead of references. It orders two numbers passed to it as arguments, exchanging them if the second is smaller than the first. Here's the listing for PTRORDER:

```
// ptrorder.cpp
// orders two arguments using pointers
#include <iostream.h>

d main()
{
    void order(int*, int*);          // prototype

    int n1=99, n2=11;                // one pair ordered, one not
    int n3=22, n4=88;

    order(&n1, &n2);                 // order each pair of numbers
    order(&n3, &n4);

    cout << endl << "n1=" << n1;     // print out all numbers
    cout << endl << "n2=" << n2;
    cout << endl << "n3=" << n3;
    cout << endl << "n4=" << n4;
}

void order(int* numb1, int* numb2)   // orders two numbers
{
    if(*numb1 > *numb2)              // if 1st larger than 2nd,
    {
        int temp = *numb1;          // swap them
        *numb1 = *numb2;
        *numb2 = temp;
    }
}
```

The function `order()` works the same as it did in REFORDER, except that it is passed the *addresses* of the numbers to be ordered, and it accesses the numbers using pointers. That is, `*numb1` accesses the number in `main()` passed as the first argument, and `*numb2` accesses the second.

Here's the output from PTRORDER:

```
n1=11        ←————— this and
n2=99        ←————— this are swapped, since they weren't in order
n3=22        ←————— this
n4=88        ←————— and this are not swapped, since they were in order
```

We'll use the `order()` function from PTRORDER in our next example program, PTRSORT, which sorts an array of integers.

```
// ptrsort.cpp
// sorts an array using pointers
#include <iostream.h>

d main()
{
    void bsort(int*, int);           // prototype
```

```
        const int N = 10;              // array size
                                       // test array
        int arr[N] = { 37, 84, 62, 91, 11, 65, 57, 28, 19, 49 };

        bsort(arr, N);                 // sort the array

        for(int j=0; j<N; j++)         // print out sorted array
            cout << arr[j] << " ";
    }

void bsort(int* ptr, int n)
    {
    void order(int*, int*);            // prototype
    int j, k;                          // indexes to array

    for(j=0; j<n-1; j++)               // outer loop
        for(k=j+1; k<n; k++)           // inner loop starts at outer
            order(ptr+j, ptr+k);       // order the pointer contents
    }

void order(int* numb1, int* numb2)    // orders two numbers
    {
    if(*numb1 > *numb2)                // if 1st larger than 2nd,
        {
        int temp = *numb1;             // swap them
        *numb1 = *numb2;
        *numb2 = temp;
        }
    }
```

The array arr of integers in main() is initialized to unsorted values. The address of the array, and the number of elements, are passed to the bsort() function. This sorts the array, and the sorted values are then printed. Here's the output of the PTRSORT:

```
11 19 28 37 49 57 62 65 84 91
```

The Bubble Sort

The bsort() function sorts the array using the *bubble sort*. This is a simple (although notoriously slow) approach to sorting. Here's how it works, assuming we want to arrange the numbers in the array in ascending order. First the first element of the array (arr[0]) is compared in turn with each of the other elements (starting with the second). If it's greater than any of them, the two are swapped. When this is done we know that at least the first element is in order; it's now the smallest element. Next the second element is compared in turn with all the other elements, starting with the third, and again swapped if it's bigger. When we're done we know that the second element has the second-smallest value. This process is continued for all the elements until the next-to-the-last, at which time the array is assumed to be ordered. Figure 12-8 shows the bubble sort in action.

The number in the first position, 37, is compared with each element in turn, and swapped with 11. The number in the second position, which starts off being 84, is compared with each element. It's swapped with 62; then 62 (which is now

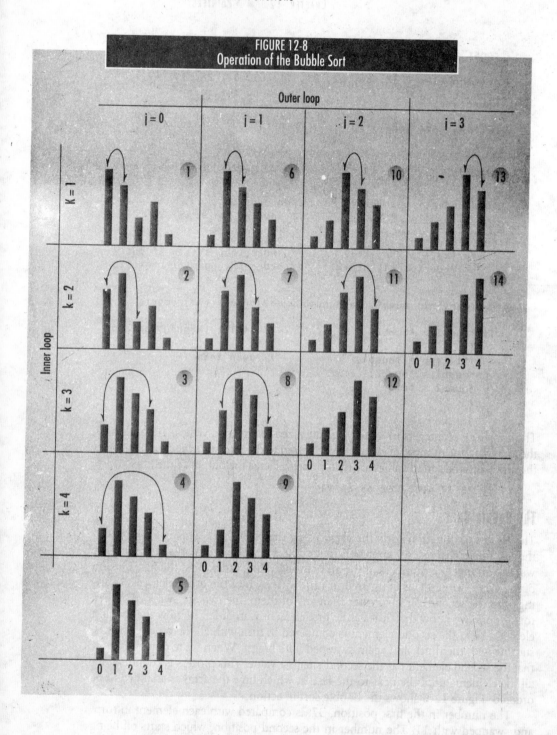

FIGURE 12-8
Operation of the Bubble Sort

in the second position) is swapped with 37, 37 is swapped with 28, and 28 is swapped with 19. The number in the third position, which is 84 again, is swapped with 62, 62 is swapped with 57, 57 with 37, and 37 with 28. The process continues until the array is sorted.

The `bsort()` function in PTRSORT consists of two nested loops, each of which controls a pointer. The outer loop uses the loop variable `j`, and the inner one uses `k`. The expressions `ptr+j` and `ptr+k` point to various elements of the array, as determined by the loop variables. The expression `ptr+j` moves down the array, starting at the first element (the top) and stepping down integer by integer until one short of the last element (the bottom). For each position taken by `ptr+j` in the outer loop, the expression `ptr+k` in the inner loop starts pointing one below `ptr+j` and moves down to the bottom of the array. Each time through the inner loop, the elements pointed to by `ptr+j` and `ptr+k` are compared, using the `order()` function, and if the first is greater than the second, they're swapped. Figure 12-9 shows this process.

The PTRSORT example begins to reveal the power of pointers. They provide a consistent and efficient way to operate on array elements and other variables whose names aren't known to a particular function.

POINTERS AND STRINGS

As we noted in the chapter on arrays, strings are simply arrays of type `char`. Thus pointer notation can be applied to the characters in strings, just as it can to the elements of any array.

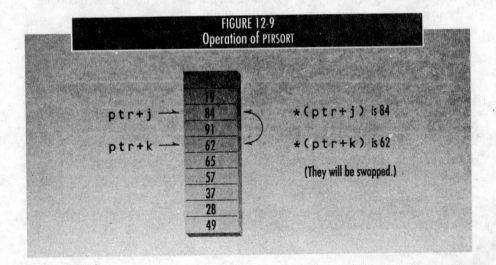

FIGURE 12-9
Operation of PTRSORT

ptr+j ⟶ 84   *(ptr+j) is 84

ptr+k ⟶ 62   *(ptr+k) is 62

(They will be swapped.)

POINTERS TO STRING CONSTANTS

Here's an example, TWOSTR, in which two strings are defined, one using array notation as we've seen in previous examples, and one using pointer notation.

```
// twostr.cpp
// strings defined using array and pointer notation
#include <iostream.h>

void main()
    {
    char str1[] = "Defined as an array";
    char* str2 = "Defined as a pointer";

    cout << endl << str1;      // display both strings
    cout << endl << str2;

// str1++;                     // can't do this; str1 is a constant
    str2++;                     // this is OK, str2 is a pointer

    cout << endl << str2;      // now str2 starts "efined..."
    }
```

In many ways these two types of definition are equivalent. You can print out both strings as the example shows, use them as function arguments, and so on. But there is a subtle difference: **str1** is an address—that is, a pointer constant—while **str2** is a pointer variable. So **str2** can be changed, while **str1** cannot, as demonstrated in the program. Figure 12-10 shows how these two kinds of strings look in memory.

We can increment **str2**, since it is a pointer, but once we do, it no longer points to the first character in the string. Here's the output of TWOSTR:

```
Defined as an array
Defined as a pointer
efined as a pointer        ←——————following str2++
```

A string defined as a pointer is considerably more flexible than one defined as an array. The following examples will make use of this flexibility.

STRINGS AS FUNCTION ARGUMENTS

Here's an example that shows a string used as a function argument. The function simply prints the string, by accessing each character in turn. Here's the listing for PTRSTR:

```
// ptrstr.cpp
// displays a string with pointer notation
#include <iostream.h>

void main()
    {
    void dispstr(char*);        // prototype
```

```
    char str[] = "Idle people have the least leisure.";

    dispstr(str);                // display the string
    }

void dispstr(char* ps)
    {
    cout << endl;                // start on new line
    while( *ps )                 // until null character,
        cout << *ps++;           // print characters
    }
```

The array address `str` is used as the argument in the call to function `dispstr()`. This address is a constant, but since it is passed by value, a copy of it is created in `dispstr()`. This copy is a pointer, `ps`. A pointer can be changed, so the function increments `ps` to display the string. The expression `*ps++` returns the successive characters of the string. The loop cycles until it finds the null character ('\0') at the end of the string. Since this has the value 0, which represents *false*, the `while` loop terminates at that point.

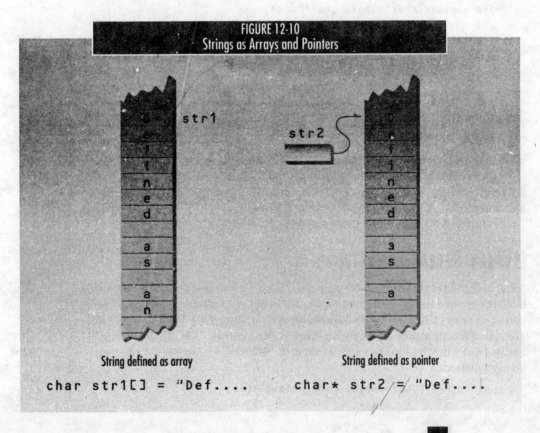

FIGURE 12-10
Strings as Arrays and Pointers

String defined as array

`char str1[] = "Def....`

String defined as pointer

`char* str2 = "Def....`

COPYING A STRING USING POINTERS

We've seen examples of pointers used to obtain values from an array. Pointers can also be used to insert values into an array. The next example, COPYSTR, demonstrates a function that copies one string to another:

```
// copystr.cpp
// copies one string to another with pointers
#include <iostream.h>

void main()
   {
   void copystr(char*, char*);    // prototype

   char* str1 = "Self-conquest is the greatest victory.";
   char str2[80];                 // empty string

   copystr(str2, str1);           // copy str1 to str2
   cout << endl << str2;          // display str2
   }

void copystr(char* dest, char* src)
   {
   while( *src )                        // until null character,
      *dest++ = *src++;                 // copy chars from src to dest
   *dest = '\0';                        // terminate dest
   }
```

Here the `main()` part of the program calls the function `copystr()` to copy `str1` to `str2`. In this function the expression

```
*dest++ = *src++;
```

takes the value at the address pointed to by `src` and places it in the address pointed to by `dest`. Both pointers are then incremented, so the next time through the loop the next character will be transferred. The loop terminates when a null character is found in `src`; at this point a null is inserted in `dest` and the function returns. Figure 12-11 shows how the pointers move through the strings.

LIBRARY STRING FUNCTIONS

Many of the library functions we have already used for strings have string arguments that are specified using pointer notation. As an example we can look at the description of `strcpy()` in the Turbo C++ documentation (or in the STRING.H header file). This function copies one string to another; we can compare it with our homemade `copystr()` function in the COPYSTR example. Here's the syntax for the `strcpy()` library function:

```
char* strcpy(char* dest, const char* src);
```

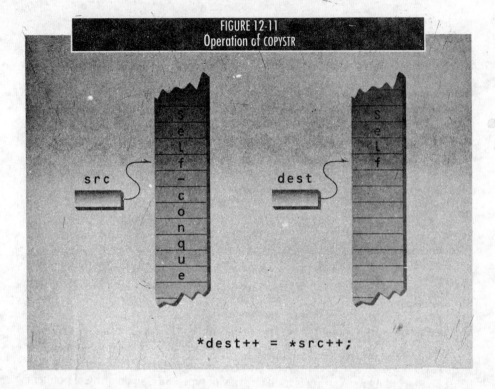

FIGURE 12-11
Operation of COPYSTR

```
*dest++ = *src++;
```

This function takes two arguments of type **char***. What is the effect of the **const** modifier in the second argument? It indicates that **strcpy()** cannot change the characters pointed to by **src**. (It does not imply that the **src** pointer itself cannot be modified. To do that the argument declaration would be **char * const src**.)

The **strcpy()** function also returns a pointer to **char**; this is the address of the **dest** string. In other respects this function works very much like our homemade **copystr()** function.

ARRAYS OF POINTERS TO STRINGS

Just as there are arrays of variables of type **int** or type **float**, there can also be arrays of pointers. A common use for this construction is an array of pointers to strings.

In Chapter 8 the STRARAY program demonstrated an array of strings. As we noted, there is a disadvantage to using an array of strings, in that the subarrays that hold the strings must all be the same length, so that space is wasted when strings are shorter than the length of the subarrays (see Figure 8-10 in Chapter 8).

Let's see how to use pointers to solve this problem. We will modify STRARAY to create an array of pointers to strings, rather than an array of strings. Here's the listing for PTRTOSTR:

441

```
// ptrtostr.cpp
// an array of pointers to strings
#include <iostream.h>
const int DAYS = 7;                     // number of pointers in array

void main()
   {                                    // array of pointers to char
   char* arrptrs[DAYS] = { "Sunday", "Monday", "Tuesday",
                           "Wednesday", "Thursday",
                           "Friday", "Saturday"  };

   for(int j=0; j<DAYS; j++)      // display every string
      cout << arrptrs[j] << endl;
   }
```

The output of this program is the same as that for STRARAY:

```
Sunday
Monday
Tuesday
Wednesday
Thursday
Friday
Saturday
```

When strings are not part of an array, C++ places them contiguously in memory, so there is no wasted space. However, to find the strings, there must be an array that holds pointers to them. A string is itself an array of type char, so an array of pointers to strings is an array of pointers to char. That is the meaning of the definition of arrptrs in PTRTOSTR. Now recall that a string is always represented by a single address: the address of the first character in the string. It is these addresses that are stored in the array. Figure 12-12 shows how this looks.

Memory Management: new and delete

We've seen many examples where arrays are used to set aside memory. The statement

```
int arr1[100];
```

reserves memory for 100 integers. Arrays are a useful approach to data storage, but they have a serious drawback: We must know at the time we write the program how big the array will be. We can't wait until the program is running to specify the array size. The following approach won't work:

```
cin >> size;      // get size from user
int arr[size];    // error; array size must be a constant
```

The compiler requires the array size to be a constant.

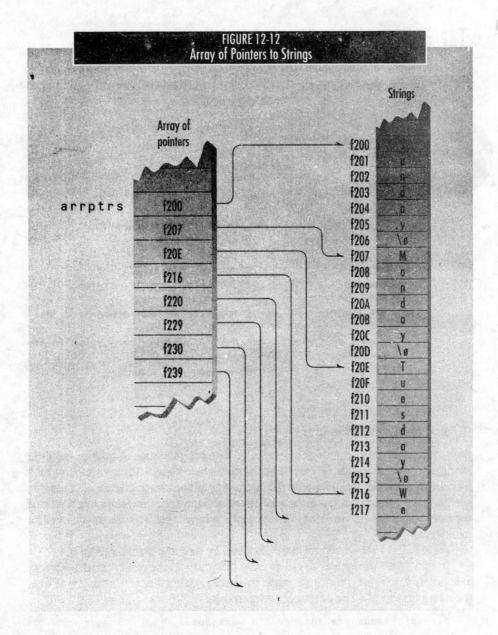

FIGURE 12-12
Array of Pointers to Strings

But in many situations we don't know how much memory we need until run time. We might want to store a string that was typed in by the user, for example. In this situation we can define an array sized to hold the largest string we expect, but this wastes memory.

THE new OPERATOR

C++ provides another approach to obtaining blocks of memory: the new operator. This operator obtains memory from the operating system and returns a pointer to its starting point. The NEWINTRO example shows how new is used:

```
// newintro.cpp
// introduces operator new
#include <iostream.h>
#include <string.h>        // for strcpy()

void main()
    {
    char* str = "Idle hands are the devil's workshop.";
    int len = strlen(str);      // get length of str

    char* ptr;                  // make a pointer to char
    ptr = new char[len+1];      // set aside memory: string + '\0'

    strcpy(ptr, str);           // copy str to new memory area ptr

    cout << endl << "ptr=" << ptr;  // show that str is now in ptr

    delete ptr;                 // release ptr's memory
    }
```

The expression

```
ptr = new char[len+1];
```

returns a pointer that points to a section of memory just large enough to hold the string str, whose length len we found with the strlen() library function, plus an extra byte for the null character '\0' at the end of the string. Figure 12-13 shows the syntax of a statement using the new operator. Remember to use brackets around the size; the compiler won't object if you use parentheses, but the results will be incorrect.

Figure 12-14 shows the memory obtained by new and the pointer to it.

In NEWINTRO we use strcpy() to copy string str to the newly created memory area pointed to by ptr. Since we made this area equal in size to the length of str, the string fits exactly. The output of NEWINTRO is:

```
ptr=Idle hands are the devil's workshop.
```

(C programmers will recognize that new plays a role similar to the malloc() family of library functions. The new approach is superior in that it returns a pointer to the appropriate data type, while malloc()'s pointer must be cast to the appropriate type.)

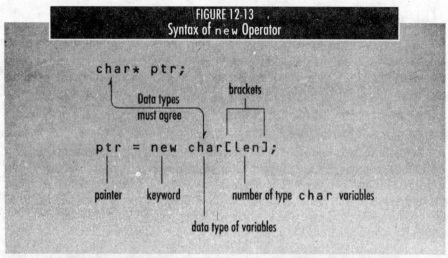

FIGURE 12-13
Syntax of new Operator

```
char* ptr;
```
Data types
must agree

brackets

```
ptr = new char[len];
```

pointer   keyword

data type of variables

number of type char variables

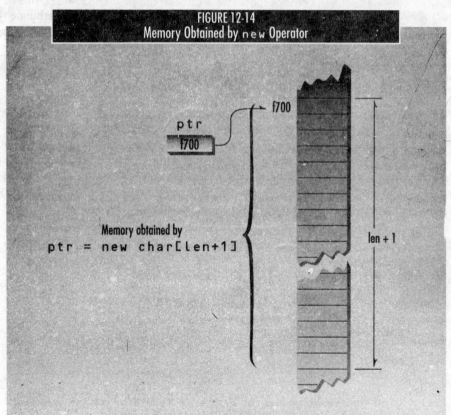

FIGURE 12-14
Memory Obtained by new Operator

f700

ptr

f700

Memory obtained by
`ptr = new char[len+1]`

len + 1

THE delete OPERATOR

If your program reserves many chunks of memory using new, eventually all the available memory will be reserved and the system will crash. To ensure safe and efficient use of memory, the new operator is matched by a corresponding delete operator that returns memory to the operating system. In NEWINTRO the statement

```
delete ptr;
```

returns to the system whatever memory was pointed to by ptr.

Actually, there is no need for this operator in NEWINTRO, since memory is automatically returned when the program terminates. However, suppose you use new in a function. If the function uses a local variable as a pointer to this memory, then when the function terminates, the pointer will be destroyed but the memory will be left as an orphan, taking up space that is inaccessible to the rest of the program. Thus it is always good practice to delete memory when you're through with it.

Deleting the memory doesn't delete the pointer that points to it (str in NEWINTRO), and doesn't change the address value in the pointer. However, this address is no longer valid; the memory it points to may be filled with something entirely different. Be careful that you don't use pointers to memory that has been deleted.

A STRING CLASS USING new

The new operator often appears in constructors. As an example, we'll modify the String class, last seen in examples such as STRPLUS in Chapter 9. You may recall that a potential defect of that class was that all string objects occupied the same fixed amount of memory. A string shorter than this fixed length wasted memory, and a longer string—if one were mistakenly generated—could crash the system by extending beyond the end of the array. Our next example uses new to obtain exactly the right amount of memory. Here's the listing for NEWSTR:

```cpp
// newstr.cpp
// using new to get memory for strings
#include <iostream.h>
#include <string.h>          // for strcpy(), etc

class String                 // user-defined string type
   {
   private:
      char* str;                         // pointer to string
   public:
      String(char* s)                    // constructor, one arg
         {
         int length = strlen(s);         // length of string argument
         str = new char[length+1];       // get memory
         strcpy(str, s);                 // copy argument to it
```

```
         }
      ~String()                          // destructor
         {
         delete str;                     // release memory
         }
      void display()                     // display the String
         {
         cout << str;
         }
   };

   void main()
      {                                   // uses 1-arg constructor
      String s1 = "Who knows nothing doubts nothing.";

      cout << endl << "s1=";             // display string
      s1.display();
      }
```

The **String** class has only one data item: a pointer to **char**, called **str**. This pointer will point to the string held by the **String** object. There is no array within the object to hold the string. The string is stored elsewhere; only the pointer to it is a member of **String**.

Constructor in NEWSTR

The constructor in this example takes a normal string as its argument. It obtains space in memory for this string with **new**; **str** points to the newly-obtained memory. The constructor then uses **strcpy()** to copy the string into this new space.

Destructor in NEWSTR

We haven't seen many destructors in our examples so far, but now that we're allocating memory with **new**, destructors become increasingly important. If we allocate memory when we create an object, it's reasonable to deallocate the memory when the object is no longer needed. As you may recall from Chapter 7, a destructor is a routine that is called automatically when an object is destroyed. The destructor in NEWSTR looks like this:

```
~String()
   {
   delete str;
   }
```

This destructor gives back to the system the memory obtained when the object was created. Objects (like other variables) are typically destroyed when the function in which they were defined terminates. This destructor ensures that memory obtained by the **String** object will be returned to the system, and not left in limbo, when the object is destroyed.

POINTERS TO OBJECTS

Pointers can point to objects as well as to simple data types. We've seen many examples of objects defined and given a name, in statements like

```
Distance dist;
```

where an object called `dist` is defined to be of the `Distance` class.

Sometimes, however, we don't know, at the time that we write the program, how many objects we want to create. When this is the case we can use `new` to create objects while the program is running. As we've seen, `new` returns a pointer to an unnamed object. Let's look at a short example program, ENGLPTR, that compares the two approaches to creating objects:

```
// englptr.cpp
// accessing member functions by pointer
#include <iostream.h>

class Distance                          // English Distance class
   {
   private:
      int feet;
      float inches;
   public:
      void getdist()                    // get length from user
         {
         cout << "\nEnter feet: ";  cin >> feet;
         cout << "Enter inches: ";  cin >> inches;
         }
      void showdist()                   // display distance
         { cout << feet << "\'-" << inches << '\"'; }
   };

void main()
   {
   Distance dist;              // define a named Distance object
   dist.getdist();             // access object members
   dist.showdist();            //    with dot operator

   Distance* distptr;          // pointer to Distance
   distptr = new Distance;     // points to new Distance object
   distptr->getdist();         // access object members
   distptr->showdist();        //    with -> operator
   }
```

This program uses a variation of the English `Distance` class seen in previous chapters. The `main()` function defines `dist`, uses the `Distance` member functions `getdist()` to get a distance from the user, and then uses `showdist()` to display it.

REFERRING TO MEMBERS

ENGLPTR then creates another object of type `Distance` using the `new` operator, and returns a pointer to it called `distptr`.

The question is, how do we refer to the member functions in the object pointed to by `distptr`? You might guess that we would use the dot (`.`) membership-access operator, as in

```
distptr.getdist();   // won't work; distptr is not a variable
```

but this won't work. The dot operator requires the identifier on its left to be a variable. Since `distptr` is a pointer to a variable, we need another syntax. One approach is to dereference (get the contents of the variable pointed to by) the pointer:

```
(*distptr).getdist();  // ok but inelegant
```

However, this is slightly cumbersome because of the parentheses. A more concise approach is furnished by the membership-access operator `->`, which consists of a hyphen and a greater-than sign:

```
distptr->getdist();   // better approach
```

As you can see in ENGLPTR, the `->` operator works with pointers to objects in just the same way that the `.` operator works with objects. Here's the output of the program:

```
Enter feet: 10          ←────────this object uses the dot operator
Enter inches: 6.25
10'-6.25"

Enter feet: 6           ←────────this object uses the -> operator
Enter inches: 4.75
6'-4.75"
```

ANOTHER APPROACH TO new

You may come across another—less common—approach to using `new` to obtain memory for objects.

Since `new` can return a pointer to an area of memory that holds an object, we should be able to refer to the original object by dereferencing the pointer. The ENGLREF example shows how this is done:

```
// englref.cpp
// defererencing pointer returned by new
#include <iostream.h>

class Distance                          // English Distance class
   {
   private:
      int feet;
      float inches;
```

```
public:
    void getdist()                      // get length from user
        {
        cout << "\nEnter feet: ";  cin >> feet;
        cout << "Enter inches: ";  cin >> inches;
        }
    void showdist()                     // display distance
        { cout << feet << "\'-" << inches << '\"'; }
    };

void main()
    {
    Distance& dist = *(new Distance);   // create Distance object
                                        // alias is "dist"
    dist.getdist();                     // access object members
    dist.showdist();                    //    with dot operator
    }
```

The expression

```
new Distance
```

returns a pointer to a memory area large enough for a **Distance** object, so we can refer to the original object as

```
*(new Distance)
```

This is the object pointed to by the pointer. Using a reference, we define **dist** to be an object of type **Distance**, and we set it equal to ***(new Distance)**. Now we can refer to members of **dist** using the dot membership operator, rather than **->**

This approach is less common than using pointers to objects obtained with **new**, or simply declaring an object, but it works in a similar way.

AN ARRAY OF POINTERS TO OBJECTS

A common programming construction is an array of pointers to objects. This arrangement allows easy access to a group of objects, and is more flexible than placing the objects themselves in an array. (For instance, in the last example in this chapter we'll see how a group of objects can be sorted by sorting an array of pointers to them, rather than sorting the objects themselves.)

Our next example, PTROBJS, creates an array of pointers to the **person** class. Here's the listing:

```
// ptrobjs.cpp
// array of pointers to objects
#include <iostream.h>

class person                            // class of persons
    {
    protected:
        char name[40];                  // person's name
```

```
      public:
          void setName(void)                  // set the name
              {
              cout << "Enter name: ";
              cin >> name;
              }
          void printName(void)                // get the name
              {
              cout << "\n    Name is: "
                   << name;
              }
      };

    void main(void)
        {
        person* persPtr[100];       // array of pointers to persons
        int n = 0;                  // number of persons in array
        char choice;

        do                                      // put persons in array
            {
            persPtr[n] = new person;            // make new object
            persPtr[n]->setName();              // set person's name
            n++;                                // count new person
            cout << "Enter another (y/n)? "; // enter another
            cin >> choice;                      // person?
            }
        while( choice=='y' );                   // quit on 'n'

        for(int j=0; j<n; j++)                  // print names of
            {                                   // all persons
            cout << "\nPerson number " << j+1;
            persPtr[j]->printName();
            }
        } // end main()
```

The class **person** has a single data item, **name**, which holds a string representing a person's name. Two member functions, **setName()** and **printName()**, allow the name to be set and displayed.

Program Operation

The **main()** function defines an array, **persPtr**, of 100 pointers to type **person**. In a **do** loop it then asks the user to enter a name. With this name it creates a **person** object using **new**, and stores a pointer to this object in the array **persPtr**. To demonstrate how easy it is to access the objects using the pointers, it then prints out the **name** data for each **person** object.

Here's a sample interaction with program:

```
Enter name: Stroustrup    ←──────── user enters names
Enter another (y/n)? y
```

```
Enter name: Ritchie
Enter another (y/n)? y
Enter name: Kernighan
Enter another (y/n)? n
Person number 1        ←————— program displays all names stored
    Name is: Stroustrup
Person number 2
    Name is: Ritchie
Person number 3
    Name is: Kernighan
```

Accessing Member Functions

We need to access the member functions `setName()` and `printName()` in the `person` objects pointed to by the pointers in the array `persPtr`. Each of the elements of the array `persPtr` is specified in array notation to be `persPtr[j]` (or equivalently by pointer notation to be `*(persPtr+j)`). The elements are pointers to objects of type `person`. To access a member of an object using a pointer, we use the `->` operator. Putting this all together, we have the following syntax for `getname()`:

```
persPtr[j]->getName()
```

This executes the `getname()` function in the `person` object pointed to by the `j`th element of the `persPtr` array. (It's a good thing we don't have to program using English syntax.)

A Linked List Example

Our next example shows a simple linked list. What is a linked list? It's another way to store data. You've seen numerous examples of data stored in arrays. Another data structure is an array of pointers to data members, as in the PTRTOSTRS and PTROBJS examples. Both the array and the array of pointers suffer from the necessity to declare a fixed-size array before running the program.

A Chain of Pointers

The linked list provides a more flexible storage system in that it doesn't use arrays at all. Instead, space for each data item is obtained as needed with `new`, and each item is connected, or *linked*, to the next data item using a pointer. The individual items don't need to be located contiguously in memory the way array elements are; they can be scattered anywhere.

In our example the entire linked list is an object of class `linklist`. The individual data items, or links, are represented by structures of type `link`. Each such structure contains an integer—representing the object's single data item—and a

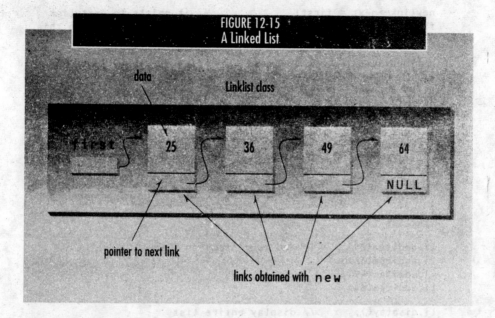

FIGURE 12-15
A Linked List

pointer to the next link. The list itself stores a pointer to the link at the head of the list. This arrangement is shown in Figure 12-15.

Here's the listing for LINKLIST:

```
// linklist.cpp
// linked list
#include <iostream.h>

struct link                              // one element of list
   {
   int data;                             // data item
   link* next;                           // pointer to next link
   };

class linklist                           // a list of links
   {
   private:
      link* first;                       // pointer to first link
   public:
      linklist()                         // no-argument constructor
         { first = NULL; }               // no first link
      void additem(int d);               // add data item (one link)
      void display();                    // display all links
   };

void linklist::additem(int d)            // add data item
   {
   link* newlink = new link;             // make a new link
   newlink->data = d;                    // give it data
```

453

```
        newlink->next = first;           // it points to next link
        first = newlink;                 // now first points to this
        }

    void linklist::display()             // display all links
        {
        link* current = first;           // set ptr to first link
        while( current != NULL )         // quit on last link
            {
            cout << endl << current->data;  // print data
            current = current->next;     // move to next link
            }
        }

    void main()
        {
        linklist li;         // make linked list

        li.additem(25);      // add four items to list
        li.additem(36);
        li.additem(49);
        li.additem(64);

        li.display();        // display entire list
        }
```

The linklist class has only one member data item: the pointer to the start of the list. When the list is first created, the constructor initializes this pointer, first, to NULL. The NULL constant is defined in the MEM.H header file (which is #included in the IOSTREAM.H file) to be 0. This value serves as a signal that a pointer does not hold a valid address. In our program a link whose next member has a value of NULL is assumed to be at the end of the list.

ADDING AN ITEM TO THE LIST

The additem() member function adds an item to the linked list. A new link is inserted at the beginning of the list. (We could write the additem() function to insert items at the end of the list, but that is a little more complex to program.) Let's look at the steps involved in inserting a new link.

First, a new structure of type link is created by the line

```
link* newlink = new link;
```

This creates memory for the new link structure with new and saves the pointer to it in the newlink variable.

Next we want to set the members of the newly created structure to appropriate values. A structure is just like a class in that, when it is referred to by pointer rather than by name, its members are accessed using the -> member-access operator. The following two lines set the data variable to the value passed as an argument to additem(), and the next pointer to point to whatever address was in first, which holds the pointer to the start of the list.

```
newlink->data = d;
newlink->next = first;
```

Finally, we want the `first` variable to point to the new link:

```
first = newlink;
```

The effect is to uncouple the connection between `first` and the old first link, insert the new link, and move the old first link into the second position. Figure 12-16 shows this process.

DISPLAYING THE LIST CONTENTS

Once the list is created it's easy to step through all the members, displaying them (or performing other operations). All we need to do is follow from one `next` pointer to another until we find a `next` that is `NULL`, signaling the end of the list. In the function `display()`, the line

```
cout << endl << current->data;
```

prints the value of the data, and

```
current = current->next;
```

moves us along from one link to another, until

```
current != NULL
```

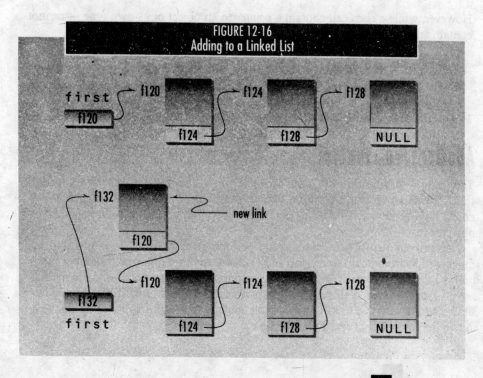

FIGURE 12-16
Adding to a Linked List

in the `while` expression becomes true. Here's the output of LINKLIST:

```
64
49
36
25
```

Linked lists are perhaps the most commonly used data storage arrangements after arrays. As we noted, they avoid the wasting of memory space engendered by arrays. The disadvantage is that finding a particular item on a linked list requires following the chain of links from the head of the list until the desired link is reached. This can be time-consuming. An array element, on the other hand, can be accessed quickly, provided its index is known in advance. We'll have more to say about linked lists and other data-storage techniques in Chapter 16.

SELF-CONTAINING CLASSES

We should note a possible pitfall in the use of self-referential classes and structures. The `link` structure in LINKLIST contained a pointer to the same kind of structure. You can do the same with classes:

```
class sampleclass
   {
   sampleclass* ptr;  // this is fine
   };
```

However, while a class can contain a *pointer* to an object of its own type, it cannot contain an *object* of its own type:

```
class sampleclass
   {
   sampleclass obj;  // can't do this
   };
```

This is true of structures as well as classes.

AUGMENTING LINKLIST

The general organization of LINKLIST can serve for a more complex situation than that shown. There could be more data in each link. Instead of an integer, a link could hold a number of data items or it could hold a pointer to a structure or object.

Additional member functions could perform such activities as adding and removing links from an arbitrary part of the chain. Another important member function is a destructor. As we mentioned, it's important to delete blocks of memory that are no longer in use. A destructor that performed this task would be a highly desirable addition to the `linklist` class. It could go through the list using `delete` to free the memory occupied by each link.

POINTERS TO POINTERS

We'll finish this chapter with an example that demonstrates an array of pointers to objects, and shows how to sort these pointers based on data in the object. This involves the idea of pointers to pointers, and may help to demonstrate why people lose sleep over pointers.

The idea in the next program is to create an array of pointers to objects of the **person** class. This is similar to the PTROBJS example, but we go farther and add variations of the **order()** and **bsort()** functions from the PTRSORT example so that we can sort a group of **person** objects based on the alphabetical order of their names. Here's the listing for PERSORT:

```cpp
// persort.cpp
// sorts person objects using array of pointers
#include <iostream.h>
#include <string.h>                 // for strcmp()

class person                        // class of persons
   {
   protected:
      char name[40];                // person's name
   public:
      void setName(void)            // set the name
         { cout << "Enter name: "; cin >> name; }
      void printName(void)          // display the name
         { cout << endl << name; }
      char* getName()               // return the name
         { return name; }
   };

void main(void)
   {
   void bsort(person**, int);       // prototype
   person* persPtr[100];            // array of pointers to persons
   int n = 0;                       // number of persons in array
   char choice;                     // input char

   do                               // put persons in array
      {
      persPtr[n] = new person;      // make new object
      persPtr[n]->setName();        // set person's name
      n++;                          // count new person
      cout << "Enter another (y/n)? "; // enter another
      cin >> choice;                //     person?
      }
   while( choice=='y' );            // quit on 'n'
```

```
        cout << "\nUnsorted list:";
        for(int j=0; j<n; j++)              // print unsorted list
           { persPtr[j]->printName(); }

        bsort(persPtr, n);                  // sort pointers

        cout << "\nSorted list:";
        for(j=0; j<n; j++)                  // print sorted list
           { persPtr[j]->printName(); }
        }  // end main()

    void bsort(person** pp, int n)          // sort pointers to persons
        {
        void order(person**, person**);  // prototype
        int j, k;                           // indexes to array

        for(j=0; j<n-1; j++)                // outer loop
           for(k=j+1; k<n; k++)             // inner loop starts at outer
              order(pp+j, pp+k);            // order the pointer contents
        }

    void order(person** pp1, person** pp2)  // orders two pointers
        {                                   // if 1st larger than 2nd,
        if( strcmp((*pp1)->getName(), (*pp2)->getName()) > 0)
           {
           person* tempptr = *pp1;          // swap the pointers
           *pp1 = *pp2;
           *pp2 = tempptr;
           }
        }
```

When the program is first executed it asks for a name. When the user gives it one, it creates an object of type **person** and sets the **name** data in this object to the name entered by the user. The program also stores a pointer to the object in the **persPtr** array.

When the user types n to indicate that no more names will be entered, the program calls the **bsort()** function to sort the **person** objects based on their **name** member variables. Here's some sample interaction with the program:

```
Enter name: Washington
Enter another (y/n)? y
Enter name: Adams
Enter another (y/n)? y
Enter name: Jefferson
Enter another (y/n)? y
Enter name: Madison
Enter another (y/n)? n

Unsorted list:
Washington
Adams
Jefferson
Madison
```

```
Sorted list:
Adams
Jefferson
Madison
Washington
```

SORTING POINTERS

Actually, we don't sort the objects themselves; we sort the pointers to the objects. This eliminates the need to shuffle the objects around in memory, which can be very time-consuming if the objects are large. The process is shown in Figure 12-17.

To facilitate the sorting activity we've added a `getName()` member function to the `person` class, so we can access the names from `order()` to decide when to swap pointers.

THE person** DATA TYPE

You will notice that the first argument to the `bsort()` function, and both arguments to `order()`, have the type `person**`. What do the two asterisks mean? These arguments are used to pass the address of the array `persPtr`, or—in the case of `order()`—the addresses of elements of the array. If this were an array of type `person`, then the address of the array would be type `person*`. However, the array is of type *pointers* to `person`, or `person*`, so its address is type `person**`. The address of a pointer is a pointer to a pointer. Figure 12-18 shows how this looks.

Compare this program with PTRSORT, which sorted an array of type `int`. You'll find that the data types passed to functions in PERSORT all have one more asterisk than they did in PTRSORT, because the array is an array of pointers.

Since the `persPtr` array contains pointers, the construction

```
persPtr[j]->printName()
```

executes the `printName()` function in the object pointed to by the `j`th element of `persPtr`.

COMPARING STRINGS

The `order()` function in PERSORT has been modified to order two strings lexigraphically—that is, by putting them in alphabetical order. To do this it compares the strings with the Turbo C++ library function `strcmp()`. This function takes the two strings `s1` and `s2` as arguments, and returns one of the following values:

Value	Condition
<0	s1 comes before s2
0	s1 is the same as s2
>0	s1 comes after s2

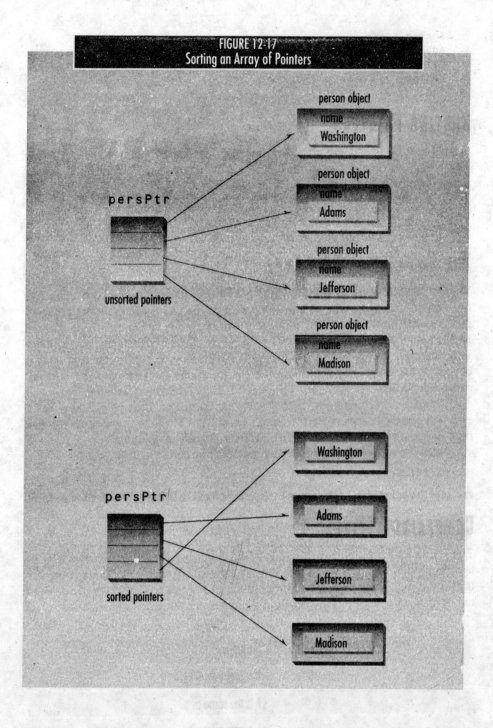

FIGURE 12-17
Sorting an Array of Pointers

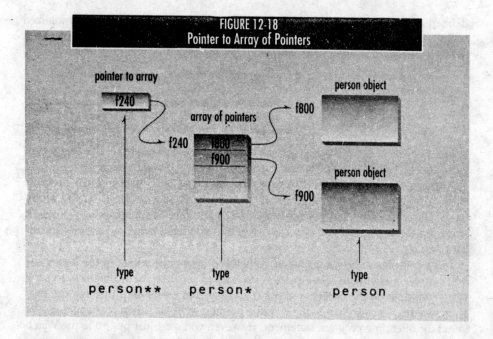

FIGURE 12-18
Pointer to Array of Pointers

pointer to array

f240

array of pointers

f240   f800
        f900

f800

f900

person object

person object

type
person**

type
person*

type
person

The strings are accessed using the syntax

```
(*pp1)->getname()
```

The argument **pp1** is a pointer to a pointer, and we want the name pointed to by the pointer it points to. The member-access operator **->** dereferences one level, but we need to dereference another level, hence the asterisk preceding **pp1**.

Just as there can be pointers to pointers, there can be pointers to pointers to pointers, and so on. Fortunately such complexities are seldom encountered.

DEBUGGING POINTERS

Pointers can be the source of mysterious and catastrophic program bugs. The most common problem is that the programmer has failed to place a valid address in a pointer variable. When this happens the pointer can end up pointing anywhere in memory. It could be pointing to the program code, or to the operating system. If the programmer then inserts a value into memory using the pointer, the value will write over the program or operating instructions, and the computer will crash or evince other uncharming behavior.

A particular version of this scenario takes place when the pointer points to address 0, which is called **NULL**. This happens, for example, if the pointer variable is defined as an external variable, since external variables are automatically initialized to 0. Instance variables in classes are considered external, so they are also initialized to 0. Here's a mini-program that demonstrates the situation:

```
int* intptr;          // external variable, initialized to 0
void main()
    {                 // failure to put valid address in intptr
    *intptr = 37;     // attempts to put 37 in address at 0
    }                 // result is "Null pointer assignment"
```

When `intptr` is defined it is given the value 0, since it is external. The single program statement will attempt to insert the value 37 into the address at 0.

Fortunately, however, the run-time error-checking unit, built into the program by the compiler, is waiting for attempts to access address 0, and will display an infamous error message: *Null pointer assignment*. If you find this message on the screen after running your program, you can guess that you have failed to properly initialize a pointer.

In a complex program it may be difficult to figure out where in the listing the null pointer assignment takes place. One way to localize the problem is to set a Watch window on the contents of the 0 address, and single-step through the program, waiting for any change in the value pointed to by 0. When it changes you've found the offending program statement. However, you can't just put `*0` in the Watch window. Here's the expression you need: `*(char *)0, 4M`. The 0 must be cast to a pointer-to-`char`. The 4M tells the debugger to display four bytes of memory. These four bytes are normally 0, so when they change to something else, you've found the problem.

SUMMARY

This has been a whirlwind tour through the land of pointers. There is far more to learn about pointers, but the topics we've covered here will provide a basis for the examples in the balance of the book, and for further study of pointers.

We've learned that everything in the computer's memory has an address, and that addresses are *pointer constants*. We can find the addresses of variables using the address operator `&`.

Pointers are variables that hold address values. Pointers are defined using an asterisk (`*`) to mean *pointer to*. A data type is always included in pointer definitions, since the compiler must know what is being pointed to, so that it can perform arithmetic correctly on the pointer. We access the thing pointed to using the asterisk in a different way, as the indirection operator, meaning *contents of the variable pointed to by*.

Array elements can be accessed using either array notation, with brackets, or pointer notation, with an asterisk. Like other addresses, the address of an array is a constant, but it can be assigned to a variable, which can be incremented and changed in other ways.

When the address of a variable is passed to a function, the function can work with the original variable. (This is not true when arguments are passed by value.) In this respect passing by pointer offers the same benefits as passing by reference, although pointer arguments must be *dereferenced* or accessed using the indirection operator. However, pointers offer more flexibility in some cases.

A string constant can be defined as an array or as a pointer. The pointer approach may be more flexible, but there is a danger that the pointer value will be corrupted. Strings, being arrays of type `char`, are commonly passed to functions and accessed using pointers.

The `new` operator obtains a specified amount of memory from the system and returns a pointer to the memory. This operator is used to create variables and data structures during program execution. The `delete` operator releases memory obtained with `new`.

When a pointer points to an object, members of the object's class can be accessed using the access operator `->`. The same syntax is used to access structure members.

Classes and structures may contain data members that are pointers to their own type. This permits the creation of complex data structures like linked lists.

There can be pointers to pointers. These variables are defined using the double asterisk: `int** pptr`.

QUESTIONS

1. Write a statement that displays the address of the variable `testvar`.
2. The contents of two pointers that point to adjacent variables of type `float` differ by _____.
3. A pointer is
   a. the address of a variable
   b. an indication of the variable to be accessed next
   c. a variable for storing addresses
   d. the data type of an address variable
4. Write expressions for the following:
   a. the address of `var`
   b. the contents of the variable pointed to by `var`
   c. the variable `var` used as a reference argument
   d. the data type pointer-to-`char`
5. An address is a _____, while a pointer is a _____.
6. Write a definition for a variable of type pointer to `float`.
7. One way pointers are useful is to refer to a memory address that has no _____.

8. If a pointer `testptr` points to a variable `testvar`, write a statement that represents the contents of `testvar` but does not use its name.

9. An asterisk placed after a data type means _____. An asterisk placed in front of a variable name means _____.

10. The expression `*test` can be said to
   a. be a pointer to `test`
   b. refer to the contents of `test`
   c. dereference `test`
   d. refer to the value of the variable pointed to by `test`

11. Is the following code correct?

```
int intvar = 333;
int* intptr;
cout << *intptr;
```

12. A pointer to `void` can hold pointers to _____.

13. What is the difference between `intarr[3]` and `*(intarr+3)`?

14. Write some code that uses pointer notation to display every value in the array `intarr`, which has 77 elements.

15. If `intarr` is an array of integers, why is the expression `intarr++` not legal?

16. Of the three ways to pass arguments to functions, only passing by _____ and passing by _____ allow the function to modify the argument in the calling program.

17. The type of variable a pointer points to must be part of the pointer's definition so that
   a. data types don't get mixed up when arithmetic is performed on them
   b. pointers can be added to one another to access structure members
   c. no one's religious conviction will be offended
   d. the compiler can perform arithmetic correctly to access array elements

18. Using pointer notation, write a prototype (declaration) for a function called `func()` that returns type `void` and takes a single argument that is an array of type `char`.

19. Using pointer notation, write some code that will transfer 80 characters from the string `s1` to the string `s2`.

20. The first element in a string is
   a. the name of the string
   b. the first character in the string
   c. the length of the string
   d. the name of the array holding the string

21. Using pointer notation, write the prototype for a function called `revstr()` that returns a string value and takes one argument that represents a string.

22. Write a definition for an array `numptrs` of pointers to the strings "One", "Two", and "Three"

464

23. The `new` operator
    a. returns a pointer to a variable
    b. creates a variable called new
    c. obtains memory for a new variable
    d. tells how much memory is available

24. Using `new` may result in less _____ memory than using an array.

25. The `delete` operator returns _____ to the operating system.

26. Given a pointer `p` that points to an object of type `upperclass`, write an expression that executes the `exclu()` member function in this object.

27. Given an object with index number 7 in array `objarr`, write an expression that executes the `exclu()` member function in this object.

28. In a linked list
    a. each link contains a pointer to the next link
    b. an array of pointers point to the links
    c. each link contains data or a pointer to data
    d. the links are stored in an array

29. Write a definition for an array `arr` of 8 pointers that point to variables of type `float`.

30. If you wanted to sort many large objects or structures, it would be most efficient to
    a. place them in an array and sort the array
    b. place pointers to them in an array and sort the array
    c. place them in a linked list and sort the linked list
    d. place references to them in an array and sort the array

EXERCISES

1. Write a program that reads a group of numbers from the user and places them in an array of type `float`. Once the numbers are stored in the array, the program should average them and print the result. Use pointer notation wherever possible.

2. Start with the `string` class from the NEWSTR example in this chapter. Add a member function called `upit()` that converts the string to all upper case. You can use the `toupper()` library function, which takes a single character as an argument and returns a character that has been converted (if necessary) to uppercase. This function uses the CTYPE.H header file. Write some code in `main()` to test this function.

3. Start with an array of pointers to strings representing the days of the week, as found in the PTRTOSTR program in this chapter. Provide functions to sort the

strings into alphabetical order, using variations of the `bsort()` and `order()` functions from the PTRSORT program in this chapter. Sort the pointers to the strings, not the actual strings.

4. Add a destructor to the LINKLIST program. It should delete all the links when a `linklist` object is destroyed. It can do this by following along the chain, deleting each link as it goes. You can test the destructor by having it display a message each time it deletes a link; it should delete the same number of links that were added to the list. (A destructor is called automatically by the system for any existing objects when the program exits.)

CHAPTER 13

VIRTUAL FUNCTIONS
AND OTHER SUBTLETIES

Now that we understand something about pointers, we can delve into more advanced C++ topics. This chapter covers a rather loosely related collection of such topics: virtual functions, friend functions, static functions, the overloaded = operator, the overloaded copy constructor, and the `this` pointer. These are advanced features; they are not necessary for every C++ program. However, they are widely used, and are essential in some situations. Studying them also casts light on the inner workings of C++.

VIRTUAL FUNCTIONS

Virtual means *existing in effect but not in reality*. A virtual function, then, is one that does not really exist but nevertheless appears real to some parts of a program.

Why are virtual functions needed? Suppose you have a number of objects of different classes but you want to put them all on a list and perform a particular operation on them using the same function call. For example, suppose a graphics program includes several different shapes: a triangle, a ball, a square, and so on, as in the MULTSHAP program in Chapter 11. Each of these classes has a member function `draw()` that causes the object to be drawn on the screen.

Now suppose you plan to make a picture by grouping a number of these elements together, and you want to draw the picture in a convenient way. One approach is to create an array that holds pointers to all the different objects in the picture. The array might be defined like this:

```
shape* ptrarr[100];   // array of 100 pointers to shapes
```

If you insert pointers to all the shapes into this array, you can then draw an entire picture using a simple loop:

```
for(int j=0; j<N; j++)
    ptrarr[j]->draw();
```

This is an amazing capability: completely different functions are executed by the same function call. If the pointer in `ptrarr` points to a ball, the function that draws a ball is called; if it points to a triangle, the triangle-drawing function is drawn. This is an important example of *polymorphism*, or giving different meanings to the same thing.

However, for this polymorphic approach to work, several conditions must be met. First, all the different classes of shapes, such as balls and triangles, must be derived from a single base class (called `shape` in MULTSHAP). Second, the `draw()` function must be declared to be `virtual` in the base class.

This is all rather abstract, so let's start with some short programs that show parts of the situation, and put everything together later.

NORMAL MEMBER FUNCTIONS ACCESSED WITH POINTERS

Our first example shows what happens when a base class and derived classes all have functions with the same name, and you access these functions using pointers but without using virtual functions. Here's the listing for NOTVIRT:

```
// notvirt.cpp
// normal functions accessed from pointer
#include <iostream.h>

class Base                          // base class
    {
    public:
        void show()                 // normal function
            { cout << "\nBase"; }
    };
class Derv1 : public Base           // derived class 1
    {
    public:
        void show()
            { cout << "\nDerv1"; }
    };
class Derv2 : public Base           // derived class 2
    {
    public:
        void show()
            { cout << "\nDerv2"; }
    };
void main()
    {
    Derv1 dv1;              // object of derived class 1
    Derv2 dv2;              // object of derived class 2
    Base* ptr;             // pointer to base class

    ptr = &dv1;            // put address of dv1 in pointer
    ptr->show();           // execute show()

    ptr = &dv2;            // put address of dv2 in pointer
    ptr->show();           // execute show()
    }
```

The `Derv1` and `Derv2` classes are derived from class `Base`. Each of these three classes has a member function `show()`. In `main()` we create objects of class `Derv1` and `Derv2`, and a pointer to class `Base`. Then we put the address of a derived class object in the base class pointer in the line

```
ptr = &dv1;  // derived class address in base class pointer
```

But wait—how can we get away with this? Doesn't the compiler complain that we're assigning an address of one type (`Derv1`) to a pointer of another (`Base`)? On the contrary, the compiler is perfectly happy, because type checking has been relaxed in this situation, for reasons that will become apparent soon. The rule is that pointers to objects of a derived class are type-compatible with pointers to objects of the base class.

Now the question is, when you execute the line

```
ptr->show();
```

what function is called? Is it `Base::show()`, or `Derv1::show()`? Again, in the last two lines of NOTVIRT we put the address of an object of class `Derv2` in the pointer, and again execute

```
ptr->show();
```

Which of the `show()` functions is called here? The output from the program answers these questions:

```
Base
Base
```

As you can see, the function in the base class is always executed. The compiler ignores the *contents* of the pointer `ptr` and chooses the member function that matches the *type* of the pointer, as shown in Figure 13-1.

Sometimes this is what we want, but it doesn't solve the problem posed at the beginning of this section: accessing objects of different classes using the same statement.

VIRTUAL MEMBER FUNCTIONS ACCESSED WITH POINTERS

Let's make a single change in our program: We'll place the keyword `virtual` in front of the declarator for the `show()` function in the base class. Here's the listing for the resulting program, VIRT:

```
// virt.cpp
// virtual functions accessed from pointer
#include <iostream.h>

class Base                          // base class
    {
    public:
        virtual void show()         // virtual function
            { cout << "\nBase"; }
    };
class Derv1 : public Base           // derived class 1
    {
    public:
```

```
        void show()
          { cout << "\nDerv1"; }
    };
class Derv2 : public Base            // derived class 2
    {
    public:
        void show()
          { cout << "\nDerv2"; }
    };
void main()
    {
    Derv1 dv1;              // object of derived class 1
    Derv2 dv2;              // object of derived class 2
    Base* ptr;              // pointer to base class

    ptr = &dv1;             // put address of dv1 in pointer
    ptr->show();            // execute show()

    ptr = &dv2;             // put address of dv2 in pointer
    ptr->show():            // execute show()
    }
```

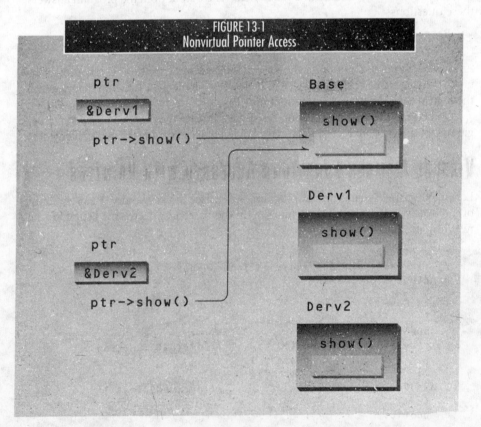

FIGURE 13-1
Nonvirtual Pointer Access

The output of this program is

```
Derv1
Derv2
```

Now, as you can see, the member functions of the derived classes, not the base class, are executed. We change the contents of **ptr** from the address of **Derv1** to that of **Derv2**, and the particular instance of **show()** that is executed also changes. So the same function call,

```
ptr->show();
```

executes different functions, depending on the contents of **ptr**. The rule is that the compiler selects the function based on the *contents* of the pointer **ptr**, not on the *type* of the pointer, as in NOTVIRT. This is shown in Figure 13-2.

LATE BINDING

The astute reader may wonder how the compiler knows what function to compile. In NOTVIRT the compiler has no problem with the expression

```
ptr->show();
```

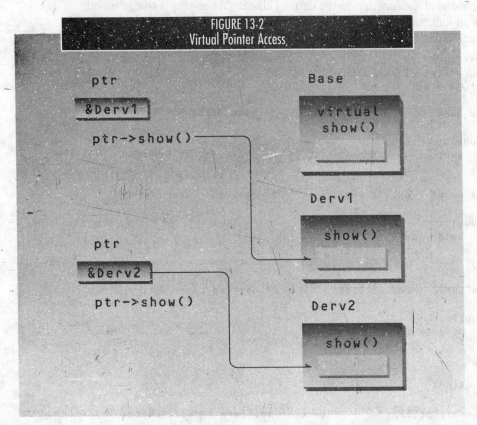

FIGURE 13-2
Virtual Pointer Access

It always compiles a call to the **show()** function in the base class. But in VIRT the compiler doesn't know what class the contents of **ptr** may contain. It could be the address of an object of the **Derv1** class or of the **Derv2** class. Which version of **draw()** does the compiler call? In fact the compiler doesn't know what to do, so it arranges for the decision to be deferred until the program is running. At run time, when it is known what class is pointed to by **ptr**, the appropriate version of **draw** will be called. This is called *late binding* or *dynamic binding*. (Choosing functions in the normal way, during compilation, is called *early*, or *static*, binding.) Late binding requires some overhead but provides increased power and flexibility.

We'll put these ideas to use in a moment, but first let's consider a refinement to the idea of virtual functions.

PURE VIRTUAL FUNCTIONS

A *pure* virtual function is a virtual function with no body (another OOP sentence that sounds as if it described an esoteric religious concept). You may have noticed in the VIRT program that **Base::show()** is never executed. This is a common situation. There is no need for the base-class version of the particular function; we only use the versions of the function in the derived classes. When this is true, the body of the virtual function in the base class can be removed, and the notation =0 added to the function declaration, as shown in the VIRTPURE example:

```
// virtpure.cpp
// pure virtual function
#include <iostream.h>

class Base                           // base class
   {
   public:
      virtual void show() = 0;       // pure virtual function
   };

class Derv1 : public Base            // derived class 1
   {
   public:
     void show()
        { cout << "\nDerv1"; }
   };

class Derv2 : public Base            // derived class 2
   {
   public:
     void show()
        { cout << "\nDerv2"; }
   };

void main()
   {
   Base* list[2];          // list of pointers to base class
```

```
    Derv1 dv1;              // object of derived class 1
    Derv2 dv2;              // object of derived class 2

    list[0] = &dv1;         // put address of dv1 in list

    list[1] = &dv2;         // put address of dv2 in list

    list[0]->show();        // execute show() in both objects
    list[1]->show();
    }
```

Now the virtual function is declared as

```
virtual void show() = 0;  // pure virtual function
```

The equals sign here has nothing to do with assignment; the value 0 is not as-signed to anything. The =0 syntax is simply how we tell the compiler that a func-tion will be pure—that is, have no body.

You might wonder, if we can remove the body of the virtual **show()** function in the base class, why we can't remove the function altogether. That would be even cleaner, but it doesn't work. Without a function **show()** in the base class, state-ments like

```
    list[0]->show();
```

would not be valid, because the pointers in the **list[]** array must point to mem-bers of class **Base**.

As you can see, we've made another, unrelated, change in VIRTPURE: The ad-dresses of the member functions are stored in an array of pointers, and accessed us-ing array elements. This works in just the same way as using a single pointer. The output of VIRTPURE is the same as VIRT:

```
    Derv1
    Derv2
```

VIRTUAL FUNCTIONS AND THE person CLASS

Now that we understand some of the mechanics of virtual functions, let's look at a situation where it makes sense to use them. Our example is an extension of the PTROBJ and PERSORT examples from Chapter 12. It uses the same **person** class but adds two derived classes, **student** and **professor**. These derived classes each con-tain a function called **isOutstanding()**. This function makes it easy for the school administrators to create a list of outstanding students and professors for the vener-able Awards Day ceremony. Here's the listing for VIRTPERS:

```
// virtpers.cpp
// virtual functions with person class
#include <iostream.h>
enum boolean { false, true };

class person                            // person class
    {
```

```
     protected:
        char name[40];
     public:
        void setName()
           { cout << "   Enter name: "; cin >> name; }
        void printName()
           { cout << "Name is: " << name << endl; }
        boolean virtual isOutstanding() = 0;  // pure virtual func
     };

class student : public person        // student class
     {
     private:
        float gpa;                    // grade point average
     public:
        void setGpa()                 // set GPA
           { cout << "   Enter student's GPA: "; cin >> gpa; }
        boolean isOutstanding()
           { return (gpa > 3.5) ? true : false; }
     };

class professor : public person      // professor class
     {
     private:
        int numPubs;                  // number of papers published
     public:
        void setNumPubs()             // set number of papers published
           {
           cout << "   Enter number of professor's publications: ";
           cin >> numPubs;
           }
        boolean isOutstanding()
           { return (numPubs > 100) ? true : false; }
     };

void main(void)
     {
     person* persPtr[100];       // list of pointers to persons
     student* stuPtr;            // pointer to student
     professor* proPtr;          // pointer to professor
     int n = 0;                  // number of persons on list
     char choice;

     do
        {
        cout << "Enter student or professor (s/p): ";
        cin >> choice;
        if(choice=='s')                      // it's a student
           {
           stuPtr = new student;             // make new student
           stuPtr->setName();                // set student name
```

```
        stuPtr->setGpa();              // set GPA
        persPtr[n++] = stuPtr;         // put pointer in list
        }
    else                               // it's a professor
        {
        proPtr = new professor;        // make new professor
        proPtr->setName();             // set professor name
        proPtr->setNumPubs();          // set number of pubs
        persPtr[n++] = proPtr;         // put pointer in list
        }
    cout << "   Enter another (y/n)? "; // do another person?
    cin >> choice;
    } while( choice=='y' );            // cycle until not 'y'

    for(int j=0; j<n; j++)             // print names of all
        {                              // persons, and
        persPtr[j]->printName();       // say if outstanding
        if( persPtr[j]->isOutstanding()==true )
            cout << "   This person is outstanding\n";
        }
    } // end main()
```

The student and professor Classes

The student and professor classes add new data items to the base class. The student class contains a variable gpa of type float, which represents the student's grade point average. The professor class contains a variable numPubs of type int, which represents the number of scholarly publications the professor has published. A student with a GPA of over 3.5, and a professor who has published more than 100 publications, are considered outstanding. (We'll refrain from comment on the desirability of these criteria for judging educational excellence.)

The isOutstanding() Function

The isOutstanding() function is declared as a pure virtual function in person. In the student class this function returns a Boolean true if the student's GPA is greater than 3.5, and false otherwise. In professor it returns true if the professor's numPubs variable is greater than 100.

The main() Program

In main() we first let the user enter a number of student and teacher names. For students, the program also asks for the GPA, and for professors it asks for the number of publications. When the user is finished, the program prints out the names of all the students and professors, noting those that are outstanding. Here's some sample interaction:

```
Enter student or professor (s/p): s
    Enter name: Timmy
```

```
    Enter student's GPA: 1.2
    Enter another (y/n)? y
Enter student or professor (s/p): s
    Enter name: Brenda
    Enter student's GPA: 3.9
    Enter another (y/n)? y
Enter student or professor (s/p): s
    Enter name: Sandy
    Enter student's GPA: 2.4
    Enter another (y/n)? y
Enter student or professor (s/p): p
    Enter name: Shipley
    Enter number of professor's publications: 714
    Enter another (y/n)? y
Enter student or professor (s/p): p
    Enter name: Wainright
    Enter number of professor's publications: 13
    Enter another (y/n)? n

Name is: Timmy
Name is: Brenda
    This person is outstanding
Name is: Sandy
Name is: Shipley
    This person is outstanding
Name is: Wainright
```

VIRTUAL FUNCTIONS IN A GRAPHICS EXAMPLE

If you have a graphics display, you can try out another example of virtual functions, this one derived from the MULTSHAP program of Chapter 11. As we noted at the beginning of this section, you may want to draw a number of shapes using the same statement. The VIRTSHAP program does this:

```
// virtshap.cpp
// virtual functions with shapes
#include <graphics.h>           // for graphics functions
#include <conio.h>              // for getche()

const int W = 50;               // size of images

class shape                     // base class
   {
   protected:
      int xCo, yCo;             // coordinates of center
      int linecolor;            // color of outline
      int fillcolor;            // color of interior
   public:
      shape()                   // no-arg constructor
         { xCo=0; yCo=0; linecolor=WHITE; fillcolor=WHITE; }
```

```
       void set(int x, int y, int lc, int fc)   // set data
          { xCo=x; yCo=y; linecolor=lc; fillcolor=fc; }
       void colorize()              // set colors
          {
          setcolor(linecolor);                         // line color
          setlinestyle(SOLID_LINE, 0, THICK_WIDTH); // line width
          setfillstyle(SOLID_FILL, fillcolor);   // set fill color
          }
       virtual void draw() = 0;       // pure virtual draw function
   };

class ball : public shape
   {
   public:
      ball() : shape()             // no-arg constr
         { }
      void set(int x, int y, int lc, int fc)    // set data
         { shape::set(x, y, lc, fc); }
      void draw()              // draw the ball
         {
         colorize();                        // set colors
         circle(xCo, yCo, W);               // draw circle
         floodfill(xCo, yCo, linecolor);    // fill circle
         }
   };

class rect : public shape
   {
   public:
      rect() : shape()             // no-arg constr
         { }
      void set(int x, int y, int lc, int fc)     // set data
         { shape::set(x, y, lc, fc); }
      void draw()              // draw the rectangle
         {
         colorize();                              // set colors
         rectangle(xCo-W, yCo-W, xCo+W, yCo+W); // draw rectangle
         floodfill(xCo, yCo, linecolor);          // fill rectangle
         moveto(xCo-W, yCo+W);                    // draw diagonal
         lineto(xCo+W, yCo-W);                    //     line
         }
   };

class tria : public shape
   {
   public:
      tria() : shape()             // no-arg constr
         { }
      void set(int x, int y, int lc, int fc)    // set data
         { shape::set(x, y, lc, fc); }
      void draw()              // draw the triangle
         {
```

```
                colorize();                     // set colors
                int triarray[] = { xCo,    yCo-W,       // top
                                   xCo+W, yCo+W,        // bottom right
                                   xCo-W, yCo+W };      // bottom left
                fillpoly(3, triarray);          // draw triangle
                }
        };

    void main()
        {
        int driver, mode;
        driver = DETECT;                // set to best graphics mode
        initgraph(&driver, &mode, "\\tc\\bgi");

        shape* ptrarr[3];               // array of pointers to shapes

        ball b1;                        // define three shapes
        rect r1;
        tria t1;
                                        // set values in shapes
        b1.set(100, 100, WHITE, BLUE);
        r1.set(100, 200, WHITE, RED);
        t1.set(100, 300, WHITE, GREEN);

        ptrarr[0] = &b1;                // put addresses in array
        ptrarr[1] = &r1;
        ptrarr[2] = &t1;

        for(int j=0; j<3; j++)          // draw all shapes
            ptrarr[j]->draw();

        getche();                       // wait for keypress
        closegraph();                   // close graphics system
        }
```

The class specifiers in VIRTSHAP are similar to those in MULTSHAP, except that the draw() function in the shape class has been made into a pure virtual function.

In main() we set up an array, ptrarr, of pointers to shapes. Next we create three objects, one of each class, and place their addresses in an array. Now it's easy to draw all three shapes. The statement

```
ptrarr[j]->draw();
```

does this as the loop variable j changes.

This is a powerful approach to combining graphics elements, especially when a large number of objects need to be grouped together and drawn as a unit.

ABSTRACT CLASSES

An *abstract class* is often defined as one that will not be used to create any objects, but exists only to act as a base class of other classes. Using this criteria, the shape

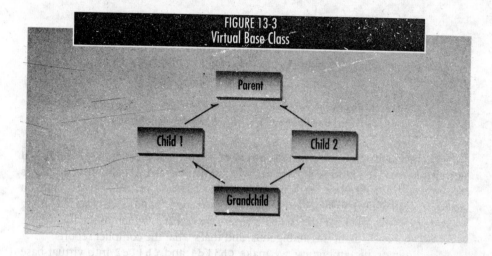

FIGURE 13-3
Virtual Base Class

class in VIRTSHAP is an abstract class. Ellis and Stroustrup (see the bibliography) tighten up this definition by requiring that, to be called abstract, a class must contain at least one pure virtual function. The **shape** class in VIRTSHAP doesn't meet this criterion, but the **person** class in VIRTPERS does.

In either case, the concept of an abstract class is an important one. We'll meet it again when we talk about the Borland class library in Chapter 15.

VIRTUAL BASE CLASSES

Before leaving the subject of virtual programming elements, we should mention *virtual base classes*.

Consider the situation shown in Figure 13-3, with a base class, **Parent**; two derived classes, **Child1** and **Child2**; and a fourth class, **Grandchild**, derived from both **Child1** and **Child2**.

In this arrangement a problem can arise if a member function in the **Grandchild** class wants to access data or functions in the **Parent** class. The NORMBASE program shows what happens:

```
// normbase.cpp
// ambiguous reference to base class

class Parent
  {
  protected:
    int basedata;
  };
class Child1 : public Parent
```

```
    { };
class Child2 : public Parent
    { };
class Grandchild : public Child1, public Child2
    {
    public:
        int getdata()
            { return basedata; }    // ERROR: ambiguous
    };
```

A compiler error occurs when the `getdata()` member function in `Grandchild` attempts to access `basedata` in `Parent`. Why? When the `Child1` and `Child2` classes are derived from `Parent`, each inherits a copy of `Parent`; this copy is called a *subobject*. Each of the two subobjects contains its own copy of `Parent`'s data, including `basedata`. Now, when `Grandchild` refers to `basedata`, which of the two copies will it access? The situation is ambiguous, and that's what the compiler reports.

To eliminate the ambiguity, we make `Child1` and `Child2` into virtual base classes, as shown by example VIRTBASE:

```
// virtbase.cpp
// virtual base classes

class Parent
    {
    protected:
        int basedata;
    };
class Child1 : virtual public Parent    // shares copy of Parent
    { };
class Child2 : virtual public Parent    // shares copy of Parent
    { };
class Grandchild : public Child1, public Child2
    {
    public:
        int getdata()
            { return basedata; }     // OK: only one copy of Parent
    };
```

The use of the keyword `virtual` in these two classes causes them to share a single common *subobject* of their base class `Parent`. Now, since there is only one copy of `basedata`, there is no ambiguity when it is referred to in `Grandchild`.

FRIEND FUNCTIONS

The concepts of encapsulation and data hiding dictate that nonmember functions should not be able to access an object's private or protected data. The policy is, if you're not a member, you can't get in. However, there are situations where such rigid discrimination leads to considerable inconvenience.

FRIENDS AS BRIDGES

Imagine that you want a function to operate on objects of two different classes. Perhaps the function will take objects of the two classes as arguments, and operate on their private data. If the two classes are inherited from the same base class, then you may be able to put the function in the base class. But what if the classes are unrelated?

In this situation there's nothing like a **friend** function. Here's a simple example, FRIEND, that shows how **friend** functions can act as a bridge between two classes:

```
// friend.cpp
// friend functions
#include <iostream.h>

class beta;                     // needed for frifunc declaration

class alpha
    {
    private:
        int data;
    public:
        alpha()  { data = 3; }                 // no-arg constructor
        friend int frifunc(alpha, beta);  // friend function
    };

class beta
    {
    private:
        int data;
    public:
        beta()  { data = 7; }                  // no-arg constructor
        friend int frifunc(alpha, beta);  // friend function
    };

int frifunc(alpha a, beta b)                // function definition
    {
    return( a.data + b.data );
    }

void main()
    {
    alpha aa;
    beta bb;
    cout << frifunc(aa, bb);                // call the function
    }
```

In this program the two classes are **alpha** and **beta**. The constructors in these classes initialize their single data items to fixed values (3 in **alpha** and 7 in **beta**).

We want the function **frifunc()** to have access to both these private data members, so we make it a **friend** function. It's declared with the **friend** keyword in both classes:

```
friend int frifunc(alphà, beta);
```

This declaration can be placed anywhere in the class; it doesn't matter if it goes in the `public` or the `private` section.

An object of each class is passed as an argument to the function `frifunc()` and it accesses the private `data` member of both classes through these arguments. The function doesn't do much: It adds the data items and returns the sum. The `main()` program calls this function and prints the result.

A minor point: Remember that a class can't be referred to until it has been declared. Class `beta` is referred to in the declaration of the function `frifunc()` in class `alpha`, so `beta` must be declared before `alpha`. Hence the declaration

```
class beta;
```

at the beginning of the program.

BREACHING THE WALLS

We should note that `friend` functions are controversial. During the development of C++, arguments raged over the desirability of including this feature. On the one hand, it adds flexibility to the language; on the other, it is not in keeping with the philosophy that only member functions can access a class's private data.

How serious is the breach of data integrity when `friend` functions are used? A `friend` function must be declared as such within the class whose data it will access. Thus a programmer who does not have access to the source code for the class cannot make a function into a `friend`. In this respect the integrity of the class is still protected. Even so, `friend` functions are conceptually messy, and potentially lead to a spaghetti-code situation if numerous `friends` muddy the clear boundaries between classes. For this reason `friend` functions should be used sparingly. If you find yourself using many `friends`, it may be that you need to rethink the design of the program.

ENGLISH DISTANCE EXAMPLE

However, sometimes `friend` functions are too convenient to avoid. One example is when `friends` are used to increase the versatility of overloaded operators. The following program shows a limitation in the use of such operators when friends are not used. This example is a variation on the ENGLPLUS and ENGLCONV programs of Chapter 9. It's called NOFRI.

```
// nofri.cpp
// limitation to overloaded + operator
#include <iostream.h>

class Distance                      // English Distance class
    {
    private:
        int feet;
        float inches;
```

```
public:
    Distance()                      // constructor (no args)
        { feet = 0; inches = 0.0; }
    Distance( float fltfeet )       // constructor (one arg)
        {                           // convert float to Distance
        feet = int(fltfeet);            // feet is integer part
        inches = 12*(fltfeet-feet);     // inches is what's left
        }
    Distance(int ft, float in)  // constructor (two args)
        { feet = ft; inches = in; }
    void showdist()                 // display distance
        { cout << feet << "\'-" << inches << '\"'; }
    Distance operator + (Distance);
    };
                                    // add this distance to d2
Distance Distance::operator + (Distance d2)    // return the sum
    {
    int f = feet + d2.feet;         // add the feet
    float i = inches + d2.inches;   // add the inches
    if(i >= 12.0)                   // if total exceeds 12.0,
        { i -= 12.0; f++; }         // less 12 inches, plus 1 foot
    return Distance(f,i);           // return new Distance with sum
    }


void main()
    {
    Distance d1 = 2.5;              // constructor converts
    Distance d2 = 1.25;             // meters to Distance
    Distance d3;
    cout << "\nd1 = "; d1.showdist();
    cout << "\nd2 = "; d2.showdist();

    d3 = d1 + 10.0;                 // distance + float: ok
    cout << "\nd3 = "; d3.showdist();
                                    // float + Distance: ERROR
//  d3 = 10.0 + d1;
//  cout << "\nd3 = "; d3.showdist();
    }
```

In this program the + operator is overloaded to add two objects of type Distance. Also, there is a one-argument constructor that converts a value of type
float, representing feet and decimal fractions of feet, into a Distance value. (That
is, it converts 10.25' into 10'-3".)

When such a constructor exists, you can make statements like this in
main():

    d3 = d1 + 10.0;

The overloaded + is looking for objects of type Distance both on its left and on
its right, but if the argument on the right is type float, the compiler will use the
one-argument constructor to convert this float to a Distance value, and then
carry out the addition.

Here is what appears to be a subtle variation on this statement:

```
d3 = 10.0 + d1;
```

Does this work? No, because the object of which the overloaded + operator is a member must be the variable to the left of the operator. When we place a variable of a different type there, or a constant, then there is no object of which + can be a member, and so there is no constructor to convert the type **float** to type **Distance**. The compiler can't handle this situation. Here's the output from NOFRI:

```
d3 = 12'-6"
```

The second addition won't compile, so these statements are commented out.

How can we write statements that have nonmember data types to the left of the operator? As you may have guessed, a **friend** can help you out of this dilemma. The FRENGL program shows how:

```
// frengl.cpp
// friend overloaded + operator
#include <iostream.h>

class Distance                        // English Distance class
    {
    private:
        int feet;
        float inches;
    public:
        Distance()                    // constructor (no args)
            { feet = 0; inches = 0.0; }
        Distance( float fltfeet )     // constructor (one arg)
            {                         // convert float to Distance
            feet = int(fltfeet);         // feet is integer part
            inches = 12*(fltfeet-feet);  // inches is what's left
            }
        Distance(int ft, float in)    // constructor (two args)
            { feet = ft; inches = in; }
        void showdist()               // display distance
            { cout << feet << "\'-" << inches << '\"'; }
        friend Distance operator + (Distance, Distance);  // friend
    };

                                      // add D1 to d2
Distance operator + (Distance d1, Distance d2)
    {
    int f = d1.feet + d2.feet;           // add the feet
    float i = d1.inches + d2.inches;     // add the inches
    if(i >= 12.0)                        // if inches exceeds 12.0,
        { i -= 12.0; f++; }              // less 12 inches, plus 1 foot
    return Distance(f,i);                // return new Distance with sum
    }

void main()
    {
```

```
Distance d1 = 2.5;                     // constructor converts
Distance d2 = 1.25;                    // float-feet to Distance
Distance d3;
cout << "\nd1 = "; d1.showdist();
cout << "\nd2 = "; d2.showdist();

d3 = d1 + 10.0;                        // distance + float: ok
cout << "\nd3 = "; d3.showdist();
d3 = 10.0 + d1;                        // float + Distance: ok
cout << "\nd3 = "; d3.showdist();
}
```

The overloaded + operator is made into a `friend`:

```
friend Distance operator + (Distance, Distance);
```

Notice that, while the overloaded + operator took one argument as a member function, it takes two as a `friend` function. In a member function, one of the objects on which the + operates is the object of which it was a member, and the second is an argument. In a `friend`, both objects must be arguments.

The only change to the body of the overloaded + function is that the variables `feet` and `inches`, used in NOFRI for direct access to the object's data, have been replaced in FRENGL by `d1.feet` and `d1.inches`, since this object is supplied as an argument.

friendS FOR FUNCTIONAL NOTATION

Sometimes a `friend` allows a more obvious syntax for calling a function than does a member function. For example, suppose we want a function that will square (multiply by itself) an object of the English `Distance` class. The MISQ example shows how this might be done with a member function:

```
// misq.cpp
// member square() function for Distance
#include <iostream.h>

class Distance                         // English Distance class
   {
   private:
      int feet;
      float inches;
   public:
      Distance()                       // constructor (no args)
         { feet = 0; inches = 0.0; }
      Distance(int ft, float in)  // constructor (two args)
         { feet = ft; inches = in; }
      void showdist()               // display distance
         { cout << feet << "\'-" << inches << '\"'; }

      Distance square();             // member function
   };
```

```
Distance Distance::square()        // return square of
    {                              // this Distance
    float fltfeet = feet + inches/12;   // convert to float
    float feetsqrd = fltfeet * fltfeet; // find the square
    int f = int(feetsqrd);              // convert back to
    float i = 12*(feetsqrd-f);          // feet and inches
    return Distance(f, i);         // return temp Distance
    }

void main()
    {
    Distance d1(3, 6.0);           // two-arg constructor
    Distance d2;                   // no-arg constructor

    d2 = d1.square();              // return square of d1
                                   // display both distances
    cout << "\nd1 = "; d1.showdist();
    cout << "\nd2 = "; d2.showdist();
    }
```

The **main()** part of the program creates a **Distance** value, squares it, and prints out the result. The output shows the original distance and the square:

```
d1 = 3'-6"
d2 = 12'-3"
```

In **main()** we use the statement

```
d2 = d1.square();
```

to find the square of **d1** and assign it to **d2**. This works all right, but if we want to work with **Distance** objects using the same syntax that we use with ordinary numbers, we would probably prefer a functional notation:

```
d2 = square(d1);
```

We can achieve this effect by making **square()** a **friend** of the **Distance** class, as shown in FRISQ:

```
// frisq.cpp
// friend square() function for Distance
#include <iostream.h>

class Distance                     // English Distance class
    {
    private:
        int feet;
        float inches;
    public:
        Distance()                 // constructor (no args)
            { feet = 0; inches = 0.0; }
        Distance(int ft, float in) // constructor (two args)
            { feet = ft; inches = in; }
```

```
        void showdist()              // display distance
           { cout << feet << "\'-" << inches << '\"'; }

        friend Distance square(Distance);  // friend function
   };

Distance square(Distance d)         // return square of
   {                                // argument
   float fltfeet = d.feet + d.inches/12;   // convert to float
   float feetsqrd = fltfeet * fltfeet;     // find the square
   int f = int(feetsqrd);                  // convert back to
   float i = 12*(feetsqrd-f);              // feet and inches
   return Distance(f, i);                  // return temp Distance
   }

void main()
   {
   Distance d1(3, 6.0);             // two-arg constructor
   Distance d2;                     // no-arg constructor

   d2 = square(d1);                 // return square of d1
                                    // display both distances
   cout << "\nd1 = "; d1.showdist();
   cout << "\nd2 = "; d2.showdist();
   }
```

Where `square()`, as a member function in MISQ, takes no arguments, it takes one as a `friend` in FRISQ. In general, the `friend` version of a function requires one more argument than when the function is a member. The `square()` function in FRISQ is similar to that in MISQ, but it refers to the data in the source `Distance` object as `d.feet` and `d.inches` instead of as `feet` and `inches`.

friend CLASSES

The member functions of a class can all be made friends at the same time when you make the entire class a friend. The program FRICLASS shows how this looks:

```
// friclass.cpp
// friend classes
#include <iostream.h>

class alpha
   {
   private:
      int data1;
   public:
      alpha() { data1 = 99; }
      friend class beta;           // beta is a friend class
   };
```

```
class beta
    {                               // all member functions can
    public:                         // access private alpha data
        void func1(alpha a)  { cout << "\ndata1=" << a.data1; }
        void func2(alpha a)  { cout << "\ndata1=" << a.data1; }
        void func3(alpha a)  { cout << "\ndata1=" << a.data1; }
    };

void main()
    {
    alpha a;
    beta b;

    b.func1(a);
    b.func2(a);
    b.func3(a);
    }
```

In class **alpha** the entire class **beta** is proclaimed a friend. Now all the member functions of **beta** can access the private data of **alpha** (in this program the single data item **data1**).

Note that in the **friend** declaration we specify that **beta** is a class using the **class** keyword:

```
friend class beta;
```

We could also have declared **beta** to be a class before the **alpha** class specifier, as in previous examples:

```
class beta;
```

and then, within **alpha**, referred to **beta** without the **class** keyword:

```
friend beta;
```

STATIC FUNCTIONS

In the STATIC example in Chapter 7 we introduced **static** member data. As you may recall, a static data member is not duplicated for each object; rather a single data item is shared by all objects of a class. The STATIC example showed a class that kept track of how many objects of itself there were. Let's extend this concept by showing how functions as well as data may be **static**. Besides showing static functions, our example will model a class that provides an ID number for each of its objects. This allows you to query an object to find out which object it is—a capability that is sometimes useful in debugging a program, among other situations. The program also casts some light on the operation of destructors. Here's the listing for STATFUNC:

```
// statfunc.cpp
// static functions and ID numbers for objects
#include <iostream.h>

class gamma
    {
    private:
        static int total;          // total objects of this class
        int id;                    // ID number of this object
    public:
        gamma()                    // no-argument constructor
            {
            total++;               // add another object
            id = total;            // id equals current total
            }
        ~gamma()                   // destructor
            {
            total--;
            cout << "\nDestroying ID number=" << id;
            }
        static void showtotal()  // static function
            {
            cout << "\nTotal is " << total;
            }
        void showid()              // non-static function
            {
            cout << "\nID number is " << id;
            }
    };

void main()
    {
    cout << endl << endl;
    gamma g1;
    gamma::showtotal();

    gamma g2, g3;
    gamma::showtotal();

    g1.showid();
    g2.showid();
    g3.showid();
    cout << "\n----------end of program----------";
    }
```

Accessing static Functions

In this program there is a static data member, total, in the class gamma. This data keeps track of how many objects of the class there are. It is incremented by the constructor and decremented by the destructor.

Suppose we want to access **total** from outside the class. We construct a function, **showtotal()**, that prints the **total**'s value. But how do we access this function?

When a data member is declared **static**, there is only one such data value for the entire class, no matter how many objects of the class are created. In fact, there may be no such objects at all, but we still want to be able to learn this fact. We could create a dummy object to use in calling a member function, as in

```
gamma dummyObj;          // make an object so we can call function
dummyObj.showtotal();    // call function
```

But this is rather inelegant. We shouldn't need to refer to a specific object when we're doing something that relates to the entire class. It's more reasonable to use the name of the class itself with the scope-resolution operator:

```
gamma::showtotal();      // more reasonable
```

However, this won't work if **showtotal()** is a normal member function; an object and the dot member-access operator is required in such cases. To access **showtotal()** using only the class name, we must declare it to be a **static** member function. This is what we do in STATFUNC. Now the function can be accessed using only the class name. Here's the output:

```
Total is 1
Total is 3
ID number is 1
ID number is 2
ID number is 3
----------end of program--------
Destroying ID number 3
Destroying ID number 2
Destroying ID number 1
```

We define one object, **g1**, and then print out the value of **total**, which is 1. Then we define two more objects, **g2** and **g3**, and again print out the total, which is now 3.

NUMBERING THE OBJECTS

We've placed another function in **gamma()** to print out the ID number of individual members. This ID number is set equal to **total** when an object is created, so each object has a unique number. The **showid()** function prints out the ID of its object. We call it three times in **main()**, in the statements

```
g1.showid();
g2.showid();
g3.showid();
```

As the output shows, each object has a unique number. The **g1** object is numbered 1, **g2** is 2, and **g3** is 3.

INVESTIGATING DESTRUCTORS

Now that we know how to number objects, we can investigate an interesting fact about destructors. STATFUNC prints an *end of program* message in its last statement, but it's not done yet, as the output shows. The three objects created in the program must be destroyed before the program terminates, so that memory is not left in an inaccessible state. The compiler takes care of this by invoking the destructor.

We can see that this happens by inserting in the destructor a statement that prints a message. Since we've numbered the objects, we can also find out the order in which the objects are destroyed. As the output shows, the last object created, g3, is destroyed first. One can infer from this last-in–first-out approach that local objects are stored on the stack.

ASSIGNMENT AND COPY-INITIALIZATION

The C++ compiler is always busy on your behalf, doing things you can't be bothered to do. If you take charge, it will defer to your judgment; otherwise it will do things its own way. Two important examples of this process are the assignment operator and the copy constructor.

You've used the assignment operator many times, probably without thinking too much about it. Suppose a1 and a2 are objects. Unless you tell the compiler otherwise, the statement

```
a2 = a1;       // set a2 to the value of a1
```

will cause the compiler to copy the data from a1, member-by-member, into a2. This is the default action of the assignment operator, =.

You're also familiar with initializing variables. Initializing an object with another object, as in

```
alpha a2(a1);   // initialize a2 to the value of a1
```

causes a similar action. The compiler creates a new object, a2, and copies the data from a1, member-by-member, into a2. This is the default action of the copy constructor.

Both these default activities are provided, free of charge, by the compiler. If member-by-member copying is what you want, you need take no further action. However, if you want assignment or initialization to do something more complex, then you can override the default functions. We'll discuss the techniques for overloading the assignment operator and the copy constructor separately, and then put them together in an example that gives a String class a more efficient way to manage memory.

OVERLOADING THE ASSIGNMENT OPERATOR

Let's look at a short example that demonstrates the technique of overloading the assignment operator. Here's the listing for ASSIGN:

```
// assign.cpp
// overloads assignment operator (=)
#include <iostream.h>

class alpha
    {
    private:
        int data;
    public:
        alpha()                         // no-arg constructor
            { }
        alpha(int d)                    // one-arg constructor
            { data = d; }
        void display()                  // display data
            { cout << data; }
        alpha operator = (alpha& a)     // overloaded = operator
            {
            data = a.data;              // not done automatically
            cout << "\nAssignment operator invoked";
            return alpha(data);         // return copy of this alpha
            }
    };

void main()
    {
    alpha a1(37);
    alpha a2;

    a2 = a1;                            // invoke overloaded =
    cout << "\na2="; a2.display();      // display a2

    alpha a3 = a2;                      // does NOT invoke =
    cout << "\na3="; a3.display();      // display a3
    }
```

The `alpha` class is very simple; it contains only one data member. Constructors initialize the data, and a member function can print out its value. The new aspect of ASSIGN is the function `operator=()`, which overloads the = operator.

In `main()` we define `a1` and give it the value 37, and define `a2` but give it no value. Then we use the assignment operator to set `a2` to the value of `a1`:

```
a2 = a1;    // assignment statement
```

This causes our overloaded `operator=()` function to be invoked. Here's the output from ASSIGN:

```
Assignment operator invoked
a2=37
a3=37
```

Initialization Is Not Assignment

In the last two lines of ASSIGN we initialize the object **a3** to the value **a2**, and display it. Don't be confused by the syntax here. The equals sign in

```
alpha a3 = a2;   // copy initialization, not an assignment
```

is not an assignment but an initialization, with the same effect as

```
alpha a3(a2);    // alternative form of copy initialization
```

This is why the the assignment operator is executed only once, as shown by the single invocation of the line

```
Assignment operator invoked
```

in the output of ASSIGN.

Taking Responsibility

When you overload the = operator you assume responsibility for doing whatever the default assignment operator did. Often this involves copying the member data from one object to another. The **alpha** class in ASSIGN has only one data item, **data**, so the **operator=()** function copies its value with the statement

```
data = a.data;
```

The function also prints the *Assignment operator invoked* message so that we can tell when it executes.

Passing by Reference

Notice that the argument to **operator=()** is passed by reference. It is not absolutely necessary to do this, but it's often a good idea. Why? As you know, an argument passed by value generates a copy of itself in the function to which it is passed. The argument passed to the **operator=()** function is no exception. If such objects are large, the copies can waste a lot of memory. Values passed by reference don't generate copies, and thus help to conserve memory.

Also, there are certain situations in which you want to keep track of the number of objects (as in the STATFUNC example, where we assigned numbers to the objects). If the compiler is generating extra objects every time you use the assignment operator, you may wind up with more objects than you expected. Passing by reference helps to avoid such spurious object creation.

Returning a Value

As we've seen, a function can return information to the calling program by value or by reference. When an object is returned by value, a new object is created and returned to the calling program. In the calling program the value of this object can be assigned to a new object, or it can be used in other ways. When an object is returned by reference, no new object is created. A reference to the original object in the function is all that's returned to the calling program.

The `operator=()` function in ASSIGN returns a value by creating a temporary `alpha` object and initializing it using the one-argument constructor in the statement

```
return alpha(data);
```

The value returned is a copy of, but not the same object as, the object of which the overloaded = operator is a member. Returning a value makes it possible to chain = operators:

```
a3 = a2 = a1;
```

However, returning by value has the same disadvantages as passing an argument by value: It creates an extra copy that wastes memory and can cause confusion. Can we return this value with a reference, using the declarator shown here for the overloaded = operator?

```
alpha& operator = (alpha& a)  // bad idea in this case
```

Unfortunately we can't use reference returns on variables that are local to a function. Remember that local (`automatic`) variables—that is, those created within a function (and not designated `static`)—are destroyed when the function returns. A return by reference returns only the address of the data being returned, and, for local data, this address points to data within the function. When the function is terminated and this data is destroyed, the pointer is left with a meaningless value. (We'll see one way to solve this problem when we talk about the `this` pointer later in this chapter.)

Not Inherited

The assignment operator is unique among operators in that it is not inherited. If you overload the assignment operator in a base class, you can't use this same function in any derived classes.

THE COPY CONSTRUCTOR

As we discussed, you can define and at the same time initialize an object to the value of another object with two kinds of statement:

```
alpha a3(a2);     // copy initialization
alpha a3 = a2;    // copy initialization, alternate syntax
```

Both styles of definition invoke a *copy constructor*: that is, a constructor that copies its argument into a new object. The default copy constructor, which is provided automatically by the compiler for every object, performs a member-by-member copy. This is similar to what the assignment operator does; the difference is that the copy constructor also creates a new object.

Like the assignment operator, the copy constructor can be overloaded by the user. The XOFXREF example shows how it's done:

```
// xofxref.cpp
// copy constructor: X(X&)
#include <iostream.h>

class alpha
    {
    private:
        int data;
    public:
        alpha()                          // no-arg constructor
            { }
        alpha(int d)                     // one-arg constructor
            { data = d; }
        alpha(alpha& a)                  // copy constructor
            {
            data = a.data;
            cout << "\nCopy constructor invoked";
            }
        void display()                   // display
            { cout << data; }
        void operator = (alpha& a) // overloaded = operator
            {
            data = a.data;
            cout << "\nAssignment operator invoked";
            }
    };

void main()
    {
    alpha a1(37);
    alpha a2;

    a2 = a1;                             // invoke overloaded =
    cout << "\na2="; a2.display();       // display a2

    alpha a3(a1);                        // invoke copy constructor
    // alpha a3 = a1;                    // equivalent definition of a3
    cout << "\na3="; a3.display();       // display a3
    }
```

This program overloads both the assignment operator and the copy constructor. The overloaded assignment operator is similar to that in the ASSIGN example. The copy constructor takes one argument: an object of type alpha, passed by reference. Here's its declarator:

```
alpha(alpha&)
```

This declarator has the form X(X&) (pronounced "X of X ref"), which is often used as a shorthand name for copy constructors. Here's the output of XOFXREF:

```
Assignment operator invoked
a2=37
Copy constructor invoked
a3=37
```

The statement

```
a2 = a1;
```

invokes the assignment operator, while

```
alpha a3(a1);
```

invokes the copy constructor. The equivalent statement

```
alpha a3 = a1;
```

could also be used to invoke the copy constructor.

We've seen that the copy constructor may be invoked when an object is defined. It is also invoked when arguments are passed by value to functions and when values are returned from functions. Let's mention these situations briefly.

Function Arguments

The copy constructor is invoked when an object is passed by value to a function. It creates the copy that the function operates on. Thus if the function

```
void func(alpha);
```

was declared in XOFXREF, and this function was called by the statement

```
func(a1);
```

then the copy constructor would be invoked to create a copy of the **a1** object for use by **func()**. (Of course, the copy constructor is not invoked if the argument is passed by reference or if a pointer to it is passed. In these cases no copy is created; the function operates on the original variable.)

Function Return Values

The copy constructor also creates a temporary object when a value is returned from a function. Suppose there were a function like this in XOFXREF:

```
alpha func();
```

and this function was called by the statement

```
a2 = func();
```

then the copy constructor would be invoked to create a copy of the value returned by **func()**, and this value would be assigned (invoking the assignment operator) to **a2**.

Why Not an X(X) Constructor?

Do we need to use a reference in the argument to the copy constructor? Could we pass by value instead? No, the compiler complains that it is *out of memory* if we try to compile

```
alpha(alpha a)
```

Why? Because when an argument is passed by value, a copy of it is constructed. What makes the copy? The copy constructor. But this is the copy constructor, so it calls itself. In fact it calls itself over and over until the compiler runs out of memory. So, in the copy constructor, the argument must be passed by reference, which creates no copies.

A MEMORY-EFFICIENT STRING CLASS

The ASSIGN and XOFXREF examples don't really need to have overloaded assignment operators and copy constructors. They use straightforward classes with only one data item, so the default assignment operator and copy constructor would work just as well. Let's look at an example where it is essential for the user to overload these operators.

Defects with the String Class

We've seen various versions of the string class in previous chapters. However, these versions are not very sophisticated. It would be nice to overload the = operator so that we could assign the value of one string object to another with the statement

```
s2 = s1;
```

If we overload the = operator, the question arises how we will handle the actual string (the array of type char), which is the principal data item in the string class.

One possibilty is for each string object to have a place to store a string. If we assign one string object to another (from s1 into s2 in the previous statement), we simply copy the string from the source into the destination object. The problem with this is that the same string now exists in two (or more) places in memory. This is not very efficient, especially if the strings are long. Figure 13-4 shows how this looks.

Instead of having each string object contain its own string, we could arrange for it to contain only a *pointer* to a string. Now, if we assign one string object to another, we need only copy the pointer from one object to another; both pointers will point to the same string. This is efficient, since only a single copy of the string itself needs to be stored in memory. Figure 13-5 shows how this looks.

However, if we use this system we need to be careful when we destroy a string object. If a string's destructor uses delete to free the memory occupied by the string, and if there are several objects with pointers pointing to the string, then these other objects will be left with pointers pointing to memory that may no longer hold the string they think it does; they become dangling pointers.

To use pointers to strings in string objects, we need a way to keep track of how many string objects point to a particular string, so that we can avoid deleteing the string until the last string that points to it is itself deleted. Our next example, STRIMEM, does just this.

499

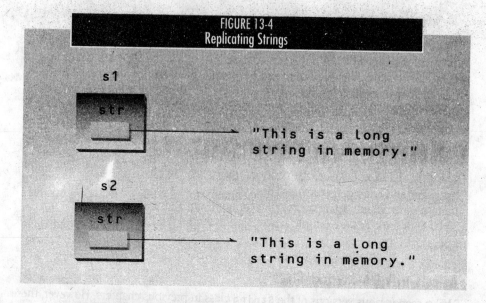

FIGURE 13-4
Replicating Strings

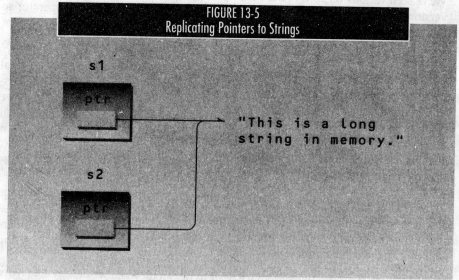

FIGURE 13-5
Replicating Pointers to Strings

A String-Counter Class

Suppose we have several `string` objects pointing to the same string and we want to keep a count of how many `strings` point to the string. Where will we store this count?

It would be cumbersome for every `string` object to maintain a count of how many of its fellow `strings` were pointing to a particular string, so we don't want to use a member variable in `string` for the count. Could we use a static variable? This

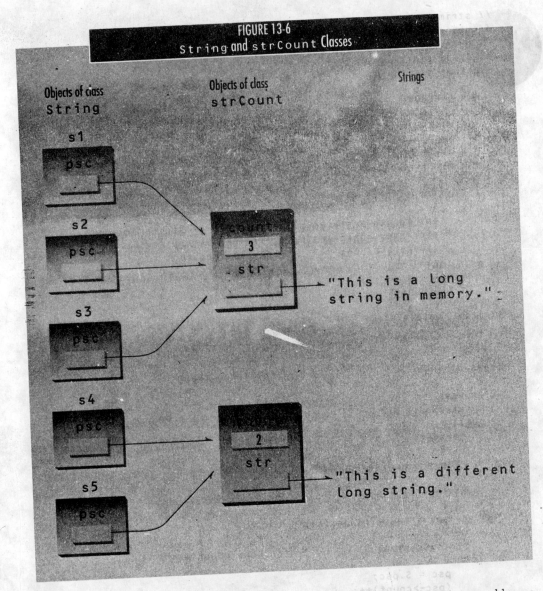

FIGURE 13-6
String and strCount Classes

is a possibility; we could create a static array and use it to store a list of string addresses and counts. However, this requires considerable overhead. It's more efficient to create a new class to store the count. Each object of this class, which we call strCount, contains a count and also a pointer to the string itself. Each String object contains a pointer to the appropriate strCount object. Figure 13-6 shows how this looks.

To ensure that String objects have access to strCount objects, we make String a friend of strCount. Here's the listing for STRIMEM:

```
// strimem.cpp
// memory-saving String class
// overloaded assignment and copy constructor
#include <iostream.h>
#include <string.h>                        // for strcpy(), etc

class strCount                             // keep track of number
   {                                       // of unique strings
   private:
      int count;                           // number of instances
      char* str;                           // pointer to string
      friend class String;                 // make ourselves available
   public:
      strCount(char* s)                    // one-arg constructor
         {
         int length = strlen(s);  // length of string argument
         str = new char[length+1];  // get memory for string
         strcpy(str, s);                   // copy argument to it
         count=1;                          // start count at 1
         }
      strCount()                           // destructor
         {
         delete str;                       // delete the string
         }
   };

class String                               // String class
   {
   private:
      strCount* psc;                       // pointer to strCount
   public:
      String()                             // no-arg constructor
         {
         psc = new strCount("NULL");
         }
      String(char* s)                      // 1-arg constructor
         {
         psc = new strCount(s);
         }
      String(String& S)                    // copy constructor
         {
         psc = S.psc;
         (psc->count)++;
         }
      ~String()                            // destructor
         {
         if(psc->count==1)                 // if this is last instance,
            delete psc;                    // release strCount
         else                              // if not last instance
            (psc->count)--;                // decrement count
         }
      void display()                       // display the String
```

```
        {
        cout << psc->str;                   // print string
        cout << " (addr=" << psc << ")";     // print address
        }
    void operator = (String& S) // assign the string
        {
        delete psc;             // delete our strCount
        psc = S.psc;            // use argument's strCount
        (psc->count)++;         // increment count
        }
    };

void main()
    {
    String s3 = "When the fox preaches, look to your geese.";
    cout << "\ns3="; s3.display();    // display s3

    String s1;                    // define String
    s1 = s3;                      // assign it another String
    cout << "\ns1="; s1.display();    // display it

    String s2(s3);                // initialize with String
    cout << "\ns2="; s2.display();    // display it
    }
```

In the main() part of STRIMEM we define a **String** object, s3, to contain the proverb "When the fox preaches, look to your geese." We define another **String** s1 and set it equal to s3; then we define s2 and initialize it to s3. Setting s1 equal to s3 invokes the overloaded assignment operator; initializing s2 to s3 invokes the overloaded copy constructor. We print out all three strings, and also the address of the **strCount** object pointed to by each object's **psc** pointer, to show that these objects are all the same. Here's the output from STRIMEM:

```
s3=When the fox preaches, look to your geese. (addr=0x8f510e00)
s1=When the fox preaches, look to your geese. (addr=0x8f510e00)
s2=When the fox preaches, look to your geese. (addr=0x8f510e00)
```

The other duties of the **String** class are divided between the **String** and **strCount** classes. Let's see what they do.

The strCount Class

The **strCount** class contains the pointer to the actual string and the count of how many **String** class objects point to this string. Its single constructor takes a pointer to a string as an argument and creates a new memory area for the string. It copies the string into this area and sets the count to 1, since just one **String** points to it when it is created. The destructor in **strCount** frees the memory used by the string.

The String Class

The **String** class uses three constructors. If a new string is being created, as in the one- and two-argument constructors, a new **strCount** object is created to hold the string, and the **psc** pointer is set to point to this object. If an existing **String** object is being copied, as in the copy constructor and the overloaded assignment operator, then the pointer **psc** is set to point to the old **strCount** object, and the count in this object is incremented. The overloaded assignment operator must also delete

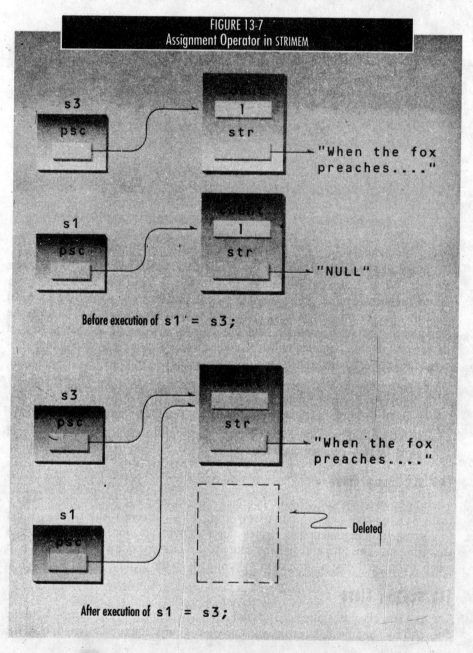

FIGURE 13-7
Assignment Operator in STRIMEM

Before execution of **s1 = s3;**

After execution of **s1 = s3;**

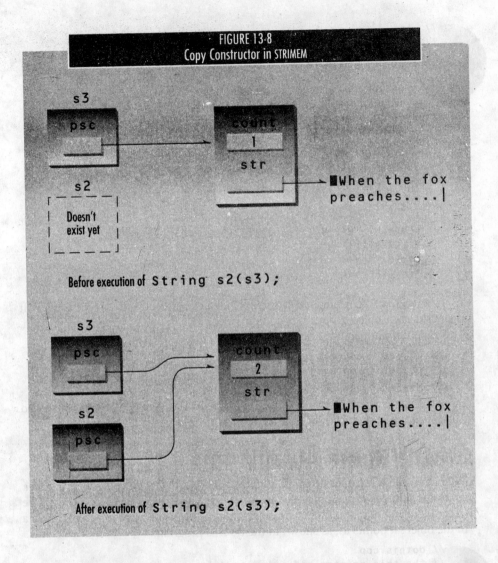

FIGURE 13-8
Copy Constructor in STRIMEM

the old **strCount** object pointed to by **psc**. Figure 13-7 shows the action of the overloaded assignment operator, and Figure 13-8 shows the copy constructor.

THE this POINTER

The member functions of every object have access to a sort of magic pointer named **this**, which points to the object itself. Thus any member function can find out the address of the object of which it is a member. Here's a short example, WHERE, that shows the mechanism:

```
// where.cpp
// the this pointer
#include <iostream.h>

class where
    {
    private:
        char charray[10];    // occupies 10 bytes
    public:
        void reveal()
            { cout << "\nMy object's address is " << this; }
    };

void main()
    {
    where w1, w2, w3;    // make three objects
    w1.reveal();         // see where they are
    w2.reveal();
    w3.reveal();
    }
```

The **main()** program in this example creates three objects of type **where**. It then asks each object to print its address, using the **reveal()** member function. This function prints out the value of the **this** pointer. Here's the output:

```
My object's address is 0x8f4effec
My object's address is 0x8f4effe2
My object's address is 0x8f4effd8
```

Since the data in each object consists of an array of 10 bytes, the objects are spaced 10 bytes apart in memory. (EC minus E2 is 10 decimal, as is E2 minus D8.)

ACCESSING MEMBER DATA WITH **this**

When you call a member function, it comes into existence with the value of **this** set to the address of the object for which it was called. The **this** pointer can be treated like any other pointer to an object, and can thus be used to access the data in the object it points to, as shown in the DOTHIS program:

```
// dothis.cpp
// the this pointer referring to data
#include <iostream.h>

class what
    {
    private:
        int alpha;
    public:
        void tester()
            {
            this->alpha = 11;    // same as alpha = 11;
            cout << this->alpha; // same as cout << alpha;
            }
```

```
};

void main()
    {
    what w;
    w.tester();
    }
```

This program simply prints out the value 11. Notice that the `tester()` member function accesses the variable `alpha` as

```
this->alpha
```

This is exactly the same as referring to `alpha` directly. This syntax works, but there is no reason for it except to show that `this` does indeed point to the object.

USING this FOR RETURNING VALUES

A more practical use for `this` is in returning values from member functions and overloaded operators.

Recall that in the ASSIGN program we could not return an object by reference, because the object was local to the function returning it, and thus was destroyed when the function returned. We need a more permanent object if we're going to return it by reference. The object of which a function is a member is more permanent than its individual member functions. An object's member functions are created and destroyed every time they're called, but the object itself endures until it is destroyed by some outside agency (for example, when it is `delete`d). Thus returning by reference the object of which a function is a member is a better bet than returning a temporary object created in a member function. The `this` pointer makes this easy.

Here's the listing for ASSIGN2, in which the `operator=()` function returns by reference the object that invoked it:

```
// assign2.cpp
// returns contents of the this pointer
#include <iostream.h>

class alpha
    {
    private:
        int data;
    public:
        alpha()                                 // no-arg constructor
            { }
        alpha(int d)                            // one-arg constructor
            { data = d; }
        void display()                          // display data
            { cout << data; }
        alpha& operator = (alpha& a)            // overloaded = operator
            {
            data = a.data;                      // not done automatically
            cout << "\nAssignment operator invoked";
            return *this;                       // return copy of this alpha
```

507

```
        }
    };

void main()
    {
    alpha a1(37);
    alpha a2, a3;

    a3 = a2 = a1;                               // invoke overloaded =
    cout << "\na2="; a2.display();  // display a2

    cout << "\na3="; a3.display();  // display a3
    }
```

In this program we can use the declaration

```
alpha& operator = (alpha& a)
```

which returns by reference, instead of

```
alpha operator = (alpha& a)
```

which returns by value. The last statement in this function is

```
return *this;
```

Since this is a pointer to the object of which the function is a member, *this is that object itself, and the statement returns it by reference. Here's the output of ASSIGN2:

```
Assignment operator invoked
Assignment operator invoked
a2=37
a3=37
```

Each time the equals sign is encountered in

```
a3 = a2 = a1;
```

the overloaded operator=() function is called, which prints the messages. The three objects all end up with the same value.

REVISED STRIMEM PROGRAM

Using the this pointer we can revise the operator=() function in STRIMEM to return a value by reference, thus making possible multiple assignment operators for String objects, such as

```
s1 = s2 = s3;
```

At the same time, we can avoid the creation of spurious objects such as those that are created when objects are returned by value. Here's the listing for STRIMEM2:

```
// strimem2.cpp
// memory-saving String class
// the this pointer in overloaded assignment
#include <iostream.h>
#include <string.h>                      // for strcpy(), etc
```

```
class strCount                              // keep track of number
    {                                       // of unique strings
    private:
        int count;                          // number of instances
        char* str;                          // pointer to string
        friend class String;                // make ourselves available
    public:
        strCount(char* s)                   // one-arg constructor
            {
            int length = strlen(s);         // length of string argument
            str = new char[length+1];       // get memory for string
            strcpy(str, s);                 // copy argument to it
            count=1;                        // start count at 1
            }
        ~strCount()                         // destructor
            {
            delete str;                     // delete the string
            }
    };

class String                                // String class
    {
    private:
        strCount* psc;                      // pointer to strCount
    public:
        String()                            // no-arg constructor
            {
            psc = new strCount("NULL");
            }
        String(char* s)                     // 1-arg constructor
            {
            psc = new strCount(s);
            }
        String(String& S)                   // copy constructor
            {
            cout << "\nCOPY CONSTRUCTOR";
            psc = S.psc;
            (psc->count)++;
            }
        ~String()                           // destructor
            {
            if(psc->count==1)               // if this is last instance,
                delete psc;                 // release strCount
            else                            // if not last instance
                (psc->count)--;             // decrement count
            }
        void display()                      // display the String
            {
            cout << psc->str;               // print string
            cout << " (addr=" << psc << ")"; // print address
            }
```

```
           String& operator = (String& S)   // assign the string
               {
               cout << "\nASSIGNMENT";
               delete psc;                    // delete our strCount
               psc = S.psc;                   // use argument's strCount
               (psc->count)++;                // increment count
               return *this;                  // return this object
               }
           };

      void main()
           {
           String s3 = "When the fox preaches, look to your geese.";
           cout << "\ns3="; s3.display();    // display s3

           String s1, s2;                     // define Strings
           s1 = s2 = s3;                      // assign them
           cout << "\ns1="; s1.display();     // display it
           cout << "\ns2="; s2.display();     // display it
           }
```

Now the declarator for the = operator is

```
String& operator = (String& S)   // return by reference
```

And, as in ASSIGN2, this function returns a pointer to this. Here's the output:

```
s3=When the fox preaches, look to your geese. (addr=0x8f640d3a)
ASSIGNMENT
ASSIGNMENT
s1=When the fox preaches, look to your geese. (addr=0x8f640d3a)
s2=When the fox preaches, look to your geese. (addr=0x8f640d3a)
```

The output shows that, following the assignment statement, all three String objects point to the same strCount object.

We should note that the this pointer is not available in static member functions, since they are not associated with a particular object.

SUMMARY

Virtual functions provide a way for a program to decide, when it is running, what function to call. Ordinarily such decisions are made at compile time. Virtual functions make possible greater flexibility in performing the same kind of action on different kinds of objects. In particular, they allow the use of functions called from an array of type pointer-to-base, that actually holds pointers to a variety of derived types. Typically a function is declared virtual in the base class, and other functions with the same name are declared in derived classes. A pure virtual function has no body in the base class.

A **friend** function can access a class's private data, even though it is not a member function of the class. This is useful when one function must have access to two or more unrelated classes and when an overloaded operator must use, on its left side, a value of a class other than the one of which it is a member. **friends** are also used to facilitate functional notation.

A **static** function is one that operates on the class in general, rather than on objects of the class. In particular it can operate on static variables. It can be called with the class name and scope-resolution operator.

The assignment operator = can be overloaded. This is necessary when it must do more than merely copy one object's contents into another. Also, the copy constructor, which creates copies during initialization, and also when arguments are passed and returned by value, can be overloaded. This is necessary when the copy constructor must do more than simply copy an object.

The **this** pointer is predefined in member functions to point to the object of which the function is a member. The **this** pointer is useful in returning the object of which the function is a member.

QUESTIONS

1. Virtual functions allow you to
   a. create an array of type pointer-to-base-class that can hold pointers to derived classes
   b. create functions that have no body
   c. group objects of different classes so they can all be accessed by the same function code
   d. use the same function call to execute member functions of objects from different classes

2. True or false: A pointer to a base class can point to objects of a derived class.

3. If there is a pointer p to objects of a base class, and it contains the address of an object of a derived class, and both classes contain a nonvirtual member function, **ding()**, then the statement **p->ding();** will cause the version of **ding()** in the _____ class to be executed.

4. Write a declarator for a virtual function called **dang()** that returns type **void** and takes one argument of type **int**.

5. Deciding—*after* a program starts to execute—what function will be executed by a particular function call statement, is called _____.

6. If there is a pointer, p, to objects of a base class, and it contains the address of an object of a derived class, and both classes contain a virtual member function, **ding()**, then the statement **p->ding();** will cause the version of **ding()** in the _____ class to be executed.

7. Write the declaration for a pure virtual function called `aragorn` that returns no value and takes no arguments.

8. A pure virtual function is a virtual function that
   a. has no body
   b. returns nothing
   c. is used in a base class
   d. takes no arguments

9. Write the definition of an array called `parr` of 10 pointers to objects of class `dong`.

10. A virtual base class is useful when
    a. different functions in base and derived classes have the same name
    b. there are multiple paths from one derived class to another
    c. the identification of a function in a base class is ambiguous
    d. it makes sense to use a base class with no body

11. True or false: A `friend` function can access a class's private data without being a member of the class.

12. A `friend` function can be used to
    a. avoid arguments between classes
    b. allow access to classes whose source code is unavailable
    c. allow one class to access an unrelated class
    d. increase the versatility of an overloaded operator

13. Write the declaration for a friend function called `harry()` that returns type `void` and takes one argument of class `george`.

14. The keyword `friend` appears in
    a. the class allowing access to another class
    b. the class desiring access to another class
    c. the private section of a class
    d. the public section of a class

15. Write a declaration that, in the class in which it appears, will make every member of the class `harry` a `friend` function.

16. A static function
    a. should be called when an object is destroyed
    b. is closely connected with an individual object of a class
    c. can be called using the class name and function name
    d. is used when a dummy object must be created

17. Explain what the default assignment operator = does when applied to objects.

18. Write a declaration for an overloaded assignment operator in class `zeta`.

19. An assignment operator might be overloaded to
    a. help keep track of the number of identical objects
    b. assign a separate ID number to each object
    c. ensure that all member data is copied exactly
    d. signal when assignment takes place

20. True or false: The user must always define the operation of the copy constructor.

21. The operation of the assignment operator and that of the copy constructor are
    a. similar, except that the copy constructor creates a new object
    b. similar, except that the assignment operator copies member data
    c. different, except that they both create a new object
    d. different, except that they both copy member data

22. Write the declaration of a copy constructor for a class called `Bertha`.

23. True or false: A copy constructor could be defined to copy only part of an object's data.

24. The lifetime of a variable that is defined as
    a. automatic in a member function coincides with the lifetime of the function
    b. external coincides with the lifetime of a class
    c. member data of an object coincides with the lifetime of the object
    d. static in a member function coincides with the lifetime of the function

25. True or false: There is no problem with returning the value of a variable defined as automatic within a member function so long as it is returned by value.

26. Explain the difference in operation between these two statements:

```
person p1(p0);
person p1 = p0;
```

27. A copy constructor is invoked when
    a. a function returns by value
    b. an argument is passed by value
    c. a function returns by reference
    d. an argument is passed by reference

28. What does the `this` pointer point to?

29. If, within a class, `da` is a member variable, will the statement `this.da=37;` assign 37 to `da`?

30. Write a statement that a member function can use to return the entire object of which it is a member, without creating any temporary objects.

EXERCISES

1. Imagine the same publishing company described in Exercise 1 of Chapter 10 that markets both book and audio-cassette versions of its works. As in that exercise, create a class called `publication` that stores the title (a string) and price (type `float`) of a publication. From this class derive two classes: `book`, which adds a page count (type `int`); and `tape`, which adds a playing time in minutes (type `float`). Each of the three classes should have a `getdata()` function to get its data from the user at the keyboard, and a `putdata()` function to display the data.

Write a `main()` program that creates an array of pointers to `publication`. This is similar to the VIRTPERS example in this chapter. In a loop, ask the user for data about a particular book or tape, and use `new` to create an object of type `book` or `tape` to hold the data. Put the pointer to the object in the array. When the user has finished entering the data for all books and tapes, display the resulting data for all the books and tapes entered, using a `for` loop and a single statement such as

```
pubarr[j]->putdata();
```

to display the data from each object in the array.

2. In the `Distance` class, as shown in the FRENGL and FRISQ examples in this chapter, create an overloaded `*` operator so that two distances can be multiplied together. Make it a `friend` function so that you can use such expressions as

```
dist1 = 7.5 * dist2;
```

You'll need a one-argument constructor to convert floating-point values into `Distance` values. Write a `main()` program to test this operator in several ways.

3. You can make a class that acts like an array. This involves overloading the subscript operator, which consists of the pair of braces: `[]`. The CLARRAY example shown here is a complete program that demonstrates how to create your own array class:

```cpp
// clarray.cpp
// creates array class
#include <iostream.h>

class Array                          // models a normal C++ array
   {
   private:
      int* ptr;                      // pointer to Array contents
      int size;                      // size of Array
   public:
      Array(int s)                   // one-argument constructor
         {
         size = s;                   // argument is size of Array
         ptr = new int[s];           // make space for Array
         }
      ~Array()                       // destructor
         { delete ptr; }
      int& operator [] (int j)       // overloaded subscript operator
         { return *(ptr+j); }
   };

void main()
   {
   const int ASIZE = 10;            // size of array
   Array arr(ASIZE);               // make an array
```

```
for(int j=0; j<ASIZE; j++)    // fill it with squares
    arr[j] = j*j;

for(j=0; j<ASIZE; j++)        // display its contents
    cout << arr[j] << "   ":
}
```

The output of this program is

```
0  1  4  9  16  25  36  49  64  81
```

Starting with CLARRAY, add an overloaded assignment operator and an overloaded copy constructor to the `Array` class. Then add statements such as

```
Array arr2(arr1);
```

and

```
arr3 = arr1;
```

to the `main()` program to test whether these overloaded operators work.

One of the advantages of making your own array class is that you can make it into a "safe" array by adding statements to the member functions to perform bounds-checking operations. In this way you can guarantee that the user of such an array doesn't write a subscript that's too big (or small) for the array and thereby cause the usual sort of catastrophe. You can create such an array class for extra credit, although we don't show this in the answers.

FILES AND STREAMS

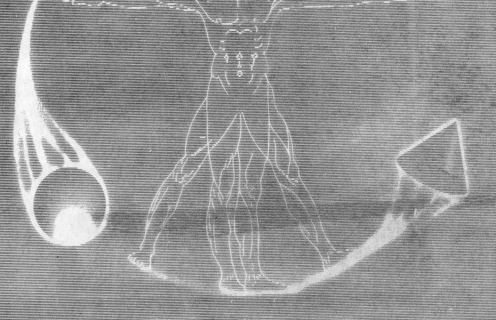

Most serious programs need to read and write data to disk files. In this chapter we describe how to perform these activities using C++ streams. We'll begin with a brief examination of the classes used in stream-oriented I/O operations in C++. Then we'll see how these classes are used for disk file I/O in various situations. We'll also examine several other features of C++ that are related to files, including redirection, command-line arguments, overloading the insertion and extraction operators, and sending data to the printer.

C programmers will note that the approach to disk I/O used in C++ is quite different from that in C. The old C functions, such as `fread()` and `fwrite()`, will still work in C++, but they are not so well suited to the object-oriented environment. The new C++ approach is considerably cleaner and easier to implement.

STREAMS

A *stream* is a general name given to a flow of data. Different streams are used to represent different kinds of data flow. Each stream is associated with a particular class, which contains member functions and definitions for dealing with that particular kind of data flow. For example, the `ifstream` class represents input disk files. Thus each file in C++ is an object of a particular stream class.

THE STREAM CLASS HIERARCHY

The stream classes are arranged in a rather complex hierarchy. You don't need to understand this hierarchy in detail to program basic file I/O, but a brief overview may be helpful. Figure 14-1 shows the arrangement of the classes used for I/O in Turbo C++.

We've already made extensive use of some of these classes. The extraction operator `>>` is a member of the `istream` class, and the insertion operator `<<` is a member of the `ostream` class. Both of these classes are derived from the `ios` class. The `cout` object, representing the standard output stream, which is usually directed to the video display, is a predefined object of the `ostream_withassign` class, which

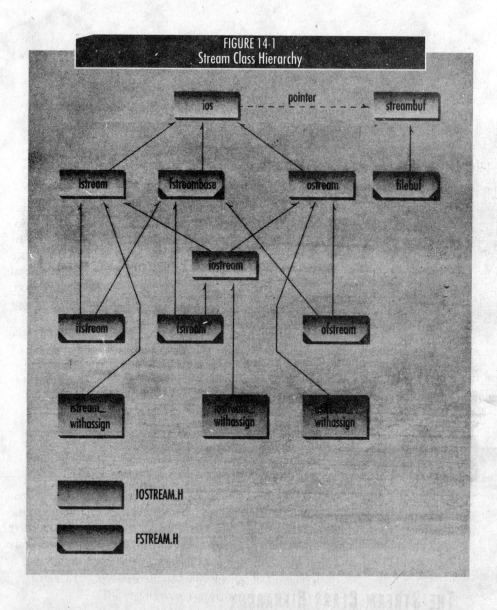

FIGURE 14-1
Stream Class Hierarchy

is derived from the `ostream` class. Similarly `cin` is an object of the `istream_withassign` class, which is derived from `istream`.

The classes used for input and output to the video display and keyboard are declared in the header file IOSTREAM.H, which we routinely included in our examples in previous chapters. The classes used for disk file I/O are declared in the file

FSTREAM.H. The figure shows which classes are in which header file. You may find it educational to print out these files and trace the relationships among the various classes. Many questions about streams can be answered by studying these class and constant declarations.

STREAM CLASSES

As you can see from Figure 14-1, the ios class is the base class for the hierarchy. It contains many constants and member functions common to input and output operations of all kinds. Some of these, such as the showpoint and fixed flags, we've seen already. It also supports some general error-status flags, which we'll look at later. The ios class contains a pointer to the streambuf class, which contains low-level routines for handling data buffers for buffered I/O.

The istream and ostream classes are derived from ios and are dedicated to input and output, respectively. Their member functions perform both formatted and unformatted operations. The istream class contains such functions as get(), getline(), read(), and overloaded extraction (>>) operators, while ostream contains put() and write, and overloaded insertion (<<) operators.

The iostream class is derived from both istream and ostream by multiple inheritance, so that other classes can inherit both of these classes from it. Three classes—istream_withassign, ostream_withassign and iostream_withassign—are inherited from istream, ostream, and iostream, respectively. They add assignment operators to these classes.

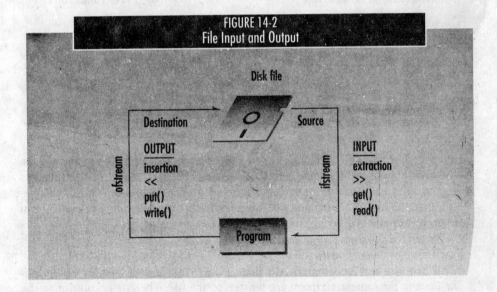

FIGURE 14-2
File Input and Output

The classes in which we are most interested for file I/O are `ifstream` for input files, `ofstream` for output files, and `fstream` for files that will be used for both input and output. These classes are derived from `istream`, `ostream`, and `iostream`, respectively, and also from `fstreambase`. Figure 14-2 shows some of the options available with the `ifstream` and `ofstream` classes.

HEADER FILES

The `ifstream`, `ofstream`, and `fstream` classes are declared in the FSTREAM.H file. This file also includes the IOSTREAM.H header file, so there is no need to include it explicitly; FSTREAM.H takes care of all stream I/O.

STRING I/O

Let's look at some simple programs that read and write disk files. We'll start by reading and writing character strings.

WRITING STRINGS

Our first program, OLINE, outputs some strings to a file.

```
// oline.cpp
// file output with strings
#include <fstream.h>                      // for file functions

void main()
   {
   ofstream outfile("TEST.TXT");          // create file for output
                                          // send text to file
   outfile << "I fear thee, ancient Mariner!\n";
   outfile << "I fear thy skinny hand\n";
   outfile << "And thou art long, and lank, and brown,\n";
   outfile << "As is the ribbed sea sand.\n";
   }
```

Here we define an object called `outfile` to be a member of the `ofstream` class. At the same time, we initialize it to the file name TEST.TXT. This initialization sets aside various resources for the file, and accesses the file of that name on the disk.

Since the insertion operator `<<` is appropriately overloaded in `ostream` (from which `ofstream` is derived), we can use it to output text to the file.

When the program terminates, the `outfile` object goes out of scope. This calls the destructor, which closes the file, so we don't need to close the file explicitly.

When you run the program, the lines of text (from Samuel Taylor Coleridge's *The Rime of the Ancient Mariner*) are written to the file. There is no output to the screen. To see that the text is in the TEST.TXT file, you can display it with the DOS *TYPE* command.

READING STRINGS

To read the same file we must create an object of class **ifstream**. We do this in the ILINE example:

```
// iline.cpp
// file input with strings
#include <fstream.h>                // for file functions

d main()
{
  const int MAX = 80;              // size of buffer
  char buffer[MAX];                // character buffer
  ifstream infile("TEST.TXT");     // create file for input
  while( infile )                  // until end-of-file
    {
    infile.getline(buffer, MAX);   // read a line of text
    cout << buffer;                // display it
    }
}
```

Here the insertion operator does not work. Instead, we read the text from the file one line at a time using the **getline()** function, which is a member of **istream** (from which **ifstream** is derived). This function reads characters until it encounters the '\n' character, and places the resulting string in the buffer supplied as an argument. The maximum size of the buffer is given as the second argument. The contents of the buffer is displayed after each line.

The output of ILINE will be the same data written to the TEST.TXT file by OLINE: the four-line Coleridge stanza.

DETECTING END-OF-FILE

An **ifstream** object, such as **infile** in this program, has a value that can be tested for various error conditions. If a condition is true, the object returns a zero value; otherwise it's nonzero. One of these conditions is the end of file (EOF). The EOF is a signal sent to the program from the hardware when a read or write operation has reached the end of the file. The program checks for the EOF in the **while** loop so that it can stop reading after the last string. (We'll see other error conditions later.) The value returned by a stream object is actually a pointer, but the "address" returned has no significance except to be tested for a zero or non-zero value.

CHARACTER I/O

The put and get() functions, which are members of ostream and istream, respectively, are used to output and input a single character at a time. Here's a program, OCHAR, that outputs a string, one character at a time:

```
// ochar.cpp
// file output with characters
#include <fstream.h>                    // for file functions
#include <string.h>                     // for strlen()

void main()
   {
   char str[] = "Time is a great teacher,\
but unfortunately it kills all its pupils.  Berlioz";

   ofstream outfile("TEST.TXT");        // create file for output
   for(int j=0; j<strlen(str); j++)     // for each character,
      outfile.put(str[j]);              // write it to file
   }
```

In this program an ofstream object is created as it was in OLINE. The length of the string is found using the strlen() function, and the characters are output using put() in a for loop. The aphorism by Hector Berlioz (a nineteenth-century composer of operas and program music) is written to the file TEST.TXT. We can read this file back in and display it using the ICHAR program:

```
// ichar.cpp
// file input with characters
#include <fstream.h>                    // for file functions

void main()
   {
   char ch;                             // character to read
   ifstream infile("TEST.TXT");         // create file for input
   while( infile )                      // read until EOF
      {
      infile.get(ch);                   // read character
      cout << ch;                       // display it
      }
   }
```

This program uses the get() function and continues reading until the EOF is reached. Each character read from the file is displayed using cout, so the entire aphorism is displayed on the screen.

Object I/O

Since C++ is an object-oriented language, it's reasonable to wonder how objects can be written to and read from disk. The next examples show the process. The **person** class, used in several previous examples, supplies the objects.

Writing an Object to Disk

Here's the listing for OPERS, which asks the user for information about an object of class **person**, and then writes this object to the disk file PERSON.DAT:

```
// opers.cpp
// saves person object to disk
#include <fstream.h>                    // for file streams

class person                           // class of persons
    {
    protected:
        char name[40];                 // person's name
        int age;                       // person's age
    public:
        void getData(void)             // get person's data
            {
            cout << "Enter name: "; cin >> name;
            cout << "Enter age: "; cin >> age;
            }
    };

void main(void)
    {
    person pers;                           // create a person
    pers.getData();                        // get data for person

    ofstream outfile("PERSON.DAT");  // create ofstream object
    outfile.write( (char *)&pers, sizeof(pers) );  // write to it
    }
```

The **getData()** member function of **person** is called to prompt the user for information, which it places in the **pers** object. Here's some sample interaction:

```
Enter name: Coleridge
Enter age: 62
```

The contents of the **pers** object are then written to disk, using the **write()** function. This function, like the other output functions we've seen, is a member of **ostream**. It takes two arguments: the address of the object to be written, and the length of the object in bytes. We use the `sizeof` operator to find the length of the `pers` object. The address of the object must be cast to type pointer to `char`.

BINARY VERSUS CHARACTER FILES

Notice that `write()`, unlike the functions we've used before, such as `<<`, `>>`, `get()`, and `put()`—operates on binary values, not on characters. That is, it treats the data stored in the object as a sequence of bytes, and makes no assumptions about how these bytes should be handled. By contrast, the character-based functions take some liberties with the data. For example, they expand the '\n' character into two bytes— a carriage-return and a linefeed—before storing it to disk. This makes the file more readable by DOS-based utilities like TYPE, but it would cause confusion if it were applied to binary file data.

READING AN OBJECT FROM DISK

Reading an object back from the PERSON.DAT file requires the `read()` member function. Here's the listing for IPERS:

```
// ipers.cpp
// reads person object from disk
#include <fstream.h>                    // for file streams

class person                           // class of persons
    {
    protected:
        char name[40];                 // person's name
        int age;                       // person's age
    public:
        void showData(void)            // display person's data
            {
            cout << "\n   Name: " << name;
            cout << "\n   Age: " << age;
            }
    };

void main(void)
    {
    person pers;                                 // create person
    ifstream infile("PERSON.DAT");               // create file
    infile.read( (char*)&pers, sizeof(pers) );   // read file
    pers.showData();                             // display person
    }
```

The output from IPERS reflects whatever data the OPERS program placed in the PERSON.DAT file:

```
Name: Coleridge
Age: 62
```

COMPATIBLE DATA STRUCTURES

To work correctly, programs that read and write objects to files, as do OPERS and IPERS, must be talking about the same class of objects. Objects of class `person` in these programs are exactly 42 bytes long, with the first 40 being occupied with a string representing the person's name, and the last two containing an `int` representing the person's age. If two programs thought the name field was a different length, for example, neither could accurately read a file generated by the other.

Notice, however, that while the `person` classes in OPERS and IPERS have the same data, they have different member functions. The first includes the single function `getData()`, while the second has only `showData()`. It doesn't matter what member functions you use, since they are not written to disk along with the object's data. The data must have the same format, but inconsistencies in the member functions have no effect. (Of course, in a more serious programming situation it would be desirable for all `person` objects to be derived from the exact same class.)

I/O WITH MULTIPLE OBJECTS

The OPERS and IPERS programs wrote and read only one object at a time. Our next example opens a file and writes as many objects as the user wants. Then it reads and displays the entire contents of the file. Here's the listing for DISKFUN.CPP:

```
// diskfun.cpp
// reads and writes several objects to disk
#include <fstream.h>              // for file streams

class person                      // class of persons
    {
    protected:
        char name[40];            // person's name
        int age;                  // person's age
    public:
        void getData(void)        // get person's data
            {
            cout << "\n   Enter name: "; cin >> name;
            cout << "   Enter age: "; cin >> age;
            }
        void showData(void)       // display person's data
            {
            cout << "\n   Name: " << name;
            cout << "\n   Age: " << age;
            }
    };

void main(void)
    {
    char ch;
```

```
person pers;                        // create person object
fstream file;                       // create input/output file
                                    // open for append
file.open("PERSON.DAT", ios::app | ios::out | ios::in );

do                                  // data from user to file
    {
    cout << "\nEnter person's data:";
    pers.getData();                 // get one person's data
                                    // write to file
    file.write( (char*)&pers, sizeof(pers) );
    cout << "Enter another person (y/n)? ";
    cin >> ch;
    }
while(ch=='y');                     // quit on 'n'

file.seekg(0);                      // reset to start of file
                                    // read first person
file.read( (char*)&pers, sizeof(pers) );
while( !file.eof() )                // quit on EOF
    {
    cout << "\nPerson:";            // display person
    pers.showData();
    file.read( (char*)&pers, sizeof(pers) );  // read another
    }                                         // person
}
```

Here's some sample interaction with DISKFUN. The output shown assumes that the program has been run before and that two **person** objects have already been written to the file.

```
Enter person's data:
    Enter name: McKinley
    Enter age: 22
Enter another person (y/n)? n

Person:
    Name: Whitney
    Age: 20
Person:
    Name: Rainier
    Age 21
Person:
    Name: McKinley
    Age: 22
```

Here one additional object is added to the file, and the entire contents, consisting of three objects, are then displayed.

The fstream Class

So far in this chapter the file objects we created were for either input or output. In DISKFUN we want to create a file that can be used for both input and output. This requires an object of the fstream class.

The open() Function

In previous examples we created a file object and initialized it in the same statement:

```
ofstream outfile("TEST.TXT");
```

In DISKFUN we use a different approach: We create the file in one statement and open it in another, using the open() function, which is a member of the fstream class.

In the open() function we include several *mode bits* to specify certain aspects of the file object we are opening. Table 14-1 shows the possibilities.

We use app because we want to preserve whatever was in the file before. That is, we can write to the file, terminate the program, and start up the program again, and whatever we write to the file will be appended to the existing contents. We use in and out because we want to perform both input and output on the file. The vertical bars between the flags cause the bits representing these flags to be logically ORed together, so that several flags can apply simultaneously.

We write one person object at a time to the file, using the write() function. When we've finished writing we want to read the entire file. Before doing this we must reset the file's current position. We do this with the seekg() function, which we'll examine in the next section, on file pointers. Then, in a while loop, we repeatedly read a person object from the file and display it on the screen.

TABLE 14-1 Mode Bits for open() Function	
Mode bit	Result
in	open for reading (default for *ifstream*)
out	open for writing (default for *ofstream*)
app	start reading or writing at end of file (*APPend*)
ate	erase file before reading or writing (*truncATE*)
nocreate	error when opening if file does not already exist
noreplace	error when opening for output if file already exists, unless *ate* or *app* is set
binary	open file in binary (not text) mode

This continues until we've read all the `person` objects—a state that we discover using `eof()`, a member function of the `ios` class. This is an alternative approach to simply checking the value of the file object itself. The `eof()` function returns a nonzero value if the EOF is encountered, and a zero otherwise. It's one of a number of stream-state functions, which we'll look at in the section on stream errors later in this chapter.

FILE POINTERS

Each file object has associated with it two integer values called the *get pointer* and the *put pointer*. These are also called the *current get position* and the *current put position*, or—if it's clear which one is meant—simply the *current position*. These values specify the byte number in the file where writing or reading will take place. (The term *pointer* in this context should not be confused with normal C++ pointers used as address variables.)

Often you want to start reading an existing file at the beginning, and continue until the end. When writing, you may want to start at the beginning, deleting any existing contents, or at the end, in which case you can open the file with the `ios::app` mode specifier. These are the default actions, so no manipulation of the file pointers are necessary. However, there are times when you must take control of the file pointers yourself so that you can read from and write to an arbitrary location in the file. The `seekg()` and `tellg()` functions allow you to set and examine the get pointer, and the `seekp()` and `tellp()` functions perform these same actions on the put pointer.

SPECIFYING THE POSITION

We saw an example of positioning the get pointer in the DISKFUN program, where the `seekg()` function set it to the beginning of the file so that reading would start there. This form of `seekg()` takes one argument, which represents the absolute position in the file. The start of the file is byte 0, so that's what we used in DISKFUN. Figure 14-3 shows how this looks.

SPECIFYING THE OFFSET

The `seekg()` function can be used in two ways. We've seen the first, where the single argument represents the position. You can also use it with two arguments, where the first argument represents an offset from a particular location in the file, and the second specifies the location from which the offset is measured. There are three possibilities for the second argument: `beg` is the beginning of the file, `cur` is the current pointer position, and `end` is the end of the file. The statement

```
seekp(-10, ios::end);
```

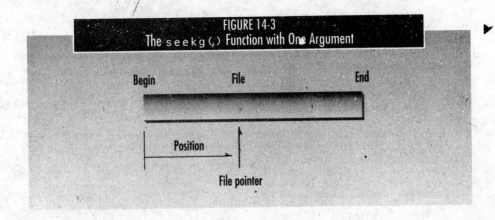

FIGURE 14-3
The seekg() Function with One Argument

for example, will set the put pointer to 10 bytes before the end of the file. Figure 14-4 shows how this looks.

Here's an example that uses the two-argument version of seekg() to find a particular person object in the PERSON.DAT file already created with DISKFUN, and to display the data for that particular person. Here's the listing for SEEKG:

```cpp
// seekg.cpp
// seeks particular person in file
#include <fstream.h>                // for file streams

class person                       // class of persons
    {
    protected:
        char name[40];             // person's name
        int age;                   // person's age
    public:
        void showData(void)        // display person's data
            {
            cout << "\n   Name: " << name;
            cout << "\n   Age: " << age;
            }
    };

void main(void)
    {
    person pers;                           // create person object
    ifstream infile;                       // create input file
    infile.open("PERSON.DAT");             // open file

    infile.seekg(0, ios::end);             // go to 0 bytes from end
    int endposition = infile.tellg();          // find where we are
    int n = endposition / sizeof(person);  // number of persons
    cout << "\nThere are " << n << " persons in file";
```

```
cout << "\nEnter person number: ";
cin >> n;
int position = (n-1) * sizeof(person);  // number times size
infile.seekg(position);                 // bytes from begin
                                        // read one person
infile.read( (char*)&pers, sizeof(pers) );
pers.showData();                        // display the person
}
```

Here's the output from the program, assuming that the PERSON.DAT file is the same as that just accessed in the DISKFUN example:

```
There are 3 persons in file
Enter person number: 2

Name: Rainier
Age: 21
```

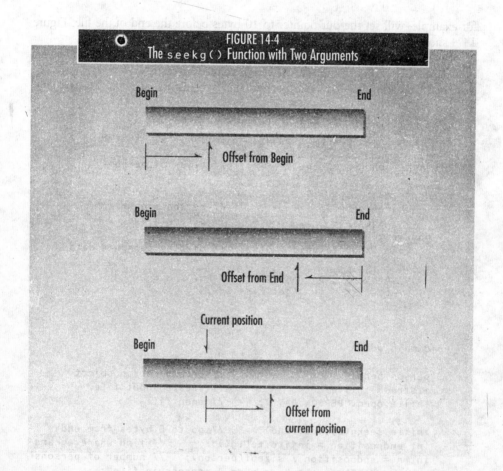

FIGURE 14-4
The seekg() Function with Two Arguments

For the user we number the items starting at 1, although the program starts numbering at 0; so person 2 is the second person of the three in the file.

THE tellg() FUNCTION

The first thing the program does is figure out how many persons are in the file. It does this by positioning the get pointer at the end of the file with the statement

```
infile.seekg(0, ios::end);
```

The tellg() function returns the current position of the get pointer. The program uses this function to return the pointer position at the end of the file; this is the length of the file in bytes. Next, the program calculates how many person objects there are in the file, by dividing by the size of a person; it then displays the result.

In the output shown, the user specifies the second object in the file, and the program calculates how many bytes into the file this is, using seekg(). It then uses read() to read one person's worth of data starting from that point. Finally, it displays the data with showData().

DISK I/O WITH MEMBER FUNCTIONS

So far we've let the main() function handle the details of stream I/O. When you use more sophisticated classes it's natural to include stream I/O operations as member functions of the class. Our next example shows how this might be done. The class consists of an array, called parr, of structures of type person. These structures hold a name and age as the person class did in previous examples, but the class group is now responsible for input and output. Here's the listing for DAROBJ:

```
// darobj.cpp
// person array object does disk I/O
#include <fstream.h>            // for file streams

struct person                   // one person
    {
    char name[40];              // person's name
    int age;                    // person's age
    };

class group                     // group of persons, in array
    {
    private:
        person parr[20];        // array of persons
        int count;              // number of persons in array
    public:
        group()                 // no-arg constructor
            { count = 0; }
        void addData();
        void showData();
```

```
        void diskIn();
        void diskOut();
    };
void group::addData()              // get one person's data
    {
    cout << "\n    Enter name: ";
    cin >> parr[count].name;
    cout << "    Enter age: ";
    cin >> parr[count++].age;
    }
void group::showData()             // display all persons in group
    {
    for(int j=0; j<count; j++)
        {
        cout << "\nPerson #" << j+1;
        cout << "\n   Name: " << parr[j].name;
        cout << "\n   Age: " << parr[j].age;
        }
    }
void group::diskIn()               // read array from file
    {
    ifstream infile;                            // make file
    infile.open("GROUP.DAT", ios::nocreate);    // open it
    if( infile )                                // if it exists,
        infile.read( (char*)this, sizeof(*this) ); // read it
    }
void group::diskOut()              // write array to file
    {
    ofstream outfile;                           // make file
    outfile.open("GROUP.DAT");                  // open it
    outfile.write( (char*)this, sizeof(*this) ); // write to it
    }

void main(void)
    {
    group grp;                  // make a group
    grp.diskIn();               // fill it with disk data (if any)
    grp.showData();             // display data for group

    char ch;
    do                          // get new persons for group
        {
        cout << "\nEnter data for person:";
        grp.addData();
        cout << "Enter another (y/n)? ";
        cin >> ch;
        }
    while(ch=='y');
    grp.showData();             // display augmented group
    grp.diskOut();              // write augmented group to disk
    }
```

The main() program creates a group object called grp. Such an object holds the data for 20 person structures. The program then displays all the persons in the group, and asks the user to enter data for an additional person. The user can enter as many persons as desired. Before terminating, the program again displays the data for all persons.

Here's some sample interaction with DAROBJ. This interaction assumes that two persons were placed in the GROUP.DAT file by a previous invocation of the program.

```
Person #1
   Name: Stimson
   Age: 45
Person #2
   Name: Hull
   Age: 58
Enter data for person:
   Enter name: Acheson
   Enter age: 63
Enter another (y/n)? y

Enter data for person:
   Enter name: Dulles
   Enter age: 72
Enter another (y/n)? n

Person #1
   Name: Stimson
   Age: 45
Person #2
   Name: Hull
   Age: 58
Person #3
   Name: Acheson
   Age: 63
Person #4
   Name: Dulles
   Age: 72
```

Besides the array of persons, group contains four member functions and a count of how many of the object spaces are actually in use.

The first function, addData(), is the only one that acts on a single person structure. It prompts the user for data, and adds a person object to the end of the array.

The other member functions act on the array as a whole. The showData() function displays the data for each of the count structures stored in the array in memory.

The diskIn() function checks to see that the GROUP.DAT file exists. If so, it opens the file and reads its entire contents into the array parr in a single statement. The infile object will return a zero value if the GROUP.DAT file does not exist, so that the statement

```
if( infile )
```

can be used to determine whether an attempt should be made to read the file. The `diskOut()` function writes the entire array **parr** from memory to the disk file GROUP.DAT.

Notice how we refer to the **group** object that we're going to write to disk with `diskOut()` and read in with `diskIn()`. In the `read()` and `write()` stream functions the address of the object to be read or written is **this** and its size is `sizeof(*this)`. The **this** pointer holds the address of the object of which `diskOut()` and `diskIn()` are members, so we can use it to read or write the entire object.

CLOSING FILES

There is no need for `diskIn()` or `diskOut()` to explicitly close the file objects **infile** or **outfile**, since they are closed automatically when the functions terminate. If it were necessary to close a file explicitly, the `close()` member function could be used:

```
file.close();
```

OTHER DATA STRUCTURES

Of course, the objects stored on disk need not be arranged as an array in memory, as they are in the DAROBJ program. They could also be read from the disk and stored in some other data structure, such as a linked list.

ERROR HANDLING

In our examples so far we have not concerned ourselves with error situations. In particular, we have assumed that the files we opened for reading already existed, and that those opened for writing could be created. In a real program it is important to verify such assumptions and take appropriate action if they turn out to be incorrect. A file that you think exists may not, or a filename that you assume you can use for a new file may already apply to an existing file. Or, perhaps there is no more room on the disk.

In previous examples we examined the error state of a stream object to find out whether we had reached the end of file. We demonstrated two approaches to finding this piece of information. First, we checked the value of the file object itself, in situations such as

```
while( infile )
        // read the next part of file
```

Here **infile** becomes zero when the EOF is reached. We also used the `eof()` member function of the **ios** class. This function returned a nonzero value when an EOF was encountered.

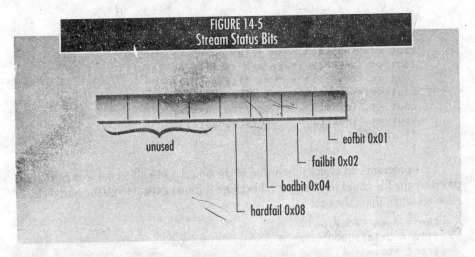

FIGURE 14-5
Stream Status Bits

- eofbit 0x01
- failbit 0x02
- badbit 0x04
- hardfail 0x08
- unused

TABLE 14-2
Stream Status Bits

Bit	Meaning
0x00	No bit set, no errors
0x01	At EOF
0x02	Read or write failed
0x04	Invalid operation (opening nonexistent file)
0x08	Hard error

Both these methods report the state of a status byte that contains several bits other than the one that reports the EOF. Figure 14-5 shows the other bits. Table 14-2 shows the meaning of these bits.

The status word can be read with `rdstate()`, a member function of `ios`. Several other member functions, including `eof()`, return the status of individual bits. Our next example demonstrates these functions.

```
// ferrors.cpp
// checks for errors opening file
#include <fstream.h>               // for file functions

void main()
    {
    ifstream file;
    file.open("GROUP.DAT", ios::nocreate);

    if( !file )
        cout << "\nCan't open GROUP.DAT";
```

```
    else
        cout << "\nFile opened successfully.";
    cout << "\nfile = " << file;
    cout << "\nError state = " << file.rdstate();
    cout << "\ngood() = " << file.good();
    cout << "\neof() = " << file.eof();
    cout << "\nfail() = " << file.fail();
    cout << "\nbad() = " << file.bad();
    file.close();
    }
```

This program first checks the value of the object `file`. If its value is zero, then probably the file could not be opened because it didn't exist. Here's the output from FERRORS when that's the case:

```
Can't open GROUP.DAT
file = 0x1c730000
Error state = 4
good() = 0
eof() = 0
fail() = 4
bad() = 4
```

The error state returned by `rdstate()` is 4. This is the bit that indicates that the file doesn't exist; it's set to 1. The other bits are all set to 0. The `good()` function returns 1 (true) only when no bits are set, so it returns 0 (false). We're not at EOF, so `eof()` returns 0. The `fail()` and `bad()` functions return nonzero, since an error occurred.

In a serious program some or all of these functions should be used after every I/O operation to ensure that things went as expected.

REDIRECTION

You can read and write to files using only the objects `cout` and `cin`. These predefined objects normally represent the display and the keyboard, but they can be redirected by the user to represent disk files. Redirection is a technique, originally imported from Unix into DOS, that allows the user considerable flexibility in the way programs are used. Redirection is supplied by DOS, not by C++; but C++ supports it, so it's interesting to see how to use it. As an example, consider the program REDIR:

```
// redir.cpp
// demonstrates redirection
// syntax: redir <source >destination
#include <iostream.h>
#include <iomanip.h>                              // for resetiosflags()

void main()
    {
```

```
char ch;
while( !cin.eof() )                       // quit on EOF
    {
    cin >> resetiosflags(ios::skipws)     // keep whitespace
        >> ch;                            // read from std input
    cout << ch;                           // send to std output
    }
}
```

ios FLAGS

Before exploring how this program can be used for redirection, we should note a peculiarity in the programming: We must reset the `skipws` flag when getting input from
`cin` in REDIR. This is necessary because `cin` normally skips over white space, which
includes spaces, newlines, and EOFs. We want to read all these characters, and fortunately `cin` has a formatting flag that allows us to disable white space skipping.

We've used a variety of other `ios` flags in previous chapters. For reference, Table
14-3 shows the complete list.

USING REDIR

When invoked in the usual way at the command line, REDIR simply echoes whatever the user types, each time (ENTER) is pressed. Here's some sample interaction
(from a poem by the sixteenth century poet Ben Jonson):

```
C>redir
Truth is the trial of itself,        ←——————— entered by user
Truth is the trial of itself,        ←——————— echoed by program
And needs no other touch;
And needs no other touch;
And purer than the purest gold,
And purer than the purest gold,
Refine it ne'er so much.
Refine it ne'er so much.
^Z
```

The user enters the (CTRL)-(Z) combination (or the (F6) function key) to terminate
the program. This character is interpreted as an EOF.

When the program is used for redirection it can take input from the keyboard
and write it to a disk file, display text from a disk file on the screen, or copy one
text file to another.

REDIRECTING OUTPUT

To redirect a program's output from the screen to a file, you use the > operator. This
is a DOS operator; it has nothing to do with C++ overloading. Here's how to invoke
REDIR to take keyboard input and redirect it to a file called SAMPLE.TXT:

```
C>redir >sample.txt
If you would avoid suspicion,              ←————— entered by user
don't lace your shoes in a melon field.   ←————— entered by user
^Z                                         ←————— entered by user
```

You can check SAMPLE.TXT with TYPE to be sure it contains this text.

REDIRECTING INPUT

To redirect a program's input so that it comes from a file and not the keyboard, you use the < operator. Here's how to invoke REDIR to take data from the file SAMPLE.TXT and use it as input to the program, which then displays it:

```
C>redir <sample.txt
If you would avoid suspicion,              ←————— displayed by program
don't lace your shoes in a melon field.   ←————— displayed by program
```

TABLE 14-3 ios Flags	
Flag	**Purpose**
skipws	Skip whitespace on input
left	Left-justify output
right	Right-justify output
internal	Use padding after sign or base indicator
dec	Decimal conversion
oct	Octal conversion
hex	Hexadecimal conversion
showbase	Use base indicator on output
showpoint	Use decimal point in floating-point output
uppercase	Uppercase hex output
showpos	Preface positive integers with '+'
scientific	Floating-point notation with E (5.4321E3)
fixed	Fixed floating-point notation (5432.1)
unitbuf	Flush all streams after insertion
stdio	Flush stdout and stderr after insertion

REDIRECTING INPUT AND OUTPUT

Both input and output can be redirected at the same time. As an example, here's how to use REDIR to copy one file to another:

```
C>redir <src.txt >dest.txt
```

Nothing is displayed, but you will find that SRC.TXT has been copied to DEST.TXT.

THE cerr AND clog OBJECTS

If you want to display a particular message even when the output of your program has been redirected to a file, you can use the `cerr` object. Insert this line into the `while` loop in REDIR:

```
cerr << ch;
```

Now try copying one file to another. Each character `ch` will be sent to the screen by `cerr`, even though the output to `cout` is going to a file. The `cerr` object is normally used to display error messages; hence the name. Another object, `clog`, is similar to `cerr` except that its output is buffered while `cerr`'s is not.

COMMAND-LINE ARGUMENTS

You are no doubt familiar with command-line arguments, used when invoking a program from DOS. They are typically used to pass the name of a data file to an application. For example, you can invoke the Turbo C++ integrated environment and a .CPP file at the same time:

```
C>tc afile.cpp
```

Here `afile.cpp` is a command-line argument. How can we get a C++ program to read the command-line arguments? Here's an example, COMLINE, that reads and displays as many command-line arguments as you care to type:

```
// comline.cpp
// demonstrates command-line arguments
#include <iostream.h>

void main(int argc, char* argv[] )
    {
    cout << "\nargc = " << argc;

    for(int j=0; j<argc; j++)
        cout << "\nArgument " << j << " = " << argv[j];
    }
```

And here's a sample interaction with the program:

```
C>comline uno dos tres

argc = 4
Argument 0 = C:\CPP\CHAP14\COMLINE.EXE
Argument 1 = uno
Argument 2 = dos
Argument 3 = tres
```

To read command-line arguments, the main() function (don't forget it's a function!) must itself be given two arguments. The first, argc (for *argument count*), represents the total number of command-line arguments. The first command-line argument is always the pathname of the current program. The remaining command-line arguments are those typed by the user; they are delimited by the space character. In the example above they are *uno*, *dos* and *tres*.

The system stores the command-line arguments as strings in memory, and creates an array of pointers to these strings. In the example the array is called argv (for *argument values*). Individual strings are accessed through the appropriate pointer, so the first string (the pathname) is argv[0], the second (*uno* in this example) is argv[1], and so on. COMLINE accesses the arguments in turn and prints them out in a for loop that uses argc, the number of command-line arguments, as its upper limit.

You don't need to use the particular names argc and argv as arguments to main(), but they are so common that any other names would cause consternation to everyone but the compiler.

Here's a program that uses a command-line argument for something useful. It displays the contents of a text file whose name is supplied by the user on the command line. Thus it imitates the DOS command *TYPE*. Here's the listing for OTYPE:

```
// otype.cpp
// imitates TYPE command
#include <fstream.h>               // for file functions
#include <process.h>              // for exit()

void main(int argc, char* argv[] )
    {
    if( argc != 2 )
        {
        cerr << "\nFormat: otype filename";
        exit(-1);
        }
    char ch;                      // character to read
    ifstream infile;              // create file for input
    infile.open( argv[1] );       // open file
    if( !infile )                 // check for errors
        {
        cerr << "\nCan't open " << argv[1];
        exit(-1);
        }
```

```
while( infile.get(ch) != 0 )    // read a character
    cout << ch;                  // display the character
}
```

This program first checks to see if the user has entered the correct number of command-line arguments. Remember that the pathname of OTYPE.EXE itself is always the first command-line argument. The second argument is the name of the file to be displayed, which the user should have entered when invoking the program:

```
C>otype ichar.cpp
```

Thus the total number of command-line arguments should equal 2. If it doesn't, the user probably doesn't understand how to use the program, and the program sends an error message via **cerr** to clarify matters.

If the number of arguments is correct, the program tries to open the file whose name is the second command-line argument (**argv[1]**). Again, if the file can't be opened, the program signals an error. Finally, in a **while** loop, the program reads the file character by character and writes it to the screen.

A value of 0 for the character signals an EOF. This is another way to check for EOF. You can also use the value of the file object itself, as we've done before:

```
while( infile )
    {
    infile.get(ch);
    cout << ch;
    }
```

PRINTER OUTPUT

Sending data to the printer is similar to sending data to a disk file. DOS predefines a number of special filenames for hardware devices. Here they are:

Name	Device
CON	Console (keyboard and screen)
AUX or COM1	First serial port
COM2	Second serial port
PRN or LPT1	First parallel printer
LPT2	Second parallel printer
LPT3	Third parallel printer
NUL	Dummy (nonexistent) device

In most systems the printer is connected to the first parallel port, so the filename for the printer should be PRN or LPT1. (You can substitute the appropriate name if your system is configured differently.) The following program, OPRINT, prints the contents of a disk file, specified on the command line, to the printer.

```
// oprint.cpp
// imitates print command
#include <fstream.h>              // for file functions
#include <process.h>             // for exit()

void main(int argc, char* argv[] )
    {
    if( argc != 2 )
        {
        cerr << "\nFormat: oprint filename";
        exit(-1);
        }
    char ch;                      // character to read
    ifstream infile;             // create file for input
    infile.open( argv[1] );      // open file
    if( !infile )                // check for errors
        {
        cerr << "\nCan't open " << argv[1];
        exit(-1);
        }
    ofstream outfile;            // make file
    outfile.open("PRN");         // open it for printer
    while( infile.get(ch) != 0 ) // read a character
        outfile.put(ch);         // write character to printer
    }
```

You can use this program to print any text file, such as any of your .CPP source files. It acts much the same as the DOS *PRINT* command.

Like the OTYPE example, this program checks for the correct number of command-line arguments, and for a successful opening of the specified file. Then it opens PRN and writes the file to it, character by character.

OVERLOADING THE EXTRACTION AND INSERTION OPERATORS

We'll finish this chapter by showing how to overload the extraction and insertion operators. This is a powerful feature of C++. It lets you treat I/O for user-defined data types in the same way as basic types like int and double. For example, if you have an object of class crawdad called cd1, you can display it with the statement

```
cout << "\ncd1=" << cd1;
```

just as if it were a basic data type.

Here's an example, ENGLIO, that overloads the insertion and extraction operators for the Distance class.

```
// englio.cpp
// overloaded << and >> operators
#include <iostream.h>

class Distance                          // English Distance class
   {
   private:
      int feet;
      float inches;
   public:
      Distance()                        // constructor (no args)
         { feet = 0; inches = 0.0; }
      Distance(int ft, float in)        // constructor (two args)
         { feet = ft; inches = in; }
      friend istream& operator >> (istream& s, Distance& d);
      friend ostream& operator << (ostream& s, Distance& d);
   };

istream& operator >> (istream& s, Distance& d)   // get Distance
   {                                             // from user
   cout << "\nEnter feet: ";  s >> d.feet;       // using
   cout << "Enter inches: ";  s >> d.inches;     // overloaded.
   return s;                                     // >> operator
   }

ostream& operator << (ostream& s, Distance& d)   // display
   {                                             // Distance
   s << d.feet << "\'-" << d.inches << '\"';     // using
   return s;                                     // overloaded
   }                                             // << operator

void main()
   {
   Distance dist1, dist2;           // define Distances
   cout << "\nEnter two Distance values:";
   cin >> dist1 >> dist2;           // get values from user

   Distance dist3(11, 6.25);        // define, initialize dist3

                                    // display distances
   cout << "\ndist1 = " << dist1 << "\ndist2 = " << dist2;
   cout << "\ndist3 = " << dist3;
   }
```

This program asks for two distance values from the user, and then prints out these values and another value that was initialized in the program. Here's a sample interaction:

```
Enter feet: 10
Enter inches: 3.5
```

```
Enter feet: 12
Enter inches: 6

dist1 = 10'-3.5"
dist2 = 12'-6"
dist3 = 11'-6.25"
```

Notice how convenient and natural it is to treat Distance objects like any other data type, using statements like

```
cin >> dist1 >> dist2;
```

and

```
cout << "\ndist1 = " dist1 << "\ndist2 = " << dist2;
```

As you can see, the << and >> operators can be chained, permitting the input or output of multiple data items in a single statement.

The operator<<() and operator>>() functions must be friends of the Distance class, since the istream and ostream objects appear on the left side of the operator. (See the discussion of friend functions in Chapter 13.) The operator<<() function takes an istream object, which will usually be cin, as its first argument, and an object of the Distance class as its second. It returns an istream so that the operator can be chained. The operator<<() function is constructed similarly but uses ostream instead of istream.

SUMMARY

In this chapter we briefly examined the hierarchy of stream classes. Then we saw how to perform disk I/O in a variety of ways. Files in C++ are objects of various classes, typically ofstream for output, ifstream for input, and fstream for both input and output. Member functions of these or base classes are used to perform I/O operations. Such functions as put() and write() are used for output, while get() and read() are used for input.

The read() and write() functions work in binary mode, so that entire objects can be saved to disk no matter what sort of data they contain. Single objects can be stored, as can arrays or other data structures of many objects.

A check for error conditions should be made after each file operation. The file object itself takes on a value of 0 if an error occurred, or nonzero otherwise. Also, several member functions can be used to determine specific kinds of errors.

Redirection provides an easily programmed (although not entirely user-friendly) approach to file I/O, using input and output to cin and cout. Sending output to the printer involves outputting to a file usually called PRN. The extraction operator >> and the insertion operator << can be overloaded so that they work with programmer-defined data types.

QUESTIONS

1. A C++ stream is
   a. the flow of control through a function
   b. a flow of data from one place to another
   c. associated with a particular class
   d. a file

2. The base class for most stream classes is the _____ class.

3. Name three stream classes commonly used for disk I/O.

4. Write a statement that will create an object called `salefile` of the `ofstream` class and associate it with a file called SALES.JUN.

5. True or false: Some streams work with input, and some with output.

6. Write an `if` statement that checks if an `ifstream` object called `foobar` has reached the end of file or has encountered an error.

7. We can output text to an object of class `ofstream` using the insertion operator `<<` because
   a. the `ofstream` class is a stream
   b. the insertion operator works with all classes
   c. we are actually outputting to `cout`
   d. the insertion operator is overloaded in `ofstream`

8. Write a statement that writes a single character to an object called `fileOut`, which is of class `ofstream`.

9. To write data that contains variables of type `float`, to an object of type `ofstream`, you should use
   a. the insertion operator
   b. `seekg()`
   c. `write()`
   d. `put()`

10. Write a statement that will read the contents of an `ifstream` object called `ifile` into an array called `buff`.

11. Mode bits such as `app` and `ate`
    a. are defined in the `ios` class
    b. can specify if a file is open for reading or writing
    c. work with the `put()` and `get()` functions
    d. specify ways of opening a file

12. Define what *current position* means when applied to files.

13. True or false: A file pointer always contains the address of the file.

14. Write a statement that moves the current position 13 bytes backward in a stream object called `f1`.

15. The statement

    `f1.write( (char*)&obj1, sizeof(obj1) );`

    a. writes the member functions of `obj1` to `f1`
    b. writes the data in `obj1` to `f1`
    c. writes the member functions and the data of `obj1` to `f1`
    d. writes the address of `obj1` to `f1`

16. Redirection redirects
    a. a stream from a file to the screen
    b. a file from a device to a stream
    c. a device from the screen to a file
    d. the screen from a device to a stream

17. Used with `cin`, what does the `skipws` flag accomplish?

18. Write a declarator for `main()` that will enable command-line arguments.

19. The printer can be accessed using the predefined filename _____.

20. Write the declarator for the overloaded `>>` operator that takes output from an object of class `istream` and displays it as the contents of an object of class `Sample`.

EXERCISES

1. Start with the `Distance` class from the ENGLCON example in Chapter 7 Using a loop similar to that in the DISKFUN example in this chapter, get a number of `Distance` values from the user and write them to a disk file. Append them to existing values in the file, if any. When the user signals that no more values will be input, read the file and display all the values.

2. Write a program that emulates the DOS *COPY* command. That is, it should copy the contents of a character file (such as any CPP file) to another file. Invoke the program with two command-line arguments—the source file and the destination file—like this:

    `C>ocopy srcfile.ext destfile.ext`

    In the program, check that the user has typed the correct number of command-line arguments, and that the files specified can be opened. Improve on the DOS *TYPE* command by having the program signal an error if the destination file already exists. This will prevent inadvertently writing over a valuable file. (Hint: Use the `noreplace` flag.)

3. Write a program that returns the size in bytes of a program entered on the command line:

    `C>filesize program.ext`

LARGER PROGRAMS

In previous chapters we've seen how the various parts of a C++ program—such as class declarations, member functions, and a `main()` function—are combined. However, the programs in these chapters all consisted of a single file. Now let's look at program organization from a more global perspective, involving multiple files.

Besides demonstrating multi-file programs, this chapter will introduce some longer and more ambitious applications. Our aim in these programs is not that you necessarily understand every detail of their operation, but that you acquire a general understanding of how the elements of larger programs relate to one another. These programs also show how classes can be used in more realistic applications than the short examples we've seen so far. On the other hand, they are not so long that it takes all spring to wade through them.

REASONS FOR MULTI-FILE PROGRAMS

There are several reasons for using multi-file programs. These include the use of class libraries, the organization of programmers working on a project, and the conceptual design of a program.

CLASS LIBRARIES

In traditional procedure-oriented languages it has long been customary for software vendors to furnish `libraries` of functions. Other programmers then combine these libaries with their own custom-written routines to create an application for the end-user.

Libraries provide ready-made functions for a wide variety of fields. For instance, a vendor might supply a library of functions for handling statistics calculations, or for advanced memory management. Libraries that provide the functions necessary to create a graphics user interface for DOS programs are popular

Since C++ is organized around classes rather than functions, it's not surprising that libraries for C++ programs consist of classes. What may be surprising is how superior a class library is to an old-fashioned function library. Because classes encapsulate both data and functions, and because they more closely model real life, the interface between a class library and the application that makes use of it can be much cleaner than that provided by a function library.

For these reasons class libraries assume a more important role in C++ programming than function libraries do in traditional programming. A class library can take over a greater portion of the programming burden. An applications programmer, if the right class library is available, may find that only a minimal amount of programming is necessary to create a final product. Also, as more and more class libraries are created, the chances of finding one that solves your particular programming problem continues to increase.

Components of a Class Library

A class library often furnishes two components: public and private. Let's see what the difference is.

Public Components

To use a class library, the applications programmer needs to access various declarations, including class declarations. These declarations can be thought of as the public part of the library and are furnished in source-code form as a header file, with the .H extension. This file is typically combined with the client's source code using an #include statement. The declarations in such a header file need to be public for several reasons. First, it's a convenience to the client to see the actual definitions rather than to read a description of them. More importantly, the client's program will need to declare objects based on these classes, and call on member functions from these objects. Only by declaring the classes in the source file is this possible.

Private Components

On the other hand, the inner workings of the member functions of the various classes don't need to be known by the client. The developers of the class library, like any other software developer, don't want to release source code if they can help it, since it might be illegally modified or pirated. Member functions—except for short inline functions—are therefore usually distributed in object form, as .OBJ files or as library (.LIB) files.

Figure 15-1 shows how the various files are related in a multi-file system.

In this chapter we'll show several larger programs organized according to these principles. The first provides a set of classes of visual screen elements, such as buttons and output windows. An application then uses these classes to create a four-function pocket calculator. The second program introduces a class of very large numbers. By *very large*, we mean numbers with an almost unlimited number of digits. Such numbers are important in various kinds of mathematics, such as calculating *pi* to thousands of digits. The third example provides classes that allow you to create your own water-distribution system. You can connect valves, tanks, pipes, and

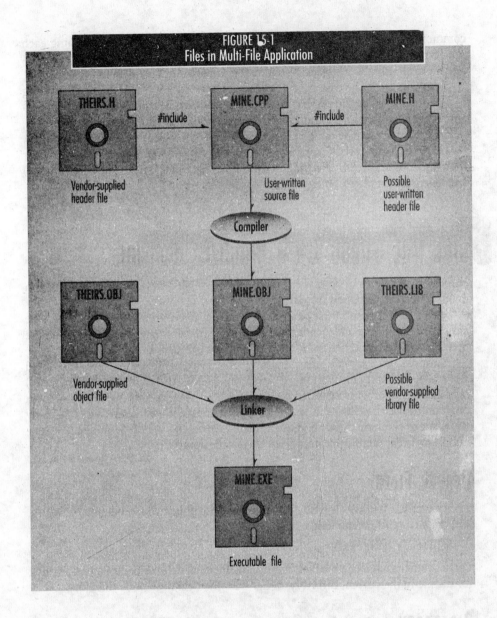

FIGURE 15-1
Files in Multi-File Application

similar components to model systems such as the cooling water system in a nuclear reactor.

OTHER REASONS FOR MULTI-FILE PROGRAMS

Programs may be broken down into multiple files for reasons other than the accommodation of class libraries. As in other programming languages, such as C, a common situation involves a project with several programmers. Confining each programmer's responsibility to a separate file helps to organize the project and define more cleanly the interface among different parts of the program.

It is also often the case that a program is divided into separate files according to functionality: One file can handle the code involved in a graphics display, for example, while another file handles mathematical analysis, and a third disk I/O. Also, in large programs, a single file may simply become too large to handle conveniently.

The techniques used for working with multi-file programs are similar, whatever the reasons for dividing the program. Let's see how Turbo C++ (or Borland C++) handles program development with multiple files.

Using the Turbo C++ Project Feature

Turbo C++ provides a sophisticated automated procedure for multi-file program development. It's accessed from the Project menu.

Here's how to combine several source or object files into one executable file. The basic idea is to create a file, called the *project file*, that contains the names for all the files that will be combined into the final executable program.

Suppose, for example, that you have purchased a prewritten class file called THEIRS.OBJ. (A library file with the .LIB extension is dealt with in much the same way.) It probably comes with a header file, say THEIRS.H. You have also written your own program to use the classes in the library; your source file is called MINE.CPP. Now you want to combine these component files—THEIRS.OBJ, THEIRS.H, and MINE.CPP—into a single executable program. Here's a simple approach.

Header Files

The header file THEIRS.H is easily incorporated into your own source file, MINE.CPP, with an #include statement:

```
#include "THEIRS.H"
```

Quotes rather than angle brackets around the filename tell the compiler to look first for the file in the current directory, rather than the default include directory.

Directory

Now, make sure the component files, THEIRS.OBJ and MINE.CPP, are in the same directory. In fact, you will probably want to create a separate directory for the project, to avoid confusion. (This isn't strictly necessary, but it's the simplest approach.) From this directory call up Turbo C++ by typing tc (or bc for Borland C++) at the DOS prompt. You don't have to open any of the component files when you call up Turbo C++; a blank screen is all you need.

OPEN A PROJECT

Now, select *Open Project* from the Project menu. A window called Load Project File will appear. This window has a text field at the top, also called Load Project File. Into this field type the name of the project file you want to create. You should give this file the same name you want to use for your final executable program, but with the extension .PRJ instead of .EXE. Thus if you want your executable file to be called MINE.EXE, type **MINE.PRJ** into the Load Project File field. (You may have to back-space to delete existing text before typing.) Then press (ENTER) or select *OK*. The Load Project File window will vanish, and another window, called Project: MINE (or what-ever name you chose), will appear at the bottom of the screen.

ENTER COMPONENT FILENAMES

You want to enter the names of your component files into this new Project window. To do this, press the (INS) key (or select *Add Item...* from the Project menu). A third window, called Add Item to Project List, will be displayed. This window has a text field called Name at the top. Into this field type the name of one of your compo-nent files—for instance, THEIRS.OBJ. Press (ENTER) or click on the Add button. You'll see the name you typed added to the Project window at the bottom of the screen. Now type the name of the next file, MINE.CPP, into the Name field (backspacing over existing text first, if necessary). This name will also appear on the Project window. You can now click on *Cancel* to make the Add Item... window go away. That's it. You've created the project file.

CREATE EXECUTABLE FILE

To create the executable file, first make sure the Project window is active. (You may have other files open on the screen.) Then select *Make EXE file* from the Compile menu. At this point the MINE.CPP file will be compiled (unless it has already been compiled and is up to date). Then the resulting MINE.OBJ file will be linked with THEIRS.OBJ, creating the executable file MINE.EXE.

To execute MINE.EXE, select *Run* from the Run menu (or press (CTRL)-(F9)). If you exit Turbo C++, you'll see MINE.EXE in your directory, where it can be executed as a stand-alone program. You'll also see the MINE.PRJ project file.

AUTOMATIC COMPILATION

Note that the project file stores the dates your files were last changed. This makes it possible for Turbo C++ to know which files need to be compiled and which don't. Thus if a source file was compiled before the executable file was created, there's no need to compile it again before relinking it. But if it has been changed since the last relinking, then Turbo C++ will cause it to be recompiled before linking its OBJ file. This automation means that as a programmer you can ignore the issue of what needs to be compiled and what doesn't, and that you can trust Turbo C++ to do the right thing when you select *Make EXE file*.

You can always compile a source file directly, using *Compile to OBJ* from the Compile menu. Each source file should compile correctly on its own. You'll probably want to do this while you're developing a set of classes or an application program that uses them. When all the source files compile correctly, you can start using the project feature to link them together and handle future changes.

Automatic Project Files

You may be surprised to find that a project file for one program is automatically loaded when in fact you want to start writing a completely different program. Why does this happen? If there is exactly one project file in a directory, Turbo C will load it automatically whenever you start it up. This may be what you want, since a directory often holds only one multi-file program. But if you want to start another project in the same directory, you may have trouble. To avoid this problem you can create a dummy (empty) .PRJ file, since if there is more than one, Turbo C++ won't automatically open any of them.

Automatic Directories

You should be aware that each project has its own default LIB and INCLUDE directories. You can see what these are by selecting *Directories...* from the Options menu. When you begin a project the IDE may be confused about what directories you want to use. If you get compiler error messages like *Unable to open include file XXX.H* or linker messages like *Unable to open file XXX.LIB*, then it may be that your default directories are incorrectly set. Change them by typing in the correct pathnames in the fields provided.

The examples in this chapter all use \TC\INCLUDE (or \BORLANDC\INCLUDE) as the include directory, and \TC\LIB (or \BORLANDC\LIB) as the library directory, so there should be no problem. However, as we'll see in the next chapter, things can get more complicated.

A Pocket Calculator: The CALC Program

Now that we know how to compile multi-file programs, let's look at our first example based on this approach. Suppose you plan to write a program that models a four-function pocket calculator, placing a picture of the calculator on the screen. However, you don't want to go to the trouble of programming the visual elements, such as push buttons and output display windows. Fortunately, you know where to obtain a set of classes designed to model the elements of screen calculators. You use these ready-made classes to model the visual elements, and write the interface and math routines yourself. In this example we'll show these two major parts of the program, and how they fit together.

The complete program puts a four-function calculator on the screen. The calculator can be used to perform arithmetic in the same way as a hand-held calculator. The program requires an EGA or VGA graphics adapter. Figure 15-2 shows how it looks on the screen.

USING THE CALCULATOR

The buttons on the calculator appear to push in when activated, as they do in Microsoft Windows and OS/2 Presentation Manager applications. This is an optical illusion, achieved by changing the shading around the edge of the button.

Different kinds of buttons are colored differently to emphasize their functions. Digits have a black background, arithmetic operators are blue, and the Clear button is red.

To use the calculator, the user types the digits of the first number, then an arithmetic operator (/, *, -, or +), then a second number, and then the equals sign (=). The answer is displayed. You can chain to another calculation: The answer automatically becomes the first operand, so you can press another arithmetic operator and key in another number to get the next answer. You can use a decimal point in the numbers you input, but not exponential notation or negative signs. The output has a fixed decimal place with two digits on its right. The equals sign and the plus sign are on the same button on the screen, and you can use either the ⊜ key or the ⊙

FIGURE 15-2
Output of CALC Program

key for either operation; the program distinguishes them by context, as on many pocket calculators.

To exit the program, press the (ESC) key.

Ideally a calculator screen-display would have its buttons activated by a mouse. However, Turbo C++ does not provide library functions for the mouse, and writing our own would make the program excessively complex. Also, not everyone has a mouse. We simulate the action of a mouse using the keyboard keys: When you type a digit, for instance, the corresponding button on the screen appears to push in. A clicking noise accompanies the "push" and "pop" of the button.

Files in the CALC Program

The CALC program consists of three files. First there is the header file, CALC.H, containing the class declarations. Next is CALC.CPP, which contains the member functions. We present this file in source form so you can read it, but if you had actually purchased it from a class library vendor it would probably be in object form, as a .LIB or .OBJ file. Finally there is CALC_APP.CPP, the file that we write ourselves.

To build this program, make sure these three files are in the same directory. Create a project called CALC_APP.PRJ. Add the files CALC.CPP and CALC_APP.CPP to the project file. When you're finished, you can compile and run the program as described at the beginning of this chapter.

Let's look first at CALC.H and CALC.CPP, the programs supplied by our mythical class vendor.

```
// calc.h
// header file for calc.cpp
#include <string.h>        // for strcpy()
#include <graphics.h>      // for graphics functions
#include <conio.h>         // for getche()
#include <dos.h>           // for delay(), sound(), etc.
#include <stdio.h>         // for sprintf()
#include <math.h>          // for atof()

class Window;                           // (needed for SCREEN)
Window* const SCREEN = (Window*)0;      // ultimate owner

enum buttonstatus { unpushed, pushed };
enum boolean { false, true };

class Window                    // parent class
    {
    protected:
        Window* ptrOwner;           // address of owner of this window
        int left, top, right, bot;  // outside edges of rectangle
        int delta;                  // distance between borders
        int deltacolor;             // color between borders
        int centercolor;            // color within inside border
```

```
    public:                    // constructor: initialize window
        Window(Window* ptro, int l, int t, int r, int b,
               int dc, int cc);
        void Display(void);      // display the window
    };

class Border : public Window    // border
    {
    public:
        Border(Window* ptro, int l, int t, int r, int b,
               int dc=BLUE, int cc=DARKGRAY)
             : Window(ptro, l, t, r, b, dc, cc)
         { }
    };

class Button : public Window    // push button
    {
    private:
        char text[20];                 // characters on button
        buttonstatus bstatus;          // pushed or unpushed
    public:
        Button(Window* ptro, int l, int t, int r, int b,
               int cc=BLACK, char* tx="")
             : Window(ptro, l, t, r, b, BLACK, cc)
          { strcpy(text, tx);  bstatus = unpushed; }
        void Click(void);              // click the button
        void Display(void);            // display the button
    };

class Output : public Window    // output window
    {
    private:
        char text[80];
    public:
        Output(Window* ptro, int l, int t, int r, int b,
               int dc=BLUE, int cc=WHITE)
             : Window(ptro, l, t, r, b, dc, cc)
          { }
        void Text(char *);     // display text sent as string
        void Number(double);   // display number
    };


// calc.cpp
// member functions for calc
#include "calc.h"              // calc header file

                              // constructor: initialize window
Window::Window(Window* ptro, int l, int t, int r, int b,
       int dc, int cc)
    {                          // set private data
```

```
        ptrOwner=ptro; left=l; top=t; right=r; bot=b;
        deltacolor=dc; centercolor=cc;
                                    // calculate delta
        delta = ((right-left)+(bot-top))/150 + 3;
        if( ptrOwner != SCREEN )    // if there is an owner,
            {                       // our coordinates
            left  += ptrOwner->left;   // start at owner's
            right += ptrOwner->left;   // upper left corner
            top   += ptrOwner->top;
            bot   += ptrOwner->top;
            }
        }

void Window::Display(void)    // display the window
    {
    setcolor(WHITE);

    int p[10];                          // draw outer rectangle and
    p[0]=left;  p[1]=top;               // fill it
    p[2]=right; p[3]=top;               // use fillpoly to clear
    p[4]=right; p[5]=bot;               // existing pattern
    p[6]=left;  p[7]=bot;               // (floodfill won't do this)
    p[8]=left;  p[9]=top;
    setfillstyle(SOLID_FILL, deltacolor);
    fillpoly(5, p);

                                        // draw inner rectangle
    rectangle(left+delta+1, top+delta,
              right-delta-1, bot-delta);
                                        // and fill it
    setfillstyle(SOLID_FILL, centercolor);
    floodfill(left+(right-left)/2, top+delta+1, WHITE );
    }

void Button::Click(void)            // click the button
    {
    bstatus = pushed;                   // push it
    Button::Display();                  // display it
    sound(500); delay(10); nosound();   // in beep
    delay(250);                         // wait 1/4 sec
    bstatus = unpushed;                 // unpush it
    Button::Display();                  // display it
    sound(400); delay(10); nosound();   // out beep
    }

void Button::Display(void)          // display the button
    {
    Window::Display();                  // display basic button
                                        // charcter on button
    moveto(left+(right-left)/2+1, top+(bot-top)/2);
    settextjustify(CENTER_TEXT, CENTER_TEXT);
    settextstyle(SANS_SERIF_FONT, HORIZ_DIR, USER_CHAR_SIZE );
```

```
    setusercharsize(5, 8, 2, 3);            // 5/8 width, 2/3 height
    setcolor(WHITE);                        // always white on black
    outtext(text);                          // write the character

    moveto(left, top);                      // upper left diagonal
    lineto(left+delta, top+delta);
    moveto(right, top);                     // upper right diagonal
    lineto(right-delta, top+delta);
    moveto(left, bot);                      // lower left diagonal
    lineto(left+delta, bot-delta);
    moveto(right, bot);                     // lower right diagonal
    lineto(right-delta, bot-delta);

    setfillstyle(SOLID_FILL, LIGHTGRAY); // illuminated edge color
    if(bstatus==unpushed)
        {                                   // shade top and left
        floodfill(left+(right-left)/2, top+1, WHITE);  // top
        floodfill(left+1, top+(bot-top)/2, WHITE);     // left
        }
    else  // pushed
        {                                   // shade bot and right
        floodfill(left+(right-left)/2, bot-1, WHITE);  // bot
        floodfill(right-1, top+(bot-top)/2, WHITE);    // right
        }
    }

void Output::Text(char *ptrstring)  // display text
    {
    Display();                              // clear output window
    moveto(right-delta, top+(bot-top)/2);
    settextjustify(RIGHT_TEXT, CENTER_TEXT);
    settextstyle(SANS_SERIF_FONT, HORIZ_DIR, USER_CHAR_SIZE );
    setusercharsize(5, 8, 1, 1);            // 5/8 width, 1/1 height
    setcolor(BLACK);                        // black text
    outtext(ptrstring);                     // insert the text
    }

void Output::Number(double d)           // display number
    {
    char buffer[80];                        // set up text buffer
    sprintf(buffer, "%16.2lf", d);          // convert number to string
    Output::Text(buffer);                   // display string
    }
```

CLASS DECLARATIONS

The CALC.H file contains the declarations of the functions. CALC.CPP contains the member functions themselves. Note that CALC.CPP #includes CALC.H. Every file that works with the classes declared in CALC.H must #include this file.

The image of the calculator has a border, an output window to display the re-sults, and 16 buttons. These three kinds of visual objects—border, output window, and buttons—have common features. They all occupy a certain position on the screen, and they all have a certain size. We make the further assumption that all these objects are created from two rectangles: an outer edge and an inner edge close to it. The space between these edges can be colored differently from the space within the inner rectangle, thus creating a picture-frame effect.

Since the image elements have common features, it's natural to put these fea-tures into a base class, and use derived classes for borders, output windows, and buttons.

THE BASE CLASS Window

In CALC.H we first declare a base class called `Window` that has the characteristics described above. Its private data includes the left, top, right, and bottom coordinates of the outside edge of the window. A variable, `delta`, specifies the distance in pix-els between the inside and outside edges. The variables `deltacolor` and `centercolor` hold the color of the space between the edges and the color of the inner rectangle, respectively.

Window Owners

In a visual image like a calculator, the graphics elements have a fixed visual relation-ship to one another; the "1" button is next to the "2" button, and so forth. Ordinarily we want to position one graphics element at a particular location on the screen, and then position other graphics elements *relative to the first*. This makes it easy to move an entire image, consisting of many elements, by changing only one set of coordi-nates. In our calculator, we want to position the border relative to the screen, and then position the buttons and the output window relative to this border. However, we might want to position a second border relative to the first (to provide visual separation for a group of buttons, for instance). Thus when we create a window—whether it is a border, a button, or an output window—we want to tell it what other window it should position itself relative to. We'll call this other window its `owner`. (We could have used the term *parent*, as is done in Microsoft Windows and OS/2 Presentation Manager programming, but this could be confused with the C++ con-cept of inheritance.)

When we create a window we'll send it a pointer to its owner so it can access the owner's coordinates and position itself relative to them. This is the variable `ptrOwner` in the declaration of the `Window` class.

Windows can own windows that own other windows. But the ultimate owner—the root of the ownership tree—is assumed to be the screen itself. In CALC.H we de-fine the variable SCREEN to be a null (0) pointer. When a window detects that the pointer to its parent has a null value, it assumes that it should position itself rela-tive to the screen, not to another window, so it treats the coordinates passed to it as absolute coordinates. Figure 15-3 shows the ownership relationship.

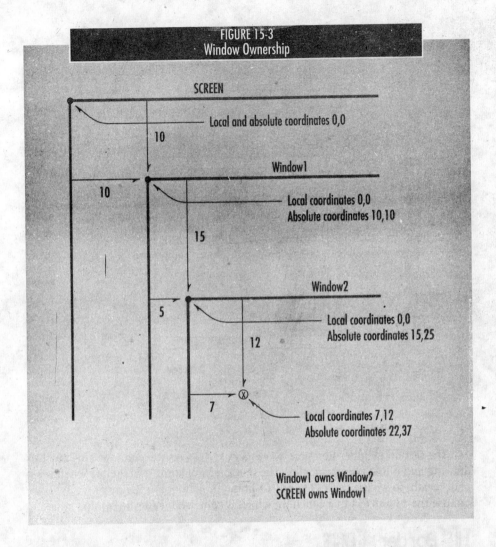

FIGURE 15-3
Window Ownership

Window1 owns Window2
SCREEN owns Window1

Window Member Functions

The member functions for the **Window** class are declared in CALC.H, but are defined in CALC.CPP. There are only two of these functions. The first is the constructor **Window()**. This function calculates the coordinates of the window, using the coordinates of the owner and the relative coordinates passed from the window definition, and then copies them into the window's protected data space. The constructor also copies the color arguments from the definition, and calculates **delta**, the distance between the inner and outer rectangles, based on the size of the window. The relationship of **delta** to the window is shown in Figure 15-4.

The value of **delta** is larger for larger windows but never smaller than 3 pixels. (The constant 150 in its definition was chosen by trial and error.)

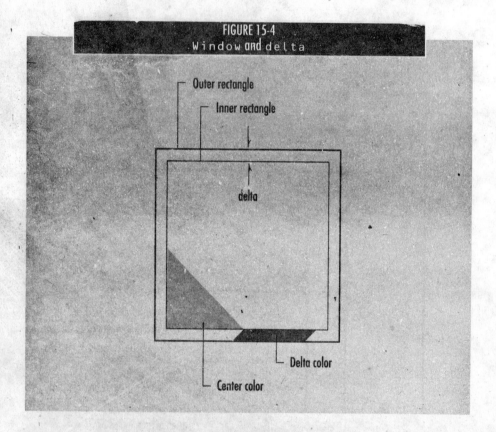

FIGURE 15-4
Window and delta

Outer rectangle

Inner rectangle

delta

Delta color

Center color

The second member function, `Display()`, displays the window. This involves drawing and filling two rectangles. The outer rectangle must obliterate whatever is underneath, so we use the `fillpoly()` library function. For the inner rectangle we can use the `floodfill()` function, which is somewhat easier to set up.

THE Border CLASS

The `Border` class is very simple, being almost identical to the `Window` class. It simply adds some optional colors, so you can declare a standard border without worrying about what colors to use. We could have dispensed with the Border class entirely, but it's conceptually cleaner to avoid creating objects of the base class and instead use it as an abstract class from which usable (or *instance*) classes are derived.

THE Button CLASS

The `Button` class adds two items of data to a window: the status of the button (whether it is pushed in or not) and the text that will appear in the center of the button. We use an `enum` to specify two possible values for the type `buttonstatus`:

unpushed and pushed. A button's text is printed in the center of the button, and is usually very short, although you could specify larger buttons that accommodated longer text.

The Button class adds three member functions, declared in CALC.H and defined in CALC.CPP. They are Click(), Display(), and the constructor Button(), which is similar to that in Border.

The Click() function depresses the button for a quarter of a second. (This is a little long if you're a fast typist, but it gives you time to see the button sink in and pop out.) It does this by changing the button status to pushed, displaying it, then changing the status back to unpushed and displaying it again. A clicking sound is added to accentuate the action.

The Display() function in the Button class first calls the Display() function in Window to draw the underlying rectangles. Note that the scope-resolution operator (::) must be used to distinguish which Display() we want. Next Display() draws the button's text. Finally it shades the button's edges—the space between the button's inner and outer rectangles.

To shade the button's edges, four short diagonal lines are drawn connecting the upper-left corner of the outer rectangle with the upper-left corner of the inner rectangle, and similarly for the other three corners. This creates four separate sections between the rectangles, around the periphery of the button: upper, lower, left, and right.

What happens next depends on the status of the button. If it is not pushed, the upper and left sections are colored light gray, and the right and lower sections remain black. If it is pushed, the coloring is reversed: The upper and left sections remain black, and the lower and right sections are colored light gray. The eye assumes that light falls from the upper left, so this scheme provides the illusion that the button protrudes from the screen when unpushed, and sinks below the screen when pushed. Figure 15-5 shows a button.

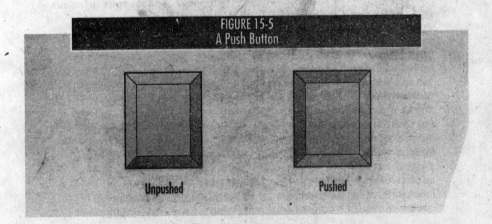

FIGURE 15-5
A Push Button

Unpushed   Pushed

THE OUTPUT WINDOW

The Output class creates the window in which the numerical results of calculations are displayed. This class adds one additional data item to Window: the text to be displayed in the output window. There are two member functions. Text() displays output provided by a string argument to the function, and Number() displays output taken from a numerical argument. Number() converts the floating-point number to a string using the sprintf() library function, and then calls Text() to display the string.

THE CALC_APP.CPP FILE

The CALC_APP.CPP file contains the code that uses the various classes to create the calculator. This code also interacts with the keyboard and performs the arithmetic requested by the user of the program. This is all handled in one function—main(). As written, the program specifies an EGA graphics adapter, but you can change it to specify VGA if you wish. The image of the calculator will be somewhat smaller, but it will work the same way.

```
// calc_app..cpp
// four-function calculator with 15 digits
// uses calc.cpp

#include "calc.h"                       // header file for calc.app

main()
    {
    int driver, mode;
    driver = EGA;                       // set graphics driver
    mode = EGAHI;                       // and graphics mode
    initgraph(&driver, &mode, "\\borlandc\\bgi");

    // this section defines the various objects
                                        // border and output windows
    Border border1(SCREEN,  240, 30, 480, 330);
    Output output1(&border1, 20, 20, 220,  60, BLUE, WHITE);
                                        // buttons
    Button button0(&border1, 30, 230, 65, 265, BLACK, "0");
    Button button1(&border1, 30, 180, 65, 215, BLACK, "1");
    Button button2(&border1, 78, 180, 113, 215, BLACK, "2");
    Button button3(&border1, 127, 180, 162, 215, BLACK, "3");
    Button button4(&border1, 30, 130, 65, 165, BLACK, "4");
    Button button5(&border1, 78, 130, 113, 165, BLACK, "5");
    Button button6(&border1, 127, 130, 162, 165, BLACK, "6");
    Button button7(&border1, 30, 80, 65, 115, BLACK, "7");
    Button button8(&border1, 78, 80, 113, 115, BLACK, "8");
    Button button9(&border1, 127, 80, 162, 115, BLACK, "9");
    Button buttonDiv(&border1, 175, 80, 210, 115, BLUE, "/");
    Button buttonMul(&border1, 175, 130, 210, 165, BLUE, "*");
```

```
Button buttonSub(&border1, 175, 180, 210, 215, BLUE, "-");
Button buttonDot(&border1, 78, 230, 113, 265, BLACK, ".");
Button buttonClr(&border1, 127, 230, 162, 265, RED, "clr");
Button buttonAdd(&border1, 175, 230, 210, 265, BLUE, "+=");

// this section displays the various objects.

border1.Display();                    // border and output windows
output1.Display();

                                      // buttons
button7.Display();      button8.Display();    button9.Display();
button4.Display();      button5.Display();    button6.Display();
button1.Display();      button2.Display();    button3.Display();
buttonSub.Display();    buttonDiv.Display();
buttonMul.Display();    buttonAdd.Display();
button0.Display();      buttonDot.Display();  buttonClr.Display();
output1.Number(0.0);                  // display 0.0

// this section handles the keyboard and activates display

const char ESC=27;               // Escape key
char dstring[80];                // string for display
char tempbuf[80];                // temp string holder
int numchars = 0;                // number of chars in dstring
char ch;                         // character read from keyboard
char oper;                       // operator: /, *, -, +
boolean isfirst = true;          // first (not second) operator
boolean chain = false;           // chaining to next number
double number1, number2;         // first and second numbers
double answer;                   // answer to arithmetic

while( (ch=getch()) != ESC )     // quit program on Escape key
   {                             // is it a digit (or dot)
   if( (ch>='0' && ch<='9') || ch=='.' )
      {
      switch(ch)
         {                       // click the button
         case '0': button0.Click(); break;
         case '1': button1.Click(); break;
         case '2': button2.Click(); break;
         case '3': button3.Click(); break;
         case '4': button4.Click(); break;
         case '5': button5.Click(); break;
         case '6': button6.Click(); break;
         case '7': button7.Click(); break;
         case '8': button8.Click(); break;
         case '9': button9.Click(); break;
         case '.': buttonDot.Click(); break;
         } // end switch
      dstring[numchars++] = ch;  // put char in buffer
      dstring[numchars] = '\0';  // put 0 at end of string
```

```
      if( atof( dstring) > 99999999999.99 ||   // if too big
              numchars > 11 )                   // or too long
          {                                     // beep
          delay(100); sound(200); delay(300); nosound();
          dstring[--numchars] = '\0';   // delete last char
          }
      output1.Text(dstring);        // send it to output window
      }  // end if (it's a digit)

                                 // if it's a valid math operator
   else if( ch=='/' || ch=='*' || ch=='-' || ch=='+' ||
          ch=='=')
      {
      strcpy(tempbuf,dstring);    // save the input string
      numchars = 0;               // empty input buffer
      dstring[numchars] = '\0';
      output1.Text(dstring);      // display empty buffer
      if( isfirst )               // if first operator
          {                       // 1st time, n1 = answer
          number1 = (chain) ? answer : atof(tempbuf);
          isfirst = false;        // next op will be second
          switch(ch)              // store the operator
              {
              case '/':  buttonDiv.Click();  oper='/';  break;
              case '*':  buttonMul.Click();  oper='*';  break;
              case '-':  buttonSub.Click();  oper='-';  break;
              case '+':                  // + and = do same thing
              case '=':  buttonAdd.Click();  oper='+';  break;
              }  // end switch (ch)
          }  // end if (first number)
      else                        // second operator
          {                       //    (should be '=')
          buttonAdd.Click();      // assume it was '='
          number2 = atof(tempbuf);  // get second number
          switch(oper)            // do the action
              {
              case '/':  answer = number1 / number2;  break;
              case '*':  answer = number1 * number2;  break;
              case '-':  answer = number1 - number2;  break;
              case '+':  answer = number1 + number2;  break;
              }
          if(answer > 99999999999.99)  // if answer too big
              output1.Text("Overflow");   // to display
          else                    // otherwise
              {                    // answer ok
              output1.Number(answer); // display the answer
              number1 = answer;
              }                     // set up to chain to
          isfirst = true;          // another 2nd operator
          chain = true;            // and another 2nd number
```

```
                }  // end else (second operator)
              }  // end else if (operator)

         else if( ch=='C' || ch=='c' )      // if it's Clear
           {
           buttonClr.Click();               // click the button
           isfirst = true;                  // next number is first
           chain = false;                   // not chaining
           numchars = 0;                    // empty input buffer
           dstring[numchars] = '\0';
           output1.Number(0.0);             // display 0.0
           }  // end else if (clear)
         else                               // it's a bad character
           {                                // beep
           delay(100); sound(200); delay(300); nosound();
           }  // end else (bad character)
       }  // end while
   closegraph();                            // shut down graphics system
   }  // end main()
```

Note that CALC_APP.CPP, like CALC.CPP, must `#include` the header file CALC.H, so that it can access the various class declarations.

In `main()` we first define all the visual elements of the calculator, then display them using each one's `Display()` function. (We could have made these display routines into a family of virtual functions, but in this particular application there was no need to do so. In a more general situation, virtual functions would provide added flexibility.)

The complicated part of `main()` involves handling the keyboard input. This is done in a large `while` loop. At the top of the loop the character is read by the `getche()` function. Pressing (ESC) terminates the loop and the program. The body of the loop is a series of `if` and `else if` constructions that decipher the character typed.

Digits

If the character is a digit or the decimal point, the appropriate button is clicked and the digit is added to the end of a character buffer called `dstring`. The '\0' character is then added in the position following the character to terminate the string. If the buffer is too full or the number too big, an error beep is generated and the offending digit is removed from the buffer (by writing over it with '\0'). The resulting buffer contents are displayed using the `Output.Text()` function.

Operators

If the character is an arithmetic operator, the string in `dstring` is saved temporarily, and `dstring` is emptied and the empty buffer displayed.

What we do next depends on whether this is the first arithmetic operator or the second. A Boolean flag variable, `isfirst`, keeps track of this state. If this flag is `true`, we know we are dealing with the first operator, which should be \, *, - or +. We save the number from `dstring` in `number1`, then click the button corresponding to the operator and save the operator for later use. (We'll ignore the possibility of chaining for the moment.)

If we've just read the second operator, it must be the = operator, so we click the += button, store the number in number2, and—using the previously stored operator—perform the corresponding arithmetic operation on number1 and number2. The result is stored in answer. If it isn't too big, we display it; otherwise we display the word *Overflow*.

Clear Button

If the character is 'C' or 'c', we click the clr button and clear the dstring buffer in preparation for starting over. We respond to any other keyboard character with an error beep but no other change.

Chaining

Often the user wants to retain the result of an operation and use it as the first operand of a second operation. This is mediated by a chain flag variable, which is set to true if we've already completed one operation. When this is the case the value to be inserted in number1 is taken from answer rather than from the user, before the indicated arithmetic is carried out.

Not a Stand-Alone File

Note that, as written, CALC.EXE is not a stand-alone program; the \TC\BGI directory specified in initgraph() must be available to the program. This directory contains the files EGAVGA.BGI (the graphics driver for EGA and VGA) and SANS.CHR (the font file for the sans serif font). We describe the procedure for creating a stand-alone graphics program in Appendix C.

Not the Windows Approach

In Windows and the OS/2 Presentation Manager, window-type objects like buttons are supplied with the operating system. The operating system also informs your program when the mouse is clicked on certain objects. For these reasons, writing a program like CALC is easier, in some ways, using Windows or PM than writing your own visual interface, as we've shown here.

A Very Long Number Class

Sometimes even the basic data type unsigned long does not provide enough precision for certain integer arithmetic operations. unsigned long is the largest integer type in Turbo C++, holding integers up to 4,294,967,295, or about ten digits. This is about the same number of digits a pocket calculator can handle. But if you need to work with numbers containing more significant digits than this, you have a problem.

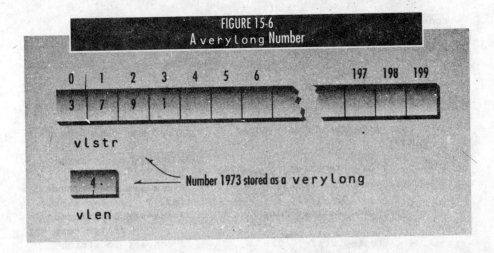

FIGURE 15-6
A verylong Number

0   1   2   3   4   5   6   197 198 199

3   7   9   1

vlstr

4. ◄——— Number 1973 *stored as a* verylong

vlen

Our next example shows a way to solve this problem. It provides a class that holds numbers up to 200 digits long. If you want to make even longer numbers, you can change a single constant in the program. Need 1000-digit numbers? No problem.

NUMBERS AS STRINGS

The verylong class stores numbers as strings of digits. This explains its large capacity; the basic types in C++ can handle long strings, since they are simply arrays. By representing numbers as strings we can make them as long as we want. There are two data members in verylong: a char array to hold the string of digits, and an int to tell how long the string is. (This length data isn't strictly necessary, but it saves using strlen() to find the string length over and over.) The digits in the string are stored in reverse order, with the least significant digit stored first, at vlstr[0]. This simplifies various operations on the string. Figure 15-6 shows a number stored as a string.

We've provided user-accessible routines for addition and multiplication of verylong numbers. (We leave it as an exercise for the reader to write subtraction and division routines.)

THE CLASS SPECIFIER

Here's the header file for VERYLONG. It shows the specifiers for the verylong class:

```
// verylong.h
// class specifier for very long integer type
#include <iostream.h>
#include <string.h>          // for strlen(), etc.
#include <stdlib.h>          // for ltoa()
```

```
const int SZ = 200;            // maximum digits in verylongs

class verylong
    {
    private:
        char vlstr[SZ];          // verylong number as a string
        int vlen;                // length of verylong string
        verylong multdigit(int);        // prototypes for
        verylong mult10(verylong);      // private functions
    public:
        verylong()                      // no-arg constructor
            { vlstr[0]='\0'; vlen=0; }
        verylong(char s[SZ])            // one-arg constructor
            { strcpy(vlstr, s); vlen=strlen(s); }   // for string
        verylong(unsigned long n)       // one-arg constructor
            {                           // for long int
            ltoa(n, vlstr, 10);         // convert to string
            strrev(vlstr);              // reverse it
            vlen=strlen(vlstr);         // find length
            }
        void putvl();                   // display verylong
        void getvl();                   // get verylong from user
        verylong operator + (verylong);  // add verylongs
        verylong operator * (verylong);  // multiply verylongs
    };
```

In addition to the data members, there are two private-member functions in class **verylong**. One multiplies a **verylong** number by a single digit, and one multiplies a **verylong** number by 10. These routines are used internally by the multiplication routine.

There are three constructors. One sets the **verylong** to 0, by inserting a terminating null at the beginning of the array and setting the length to 0. The second initializes it to a string (which is in reverse order), and the third initializes it to a **long int** value.

The **putvl()** member function displays a **verylong**, and the **getvl** gets a **verylong** value from the user. You can type as many digits as you like, up to 200. Note that there is no error checking in this routine; if you type a nondigit the results will be inaccurate.

Two overloaded operators, **+** and *****, perform addition and multiplication. You can use expressions like

```
alpha = beta * gamma + delta;
```

to do **verylong** arithmetic.

THE MEMBER FUNCTIONS

Here's VERYLONG.CPP, the file that holds the member function definitions:

```
// verylong.cpp
// implements very long integer type
#include "verylong.h"            // header file for verylong

    d verylong::putvl()                  // display verylong
        {
        char temp[SZ];
        strcpy(temp,vlstr);              // make copy
        cout << strrev(temp);            // reverse the copy
        }                                // and display it

void verylong::getvl()                   // get verylong from user
        {
        cin >> vlstr;                    // get string from user
        vlen = strlen(vlstr);            // find its length
        strrev(vlstr);                   // reverse it
        }

verylong verylong::operator + (verylong v)  // add verylongs
        {
        char temp[SZ];
                                         // find longest number
        int maxlen = (vlen > v.vlen) ? vlen : v.vlen;
        int carry = 0;                   // set to 1 if sum >= 10
        for(int j = 0; j<maxlen; j++)    // for each position
            {
            int d1 = (j > vlen-1)   ? 0 : vlstr[j]-'0';   // get digit
            int d2 = (j > v.vlen-1) ? 0 : v.vlstr[j]-'0'; // get digit
            int digitsum = d1 + d2 + carry;              // add digits
            if( digitsum >= 10 )         // if there's a carry,
                { digitsum -= 10; carry=1; } // decrease sum by 10,
            else                         // set carry to 1
                carry = 0;               // otherwise carry is 0
            temp[j] = digitsum+'0';      // insert char in string
            }
        if(carry==1)                     // if carry at end,
            temp[j++] = '1';             // last digit is 1
        temp[j] = '\0';                  // terminate string
        return verylong(temp);           // return temp verylong
        }

verylong verylong::operator * (verylong v)  // multiply verylongs
        {
        verylong pprod;                  // product of one digit
        verylong tempsum;                // running total
        for(int j=0; j<v.vlen; j++)      // for each digit in arg
            {
            int digit = v.vlstr[j]-'0';  // get the digit
            pprod = multdigit(digit);    // multiply this by digit
```

```
      for(int k=0; k<j; k++)              // multiply result by
         pprod = mult10(pprod);           //    power of 10
      tempsum = tempsum + pprod;          // add product to total
      }
   return tempsum;                        // return total of prods
   }

verylong verylong::mult10(verylong v)     // multiply argument by 10
   {
   char temp[SZ];
   for(int j=v.vlen-1; j>=0; j--)         // move digits one
      temp[j+1] = v.vlstr[j];             //    position higher
   temp[0] = '0';                         // put zero on low end
   temp[v.vlen+1] = '\0';                 // terminate string
   return verylong(temp);                 // return result
   }

verylong verylong::multdigit(int d2)      // multiply this verylong
   {                                      // by digit in argument
   char temp[SZ];
   int carry = 0;
   for(int j = 0; j<vlen; j++)            // for each position
      {                                   // in this verylong
      int d1 = vlstr[j]-'0';              // get digit from this
      int digitprod = d1 * d2;            // multiply by that digit
      digitprod += carry;                 // add old carry
      if( digitprod >= 10 )               // if there's a new carry,
         {
         carry = digitprod/10;            // carry is high digit
         digitprod -= carry*10;           // result is low digit
         }
      else
         carry = 0;                       // otherwise carry is 0
      temp[j] = digitprod+'0';            // insert char in string
      }
   if(carry != 0)                         // if carry at end,
      temp[j++] = carry+'0';              // it's last digit
   temp[j] = '\0';                        // terminate string
   return verylong(temp);                 // return verylong
   }
```

The putvl() and getvl() functions are fairly straightforward. They use the strrev() library function to reverse the string, so it is stored in reverse order but input is displayed normally.

The operator+() function adds two verylongs and leaves the result in a third verylong. It does this by considering their digits one at a time. It adds digit 0 from both numbers, storing a carry if necessary. Then it adds the digits in position 1, adding the carry if necessary. It continues until it has added all the digits in the larger of the two numbers. If the numbers are different lengths the nonexistent digits in the shorter number are set to 0 before being added. Figure 15-7 shows the process.

Multiplication uses the `operator*()` function. This function performs multiplication by multiplying the multiplicand (the top number when you write it by hand) by each separate digit in the multiplier (the bottom number). It calls the `multdigit()` routine to this. The results are then multiplied by 10 an appropriate number of times to shift the result to match the position of the digit, using the `mult10()` function. The results of these separate calculations are then added together using the `operator+()` function.

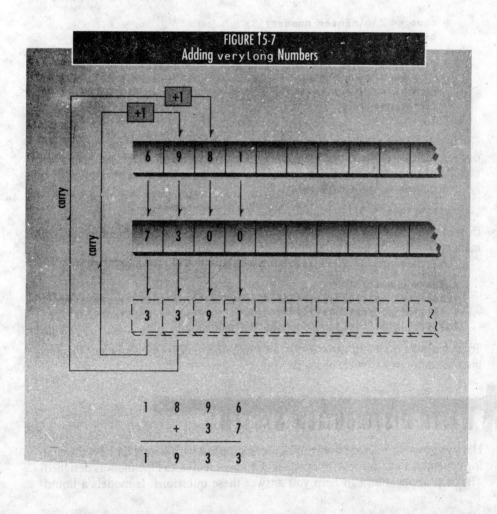

FIGURE 15-7
Adding `verylong` Numbers

THE APPLICATION PROGRAM

To test the verylong class we use a variation of the FACTOR program from Chapter 4 to calculate the factorial of a number entered by the user. Here's the listing for VL_APP.CPP:

```
// vl_app.cpp
// calculates factorials of larger numbers using verylong class
#include "verylong.h"                    // verylong header file
   main()
{
   unsigned long numb, j;
   verylong fact=1;                      // initialize verylong

   cout << "\n\nEnter number: ";
   cin >> numb;                          // input a long int

   for(j=numb; j>0; j--)                 // factorial is numb *
      fact = fact * j;                   //     numb-1 * numb-2 *
   cout << "Factoral is ";               //     numb-3 and so on
   fact.putvl();                         // display factorial
   }
```

In this program fact is a verylong variable. The other variables, numb and j, don't need to be verylongs because they don't get so big. To calculate the factorial of 200, for example, numb and j require only three digits, while fact requires 158.

Notice how, in the expression

```
fact = fact * j;
```

the long variable j is automatically converted to verylong, using the one-argument constructor, before the multiplication is carried out.

Here's the output when we ask the program to find the factorial of 100:

```
Enter number: 100
Factoral is 93326215443944152681699238856266700490071596826438162
1468592963895217599993229915608941463976156518286253697920827223
758251185210916864000000000000000000000000000
```

Try *that* using type long variables! Surprisingly, the routines are fairly fast; this program executes in a fraction of a second.

A WATER-DISTRIBUTION SYSTEM

Have you ever wondered how your house is supplied with water? Or how the cooling system in a nuclear reactor operates? Or how the Alaska Pipeline was designed? The next application can help you answer these questions. It models a liquid-distribution system, consisting of pipes, valves, tanks, and other components. This example shows how easy it is to create a set of classes for a specialized situation. A similar approach could be used in other process-control applications, such as the hydraulic systems used to operate aircraft. The general approach is even applicable to electrical distribution systems, or economic systems that track the flow of money.

Figure 15-8 shows a water-distribution system for a small community built on a hillside. This water system will be modeled in the PIPES program.

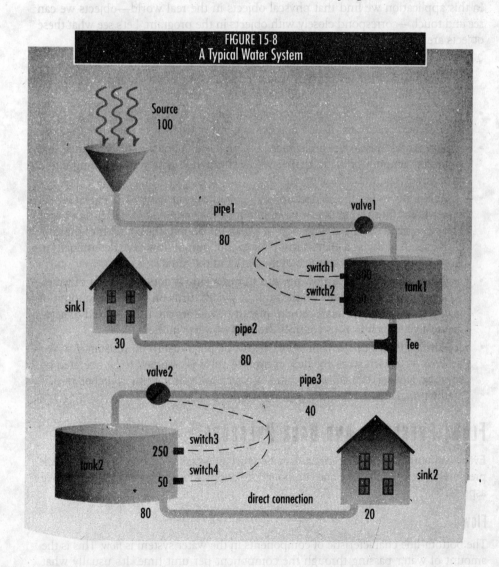

FIGURE 15-8
A Typical Water System

As in the previous program, we'll break this program into three files. PIPES.H will contain the class declarations, and PIPES.CPP will contain the definitions of the member functions. These files can be assumed to be provided by a vendor of class libraries. The PIPE_APP.CPP file is the one we write ourselves to specify a water system with a particular arrangement of tanks, valves, and pipes.

COMPONENTS OF A WATER SYSTEM

In this application we find that physcal objects in the real world—objects we can see and touch—correspond closely with objects in the program. Let's see what these objects are.

- A *source* supplies water to the system. In the real world it might correspond to a spring, well, or reservoir. The water from the source is assumed to be always available but cannot be supplied faster than a certain fixed rate.

- A *sink* is a user of water. It represents a house, factory, or farm, or a group of such water consumers. A sink absorbs water from the system at a fixed rate.

- A *pipe* carries water over a distance. A pipe has a characteristic resistance that limits the amount of water that can flow through it. The water flowing into a pipe equals the water flowing out.

- A *tank* stores water. It also decouples the input/output flows: The rate at which water flows into the tank can be different from the rate at which it flows out. For example, if the input flow is greater than the output, the contents of the tank increases. A tank has a characteristic maximum output flow rate, determined (in this model, at least) by the size of the outlet in the tank.

- To keep a tank from overflowing, and to make sure it doesn't run out of water, we can associate *switches* with the tank. A switch turns on when the amount of water in the tank reaches a certain quantity. Switches are usually used to actuate a valve, which in turn controls the level of water in the tank.

- A *valve* regulates the flow of water. It can be on, causing no resistance to the flow, or off, which stops the flow entirely. A valve is assumed to be operated by some sort of servo-mechanism, and is typically controlled by switches associated with a tank.

FLOW, PRESSURE, AND BACK PRESSURE

Every component in the system has three important aspects: flow, pressure, and back pressure. When we connect one component to another, we're connecting these three aspects.

Flow

The bottom-line characteristic of components in the water system is *flow*. This is the amount of water passing through the component per unit time. It's usually what we're interested in measuring when we model a system.

Often the flow into a component is the same as the flow out. This is true of pipes and of valves. However, as noted above, it is not true of tanks.

Pressure

Flow isn't the whole story. For example, when a valve is turned off, the flow both into it and out of it stops, but water may still be *trying* to flow through the valve. This potential for flow is *pressure*. A source or a tank provides water at a certain pressure. If the rest of the system permits, this pressure will cause a proportional flow: The greater the pressure, the greater the flow. But if a valve is turned off, the flow will stop, regardless of what the pressure is. Pressure, like flow, is transmitted downstream from one component to another.

A tank decouples pressure as well as flow. The pressure downstream from a tank is determined by the tank, not by the upstream pressure.

Back Pressure

In opposition to pressure is *back pressure*. This is caused by the resistance to flow of some components. A small-diameter pipe, for instance, will slow the flow of water, so that no matter how much pressure is supplied, the flow will still be small. This back pressure will slow the flow not only into the component causing the back pressure but into all components upstream.

Back pressure goes the opposite way from flow and pressure. It's transmitted from the downstream component to the upstream component. Tanks decouple back pressure as they do pressure and flow.

COMPONENT INPUT AND OUTPUT

Sometimes the flow, pressure, or back pressure are the same on both ends of a component. The flow into one end of a pipe, for example, is the same as the flow out the other end (we assume no leaks). However, these characteristics can also be different on the upstream and downstream sides. When a valve is turned off, the pressure on its downstream side becomes zero, no matter what the pressure on the upstream side is. The flow into a tank may be different from the flow out; the difference between input and output flow is reflected in changes to the contents of the tank. The output pressure of a pipe may be less than the input pressure because of the pipe's resistance.

Thus each component, at any given instant, can be characterized by six values. There are three inputs: pressure (from the upstream component), back pressure (from downstream), and flow (from upstream). There are also three outputs: pressure (on the downstream component), back pressure (on the upstream component), and flow (to the downstream component). This situation is shown in Figure 15-9.

The outputs of a component are calculated from its inputs, and also from the internal characteristics and state of the component, such as the resistance of a pipe, or whether a valve is open or closed. A member function of each component, called Tick() because it occurs at fixed time intervals, is used to calculate the components'

579

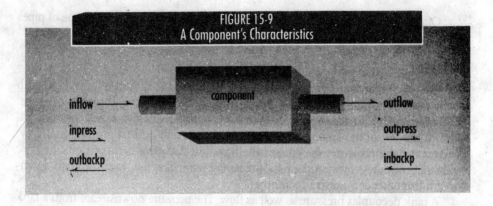

FIGURE 15-9
A Component's Characteristics

inflow → component → outflow

inpress outpress

outbackp inbackp

output based on its input and internal characteristics. If the input pressure to a pipe is increased, for example, the flow will increase correspondingly (unless the back pressure caused by the pipe's resistance and other components beyond it in the line is too high).

MAKING CONNECTIONS

To create a water system we need to connect the various components together. It should be possible to connect any component to any other component so that water flows from one to another. (Switches are not connected in this way, since they don't carry water.) Besides flow, both pressure and back pressure must be connected, since they are also transmitted from component to component.

Thus, making a connection means setting the output pressure and output flow from the upstream object to the input pressure and input flow of the downstream object, and setting the output back pressure from the downstream object to the input back pressure of the upstream object. This is shown in Figure 15-10.

SIMPLIFYING ASSUMPTIONS

To avoid complex mathematics we've made some simplifying assumptions.

What we call back pressure in the program should probably be called something like *ease of flow*. The values we use for this characteristic are *proportional* to the resulting flow, being small if only a small amount can flow, and large when the flow can be large. Real back pressure would be the reciprocal of the resulting flow, but this would complicate the program unduly.

Both pressure and back pressure are assumed to be measured in the same units as flow. To calculate the flow, we examine the pressure pushing water into the system, and the back pressure resisting its flow. The resulting flow is the smallest of these two numbers. Thus if a source provides 100 gallons/minute, and a pipe has

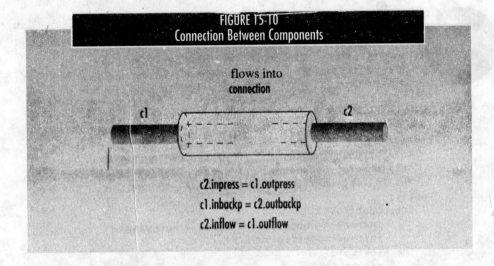

FIGURE 15-10
Connection Between Components

flows into
connection

c1   c2

c2.inpress = c1.outpress
c1.inbackp = c2.outbackp
c2.inflow = c1.outflow

a resistance of 60 gallons/minute, which causes a back pressure of 60 gallons/minute, the flow will be 60 gallons/minute.

These assumptions don't model exactly the real world of hydraulic flow, in which flow is determined by complex formulas relating pressure and back pressure, but they do provide a good first approximation.

We assume the output pressure of a tank is a constant. In reality it would depend on the contents of the tank. However, for tanks considerably higher in elevation than the sink, this is a reasonable approximation.

There is also an unavoidable built-in kind of imperfection in our approach to this problem. The physical system we are modeling is an analog system that changes continuously with time. But our model is "digital": it samples the state of the components at discrete "ticks," or time intervals. Thus when something changes, like a valve opening, it may take several loop cycles for the resulting pressure and flow changes to propagate throughout the system. These transients can be ignored in analyzing the system's behavior.

PROGRAM DESIGN

Our goal in this program is to create a family of classes that make it easy to model different water-distribution systems. In this application it's easy to see what the classes should represent. We create a class for each kind of component—a valve class, a tank class, a pipe class, and so on. Once these classes are established, the programmer can then connect components as necessary to model a specific system.

Here are the listings for the PIPES.H and PIPES.CPP files. We assume these files are supplied by a class software vendor.

```
// pipes.h
// header file for pipes

const int infinity = 32767;     // infinite back pressure
enum offon { off, on };         // status of valves and switches
class Tank;                     // for using Tank in Switch

class Component                 // components (Pipe, Valve, etc.)
   {
   protected:
      int inpress, outpress;    // pressures in and out
      int inbackp, outbackp;    // back pressures in and out
      int inflow, outflow;      // flow in and out
   public:
      Component(void)
         { inpress = outpress = inbackp = outbackp =
           inflow = outflow = 0; }
      int Flow(void)
         { return inflow; }
      friend void operator >= (Component&, Component&);
      friend void Tee(Component&, Component&, Component&);
   };

class Source : public Component     // flow begins here
   {
   public:
      Source(int outp)
         { outpress = inpress = outp; }
      void Tick(void)                   // update
                                        // output pressure fixed
         {
         outbackp = inbackp;
         outflow = (outpress < outbackp) ? outpress : outbackp;
         inflow = outflow;
         }
   };

class Sink : public Component       // flow ends here
   {
   public:
      Sink(int obp)                     // initialize backpressure
         { outbackp = inbackp = obp; }
      void Tick(void)                   // update
                                        // output back pressure fixed
         {
         outpress = inpress;
         outflow = (outbackp < outpress) ? outbackp : outpress;
         inflow = outflow;
         }
   };
```

```
class Pipe : public Component          // connects other components,
    {                                  // has resistance to flow
    private:
        int resist;
    public:
        Pipe(int r)           // initialize
            { inbackp = resist = r; }
        void Tick(void);  // update
    };

class Valve : public Component        // turns flow on or off
    {
    private:
        offon status;                  // on (open) or off (closed)
    public:
        Valve(offon s)
            { status = s; }
        offon& Status(void)
            { return status; }
        void Tick(void);
    };

class Tank : public Component         // stores water
    {
    private:
        int contents;                  // water in tank (gals)
        int maxoutpress;               // max output pressure
    public:
        Tank(int mop)                  // initialize to empty tank
            { maxoutpress = mop; contents = 0; }
        int Contents(void)             // get contents
            { return(contents); }
        void Tick(void);
    };

class Switch                          // activated by tank level
    {                                 // can operate valves
    private:
        offon status;     // 'on' if contents > triggercap
        int cap;          // capacity where switch turns on
        Tank* tankptr;    // pointer to owner tank
    public:
        Switch(Tank *tptr, int tcap)   // initialize
            { tankptr = tptr; cap = tcap; status = off; }
        int Status(void)               // get status
            { return(status); }
        void Tick(void)                // update status
            { status = (tankptr->Contents() > cap) ? on : off; }
    };
```

```
// pipes.cpp
// function definitions for pipes

#include "pipes.h"                    // needed for class definitions

                                      // "flows into" operator: c1 >= c2
void operator >= (Component& c1, Component& c2)
   {
   c2.inpress = c1.outpress;
   c1.inbackp = c2.outbackp;
   c2.inflow =  c1.outflow;
   }

                                      // "tee" divides flow into two
void Tee(Component& src, Component& c1, Component& c2)
   {
                                      // avoid division by 0
   if( (c1.outbackp==0 && c2.outbackp==0) ||
      (c1.outbackp==0 && c2.outbackp==0) )
      {
      c1.inpress = c2.inpress = 0;
      src.inbackp = 0;
      c1.inflow = c2.inflow = 0;
      return;
      }                               // proportion for each output
   float f1 = (float)c1.outbackp / (c1.outbackp + c2.outbackp);
   float f2 = (float)c2.outbackp / (c1.outbackp + c2.outbackp);
                                      // pressures for two outputs
   c1.inpress = src.outpress * f1;
   c2.inpress = src.outpress * f2;
                                      // back pressure for single input
   src.inbackp = c1.outbackp + c2.outbackp;
                                      // flow for two outputs
   c1.inflow = src.outflow * f1;
   c2.inflow = src.outflow * f2;
   }

void Pipe::Tick(void)                 // update pipes
   {
   outpress = (inpress < resist) ? inpress : resist;
   outbackp = (inbackp < resist) ? inbackp : resist;

   // outflow is the lesser of outpress, outbackp, and resist
   if(outpress < outbackp && outpress < resist)
      outflow = outpress;
   else if(outbackp < outpress && outbackp < resist)
      outflow = outbackp;
   else
      outflow = resist;
   }
```

```
void Valve::Tick(void)                  // update valves
{
    if(status==on)                      // if valve open
    {
        outpress = inpress;
        outbackp = inbackp;
        outflow = (outpress < outbackp) ? outpress : outbackp;
    }
    else                                // if valve closed
    {
        outpress = 0;
        outbackp = 0;
        outflow = 0;
    }
}


void Tank::Tick(void)                   // update tanks
{
    outbackp = infinity;                // will take all the flow
                                        // you can give it
    if( contents > 0 )                  // if not empty
    {
        outpress = (maxoutpress<inbackp) ? maxoutpress : inbackp;
        outflow = outpress;
    }
    else                                // if empty
    {
        outpress = 0;                   // no out pressure,
        outflow = 0;                    // no flow
    }
    contents += inflow - outflow;       // always true
}
```

PROGRAMMING THE CONNECTIONS

A key part of program usability is a simple, intuitive way of describing connections in the program. We could use a function, such as

```
Connect(valve1, tank1);
```

However, this can be confusing: Is the upstream component the right argument or the left?

A better approach is to overload an operator to represent connections between components. We'll choose the greater-than-or-equal-to operator, >=, which provides a visual indication of flow direction from left to right. We can call it the *flows into* operator. A program statement establishing a connection would look like this:

```
valve1 >= tank1;
```

meaning that water from valve1 *flows into* tank1.

Base and Derived Classes

When designing our program we look first for similarities among the various objects. The common attributes can be placed in a base class, while the individual features that distinguish the components can be placed in derived classes.

The Component Base Class

In this application we note that all the objects (except switches) have water flowing through them and can be connected to each other. We will therefore create a base class that permits connections. We'll call it `Component`.

```
class Component                    // components (Pipe, Valve, etc.)
   {
   protected:
      int inpress, outpress;      // pressures in and out
      int inbackp, outbackp;      // back pressures in and out
      int inflow, outflow;        // flow in and out
   public:
      Component(void)
         { inpress = outpress = inbackp = outbackp =
           inflow = outflow = 0; }
      int Flow(void)
           { return inflow; }
      friend void operator >= (Component&, Component&);
      friend void Tee(Component&, Component&, Component&);
   };
```

A component has pressure, back pressure, and flow. These all have two values: input to the component, and output from it. For input we have the flow into the object from upstream, the pressure exerted by objects on its upstream side, and the back pressure exerted by objects on the downstream side. For output there is the flow out of the object, the pressure it transmits to the downstream object, and the back pressure it transmits to the upstream object. These values are all stored in objects of the Component class. A constructor for this class initializes all the data items to 0, and another member function returns the flow, which is, for most components, what we want to measure to see how the system is working.

The *Flows Into* Operator

The *flows into* operator, `>=`, connects an upstream component with a downstream component. Three inputs (the downstream object's pressure and flow and the upstream object's back pressure) are set equal to three outputs (the upstream object's pressure and flow and the downstream object's back pressure).

```
// "flows into" operator: c1 >= c2
void operator >= (Component& c1, Component& c2)
    {
    c2.inpress = c1.outpress;
    c1.inbackp = c2.outbackp;
    c2.inflow =  c1.outflow;
    }
```

The `>=` operator is defined as a `friend` of the `Component` class. It could also be defined as a member class, but another kind of connection, the `Tee()` function, must be a `friend`, so we'll make `>=` a `friend` for consistency. Both arguments to `>=` are passed by reference, since the original arguments must both be modified.

Since the `>=` operator applies to objects of the base class `Component`, it works on objects of the derived classes, such as tanks, valves, and pipes. This saves you from having to write a separate function to handle each kind of connection, such as

```
friend void operator >= (Pipe&, Valve&);
friend void operator >= (Valve&, Tank&);
friend void operator >= (Tank&, Sink&);
```

and so on *ad infinitum*.

DERIVED CLASSES

The classes that model the physical objects in the system are derived from the base class `Component`. These are `Source`, `Sink`, `Pipe`, `Valve`, and `Tank`. Each has specific characteristics. A source has a fixed input pressure. A sink has a fixed back pressure. A pipe has a fixed internal resistance; its output back pressure can never be greater than a fixed value. A valve has a status of type `offon`, `off`, or `on` (defined in an `enum` statement). A tank has contents—how full it is. A valve's status and a tank's contents change as the program runs.

Variables that will be constant throughout the program, such as the resistance of a pipe, or the output pressure of a tank, are initialized when the object is first created.

As we noted, all these derived classes, and the `switch` class as well, include member functions called `Tick()`. This function is called for each object in the system—once each time period—to update the internal state of the object and to calculate the three outputs (pressure, back pressure, and flow) from the three inputs.

The Tee() Function

The `Tee()` function divides a single input flow into two output flows. The proportion of flow going into each downstream component is proportional to the back pressure of each component. A pipe with a lot of resistance will get a smaller proportion of the flow than one with low resistance. (See the listing for this function.)

`Tee()` is called with three arguments: the source component and the two downstream components, in order:

```
Tee(input, output1, output2);
```

It would be nice to use a more intuitive operator than a function with three parameters to connect three components. For instance,

```
input >= output1 + output2;
```

Unfortunately there is no ternary operator (one that takes three arguments) that can be overloaded in C++.

The Switch Class

The Switch class has a special relationship to the Tank class. Each tank is typically associated with two switches. One switch is set to turn on when the tank level is above a certain minimum value (when the tank is almost empty). The other turns on when the level is above a certain maximum value (when the tank is full). This maximum determines the capacity of the tank.

Let's define the relationship between switches and tanks by saying that a switch is "owned" by a tank. When a switch is defined, it's given two values. One is the address of the tank that owns it. The other is the contents level at which it will turn on. The Tick() member function in Switch uses the address of its owner tank to directly access the tank contents. This is how it figures out whether to turn itself on or off.

Switches are typically used to control a valve that regulates the flow of water into a tank. When the tank is full, the valve turns off; when it's nearing empty, the valve turns on again.

THE PIPE_APP.CPP FILE

The main() part of the program would be written by an application programmer to model a specific water system. Here's the listing for PIPE_APP.CPP. This file contains only one function: main().

```
// pipe_app.cpp
// models a water supply system

#include "pipes.h"        // for pipes header file
#include <iostream.h>     // for cout, etc.
#include <iomanip.h>      // for setw
#include <conio.h>        // for kbhit()

main()
   {
   Source src(100);             // source(maximum capacity)
   Pipe pipe1(80);              // pipe(resistance)
   Valve valve1(on);            // valve(initially on)

   Tank tank1(60);              // tank1(maximum outflow)
   Switch switch1(&tank1, 300); // tank1 high switch
   Switch switch2(&tank1, 50);  // tank1 low switch
```

```
    Pipe pipe2(80);              // pipe
    Sink sink1(30);              // sink(maximum capacity)
    Pipe pipe3(40);              // pipe
    Valve valve2(on);            // valve

    Tank tank2(80);              // tank2
    Switch switch3(&tank2, 250); // tank2 high switch
    Switch switch4(&tank2, 50);  // tank2 low switch

    Sink sink2(20);              // sink

    while( !kbhit() )            // quit on keypress
      {                          // make connections
      src >= pipe1;              //    source flows into pipe1
      pipe1 >= valve1;           //    pipe1 flows into valve1
      valve1 >= tank1;           //    valve1 flows into tank1
      Tee(tank1, pipe2, pipe3);  //    output of tank1 splits
      pipe2 >= sink1;            //    pipe2 flows into sink1
      pipe3 >= valve2;           //    pipe3 flows into valve2
      valve2 >= tank2;           //    valve2 flows into tank2
      tank2 >= sink2;            //    tank2 flows into sink2

      src.Tick();                // update all components
      pipe1.Tick();              //    and switches
      valve1.Tick();
      tank1.Tick();
      switch1.Tick();
      switch2.Tick();
      pipe2.Tick();
      sink1.Tick();
      pipe3.Tick();
      valve2.Tick();
      tank2.Tick();
      switch3.Tick();
      switch4.Tick();
      sink2.Tick();
                                 // if tank1 gets too high
      if( valve1.Status()==on && switch1.Status()==on )
        valve1.Status() = off;
                                 // if tank1 gets too low
      if( valve1.Status()==off && switch2.Status()==off )
        valve1.Status() = on;
                                 // if tank2 gets too high
      if( valve2.Status()==on && switch3.Status()==on )
        valve2.Status() = off;
                                 // if tank2 gets too low
      if( valve2.Status()==off && switch4.Status()==off )
        valve2.Status() = on;
                                 // output
      cout << "  Src=" << setw(2) << src.Flow();
```

```
cout << "   P1=" << setw(2) << pipe1.Flow();
if( valve1.Status()==off )
    cout << "   V1=off";
else
    cout << "   V1=on ";
cout << "   T1=" << setw(3) << tank1.Contents();
cout << "   P2=" << setw(2) << pipe2.Flow();
cout << "   Snk1=" << setw(2) << sink1.Flow();
cout << "   P3=" << setw(2) << pipe3.Flow();
if( valve2.Status()==off )
    cout << "   V2=off";
else
    cout << "   V2=on ";
cout << "   T2=" << setw(3) << tank2.Contents();
cout << "   Snk2=" << setw(2) << sink2.Flow();
cout << "\n";
    }
}
```

Declaring the Components

In `main()` the various components—pipes, valves, tanks, and so on, are first declared. At this time their fixed characteristics are initialized: A pipe is given a fixed resistance, and a tank's contents are initialized to empty.

Connecting and Updating

The bulk of the work in `main()` is carried out in a loop. Each time through the loop represents one time period, or tick of the clock. Pressing any key causes an exit from the loop and terminates the program.

The first business in the loop is to connect the various components. The source `src` is connected to `pipe1`, `pipe1` is connected to `valve1`, and so on. The resulting system was shown in Figure 15-8.

Once the connections are made, the internal states of all the components are updated by calling their `Tick()` functions.

Valves are opened and closed in `if` statements, based on the previous state of the valves and on switches. The goal is to keep the contents of the tank between the upper switch and the lower switch by opening and closing the valve as appropriate. When the tank contents reach the high switch, this switch is turned on, and the `if` statement causes the valve to close. When the contents drop below the bottom switch, turning it off, the valve is opened.

Output

To see what's happening in the system, we use `cout` statements to print out the flow of various components, the capacity of the tanks, and the status of the valves as they change with time. Figure 15-11 shows some sample output.

FIGURE 15-11
Output of PIPES Program

```
Src=80  P1=80  V1=on   T1=300  P2=30  Snk1=30  P3= 0  V2=off  T2=172  Snk2=20
Src=80  P1=80  V1=off  T1=350  P2=30  Snk1=30  P3= 0  V2=off  T2=152  Snk2=20
Src=80  P1=80  V1=off  T1=400  P2=30  Snk1=30  P3= 0  V2=off  T2=132  Snk2=20
Src=80  P1=80  V1=off  T1=370  P2=30  Snk1=30  P3= 0  V2=off  T2=112  Snk2=20
Src= 0  P1=80  V1=off  T1=340  P2=30  Snk1=30  P3= 0  V2=off  T2= 92  Snk2=20
Src= 0  P1= 0  V1=off  T1=310  P2=30  Snk1=30  P3= 0  V2=off  T2= 72  Snk2=20
Src= 0  P1= 0  V1=off  T1=280  P2=30  Snk1=30  P3= 0  V2=off  T2= 52  Snk2=20
Src= 0  P1= 0  V1=off  T1=250  P2=30  Snk1=30  P3= 0  V2=on   T2= 32  Snk2=20
Src= 0  P1= 0  V1=off  T1=220  P2=30  Snk1=30  P3= 0  V2=on   T2= 12  Snk2=20
Src= 0  P1= 0  V1=off  T1=190  P2=30  Snk1=30  P3= 0  V2=on   T2= -8  Snk2=20
Src= 0  P1= 0  V1=off  T1=130  P2=12  Snk1=30  P3=17  V2=on   T2= -8  Snk2=20
Src= 0  P1= 0  V1=off  T1= 70  P2=25  Snk1=12  P3=34  V2=on   T2= -8  Snk2= 0
Src= 0  P1= 0  V1=on   T1= 10  P2=25  Snk1=25  P3=34  V2=on   T2=  9  Snk2= 0
Src= 0  P1= 0  V1=on   T1=-50  P2=25  Snk1=25  P3=34  V2=on   T2= 23  Snk2= 0
Src= 0  P1= 0  V1=on   T1= 30  P2=25  Snk1=25  P3=34  V2=on   T2= 37  Snk2=20
Src=80  P1= 0  V1=on   T1= 50  P2= 0  Snk1=25  P3= 0  V2=on   T2= 51  Snk2=20
Src=80  P1=80  V1=on   T1= 70  P2=25  Snk1= 0  P3=34  V2=on   T2= 65  Snk2=20
Src=80  P1=80  V1=on   T1= 90  P2=25  Snk1=25  P3=34  V2=on   T2= 45  Snk2=20
Src=80  P1=80  V1=on   T1=110  P2=25  Snk1=25  P3=34  V2=on   T2= 59  Snk2=20
Src=80  P1=80  V1=on   T1=130  P2=25  Snk1=25  P3=34  V2=on   T2= 73  Snk2=20
Src=80  P1=80  V1=on   T1=150  P2=25  Snk1=25  P3=34  V2=on   T2= 87  Snk2=20
Src=80  P1=80  V1=on   T1=170  P2=25  Snk1=25  P3=34  V2=on   T2=101  Snk2=20
Src=80  P1=80  V1=on   T1=190  P2=25  Snk1=25  P3=34  V2=on   T2=115  Snk2=20

C:\WORK\PIPES>
```

Notice in this figure that some values occasionally fall below zero. This is due to the digital nature of the simulation, mentioned earlier. Such transients can be ignored.

The goal of most water systems is to supply a continuous flow of water to the various sources. The output of PIPES shows that there are some problems in the system modeled. The flow to **sink1** alternates between 25 and 30 gallons/minute, depending on whether **tank2** is filling or not. The water-system client would probably prefer that the supply was constant. Even worse, **sink2** experiences periods of no flow at all. It would seem that some components of the system need to be resized to eliminate these defects.

Of course **cout** provides a very unsophisticated output system. It would be easy to provide a graphic output, where pictures of the components appear on the screen. A **Display()** function built into each component would draw a picture of that component. Pictures would be connected as they are in the program—valve to tank, tank to pipe, and so on. The user could watch tanks fill and empty and valves open and close. Numbers beside pipes could display the flow within. This would make it easier to interpret the system's operation. It would also make the program larger and more complicated, which is why it is not implemented here.

SUMMARY

Vendor-provided object libraries are often distributed as a public component containing class declarations in a .H header file, and a private component containing member function definitions in a .OBJ object file or .LIB library file.

The Turbo C++ project feature can be used to combine several source or object files into a single executable file. This permits files provided by one vendor to be combined with user-written files to create a final application. The project feature simplifies keeping track of what files need to be compiled. It compiles any source file that has been modified since the last linking, and links the resulting object files.

QUESTIONS

1. Breaking a program into several files is desirable because
   a. some files don't need to be recompiled each time
   b. a program can be divided functionally
   c. files can be marketed in object form
   d. each programmer can work on a separate file
2. A .H file is attached to a .CPP file using the _____.
3. A .OBJ file is attached to a .CPP file using _____.
4. A *project* file
   a. examines the contents of the files in the project
   b. examines the dates of the files in the project
   c. contains instructions for compiling and linking
   d. contains definitions for C++ variables
5. A group of related classes, supplied as a separate product, is often called a

   _____.
6. True or false: A header file may need to be accessed by more than one source file in a project.
7. The so-called private files of a class library
   a. require a password
   b. can be accessed by **friend** functions
   c. help prevent code from being pirated
   d. contain object code
8. True or false: Class libraries can be more powerful than function libraries.

9. To create a project file, you must
   a. close all other project files in your directory
   b. put all the relevent filenames into a project file
   c. put the dates of the relevant files into a project file
   d. start by selecting *Open Project* from the Project menu
10. The public files in a class library usually contain
    a. constant definitions
    b. member function definitions
    c. class declarations
    d. variable definitions

PROJECTS

Unfortunately, we don't have room in this book for exercises that involve the kind of larger programs discussed in this chapter. However, here are some suggestions for projects you may wish to pursue on your own.

1. Using the `Window` and related classes from the CALC example, write a new `main()` program that models a hexadecimal calculator. Or, create a scientific calculator with trigonometric (sine, cosine, and tangent), exponential, and similar function keys.

2. Create member functions to perform subtraction and division for the `verylong` class in the VERYLONG example. These should overload the – and / operators. Warning: There's some work involved here. When you include subtraction, you must assume that any `verylong` can be negative as well as positive. This complicates the addition and multiplication routines, which must do different things depending on the signs of the numbers.

   To see one way to perform division, do a long-division example by hand and write down every step. Then incorporate these steps into a division member function. You'll find that you need some comparisons, so you'll need to write a comparison routine, among other things.

3. Add a pump class to the PIPES example, so you can model water systems that don't rely on gravity. Create a water system that incorporates such a class. (Hint: A pump should derive its input from a tank.)

4. Create a class library that models something you're interested in. Create a `main()` or "client" program to test it. Market your class library and become rich and famous.

THE TURBO C++ CLASS LIBRARY

Turbo C++ and Borland C++ come with a library of classes. These classes consist mostly of *container classes*—that is, classes that can contain objects of other classes. This chapter describes the Borland class library and how it's used.

REINVENTING THE WHEEL

A common programming task is setting up data structures such as stacks, queues, and linked lists. Most substantial programs require several such data structures, so their creation can be a major part of a programming effort. In old-fashioned procedural programs it was common to create each data structure from the ground up. Each time you needed a linked list, for example, you probably started from scratch to put together the various structures and functions that allowed you to insert and delete elements in the list. Even if you cut-and-pasted code from previous projects, it probably still needed extensive revision before it would work in the new environment. Creating similar data structures over and over is inefficient. Is there a way to avoid reinventing the wheel?

OOP To The Rescue

Borland's class library provides a solution to this problem. By using an object-oriented approach, the data structures in the class library can be used with a wide variety of data without being rewritten. If you need a linked list, you no longer need to write your own; use a Borland List class, and put any objects in it you want.

The Borland class library data structures are useful in the same situations your own homemade structures would be. The Array may be appropriate for matrix analysis. You might use the Stack class for parsing an expression in a programming or natural language. Objects in a List could represent lines of text in a word processor, and so forth.

ADVANCED COURSE

In addition to being a useful source of ready-made data structures, the Borland container class library provides a sophisticated example of a class hierarchy. Source code is supplied, and assiduous study of it can provide an advanced course in the application of object-oriented programming.

In this chapter we'll introduce the Borland class library. We won't cover all the classes in detail: our goal is to get you started.

We should note that, as of this writing, some of the routines in the Borland class library that is distributed with the Turbo C++ version 1.0 product are a bit buggy. These problems have been corrected in version 1.01 of Turbo C++ and in Borland C++, so you should use the class libraries from these produects if at all possible.

In this chapter we'll refer to the class library as the Borland class library, whether it is distributed with Turbo C++ or Borland C++.

DEVELOPING PROGRAMS FOR THE CLASS LIBRARY

Setting up the programming environment to develop programs that use the Borland class library requires some extra steps.

CREATING CLASS LIBRARY FILES

The Borland class library has its own subdirectory, normally called CLASSLIB, in the TC directory (or, if you're using Borland C++, the BORLANDC directory). CLASSLIB contains various subdirectories, including INCLUDE and LIB. (Note that these are not the same as the INCLUDE and LIB directories that are direct descendants of the TC or BORLANDC directory.) There is also a directory of example programs, called EXAMPLES, and a directory of source code for class member functions, called SOURCE.

Before using the class library you must run a batch file called BUILD.BAT, which is located in the \TC\CLASSLIB\SOURCE (or \BORLANDC\CCLASSLIB\SOURCE) directory. The object files for the Borland library classes must be combined into a file called TCLASSx.LIB, where 'x' stands for S, C, M, L, or H, depending on whether you need the Small, Compact, Medium, Large, or Huge memory model. When you run BUILD you should enter one or more of these letters (or "all" for all the models) on the command line. The programs in this book require only the small model, so you would enter

```
C>build s
```

This constructs the file TCLASSS.LIB, which you will link to the object file created from your own source file.

WRITE THE SOURCE FILES

Start up the IDE in the directory where you want to develop your program. Write the source file and give it the .CPP extension (as in MYPROG.CPP). This file should #include header files for all the class libraries you intend to use. For instance, if you use the `String` class you should include STRNG.H, and if you use the `Stack` class you should include STACK.H. You can do a DIR of \TC\CLASSLIB\INCLUDE (or \BORLANDC\CLASSLIB\INCLUDE) to see what files are available. In general the filenames closely match the corresponding class names.

You can separate your program into a header file and a program file (MYPROG.H and MYPROG.CPP), as we discussed in the last chapter. (This is how the Borland classes are arranged.) However, for short experimental programs it's easier to keep your entire program in one file; that's the approach we take in this chapter. You can use a separate directory for each of your programs, or you can put several programs in one directory.

CREATE A PROJECT FILE

Programs that use the Borland class library consist of multiple files, so you'll need to use the project feature described in Chapter 15. Use the IDE to create a project, say MYPROG.PRJ, that contains your source file MYPROG.CPP, and (assuming you use the Small memory model) the library file TCLASSS.LIB. For the examples in this chapter these two files are the only ones you need in the project file.

SET THE DIRECTORIES

The IDE needs to know where the INCLUDE and LIB subdirectories are, or it won't be able to find the necessary include and library files. The most straightforward approach is to enter the pathnames of these directories into the box provided by the *Directories...* selection in the Options menu. You need the INCLUDE and LIB directories from both the \TC\CLASSLIB (or \BORLANDC\CLASSLIB) directory and the ones directly under the TC (or BORLANDC) directory. Separate the pathnames with semicolons. That is, in the *Include Directories* field enter

```
C:\TC\CLASSLIB\INCLUDE;C:\TC\INCLUDE
```

or, if you're using Borland C++,

```
C:\BORLANDC\CLASSLIB\INCLUDE;C:\BORLANDC\INCLUDE
```

In the *Library Directories* field enter

```
C:\TC\CLASSLIB\LIB;C:\TC\LIB
```

or, if you're using Borland C++,

```
C:\BORLANDC\CLASSLIB\LIB;C:\BORLANDC\LIB
```

Now, once you've invoked the appropriate project file, you can compile, link, and run your program, as described in the last chapter.

A Simple Example Using the String Class

Here's a simple example program that uses one of the classes in the Borland library: **String**. This class is somewhat like the various **string** classes that we've seen in previous examples in this book. It lets you store strings of characters. It overloads the = operator so that you can set one **String** object equal to another, and provides other useful functions.

String is not a full-blown container class, but it's fairly simple and serves as a convenient introduction to programming with the Borland class library.

Here's an example, STRTEST, that exercises some of the **String** member functions:

```
// strtest.cpp
// tests the String class
#include <iostream.h>
#include <strng.h>                          // for String class

void main()
    {
    String str1("Babbage");                 // initialize two Strings
    String str2("Boole");

    cout << "\nstr1=";  str1.printOn(cout);
    cout << "\nstr2=";  str2.printOn(cout);

    str1 = str2;                            // overloaded =

    cout << "\nstr1=";  str1.printOn(cout);

    String str3(str2);                      // copy constructor

    if( str2.isEqual(str3) )
        cout << "\nstr2 equals str3";
    }
```

Notice that, since it uses the **String** class, the program includes the STRNG.H header file. (It can't be called STRING.H, which is already the name of the header file that handles ordinary string operations.)

The **String** class has a constructor that converts a string of type **char*** into a **String**, so in STRTEST we initialize **str1** and **str2** with strings.

The member function **printOn()** is used to print out the values of these objects. This member function is common to all the classes in the hierarchy; it will appear often in the example programs. The use of the overloaded = operator is demonstrated by setting **str1** equal to **str2** and displaying the new value of **str1**.

The **String** class has a copy constructor, so we demonstrate that it works by initializing a new **String**—**str3**—with **str2**. We then test the **isEqual()** member function by checking if **str2** is equal to **str3**. It is, of course, since we just initialized the one with the other, so the body of the **if** statement executes. Here's the output of STRTEST:

```
str1=Babbage
str2=Boole
str1=Boole
str2 equals str3
```

So far this should not look too radical. We have already seen how to write our own **String** classes with similar capabilities. However, we're just getting started.

A CONTAINER CLASS: Stack

There are two kinds of classes in the Borland class library: container classes and noncontainer classes. The **string** class is not a container class, since an object of class **String** cannot hold objects of other classes. It is in the container classes that the real power of the Borland class library lies. There are many container classes, but let's focus for a moment on the **Stack** class. As we've seen in previous chapters, a stack is a structure that stores data on a first-in–last-out basis, like a stack of dishes. Figure 16-1 shows the **Stack** class.

When you write your own stack class, you normally configure it to hold a particular kind of data—objects of a specific class, say. The container classes in the Borland class library, on the other hand, are versatile enough to hold any kind of data, providing the data consists of objects from a class derived from the base class

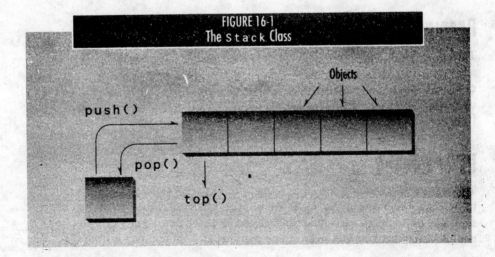

FIGURE 16-1
The **Stack** Class

Object, which is declared in the Borland class library. Fortunately the **String** class is derived (indirectly) from **Object**, so we can store objects of class **String** in an object of class **Stack**. The STAKSTR example shows how this looks:

```
// stakstr.cpp
// a Stack object holds four String objects

#include <iostream.h>
#include <stack.h>                    // for Stack class
#include <strng.h>                    // for String class

void main()
    {
    Stack stk;                        // make a Stack

    String s1("Bart");                // make four Strings
    String s2("Casey");
    String s3("Mike");
    String s4("Slade");

    stk.push(s1);                     // push the Strings on the Stack
    stk.push(s2);
    stk.push(s3);
    stk.push(s4);

    while( !stk.isEmpty() )           // until Stack is empty,
        {
        String& temp = (String&)stk.pop(); // pop top into temp
        temp.printOn(cout);                // display temp
        cout << endl;
        }
    }
```

PUSHING AND POPPING IN THE Stack CLASS

Two important member functions in the class **stack** are (not surprisingly) **push()** and **pop()**. In this example we create an object of class **stack** and four objects of class **String** (named after the desperados who get drunk and wreck the saloon in old western movies). Then we push each **String** onto the **stack** with the **push()** function.

IS IT EMPTY?

The **Stack** class contains a member function, **isEmpty()**, which returns nonzero if there are no objects in the stack. We use this function as the conditional expression in a **while** loop. Each time through the loop, we pop a **String** using **pop()**, and display it using **printOn()**. Since popping an item removes it from the stack, when we've popped all four items the stack is empty and the loop exits. Here's the output from STAKSTR:

```
Slade
Mike
Casey
Bart
```

The items are popped off in reverse order, as in all stacks.

Note that we could have combined the first two lines in the `while` body into a single line:

```
stk.pop().printOn(cout);
```

This has the same effect but eliminates the temporary `string` variable `temp`.

THE CONTAINER CLASS HIERARCHY

As we've noted, most of the classes in the Borland class library are related in one large hierarchy. We've seen two of these classes so far, `String` and `Stack`. Now let's look at all the classes together, as shown in Figure 16-2.

The major classes are derived from a single base class, `Object`. Most of these classes are container classes, which are derived from class `Container`, which is derived from `Object`. The class `Stack`, which we've used already, is such a container class. Class `String` is a noncontainer class derived from `Sortable`, which is derived from `Object`.

INSTANCE AND ABSTRACT CLASSES

Not all classes are intended for the creation of objects. Those that are, are called *instance* classes. In the figure they're shown with diagonal lines in the box corners. The `String` and `Stack` classes are examples of instance classes. Another group of classes serve only as base classes for instance classes. As we mentioned earlier, these are called abstract classes. In the figure they're shown with plain box corners.

Table 16-1 provides a brief description of the container instance classes.

It's beyond the scope of this book to delve deeply into the relative merits of these data structures in different situations. For a serious book on the subject try *Algorithms*, by Robert Sedgewick, listed in the bibliography.

MEMBER FUNCTIONS

Since each container class is derived from several other classes, you can use functions that are members, not only of the class you're using, but of its ancestors as well. Figuring out what functions are available to a given class requires looking at all the classes above it in the hierarchy.

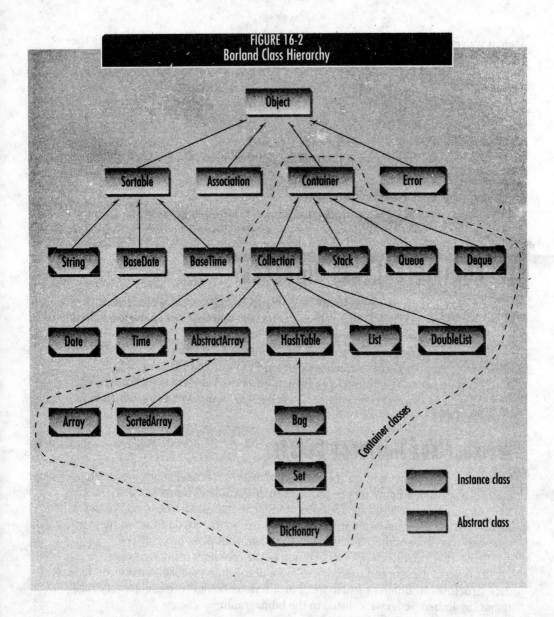

FIGURE 16-2
Borland Class Hierarchy

For containers, the most interesting member functions are those that access the data in the container, since they define how the data structure is used. Table 16-2 shows these functions.

	TABLE 16-1
	Container Instance Classes
Class	**Purpose**
Association	Groups a key (like a word) and a value (like a definition).
Array	Useful when each item can be given an index number and specific items must be quickly accessed. Difficult to expand and contract as number of items changes. Items not ordered.
SortedArray	Similar to Array, but items are stored in sorted order.
HashTable	Fast to find a particular item but slow to iterate through all items. Items are inserted and deleted using a key, or hash code, derived from the item. Items are not accessible by index. Same item may appear more than once.
Bag	Like HashTable.
Set	Like HashTable, but item may appear only once.
Dictionary	A Set containing Associations.
List	A linked list. Items are inserted and deleted only at head of list. Expands and contracts to hold changing number of items. Fast to iterate through list; slow to access a particular item.
DoubleList	Linked list; items inserted and deleted from both ends of list.
Stack	Items accessed only at top of stack; pushed down and popped off on last-in–first-out basis.
Queue	Items in at one end of queue, out at the other, on first-in–first-out basis.
Deque	Double-ended queue, combination of stack and queue; items pushed or popped on either end of deque (a special kind of double list).

Remember that each class can access the member functions of classes above it in the hierarchy, as well as those shown in Table 16-2. The purpose of these functions will become clearer as we see more examples.

HEADER FILES

You should examine the header files, and sometimes the source files, for the classes you use and for their ancestor classes. In the directory \TC\CLASSLIB\INCLUDE (or \BORLANDC\CLASSLIB\INCLUDE) you will find, for example, STACK.H, the header file for

TABLE 16-2
Data-Access Functions

Class	Function	Purpose
Container	firstThat()	Find first object satisfying condition
	lastThat()	Find last object satisfying condition
Stack	push()	Add object to top of stack
	pop()	Remove object from top of stack
	top()	Examine object at top of stack
Queue	put()	Add object to head of queue
	get()	Remove object from head of queue
	peekLeft()	Examine object at head of queue
	peekRight()	Examine object at tail of queue
Deque	putLeft()	Add object to left end of deque
	putRight()	Add object to right end of deque
	getLeft()	Remove object from left end of deque
	getRight()	Remove object from right end of deque
	peekLeft()	Examine object on left end of deque
	peekRight()	Examine object on right end of deque
Collection	add()	Add object to collection
	detach()	Remove object from collection
	destroy()	Remove object from collection and delete it from memory
	hasMember()	Check collection for specified object
	findMember()	Return position of specified object
List	add()	Add object to head of list
	detach()	Remove object from head of list
	destroy()	Remove object from head of list and delete it
	peekHead()	Examine object at head of list
DoubleList	addAtHead()	Add object to head of list
	add()	Same as addAtHead()
	addAtTail()	Add object to tail of list
	detachFromHead()	Remove object from head of list
	detachFromTail()	Remove object from tail of list
	destroyFromHead()	Remove object from head of list and delete it
	destroyFromTail()	Remove object from tail of list and delete it
	peekAtHead()	Examine object at head of list
	peekAtTail()	Examine object at tail of list
Array	add()	Add object at end of array
	addAt()	Replace object at specified position
	[]	Return reference to specified object

		TABLE 16-2 Data-Access Functions (continued)
SortedArray	add()	Add object at sorted position
	detach()	Remove object, reposition remaining objects to fill position
	[]	Return reference to specified object
HashTable	add()	Add object at coded position
	detach()	Remove specified object
	findMember()	Find specified object
Bag	see HashTable	
Set	add()	Add object to set only if it is not already there
Dictionary	add()	Add association to dictionary
	lookup()	Return specified association

the **Stack** class, and in \TC\CLASSLIB\SOURCE (or \BORLANDC\CLASSLIB\SOURCE) you will find STACK.CPP. Going up the hierarchy you will also find CONTAIN.H and CONTAIN.CPP, the files for the **Container** class, the base class for **Stack**; and OBJECT.H and OBJECT.CPP, the files for **Object**, the base class for **Container**. You'll need to look at all these files to see the complete set of member functions available for the **Stack** class.

Note that each header file **#include**s the header files for the classes above it in the hierarchy. For example, the STRNG.H header file includes the header files SORTABLE.H and OBJECT.H, which correspond to its ancestor classes **Sortable** and **Object**. This permits objects of class **String** to access member functions whether they are defined in **String** or in classes further up the hierarchy.

CORE MEMBER FUNCTIONS

A handful of member functions are declared to be pure virtual functions in **Object**. These functions must therefore be replicated in all classes. We've used two of these, **printOn()** and **isEqual()**, already. Table 16-3 shows these functions.

Let's look at a short program example, STANDARD, which shows how the remainder of the pure virtual functions in **Object** are used.

```
// standard.cpp
// tests standard Object functions
#include <iostream.h>
#include <strng.h>

void main()
    {
    String str1("Babbage");                    // initialize a String
```

```
    cout << "\nstr1 has a class ID of ";
    cout << str1.isA();                        // find class ID number

    cout << "\nstr1 is a member of the class ";
    cout << str1.nameOf();                     // find class name

    cout << "\nstr1 has a hash value of ";
    cout << str1.hashValue();                  // find item's hash value
    }
```

In this program we create a single object of type `String` and apply the functions to it. Here's the output of STANDARD:

```
str1 has a class ID of 3
str1 is a member of the class String
str1 has a hash value of 25340
```

These functions are used internally by various member functions, but you may find uses for them yourself, as we'll discuss when we create our own derived classes.

	TABLE 16-3 Pure Virtual Functions in `Object`
Function	**Purpose**
`isA()`	Returns the class of the object. This is type `classType`, which is the same as `unsigned int`. The codes for the classes in the library are selected from the list in CLSTYPES.H. User-written classes start at `__firstUserClass`.
`nameOf()`	Returns a character representation of the class name. If your class is named *Sample*, it should return a pointer to the string "Sample".
`printOn()`	Displays the contents of an object in a format suitable for that object. This is up to whoever invents the object. A String displays a string, but a more complex class will require a more complex display.
`hashValue()`	Returns a unique key based on the object. This is type `hashValueType`, which is the same as `unsigned int`. The key should be as unique as possible, and so should be derived from all the object's data, distilled into a single number.
`isEqual()`	Determines whether an object is equal to another object. Returns an `int` representing a Boolean value (0 or 1). What constitutes equality depends on the object.

THE Date CLASS

There are two other non-container classes that we can use to provide sample items to put in the container classes. (We'll see how to create our own classes, derived from Object, later on.) These are the Date and Time classes. Let's look at an example of the Date class in use, in the DATETEST example:

```
// datetest.cpp
// the Date class
#include <iostream.h>
#include <ldate.h>              // for Date class
void main()
{
Date da1;                       // create a Date
da1.SetMonth(2);                // set its values
da1.SetDay(14);
da1.SetYear(1993);

cout << "\nda1=";               // display it
da1.printOn(cout);

Date da2(12, 25, 1994);         // initialize a Date
cout << "\nda2=";               // display it
da2.printOn(cout);

cout << "\nMonth=" << da2.Month();   // display its values
cout << "\nDay=" << da2.Day();
cout << "\nYear=" << da2.Year();
                                // do comparisons
cout << "\nda1=da2: " << da1.isEqual(da2);
cout << "\nda1<da2: " << da1.isLessThan(da2);
cout << "\nda2<da1: " << da2.isLessThan(da1);
}
```

In this program we create a Date object called da1, and use the member functions SetMonth(), and so on, to set values for the month, day, and year. The printOn() function then displays this object. A three-argument constructor initializes another Date—da2—and the printOn() displays it.

Individual items in da2 are displayed using the member functions Month(), Day(), and Year(). Finally we exercise the isEqual() function and another function called isLessThan() to compare da1 and da2; we display the Boolean value of the relationship—0 for false and 1 for true. Here's the output from DATETEST:

```
da1=February 14,1993
da2=December 25,1994
Month=11
```

```
Day=25
Year=1994
da1=da2: 0
da1<da2: 1
da2<da1: 0
```

(Note that 11 represents December, since January is 0.)

THE Array CLASS

Arrays are common data structures that are supported directly by C++, as we've seen in numerous examples. However, C++ arrays have some weaknesses. Perhaps most importantly, they give you no warning if you attempt to access elements that are outside the bounds of the array. The Borland **Array** class attempts to correct such defects. Figure 16-3 shows the **Array** class.

Our next example, ARRDATE, shows an **Array** object that contains both **Date** and **String** objects:

```
// arrdate.cpp
// Array of Dates and Strings
#include <array.h>                      // for Array class
#include <ldate.h>                      // for Date class
#include <strng.h>                      // for String class
void main()
    {
    Array arr(4);                       // create an Array,
                                        //    index from 0 to 4
    Date* ptrd1 = new Date(12, 7, 1941);  // create three Dates
    Date* ptrd2 = new Date(5, 8, 1945);   // and two strings
    Date* ptrd3 = new Date(9, 2, 1945);
    String* ptrs1 = new String("Franklin Delano Roosevelt");
    String* ptrs2 = new String("Winston Churchill");

    arr.add(*ptrd1);                    // put Dates and Strings
    arr.add(*ptrd2);                    // in Array
    arr.add(*ptrd3);
    arr.add(*ptrs1);
    arr.add(*ptrs2);

    cout << "\nEntire array:\n";
    arr.printContentsOn(cout);          // display Array

    cout << "\nIndividual elements:";   // display elements
    for(int j=0; j<arr.arraySize(); j++)
        {
        cout << "\nElement number " << j << " is ";
        arr[j].printOn(cout);
        }
```

```
Date* ptrd4 = new Date(4, 31, 1943);   // make another Date
arr.addAt(*ptrd4, 1);                  // put in array at [1]
                                       // make another String
String* ptrs3 = new String("Douglas MacArthur");
arr.addAt(*ptrs3, 2);                  // put in array at [2]

cout << "\n\nEntire array:\n";
arr.printContentsOn(cout);             // display Array
}
```

This program creates an `Array` object `arr`. The argument in this constructor represents the upper bound, not the array size. Thus `arr` has a size of 5; it holds objects with subscripts 0, 1, 2, 3, and 4.

The program creates three pointers to `Date` objects and two pointers to `String` objects, all created with `new`. This pointer approach sometimes leads to more robust programs than does defining the objects themselves.

Notice that there is no problem in putting different classes of objects in the same container. As long as the objects are all derived from `Object`, they are perfectly compatible.

ADDING ELEMENTS TO ARRAYS

The five objects (the contents of the pointers) are then placed in the array using the `add()` member function. We can now print out the contents of the entire `Array` using `printContentsOn()`, a special member function for arrays.

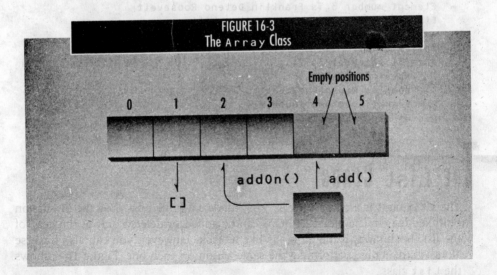

FIGURE 16-3
The Array Class

ARRAY NOTATION IN CLASS Array

Since the [] operator is overloaded in Array, we can access individual array elements using standard array notation:

```
arr[j].printOn(cout);
```

This statement causes element j to display itself.

INSERTING ARRAY ELEMENTS

While the add() function always inserts an object at the next unused position in the array, another function, addOn(), can write over existing elements. You supply this function with the element to be added and the position it will be added to. In ARRDATE we insert a new date and a new string at positions 1 and 2, respectively, and then display the entire array again. Here's the output:

```
Entire array:
Array ( December 7,1941,
     May 8,1945,
     September 2,1945,
     Franklin Delano Roosevelt,
     Winston Churchill )

Individual elements:
Element number 0 is December 7,1941
Element number 1 is May 8,1945
Element number 2 is September 2,1945
Element number 3 is Franklin Deleno Roosevelt
Element number 4 is Winston Churchill

Entire array:
Array ( December 7,1941,
     April 31,1943,
     Douglas MacArthur,
     Franklin Delano Roosevelt,
     Winston Churchill )
```

THE List CLASS

The List class is a container class that models a linked list. (See the discussion of linked lists in Chapter 12.) Items can be added or deleted only at the head of the list. In this way a linked list is like a stack. However, you can also traverse along all the items, performing the same action on each one. Figure 16-4 shows the List class.

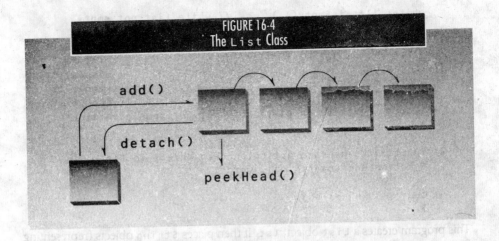

FIGURE 16-4
The List Class

The LISTSTR program demonstrates a List of String objects.

```
// liststr.cpp
// List of Strings

#include <iostream.h>
#include <list.h>                    // for List class
#include <strng.h>                   // for String class

void main()
   {
   void actionFunc(Object&, void*);  // prototype
   List lst;                         // make a List

   String s1("Hawthorne");           // make four Strings
   String s2("Melville");
   String s3("Poe");
   String s4("Stevenson");

   lst.add(s1);                      // add the Strings to the List
   lst.add(s2);
   lst.add(s3);
   lst.add(s4);
                                     // say how many items in List
   cout << "\nItems in List: " << lst.getItemsInContainer();

   lst.forEach(actionFunc, 0);       // perform action on each item

   cout << "\nItems in List: " << lst.getItemsInContainer();
```

```
while( !lst.isEmpty() )          // while list not empty
   {
   String& temp = (String&)lst.peekHead();  // get a String,
   cout << endl;
   temp.printOn(cout);                      // display it,
   lst.detach(temp);                        // remove it
   }                                        // from list
cout << "\nItems in List: " << lst.getItemsInContainer();
}

// function to perform action on each object in list
void actionFunc(Object& obj, void*)
   {
   cout << "\n" << obj;
   }
```

This program creates a **List** object, **lst**. It then places **String** objects (representing four nineteenth-century authors) in the list, using the **add()** member function.

HOW MANY OBJECTS IN A CONTAINER?

The program uses a new member function, **getItemsInContainer()**, to report the number of items currently on the list: This function returns an integer.

ITERATING THROUGH THE OBJECTS

The Borland class library includes a powerful capability for iterating through all the objects in a container. This is similar to the way a **for** loop can iterate through all the elements in a normal C++ array. Member functions of Borland container classes make use of this iteration facilty to perform a similar action on all items in a container, or to check each item for particular characteristics. The member function that performs the same action on each item is called **forEach()**. We use it in LISTSTR to cause each item to display itself. The **forEach()** function is unusual in that it requires you to tell it what action you want to perform on each item. You do this by passing it the address of a function as an argument. This function will be called to carry out the desired action. A function's address is represented by its name alone, with no parentheses.

In LISTSTR the function that performs the desired action is **actionFunc()**. A single call to **forEach()** causes **actionFunc()** to be called for each object on the list. If there are four objects, **actionFunc()** will be called four times. Each object is passed to **actionFunc()** as an argument. In LISTSTR this function simply displays the **String** object with **cout**.

Iteration involves the use of iterator classes. These classes are friends of the container classes. They contain the mechanism to implement **forEach()** and similar functions. For instance, there is a **ListIterator** class to go with the **List** class. You don't need to know how these classes work to use **forEach()** (although you would need to provide an iteration class if you wanted `forEach()` to work with a container class you created yourself). Figure 16-5 shows the hierarchy of the iterator classes.

PEEKING AT THE HEAD OF THE LIST

In the LISTSTR example the `peekHead()` function (a member function of `List`) allows you to examine the object at the head of the list. It doesn't remove the item from the list but returns a reference to it. We use it to display the item. Notice that this function returns type `Object&`. Since we're dealing with `String` objects we must cast the return value from the function to type `String&`. We store the value in `temp` and print it out using `printOn()`.

DETACHING OBJECTS

You can remove an item from a `List` by using the `detach()` member function. This function does not destroy the object itself. Another function, `destroy()`, can be used to remove an item and simultaneously destroy it. We use `detach()` in the `while` loop to remove the item from the head of the list. At the end of the `while` loop we check how many items are left on the list; there should be none. Here's the output from LISTSTR:

```
Items in List: 4
Stevenson                 ←——————— displayed by forEach()
Poe
Melville
Hawthorne
Items in List: 4
Stevenson                 ←——————— displayed by peekHead() in while loop
```

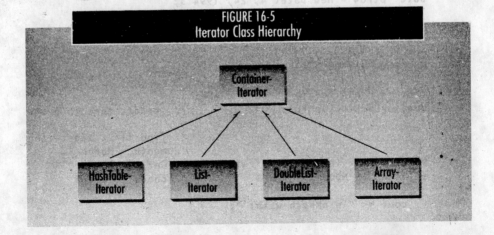

FIGURE 16-5
Iterator Class Hierarchy

```
Poe
Melville
Hawthorne
Items in List: 0        ←———— now the list is empty
```

THE Queue CLASS

A queue is like the line of people waiting at the teller's window in the bank. Items are placed in the queue at one end and removed from the other, on a first-in–first-out basis. Figure 16-6 shows the `Queue` class.

Queues are useful when one part of a program generates data faster than another part can handle it. The first part can store the data in a queue, and the second part can remove the data when it has time.

Our next example, QUEDATE, shows a `Queue` object that contains `Date` objects.

```cpp
// quedate.cpp
// Queue and Date classes
#include <iostream.h>
#include <ldate.h>                 // for Date class
#include <queue.h>                 // for Queue class

int main()
    {
    void actionFunc(Object&, void*);     // prototypes
    int testFunc(const Object& obj, void*);

    Queue que;                           // create a Queue

    Date* ptrd1 = new Date( 1, 21, 1991 );  // create four
    Date* ptrd2 = new Date( 2, 22, 1992 );  // pointers to Dates
    Date* ptrd3 = new Date( 3, 23, 1993 );
    Date* ptrd4 = new Date( 4, 24, 1994 );

    que.put( *ptrd1 );                   // put Dates
    que.put( *ptrd2 );                   // in queue
    que.put( *ptrd3 );
    que.put( *ptrd4 );

    cout << "\n\nIterate through queue:";
    que.forEach(actionFunc, 0);          // iterate through queue

                                         // find first Date with
                                         // month = March
    Date& temp = (Date&)que.firstThat(testFunc, 0);
    if( temp != NOOBJECT )               // check if match
        {
        cout << "\n\nMatch with: ";
```

```
        temp.printOn(cout);
        }
    else
        cout << "\n\nNo match.";

    cout << "\n\nRemove items from queue:";
    while( !que.isEmpty() )                  // until queue empty
        {
        Date& temp = (Date&)que.get();       // get Date, put in temp
        cout << endl;
        temp.printOn(cout);                  // print temp
        delete &temp;                        // delete temp
        }
    }

// function to perform action on each item in queue
void actionFunc(Object& obj, void*)
    {
    cout << endl;
    obj.printOn(cout);                       // display argument
    }

// function to test each item in queue
int testFunc(const Object& obj, void*)
    {
    Date& temp = (Date&)obj;                 // make a Date
    return (temp.Month() == 2) ? 1 : 0;      // return 1 if month
    }                                        // is March
```

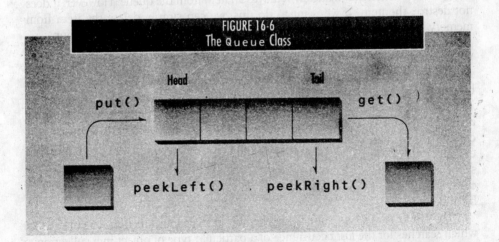

FIGURE 16-6
The Queue Class

THE put() AND get() FUNCTIONS

Objects are placed in the head of the queue using the put() member function, and removed from the tail using the get() member function. In QUEDATE we put four dates in the queue. Then, as in the previous example, we use forEach() to cause each date to print itself.

THE firstThat() FUNCTION

Suppose we want to search through a data structure, looking for items with a particular characteristic. To accomplish this we can use the firstThat() function. This function, like forEach(), uses an iterator class to operate on each item in a data structure. The firstThat() function takes two arguments. The first is the address of the function to be used to test the object. The second is the address of a list of parameters to this function. We don't need any parameters in this case, so we set this argument to 0.

In the QUEDATE example the test function is called testFunc(). It checks each Date object to see if its Month field is 2 (which represents March, since January is 0), using the Month() member function. It returns 0 if the object fails the test, and 1 otherwise. If testFunc() returns 1, indicating a match, then firstThat() returns a reference to the Date object that passed the test. The program then prints Match with: and the object. Otherwise, firstThat() returns a special object called NOOBJECT, which represents an object that doesn't exist. Finding this object causes the program to print No match.

OWNERSHIP AND DELETING ITEMS

The get() function automatically removes an item from the queue. However, it does not destroy the item. If we want to do this, we can simply delete the item from memory, using the delete operator. This is what happens in the while loop.

Notice that it would be bad form to delete an item that was still in the queue. When an item is placed in a container it is said to be *owned* by the container. Destroying an item that is owned by any container will lead to trouble, since there will be pointers in the container pointing to objects that no longer exist.

To avoid such problems it is important to ensure that an item is removed from a container before it is destroyed. Sometimes this isn't obvious. For example, if a container is defined as a global variable, and you define an item and put it into this container using a function, then when the function returns, the item will go out of scope and be deleted. The container, however, being global, continues to exist and continues to believe that it owns the item. Trouble swiftly follows, and the bug can be difficult to find.

The firstThat() function is matched by an analogous function, lastThat(), which searches for the *last* occurrence of a particular type of object in a collection.

USER-DEFINED CLASSES

So far we've stored only **String**, **Date**, and **Time** objects in container classes. This is rather limiting. The real power of the Borland class library becomes apparent when you are able to store objects from classes that you create yourself.

The next example shows a minimal example of a user-defined class. This class, **Sample**, has only a single data item—a variable called **data**. **Sample** is derived from class **Object**; this is necessary if its objects are to be stored in containers.

The example, ARRSAMP, consists of an **Array** object that holds a number of **Sample** objects. Here's the listing:

```
// arrsamp.cpp
// Array and user-defined class Sample

#include <array.h>                              // for Array class
#define sampleClass __firstUserClass            // (see CLSTYPES.H)

class Sample : public Object                    // user-defined class
    {
    private:
        int data;
    public:
        Sample(const int d)                     // constructor
            { data = d; }
        ~Sample()                               // destructor
            { }
        Sample(const Sample& sourceSample)  // copy constructor
            { data = sourceSample.data; }
        classType isA() const                   // isA()
            { return sampleClass; }
        char* nameOf() const                    // nameOf()
            { return "sample"; }
        void printOn( ostream& outputStream ) const // printOn()
            { outputStream << "**" << data << "**"; }
        hashValueType hashValue() const         // hashValue()
            { hashValueType value = data; return value; }
        int isEqual( const Object& testSample ) const // isEqual()
            { return (data == ((Sample &)testSample).data); }
    };

void main()
    {
    Array arr(3);                               // create Array,
                                                //    index from 0 to 3
    Sample* s1 = new Sample(99);                // create four Samples
    Sample* s2 = new Sample(101);
    Sample* s3 = new Sample(111);
    Sample* s4 = new Sample(113);
```

```
    arr.add(*s1);                          // put Samples in Array
    arr.add(*s2);
    arr.add(*s3);
    arr.add(*s4);

    cout << "\nArray contents:\n";
    arr.printContentsOn(cout);             // display Array
    cout << endl;

    cout << "Elements:\n";
    for(int j=0; j<arr.arraySize(); j++)   // access elements
        {
        arr[j].printOn(cout);              // display each one
        cout << endl;
        }
    arr.detach(1);                         // remove two Samples
    arr.detach(2);                         // from Array
    cout << "\nArray contents:\n";
    arr.printContentsOn(cout);             // display smaller Array
    }
```

THE Sample CLASS

The Sample class in this program includes a constructor and a destructor. As we noted earlier, classes derived from Object must supply certain member functions that are declared as pure virtual functions in Object: isA(), nameOf(), printOn(), hashValue(), and isEqual(). You may wonder about the const keyword in the definition of these functions in ARRSAMP. This keyword is necessary to match the declarations in Object. It has the effect of redefining the type of the this pointer from (in this example) Sample* const, a constant pointer to Sample, to const Sample* const, a constant pointer to a constant Sample.

The hashValue() function in Sample simply returns the data item; this is an easy way to make a hash value. The isEqual() function checks to see if the data items in the two objects are equal; if so, the objects are considered equal.

If we were creating a container class, we would need to add several other functions. These are forEach(), firstThat(), lastThat(), isSortable() (which returns 0 or 1, depending on whether the class is derived from Sortable), and isAssociation() (which returns 0 or 1, depending on whether the class is derived from Association). However, the Sample class is not a container class and doesn't need these functions.

The class number is obtained from constants in the file CLSTYPES.H. This file #defines a constant called __firstUserClass. We set the number of our class, sampleClass, equal to this constant. If we defined other user classes, they could be numbered __firstUserClass+1, __firstUserClass+2, and so on.

THE main() PROGRAM

The main() program in ARRSAMP creates an object of class Array and four objects of class Sample. It puts the Samples in the Array with the put() member function, and then prints the contents of Array using, first, printContentsOn() for arr, and then printOn() for each element. Both approaches end up by invoking the printOn() function defined in the Sample class.

The program uses the detach() member function to remove two items from the array, and then prints the array contents again. Here's the output of ARRSAMP:

```
Array contents:
Array { **99**,
    **101**,
    **111**,
    **113** }

Elements:
**99**
**101**
**111**
**113**

Array contents:
Array { **99**,
    **113** }
```

A Bag OF Persons

A bag is an unordered collection of items. The class Bag is derived from the class HashTable, and is functionally equivalent to it. A hash table is a data structure in which each item stored in the structure can be accessed using a code. The code is an integer derived from the data in a particular object (the data is "hashed," or compacted together, to create the code; hence the name). The method used to derive the hash code depends on the data. Often objects have unique hash codes, but sometimes two or more objects will share the same code. Figure 16-7 shows the Bag class.

Bags and hash tables offer a good way to store data when you want to recall a random item quickly and don't need to iterate quickly through successive items, as in an array.

In previous chapters we saw examples of a Person class. The current program demonstrates a Bag of Person objects. Here's the listing for BAGPERS:

```
// bagpers.cpp
// Bag and user-defined Person class

#include <bag.h>              // for Bag class
#include <string.h>           // for strlen(), strcpy()
#define personClass __firstUserClass  // (see CLSTYPES.H)
```

USER-DEFINED CLASSES

```
class Person : public Object              // user-defined class
    {
private:
    char* name;
    int age;
public:
    Person()                              // constructor
        {
        name = new char;
        name[0] = '\0';
        age = 0;
        }
    Person(const char* str, const int a)  // constructor
        {
        name = new char[ strlen(str)+1 ];
        strcpy(name, str);
        age = a;
        }
    Person(const Person& sourcePerson)    // copy constructor
        {
        name = new char[ strlen(sourcePerson.name)+1 ];
        strcpy(name, sourcePerson.name);
        age = sourcePerson.age;
        }
    ~Person()                             // destructor
        { delete name; }
    classType isA() const                 // isA()
        { return personClass; }
    char* nameOf() const                  // nameOf()
        { return "Person"; }
    void printOn( ostream& outputStream ) const  // printOn()
        {
        outputStream << "(Name=" << name;
        outputStream << ", Age=" << age << ")";
        }
    hashValueType hashValue() const       // hashValue()
        {
        hashValueType hvalue = name[0] + age;
        return hvalue;
        }
    int isEqual( const Object& testPers ) const  // isEqual()
        {
        return age == ((Person &)testPers).age &&
                !strcmp(name, ((Person &)testPers).name);
        }
    };

void main()
    {
    Bag bg;                               // create default-size Bag
```

```
Person* ptrp1 = new Person("Bart", 23);   // create three
Person* ptrp2 = new Person("Casey", 25);  // Persons
Person* ptrp3 = new Person("Slade", 27);

bg.add(*ptrp1);                      // put Persons in Bag
bg.add(*ptrp2);
bg.add(*ptrp3);

cout << "\nContents of: ";           // display contents of Bag
bg.printOn(cout);

                                     // see if *ptrp2 is in Bag
Person testPerson = (Person&)bg.findMember( *ptrp2 );
if( testPerson == NOOBJECT )
   cout << "\nCan't find Person";
else
   {
   cout << "\nFound Person: ";
   testPerson.printOn(cout);         // display Person
   bg.detach(testPerson);            // remove Person from Bag
   }
cout << "\n\nContents of: ";         // display contents of Bag
bg.printOn(cout);
}
```

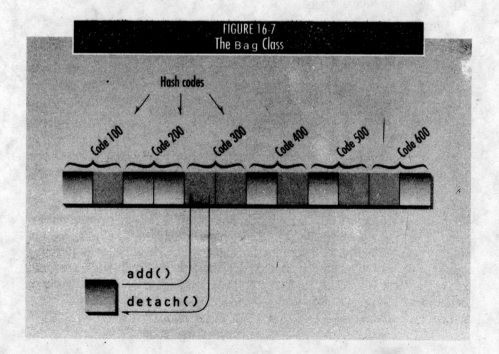

FIGURE 16-7
The Bag Class

THE Person CLASS

Like the Sample class in the previous example, the Person class has been augmented with the obligatory isA() and similar functions. Some of these functions, such as printOn() and isEqual(), must now operate on two pieces of data: the name and age of the Person.

THE main() PROGRAM

The main() program creates a Bag and three Person objects. It puts the Person objects in the Bag using the add() member function, and then displays the Bag using printOn().

THE findMember() FUNCTION

The findMember() function is then called to search the entire bag for a specific item. This item is ("Casey", 25), which is used as an argument to the function. The function returns the found object if there is a match but returns NOOBJECT otherwise. The program prints an appropriate message. In BAGPERS there is a match, and the program prints out the matching record and then removes it from the bag with detach(). A final display of the bag's contents reveals that the item is indeed gone. Here's the output from BAGPERS:

```
Contents of: Bag { (Name=Bart, Age=23),
    (Name=Casey, Age=25),
    (Name=Slade, Age=27) }

Found Person: (Name=Casey, Age=25)

Contents of: Bag { (Name=Bart, Age=23),
    (Name=Slade, Age=27) }
```

Using findMember() and similar functions can create complications. If you put objects of several different classes in the same container, and you're testing them for a particular condition, you may need to check what kind of object each one is before you perform a particular test. For instance, if you have String objects and Date objects in a container, you don't want to test the String objects with the Month() member function. To avoid such inappropriate tests, you can use the isA() function to determine the class of the object before performing class-specific tests on it. Similarly, you don't want to try to sort objects that are not part of the Sortable class, so you should use isSortable() before trying to sort objects.

SUMMARY

The Borland class library contains a number of container classes that can be used to hold objects of other classes. This simplifies the creation of data structures: You can use the Borland classes instead of writing your own. The Borland container classes are arranged in a hierarchy. The class **Object** is the base class for the hierarchy. Objects to be placed in containers must be members of classes derived from **Object**. You can modify your own classes to be derived from the **Object** class; then their objects can be stored in the different Borland container classes.

QUESTIONS

1. The Borland Class library is useful because it
   a. is graphics-based
   b. helps you avoid writing the same data structure **many times**
   c. demonstrates a complex class hierarchy
   d. undermines your faith in humanity

2. The Borland class library .LIB files are in the _____ directory.

3. True or false: You must use a BUILD program to create Borland class library files.

4. If you're writing a program called MYPROG that uses Borland class libraries, two files you must have in your project file are _____ and
   _____.

5. The **String** class is useful because
   a. it is an example of a container class
   b. **String** objects can be placed in containers
   c. it simplifies some string operations
   d. **Dates** and **Times** are derived from it

6. Write a statement that causes an object **st** of class **String** to display itself.

7. An object of the **Stack** class can hold data that
   a. is an object of a class derived from **Object**
   b. is an object of a container class
   c. is an object of a noncontainer class
   d. contains the member function **isClass()**

8. Write two statements that put an object called **obj1** on a **stack** called **stack1** and then remove it.

9. Write a **while** loop that terminates when a **Stack** object called **stack1** is empty.

10. True or false: A **stack** object is a container.

11. An object in the Borland class hierarchy can access member functions
    a. only in its own class
    b. in any container class
    c. in its own class and in any classes it's derived from
    d. in any class derived from **Object**

12. Write a statement that will put an object called **obj1** into an object called **array1** of class **Array**, at position 3.

13. True or false: An object of class **Array** will hold objects from only one class.

14. The statement **Array a(7);** creates space for _____ objects.

15. The **forEach()** member function
    a. calls a user-written function
    b. is a member of an iterator class
    c. must be defined differently for every object
    d. causes the same action to be performed on each object in a container

16. Explain the difference between an *instance* class and an *abstract* class.

17. Write an expression that returns the number of objects in the **List** object **list1**.

18. What member function can you use to search a **List** for an object that has a certain value?

19. If you write your own class so that its objects can be stored in Borland containers, you will probably need to
    a. create your own **printOn()** function
    b. ensure that your class can store **Date** objects
    c. derive your class from the **Container** class
    d. overload the **hashValue()** member function in **Object**

20. True or false: You should not destroy an object that's stored in a container without first removing the object from the container.

EXERCISES

1. Create four objects of class **Time**, and an object of class **Array**. Put the **Time** objects in the **Array**. Then display the contents of the array, first using **printContentsOn()** for the entire **Array**, and then **printOn()** for each element.

2. Create some objects of the `String` class, and put them in a `Deque`—some at the head of the `Deque` and some at the tail. Display the contents of the `Deque` using the `forEach()` function and a user-written display function. Then search the `Deque` for a particular `String`, using the `firstThat()` function, and display any `Strings` that match. Finally remove all the items from the `Deque` using the `getLeft()` function, and display each item. Notice the order in which the items are displayed: Using `getLeft()`, those inserted on the left (head) of the `Deque` are removed in last-in–first-out order, while those put on the right side are removed in first-in–first-out order. The opposite would be true if `getRight()` were used.

3. Create some objects of the `Person` class (from the BAGPERS example), and put them on a `List`. Display the contents of the resulting list in three ways: (1) Use `printOn()` for the entire list, (2) use `forEach()` to call a user-written display function, and (3) use the `peekHead()` function in a `while` loop with a `detach()` function that removes each `Person` after it's displayed.

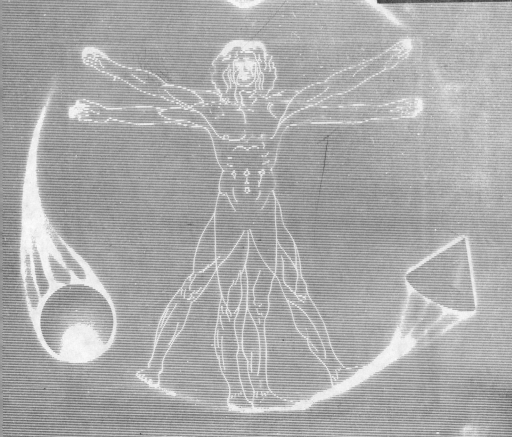

CHAPTER **17**

JUST FOR FUN

This chapter contains several programs that are more complex or idiosyncratic than those we've seen earlier in this book. Nevertheless, they demonstrate some interesting ways that classes can be used in C++ programming. (These programs are also fun to use, even for people who don't know anything about C++.)

There are three programs. The first uses fractals to generate flowers, the second is an OOP version of Conway's game of Life, and the third is a program that will probably beat (or at least tie) you in tic-tac-toe. The fractal program requires a graphics display, but the other two programs require only a character display, and so will run on any MS-DOS computer.

FRACTAL FLOWERS

Fractals are mathematical graphics constructions with the property of self-similarity. This means that a part has the same appearance as the whole, a part of a part has the same appearance as a part, and so on. The best way to understand fractals is to see an example. Our program, TENDRILS, uses fractals to create a flowering plant. Figure 17-1 shows the output of the program.

Every time you run TENDRILS the output is different. Some plants look fairly regular; others are weird and distorted. You can create an entire jungle of plants, each completely unique.

Fractal Fundamentals

Fractals start with a simple graphics element and duplicate this element at various scales to build up the final image. In TENDRILS the fundamental graphics element is a series of short line segments that form a curved line. Each segment is connected to the next at a slight angle, so the result is a line with a curving shape and a fixed length, which we'll call a *tendril*. This is shown in Figure 17-2.

When fractals are used to imitate natural phenomena such as flowers (or mountains or clouds or similar forms), an element of randomness is commonly introduced into the creation of the fundamental graphics elements so that the image will display natural-looking variations. We introduce randomness by deciding in a random

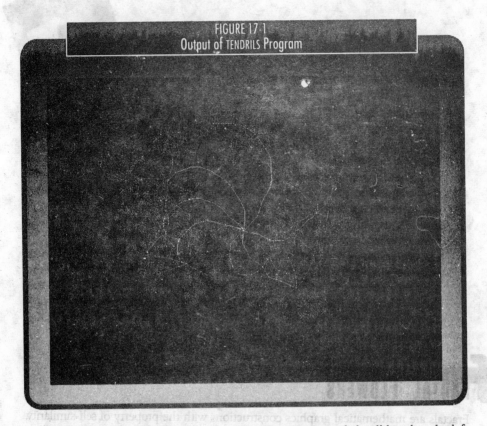

FIGURE 17-1
Output of TENDRILS Program

way whether the angle that joins any two segments in a tendril will bend to the left or to the right. We also arrange things so that the angle is more likely to turn to the left than to the right. This generates tendrils that tend to curve leftward but do so in an irregular way.

A number of tendrils are grouped together to form a cluster. The tendrils in a cluster all start at the same point and radiate from this point at equally spaced angles. However, their random bending soon destroys this initial symmetry.

Here's the listing for TENDRILS:

```
// tendrils.cpp
// draws "biological" forms
#include <graphics.h>      // for graphics functions
#include <stdlib.h>        // for randomize(), rand()
#include <time.h>          // for randomize()
#include <math.h>          // for sin(), cos()
#include <conio.h>         // for getch()

const int   X0=320;        // center of screen
const int   Y0=240;
const float PI=3.14159;    // pi
const int   NUME=30;       // numerator of probability
```

```
const int    DENOM=100;           // denomenator of probability
const int    NUMBER = 7;          // number of tendrils per cluster
const float RAD = 3.0;            // length of straight line segments
const float DELTHETA = 0.1;       // change in theta (radians)
const int    SEGS = 60;           // max line segments per tendril
const int    REDUX = 3;           // how much to divide # of segments
const int    MIN = 1;             // minimum number of line segments

class cluster
   {
   public:
      void display(int size, int x, int y);
   };

class tendril
   {
   public:
      void display(int size, float theta, int x, int y);
   };

void cluster::display(int size, int x0, int y0)
   {
   if( kbhit() )
      exit(0);
   for(int i=0; i<NUMBER; i++)          // for each tendril
      {
      float theta = i * 2*PI/NUMBER;
      int x=x0, y=y0;
      moveto(x, y);
      tendril t;                        // make a tendril
      t.display(size, theta, x, y);     // display it
      }
   }

void tendril::display(int size, float theta, int x, int y)
   {
   for(int j=0; j<size; j++)
      {                                 // left or right
      int chng = ( random(DENOM)<NUME ) ? -1 : 1;
      theta = theta + chng*DELTHETA;    // new angle
      x = x + RAD*sin(theta);           // x and y of
      y = y + RAD*cos(theta);           //    next point
      if(size < 4) setcolor(RED);
      else if(size < 13) setcolor(GREEN);
      else if(size < 40) setcolor(LIGHTGREEN);
      else setcolor(YELLOW);
      lineto(x, y);                     // draw line
      }
   if( size > MIN )
      {                                 // if tendril long enough
      cluster c;                        // make a new cluster
```

```
    int newsize = size / REDUX;    // but smaller than before
    c.display(newsize, x, y);      // display it
    }
  }

void main()
  {
  int driver, mode;
  driver = VGA;          // set graphics driver
  mode = VGAHI;          // and graphics mode
  initgraph(&driver, &mode, "\\tc\\bgi");
  randomize();           // seed random number generator

  int x=X0, y=Y0;        // set origin of cluster
  int size = SEGS;
  cluster c;             // define a cluster
  c.display(size, x, y); // display the cluster
  getch();               // hold image until keypress
  closegraph();          // reset graphics system
  }
```

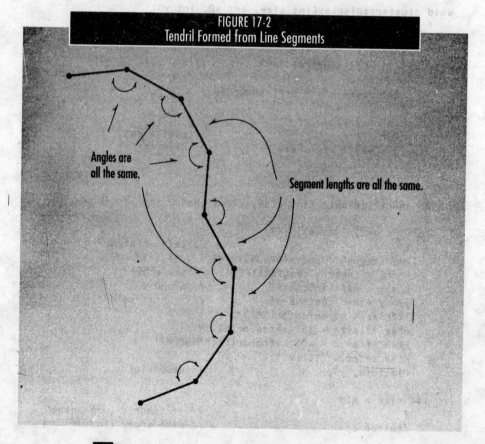

FIGURE 17-2
Tendril Formed from Line Segments

Angles are
all the same.

Segment lengths are all the same.

There are two classes in TENDRILS. The class `cluster` models a group or cluster of tendrils, and the class `tendril` models a single tendril. Each class has only one member function: `display`. After a `tendril` or `cluster` object draws itself, it is not used again in the program. Since it doesn't need to remember anything, it has no need of any data items; thus there is no private data in either class.

The main program creates a single object of class `cluster` and displays it. This cluster object in turn creates a series of tendril objects, all starting at the same place but at different angles. The cluster object displays each one. Each of these tendril objects, in the course of displaying itself, draws the series of line segments that form its body, and then—at the end of the tendril—it creates an object of type cluster but with a smaller size. It then tells this cluster to display itself. Figure 17-3 shows how this looks.

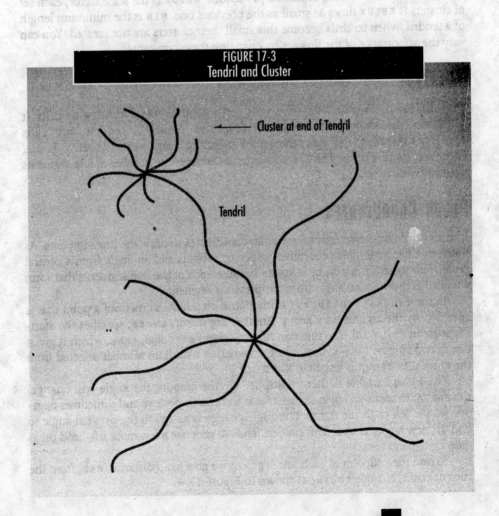

FIGURE 17-3
Tendril and Cluster

Cluster at end of Tendril

Tendril

Tendrils create clusters, and clusters create tendrils, until the tendrils are too short to be usefully displayed. At this point each tendril creates itself but no cluster, and the program ends. The result is a screen display that looks like some sort of exotic flowering plant.

CONSTANTS

The program starts with a series of constant definitions. These constants are used to control the appearance of the flowers generated by the program. NUME divided by DENUM specifies the probability that a segment will bend to the right. NUMBER is the number of tendrils in a cluster. RAD is the length of a straight line segment. DELTHETA is the change in angle between one line segment of a tendril and the next. SEGS is the number of line segments per tendril. REDUX is the scale factor; each set of clusters is REDUX times as small as the previous one. MIN is the minimum length of a tendril; when tendrils become this small their clusters are not created. You can vary the appearance of the flowers by changing these constants.

CLUSTERS

The cluster::display() function uses a for loop to create NUMBER tendrils. It calculates the angle of each tendril (theta), creates a tendril, and calls tendril::display() to display the tendril—sending it arguments to specify its size, angle, and starting point. The size parameter determines the number of line segments used to create a tendril.

POLAR COORDINATES

It turns out to be convenient to use polar coordinates to draw the line segments. As noted in Chapter 9, polar coordinates specify a radius and an angle from a central point. This system is useful in TENDRILS because each of the line segments that form a tendril is drawn at an angle from the previous segment.

In the tendril::display() function each tendril starts from a point that is specified by the arguments x and y. Another argument, theta, specifies the starting angle of the tendril. The function first calculates a variable, chng, which is given one of two values, 1 or −1, depending on whether a random number selected from the range 0 to DENUM is less than NUME.

The chng variable is then multiplied by the amount the angle will change, DELTHETA, to create an angle change that is sometimes positive and sometimes negative (to the left or to the right). The angle change is added to the original angle to find the new angle, theta. This process tends to generate a few more left-hand turns than right-hand turns.

To find the endpoint of each line segment we go a fixed distance, RAD, from the current point, at angle theta, as shown in Figure 17-4.

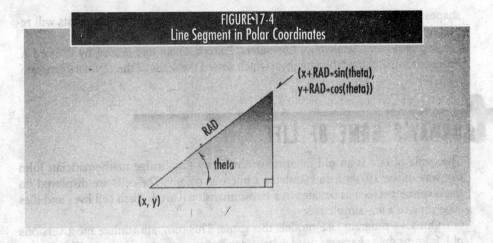

FIGURE 17-4
Line Segment in Polar Coordinates

To draw the line segment, we use the graphics function `lineto()`, which requires rectangular (x,y) coordinates. These can be calculated from the formulas

```
x = x + RAD*sin(theta);
y = y + RAD*cos(theta);
```

Depending on the size of the tendril, the function then selects an appropriate color and draws the segment.

RECURSION

When all the line segments that constitute the tendril have been drawn, `tendril::display()` then creates a cluster, using a size REDUX times as small as its own size.

Since a `tendril` object is created by a `cluster` object, and a `cluster` object is created by a `tendril` object, the program is *recursive*. This nesting of one object within another, like Chinese boxes, must terminate at some point, or the program will run forever, generating ever more microscopic tendrils. This terminating point is determined by the `if` statement in `tendril::display()`, which decides whether to create a cluster, based on the current tendril size. If the size is smaller than the MIN constant, the recursion stops.

The TENDRILS program could easily be written without classes, as a series of nested `for` loops. Using classes, however, makes clearer the association between the parts of the program (class `tendril` and class `cluster`) and the specific graphics elements they display.

You can cause radical alterations in the appearance of the flowers generated by the TENDRILS program by altering the constants at the start of the program. For example, by causing all the tendrils to branch upward in each cluster, you can create shapes that look like trees rather than flowers. Fine tuning of the constants will reveal different kinds of trees, from poplars to evergreens.

For more on fractals read *Computers, Pattern, Chaos and Beauty*, by Clifford A. Pickover (listed in the bibliography), which sowed the seeds of the TENDRILS program.

CONWAY'S GAME OF LIFE

The game of Life is an old favorite, invented by Cambridge mathematician John Conway in the 1970s. Life simulates a microbe colony. The cells are displayed on the computer screen as squares in a two-dimensional array. Each cell lives and dies according to a few simple rules.

Our C++ program LIFE models this game. This program (unlike most versions of Life) runs on a character display; you don't need a graphics monitor. The display routine in this program uses a somewhat unusual approach to displaying the cells. To make the cells square instead of oblong, and to increase the number of cells, we put two cells in each character position, one over the other, as shown in Figure 17-5. An 80x25-character screen can thus display an array of 80x50 cells—enough for most Life demonstrations.

RULES OF LIFE

A cell can be either alive (displayed as a white square) or dead (a dark or empty square). Each cell has eight potential neighbors: those cells above and below it, those to its left and right, and the four diagonal cells. If an empty (dead) cell has exactly

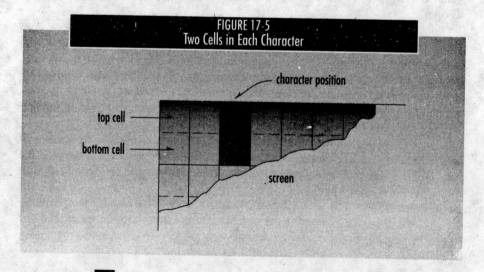

FIGURE 17-5
Two Cells in Each Character

character position

top cell

bottom cell

screen

three neighbors, it becomes alive (is born). If a living cell has either two or three neighbors, it continues to live. But if a living cell has fewer than two neighbors, it dies (presumably from loneliness), and if it has more than three neighbors it also dies (from overcrowding).

The program calculates the fate of all the cells and then changes the cells to their new states and displays them. Some cells are born, others die, others continue to live. Each calculation-display sequence is called a generation.

The fascinating thing about Life is that these simple rules can give rise to very complex displays of pattern growth and change from generation to generation. Some simple patterns behave in predictable ways. For example, a four-by-four block of living cells is stable; since every cell has three living neighbors, they all continue to live. However, a line of three cells (called a *semaphore*) will flip back and forth between vertical and horizontal; the cell in the middle lives, the ones at the ends die, and new cells are born next to the middle. Other fairly simple patterns, such as the

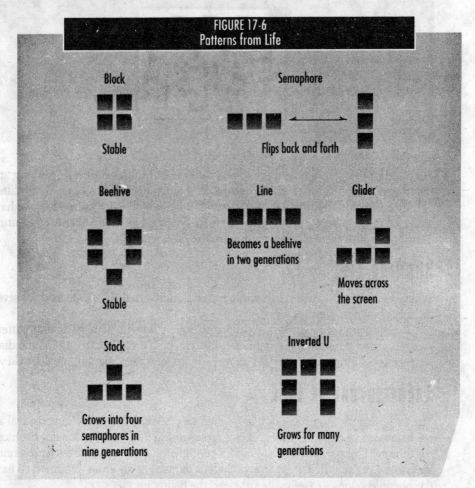

FIGURE 17-6
Patterns from Life

Block
Stable

Semaphore
Flips back and forth

Beehive
Stable

Line
Becomes a beehive
in two generations

Glider
Moves across
the screen

Stack
Grows into four
semaphores in
nine generations

Inverted U
Grows for many
generations

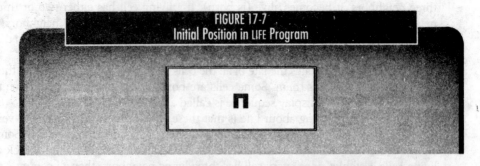

FIGURE 17-7
Initial Position in LIFE Program

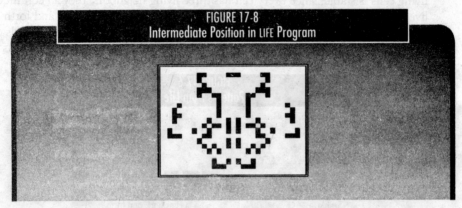

FIGURE 17-8
Intermediate Position in LIFE Program

one used in the program, can grow into patterns of hundreds of cells, shifting and moving in fantastic kaleidoscopic animation. Figure 17-6 shows some possibilities.

Considerable research has been done on Life, which is far richer than we have space to discuss here. To learn more, read *Wheels, Life, and Other Mathematical Amusements*, by Martin Gardner (listed in the bibliography).

RUNNING LIFE

When you start LIFE you'll see a simple pattern: an inverted "U" shape made of seven cells, as shown in Figure 17-7.

Pressing any key causes this pattern to start evolving. This particular pattern grows for several hundred generations before reaching a stable state. An intermediate state in its evolution is shown in Figure 17-8. To stop the program, press any key.

ARCHITECTURE OF LIFE

The LIFE program uses only one class, called **cell**. We define a two-dimensional array of objects of this class, each object representing a cell on the screen. Each cell has four items of private data: its X and Y coordinates, and two variables representing the **state** of the cell. The **state** variable is defined in an **enum** definition to have the possible values **alive** or **dead**. Here' the listing for LIFE.CPP:

```cpp
// life.cpp
// recreates Conway's "Game of Life"
#include <conio.h>                     // for kbhit(), getch(), etc.
const unsigned char top = '\xDF';   // square in upper half
const unsigned char bot = '\xDC';   // square in lower half
const unsigned char both = '\xDB';  // square in both halves
const unsigned char none = '\x20';  // square in neither half
const int maxCols = 80;             // screen width
const int maxRows = 50;             // two squares per character
const int maxRealRows = 25;         // really only 25 rows

enum state { dead, alive };

class Cell
   {
   private:
      int xCo, yCo;                    // coordinates of cell
      state oldState, newState;        // dead or alive
   public:
      void InitCell(int, int);         // initialize cell
      void SetLive(void);              // to set initial pattern
      state GetState(void);            // to check neighbors
      void Calc(void);                 // calculate new state
      void Display(void);              // display the cell
   };

Cell c[maxCols][maxRows];              // define array of cells

void Cell::InitCell(int x, int y)      // initialize cell
   {
   xCo = x;                            // set coordinates
   yCo = y;
   oldState = newState = dead;         // set to dead
   }

void Cell::SetLive()                   // set cell to alive
   {
   newState = alive;
   }

state Cell::GetState(void)             // get state of cell
   {
   return(oldState);
   }

void Cell::Calc()                                  // calculate new state
   {                          // find number of neighbors alive
   int neighbors = c[xCo-1][yCo-1].GetState() +    // nw
                   c[xCo  ][yCo-1].GetState() +    // n
                   c[xCo+1][yCo-1].GetState() +    // ne
                   c[xCo-1][yCo  ].GetState() +    // w
```

```
                        c[xCo+1][yCo  ].GetState() +    // e
                        c[xCo-1][yCo+1].GetState() +    // sw
                        c[xCo  ][yCo+1].GetState() +    // s
                        c[xCo+1][yCo+1].GetState();     // se

   newState = dead;          // cell is dead unless
                             // it's alive and has 2 or 3 neighbors
   if( oldState==alive && (neighbors==2 || neighbors==3) )
      newState = alive;

                             // or it's dead and has 3 neighbors
   else if( oldState==dead && neighbors==3 )
      newState = alive;
   }


// display the cell
// ( yCo goes from 0 to 49, screenRow from 0 to 24 )
void Cell::Display(void)
   {
   char chbuff[1];           // one-character buffer
   oldState = newState;      // update oldState

   if( newState==alive )     // if cell is alive, display it
      {
      int screenRow = yCo / 2;  // find actual row on screen
      int botrow = yCo % 2;     // top row = 0, bottom row = 1
                                // get screen character (two cells)
      gettext(xCo, screenRow, xCo, screenRow, chbuff);
      int ch = chbuff[0];
                                // find character (two cells)
      if(botrow)                      // if our cell on bottom row,
         if(ch==none || ch==bot)      // and if neither or bottom,
            ch = bot;                 //     set bottom only
         else                         // if both or top,
            ch = both;                //     set both
      else                            // if our cell on top row,
         if(ch==none || ch==top)      // and if neither or top half,
            ch = top;                 //     set top only
         else                         // if both or bottom halves,
            ch = both;                //     set bottom
                                // set new screen character
      gotoxy(xCo, screenRow);   // move cursor
      putch(ch);                // insert character
      }
   }

main()
   {
   int x, y;
   clrscr();                         // clear screen
   _setcursortype(_NOCURSOR);        // turn off cursor
```

```
for(x=0; x<maxCols; x++)              // initialize to dead
   for(y=0; y<maxRows; y++)
      c[x][y].InitCell(x, y);

c[39][24].SetLive();                  // set inverted U pattern
c[40][24].SetLive();
c[41][24].SetLive();
c[39][25].SetLive();
c[41][25].SetLive();
c[39][26].SetLive();
c[41][26].SetLive();

for(x=0; x<maxCols; x++)              // display initial cells
   for(y=0; y<maxRows; y++)
      c[x][y].Display();

getch();                             // wait for keypress

while( !kbhit() )                    // continue until keypress
   {
   for(x=1; x<maxCols-1; x++)        // find new states
      for(y=1; y<maxRows-1; y++)
         c[x][y].Calc();

   clrscr();                         // erase screen

   for(x=0; x<maxCols; x++)          // display cells
      for(y=0; y<maxRows; y++)
         c[x][y].Display();
   } // end while
_setcursortype(_NORMALCURSOR);       // restore cursor
} // end main()
```

Two states, represented by oldState and newState, are necessary for each cell, because calculating the new state of all the cells is a two-step process. First the new state of each cell is calculated, based on the old state of its neighbors. Until this is carried out for all cells, no cell may change its old state. Then the old state is set to the value of the new state, and all the old states are displayed.

Initializing the Cells

Each cell must know where it is so that it knows what neighbors to query to find out if it lives or dies. A member function, InitCell(), executed once for each cell at the beginning of the program, tells each cell its coordinates and sets its states to dead. (A constructor can't be used because you can't pass arguments when initializing array members in a constructor.)

Getting and Setting the State

The member function GetState() returns the state, alive or dead, of a cell. It's used to calculate the number of living neighbors. The SetAlive() function sets the new state of the cell to *alive*, and is used in main() to set the initial cell pattern.

Calculating the New State

The member function `Calc()` determines whether the cell will live or die. This function finds the state of all eight neighboring cells and adds them together to obtain the number of living neighbors. A living cell will die unless it has two or three living neighbors, and a dead cell will be born if it has three neighbors. This function changes the cell's `newState` variable accordingly. The `Calc` member function is unusual in that it assumes the existence of objects of its own class, namely `c[x][y]`.

Displaying the Cell

Before displaying the cell, the `Display()` function first sets the `oldState` variable equal to `newState`. It can do this because it knows that `Calc()` has finished calculating the new state for all the variables. `Display()` uses the library function `gotoxy()` to cause a cell to display itself at the correct position.

Because the screen is erased just before all the cells display themselves, they need do nothing if they are dead. If a cell is alive, it must figure out what character on the screen to modify. It determines the existing character with the `gettext()` function.

Since each character has two cell positions, some logic is devoted to figuring out the correct graphics character to insert. There are four possibilities: a blank character (a space), a character with a cell on the bottom but not on the top, a character with a cell on the top but not on the bottom, and a character with cells on both the top and the bottom. The choice depends on the character that was there before (stored in the variable `ch`) and whether the cell that we want to display is on the top row of the character or on the bottom row. The nested `if else` statements take care of this. Figure 17-9 shows the possibilities.

THE main() FUNCTION

The `main()` function erases the screen, using the `clrscr()` function. Then it initializes all the cells to *dead*, and sets some of them back to *alive* to form the initial pattern. It displays this initial pattern and waits for a keypress.

Following this keypress, the program enters a loop (which can be terminated with a second keypress). Three actions take place in the loop. First the new state of all the cells is found, using `Calc()`. Notice that the cells on the outer edges of the array are not calculated (the index variables go from 1 to the maximum-1). This avoids out-of-bounds array references when a cell examines its neighbors. Next the screen is erased, and finally all cells are displayed using `Calc()`.

The present version of LIFE requires you to rewrite the calls to `SetLive()` in `main()` if you want to change to a new initial pattern. This simplifies the program but makes it rather inflexible. It would be easy to modify this program so the user could type in initial patterns using cell coordinates. This would give it much more flexibility. Even better would be a routine that allowed the user to input cell positions using the cursor keys.

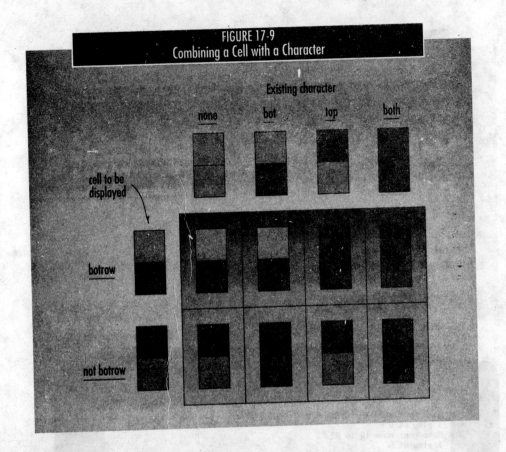

FIGURE 17-9
Combining a Cell with a Character

Existing character

none   bot   top   both

cell to be
displayed

botrow

not botrow

A TIC-TAC-TOE PROGRAM

Tic-tac-toe is a classic pencil-and-paper game in which each of two opponents tries
to get three marks, usually represented by O and X, in a row. Figure 17-10 shows
such a game, where X (due to an unfortunate lapse in concentration by O) wins.

The next program, TICTAC, enables the computer to play tic-tac-toe against a
human opponent. This program actually demonstrates a minor form of artificial in-
telligence. In terms of OOP, it provides another example of recursion. A member
function in one object creates another object of the same type, the same member
function in the second object creates a third object, and so on.

You may think that tic-tac-toe is too simple a game to merit serious analysis.
However, the approach used in TICTAC is fundamentally the same as that of programs
that play other, more challenging, games, such as checkers, chess, go, and bridge.
It uses the same strategy of recursively evaluating positions on a game tree, following the tree from a few initial branches to hundreds or thousands of subbranches.

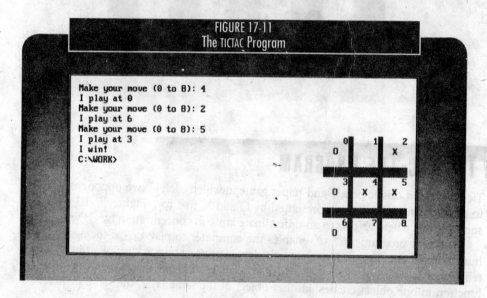

FIGURE 17-10
Moves in a Typical Tic-Tac-Toe Game

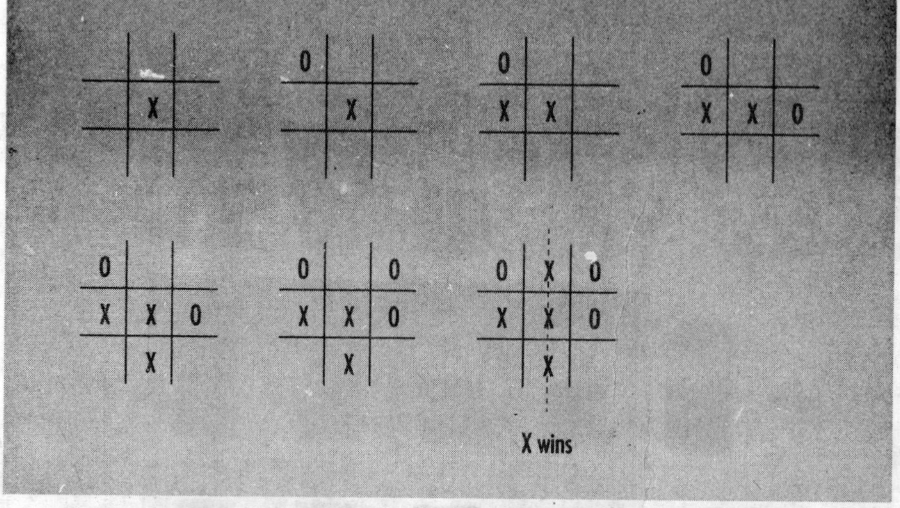

X wins

FIGURE 17-11
The TICTAC Program

```
Make your move (0 to 8): 4
I play at 0
Make your move (0 to 8): 2
I play at 6
Make your move (0 to 8): 5
I play at 3
I win!
C:\WORK>
```

TICTAC "thinks ahead" all the way to the end of the game, so it plays as well as, or better than, many humans. Figure 17-11 shows the screen display after several moves.

Here's the listing for TICTAC.CPP:

```
// tictac.cpp
// tic-tac-toe game
#include <iostream.h>    // for cout, etc
#include <conio.h>       // for gotoxy()
#include <process.h>     // for exit()

enum whoplays { human, machine };
enum cell { empty, full };
enum boolean { false, true };

int deep = 0;            // recursion depth

class Position           // represents one board position
   {
   private:
      cell mcell[9];     // cells marked with machine moves
      cell hcell[9];     // cells marked with human moves
      whoplays player;   // human or machine to play next
   public:
      Position();                   // constructor
      boolean IsWin();              // win in this position?
      boolean IsLegal(int);         // move is legal?
      void MakeMove(int);           // make move
      void SetPlayer(whoplays);     // swap player and machine
      static void InitDisplay();    // displays lines & numbers
      void Display();               // display board position
      int Evaluate(int&);           // score this position
   };

// Position()
// constructor: reset all cells to empty
Position::Position()
   {
   for( int j=0; j<9; j++ )
      mcell[j] = hcell[j] = empty;
   }

// IsWin()
// see if the current position is a win for player
boolean Position::IsWin()
   {
   cell *ptr;           // pointer to cells
   if( player==human ) // point to appropriate array
      ptr = hcell;
   else
      ptr = mcell;
                        // check for a 3-in-a-row
   if( (ptr[0] && ptr[1] && ptr[2]) ||  // horizontal
       (ptr[3] && ptr[4] && ptr[5]) ||
       (ptr[6] && ptr[7] && ptr[8]) ||
```

```
            (ptr[0] && ptr[3] && ptr[6]) ||  // vertical
            (ptr[1] && ptr[4] && ptr[7]) ||
            (ptr[2] && ptr[5] && ptr[8]) ||
            (ptr[0] && ptr[4] && ptr[8]) ||  // diagonal
            (ptr[2] && ptr[4] && ptr[6]) )
         return(true);
      else
         return(false);
      }


// IsLegal()
// find if move is legal in this position
boolean Position::IsLegal(int move)
      {
      if( move>=0 && move<=8 &&
                    mcell[move]==empty && hcell[move]==empty )
         return(true);
      else
         return(false);
      }


// MakeMove()
// make move in current position with current player
void Position::MakeMove(int move)
      {
      if( player==human )        // player is human
         hcell[move] = full;
      else                       // player is machine
         mcell[move] = full;
      }


// SetPlayer()
// set player to human or machine
void Position::SetPlayer(whoplays p)
      {
      player = p;
      }


// InitDisplay()
// Draws lines, numbers squares
void Position::InitDisplay()
      {
      const unsigned char block = '\xB2';        // gray block

      void Insert(unsigned char, int, int);      // prototype
      int row, col;

      clrscr();                                  // clear screen
      for(row=0; row<11; row++)                  // vertical lines
         {
```

```
      Insert( block,  5, row);
      Insert( block, 11, row);
      }
   for(col=0; col<17; col++)                    // horizontal lines
      {
      Insert( block, col, 5);
      Insert( block, col, 7);
      }
   for(int j=0; j<9; j++)                    .. number squares
      Insert( (char)(j+'0'), (j%3)*6+4, (j/3)*4 );
   } // end InitDisplay()

// Display()
// displays board
void Position::Display()
   {
   void Insert(unsigned char, int, int);     // prototype
   int row, col;

   for(int j=0; j<9; j++)                     // for each square
      {
      if( hcell[j] )                          // human move
         Insert('X', (j%3)*6+2, (j/3)*4+1);
      else if( mcell[j] )                     // machine move
         Insert('0', (j%3)*6+2, (j/3)*4+1);
      else                                    // no move
         Insert(' ', (j%3)*6+2, (j/3)*4+1);
      }
   gotoxy(1, 23);                             // restore cursor pos
   } // end Display()

// Insert()
// inserts character ch at col, row
void Insert(unsigned char ch, int col, int row)
   {
   // start 5 lines down, 50 cols over
   gotoxy(col+50+1, row+5+1);                 // insert the character
   putch(ch);
   }

// Evaluate()
// set score to chance of win, return the best move
int Position::Evaluate( int& score )
   {
   int const winscore = 100;       // score for a win (lose=0)
   int const drawscore = 50;       // score for a draw
   int returnmove;                 // move to be returned
   Position *posptr;               // pointer to new position
   int legalmoves = 0;             // count legal moves
   int totalscore = 0;             // cumulative score
   int highscore = 0;              // highest score to date
```

```
int avgscore;                       // average score,
int score2;                         // score from recursive call
boolean waswin = false;             // true if at least one win
boolean wasother = false;           // if at least one non-win


++deep;                             // down one recursion level
for(int move=0; move<9; move++)     // for each of 9 moves
   {                                // 'player' can make
   if( IsLegal(move) )              // if no one played there yet
      {
      if( legalmoves==0 )           // set returnmove to first
         returnmove = move;         //    legal move
      ++legalmoves;                 // count a legal move
      posptr = new Position;        // make new position
                                    //    for this move
      *posptr = *this;              // transfer this pos to posptr
      posptr->MakeMove(move);       // make the move
      if (deep < 3)                 // display, if in first two
         posptr->Display();         // levels of recursion
      if( posptr->IsWin() )         // check if it's a win
         {
         waswin = true;             // there was a win
         highscore = winscore;      // win is highest score
         totalscore += winscore;    // update total
         returnmove = move;         // return this move
         }
      else                          // no win, so check deeper
         {
                                    // swap human/machine
         whoplays newp = (player==machine) ? human : machine;
         posptr->SetPlayer(newp);   // in new position


                                    // recursive call
         posptr->Evaluate(score2);  // to new position

         if(score2==winscore)       // if wining score,
            waswin = true;          // remember there was a win
         else
            wasother = true;        // remember non-win
         totalscore += score2;      // add new score to total
         if( score2 > highscore )   // remember the move that
            {                       // produced the
            highscore = score2;     // highest score, and
            returnmove = move;      // the score
            }
         } // end else (no win)
      delete posptr;                // delete the position
      } // end if IsLegal
   } // end for
                                    // summarize results of all moves
```

```
        if( legalmoves==0 )      // if there are no legal moves
            {
            score = drawscore;    // it must be a draw
            --deep;               // go up one recursion level
            return(99);           // return nonsense move
            }
        else                                // there were some legal moves
            {
            avgscore = totalscore / legalmoves;    // find average
            if( waswin && wasother )               // if wins and non-wins,
                score = winscore - (winscore-avgscore)/5;  // favor wins
            else
                score = avgscore;  // otherwise, use the average score
            score = 100 - score;  // invert: bad for them, good for us
            --deep;               // go up one recursion level
            return(returnmove);   // return best move
            } // end else (legal moves)
    } // end Evaluate()


// main()
// get human move, get machine move, etc.
void main(void)
    {
    int move;                     // store moves
    int sc;                       // for Evaluate()
    int movecount = 0;            // number of move-pairs
    Position current;             // create current position
    int cursrow = 0;              // cursor row for text

    Position::InitDisplay();      // display the board
    while(1)                      // cycle until game over
        {
        current.SetPlayer(human); // set player to human
        current.Display();        // display the position
        gotoxy(1, ++cursrow);
        cout << "Make your move (0 to 8): ";  // get human move
        cin >> move;
        if( ! current.IsLegal(move) )
            {
            gotoxy(1, ++cursrow);
            cout << "Illegal move.";
            continue;             // return to top of loop
            }
        current.MakeMove(move);   // make human move
        current.Display();
        if( current.IsWin() )     // check for human win
            {
            gotoxy(1, ++cursrow);
            cout << "You win!";
            exit(0);
            }
```

```
        if( ++movecount==5 )            // if human move was
          {                             // the last possible move
          gotoxy(1, ++cursrow);
          cout << "It's a draw";
          exit(0);
          }                             // now machine can play
        current.SetPlayer(machine);     // set player to machine
        move = current.Evaluate(sc);    // get machine move
        gotoxy(1, ++cursrow);
        cout << "I play at " << move;
        current.MakeMove(move);         // make machine move
        current.Display();
        if( current.IsWin() )           // check for machine win
          {
          gotoxy(1, ++cursrow);
          cout << "I win!";
          exit(0);
          }
        }  // end while
     }  // end main()
```

THE Position CLASS

TICTAC uses objects of the class **Position**. Each object of this class represents a board position—that is, some arrangement of Xs and Os on the 3-by-3 matrix of squares. Besides recording the X and O moves made to date, a **Position** object also includes a variable that specifies the player with the next turn.

The **main()** program creates a single object of class **Position** called **current**. This position records the current state of the game, and is displayed so the user can see what's happening.

MEMBER FUNCTIONS OF Position

Let's look at each member function of **Position** in turn. This will serve to explain how TICTAC works.

The Position() Constructor

The constructor for **Position** initializes all the cells in a given position to **empty**. A single array could be used to represent the board, but it turns out to be simpler to use two arrays: one for human moves (**hcell**) and one for machine moves (**mcell**). The elements of these arrays are of type **cell**, which is declared in an **enum** statement to have two possible values: **empty** and **full**.

The cells are numbered from 0 in the upper-left corner down to 8 in the lower-right corner.

The IsWin() Function

The isWin() function figures out if a particular position represents a win. If the human is playing, a win is three hcell (for *human cell*) elements in a row; if the player is the machine, it's three mcell elements. IsWin() sets a pointer to the appropriate array, and then checks each of the eight possible three-in-a-rows to see if its cells are occupied. It returns the Boolean value of true if it finds a win, or false if it doesn't.

The IsLegal() Function

The IsLegal() function checks to see if a move, sent to it as an argument, is legal. A move is legal if it is a number between 0 and 8 and if neither human nor machine has already played in the specified cell.

The MakeMove() Function

The MakeMove() function changes the contents of the specified cell from empty to full. This happens in mcell or in hcell, depending on whether the player in the position is the machine or the human.

The SetPlayer() Function

The SetPlayer() function changes the player in a particular position. The main() program uses it to switch back and forth between the human—who always plays first—and the machine, as they alternate moves in the current position.

The InitDisplay() Function

When the program is first executed, it calls InitDisplay() to draw the crossed lines that form the tic-tac-toe game board, and to number each of the resulting nine squares, so the human knows what they are. The squares are numbered from 0 to 8, as shown in the program output. InitDisplay() starts by clearing the screen with clrscr() It uses the Insert() function to actually place characters on the screen.

The Display() Function

The main() program displays the moves made on the board by calling Display() as a member function of the current position. This function translates the contents of hcell and mcell into the X and O display. Display() is also used by the Evaluate() function to show—very briefly—the positions it's thinking about as it looks ahead. Display() places characters on the screen by calling the Insert() function.

The Insert() Function

The Insert() function inserts a character at a fixed column-row position on the screen, using the gotoxy() and putch() library functions. Insert() uses a coordinate system that starts 5 lines down and 50 columns over from the upper-left corner of the screen; that's where the game board is drawn.

The Evaluate() Function

We now come to the "brains" of the program. The Evaluate() function evaluates a particular position to see how likely it is to lead to a win for a particular player. It also returns the best move in a particular position.

The main() function calls Evaluate to determine the best machine move, and makes the machine's move based on the recommendations of this function. How does Evaluate() figure out the best move? Its overall strategy is to create a new Position object (using new) for each move that can be legally made from its position. Each of these positions is then evaluated. For instance, the human has the first move and selects one of the nine choices. Thus on its first move the machine is faced with eight possible moves. Which is the best? To decide, it evaluates each of the eight moves. For each of the eight moves it creates a new Position. From this position it then calculates a score, based on how likely the move is to lead to a win. When all possible moves have been evaluated, it returns the move with the highest score, and main() then executes this move.

How is each of the eight possible moves evaluated? For the position corresponding to each move, Evaluate() calls itself again. For each of the eight moves the machine can make, the human has seven possible responses. When Evaluate() is called for one of the machine's eight moves, it generates a position for each of the seven possible human responses. Each of these seven positions then uses Evaluate again to determine the best move. This involves creating six positions for each possible machine move, and calling Evaluate() for each of the six moves. The resulting branching of nine initial moves, each with eight responses, and so on, is partially shown in Figure 17-12. Since there are 9! (9 factorial, or 9*8*7*6*5*4*3*2*1, or more than 300,000) possible move combinations, we can't show them all. We show the first few, and several toward the end of the tree.

Eventually, as the Evaluate() function works its way down lower and lower into the move tree, one of several things happens. The first possibility is that somebody wins—that is, they get three-in-a-row. This is the end of that branch of the move tree, since the game ends at that point. (Thus there are actually somewhat fewer possible positions than 9!, since the tree stops branching when there's a win, although this does not reduce the size of the tree substantially.) The Evaluate() function assigns a number, called a *score*, to each possible outcome so that the various moves can be compared. A win results in a score of 100; this is the highest score. A score of 0 represents a loss.

The other possibility when the move tree is followed to the end is that no more moves can be made; all the squares have been filled by Xs or Os, and the game is a draw. A draw results in a score of 50.

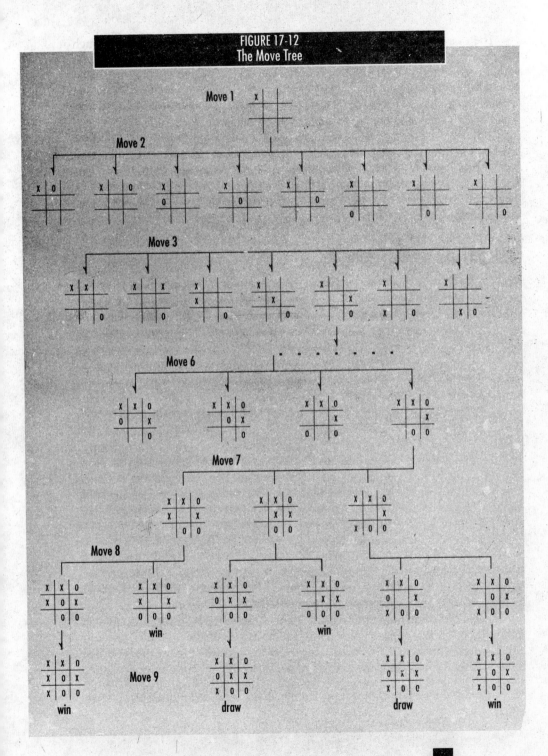

FIGURE 17-12
The Move Tree

The Evaluate() function is set up in the form of a loop that cycles through nine possible moves. In each cycle through the loop, it checks to see if the move is legal. If so, it creates a new position, transfers the current position into it, and makes the move in the new position. It then checks to see if making this move results in a win. If so, it places 100 in the highscore variable, and adds 100 to a running total. It also remembers the move that generated the score.

If the move didn't generate a win, Evaluate() must look deeper, so it calls the Evaluate() function that is a member of the new position. This function will eventually return a score, either because there's a win or because the game ends. This score is again added to the running total. If the score is the highest seen so far, it is placed in the highscore variable, and the return move is set to this new high-scoring move.

EVALUATING A POSITION

When all the moves have been evaluated, the loop ends, and Evaluate() figures out a total score for its position. You can approximate this calculation by saying that it averages the scores of the opponent's moves. Evaluate() then inverts the average to obtain the score. The inversion is necessary because a win for our opponent is a loss for us. For instance, if our opponent has four moves—say three wins and a draw—the total score is close to 100 for him, but close to 0 for us, since there's a good chance we'll lose. A draw, on the other hand, is a draw for both players, and 50 subtracted from 100 is still 50.

This inversion of the score each time the player changes is called the *minmax* approach. We assume we'll do what's good for us, but we also assume our opponent will do what's bad for us.

Combining several scores into one is actually a little more complicated than simply averaging them. To see the reason for this, imagine that our opponent can make one of four moves. One of the moves leads to a win for him, and three lead to losses for him. What's the score for these four moves? The average would be 100+0+0+0, or 25, which is less than a draw. However, our opponent won't choose one of the moves at random; he'll choose the best one for him. So the score for him is close to 100. It's not quite 100, since it's not quite as good as four wins (which would score 100), but it's still up there. For us (as opposed to our opponent) the situation is reversed. We don't want to make the move that will lead to our opponent having four possible moves, one of which is a win, so we score the move close to 0.

These considerations—and trial and error—lead to the following scoring algorithm: If our opponent has some wins and some other outcomes (draws, losses, or other scores), then we start with 100 (the winscore constant in the program) and subtract from it 100 minus the average score, divided by 5. For the win and three losses described above, the average is 25, so the score is 100 – (100–25)/5, or 85. For a win and three draws, the average is 62, so the score would be 100 – (100–62)/5, or 92.

If there are no wins, or all wins, the average can be used without modification. Four draws is 50, two losses and two draws is 25 (75 for us), four wins is 100 (0 for us), and so on.

THE main() FUNCTION

The main() function cycles around a loop. It asks the user for his move, and makes it on the current position. It then displays this position, calls Evaluate() to find the best response, makes this move, displays it, and returns to the top of the loop to ask for the next human move. After either a human or a machine move, the current position is checked for a win. If the human has made his or her fifth move, the game is a draw. Messages are printed for these three outcomes.

FURTHER THOUGHTS

You may have noticed how long it takes the program to make its first move (actually the second move of the game) when it has 8 choices, and how much more quickly it figures out its next move (the fourth move of the game) when it has only 6 choices. Not only is 8 larger than 6, but the branches of the move tree that start at the second move are far larger than those starting at the fourth move. There are about 8! choices for the second move, but only 6!, or 56 times fewer, for the fourth. If we changed the program to let the machine play first, its first move would take nine times as long as the current first move.

Thus you can see that if the tic-tac-toe game were even slightly more complicated than it is, we could not use the approach of following the move tree to the end. For more complex games a different strategy must be used. One approach is to follow the move tree downward only a fixed number of moves. At an appropriate depth no more positions are created. Instead, the position is evaluated in other ways. In a chess game, for example, an evaluation is based on such factors as the number of pawns occupying center squares and the total value of the pieces on the board. Also, branches that lead to unlikely situations are not explored; this is called "pruning" the tree. Such topics are beyond the scope of this book.

SUMMARY

This chapter has explored some diverse applications of C++ programming. If nothing else, these examples should demonstrate that the uses to which you can put C++ are limited only by your imagination (or perhaps the spur of necessity). The object-oriented approach can be applied to most programming problems. Now that you understand how to use this new approach, as embodied in C++, you have at your disposal one of the most powerful programming tools yet created. We hope you enjoyed this introduction to OOP and C++, and that your use of these tools is amusing as well as profitable.

QUESTIONS AND EXERCISES

Because this chapter is just for fun, there are no questions or exercises.

COMPLETE FUNCTION REFERENCE

The **Prototype**s of Standard functions are being discussed in the alphabetical order of their names.

► abort ►

Prototype	:	void abort(void);
abort	:	Abnormally terminates a process and returns control back to calling program.
Prototype in	:	process.h and stdlib.h

► abs ►

Prototype	:	int abs(int x);
abs	:	The absolute value of integer x is returned.
Prototype in	:	math.h and stdlib.h

► absread/abswrite ►

Prototype	:	int absread / abswrite (int drive, int nsects,int lsect, void *buffer);
absread/ abswrite	:	Reads / Writes disk sectorwise. Drive is specified as abswrite int drive (where 0 = A, 1 = B etc.) nsects no. of sectors startingfrom logical sector no. lsect(0 based; 1st sector is numbered logical 0) are read & stored to, or written from memory pointed to by buffer.

The largest amount of memory that can be read/written in per call is limited to the memory available in the segment of buffer.

Returns 0 for success; on error, returns -1 and sets errno.

Prototype in	:	dos.h

► access ►

Prototype	:	int access(const char *filename, int amode);
access	:	Determines accessibility of a file as per amode. If the requested access is allowed, 0 is returned; otherwise, a value of -1 is returned and errno is set. Value of amode determines what is to be checked for :

amode Checks for

0	file existence
2	write permission
4	read permission
6	read and write permission

Prototype in	:	io.h

► acos ►

Prototype	:	double acos(double x);
acos	:	Returns Arc Cosine of x. Value returned is angle in Radians.
Prototype in	:	math.h

► allocmem ►

Prototype	:	int allocmem(unsigned size, unsigned *segp);
allocmem	:	Allocates DOS memory segment of size paragraphs and stores the segment part of allocated address at segp; the offset is 0.
		Returns -1 on success. On failure, sets _doserrno and errno and returns the size of the largest available memory block.
Prototype in	:	dos.h

► asin ►

Prototype	:	double asin(double x);
asin	:	Returns Arc Sine of x. Value returned is angle in Radians.
Prototype in	:	math.h

► atan ►

Prototype	:	double atan(double x);
atan	:	Returns Arc tangent of x. Value returned is angle in Radians.
Prototype in	:	math.h

► atan2 ►

Prototype	:	double atan2(double num, double denum);
atan2	:	Returns Arc tangent of num / denum Value returned is angle in Radians.
Prototype in	:	math.h

► atexit ►

Prototype	:	int atexit(atexit_t func);
atexit	:	Registers func as the function which will be called before termination caused by exit function. Returns 0 on success; nonzero otherwise.
Prototype in	:	stdlib.h

► atof ►

Prototype	:	double atof(const char *string);
atof	:	Converts a string to a floating point and returns the converted value. 0 as return value signifies that the string cannot be converted.
Prototype in	:	math.h and stdlib.h

► atoi / atol ►

Prototype	:	int atoi(const char *s); long atol(const char *s);

atoi / atol	:	These macros convert string s of digits and/or decimal point to integer (atoi) or long integer (atol : used for value greater than int range) described by the string. The converted value or 0 (if the string cannot be converted) is returned.
Prototype in	:	stdlib.h

► asctime ►

Prototype	:	char *asctime(const struct tm *tblock);
asctime	:	The date and time passed as per format of struct tm is converted to an ASCII string which is overwritten with each call. The string contains date and time & a pointer to this character string is returned.
Prototype in	:	time.h

► assert ►

Prototype	:	void assert(int testexpression);
assert	:	It is used for diagnostic purposes. If TestExpression evaluates to Zero, a messege is printed on the stderr device (giving indication of line number & file where the assertion failed) and function abort() is called. Calling of abort() can be blocked by having NDEBUG defined.
Prototype in	:	assert.h

► bdos ►

Prototype	:	int bdos(int func, unsigned dx,unsigned al);
bdos	:	It works as interface to DOS system calls through INT 21H. The function no. func of int 21h is called with dx & al registers set to the arguments. Returns the value of AX set by int 21h.
Prototype in	:	dos.h

► bdosptr ►

Prototype	:	int bdosptr(int fun, void *argument, unsigned alval);

bdosptr : It works as interface to those DOS system calls through INT 21H which are called with some ASCIIZ string as argument. Function no. func of int 21h is called with ds:dx pointing to argument & al set to alval. Returns -1 on failure or the value of AX set by int 21h on success. On failure, errno and _doserrno are also set.

Prototype in : dos.h

► bioscom ►

Prototype : int bioscom(int command, char cntrlbyte, int port);

bioscom : It is the interface provided by C to the BIOS interrupt 14 hex (20) dealing with Serial communications.
Command values are as follows:

0 Initialise communication parameters as per cntrlbyte

1 Transmit cntrlbyte out from port

2 Receive a byte as a char (in low 8 bits of the return value)

3 Get status of port port is designator of com port

0 COM1

1 COM2 etc.

It returns an int as a 16 bit word. Upper 8 bits are status bits. Lower 8 bits depend on command specified.

Status bits are interprated as under :

bit no.   Set to 1 means

0 Receiving Data is Ready

1 Overrun Error

2 Parity Error

3 Framing Error

4 Break has been detected

5 Transmit Hold Register is Empty

6 Transmit Shift Register is Empty

7   Time Out

command = 0

cntrlbyte will be so formed that required initialisation parameters are depicted.

Format is : Bit 0 = LSB Bit 7 = MSB such that

Bit no. :   7 6 5   4 3   2   1 0

Used for :   Baud Rate Parity Stop Bit Count Word Size

Values
& Meaning   : 111 : 9600 11 : Even 1 : 2 bits 11 : 8 bits
                     110 : 4800 10 : None 0 : 1 bit 10 : 7 bits
                     101 : 2400 01 : Odd 01 : Not used
                     100 : 1200 00 : None 00 : Not used
          command = 1
          cntrlbyte will be the character to be transmitted to port.
          command = 2 & 3

          cntrlbyte is insignificant and can be set zero.

Prototype in   :   bios.h

▶ biosdisk ▶

Prototype   :   int biosdisk(int func, int drive, int head, int track, int sector,
                      int numsectrs, void *databuffer);

biodisk   :   It is the interface provided by C to the BIOS interrupt 13
                      hex (19) dealing with Disk Services.

                      Possible func values (functions of int 13 h) are many and
                      their discussion is best left to books on assembly language
                      programming.
                      Return a value depending upon return value of asked BIOS
                      function.
                      The arguments are :
                      func   : The desired function of int 13H
                      drive   : Disk drive A = 0, B = 1 etc.
                                   80 onward for Fixed disk
                      head   : Head number of drive 0, 1 etc.
                      track   : Track / Cylinder number 0, 1...
                      sector   : Sector number 0, 1....
                      numsectrs : Number of Sectors
                      databuffer : A buffer to hold data viz. to hold data to
                                   be written to disk

Prototype in   :   bios.h

▶ biosequip ▶

Prototype   :   int biosequip(void);

biosequip   :   It gives the primitive indication of equipments installedin
                      the computer system. Returns the BIOS equipment flags
                      which is also stored by BIOS on the System Power On

at BIOS Data Area 0040:0010 H by obtaining it on execution of Int 11H.

The Return Value is interprated as follows :

Bit No. Meaning

Bit No.	Meaning
0	1 :Floppy disk drive (s) installed
1	1 :Math Coprocessor installed
4-5	Video Mode
	01 : 40 X 25 colour
	10 : 80 X 25 colour
	11 : 80 X 25 mono
6-7	No. of Floppy Drives installed (if any)
	00 = 1 drive 01 = 2 10 = 3 11 = 4
	9-11 No. of Serial ports installed
	14-15 No. of Printers installed

Prototype in : bios.h

► bioskey ►

Prototype : int bioskey(int cmd);

bioskey : Provides an interface to the Keyboard where the commnds given as cmd have meanings as below:

cmd	Action
0	Returns scancode from buffer, key is deleted from the keyboard buffer. Waits for keypress if buffer is empty.
1	Returns scancode from buffer, but key is not deleted from the buffer. Does not wait for keypress and returns 0 if the buffer is empty.
2	Returns the shift status flags as stored by BIOS in its data area.

The status is a 16 bit word where each bit when set, means as below :

Bit	Meaning, if bit = 1
0	Right Shift Key Pressed
1	Left Shift Key Pressed
2	Control(^) Key Pressed
3	Alternate Key Pressed
4	Scroll Lock Toggled
5	Numeric Lock Toggled

6	Caps Lock Toggled
7	Insert mode Toggled
8	Left Ctrl Key Pressed
9	Left Alt Key Pressed
10	Sys Req Key Pressed
11	Ctrl Num Lock Pressed
12	Scroll Lock Key Pressed
13	Num Lock Key Pressed
14	Caps Lock Key Pressed
15	Insert Key Pressed

Prototype in : bios.h

► biosmemory ►

Prototype : int biosmemory(void);

biosmemory : Returns size of conventional system memory Kilobytes.

Prototype in : bios.h

► brk ►

Prototype : int brk(void *address);

brk : Changes space allocation in the data-segment

Prototype in : alloc.h

► bsearch ►

Prototype : void *bsearch(const void *key, const void *base, size_t *nelem, size_t width, int (*fcmp)(const void*, const void*));

bsearch : The first entry in the table matching the search key is searched for and returns the address of the same if found or NULL otherwise. It may be noted that this uses binary search algorithm and so the table must be in ascending order. key is pointer to search key, base is the start address of table, width is size of each element and nelem points to number of elements in the table. The function fcmp has to be designed so that its return value is:

Less than 0 if *elem1 is Less than *elem2
0 if *elem1 equals *elem2
More than 0 if *elem1 is more than *elem2

Prototype in	:	stdlib.h

▶ cabs ▶

Prototype	:	double cabs(struct complex z);
cabs	:	Returns a double being the absolute value of complex number z.
Prototype in	:	math.h

▶ calloc ▶

Prototype	:	void *calloc(size_t numitems, size_t sizek);
calloc	:	Allocates space for numitems items of sizek each and stores zero in the area. Returns a pointer to the newly allocated block.Return value is NULL if enough space is not available.
Prototype in	:	alloc.h and stdlib.h

▶ ceil ▶

Prototype	:	double ceil(double x);
ceil	:	Returns the smallest integer not less x.
Prototype in	:	math.h

▶ cgets ▶

Prototype	:	char *cgets(char *str)
cgets	:	Reads string from console. Before call to cgets, the char str[0] must be set to contain the maximum length of the string to be read. On return, str[1] is holds the number of characters actually read. The string begins at str[2] whose addressis returned.
Prototype in	:	conio.h

▶ chdir ▶

Prototype	:	int chdir(const char *path);
chdir	:	Current directory is changed to path & 0 is returned success. On failure, -1 is returned and errno is set.

Prototype in : dir.h

► chmod ►

Prototype : int chmod(const char *path, int amode);

chmod : Changes access mode to amode & returns 0 on success whereas -1 is returned otherwise.

Prototype in : io.h

► _chmod ►

Prototype : int _chmod(const char *path,int func [,int attrib]);

_chmod : The file attribute is accessed for view /change of the access mode. If func is 0, _chmod returns the file's attributes. If func is 1, the attributes are set. _chmod returns the file attribute word on success; otherwise -1 is returned and errno is set. The parameter attrib is to be supplied in case of func=1 only.

Prototype in : io.h

► chsize ►

Prototype : int chsize(int handle, long size);

chsize : Size of file specified by handle is changed to size bytes. 0 is returned on success. On failure, it returns -1 and sets errno.

Prototype in : io.h

► _clear87 ►

Prototype : unsigned int _clear87 (void)

_clear87 : Clears 80x87 floating-point status and returns an int the bits of which indicate the old status. The bit pattern may be interpreted as below :
Bit 0 : Invalid Operation   Bit 1 : DeNormalised Operand
Bit 2 : Zero Devide Error Bit 3 : Overflow Error
Bit 4 : Underflow Error   Bit 5 : Precision Error
Bit 6 : Reserved   Bit 7 :Interrupt Request
Bit 8,9,10 & 14: Condition Code bits 0,1,2,3

Bit 11,12,13 : Stack top Pointer bits 0,1,2
Bit 15 :Busy Flag

| Prototype in | : | float.h |

► clearerr ►

Prototype	:	void clearerr(FILE *fp);
clearerr	:	The error (& EOF) indicators occured on any operation involving a file fp is cleared.
Prototype in	:	stdio.h

► clock ►

Prototype	:	clock_t clock(void);
clock	:	The processor time used upto this call since the beginning of program execution is returned in clock ticks (CLK_TCK clock ticks = 1 second).
Prototype in	:	time.h

► _close/close ►

Prototypes	:	int _close(int handle); int close (int handle);
_close/close	:	Both are used to close a file specified by handle On success, these return 0; otherwise, they return -1 and set errno.
Prototype in	:	io.h

► clreol ►

Prototype	:	void clreol(void);
clreol	:	All characters from the current cursor position to the end of the line are cleared, without moving the cursor.
Prototype in	:	conio.h

► clrscr ►

Prototype	:	void clrscr(void);
clrscr	:	The text mode window of screen is cleared.
Prototype in	:	conio.h

► _control87 ►

Prototype	:	unsigned int _control87(unsigned int newcw, int mask);

_control87 : The existing 80x87 control word may be changed by this function.The bits of control word are made equal to corresponding bit of the newcw provided that the corresponding bit of mask is 1. (If a bit in mask is 1, corresponding bit in newcw is made the new value for the same bit in the control word. If mask bit is 0, the control word is not altered.). The resulting new control word is returned.

The names defined in float.h may be used as mask or newcw but for better understanding, we will see the control word format of 80x87 as below :

Bit 0 : Invalid Operation   Bit 1 : DeNormalised Operand
Bit 2 : Zero Divide Error   Bit 3 : Overflow Error
Bit 4 : Underflow Error   Bit 5 :Precision Error
Bits 0-5 are to mask these Errors 1 means that the corresponding error will be masked.
Bit 6 : Reserved   Bit7 : Interrupt Enable (0=Enable)
Bit 8-9: Precision Control bits 0,1
00 = 24bit 11 = 64bits 10(bit 8 =0) = 53 bits 01 Not Used
Bit 10-11 : Rounding Control bit 0,1
00 =Round to Nearest 11 =Chop up to precision size
01 (bit10 =1) =Round Down 10 = Round Up
Bit 12 :Infinity Control 0= Projective 1= Affine
Bit 13-15 :Reserved

Prototype in : float.h

► coreleft ►

Prototype : unsigned coreleft(void);
in Tiny, small,and medium models: unsigned long coreleft(void);
in Compact, large, and huge models:

coreleft : Returns a measure of memory available (unused).

Prototype in : alloc.h

► cos ►

Prototype : double cos(double x);

cos	:	Returns requested trigonometric ratio of the angle x where x is in radians.
Prototype in	:	math.h

► cosh ►

Prototype	:	double cosh(double x);
cosh	:	Returns requested trigonometric ratio of the angle x where x is in radians.
Prototype in	:	math.h

► country ►

Prototype	:	struct country *country(int ctrycod,struct country *cp);
country	:	Returns a pointer to struct cp wherein the country specific information for the country specified by ctrycod is stored by it.
Prototype in	:	dos.h

► cprintf ►

Prototype	:	int cprintf(const char *format[,argument,...]);
cprintf	:	Writes formatted output to the text window on the screen and returns the number of bytes output. Format is same as in case of printf discussed later. Please note that \n in cprintf does not result in both CR & LF but only LF; so use \r for CR.
Prototype in	:	conio.h

► cputs ►

Prototype	:	int cputs(const char *str);
cputs	:	Writes a string to the text window on the screen & returns the last character printed.
Prototype in	:	conio.h

► _creat/creat ►

Prototypes	:	int _creat(const char *path, int attrib); int creat(const char *path, int amode);
_creat/creat	:	A new file is created or if specified file exists, that is truncated for being overwritten. creat opens the file in the mode given by _fmode with permissions given by amode as detailed in 3.9.1. _creat always opens file in binary mode with given attribute. On success, the new file handle is returned; otherwise -1 is returned and errno is set.
Prototype in	:	io.h

► creatnew ►

Prototype	:	int creatnew(const char *path, int mode);
creatnew	:	Creates a new file as done by _creat. The only difference is that an error is returned if the file already exists.
Prototype in	:	io.h

► creattemp ►

Prototype	:	int creattemp(char *path, int attrib);
creattemp	:	Creates a unique file in the directory given by path. The action is similar to _creat, except that path is a path name only (ending with a \ ) without filename but sufficient in size to hold the resulting unique filename created by it. path is modified to hold complete filename with path. 0 is returned on success. -1 on failure when errno is also set.
Prototype in	:	io.h

► cscanf ►

Prototype	:	int cscanf(char *format [, address,...]);
cscanf	:	Scans and formats input from console & returns the number of input fields successfully processed. If attempted to read at the end-of-file, the return value is EOF. Format is same as in case of scanf discussed later.
Prototype in	:	conio.h

► ctime ►

Prototype	:	char *ctime(const time_t *time);
ctime	:	Converts the date and time to a string & returns a pointer to the character string which is overwritten with each call.
Prototype in	:	time.h

► ctrlbrk ►

Prototype	:	void ctrlbrk(int (*handler)(void));
ctrlbrk	:	Sets control-break handler from default to the new function pointed to by handler.The handler function should be designed to return 0 to abort the current program.
Prototype in	:	dos.h

► delay ►

Prototype	:	void delay(unsigned duration);
delay	:	Suspends execution for duration milliseconds.
Prototype in	:	dos.h

► delline ►

Prototype	:	void delline(void);
delline	:	Deletes the current line in the text window.
Prototype in	:	conio.h

► difftime ►

Prototype	:	double difftime(time_t time2, time_t time1);
difftime	:	The difference between two times is computed and the elapsed time from time1 to time2 is returned in seconds.
Prototype in	:	time.h

► disable ►

Prototype	:	void disable(void);

disable   :   All hardware interrupts except NMI are disabled.

Prototype in   :   dos.h

▶ div or ldiv ▶

Prototype   :   div_t div(int num, int denom);
                            ldiv_t ldiv(long int num, long int denom);

div or ldiv   :   division of two integers (div) or longs (ldiv) is performed
                            and the quotient and the remainder are returned as div_t
                            or ldiv_t type defined in stdlib.h. num and denom are the
                            numerator and the denominator, respectively.

Prototype in   :   stdlib.h

▶ dosexterr ▶

Prototype   :   int dosexterr(struct DOSERROR *eblkp);

dosexterr   :   The extended error information based on the last DOS call
                            is filleds in the structure pointed to by eblkp and the value
                            of the structure field de_exterror is returned.

Prototype in   :   dos.h

▶ dostounix ▶

Prototype   :   long dostounix(struct date *d, struct time *t);

dostounix   :   Returns UNIX version (i.e number of seconds since
                            00:00:00 GMT on 1.1.1970) of the date and time parameters
                            supplied in the structs as in DOS style.

Prototype in   :   dos.h

▶ dup ▶

Prototype   :   int dup(int handle);

dup   :   Returns duplicate file handle for the handle passed. -1 is
                            returned and errno is set on error.

Prototype in   :   io.h

► dup2 ►

Prototype	:	int dup2(int oldh, int newh);
dup2	:	Existing file handle oldh is duplicated onto another existing file handle newh. oldh then behaves as if it were newh. Used for Redirection purposes. Returns 0 on success & -1 on error.
Prototype in	:	io.h

► ecvt or fcvt ►

Prototypes	:	char *ecvt(double value, int ndig, int *dec, int *sign); char *fcvt(double value, int ndig, int *dec, int *sign);
ecvt or fcvt	:	These convert floating-point number passed as value to the corresponding string. For ecvt, ndig gives the number of digits to store, while for fcvt it is the number of digits to store after the decimal point. The return value points to converted data. value can also be supplied in scientific notation.
Prototype in	:	stdlib.h

► __emit__ ►

Prototype	:	void __emit__(argument,...);
__emit__	:	The arguments are directly put into the compiled code. viz. if int 05 (PrtSc service) is required at any place in code, it may be achieved by having m/c code for int 05 (i.e. CDh 05h in Assembly) in the code at the place. This can be achieved by __emit__(0xcd,0x05);.
Prototype in	:	dos.h

► enable ►

Prototype	:	void enable(void);
enable	:	Enables hardware interrupts earlier disabled by software.
Prototype in	:	dos.h

► eof ►

Prototype	:	int eof(int handle);
eof	:	Checks whether the position marker in the file given by its handle is at the end-of-file. If yes, returns 0. 1 is returned if position marker is NOT at eof & an error is indicated by setting of errno & return value of -1.
Prototype in	:	io.h

► exit / _exit ►

Prototype	:	void exit(int status); void _exit(int status);
exit / _exit	:	The program is terminated and status is returned to caller as return value of program. Before terminating, buffered output is flushed, files are closed, and exit functions (also the one defined by atexit()) are called.
Prototype in	:	process.h and stdlib.h

► exec... functions ►

Prototypes	:	int execl(char *path, char *arg0,.., NULL);
		int execle(char *path, char *arg0,.., NULL, char **env);
		int execlp(char *path, char *arg0,..);
		int execlpe(char *path, char *arg0,.., NULL, char **env);
		int execv(char *path, char *argv[]);
		int execve(char *path, char *argv[], char **env);
		int execvp(char *path, char *argv[]);
		int execvpe(char *path, char *argv[], char **env);

exec.... **functions**	:	functions that load and run other programs.
Prototype in	:	process.h

► exp ►

Prototype	:	double exp(double n);
exp	:	Returns e raised to the nth power.
Prototype in	:	math.h

▶ fabs, labs ▶

Prototypes	:	double fabs(double x); long int labs(long int x);
fabs, labs	:	Return absolute value of floating-point number (fabs) or long int number.
Prototype in	:	math.h

▶ farcalloc ▶

Prototype	:	void far *farcailoc(unsigned long numunits,unsigned long unitsize);
farcalloc	:	Allocates space from far heap,for numunits items of unitsize bytes each. Returns a pointer to the newly allocated block. If enough space does not exist,NULL is returned.
Prototype in	:	alloc.h

▶ farcoreleft ▶

Prototype	:	unsigned long farcoreleft(void);
farcalloc	:	Returns the total amount of space left (in bytes) between the highest allocated block and the end of memory.
Prototype in	:	alloc.h

▶ farfree ▶

Prototype	:	void farfree(void far *block);
farfree	:	Frees a block allocated earlier from far heap
Prototype in	:	alloc.h

▶ farheapcheck ▶

Prototype	:	int farheapcheck(void);
farheapcheck	:	This function checks the far heap. The size, pointer, and other critical attributes of every block in the far heap is examined. A value less than Zero is returned in case of an error; otherwise the return value is greater than Zero. The return values are defined as symbols.

Prototype in   :   alloc.h

► farheapcheckfree ►

| Prototype | : | int farheapcheckfree(unsigned int fillerval); |

farheapcheckfree :   All the free blocks on the far heap are checked for presence of a constant value passed to the function as fillerval. The return value is greater than zero if fillerval is found and less than zero for an error.

Prototype in   :   alloc.h

► farheapchecknode ►

| Prototype | : | int farheapchecknode(void *node); |

farheapchecknode: Checks and verifies a single node on the far heap. Returnvalue is indicator of the status of the block pointed to by node.

Prototype in   :   alloc.h

► farheapfillfree ►

| Prototype | : | int farheapfillfree(unsigned int filler); |

farcheapfillfree   :   Fills the free block on the far heap with a constant passed to the function as "filler". The return value is less than zero for an error. Success is indicated by a return value greater than zero.

Prototype in   :   alloc.h

► farheapwalk ►

| Prototype | : | int farheapwalk(struct farheapinfo *hi); |

farheapwalk   :   The far heap is examined node by node and the pointer,size and use status are checked and filled in the structure hi. _HEAPOK is returned with the last block on the heap._HEAPEND will be returned on the next call to this function.

Note:

1. Before using farheapwalk, farheapcheck must be used to verify the heap because farheapwalk assumes the heap as correct.

2. farheapwalk receives a pointer to a structure of type heapinfo. For the first call to heapwalk, the hi.ptr field should be set to null. On return, hi.ptr contains the address of the first block. hi.size contains the size of the block in bytes and hi.in_use will be set if the block is currently in use.

Prototype in	:	alloc.h

► farmalloc ►

Prototype	:	void far *farmalloc(unsigned long number);
farmalloc	:	Allocates number bytes from far heap and Returns a pointer to the allocated block. NULL is returned if space for the new block is not available.
Prototype in	:	alloc.h

► farrealloc ►

Prototype	:	void far *farrealloc(void far *oldblockptr, unsigned long nbytes);
farrealloc	:	Allocated block in far heap is adjusted for alteration in size to new size of nbytes bytes. Name of the old pointer may be preserved but value of the pointer may change if enough memory for new size can not be achieved from the same memory address as pointed to by the pointer oldblockptr. Returns the address of the reallocated block. NULL is returned in case of failure.
Prototype in	:	alloc.h

► fclose ►

Prototype	:	int fclose(FILE *fp);
fclose	:	Closes the file pointed to by fp & returns 0 on success. EOF is returned in case of error.
Prototype in	:	stdio.h

► fcloseall ►

Prototype	:	int fcloseall(void);
fcloseall	:	Closes all open streams (Except stdin, stdout, stderr, and stdaux). Returns number of streams closed, or EOF in case of error.
Prototype in	:	stdio.h

► fdopen ►

Prototype	:	FILE *fdopen(int handle, char *type);
fdopen	:	A FILE structure is created to for the file referred to by the handle. Returns a pointer to the newly opened stream or NULL in case of error. type is as used in case of fopen.
Prototype in	:	stdio.h

► feof ►

Prototype	:	int feof(FILE *stream);
feof	:	It is a macro to return nonzero if end-of-file has been reached on the stream.
Prototype in	:	stdio.h

► ferror ►

Prototype	:	int ferror(FILE *stream);
ferror	:	This macro returns nonzero if an error has occurred on stream.
Prototype in	:	stdio.h

► fflush ►

Prototype	:	int fflush(FILE *stream);
fflush	:	Flushes the stream (i.e. the internal buffer for the stream is written to disk file). Returns EOF in case of any error.
Prototype in	:	stdio.h

► fgetc/getc ►

Prototype	:	int fgetc(FILE *stream); int getc(FILE *stream);
fgetc / getc	:	Reads a character from stream and returns the same after converting it to an int without sign extension.. EOF is returned on error or when end of file is encountered. fgetc is function version of the macro getc.
Prototype in	:	stdio.h

► fgetchar/getchar ►

Prototype	:	int fgetchar(void);
fgetchar/ getchar	:	These are equivalent to fgetc (stdin) / getc (stdin).
Prototype in	:	stdio.h

► fgetpos ►

Prototype	:	int fgetpos(FILE *stream, fpos_t *pos);
fgetpos	:	Gets the current position of file pointer and stores it in memory pointed to by pos. Returns 0 on success; otherwise nonzero.
Prototype in	:	stdio.h

► fgets ►

Prototype	:	char *fgets(char *s, int n, FILE *stream);
fgets	:	The function fgets gets a string (of size n bytes) from the file pointed to by stream and returns pointer to the target string s on success, or NULL on end-of-file or error.
Prototype in	:	stdio.h

► filelength ►

Prototype	:	long filelength(int handle);
filelength	:	Returns the size of file in bytes. An error is indicated by setting of errno & return value of -1.
Prototype in	:	io.h

► floor ►

Prototype	:	double floor(double x);
floor	:	Returns largest integer not more than x.
Prototype in	:	math.h

► fmod ►

Prototype	:	double fmod(double x, double y);
fmod	:	Returns the remainder of x/y
Prototype in	:	math.h

► FP_OFF, FP_SEG, and MK_FP macros►

Prototypes	:	unsigned FP_OFF(void far *p); unsigned FP_SEG(void far *p); void far *MK_FP(unsigned seg, unsigned ofs);
FP_OFF, FP_SEG, and MK_FP macros	:	These Macros are used to

FP_OFF	:	return offset of the far address argument
FP_SEG	:	return segment of the far address argument
MK_FP	:	return complete far address pointer from the segment & offset given in the argument.

Prototype in	:	dos.h

► _fpreset ►

Prototype	:	void _fpreset(void);
_fpreset	:	The implementation bundled floating-point math package is reinitialised. In case of the exec and spawn system functions child process might alter the parent process's floating-point state & so this function may be required to be used in conjunction with those.
Prototype in	:	float.h

▶ free ▶

Prototype	:	void free(void *block);
free	:	Frees a block allocated earlier with malloc or calloc
Prototype in	:	alloc.h
		stdlib.h

▶ frexp ▶

Prototype	:	double frexp(double x, int *exponent);
frexp	:	Calculates a and n, such that
		$0.5 =< a <1$ and
		$x = a * (2 ** n)$.
		Stores n in the integer pointed to by exponent. Returns a.
Prototype in	:	math.h

▶ fileno ▶

Prototype	:	int fileno(FILE *stream);
fileno	:	This macro returns the file handle associated with the file a stream.
Prototype in	:	stdio.h

▶ findfirst/findnext ▶

Prototype	:	int findfirst(const char *pathname, struct ffblk *ffblk, int attrib);int findnext(struct ffblk *ffblk);
findfirst/	:	Disk & directory given by pathname are searched for the findnext matching filename having attribute specified by attrib. The details are stored in structure ffblk pointed to in argument. findfirst must be used to find first occurance of matching file. findnext uses the same memory area for ffblk as used by findfirst and may be called accordingly to find next occurances. Wildcards (? & *) may be used in file specification. Returns 0 on success; -1 is returned on no match or error in which case errno is set.
Prototype in	:	dir.h

► flushall ►

Prototype	:	int flushall(void);
flushall	:	For all the open streams, buffers are flushed (buffers for input streams are cleared and those for output streams are written to files) and the number of open streams is returned.
Prototype in	:	stdio.h

► fnmerge ►

Prototype	:	void fnmerge(char *path, const char *drive, const char *directory, const char *filename, const char *extension);
fnmerge	:	Using the components given in argument, the full pathname is formed and stored at path as a null terminated string.
Prototype in	:	dir.h

► fnsplit ►

Prototype	:	int fnsplit(const char *path, char *drive, char *directory, char *filename, char *extension);
fnsplit	:	Given path name is used to find out component parts and those are stored at strings pointed to in argument.
Prototype in	:	dir.h

► fopen ►

Prototype	:	FILE *fopen(const char *filename, const char *mode);
fopen	:	Opens the stream filename in the mode mode & if succeeded, Returns a pointer to the newly open stream; or NULL otherwise.
Prototype in	:	stdio.h

► fprintf ►

Prototype	:	int fprintf(FILE *stream, const char *format[,argument,....]);
fprintf	:	Sends formatted output to a stream. Uses the same format specifiers as printf, but sends output to the specified stream. Returns the number of bytes output or EOF in case of error.

Prototype in   :   stdio.h

▶ fputc/putc ▶

Prototype	:	int fputc(int c, FILE *stream); int putc(int c, FILE *stream);
fputc/putc	:	The character c is output to stream & returns the same on success, or EOF on error. fputc is the function version of putc macro.
Prototype in	:	stdio.h

▶ fputchar/putchar ▶

Prototype	:	int fputchar(int c); int putchar(int c);
fputchar/	:	These are same as fputc /putc except that the stream is implicit putchar to be stdout. fputchar is the function version of putchar macro.
Prototype in	:	stdio.h

▶ fputs/puts ▶

Prototype	:	int fputs(const char *s, FILE *stream);
fputs/puts	:	The string s is output to stream (In case of fputs) or stdout (In case of puts).
Prototype in	:	stdio.h

▶ fread ▶

Prototype	:	size_t fread(void *ptr, size_t size, size_t n, FILE *stream);
fread	:	Reads n items of size bytes each from the stream and stores in memory pointed to by ptr. Returns the number of items (not bytes) actually read.
Prototype in	:	stdio.h

▶ freemem ▶

Prototype	:	int freemem(unsigned segx);

freemem   :   Frees a DOS memory block previously allocated with allocmem at address seg:offset = segx:0000.Returns 0 on success. On failure, errno is set & -1 returned.

Prototype in   :   dos.h

► freopen ►

Prototype   :   FILE *freopen(const char *pname, const char *mode, FILE *oldstream);

freopen   :   Associates a new file with an open stream pointed to by oldstream. The oldstream is closed. The file named by pname is opened in mode given as mode and is associated with oldstream. Returns oldstream on success, or NULL on failure.

Prototype in   :   stdio.h

► fscanf ►

Prototype   :   int fscanf(FILE *strinp, const char *format[, address,...]);

fscanf   :   Performs formatted input from the stream strinp, converts as per format and stores at the addresses given in argument. format is as explained before discussions regarding fprintf. Returns the number of input fields successfully scanned, converted, and stored. Return value doesn't include unstored scanned fields.

Prototype in   :   stdio.h

► fseek ►

Prototype   :   int fseek(FILE *stream, long offset, int whence);

fseek   :   The file pointer for the stream is positioned at offset number of bytes calculated from the position specified by whence. offset may be zero, negative, or positive. The defined symbols SEEK_CUR, SEEK_SET, & SEEK_END are used as whwnce specifiers to indicate current position, BOF & EOF respectively. Returns 0 if successful or nonzero on failure.

Prototype in   :   stdio.h

► fsetpos ►

Prototype	:	int fsetpos(FILE *fp, const fpos_t *pos);
fsetpos	:	Positions the position marker (file pointer) of file pointed to by fp to the new position pointed to by pos which is of the type returned by call to fgetpos. Returns 0 on success, nonzero otherwise.
Prototype in	:	stdio.h

► fstat ►

Prototype	:	int fstat(int handle, struct stat *statbuf);
fstat	:	Gets information regarding the open file whose handle is passed to it. Stores information in statbuf in the structure defined as stat. Returns 0 on success while -1 is returned and errno is set on error.
Prototype in	:	stat.h

► ftell ►

Prototype	:	long ftell(FILE *stream);
ftell	:	Returns the current file pointer position on success or -1L on error.
Prototype in	:	stdio.h

► ftime ►

Prototype	:	void ftime(struct timeb *buf);
ftime	:	Current system time is stored by this function in the structure timeb at buf. The timeb structure contains time as a count of seconds since January 1, 1970. A separate milliseconds field is also there. The local time zone and a flag for daylight savings flag are also stored.
Prototype in	:	timeb.h

► fwrite ►

Prototype	:	size_t fwrite(const void *ptr, size_t size, size_t n, FILE*stream);

fwrite	:	Writes n items of size bytes from memory pointed to by ptr to file pointed to by stream. Returns the number of items (each of size bytes) actually written.
Prototype in	:	stdio.h

► getw ►

Prototype	:	int getw(FILE *stream);
getw	:	Gets integer from stream and returns the same. Returns EOF on both end-of-file or error. feof or ferror may have to be used to find out exact reason of return value = EOF.
Prototype in	:	stdio.h

► gcvt ►

Prototype	:	char *gcvt(double value, int ndec, char *buf);
gcvt	:	Converts given floating-point number, value, to a string of corresponding value with ndec no. of places after dec. point, stores at buf and returns the address of the string pointed to by buf. value can also be supplied in scientific notation.
Prototype in	:	stdlib.h

► geninterrupt ►

Prototype	:	void geninterrupt(int intr_num);
geninterrupt	:	This is a macro which generates a software interrupt.
Prototype in	:	dos.h

► getcbrk ►

Prototype	:	int getcbrk(void);
getcbrk	:	Checks for active control-break setting. Returns 0 if control-break checking is off (program will check for Ctrl-Break only on console, printer, and communications I/O calls); and 1 if checking is on (program will check for pressing of ctrl-break key on every system call).

Prototype in   :   dos.h

▶ getch/getche ▶

Prototype	:	int getch(void); int getche(void);
getch/getche	:	Gets a character from console, with echoing to screen in case of getche, or without echoing in case of getch. Both functions return the character read. Buffering of whole lines is not done.
		It may be noted that the Special keys such as function keys and arrow keys are represented by a two-character sequence (a zero character as ASCII code followed by the scan code for the particular key pressed); so the program using these functions should take care for reinvoking the function in case zero is read in.
Prototype in	:	conio.h

▶ getcurdir ▶

Prototype	:	int getcurdir(int drive, char *directory);
getcurdir	:	Current directory for specified drive is stored in **array** directory. Drive is denoted as 0 for the default drive, A=1, B=2 & so on. Returns 0 on success; -1 on error.
Prototype in	:	dir.h

▶ getcwd ▶

Prototype	:	char *getcwd(char *buf, int buflen);
getcwd	:	Finds out current working directory, stores it in buf as an array and size of array in buflen. Returns a pointer to buf. On error, errno is set & NULL is returned.
Prototype in	:	dir.h

▶ getdate/gettime ▶

Prototypes	:	void getdate(struct date *datep); void gettime(struct time *timep);
getdate/gettime	:	Gets system date / time and stores at specified memory in struct date / time.

Prototype in	:	dos.h

► getdfree ►

Prototype	:	void getdfree(unsigned char dr,struct dfree*dtbl);
getdfree	:	Gets free space on disk specified as dr (A = 1) and stores the data in struct dfree at memory pointed to by dtbl. In case of error, df_sclus in the dfree structure is set to 0xFFFF.
Prototype in	:	dos.h

► getdisk ►

Prototype	:	int getdisk(void);
getdisk	:	Returns the current drive as an int where Drive A=0, B=1 etc.
Prototype in	:	dir.h

► getdta ►

Prototype	:	char far *getdta(void);
getdta	:	Gets address of current disk transfer area & returns a pointer to it.
Prototype in	:	dos.h

► getenv ►

Prototype	:	char *getenv(const char *name);
getenv	:	Gets string defining name from the environment. Returns a pointer to the value associated with name or NULL if the name is not defined in the environment.
Prototype in	:	stdlib.h

► getfat/getfatd ►

Prototype	:	void getfat(unsigned char drive,struct fat info *dtable);
getfat/getfatd	:	Stores the FAT information for given drive (A =1), or current drive in case of getfatd, in the structure fatinfo.
Prototype in	:	dos.h

▶ getftime ▶

Prototype	:	int getftime(int handle, struct ftime *fdtp);
gettime	:	The date and time of file specified by handle is stored in struct ftime & 0 is returned on success. Otherwise -1 is returned and errno is set. **Prototype** is also declared in io.h, But ftime is not defined in dos.h. So to use it io.h should be #includeD.
Prototype in	:	dos.h

▶ getpass ▶

Prototype	:	char *getpass(const char *prompt);
getpass	:	Displays the prompt string and then reads the password without echoing. Returns a pointer to a static string containing the input password.
Prototype in	:	conio.h

▶ getpsp ▶

Prototype	:	unsigned getpsp(void);
getpsp	:	Returns the program segment prefix address.
Prototype in	:	dos.h

▶ gets ▶

Prototype	:	char *gets(char *s);
gets	:	gets is fgets with file = stdin. It gets a string from stdin. In contrast to fgets, n is not specified because gets goes on taking input from stdin until it finds a newline character.
Prototype in	:	stdio.h

▶ gettext ▶

Prototype	:	int gettext(int left, int top, int right, int, void *destin);
gettext	:	The text is copied from text-mode screen to memory at the address destin. Returns nonzero on success. Coordinates give the boundry on the screen from within which the text is to be copied.

Prototype in   :   conio.h

► gettextinfo ►

Prototype	:	void gettextinfo(struct text_info *r);
gettextinfo	:	Gets text-mode video information and stores results in struct text_info pointed to by r.
Prototype in	:	conio.h

► getvect ►

Prototype	:	void interrupt (*getvect(int interrupno))();
getvect	:	Gets the interrupt vector for interrupno and returns the 4-byte value as a pointer to a function of interrupt type returning nothing (void).
Prototype in	:	dos.h

► getverify ►

Prototype	:	int getverify(void);
getverify	:	Returns 1 if the verify flag is on (system verifies the correctness of each disk write operation after writing). 0 is returned otherwise.
Prototype in	:	dos.h

► gmtime ►

Prototype	:	struct tm *gmtime(const time_t *timer);
gmtime	:	Converts date and time to Greenwich Mean Time and returns a pointer to the broken-down time structure,which is overwritten with each call to gmtime.
Prototype in	:	time.h

► gotoxy ►

Prototype	:	void gotoxy(int x, int y);
gotoxy	:	Positions cursor in text window to column x of row y.
Prototype in	:	conio.h

► harderr ►

Prototype	:	void harderr(int (*crhand)());
harderr	:	When DOS encounters a critical error (INT 0x24), it enters the system defined critical error handler i.e. the ISR for INT 24h. This function establishes another function (returning int & pointed to by crhand) that will be called instead of the system defined critical error handler.
Prototype in	:	dos.h

► hardresume ►

Prototype	:	void hardresume(int axret);
hardresume	:	If the error handler (established by harderr) needs to return control to the DOS routine which caused the critical error; this function can be used. The value axret will be returned to DOS routine through AX register as the return value of critical error handler. It may be noted that the meanings of return values are interprated by DOS as :0,1,2 = ignore, retry, abort respectively.
Prototype in	:	dos.h

► hardretn ►

Prototype	:	void hardretn(int retn);
hardretn	:	If the error handler (established by harderr) needs to return control to the Application program directly instead of the DOS routine (called by application) which caused the critical error; this function can be used. The value retn will be returned to the Application instead of the normal return value of the DOS routine which caused the critical error.
Prototype in	:	dos.h

►heapcheck, heapcheckfree, heapchecknode and heapwalk►

All these functions are analogous to their far counterparts (viz. farheapcheck) except that

1. These work on near heaps in tiny / small data models

2. These map to their far counterparts in large models.

Prototype in   :   alloc.h

► highvideo ►

Prototype	:	void highvideo(void);
highvideo	:	Subsequent calls to text functions (viz.putch and cprintf) result in display of text in high-intensity.
Prototype in	:	conio.h

► hypot ►

Prototype	:	double hypot(double b, double p);
hypot	:	Returns hypotenuse of right triangle having base = b and perpendicular = p.
Prototype in	:	math.h

► ldexp ►

Prototype	:	double ldexp(double m, int exp);
ldexp	:	It is reverse of frexp. It calculates m * (2 ** exp) and returns the value.
Prototype in	:	math.h

► inp ►

Prototype	:	int inp(int portid);
inp	:	This is a macro to read a byte from hardware port portid and returns the same as an int.
Prototype in	:	dos.h

► inportb ►

Prototype	:	unsigned char inportb (int portid);
inportb	:	This is a true function to read a byte from hardware port portid and returns the same as an unsigned char.
Prototype in	:	dos.h

► insline ►

Prototype	:	void insline(void);
insline	:	A blank line is inserted in text window at the current cursor position — thereby shifting down the lines below the cursor position and the causing loss of last line.
Prototype in	:	conio.h

► int86 ►

Prototype	:	int int86 (int intno, union REGS *inr, union REGS *outr);
int86	:	CPU registers are loaded with the values stored in inr and the software interrupt intno is issued. The resulting CPU register values after execution of interrupt are stored in outr.
Prototype in	:	dos.h

► int86x ►

Prototype	:	int int86x (int intno, union REGS *inregs, union REGS *outregs, struct SREGS *segregs);
int86x	:	CPU registers are loaded with the values stored in inregs and segregs then the software interrupt intno is issued and the resulting CPU register values after execution of interrupt are stored in outregs & segregs. Please note that software interrupts using segment registers of CPU can be accessed by int86x but not int86 function.
Prototype in	:	dos.h

► intdos ►

Prototype	:	int intdos(union REGS *in, union REGS *out);
intdos	:	It is int86 with intno = 21h (33).
Prototype in	:	dos.h

► intdosx ►

Prototype	:	int intdosx(union REGS *inregs, union REGS *outregs, struct SREGS *segregs);

intosx	:	It is int86x with intno = 21h (33).
Prototype in	:	dos.h

▶ intr ▶

Prototype	:	void intr(int intno, struct REGPACK *preg);
intr	:	It is an alternate 8086 software interrupt interface which loads the CPU registers with the values stored in preg, then issues the interrupt intno, and finally stores the resulting CPU register values in back in preg.
Prototype in	:	dos.h

▶ ioctl ▶

Prototype	:	int ioctl(int handle, int func [, void *argdx, int argcx]);
ioctl	:	It provides communication between the Application & Device driver using DOS INT 21H, Service 44H (IOCTL Call). The func is the Subfunction no. of IOCTL call, handle is device/file handle no. & argdx/ argcx are the values to be loaded in CPU registers DX/CX before requesting DOS system call. Although efficient use of this function calls for in-depth understanding of DOS device drivers, a general level detail follows :

func = 0 / 1

used to get /set the device information word (in case of func=1 the word to be set is the argdx, while in func 0 argdx may be 0). The value in DX of the IOCTL call is returned.

The device information word is made /interpreted as below:
For file — Bits 0-5 :Drive no. (A=0),
Bit 6: 0 if file was written
Bit 7: 0 Bits 8-15: Insignificant
For Device — Bit 0 : 1 if stdin, Bit 1 : 1 if stdout
Bit 2 : 1 if NUL device, Bit 3 : 1 if clock
Bit 5 : 0 if ASCII 1 if binary, Bit 6 : 0 if eof input
Bit 7 : 1, Bit 14: 1 if func 2 & 3 supported else 0
Other bits are insignificant.

func 2 & 3

Used to get (func 2) or request (func 3) hardware dependent status and availability information /operation from the character device driver provided that the driver supports these functions. argcx holds the no. of bytes to be read from /written to control channel of device data into / from the buffer pointed to by argdx. Return value is the no. of bytes actually transferred.

func 4 & 5 : Exactly similar to 2 & 3, but for Block device.

func 6 & 7 : Return the device status for Input/Output.

func 8 : Returns 0 if requested handle is for removable drive. argdx & argcx are insignificant. Handle is 0=Default drive, 1=A etc.errno is set & -1 is returned in all the function if error occurs.

Prototype in : io.h

► is* ►

Prototype : Following is the macro names/prototypes and the condition when macro test evaluates to true.

isalnum(c)	if c is a letter or digit
isalpha(c)	if c is a letter
isdigit(c)	if c is a digit
iscntrl(c)	if c is an ordinary control character
isascii(c)	if c is a valid ASCII character
isprint(c)	if c is a printable character
isgraph(c)	if c is a printable non space character
islower(c)	if c is in lowercase
isupper(c)	if c is in uppercase
ispunct(c)	if c is a punctuation character
isspace(c)	if c is a whitespace

i.e. space, tab, carriage return, newline, vertical tab, or form-feed

isxdigit(c)	if c is a hexadecimal digit
is* :	character classification macros

Prototype in : ctype.h

▶ isatty ▶

Prototype	:	int isatty(int handle);
isatty	:	The type of device associated with handle is checked and a nonzero integer is returned If the device is a character device.
Prototype in	:	io.h

▶ itoa ▶

Prototype	:	char *itoa(int value, char *string, int radix);
itoa	:	Pl. see ultoa/ ltoa. This converts an integer to string. Returns a pointer to the target string.
Prototype in	:	stdlib.h

▶ kbhit ▶

Prototype	:	int kbhit(void);
kbhit	:	Checks for available keystroke waiting to be read. If a keystroke is available(key has been pressed), kbhit returns a nonzero integer; otherwise returns 0.
Prototype in	:	conio.h

▶ keep ▶

Prototype	:	void keep(unsigned char status, unsigned size);
keep	:	This function causes exit from the program returning status to DOS as the exit value, and size paragraphs of the program from begining is put resident in memory (a TSR behaviour).
Prototype in	:	dos.h

▶ lfind or lsearch ▶

Prototypes	:	void *lfind(const void *key, const void *base, size_t *nelem, size_t width, int (*fcmp)(const void *, const void*));
		void *lsearch(const void *key, void *base, size_t *nelem, size_t width, int (*fcmp)(const void *, const void*));

lfind or lsearch : These functions use linear search algorithm in an array of sequential records & return the address of the first entry in the table that matches the search key. If no match is found, lsearch appends it to the list; while lfind returns 0. key is pointer to search key, base is the start address of table, width is size of each element and nelem points to number of elements in the table. The function fcmp has to be designed so that its return value is as in bsearch.

Prototype in : stdlib.h

► localeconv ►

Prototype : struct lconv *localeconv(void);

localeconv : The country-specific monetary and other numeric formats are set up form the current locale structure lconv; a pointer to which is returned.

Prototype in : locale.h

► localtime ►

Prototype : struct tm *localtime(const time_t *timer);

localtime : Converts date and time (type time_t) to structure tm and returns the tm structure, which is overwritten with each call.

Prototype in : time.h

► lock ►

Prototype : int lock(int handle, long offset, long length);

lock : The file-sharing (concurrent file access) is locked, thereby preventing read /write access (in the file associated with handle) by another program to the region starting at the address offset for length bytes. Returns 0 on success, -1 on error.

Prototype in : io.h

► log ►

Prototype : double log(double x);

log	:	Returns the natural Logarithm of x i.e. ln(x).
Prototype in	:	math.h

▶ log10 ▶

Prototype	:	double log10(double x);
log10	:	Returns the Logarithm of x at base 10 i.e. log(x).
Prototype in	:	math.h

▶ longjmp ▶

Prototype	:	void longjmp(jmp_buf jmpbuf, int retval);
longjmp	:	Non local jump is performed. Control is transferred to the statement where the call to setjmp was made. Execution continues at this point assuming setjmp to have returned the value passed as retval. setjmp initialises the jmpbuf. longjmp cannot return the value 0; if 0 is passed in retval, longjmp will return 1.
Prototype in	:	setjump.h

▶ lowvideo ▶

Prototype	:	void lowvideo(void);
lowvideo	:	Subsequent calls to text functions (viz.putch and cprintf) result in display of text in low-intensity.
Prototype in	:	conio.h

▶ _lrotl, _lrotr, _rotl and _rotr ▶

Prototypes	:	unsigned long _lrotr(unsigned long val, int count); unsigned long _lrotl(unsigned long val, int count);unsigned _rotl(unsigned val, int count); unsigned _rotr(unsigned val, int count);
_lrotl, _lrotr, _rotl and _rotr	:	Both these functions return the value of val rotated by count bits to left (_lrotl /_rotl) or right (_lrotr / _rotr).
Prototype in	:	stdlib.h

► lseek ►

Prototype	:	long lseek(int handle, long xbytes, int frompos);
lseek	:	The read/write file pointer for the file associated with handle is moved xbytes bytes calculated from the position frompos. xbytes may be a negative no. too and frompos is SEEK_CUR, SEEK_SET, or SEEK_END (current position, BOF, or EOF). The new file position (no. of bytes from BOF) is returned on success, while errno is set & -1L is returned on error.
Prototype in	:	io.h

► ltoa/ultoa ►

Prototype	:	char *ultoa(unsigned long value,char *string, int radix);char *ltoa(long value, char *string, int radix);
ltoa or ultoa	:	ultoa/ ltoa converts an unsigned long /long to a string. Returns a pointer to string. There is no error return. In decimal representation, radix=10. For hexadecimal, radix=16.
Prototype in	:	stdlib.h

► malloc ►

Prototype	:	void *malloc(size_t size);
malloc	:	allocates main memory
Prototype in	:	alloc.h and stdlib.h

► matherr ►

Prototype	:	int matherr(struct exception *excp);
matherr	:	Math library has its own error handler. This function provides a hook into that error handler so that the handling of errors detected by the math library may be controlled. The function matherr may be coded for that purpose.It can also be made to modify the excp->retval to control the return value returned by the function which generated error to its caller. matherr should be coded such as to return nonzero to indicate that the problem has been resolved; otherwise it should return 0.

Prototype in	:	math.h

► max/min ►

Prototypes	:	max(a,b); min(a,b);
max/min	:	These macros find the maximum/minimum value of a&b
Prototype in	:	stdlib.h

► memccpy ►

Prototype	:	void *memccpy(void *dest, const void *src, int c, size_tn);
memccpy	:	Copies a block of atmost n bytes from src to dest. This function stops after copying a byte that matches c and returns a pointer to the byte in dest immediately following c; otherwise it returns NULL.
Prototype in	:	mem.h

► memchr ►

Prototype	:	void *memchr(const void *s, int c, size_t n);
memchr	:	Searches the first n bytes of array s for character c and returns a pointer to the first occurrence of c in s. If c does not occur in array s; NULL is returned.
Prototype in	:	mem.h

► memcmp/memicmp ►

Prototype	:	int memcmp (const void *s1, const void *s2, size_t n); int memicmp(const void *s1, const void *s2, size_t n);
memcmp/ memicmp	:	A length of exactly n bytes of two strings, s1 and s2, are compared and a value LESS THAN, EQUAL TO or GREATER THAN 0 is returned respectively in cases of s1 < s2, s1 = s2 or s1 > s2 as per the byte by byte comparison. Note that memicmp ignores case of characters in the two strings.
Prototype in	:	mem.h

► memcpy ►

Prototype	:	void *memcpy (void *dest, const void *src, size_t n);
memcpy	:	n bytes are copied from src to dest and dest is returned.
Prototype in	:	mem.h

► memmove ►

Prototype	:	void *memcpy (void *dest, const void *src, size_t n);
memmove	:	n bytes are copied from src to dest and dest is returned.
Prototype in	:	mem.h

► memset ►

Prototype	:	void *memset(void *s, int c, size_t n);
memset	:	n bytes of s are set to byte c and returns s.
Prototype in	:	mem.h

► mkdir ►

Prototype	:	int mkdir(const char *path);
mkdir	:	The directory specified by path is created & 0 is returned on success. errno is set and -1 returned on error.
Prototype in	:	dir.h

► mktemp ►

Prototype	:	char *mktemp(char *template);
mktemp	:	Directory is scanned and a unique filename matching the template is created & stored at the string template whose address is returned.
Prototype in	:	dir.h

► modf ►

Prototype	:	double modf(double x, double *integerprt);
modf	:	The integer and fraction parts of the argument x are separated.The integer part is stored in memory pointed to by integerprt and the fraction is returned.

Prototype in : math.h

▶ movedata ▶

Prototype : void movedata(unsigned srcseg, unsigned srcoff, unsigned destseg, unsigned destoff, size_t n);

movedata : Copies n bytes from sreseg:srcoff to destseg:destoff.

Prototype in : mem.h

▶ movetext ▶

Prototype : int movetext(int left, int top, int right, int bottom, int destleft, int desttop);

movetext : Text is copied from one rectangle to another on the text mode screen. Source rectangle is defined by the coordinates left, right, top & bottom while destination is given by its top left point through destleft & desttop. Returns nonzero on success.

Prototype in : conio.h

▶ movmem ▶

Prototype : void movmem(void *src, void *dest, unsigned length);

movmem : Moves a block of length bytes from src to dest where both are in same segment.

Prototype in : mem.h

▶ normvideo ▶

Prototype : void normvideo(void);

normvideo : Subsequent calls to text functions (viz.putch and cprintf) result in display of text in normal intensity.

Prototype in : conio.h

▶ nosound ▶

Prototype : void nosound(void);

nosound : Turns off the speaker of the PC. When speaker is made on by a function; it needs to be made off by this function.

Prototype in : dos.h

▶ open ▶

Prototype : int open(const char *path, int access [,unsigned mode]);

open : opens a file for reading or writing.

Prototype in : io.h

▶ outp/outportb/outport ▶

Prototypes : int outp(int portid,int byte_value); void outportb(int portid, unsigned char value); void outport(int portid, int value);

outp/outportb/ : outp is a macro while outportb is a function. Both output outport (write) a byte given as value to the hardware port no. portid. outport writes a word rather than a byte to port.

Prototype in : dos.h

▶ parsfnm ▶

Prototype : char *parsfnm (const char *cmd,struct fcb *f, int opt);

parsfnm : Parses the filename pointed to by cmd and builds a File Control Block (FCB) for the same. opt is the value determining the method of parsfname working.

opt	significance
1	Leading separators to be scanned off the cmd
2	If cmd does not have explicit drive specifier assume no change in previous drive specifier of the FCB
4	If cmd does not have explicit filename specifier assume no change in previous filename member of the FCB
8	If cmd does not have explicit extension specifier assume no change in previous extension member of the FCB

On successfull parsing, parsfnm returns a pointer to the next byte after the end of the file name. 0 is returned on error.

Prototype in : dos.h

► peek ►

Prototype	:	int peek(unsigned segment, unsigned offset);
peek	:	Reads a word begining from the memory location specified by address segment:offset and returns the same as an int.
Prototype in	:	dos.h

► peekb ►

Prototype	:	char peekb(unsigned segment, unsigned offset);
peekb	:	Reads a single byte from memory location specified by address segment:offset and returns the same as a char.
Prototype in	:	dos.h

► perror ►

Prototype	:	void perror(const char *s);
perror	:	Prints modified version of system error message to stderr. First the argument string is printed followed by a colon & then a message corresponding to the current value of errno is printed. The newline character is added at end.
Prototype in	:	stdio.h

► poke/pokeb ►

Prototypes	:	void poke(unsigned seg, unsigned off, int val); void pokeb(unsigned seg, unsigned off, char val);
poke/pokeb	:	poke (pokeb) write a word (byte) begining from (at) the memory location specified by address seg:off.
Prototype in	:	dos.h

► poly ►

Prototype	:	double poly(double x, int dgri,double coeff[]);
poly	:	Generates a polynomial in x, of degree dgri and with coefficients given by array coeff. Returns the value of the polynomial at given value of x.
Prototype in	:	math.h

► pow ►

Prototype	:	double pow(double x, double y);
pow	:	Returns x raised to power y.
Prototype in	:	math.h

► pow10 ►

Prototype	:	double pow10(int n);
pow10	:	Returns value of 10 raised to the power n.
Prototype in	:	math.h

► printf ►

Prototype	:	int printf(const char *format [, argument,...]);
printf	:	It is equivalent to call to the function printf(stdout, const char *format[, argument,...]); and is used for formatted output to the standard output.
Prototype in	:	stdio.h

► putch ►

Prototype	:	int putch(int ch);
putch	:	The int ch is output to the text window on the screen as a character in the current display attribute. Returns c if the character is displayed & EOF On error.
Prototype in	:	conio.h

► putenv ►

Prototype	:	int putenv(const char *name);
putenv	:	Adds string name to current environment & returns 0 on success, -1 on failure.
Prototype in	:	stdlib.h

► puttext ►

Prototype	:	int puttext(int left, int top, int right, int bottom, void *source); puttext : The text is copied to text-mode screen

from memory at the address source. Returns nonzero on success. Coordinates give the boundry on the screen within which the text is to be copied.

Prototype in : conio.h

▶ putw ▶

Prototype : int putw(int w, FILE *stream);

putw : Outputs integer w to stream and returns the integer w. On error, returns EOF.

Prototype in : stdio.h

▶ qsort ▶

Prototype : void qsort(void *base, size_t nelem, size_t width, int(*fcmp)(const void *, const void *));

qsort : Parameters mean same as bsearch. fcmp also same as in bsearch. Sorts the table using the quicksort algorithm.

Prototype in : stdlib.h

▶ raise ▶

Prototype : int raise(int sigint);

raise : The default handler (or the one installed by signal) for the signal type sigint, is executed. Signal types for sigint (viz. SIGFPE)are defined in signal.h. It can also be used by a program to send signals to itself. Returns 0 on success.

Prototype in : signal.h

▶ rand ▶

Prototype : int rand(void);

rand : Returns random numbers from 0 to RAND_MAX.

Prototype in : stdlib.h

▶ randbrd ▶

Prototype : int randbrd(struct fcb *fcb, int rcnt);

randbrd	:	rcnt number of records are tried to be read from the file specified in the FCB and read records are copied in the DTA. The int returned may have the following values and are interpreted as below to indicate the result of operation:

0	All records could be read
1	End-of-file; last record read completely
2	Not enough space in DTA to read all records
3	End-of-file; last record read is incomplete

Prototype in   :   dos.h

► randbwr ►

Prototype   :   int randbwr(struct fcb *fcb, int rcnt);

randbwr   :   rcnt number of records are tried to be written to the file specified in the FCB from the records available in the DTA. The int returned may have the following values and are interprated as below to indicate the result of operation :

0	All records are written
1	Insufficient disk space
2	Insufficient DTA space

Prototype in   :   dos.h

► random ►

Prototype   :   int random(int num);

random   :   This is a macro that returns a random integer between 0 and (num-1).

Prototype in   :   stdlib.h

► randomize ►

Prototype   :   randomize(); / void randomize(void);

randomize   :   Initializes the random number generator with a random value. It uses the time function, so you should include time.h when using this routine.

Prototype in   :   stdlib.h

► read ►

Prototype	:	int read(int handle, void *buf, unsigned len);
read	:	Reads len bytes from file associated with handle & stores the bytes in buffer pointed to by buf. On success, the count of bytes placed in the buffer (excluding carriage returns or Ctrl-Z characters, if the file was opened in text mode) is returned. On error, it returns -1 and sets errno.
Prototype in	:	io.h

► _read ►

Prototype	:	int _read(int handle, void *buf, unsigned len);
_read	:	Same as read().
Prototype in	:	io.h

► realloc ►

Prototype	:	void *realloc(void *block, size_t size);
realloc	:	allocates main memory
Prototype in	:	alloc.h and stdlib.h

► remove ►

Prototype	:	int remove(const char *filename);
remove	:	This macro removes the file whose name is passed as the argument to it by using a call to unlink. Returns 0 on success. On error, -1 is returned and errno is set.
Prototype in	:	stdio.h

► rename ►

Prototype	:	int rename(const char *old, const char *newname);
rename	:	Renames file old to newname. Returns 0 on success & on error, it returns -1 besides setting errno.
Prototype in	:	stdio.h

▶ rewind ▶

Prototype	:	void rewind(FILE *stream);
rewind	:	The file pointer is positioned to stream's beginning.
Prototype in	:	stdio.h

▶ rmdir ▶

Prototype	:	int rmdir(const char *path);
rmdir	:	The directory specified by path is removed & 0 is returned on success. errno is set and -1 returned on error.
Prototype in	:	dir.h

▶ sbrk ▶

Prototype	:	void *sbrk(int increment);
sbrk	:	Adds increment bytes to the break value; thereby changing the top of data segment space allocation to increment bytes higher.Old break value is returned by sbrk on success, while failure is indicated by -1 being the return value and errno set. Comparison with brk is suggested for a better grasp.
Prototype in	:	alloc.h

▶ scanf ▶

Prototype	:	int scanf(const char *format [,...]);
scanf	:	It is equivalent to call to the functionfscanf(stdin, const char *format[,address,...]); and is used for formatted input from the standard input. Returns the number of inputs processed successfully. It processes input according to the format and places the results in the memory locations pointed to by the arguments.
Prototype in	:	stdio.h

▶ searchpath ▶

Prototype	:	char *searchpath(const char *file);
searchpath	:	Returns a pointer to a string having the complete path of file. On failure NULL is returned.

Prototype in   :   dir.h

► segread ►

| Prototype | : | void segread(struct SREGS *segp); |
| segread | : | Values in the CPU segment registers are read and stored in the structure pointed to by segp. |

Prototype in   :   dos.h

► setblock ►

| Prototype | : | int setblock(unsigned segx,unsigned nsiz); |
| setblock | : | The size of memory block previously allocated at segment segx is adjusted to the new size of nsiz paragraphs.Returns -1 on success while on failure,_doserrno is set and size of the largest possible block is returned. |

Prototype in   :   dos.h

► setbuf ►

| Prototype | : | void setbuf(FILE *stream, char *buf); |
| setbuf | : | Assigns buffering to stream and sets buf as pointer to start of buffer for the stream. If buf is NULL, I/O for the file will be unbuffered; otherwise, it is buffered. The buffer will be BUFSIZ bytes long. |

Prototype in   :   stdio.h

► setcbrk ►

| Prototype | : | int setcbrk(int cvalue); |
| setcbrk | : | The control-break setting is made on / off depending upon whether cvalue is 1 / 0. cvalue is returned. If cvalue is 1, Ctrl-Break is checked on every system call. If it is 0, checking done only on console, printer, and communications I/O calls. |

Prototype in   :   dos.h

► setvbuf ►

Prototype	:	int setvbuf(FILE *stream, char *buf, int type, size_t size);
setvbuf	:	It is similar to setbuf except that type & size of assigned buffer is controllable. size is the buffer size in bytes. Returns 0 on success; otherwise nonzero.
Prototype in	:	stdio.h

► _setcursortype ►

Prototype	:	void _setcursortype(int cur_t);
_setcursortype	:	Appearance of cursor is on the screen is selected as per cur_t. Values of cur_t can be _NOCURSOR, _SOLIDCURSOR or _NORMALCURSOR to get the cursor turned off, appear as a solid block or as the normal underscore respectively.
Prototype in	:	conio.h

► setdate ►

Prototype	:	void setdate(struct date *datep);
setdate	:	System date is set to the parameter passed.
Prototype in	:	dos.h

► setdisk ►

Prototype	:	int setdisk(int drive);
setdisk	:	Current disk drive is set to specified drive where 0 = A, 1 = B & so on. Returns the total number of drives available on system.
Prototype in	:	dir.h

► setdta ►

Prototype	:	void setdta(char far *newdta);
setdta	:	The default disk-transfer area is changed to the memory area pointed to by newdta.
Prototype in	:	dos.h

► setftime ►

Prototype	:	int setftime(int handle, struct ftime *ftimep);
setftime	:	The date/time stamp of given file is set to the value stored in structure pointed to by ftimep. Returns 0 on success; otherwise -1.
Prototype in	:	io.h

► setjmp ►

Prototype	:	int setjmp(jmp_buf jmpb);
setjmp	:	Non local jump is Set up. setjmp initialises the jmpbuf and stores relevant information (register values and flag status) in it to enable lomgjmp to return control to the statement following setjmp. Returns 0 when it is initially called.
Prototype in	:	setjump.h

► setlocale ►

Prototype	:	char *setlocale(int catcode, char *locode);
setlocale	:	If supported by the implementation, this function selects a locale from the implementation defined character code locode. Those country dependent expression formats which fall within the category catcode, are modified to match the selected locale. catcode may be any of the defined categories viz. LC_MONETARY, LC_NUMERIC, LC_TIME, LC_COLLATE, LC_CTYPE or LC_ALL.
Prototype in	:	locale.h

► setmem ►

Prototype	:	void setmem(void *dest, int length,char value);
setmem	:	The char (byte) value is filled in length byte long range of memory starting from address pointed to by dest.
Prototype in	:	mem.h

► setmode ►

Prototype	:	int setmode(int handle, int amode);

| setmode | : | Sets mode of an open file to amode & returns 0 on success; otherwise -1. amode is as defined oflags in fcntl.h. |
| Prototype in | : | io.h |

► settime ►

Prototype	:	void settime(struct time *tp);
settime	:	System time is set to the parameter passed.
Prototype in	:	dos.h

► setvect ►

Prototype	:	void setvect(int intno, void interrupt (*isr) ());
setvect	:	The vector entry in the system table for interrupt no. intno is set to the pointer to a function isr. isr will be called when interrupt number intno occurs. It may be noted that a C function intended to serve as an ISR (Interrupt Service Routine) needs to be defined with the keyword interrupt.
Prototype in	:	dos.h

► setverify ►

Prototype	:	void setverify(int value);
setverify	:	Verify state is set to value. Verify state =1 means that a read operation should follow every disk write operation to insure correctness of latter. 0 means that reading after each write will not be done.
Prototype in	:	dos.h

► signal ►

Prototype	:	void (*signal(int sig, void (*func)int sig[,int subcode])))(int);
signal	:	The signal-handling actions are specified by it. Signals are raised by calling raise or when an exception condition occurs. When a signal of type sig is raised, the function pointed to by func will be called.
Prototype in	:	signal.h

► sin ►

Prototype	:	double sin(double x);
sin	:	Returns requested trigonometric ratio of the angle x where x is in radians.
Prototype in	:	math.h

► sinh ►

Prototype	:	double sinh(double x);
sinh	:	Returns requested trigonometric ratio of the angle x where x is in radians.
Prototype in	:	math.h

► sleep ►

Prototype	:	void sleep(unsigned timecount);
sleep	:	Suspends execution for an interval of timecount seconds. It is as if computer system is sleeping for that interval.
Prototype in	:	dos.h

► sopen ►

Prototype	:	sopen(char *path, int access, int shflag, int mode);
sopen	:	This is not a true function but a macro which opens a file given by path in the shared mode. access is as defined in fcntl.h, mode is as in sys/stat.h and sharing flags as in share.h are used for shflag — these determine the actual mode/status of opened file.
Prototype in	:	io.h

► sound ►

Prototype	:	void sound(unsigned frequency);
sound	:	The speaker of the PC is turned on to emit sound at the specified frequency (in Hertz).
Prototype in	:	dos.h

► spawn...functions ►

Prototypes	:	int spawnl (int mode, char *path, char *arg0,..., NULL);
		int spawnle(int mode, char *path,char *arg0,..., NULL, char*envp[]);
		int spawnlp (int mode, char *path, char *arg0,..., NULL);
		int spawnlpe(int mode, char *path, char*arg0,..., NULL, char*envp[]);
		int spawnv(int mode, char *path, char *argv[]);
		int spawnve(int mode, char *path,char *argv[], char *envp[]); int spawnvp(int mode, char *path,char *argv[]);
		int spawnvpe(int mode, char *path,char *argv[], char *envp[]);

spawn...functions : functions that create and run other programs.

Prototype in : process.h

► sprintf ►

Prototype : int sprintf(char *buffer, const char *format [, argument,...]);

sprintf : It is similar to fprintf except that here file is not used for storing output to but a string (i.e. memory) pointed to by buffer is used for that purpose. Returns the number of bytes output, or EOF on error.

Prototype in : stdio.h

► sqrt ►

Prototype : double sqrt(double x);

sqrt : Returns the square root of x.

Prototype in : math.h

► srand ►

Prototype : void srand(unsigned seed);

srand : Initializes random number generator using seed as seed for random no. generation. randomise uses predefined seed. It also uses the time function, so you should include time.h when using this routine.

Prototype in   :   stdlib.h

► sscanf ►

Prototype	:	int sscanf(const char *buffer,const char *format [, address,...]);
sscanf	:	It is similar to fscanf except that here file is not used for getting output from but a string (i.e. memory) pointed to by buffer is used for that purpose. Returns the number of input fields successfully scanned, converted, and stored. Attempts to read past end of buffer, results in EOF being returned.
Prototype in	:	stdio.h

► stat ►

Prototype	:	int stat(char *path, struct stat *statbuf);
stat	:	Gets information regarding the open file whose specification including path is passed to it. Stores information in statbuf in the structure defined as stat. Returns 0 on success while -1 is returned and errno is set on error.
Prototype in	:	stat.h

► _status87 ►

Prototype	:	unsigned int _status87(void);
_status87	:	The floating-point status is read & bits in the return value give the floating-point status to be interprated as given in _clear87.
Prototype in	:	float.h

► stime ►

Prototype	:	int stime(time_t *tp);
stime	:	Sets system date and time to tp and returns 0.
Prototype in	:	time.h

► stpcpy ►

Prototype	:	char *stpcpy(char *dest, const char *src);
stpcpy	:	stpcpy is same as strcpy, except that it returns a value given by (dest + strlen (src)).
Prototype in	:	string.h

► strcat/strncat ►

Prototype	:	char *strcat(char *dest, const char *src);
		char *strncat(char *dest, const char *src, size_t maxlen);
strcat/strncat	:	In strcat entire src is appended to end of dest by removing NULL terminator of latter and dest is returned while strncat appends at most maxlen characters of src to dest.
Prototype in	:	string.h

► strchr/strrchr ►

Prototypes	:	char *strchr (const char *s, int c);
		char *strrchr(const char *s, int c);
strchr/strrchr	:	In case c does not occur in s, NULL is returned; otherwise the pointer to the first (last) occurrence of c in s is returned by strchr (strrchr).
Prototype in	:	string.h

► strcmp/strncmp ►

Prototypes	:	int strcmp(const char *s1, const char *s2);
		int strncmp(const char *s1, const char *s2, size_t maxlen);
strcmp/strncmp	:	strcmp compares one string to another; while strncmp takes up at most maxlen characters of strings for comparison. Returns indicator of S1-S2 (i.e. less than 0 if s1 is less than s2).
		Note that the comparisons are done starting with the first character in each string and continuing with subsequent characters until occurance of different corresponding characters is detected (or until a number of n characters have been examined, if relevant).
Prototype in	:	string.h

► strcmpi ►

Prototype	:	int strcmpi(const char *s1, const char *s2)
strcmpi	:	strcmpi is a macro to compare strings ignoring case.
Prototype in	:	string.h

► strcpy ►

Prototypes	:	char *strcpy(char *dest, const char *src);
strcpy	:	strcpy copies entire string src to dest and returns dest.
Prototype in	:	string.h

► strcspn ►

Prototype	:	size_t strcspn(const char *s1, const char *s2);
strcspn	:	Returns the length of the initial part of s1 that consists entirely of those characters which are NOT used in s2.
Prototype in	:	string.h

► strdup ►

Prototype	:	char *strdup(const char *s);
strdup	:	Copies s to new location & returns pointer to duplicated s, (or NULL if space could not be allocated for the copy). Tries to allocate memory for duplicate s. freeing the space allocated by strdup is to be done subsequently by application.
Prototype in	:	string.h

► _strerror ►

Prototype	:	char *_strerror(const char *s);
_strerror	:	_strerror is used to construct a customized error message using the string s followed respectively by a colon, a space, the most recently generated system error message, and a newline. The string s should be less than 95 characters long. It returns a pointer to the generated error message string.
Prototype in	:	string.h

► strerror ►

Prototype	:	char *strerror(int errnum);
strerror	:	strerror returns a pointer to the error message associated with the error number errnum.
Prototype in	:—	string.h

► stricmp ►

Prototype	:	int stricmp(const char *s1, const char *s2);
stricmp	:	stricmp is function version of the macro strcmpi.
Prototype in	:	string.h

► strlen ►

Prototype	:	size_t strlen(const char *s);
strlen	:	Returns the length of string s as number of characters.Does not count the null terminator.
Prototype in	:	string.h

► strlwr ►

Prototype	:	char *strlwr(char *s);
strlwr	:	strlwr converts s to string having all characters convrted to lower case and returns pointer to s.
Prototype in	:	string.h

► strncmpi ►

Prototype	:	int strncmpi(const char *s1, const char *s2, size_t n);
strncmpi	:	strncmpi works as strcmpi but for a maximum length of n bytes.
Prototype in	:	string.h

► strncpy ►

Prototype	:	char *strncpy(char *dest, const char *src, size_t maxlen);

| strncpy | : | strncpy copies entire src if it is smaller than maxlen characters or else it copies only maxlen characters from src to dest. If maxlen characters get copied, no null character is appended by strncpy. Returns dest. |
| Prototype in | : | string.h |

► strnicmp ►

Prototype	:	int strnicmp(const char *s1, const char *s2,size_t maxlen);
strnicmp	:	strnicmp is function version of macro strncmpi.
Prototype in	:	string.h

► strpbrk ►

Prototype	:	char *strpbrk(const char *s1, const char *s2);
strpbrk	:	Scans string s1 for the first occurrence of any character that is present in string s2 and returns a pointer to the character in s1 which was the first amongst those which occurred in s2. If none of the characters of s2 occurs in s1, NULL is returned.
Prototype in	:	string.h

► strrev ►

Prototype	:	char *strrev(char *s);
strrev	:	Reverses all characters in s and returns a pointer to the reversed string.
Prototype in	:	string.h

► strset/strnset ►

Prototypes	:	char *strset(char *s, int ch); char *strnset(int *s, int ch, size_t n);
strset/strnset	:	strset (strnset) sets all (at most the first n) characters of s to ch. null character is found.
Prototype in	:	string.h

► strspn ►

Prototype	:	size_t strspn(const char *s1, const char *s2);
strspn	:	Scans string s1 to find out a segment that consists of only those characters which form a subset of the set of characters specified by s2. Returns the length of such initial segment of s1.
Prototype in	:	string.h

► strstr ►

Prototype	:	char *strstr(const char *s1, const char *s2);
strstr	:	Finds the first occurrence of complete s2 string in the string s1 and returns a pointer to the start of s2 in s1 or NULL if s2 does not occur in s1.
Prototype in	:	string.h

► strtod ►

Prototype	:	double strtod(const char *s, char **endptr);
strtod	:	Converts string to double floating point and returns the value of s as a double, where s is a sequence of characters. The string must match the following format:

[ws] [sn] [ddd] [.] [ddd] [fmt[sn]ddd]

where :
ws = whitespace
sn = sign (+ or -) All elements
ddd = digits in [ ]
fmt = e or E are optional endptr is address past the end of string.

Prototype in	:	stdlib.h

► strtok ►

Prototype	:	char *strtok(char *s1, const char *s2);
strtok	:	Scans s1 to find out the first occurance of any token not contained in s2. If the token is found, a null character is written into s1 after that token, and pointer to the token is returned.

NULL is returned if no such token is found in s1.

Prototype in	:	string.h

► strtol/strtoul ►

Prototype	:	long strtol(const char *s, char **ptr, int radix); unsigned long strtoul (const char *s, char **ptr, int radix);
strtol/strtoul	:	Converts string s to a long / unsigned long (strol/ stroul) using the given radix (10 for decimal, 8 for octal).Returns the converted value of s, or 0 on error. The string must match the following format: [ws] [sn] [0] [x] [ddd] where : ws = whitespace All elements sn = sign (+ or -)in [ ] ddd = digits are optional ptr is address past the end of string.
Prototype in	:	stdlib.h

► strupr ►

Prototype	:	char *strupr(char *s);
strupr	:	strupr converts s to string having all characters convrted to upper case and returns pointer to s.
Prototype in	:	string.h

► swab ►

Prototype	:	void swab(char *frm, char *todest, int nbytes);
swab	:	nbytes bytes starting from address frm are taken, odd and even bytes are exchanged and resulting swapped bytes of string are stored at todest. frm[0] becomes todest[1] and frm[1] becomes todest[0]. nbytes should be an even number.
Prototype in	:	stdlib.h

► system ►

Prototype	:	int system(const char *command);
system	:	A DOS command is issued to environment for execution.It may be an internal DOS command, or a.COM/.EXE/.BAT batch file. Returns 0 on success, -1 on failure.

Prototype in	:	process.h and stdlib.h

► tan ►

Prototype	:	double tan(double x);
tan	:	Returns requested trigonometric ratio of the angle where x is in radians.
Prototype in	:	math.h

► tanh ►

Prototype	:	double tanh(double x);
tanh	:	Returns requested trigonometric ratio of the angle x where x is in radians.
Prototype in	:	math.h

► tell ►

Prototype	:	long tell(int handle);
tell	:	Returns current position of file pointer in no. of bytes from BOF. A return value of -1 indicates error.
Prototype in	:	io.h

► textattr ►

Prototype	:	void textattr(int newattr);
textattr	:	Sets text attribute to newattr for text functions. The attributes are intrprated bitwise as by DOS i.e. MSB =1 gives blink, LSB(bit 0) bit 1 & bit 2 are for rgb of foreground,bit 3 =1 means high intensity, bit 4,5,6 specify rgb colours for background. So 00000111B = 07 will mean no blink, black background, no high intensity & white foreground color for character.
Prototype in	:	conio.h

► textbackground ►

Prototype	:	void textbackground(int newcolor);

| textbackground | : | Selects new text background color and keeps the foreground i.e. colour of character unchanged. |
| Prototype in | : | conio.h |

► textcolor ►

Prototype	:	void textcolor(int newcolor);
textcolor	:	Selects new character color in text mode without altering background colour.
Prototype in	:	conio.h

► textmode ►

Prototype	:	void textmode(int newmode);
textmode	:	Video mode of screen in text mode is changed to newmode. Cant be used to change from graphics to text mode. newmode may be any of predefined symbolic constants (viz. BW40) discussed earlier in the text.
Prototype in	:	conio.h

► time ►

Prototype	:	time_t time(time_t *t);
time	:	Gets the time elapsed since 00:00:00 GMT of 1.1.1970 till the moment, in seconds. This value is returned as well as stored in the location pointed to by t.
Prototype in	:	time.h

► tmpfile ►

Prototype	:	FILE *tmpfile(void);
tmpfile	:	Opens a temporary file in binary mode and returns a pointer to the stream of the temporary file created; OR NULL if the file can't be created.
Prototype in	:	stdio.h

► tmpnam ►

Prototype	:	char *tmpnam(char *sptr);
tmpnam	:	Creates a unique file name (as 8 character name, dot, and a three character extension) and stores that as a NULL terminated string in memory pointed to by sptr. If sptr is NULL, tmpnam returns a pointer to an internal static object;otherwise it returns sptr.
Prototype in	:	stdio.h

► toascii ►

Prototype	:	int toascii(int c);
toascii	:	translates characters to ascii format
Prototype in	:	ctype.h

► _tolower ►

Prototype	:	int _tolower(int c);
_tolower	:	translates characters to lowercase.
Prototype in	:	ctype.h

► _toupper ►

Prototype	:	int _toupper(int c);
_toupper	:	translates characters to uppercase.
Prototype in	:	ctype.h

► tolower ►

Prototype	:	int tolower(int ch);
tolower	:	This is function form of macro _tolower. It returns the lowercase converted value of ch if it's some uppercase character; otherwise ch is returned unchanged.
Prototype in	:	ctype.h

► toupper ►

Prototype	:	int toupper(int ch);
toupper	:	This is function form of macro _toupper. It returns the uppercase converted value of ch if it's some lowercase character; otherwise ch is returned unchanged.
Prototype in	:	ctype.h

► tzset ►

Prototype	:	void tzset(void);
tzset	:	Sets global variables daylight, timezone, and tzname for UNIX time compatibility.An environment string of the form TZ=... to define the time zone is expected by tzset.
Prototype in	:	time.h

► ungetc ►

Prototype	:	int ungetc(int c, FILE *str);
ungetc	:	Pushes the character c back into input stream str, so that the next call to any stream input functions (viz. getc) for stream will return c. Returns the c if successful; EOF otherwise.
Prototype in	:	stdio.h

► ungetch ►

Prototype	:	int ungetch(int ch);
ungetch	:	Pushes a character back to the keyboard buffer thereby ensuring that the next call to getch or other console input functions will get ch as a keyboard input. Returns ch on success and EOF on error.
Prototype in	:	conio.h

► unixtodos ►

Prototype	:	void unixtodos(long time, struct date *d, struct time *t);
unixtodos	:	The date and time are converted from UNIX format to DOS format. 3.7.11 (dostounix) may also be referred to.

Prototype in : dos.h

► unlink ►

Prototype : int unlink(const char *filename);

unlink : Deletes the given file if the attribute is not Read Only. Returns 0 on success and -1 on error.

Note : Prototype appears in dos.h, io.h & also stdio.h

Prototype in : dos.h

► unlock ►

Prototype : int unlock(int handle, long offset, long length);

unlock : The file-sharing lock set by lock() is released. The file selected is the one associated with handle. Unlocking occurs for length bytes in the file from the position given as offset bytes from BOF. Returns 0 on success; -1 on error.

Prototype in : io.h

► va_end ►

Prototype : void va_end(va_list ap);

va_end : It is a macro that ends access to variable argument

Prototype in : stdarg.h

► va_start ►

Prototype : void va_start(va_list ap, lastfix);

va_start : It is a macro that begins access to variable argument

Prototype in : stdarg.h

► vfprintf ►

Prototype : int vfprintf(FILE *fp, const char *fstr, va_list arglist);

vfprintf : Sends formatted output (as per format string fstr — same as used in printf) to the stream (pointed to by fp) using argument list arglist. Returns the number of bytes output; or EOF in case of error. It is fprintf with variable no. of arguments.

Prototype in   :   stdio.h

► vfscanf ►

Prototype	:	int vfscanf(FILE *sptr, const char *format, va_list arglist);
vfscanf	:	Scans formatted input (as per format string fstr — same as used in printf) from the stream (pointed to by sptr) using argument list arglist. Returns the number of input fields scanned, converted, and stored. It is fscanf with variable no. of arguments.

Prototype in   :   stdio.h

► vprintf ►

Prototype	:	int vprintf(const char *format, va_list arglist);
vprintf	:	Sends formatted output to stdout using argument list. Returns the number of bytes output or NULL in case of error. It may be considered as vfprintf with stream being stdout.

Prototype in   :   stdio.h

► vscanf ►

Prototype	:	int vscanf(const char *format, va_list arglist);
vscanf	:	Scans formatted output from stdin using argument list. Returns number of input fields scanned, converted, and stored. Returns EOF when End-of-file is encountered. It may be considered as vfscanf with stream being stdin.

Prototype in   :   stdio.h

► vsprintf ►

Prototype	:	int vsprintf(char *buffer, const char *format. va_list arglist);
vsprintf	:	Sends formatted output to a string using argument list. Returns the number of bytes output or EOF in case of error.

Prototype in   :   stdio.h

► vsscanf ►

Prototype	:	int vsscanf(const char *buffer, const char *format,va_list arglist);
vsscanf	:	Performs formatted input from a string using argument list. Returns number of input fields scanned, converted, and stored. On reaching end-of-file, it returns EOF.
Prototype in	:	stdio.h

► wherex/wherey ►

Prototype	:	int wherex(void); int wherey(void);
wherex/	:	wherex(wherey) give column (row) number of current cursor wherey position within the current text window. Returns an integer in the range 1 to 80 (1 to 25).
Prototype in	:	conio.h

► window ►

Prototype	:	void window(int left, int top, int right, int bottom);
window	:	Defines active text-mode window bounded by coordinates passed where the top left corner of the screen is (1,1).
Prototype in	:	conio.h

► write/_write ►

Prototypes	:	int write (int handle, void *buf, unsigned len); int _write(int handle, void *buf, unsigned len);
write/_write	:	len bytes are written from memory pointed to by buf to the file associated with handle. Return value is the number of bytes written, or -1 in case of error.
Prototype in	:	io.h

THE VISUAL C++

Introduction

The Visual C ++ provides you with a comprehensive, up-to-date production-level development environment for developing all windows applications. Version 4.0 of Visual C++ provides a powerful 32-bit compiler to help you develop Win32 applications for Windows 95 and Windows NT operating systems. Version 2.0 of Visual C++ provides a 16-bit compiler for developing 16-bit Win32s application for windows 3.x and MS-DOS environments. The Microsoft Visual C++ compiler package also provides tools for building Windows programs for Windows 3.x, Windows 95 and Windows NT environments. The C++ compiler includes all the header files, libraries, dialog and resource editors necessary to create a truly robust windows application. Microsoft has also incorporated the resource editors for bit maps, icons, cursors, menus, and dialog boxes directly into the integrated environment. New Class Wizards helps you to build object linking and embedding (OLE) applications using Microsoft Foundation class (MFC) libraries in record time.

Hardware and Software Requirements:

The following minimum hardware and software is required to run the 16-bit- or 32-bit version of the Microsoft Visual C++ compiler package

- An 80386 based PC
- Minimum 16 MB RAM
- 10 MB of free hard disk space is required for minimum installation.
- VGA Monitor
- Mouse
- Microsoft Windows 95 or Windows MT for Win 32 development.

Minimal hardware and software requirements are not always the optimal choice because you will want a fast microprocessor that can handle the size and complexity of advanced

Windows applications. You can also obtain these performance enhancements by having a large amount of free disk space and by having a lot of memory maximizes the overall performance of both Microsoft Visual C++ and the Windows environment. So it is recommend that the following hardware and software is required to optimize the development cycle of C and C++ programs:

- A Pentium based PC
- Speed 90 MHz or higher
- 100 MB of free hard disk space
- A Super VGA Monitor
- Mouse
- 20 MB RAM
- Microsoft Windows 95 or Windows NT for Win32 development.

The improvements made to Windows MT and Windows 95 provide you with the features and performance necessary to create state-of-art Windows applications. Buy a monitor with as large a screen as possible because your eyes will appreciate super-VGA resolution monitors as you develop these applications in a graphical environment.

NOTE

1. If you are developing applications targeted for 32-bit operating systems, such as Windows 95 and Windows NT, you will only need the 32-bit version of the compiler.

2. If you are developing application for the 16-bit Windows 3x and MS-DOS environments, you will only need to install the 16-bit version of the version 2.0 compiler.

3. If you are developing applications that will cross all of these software platforms, you will have to have both the 16-bit and 32-bit versions of the compiler.

Installation Procedure

The Microsoft Visual C++ Compiler package installs almost automatically except answering some questions. Here, we will lists the steps of typical installation of 32-bit version of Visual C++(Ver 4.0). Installation steps for 16-bit version of Visual C++ (Ver 2.0) follows similar steps.

1   Insert the first disk or CD-ROM of Visual C++ and run the SETUP.EXE program.

2   You will be prompt to choice a install options, such as Typical, Custom, Minimum or CD-ROM. The amount of the hard disk you must have depends upon the option you chose.

3   After that you will prompted for your Name, Organization, and Product ID. Supply this information.

4   Now, it will start the installation. You can see the progress by watching File Copy Process dialog box. Installation takes about 15 minutes on a Pentium machine with 90 MHz.

5   After copying all the files, you will be prompt "Whether your configuration should be changed now or later". Choose first option: "Make changes now and backup current version."

6   You will be prompt to register environment variables. This is in the form of a check box, with the box already checked. Accept the default and register the environment variables at the time. By registering the environment variables, you provide your compiler with important information about your system.

7   After completing the installation, reboot your system so that your new created configuration file should be effected.

You will find a several sub-directory in the visual C++ directory:

Sub-directories		Description
BIN	–	Executable files and build tools needed to build 32-bit applications
OLE	–	Files for building OLE applications
SAMPLES	–	Contains Sample Programs
MFC	–	Microsoft Foundation Class (MFC) library files
INCLUDE	–	C++ run-time and header files
LIB	–	C+++ run-time and Win32 SDK libraries.
HELP	–	Contains Help Files

Note that you will also find several README files in the subdirectory, which provides the latest release information for the compiler.

Starting Visual C++ 32-bit IDE (Integrated Development Environments)

To invoke the Visual C++, double click the Visual C++ icon from the Microsoft Visual C++ group. Alternatively, you can access the Windows Run Command, from the keyboard, and enter the following command:

C: MSDEV.EXE

The Visual C++ system can be classified into four parts:

- Menu Bar
- Menu Pad
- Menus
- Menu Options
- Tool bar

Menu Bar: A Menu Bar displays the titles for menu and it is located at the top of the screen. The content of the menu bar changes when you move to the other part of the menu bar.

Menu Pads: Menu Pads occurs on the menu bar and displays the title of menus. These titles on the menu bar are called menu pads. Mouse and keyboard can be used to display the menu associated with each menu pad. To access the menu bar from the mouse, click on the title of the menu you want to use. To access the menu bar from Keyboard, press <ALT> key or <F10> key and then type the underlined letter for the menu you want to use or press the Right and Left arrow keys to move from menu pad to menu pad, and press <Enter> key.

Note that some menu pads appear dimmed and cannot be chosen. These menu pads are disabled. You can not display the menu if the menu pad is disabled.

Menus: When you choose a menu pad from the menu bar, Visual C++ displays a menu. A menu is a list of related options. When you choose an option from a menu, you are telling Visual C++ what action to take. Choose menus to activate a highlighted option by clicking with mouse or pressing the <Spacebar> key or <Enter> key.

Menu Options: When you choose a menu pad from the member, Visual C++ display a menu. A menu contains options. The options on each menu are logically related to menu pad.

To choose a menu option you want, use one of the following techniques:

- Move to the menu pad and click. The menu appears. Click on the desired option you want.

- Press <Alt> Key or <Fio> key and then press the hot key (underlined letter) in the menu pad name. Type the hot key for the menu option you want.

Press \<ALT\> or \<Fio\> key then use the Left and Right arrow keys to the menu pad you want to use and then press \<Enter\> key. Use the Up and Down arrow Keys to select the desired option and then press the \<Enter\> or \<Spacebar\> key.

Certain menu options have an ellipsis (...) after the option. This tells you that the option will open a dialog box. A dialog box appears to request the additional information.

Toolbar: The Toolbar occur below the menu bar and displays the icons. To access the Toolbar from the mouse, click on the icon you want to use.

Dialog Controls

The Dialog controls and their uses are as follows:

1 Focus Rectangle:- A dotted **rectangle** around a control, called a focus rectangle, indicates the current control in the dialog.

2. Check Box: A **check box** is a hollow box followed by text. Turn features on and off. When a check box followed by text. Turn features on and off. When a check box is on or selected, it has a check work. Multiple check boxes can be selected in a group.

3. Push Button : A **Push button** contains key words or pictures that describe the action it triggers. The action related with a push button occurs immediately when you click (or press \<RETURN\> key) a push button unless it contains an ellipsis (...). A push button has an ellipsis (...), indicating that another dialog box will appear. A Push button contains a double greater-than sign (>>). Expand the current dialog box so you can see additional controls.

The default push button in each dialog box has a darker border than the other push buttons. To choose the default push button, you can click it with the mouse or press \<RETURN\> key at any time in the dialog box.

4. Radio Button: A **radio button** is a hollow circle followed by text. Turn features on and off. When a radio button is selected, it appears filled and the previously selected radio button in a group becomes deselected. Only one radio button can be selected in a group at a time.

5. Spinners: A **spinners** control occurs in dialog locations, when you are required to increment or decrement a numeric value. To use a spinner control, click on the Up arrow to increase the numeric value, and click on the down arrow to decrease the numeric value.

6. Text Box: The **rectangle** box indicates an editable text region, where you can enter text. To enter text in a **text box,** click on the text box to position the cursor, or press <Tab> key and then enter the text.

7. List Box : A **list box** contains a list of items like files, fields, and directories. To select the listed items, click on the arrow at end of the scroll box to move through the list and then click on the desired item.

To use the keyboard to choose a item in a list, press the <Tab> key to move the list box. Once you Tab to the list, you can move through the list in the following ways:

- To move through the list item by item, press Up and Down Arrow keys.

- To display the previous or next window of the list options, press <pgUp> and <pgDn> keys.

- To choose the first or last item in the list, press <Home> and <End> keys.

8. Popup (Combo Box) : A **popup** control is a rectangle with an underlined arrow, that you an choose to display the associated popup. To choose the option from popup with the mouse. click on the popup control, and then click on appropriate option. To select the option from the popup with the keyboard, press <Tab> key to move the popup control and press the <Spacebar> or press <Alt+Up Arrow> or <Alt+Down Arrow> keys. Now you can use the arrow keys to move the appropriate option and then press <RETURN> key or <Spacebar> key.

Text Editor

The Visual FoxPro text editor allows you to create and modify text. The following keys can be used for selection and editing text.

Key(s)	Action
Cursor Movement	
Right Arrow	To move the cursor one character to the right.
Left Arrow	To move the cursor one character to the left.
Up Arrow	To move the cursor up one line.
Down Arrow	To move the cursor down one line.
Home	To move the cursor to the beginning of the current line.
End	To move the cursor to the end of the current line.
PgUp	To move the cursor up the height of the current window.
PgDn	To move the cursor down the height of the current window.
Ctrl+Home	To move the cursor to the beginning of the current text.
Ctrl+End	To move the cursor to the end of the current text.
Ctrl+Right Arrow	To move the cursor one word to the right.
Ctrl+Left Arrow	To move the cursor one word to the left.
Selecting Text	
Shift+Right Arrow	To select one character to the right of the cursor.
Shift+Left Arrow	To select one character to the left of the cursor.
Shift+Up Arrow	To select one line up to the cursor.
Shift+Dn Arrow	To select one line down to the cursor.
Shift+Ctrl+Right Arrow	To select one word to the right of the cursor.
Shift+Ctrl+Left Arrow	To select one word to the left of the cursor.
Shift+Ctrl+Home	To select from the cursor to the beginning of text.
Shift+Ctrl+End	To select from the cursor to the end of text.
Ctrl+A	To select all text.
Deleting Text	
Backspace	To delete the selected text or the character to the left of the cursor if no text is selected.

Key(s)	Action
Del	To delete selected text or the character to the right of the cursor.
Ctrl+Backspace	To delete the word to the left of the cursor including any spaces between the cursor and the word.

Inserting Text

Ins	To switch between insert and overwrite mode.

Visual C++ Menu System

The visual C++ menu system makes it easy to communicate without programming. The titles of the menu system are described below:

File Menu:

The Visual C++ IDE **File** menu localizes the standard set of file manipulation commands common to many Windows applications. The command options available from the **File** menu are:

File

New...	Ctrl+N
Open...	
Close	
Open Workspace...	
Close Workspace...	
Save	Ctrl+S
Save As...	
Save All	
Find in Files...	
Page Setup...	
Print...	Ctrl+P
Exit	

The **File** menu options are described as follows:

Option	Description
New...	Opens a new Edit dialog box. You usually begin any new application at this point. The IDE (Integrated Development Environment automatically titles and numbers each window you open.
Open...	Allows you to open any type of existing files. The standard Open File dialog box displays the default drive, path, and file search parameter and allows you to select your own parameters.
Close	Closes the current windows. If the window's contents have changed, you will be asked to save the charges.
Open Workspace	Project workspaces contain projects that you can build. A project consists of a single set of files and a set of one or more project configuration. Each project configuration, together with the set of files, determines the binary output file that you create. You use the open Workspace option to retrieve a preciously defined workspace.
Close Workspace	Closes an opened workspace. This allows you to open another workspace and begin developing a separate application.
Save	Allows you to save the content of the active window to the file specified.
Save As...	Allows you to save a copy of the active window's contents under a new name.
Save All	If you have never written a C, C++ Windows 95, or Windows NT application, you will be stunned at the actual number of files involved in creating a project's executable file. The problem with the save option Saves is that it only saves the active window's contents. The Save All option saves every window's contents. Note that if any window contains previously unsaved text, the Save All option will automatically invoke the Save As dialog box, prompting you for a valid filename for each windows.
Find in Files...	Allows you to search for a sequence of characters in one or more files. Specify which files to search by indicating the type of file and the folder names. The search results are displayed in the Output Window. When the search is complete, you can open a file containing a match by double-clicking the entry in the Output window.

Print Setup...	Allows you to select the printer you want to use and other several options about the printer.
Print...	Allows you to print only the sources listed below: –The contents of the window –The contents of a file that is not currently open. –The contents of ASCII file or clipboard –The contents of any open Editing window.
Exit	Allows you to leave Visual C++ IDE and returns you to the windows desktop. Don't worry if you have forgotten to save a window's contents before selecting Exit. IDE will automatically display a warning message for each window containing unsaved text, allowing you to save the information before exiting.

Edit Menu

The Visual C++ IDE Edit menu allow you to quickly edit or search through an active window's contents in much the same way you would with any standard word processor. The command options available from the **Edit** menu are:

The **Edit** menu options are described as follows:

Edit	
Undo	Ctrl+Z
Redo	Ctrl+A
Cut	Ctrl+X
Copy	Ctrl+C
Past	Ctrl+V
Delete	Del
Select All	
Find	
Replace	
Go To...	
InfoViewer Bookmarks...	
Bookmark...	
Breakpoints...	Ctrl+B
Properties	Altr+Enter

Option	Description
Undo	– Allows you to reverse the last action you have performed on any text within a field, record or file, and in text editing regions in dialogs.
Redo	– Allows you to restore the last action after it was undo.
Cut	– Allows you to remove selection and put it on the clipboard.
Copy	– Allows you to copy selection and put it on the clipboard.
Paste	– Allows you to place a copy of the clipboard contents at the current insertion point(Cursor).
Delete	– Deletes selected text without copying the information to the clipboard. Even though deleted text is not copied to the clipboard, you can still undo a Delete by choosing the Edit/Undo command.
Select All	– Allows you to select the entire contents of the active window for cutting. copying or deleting.
Find...	– Allows you to search for specified text.
Replace...	– Allows you to replace specified text.
Go To...	– Once again Visual C++ IDE comes to your rescue. With the typical Windows application frequently including dozens of files, it becomes no minor task to locate an object's point of declaration. The Go To... option does that for you.
InfoViewer Bookmarks...	– Shows organisation of Books Online. You can display any topic in its hierarcy.
Bookmark	– Sets or removes a bookmark. You can use bookmarks, to mark certain code lines you wish to refer back to within you program. Bookmarks can also be set manually with this option, as well as with the set Bookmark option from within the Find.... option.
Breakpoints	– Break points are used by the **Go** menu item by first selecting the Breakpoints... Option. This opens up the Breakpoints dialog box, which allows you to add, delete, disable, and clear all Breakpoints.
Properties...	– Allows you to specify the active window's characteristics. For instance, the active window can be designates as a read-only file, or it can be limited to allow it to contain C syntax but not C++ syntax. The Read only option allows you to

charge the active window's read-only status. This option toggles the file's status. If the file is not currently read-only, the command will make it read-only. If the file was previously designed as read-only, the command will remove the designation, allowing you to update and save any editing changes; check this option if you want to active file to be marked as a read-only status.

View Menu

The View menu provides access to those commands involved in displaying the current project's various Views. Views include Help file windows, Book online windows, and a selection of other windows that are helpful in debugging applications. The command options available with the **View** menu item are:

View

ClassWizard	
Resource Symbols	
Resource Includes	
Full Screen	
Toolbars...	
InfoViewer Query Results	Ctrl+Shift+K
InfoViewer History List	Ctrl+Shift+L
Project Workspace	Alt+0
InfoViewer Topic	Alt+1
Output	Alt+2
Watch	Alt+3
Variables	Alt+4
Registers	Alt+5
Memory	Alt+6
Call Stack	Alt+7
Disassembly	Alt+8

The View menu options are described as follows:

Option	Description
ClassWizard –	Provides an advanced programming tool that allows you to declare new Microsoft Foundation Class (MFC) - based classes or add new message-response member function to an existing MFC - based object.
Resource Symbols... –	Displays an outline of all the symbols in a specific source file and filter the information that is displayed.
Resource Includes... –	Modifies Microsoft Developer Studio's normal working arrangement of storing all resources in the project. RC file and all symbols in RESOURCE.H
Full Screen –	You can use the text editor and other resource editors in Full screen mode. When you initially select Full screen mode, a toolbar button with a small graphic of a computer screen in displayed.
Toolbars... –	Allows you to select the toolbars that will be displayed in the Visual C++ IDE.
InfoViewer Query Results –	Displays a list of previously answered InfoViewer Queries
Info Viewer History List –	Displays a History List of Previous Views requested
Project Workspace –	Displays a window with additional tabbel windows currently active for the selected Project workspace
Output –	Activates the project Output window.
Watch –	Allows you to watch variables previously selected by the programmer.
Variables –	Opens the variables watch window, allowing you to view currently active variables, local variables, or an object's this pointer
Registers –	Brings the Register window to the foreground. This read-only window displays the current state of the microprocessor, including Register contents and flags status.
Memory –	Opens the memory dump window starting at a specified address, which allows you to scroll through memory to view memory locations in the program's available address space.

| Call Stack | – | Displays the sequence of function calls leading up to the current line of code highlighted by the debugger. The reverse-order list works like a data structure's stack: the last function called is at the top of the list and the first function called is at the bottom. |
| Disassembly | – | Opens the disassembly window, which allows you to view the assembly-language code generated by your source code. |

Insert Menu

The **Insert** Menu of Visual C++, allows you to access options involved with inserting:

> File
> **R**esource....
> Resource Copy.....
> Files into Project.....
> Project....
> Component...

The above options are self explanatory and does not require any further clarification.

Build Menu

The Build Menu of Visual C++, contains many of the commands necessary to generate the application's executable file, *.EXE. The command options available with Build menu are as follows:

Build

Compile	Ctrl+F8
Build	Shift+F8
Rebuild All	Alt+F8
Batch Build...	
Stop Build	Ctrl+Back
Update All Dependencies	
Debug	
Execute	Ctrl+F5
Setting...	
Configurations...	
Subprojects...	
Set Default Configuration...	

The options available with Build menu are described as follows:

Option	Description
Compile	Signals the compiler to compile the source code in the active window. Compiling a file is a useful development phase, since it is here that you learn whether the file in question contains any syntax errors. For this reason, it is possible to compile header (*.H) files even through header files cannot be executed. If the compile process detects any syntax errors, either nonfatal warnings or fatal errors, they are displayed in the Output window.
Build	Examines all of the files in the project and then compiles and links only those dependent files displaying dates and times more recent than the project's executable file.
	Note that typical C/C++ programs are comprised of many files. Some of these files may be supplied by the compiler, the operating system, the programmer, or even third-party vendors. It can get even more complicated if the project's files are created by several programming teams. Because there can be so many files, and because the compile process can take a very long time, the Build option becomes an extremely useful tool.
Rebuild All	The only difference between Build and Rebuild All is that Rebuild All ignores the dates of all of a project's files and painstakingly compiles and links all of them.
Batch Build...	It is similar to the Build option except that it builds multiple project targets.
Stop Build	Allow you to stop a Build or Rebuild All action.
Update All Dependencies	Allows you to append the current active window's filename to the project files.
	Note that most windows applications are made up of multiple source code files, header files, and resource files. Select this option whenever you wish to update the list of included files for the project.
Debug	Activates the integrated debugger
Execute	Allows you to run your program
Settings..	Allows you to select the project configuration. You can also select multiple project configurations, and specify settings common to all the configurations.

Configurations...	–	Allows you to modify or specify the configuration already set by Developer Studio in default.
Sub projects...	–	Allows you a include one project to other projects. This option gives you access to these previously defined workspaces.
Set Default Configuration...	–	You can specify specific optimization settings - or the setting for no optimization at all - for any individual files in the configuration. The settings that you specify at the file level in the project configuration override options set at the configuration level. You can specify some types of settings, such as linking, only at the project configuration level.

Tools Menu

The **Tools** menu of Visual C++, provides access to many helpful IDE utilities designed to make developing and controlling various object-oriented windows-applications as easy as possible. The options available with Tools menu are:

```
Tools
┌─────────────────────────────────────────────────────┐
│ Browse...                         Ctrl+Fll           │
│ Close Browse Info Fill                               │
├─────────────────────────────────────────────────────┤
│ Profile...                                           │
│ Remote Connection...                                 │
│ Customize...                                         │
│ Options...                                           │
├─────────────────────────────────────────────────────┤
│ Record Keystrokes                                    │
│ Playback Recording                                   │
├─────────────────────────────────────────────────────┤
│ Spy++                                                │
│ MFC Tracer                                           │
│ Register Control                                     │
│ OLE Contrl Test Container                            │
│ OLE Object Views                                     │
└─────────────────────────────────────────────────────┘
```

The options available with Tools menu are described as follows:

Option	Description
Browse...	– Keeps a history list of all object definitions or references that have been previously searched for. This history list work like a stack data structure, with the last item entered being the first item removed.
Close Browse Info File	
	– Use the Close Browse Info file option to close the Browse Info file.
Profile...	– Opens the Profile dialog box, which allows you to view the current application's performance.
Remote Connection...	– Activates the Remote Connection option allowing you full remote access to the IDE.
Customize..	– Allows you to add, delete, and customize tools used by the Tools menu. Additional options allow you to assign shortcut keys to various commands.
Options...	– Offers commands to automize the Visual C++ IDE itself or modify how your appliction is developed. If you are a first-time user of Microsoft Visual C++, feel free to examine the contents of options sub menu. However until you fully understand the ramifications of changing install defaults, look but do not touch.
Record Keystrokes	– Allows you to record Keystrokes in the current editor view. This options lets you save frequently used command sequences to be played back later.
Playback Recording	– Plays back previously recorded keystrokes in the current editor view.
Spy ++, MFC Tracer	– Provide instant access to Microsoft Spy++ and MFC Tracer debugging utilities.
OLE Control Test Container	
	– Allows you to access to the supplied OLE control Test container. An OLE control container is a container that fully supports OLE controls and can incorporate them into its own window.
	An OLE control is a reusable software element that you can use in many development projects. Controls allow your

user to access databases, monitor data, and make various selections within an applications.

OLE Object View   –   Activates the OLE Object Viewer. The OLE 2.0 object Viewer is a tool designed to help implementors of OLE2.0 enabled applications better understand what is happening in their systems. It is a powerful testing tool that lets you verify that your objects and interfaces are be having exactly as you planned.

Window Menu

The **Window** menu option of Visual C++, allows you to control the visibility of the various windows involved in an application's development cycle. It also allows you to see the input focus by deciding which window is active.

The options available a with **Window** item are:

```
Window

 New Window
 Split
 Hide                Shift+ESc
 Cascade
 Title Horizontally
 Title Vertically
 Close All
 Windows
```

The option available with this item are described as follows:

Option		Description
New Window	–	Allows you to open a new window for the current project
Split	–	Splits the active window into panes
Hide	–	Hides the active window
Cascade	–	This option will take all the windows currently open, and skew them down the display screen like a deck of cards.
Title Horizontally, Title Vertically	–	Instruct the integrated environment to equally subdivide the visual workspace so that each open window is the same

shaped size. The advantage of this visual arrangement is that you can see the contents of all open windows simultaneously.

Close All... – Closes All open Windows.

Windows – Opens up a history list of all currently open windows allowing you to quickly switch the file of interest.

Help Menu

The **Help** menu of Visual C++, Subdivides the database into categories. Each command opens up a standard Help dialog box allowing you to specify search patterns, move forward and backward through nested Help windows, and select high-level views of Help topics.

The Development System

The Microsoft 32-bit Visual C++ compiler for Windows 95 and Windows NT incorporates new, fully integrated Windows development tools and a visual interface. The following sections list those stand-alone utilities that are now incorporated in the Microsoft Visual C++ compiler.

New Integrated Debugger

Microsoft pulls the horsepower of its original Code View debugger directly in the Visual C++ platform with its new integrated debugger. The debugger is accessed from the Build menu. The integrated debugger allows you to execute programs in single steps, view and change variable contents, and even back out of code sections. You will find it to be a big help when programs compile but don't seem to perform as expected.

New Integrated Resource Editors

These editors are accessed from the Insert menu. The resource editors allow you to design and create Windows resources, such as bitmaps, cursors, icons, menus, and dialog boxes. Resources allow you to create visually appealing user interfaces to your applications. The following is the most popular resource editors.

1. Dialog Box Editor

The Dialog Box editor is slick graphical development tool which allows you to easily and quickly create professional-looking dialog boxes. The Dialog Box editor allows you to customize a dialog box's labels, framing, option and check box selections, text windows, and scroll bars. The Dialog Box editor allows you to combine numerous controls into your custom dialog boxes. Controls combine a visual graphical representation of some feature with a predefined set of properties that you can customize. For instance, check boxes, radio buttons, and list boxes are all forms of Windows controls.

2. Graphical Image Editors

The Graphical Image editors allow you to easily create custom bitmaps, icons, and cursors. An icon is a small color image used to represent an application when it has been minimized. Visual C++ even allows you to use an Image Editor to create custom cursors.

Additional Tools

The Additional Visual C++ tools are integrated into the compiler's package, and located under the Tools menu. These include Spy++, MFC Tracer, and the Test Container. You will find the Spy++ utility a great help when working on 32-bit Windows applications.

1. Spy++

Spy++ gives a graphical view of the system's processes, threads, windows and windows messages.

2 MFC Tracer

MFC Tracer allows the programmer to set the trace flags in AFX.INI. These flags are used to define the category of Trace messages that are sent from the MFC (Microsoft Foundation Class) application to the debugging window. Tracer is thus a debugging tool. You will want to use the MFC Tracer tool when you build MFC applications.

3. Test Container

The Test Container tool allows you to quickly test custom controls. Properties and features of the control can be altered while in the test container.

Outside the Integrated Environment

There are various tools located outside the integrated environment. Some tools, such as Spy++ and MFC Tracer, and available within and outside the compiler's Integrated Development Environment (IDE).

1. The Process Viewer (PView)

The Process Viewer allows you to quickly set and view all of the options necessary to track current processes, threads, and processor time-slicing. To start the Process Viewer, simply double-click on the PView icon in the Visual C++ group box.

The Process Viewer can shows the following information:

a. What percentage of time is spend running API calls'.

b. What happens if a thread or process stops responding to DDE, OLE, or pipe I/O?

c. Which processes and threads are using the most CPU time?

d. How much memory is being paged out?

e. How does the program run at different system priorities?

f. How much memory does the program allocate at various points in its execution?

WinDiff

The WinDiff utility allows you to graphically compare and modify two files or two directories. All of the options within WinDiff operate much like their counterpart commands in the Windows 95 Explorer or the Windows NT File Manager.

Compiler Features

The Visual C++ compiler package contains many useful enhancements, new features, and options. The following sections explain them briefly.

P-Code

P-code, short for "packed code", is used toward optimizing code speed and size. P-code can significantly reduce a program's size and execution speed by as much as 60 percent. All of this is accomplished simply by turning on the specific compiler option. This means that any code written in C or C++ can be compiled either normally or with p-code.

The P-code compiles an application's source code into "interpreted object code," which is a higher-level and more condensed representation of object code. The process is completed when a small interpreter module is linked into the application.

The most significant use of this technology does require some expertise. Since the interpreter generates object code at run time, p-code runs more slowly than native object code. With careful use of the **#pragma** directive, an application can generate p-code for space-critical functions, and switch back to generating native code for speed-critical functions.

The best candidates for p-code generation are those routines that deal with the user interface; and because many Windows applications spend 50 percent of their time handling the user interface, p-code provides the optimum performance characteristics.

Precompiled Headers and Types

The Visual C++ places generic types, function prototypes, external references, and member function declarations in special files called header files. These header files contain many of the critical definitions needed by the multiple source files that are pulled together to create the executable version of your program. Portions of these header files are typically recompiled for every module that includes the header. Unfortunately, repeatedly compiling portions of code can cause the compiler to slow down.

Visual C++ speeds up the compile process by allowing you to precompiled your header files. Precompilation saves the state of an applications compilation to a certain point and represents the relationship that is set up between the source file and the precompiled header. It is possible to create more than one precompiled header file per source file.

One of the best applications of this technology involves the development cycle of an application that has frequent code changes but not frequent base class definitions. If the header file is precompiled, the compiler can concentrate its time on the changes in the source code. Precompiled headers also provide a compile time boost for applications with headers that comprise large portions of code for a given module, as often happens with C++ programs.

Unlike many popular C++ compilers, the Microsoft C++ compiler does not restrict precompilation to header files. Since the process allows you to precompile a program up to a specified point, you an even precompile source code. This is extremely significant for C++ programs that contain most of their member function definitions in header files. In general, precompilation is reserved for those portions of your program that are considered stable; it is designed to minimize the time needed to compile the parts of your program under development.

MFC Library

The MFC library features classes for managing Windows objects and offers a number of general-purpose classes that can used in both MS-DOS and Windows application, For instance, there are classes for creating and managing files, strings, time, persistent storage, and exception handling.

In effect, the Microsoft Foundation Class library represents virtually every Windows API feature and includes sophisticated code that streamlines message processing, diagnostics, and other details that are a normal part of all Windows applications. The logical combination and enhancement of Windows API functions has following key advantages:

(i) The Encapsulation of Windows API is Logical and Complete

The MFC library provides support for all of the frequently used Windows API functions, including windowing functions, messages, controls, menus, dialog boxes, graphics device interface (GDI) objects (font, brushes, pens, and bitmaps), object linking, and the multiple document interface (MDI).

(ii) The MFC Functions are Easy to Learn

Microsoft has made a concerted effort to keep the names of the MFC functions and associated parameters as similar as possible to their Windows API parent classes. This minimizes the confusion for experienced Windows programmers wanting to take advantage of the simplified MFC platform. If also makes it very easy for a beginning Windows programmer to grow into the superset of Windows API functions when they are ready or when the application requires it.

(iii) The C++ Code is More Efficient

An application will consume only a little extra RAM when using the classes in the MFC library compiled under the small memory model. The execution speed of an MFC application is almost identical to that of the same application written in C using the standard Windows API.

(iv) The MFC Library Offers Automatic Message Handling

The MFC library eliminates one frequent source of programming errors, the Windows API message loop. The MFC classes are designed to automatically handle every one of the Windows messages. Instead of using the standard switch-case statements, each Window message is mapped directly to a member function, which takes the appropriate action.

(v) The MFC Library Allows Self-Diagnostics

Incorporated into the MFC library is the ability to perform self-diagnostics. This means that you can dump information about various objects to a file and validate an object's member variables, all in an easily understood format.

(vi) The MFC Library Incorporates a Robust Architecture

Anticipating the much-needed ANSI C throw / catch standard, the MFC library already incorporates an extensive exception-handling architecture. This allows an MFC object to eloquently recover from standard error conditions such as "out of memory" errors, invalid option selection, and file or resource loading problems. Every component of the architecture is upward compatible with the proposed ANSI C recommendations.

(vii)The MFC Library Offers Dynamic Object Typing

This extremely powerful feature delays the typing of a dynamically allocated object until run time. This allows you to manipulate an object without having to worry about its underlying data type. Because information about the object type is returned at run time, the programmer is freed from one additional level of detail.

(viii) The MFC Library can Harmoniously Co-Exist with C-based Windows Applications.

The most important feature of the MFC library is its ability to co-exist with C-based Windows applications that use Windows APL Programmers can use a combination of MFC classes and Windows API calls within the same program. This allows an MFC application to easily evolve into true C++ object oriented code as experience or demand requires. This transparent environment is possible because of the common naming conventions between the two architectures. The means that MFC headers, types, and global definitions do not conflict with Windows API names. Transparent memory management is another key component to the successful relationship.

(ix) The MFC Library Can Be used with MS-DOS

The MFC library was designed specifically for developing Windows applications. However, many of the classes provide frequently needed objects used for file I/O and string manipulation. For this reason, these general-purpose classes can be used by both Windows and MS-DOS developers.

(x) The MFC Library and Wizards.

The ClassWizard and ControlWizard only create code compatible with the MFC. These dynamic program developers are a must when developing OLE applications.

Function Inlining

The Microsoft Visual C++ compiler supports complete function inlining. The functions of any type or combination of instructions can be expanded in line. Many popular C++ compilers restrict inlining to certain types of statements or expressions. The Visual C++ compiler allows you to inline your most speed-critical routines without restricting their content. This option is set from the Project menu by selecting Settings..., then the C/C++ folder, and finally Optimizations from the Category list.

Microsoft Visual C++ Compiler Options

Microsoft Visual C++ compilers allow you to take advantage of several speed or code size options for every type of program development. Here, we will discuss those options directly related to the 32-bit, version 4.0, Microsoft C++ compiler. If you are using the 16-bit or 32-bit version 2.0 compiler, your options will be similar, but located under different tabs.

The following compiler options allow you to optimize your code for executable size, speed, or build time. All options are set from the Build menu by selecting the Settings menu item.

General

Allows you to specify the use, or nonuse, of the Microsoft Foundation Class library. Output directories can also be given for intermediate and final C/C++ compiled files.

Debug

The location of the executable file can be specified along with the working directory, optional program arguments and a remote executable path and file name. By using the Category list you can specify extra Dynamic Link Libraries (DLLs).

Custom Build

Allows you can specify custom tools for use in building projects. This includes tools to run on the output file of the project configuration.

C/C++

The C\C++ tab allows you to select from the following categories:

- General
- C++ Language
- Code Generation
- Customization
- Listing files
- Optimizations
- Precompiled headers
- Preprocessor

The General category allows the warning error level to be set, debug information to be specified, compiler optimizations to be set, preprocessor definitions to be given, and project options listed.

The C++ Language category allows the representation method to be specified, exception handling to be set, run time information to beset, construction displacements to be set, and project options to be listed.

The Code Generation category allows the microprocessor to be targeted, calling conventions given, run time library specified, and structure member alignment to be noted. Project options are, again, listed.

The Customization category allows the following items to be enabled or disabled:

(*i*) language extensions

(*ii*) function-level linking

(*iii*) duplicate strings

(*iv*) minimal rebuild

(*v*) incremental compilation

(*vi*) banner and information message suppression

The listing files category allows the generation of browse information. The Browse file destination can be set. Local variables are allowed in the Browse file. The file types can also be set optionally. Project options are listed.

The Optimizations category allows various code optimizations to be set, such as speed and size. In line function expansion is also given. Project options are listed.

The Precompiled headers category allows the use of precompiled header files. These are files with .PCH extensions. Precompiled header files speed the compile and link process, but should be eliminated from you directory upon project completion because of their large size. Project options are listed.

The Preprocessor category allows preprocessor definitions to be given. It is also possible to include additional directories and ignore standard paths. Project options are listed.

Link

The Link tab allows you to select from the following categories.

(i) General: From the General category the name of the file and extension can be specified. Most frequently the extension will be an .EXE file extension. However, you'll learn how to develop applications with .DDL and .SCR file extensions in this text. Object/library modules can also be entered. These modules are important for multimedia applications where specific libraries are not assumed. The following items can also be included.

    (a) profiling

    (b) incremental linking

    (c) ignoring default libraries

    (d) map file generation

    (e) debug information

(ii) Customization: The Customization category allows the following items to be included:

    (a) program database

    (b) output file name

    (c) process message printing

    (d) startup banner

    (e) incremental linking

(iii) Debug The Debug category information in various formats.

(iv) Input The Input category allows the specification of Object/library modules. Additionally, symbol references and MS-DOS stub file names are given.

(v) Output The Output category allows the base address, entry point, stack allocation, and version information for the project to be set.

Resources

The Resource tab permits the resource file to be given. Additional features include language, resource directories, and preprocessor definitions.

OLE Types

The OLE types tab permits the output file name, the output header file name, preprocessor definitions, and startup banner to be specified.

Browse Info

The Browse info tab allows the Browse info file name to be specified. Additionally, the Browse info file and startup banner can be checked.

Advanced Features of Visual C++

The Microsoft Visual C++ compiler includes several advanced tools that are useful for program development.

> *(i)* The creation of bitmaps cursors, icons from within the Visual C++ Integrated Development Environment (IDE),
>
> *(ii)* Books Online
>
> *(iii)* Debugging and Testing.

As you begin developing programs in C, C++, and Windows, you will find that the Visual C++ compiler helps you locate syntax errors during the build operation. Syntax errors are often the easiest errors to fix because of the detailed help provided by online help facilities. However, just because an application is free of syntax errors does not mean that it will perform as expected.

Custom Icons, Cursors, and Bitmaps

Customizing a Windows application with your own icons, cursors, bitmaps, and dialog boxes is easy with Microsoft's Visual C++ Integrated Development Environment (IDE), sometimes called the Developer Studio. The Visual C++ IDE is not just a compiler. It is also an easy-to-use, powerful resource editor.

How to use the Visual C++ IDE to draw a bitmap. All other graphic figures, such as icons and cursors, can be createdin a similar manner. The Visual C++ IDE allows you to design device-independent color bitmap images. These bitmaps are functionally device independent in respect to resolution. The image file format allows you to create a bitmap that always looks the same, regardless of the resolution of the display on which it appears.

For instance a single bitmap might consist of four definitions (DIBs).

> *(i)* one designed for monochrome displays.
>
> *(ii)* one for CGs.
>
> *(iii)* one for EGAs.
>
> *(iv)* one for VGAs.

Whenever the application displays the bitmap, it simply refers to it by name; Windows automatically selects the icon image that is best suited to the current display.

The first step you must take to create an application resource such as a bitmap is to click on the File menu and choose New...menu item.

The resulting dialog box, displays the drop-down list box as shown below with New or available resources.

Text Fill

Project Workspace

Resource Script

Resource Template

Binary File

Bitmap File

Icon File

Cursor File

Because we want to create a bitmap, this resource is highlighted. Simply press ENTER to confirm your selection.

Creating a bitmap with the Visual C++ resource editor is just about as easy as creating a picture with Windows Paintbrush. The Visual C++ resource editor first presents you with a blank bitmap grid and the drawing tools toolbar.

You use the toolbar to select the brush size, the brush color, and various drawing modes, such as fills and predefined shapes.

To set resource's properties, begin by pressing ALT-ENTER. The step displays the particular resource's Properties dialog box. The following illustration shows the Bitmap Properties dialog box with the details of the bitmap's width, height, colors, file name, and Save compressed properties.

The initial steps required for creating a dialog box resource are identical to those described previously for creating a bitmap resource. First, choose the kind of resource you wish to create.

The objects toolbox allows you to place a variety of controls in your dialog box design. These include:

(i) bitmap

(ii) label

(iii) edit box

(iv) frame

(v) button

(vi) check box

   (vii)   radio button

   (viii)   combo box

   (ix)   list box

   (x)   horizontal scroll bar

   (xi)   vertical scroll bar

   (xii)   user-defined control.

A cursor resource differs slightly from a bitmap or an icon resource in that it can contain a hotspot. A cursor's hotspot represents the part of the image that registers the cursor's screen coordinates.

Creating a cursor involves the same initial steps used for creating bitmaps and dialog boxes. The process is started by first selection the File menu and choosing New...menu item command, and then choosing the Cursor File resource.

A cursor's hotspot is set by first clicking on the hotspot button to the right of the Hotspot; label in the design toolbar. Once you have clicked on the button, simply move the mouse pointer into the cursor's bitmap design and click on the appropriate cell.

Books Online

Books Online has an easy-to-use graphical interface that allows you to access hundreds of pages of Microsoft Magazine and book articles.

Notice that each entry has a closed-book icon followed by the book's title. Part of doing an efficient topic search, such as looking up keywords or C/C++ topics, involves knowing the type of information that is available.

One way to do a topic search to first double-click on the book title you are interested in.

When you double-click on a book's title, the graphical display of the Books Online dialog box changes. First, the closed-book icon to the left of the book's title turns into an open book. Listed underneath the title is an expanded drop-down list of associated titles.

Notice that the subtitle's icon changes to an open book. Listed underneath this subtitle are all the names for the pages or chapters available. At this point, once you have found a page or chapter of interest, simply double-click on the item's title.

The new interactive Visual C++ Help Window is brought to the foreground by clicking on the book title *New Features in Visual* C++, and has hot-links to related topics accessed by clicking the mouse over items of interest.

A second approach to executing a search begins with double-clicking on the Help menu and choosing Search button. When you select this option, the dialog box presents you with a standard Windows Search dialog box.

Simply select the **Lifst Books** button to update the workspace to show the requested topic.

Although it is definitely true that Books Online and its associated views make for efficient searches, the utility pair may leave your eyes crossed. Besides, what if you want some hard copy documentation, or you want to further analyze something after your system is shut down? For these and other reasons, many people still prefer reading a printed page over staring endlessly at a computer monitor. Books Online uses a straightforward approach to document printing. Simply click the right mouse button on the help window and choose the Print Topic option. Books Online will print the topic that is displayed in the active window when this command is selected.

Often you will not need to print an entire topic, especially if the selected title is an entire chapter. By choosing the Copy command, you can decide which portions of a topic to print. First select the portion of the help text that you want to print. First select the portion of the help text that you want to print. You select text by placing the mouse pointer inside the text window at the beginning of the text you want to select, holding down the left mouse button, an dragging the mouse until it highlights the desired text. Click the right mouse button inside the help window and choose the Copy button to complete the operation. Copy places the information on the Windows Clipboard. Clipboard contents can be pasted into any Windows-based word processor for printing and editing.

Debugging and Testing

The use of Microsoft's debugging and testing utilities. These utilities are used to locate an application's logical error or errors that are generated when the application is executed simultaneously with other programs.

Syp++ is one of the most dynamic tools shipped with Microsoft Visual C/C++. This utility allows you to "spy" on one or all of the currently loaded Windows applications. This utility's Window option allows you to view each application's name class, module, parent, display window's rectangular screen coordinates, window style and window ID number.

Spp++ also lets you view the messages being sent throughout the environment. There are nine check boxes that allow you to predefine the reported message types:

    (i) Mouse

    (ii) Window

    (iii) Other

    (iv) Input

    (v) Init

    (vi) DDE

(vii) System

(viii) Clipboard

(ix) Non-client

Generate output can be displayed in synchronous or asynchronous mode and sent to a Spy++ window, a file, or to COM1 for remote debugging.

After you have selected the types of windows you want to watch, you use the Window menu to decide if these messages are to be watched for one window only or for all windows. If you choose the Window menu and choosing Window....command, Spy++ waits for you to click the mouse over the window you want to watch.

The Process Viewer dialog box allows you to quickly set and view all of the options necessary to track current processes, threads, and processor timeslicing.

To start the Process Viewer, simply double-click on the PView icon in the Visual C++ group. The Process Viewer can shows the following information:

(a) What happens if a thread or process stop responding to DDE, OLE, or pipe I/O?

(b) How does the program run at different system priorities?

(c) Which processes and threads are using the most CPU time?

(d) What percentage of time is spent running API calls?"

(e) How much memory does the program allocate at various points in its execution, and how much memory is being paged out?

The WinDiff utility, found in the Visual C++ group, allows you to graphically compare and modify two files or two directories. All of the options within WinDiff operate in the manner similar to those commands found in the File Manager.

APPENDICES

APPENDICES

ASCII TABLE

IBM Character Codes			
DEC	HEX	Symbol	Key
0	00	(NULL)	CTRL 2
1	01	☺	CTRL A
2	02	●	CTRL B
3	03	♥	CTRL C
4	04	♦	CTRL D
5	05	♣	CTRL E
6	06	♠	CTRL F
7	07	•	CTRL G
8	08	◘	BACKSPACE
9	09	○	TAB
10	0A	◙	CTRL J
11	0B	♂	CTRL K
12	0C	♀	CTRL L
13	0D	♪	ENTER
14	0E	♫	CTRL N
15	0F	¤	CTRL O
16	10	►	CTRL P
17	11	◄	CTRL Q
18	12	↕	CTRL R
19	13	‼	CTRL S
20	14	¶	CTRL T
21	15	§	CTRL U
22	16	■	CTRL V
23	17	↨	CTRL W
24	18	↑	CTRL X
25	19	↓	CTRL Y
26	1A	→	CTRL Z
27	1B	←	ESC
28	1C	∟	CTRL \

IBM Character Codes			
DEC	HEX	Symbol	Key
29	1D	↔	CTRL]
30	1E	▲	CTRL 6
31	1F	▼	CTRL -
32	20		SPACEBAR
33	21	!	!
34	22	"	"
35	23	#	#
36	24	$	$
37	25	%	%
38	26	&	&
39	27	'	'
40	28	(	(
41	29	)	)
42	2A	*	*
43	2B	+	+
44	2C	,	,
45	2D	-	-
46	2E	.	.
47	2F	/	/
48	30	0	0
49	31	1	1
50	32	2	2
51	33	3	3
52	34	4	4
53	35	5	5
54	36	6	6
55	37	7	7
56	38	8	8
57	39	9	9

IBM Character Codes			
DEC	HEX	Symbol	Key
58	3A	:	⊡
59	3B	;	⊡
60	3C	<	⊙
61	3D	=	⊙
62	3E	>	⊙
63	3F	?	⊙
64	40	@	⊙
65	41	A	Ⓐ
66	42	B	Ⓑ
67	43	C	Ⓒ
68	44	D	Ⓓ
69	45	E	Ⓔ
70	46	F	Ⓕ
71	47	G	Ⓖ
72	48	H	Ⓗ
73	49	I	Ⓘ
74	4A	J	Ⓙ
75	4B	K	Ⓚ
76	4C	L	Ⓛ
77	4D	M	Ⓜ
78	4E	N	Ⓝ
79	4F	O	Ⓞ
80	50	P	Ⓟ
81	51	Q	Ⓠ
82	52	R	Ⓡ
83	53	S	Ⓢ
84	54	T	Ⓣ
85	55	U	Ⓤ
86	56	V	Ⓥ
87	57	W	Ⓦ
88	58	X	Ⓧ
89	59	Y	Ⓨ
90	5A	Z	Ⓩ
91	5B	[	⊙
92	5C	\	⊙
93	5D	]	⊙
94	5E	^	⊙
95	5F	_	⊙
96	60	`	⊙

IBM Character Codes			
DEC	HEX	Symbol	Key
97	61	a	⊙
98	62	b	ⓑ
99	63	c	ⓒ
100	64	d	ⓓ
101	65	e	⊙
102	66	f	ⓕ
103	67	g	ⓖ
104	68	h	ⓗ
105	69	i	ⓘ
106	6A	j	ⓙ
107	6B	k	ⓚ
108	6C	l	ⓛ
109	6D	m	ⓜ
110	6E	n	ⓝ
111	6F	o	ⓞ
112	70	p	ⓟ
113	71	q	ⓠ
114	72	r	ⓡ
115	73	s	ⓢ
116	74	t	ⓣ
117	75	u	ⓤ
118	76	v	ⓥ
119	77	w	ⓦ
120	78	x	ⓧ
121	79	y	ⓨ
122	7A	z	ⓩ
123	7B	{	⊙
124	7C	¦	⊙
125	7D	}	⊙
126	7E	~	⊙
127	7F	Δ	CTRL ←
128	80	Ç	ALT 128
129	81	ü	ALT 129
130	82	é	ALT 130
131	83	â	ALT 131
132	84	ä	ALT 132
133	85	à	ALT 133
134	86	å	ALT 134
135	87	ç	ALT 135

IBM Character Codes

DEC	HEX	Symbol	Key	
136	88	ê	ALT	136
137	89	ë	ALT	137
138	8A	è	ALT	138
139	8B	ï	ALT	139
140	8C	î	ALT	140
141	8D	ì	ALT	141
142	8E	Ä	ALT	142
143	8F	Å	ALT	143
144	90	É	ALT	144
145	91	æ	ALT	145
146	92	Æ	ALT	146
147	93	ô	ALT	147
148	94	ö	ALT	148
149	95	ò	ALT	149
150	96	û	ALT	150
151	97	ù	ALT	151
152	98	ÿ	ALT	152
153	99	Ö	ALT	153
154	9A	Ü	ALT	154
155	9B	¢	ALT	155
156	9C	£	ALT	156
157	9D	¥	ALT	157
158	9E	Pt	ALT	158
159	9F	ƒ	ALT	159
160	A0	á	ALT	160
161	A1	í	ALT	161
162	A2	ó	ALT	162
163	A3	ú	ALT	163
164	A4	ñ	ALT	164
165	A5	Ñ	ALT	165
166	A6	ª	ALT	166
167	A7	º	ALT	167
168	A8	¿	ALT	168
169	A9	⌐	ALT	169
170	AA	¬	ALT	170
171	AB	½	ALT	171
172	AC	¼	ALT	172
173	AD	¡	ALT	173
174	AE	«	ALT	174

IBM Character Codes

DEC	HEX	Symbol	Key	
175	AF	»	ALT	175
176	B0	░	ALT	176
177	B1	▒	ALT	177
178	B2	▓	ALT	178
179	B3	│	ALT	179
180	B4	┤	ALT	180
181	B5	╡	ALT	181
182	B6	╢	ALT	182
183	B7	╖	ALT	183
184	B8	╕	ALT	184
185	B9	╣	ALT	185
186	BA	║	ALT	186
187	BB	╗	ALT	187
188	BC	╝	ALT	188
189	BD	╜	ALT	189
190	BE	╛	ALT	190
191	BF	┐	ALT	191
192	C0	└	ALT	192
193	C1	┴	ALT	193
194	C2	┬	ALT	194
195	C3	├	ALT	195
196	C4	─	ALT	196
197	C5	┼	ALT	197
198	C6	╞	ALT	198
199	C7	╟	ALT	199
200	C8	╚	ALT	200
201	C9	╔	ALT	201
202	CA	╩	ALT	202
203	CB	╦	ALT	203
204	CC	╠	ALT	204
205	CD	═	ALT	205
206	CE	╬	ALT	206
207	CF	╧	ALT	207
208	D0	╨	ALT	208
209	D1	╤	ALT	209
210	D2	╥	ALT	210
211	D3	╙	ALT	211
212	D4	╘	ALT	212
213	D5	╒	ALT	213

663

IBM Character Codes

DEC	HEX	Symbol	Key	DEC	HEX	Symbol	Key
214	D6	π	(ALT) 214	235	EB	δ	(ALT) 235
215	D7	⫟	(ALT) 215	236	EC	∞	(ALT) 236
216	D8	⧖	(ALT) 216	237	ED	φ	(ALT) 237
217	D9	⌐	(ALT) 217	238	EE	ε	(ALT) 238
218	DA	⌐	(ALT) 218	239	EF	∩	(ALT) 239
219	DB	■	(ALT) 219	240	F0	≡	(ALT) 240
220	DC	▬	(ALT) 220	241	F1	±	(ALT) 241
221	DD	▍	(ALT) 221	242	F2	≥	(ALT) 242
222	DE	▐	(ALT) 222	243	F3	≤	(ALT) 243
223	DF	▀	(ALT) 223	244	F4	⌠	(ALT) 244
224	E0	α	(ALT) 224	245	F5	⌡	(ALT) 245
225	E1	β	(ALT) 225	246	F6	÷	(ALT) 246
226	E2	Γ	(ALT) 226	247	F7	≈	(ALT) 247
227	E3	π	(ALT) 227	248	F8	°	(ALT) 248
228	E4	Σ	(ALT) 228	249	F9	•	(ALT) 249
229	E5	σ	(ALT) 229	250	FA		(ALT) 250
230	E6	μ	(ALT) 230	251	FB	√	(ALT) 251
231	E7	τ	(ALT) 231	252	FC	η	(ALT) 252
232	E8	Φ	(ALT) 232	253	FD	²	(ALT) 253
233	E9	Θ	(ALT) 233	254	FE	■	(ALT) 254
234	EA	Ω	(ALT) 234	255	FF	(blank)	(ALT) 255

Note that IBM Extended ASCII characters can be displayed by pressing the (ALT) key and then typing the decimal code of the character on the keypad.

TURBO C++ KEYWORDS

Keywords implement specific C++ language features. They cannot be used as names for variables or other user-defined program elements. Most of the keywords are common to both C and C++, but some are specific to C++. A few are specific to MS-DOS computers and are not found in other C++ implementations, such as Unix.

asm	_far	public
auto	far	register
break	float	return
case	for	_saveregs
catch	friend	_seg
_cdecl	goto	short
cdecl	huge	signed
char	if	sizeof
class	inline	_ss
const	int	static
continue	interrupt	struct
_cs	_loadds	switch
default	long	template
do	_near	this
double	near	typedef
_ds	new	union
else	operator	unsigned
enum	_pascal	virtual
_es	pascal	void
_export	private	volatile
extern	protected	while

CREATING STAND-ALONE GRAPHICS PROGRAMS

In Chapter 11, on graphics, we described a simple approach to creating graphics programs. Unfortunately, in order for a program to run, this approach requires the existence of the Turbo C++ or Borland C++ development system on your computer's hard disk. This is not very satisfactory if you plan to distribute a program to users who are not running Turbo C++ or Borland C++.

However, by using the project feature, described in Chapter 15, we can make *stand-alone* graphics programs—that is, graphics programs that run on any MS-DOS computer, not just one in which the Turbo development system is installed.

SPECIAL FILES

The approach to graphics that we used in Chapter 11 relies on the existence of the directory \TC\BGI (or \BORLANDC\BGI, if you're using Borland C++) in the system. The last argument to the `initgraph()` function specifies the path to this directory, and the graphics functions expect to find various files there. One of these files is the graphics driver. If you're using an EGA or VGA display mode, then this driver is the file EGAVGA.BGI. If you're using CGA, it's CGA.BGI.

If you're using fonts, then your program will need other files from \TC\BGI. These files have the .CHR extension. TRIP.CHR is necessary if you use the triplex font, LITT.CHR for the small font, SANS.CHR for the sans serif font, and GOTH.CHR for the Gothic font. Since your program depends on one or more of these files, it won't run in a computer that doesn't already have them installed in the appropriate directory.

There are several ways to create a stand-alone program that will run on any machine. Here's one of the simplest.

Three steps are necessary. First you insert into your source file certain functions to *register* the drivers and fonts you use. Next you convert any .BGI or .CHR files your program needs to .OBJ files. And finally you link these .OBJ files to your program using the Turbo C++ project facility. Let's look at these steps in more detail.

REGISTERING DRIVERS AND FONTS

To create a stand-alone program you must link various files together. Some of these files are derived from the drivers and font files that are normally in the BGI directory. The graphics system must be told that these files are supplied at link time and are therefore not found in the BGI directory. Telling this to the graphics system is called *registering* the files.

Two functions are used for this purpose. The `registerbgidriver()` function registers drivers like CGA.BGI and EGAVGA.BGI. However, these filenames themselves are not used as arguments to this function. What Borland calls *symbolic* filenames are used instead. For the files shown, these are `CGA_driver` and `EGAVGA_driver`.

The `registerbgifont()` function registers font files like SANS.CHR. Table C-1 shows the correspondence between the filenames and the names to be supplied to this function. The registration functions go just before `initgraph()`.

Let's assume that we want to create a stand-alone version of the CALC program presented in Chapter 15. (The process would be similar with other graphics programs.) Here's how to rewrite the CALC_APP.CPP file:

```
registerbgidriver(EGAVGA_driver); // register driver
registerbgifont(sansserif_font);  // register font
int driver, mode;
driver = EGA;
mode = EGAHI;
initgraph(&driver, &mode, "");     // initialize graphics system
```

The pathname in `initgraph()` is not necessary when the driver is registered, and can be left blank as shown.

TABLE C-1 Symbolic Font Names	
Filename	Symbolic name
TRIP.CHR	triplex_font
LITT.CHR	small_font
SANS.CHR	sansserif_font
GOTH.CHR	gothic_font

CONVERTING THE .BGI AND .CHR FILES

In order for drivers and font files to be linked with your application files, they must be converted to object form. You use the BGIOBJ.EXE utility to convert .BGI or .CHR files to .OBJ files. Simply enter **BGIOBJ**, followed by the name of the file, without the extension. In CALC we convert EGAVGA.BGI to EGAVGA.OBJ, and SANS.CHR to SANS.OBJ. You would enter

```
C>bgiobj egavga
```

and

```
C>bgiobj sans
```

LINKING MULTIPLE FILES

Now we're ready to compile and link the various files we've created into a final executable file, using the project facility. Make sure all the files you need are in the same directory. (Actually you can put the files wherever you want, but it's simpler if they're all in one place.) These files include all the .OBJ files generated from .BGI and .CHR files, and the .CPP source file (or files) for your program. In CALC these are CALC.CPP, CALC_APP.CPP, EGAVGA.OBJ, and SANS.OBJ.

Create a project file for these files, as described in Chapter 15. Give it the name of your main .CPP file, such as CALC_APP.PRJ. Then create the final .EXE file by selecting *Make EXE File* from the Compile menu. In the CALC example you'll emerge with a CALC_APP.EXE file that can be executed on any MS-DOS computer (provided it has an EGA or VGA display).

ANSWERS TO QUESTIONS AND EXERCISES

Chapter 1
Answers to Questions

1. procedural, object-oriented
2. b
3. data, act on that data
4. a
5. data hiding
6. a, d
7. objects
8. false; the organizational principles are different
9. encapsulation
10. d
11. false; most lines of code are the same in C and C++
12. polymorphism
13. d
14. b

Chapter 3
Answers to Questions

1. b, c
2. parentheses
3. braces { }
4. It's the first function executed when the program starts
5. statement

6. ```
// this is a comment
/* this is a comment */
```

7. a, d

8. a. 2
   b. 10
   c. 4
   d. 4

9. false

10. a. integer constant
    b. character constant
    c. floating-point constant
    d. variable name (could also be something else)
    e. function name

11. a. `cout << 'x';`
    b. `cout << "Jim";`
    c. `cout << 509;`

12. false; they're not equal until the statement is executed

13. `cout << setw(10) << george;`

14. IOSTREAM.H

15. `cin >> temp;`

16. IOMANIP.H

17. string constants, preprocessor directives, comments

18. true

19. 2

20. assignment (=) and arithmetic (like + and *)

21. ```
temp += 23;
temp = temp + 23;
```

22. 1

23. 2020

24. to provide declarations and other data for library functions, overloaded operators, and objects

25. CS.LIB

Solutions to Exercises

1. ```
// ex3_1.cpp
// converts gallons to cubic feet
#include <iostream.h>

void main()
   {
   float gallons, cufeet;
```
```

```
        cout << "\nEnter quantity in gallons: ";
        cin >> gallons;
        cufeet = gallons / 7.481;
        cout << "Equivalent in cublic feet is " << cufeet;
        }
```

2.
```
// ex3_2.cpp
// generates table
#include <iostream.h>
#include <iomanip.h>

main()
    {
    cout << endl << 1990 << setw(8) << 135
         << endl << 1991 << setw(8) << 7290
         << endl << 1992 << setw(8) << 11300
         << endl << 1993 << setw(8) << 16200;
    }
```

3.
```
// ex3_3.cpp
// exercises arithmetic assignment and decrement
#include <iostream.h>

void main()
    {
    int var = 10;
    cout << endl << var;        // var is 10
    var *= 2;                   // var becomes 20
    cout << endl << var--;      // displays var, then decrements it
    cout << endl << var;        // var is 19
    }
```

Chapter 4

Answers to Questions

1. b, c
2. `george != sally`
3. -1 is true; only 0 is false.
4. The initialize expression initializes the loop variable, the test expression tests the loop variable, and the increment expression changes the loop variable.
5. c, d
6. true
7.
```
for(int j=100; j<=110; j++)
    cout << endl << j;
```
8. braces (curly brackets)
9. c

10.
```
int j = 100;
while( j <= 110 )
    cout << endl << j++;
```
11. false
12. at least once
13.
```
int j = 100;
do
    cout << endl << j++;
while( j <= 110 );
```
14.
```
if(age > 21)
    cout << "Yes";
```
15. d
16.
```
if( age > 21 )
    cout << "Yes";
else
    cout << "No";
```
17. a, c
18. '\r'
19. preceding, surrounded by braces
20. reformatting
21.
```
switch(ch)
    {
    case 'y':
        cout << "Yes";
        break;
    case 'n':
        cout << "No";
        break;
    default:
        cout << "Unknown response";
    }
```
22. `ticket = (speed > 55) ? 1 : 0;`
23. d
24. `limit == 55 && speed > 55`
25. unary, arithmetic, relational, logical, conditional, assignment
26. d
27. the top of the loop
28. b

Solutions to Exercises

1.
```
// ex4_1.cpp
// displays multiples of a number
#include <iostream.h>
#include <iomanip.h>                    // for setw()
```

```
    void main()
        {
        unsigned long n;                        // number

        cout << "\nEnter a number: ";
        cin >> n;                               // get number
        for(int j=1; j<=200; j++)               // loop from 1 to 200
            {
            cout << setw(5) << j*n << "  ";     // print multiple of n
            if( j%10 == 0 )                     // every 10 numbers,
                cout << endl;                   // start new line
            }
        }
```

2. `// ex4_2.cpp`

```
    // converts fahrenheit to centigrad, or
    // centigrad to fahrenheit
    #include <iostream.h>

    void main()
        {
        int response;
        double temper;

        cout << "\nType 1 to convert fahrenheit to celsius,"
             << "\n     2 to convert celsius to fahrenheit: ";
        cin >> response;
        if( response == 1 )
            {
            cout << "Enter temperature in fahrenheit: ";
            cin >> temper;
            cout << "In celsius that's " << 5.0/9.0*(temper-32.0);
            }
        else
            {
            cout << "Enter temperature in celsius: ";
            cin >> temper;
            cout << "In fahrenheit that's " << 9.0/5.0*temper + 32.0;
            }
        }
```

3. `// ex4_3.cpp`

```
    // makes a number out of digits
    #include <iostream.h>
    #include <conio.h>                          // for getche()

    void main()
        {
        char ch = 'a';                          // ensure it isn't '\r'
        unsigned long total = 0;                // this holds the number

        cout << "\nEnter a number: ";
        while( (ch=getche()) != '\r' )          // quit on Enter
```

```
              total = total*10 + ch-'0';        // add digit to total*10
          cout << "\nNumber is: " << total;
          }
  4. // ex4_4.cpp
     // models four-function calculator
     #include <iostream.h>
     #include <conio.h>                    // for getche()

     void main()
         {
         double n1, n2, ans;
         char oper, ch;
         do
             {
             cout << "\nEnter first number, operator, second number: ";
             cin >> n1 >> oper >> n2;
             switch(oper)
                 {
                 case '+':  ans = n1 + n2;  break;
                 case '-':  ans = n1 - n2;  break;
                 case '*':  ans = n1 * n2;  break;
                 case '/':  ans = n1 / n2;  break;
                 default:   ans = 0;
                 }
             cout << "Answer = " << ans;
             cout << "\nDo another (y/n)? ";
             ch = getche();
             } while( ch != 'n' );

         }
```

Chapter 5

Answers to Questions

1. b, d
2. true
3. semicolon
4. ```
   struct time
       {
       int hrs;
       int mins;
       int secs;
       };
   ```
5. false; only a variable definition creates space in memory
6. c
7. `time2.hrs = 11;`
8. 18 (3 structures times 3 integers times 2 bytes)
   ```

9. `time time1 = { 11, 10, 59 };`

10. true

11. `temp = fido.dog.paw;`

12. c, d

13. `enum players { B1, B2, SS, B3, RF, CF, LF, C, P };`

14. `players joe, tom;`
    `        joe = LF;`
    `        tom = P;`

15. a. no
    b. yes
    c. no
    d. yes

16. 0, 1, 2

17. `enum speeds { obsolete=78, single=45, album=33 };`

18. Because `false` should be represented by 0.

Solutions to Exercises

1.
```
// ex5_1.cpp
// uses structure to store phone number
#include <iostream.h>

struct phone
   {
   int area;          // area code (3 digits)
   int exchange;      // exchange (3 digits)
   int number;        // number (4 digits)
   };

void main()
   {
   phone ph1 = { 212, 767, 8900 };  // initialize phone number
   phone ph2;                       // define phone number
                                    // get phone no from user
   cout << "\nEnter your area code, exchange, and number: ";
   cin >> ph2.area >> ph2.exchange >> ph2.number;

   cout << "\nMy number is "        // display numbers
        << '(' << ph1.area << ") "
        << ph1.exchange << '-' << ph1.number;

   cout << "\nYour number is "
        << '(' << ph2.area << ") "
        << ph2.exchange << '-' << ph2.number;
   }
```

```
2. // ex5_2.cpp
   // structure models point on the plane
   #include <iostream.h>

   struct point
      {
      int xCo;        // X coordinate
      int yCo;        // Y coordinate
      };

   void main()
      {
      point p1, p2, p3;                             // define 3 points

      cout << "\nEnter coordinates for p1: ";       // get 2 points
      cin >> p1.xCo >> p1.yCo;                      // from user
      cout << "Enter coordinates for p2: ";
      cin >> p2.xCo >> p2.yCo;

      p3.xCo = p1.xCo + p2.xCo;                     // find sum of
      p3.yCo = p1.yCo + p2.yCo;                     // p1 and p2

      cout << "Coordinates of p1+p2 are: "          // display the sum
           << p3.xCo << ", " << p3.yCo;
      }
```

```
3. // ex5_3.cpp
   // uses structure to model volume of room
   #include <iostream.h>

   struct Distance
      {
      int feet;
      float inches;
      };

   struct Volume
      {
      Distance length;
      Distance width;
      Distance height;
      };

   void main()
      {
      float l, w, h;
      Volume room1 = { { 16, 3.5 }, { 12, 6.25 }, { 8, 1.75 } };

      l = room1.length.feet + room1.length.inches / 12.0;
      w = room1.width.feet  + room1.width.inches  / 12.0;
      h = room1.height.feet + room1.height.inches / 12.0;

      cout << "\nVolume = " << l*w*h << " cubic feet";
      }
```

Chapter 6

Answers to Questions

1. d (half credit for b)
2. definition
3. ```
   void foo()
       {
       cout << "foo";
       }
   ```
4. declaration, prototype
5. body
6. call
7. declarator
8. c
9. false
10. to clarify the purpose of the arguments
11. a, b, and c
12. empty parentheses mean the function takes no arguments
13. one
14. true
15. at the beginning of the declaration and declarator
16. `void`
17. ```
    main()
        {
        int times2(int);          // prototype
        int alpha = times2(37);   // function call
        }
    ```
18. a
19. to modify the original argument
20. a, c
21. ```
    int bar(char);
    int bar(char, char);
    ```
22. faster, more
23. `inline float foobar(float)`
24. a, b
25. `char blyth(int, float=3.14159);`
26. visibility, lifetime
27. those functions defined following the variable definition
28. the function in which it is defined
29. b, d
30. on the left side of the equals sign
    ```

Solutions to Exercises

1.
```cpp
// ex6_1.cpp
// function finds area of circle
#include <iostream.h>

float circarea(float radius);

void main()
    {
    double rad;
    cout << "\nEnter radius of circle: ";
    cin >> rad;
    cout << "Area is " << circarea(rad);
    }

float circarea(float r)
    {
    const float PI = 3.14159;
    return r * r * PI;
    }
```

2.
```cpp
// ex6_2.cpp
// function raises number to a power
#include <iostream.h>

double power( float n, int p=2);      // p has default value 2

void main()
    {
    double number, answer;
    int pow;
    char yeserno;

    cout << "\nEnter number: ";        // get number
    cin >> number;
    cout << "Want to enter a power (y/n)? ";
    cin >> yeserno;
    if( yeserno == 'y' )               // user wants a non-2 power?
        {
        cout << "Enter power: ";
        cin >> pow;
        answer = power(number, pow);   // raise number to pow
        }
    else
        answer = power(number);        // square the number
    cout << "Answer is " << answer;
    }

// power()
// returns number n raised to a power p
double power( float n, int p )
```

```
     {
     double result = 1.0;              // start with 1
     for(int j=0; j<p; j++)            // multiply by n
        result *= n;                   // p times
     return result;
     }
```

3. `// ex6_3.cpp`

```
// function sets larger of two numbers to 0
#include <iostream.h>

void main()
     {
     void zeroSmaller(int&, int&);
     int a=4, b=7, c=11, d=9;

     zeroSmaller(a, b);
     zeroSmaller(c, d);
     cout << "\na=" << a << " b=" << b
          << " c=" << c << " d=" << d;
     }

// zeroSmaller()
// sets the smaller of two numbers to 0
void zeroSmaller(int& first, int& second)
     {
     if( first < second )
        first = 0;
     else
        second = 0;
     }
```

4. `// ex6_4.cpp`

```
// function returns larger of two distances
#include <iostream.h>

struct Distance                        // English distance
     {
     int feet;
     float inches;
     };
                                       // declarations
Distance bigengl(Distance, Distance);
void engldisp(Distance);

void main()
     {
     Distance d1, d2, d3;              // define three lengths
                                       // get length d1 from user
     cout << "\nEnter feet: ";  cin >> d1.feet;
     cout << "Enter inches: ";  cin >> d1.inches;
                                       // get length d2 from user
```

```
      cout << "\nEnter feet: ";   cin >> d2.feet;
      cout << "Enter inches: ";   cin >> d2.inches;

      d3 = bigengl(d1, d2);          // d3 is larger of d1 and d2
                                     // display all lengths
      cout << "\nd1="; engldisp(d1);
      cout << "\nd2="; engldisp(d2);
      cout << "\nlargest is "; engldisp(d3);
      }

// bigengl()
// compares two structures of type Distance, returns the larger
Distance bigengl( Distance dd1, Distance dd2 )
      {
      if(dd1.feet > dd2.feet)        // if feet are different, return
         return dd1;                 // the one with the largest feet
      if(dd1.feet < dd2.feet)
         return dd2;
      if(dd1.inches > dd2.inches)    // if inches are different,
         return dd1;                 // return one with largest
      else                           // inches, or dd2 if equal
         return dd2;
      }

// engldisp()
// display structure of type Distance in feet and inches
void engldisp( Distance dd )
      {
      cout << dd.feet << "\'-" << dd.inches << "\"";
      }
```

Chapter 7

Answers to Questions

1. A class specifier describes how objects of a class will look when they are created.

2. class, object

3. c

4. ```
   class leverage
      {
      private:
         int crowbar;
      public:
         void pry();
      };
   ```

5. false; both data and functions can be private or public
   ```

6. `leverage lever1;`

7. d

8. `lever1.pry();`

9. inline (also **private**)

10. `int getcrow()`
       `{ return crowbar; }`

11. defined (created)

12. the class of which it is a member

13. `leverage()`
       `{ crowbar = 0; }`

14. true

15. a

16. `int getcrow();`

17. `int leverage::getcrow()`
       `{ return crowbar; }`

18. Member functions and data are, by default, public in structures but private in classes.

19. three, one

20. calling one of its member functions

21. b, c, d

22. false; trial and error may be necessary

Solutions to Exercises

```
1. // ex7_1.cpp
   // uses a class to model an integer data type
   #include <iostream.h>

   class Int                          // (not the same as int)
      {
      private:
         int i;
      public:
         Int()                        // create an Int
            { i = 0; }
         Int(int ii)                  // create and initialize an Int
          { i = ii; }
         void add(Int i2, Int i3)     // add two Ints
            { i = i2.i + i3.i; }
         void display()               // display an Int
            { cout << i; }
      };

   void main()
      {
```

```
    Int Int1(7);                // create and initialize an Int
    Int Int2(11);               // create and initialize an Int
    Int Int3;                   // create an Int

    Int3.add(Int1, Int2);               // add two Ints
    cout << "\nInt3 = "; Int3.display();  // display result
    }
```

2.
```
// ex7_2.cpp
// uses class to model toll booth
#include <iostream.h>
#include <conio.h>

const char ESC = 27;        // escape key ASCII code
const double TOLL = 0.5;    // toll is 50 cents

class tollBooth
    {
    private:
        unsigned int totalCars;   // total cars passed today
        double totalCash;         // total money collected today
    public:
        tollBooth()                             // constructor
            { totalCars = 0; totalCash = 0.0; }
        void payingCar()                        // a car paid
            { totalCars++; totalCash += TOLL; }
        void nopayCar()                         // a car didn't pay
            { totalCars++; }
        void display()                          // display totals
            { cout << "\nCars=" << totalCars
                   << ", cash=" << totalCash; }
    };

void main()
    {
    tollBooth booth1;           // create a toll booth
    char ch;

    cout << "\nPress 0 for each non-paying car,"
         << "\n      1 for each paying car,"
         << "\n      Esc to exit the program.\n";
    do
        {
        ch = getche();          // get character
        if( ch == '0' )         // if it's 0, car didn't pay
            booth1.nopayCar();
        if( ch == '1' )         // if it's 1, car paid
            booth1.payingCar();
        } while( ch != ESC );   // exit loop on Esc key
    booth1.display();           // display totals
    }
```

3. // ex7_3.cpp
```cpp
// uses class to model a time data type
#include <iostream.h>

class time
    {
    private:
        int hrs, mins, secs;
    public:
        time()                             // no-arg constructor
            { hrs = mins = secs = 0; }

        time(int h, int m, int s)          // 3-arg constructor
            { hrs=h; mins=m; secs=s; }

        void display()                     // format 11:59:59
            { cout << hrs << ":" << mins << ":" << secs; }

        void add_time(time t1, time t2)    // add two times
            {
            secs = t1.secs + t2.secs;      // add seconds
            if( secs > 59 )                // if overflow,
                { secs -= 60; mins++; }    //    carry a minute
            mins += t1.mins + t2.mins;     // add minutes
            if( mins > 59 )                // if overflow,
                { mins -= 60; hrs++; }     //    carry an hour
            hrs += t1.hrs + t2.hrs;        // add hours
            }
    };

void main()
    {
    time time1(5, 59, 59);                 // creates and initialze
    time time2(4, 30, 30);                 //     two times
    time time3;                            // create another time

    time3.add_time(time1, time2);          // add two times
    cout << "\ntime3 = "; time3.display(); // display result
    }
```

Chapter 8

Answers to Questions

1. d
2. same
3. `double doubleArray[100];`
4. 0, 9
5. `cout << doubleArray[j];`

6. c

7. `int coins[] = { 1, 5, 10, 25, 50, 100 };`

8. d

9. `twoD[2][4]`

10. true

11. `float flarr[3][3] = { {52,27,83}, {94,73,49}, {3,6,1}, };`

12. memory address

13. a, d

14. an array with 1000 elements of structure or class `employee`.

15. `emplist[17].salary`

16. c

17. `bird manybirds[50];`

18. false

19. `manybirds[27].cheep();`

20. array, `char`

21. `char city[21]` (An extra byte is needed for the null character.)

22. `char dextrose[] = "C6H1206-H2O";`

23. true

24. d

25. `strcpy(blank, name);`

26.
```
class dog
    {
    private:
        char breed[80];
        int age;
    }
```

Solutions to Exercises

1.
```
// ex8_1.cpp
// reverses a string
#include <iostream.h>
#include <string.h>                    // for strlen()

const int MAX = 80;

void main()
    {
    void reversit( char[] );           // prototype
    char str[MAX];                     // string

    cout << "\nEnter a string: ";      // get string from user
    cin.get(str, MAX);
```

```
    reversit(str);                        // reverse the string

    cout << "Reversed string is: ";  // display it
    cout << str;
    }

// reversit()
// function to reverse a string passed to it as an argument
void reversit( char s[] )
    {
    int len = strlen(s);                 // find length of string
    for(int j = 0; j < len/2; j++)       // swap each character
        {                                //    in first half
        char temp = s[j];                //    with character
        s[j] = s[len-j-1];               //    in second half
        s[len-j-1] = temp;
        }
    }
```

2.
```
// ex8_2.cpp
// employee object uses a string as data
#include <iostream.h>

const int LEN = 80;

class employee
    {
    private:
        char name[LEN];
        long number;
    public:
        void getdata()                          // get data from user
            {
            cout << "\nEnter name: ";  cin >> name;
            cout << "Enter number: "; cin >> number;
            }
        void putdata()                          // display data
            {
            cout << "\n   Name: " << name;
            cout << "\n   Number: " << number;
            }
    };

void main()
    {
    employee emparr[100];          // an array of employees
    int n = 0;                     // how many employees
    char ch;                       // user response

    do                             // get data from user
        {
        cout << "\nEnter data for employee number " << n+1;
```

687

```
        emparr[n++].getdata();
        cout << "Enter another (y/n)? "; cin >> ch;
        }
     while( ch != 'n' );

     for(int j=0; j<n; j++)          // display data in array
        {
        cout << "\nEmployee number " << j+1;
        emparr[j].putdata();
        }
     }
```

3. `// ex8_3.cpp`

```cpp
// ex8_3.cpp
// averages an array of Distance objects input by user
#include <iostream.h>

class Distance                          // English Distance class
   {
   private:
      int feet;
      float inches;
   public:
      Distance()                        // constructor (no args)
         { feet = 0; inches = 0; }
      Distance(int ft, float in)  // constructor (two args)
         { feet = ft; inches = in; }

      void getdist()                    // get length from user
         {
         cout << "\nEnter feet: ";  cin >> feet;
         cout << "Enter inches: ";  cin >> inches;
         }

      void showdist()                   // display distance
         { cout << feet << "\'-" << inches << '\"'; }

      void add_dist( Distance, Distance );    // declarations
      void div_dist( Distance, int );
   };
                                        // add Distances d2 and d3
void Distance::add_dist(Distance d2, Distance d3)
   {
   inches = d2.inches + d3.inches;  // add the inches
   feet = 0;                        // (for possible carry)
   if(inches >= 12.0)               // if total exceeds 12.0,
      {                             // then decrease inches
      inches -= 12.0;               // by 12.0 and
      feet++;                       // increase feet
      }                             // by 1
   feet += d2.feet + d3.feet;       // add the feet
   }

                                    // divide Distance by int
```

```
void Distance::div_dist(Distance d2, int divisor)
    {
    float fltfeet = d2.feet + d2.inches/12.0;   // convert to float
    fltfeet /= divisor;                          // do division
    feet = int(fltfeet);                         // get feet part
    inches = (fltfeet-feet) * 12.0;              // get inches part
    }


void main()
    {
    Distance distarr[100];          // array of 100 Distances
    Distance total, average;        // other Distances
    int count = 0;                  // counts Distances input
    char ch;                        // user response character
    do
        {
        cout << "\nEnter a Distance";           // get Distances
        distarr[count++].getdist();             // from user, put
        cout << "\nDo another (y/n)? ";         // in array
        cin >> ch;
        }
    while( ch != 'n' );

    for(int j=0; j<count; j++)                   // add all Distances
        total.add_dist( total, distarr[j] );     // to total
    average.div_dist( total, count-1 );          // divide by number

    cout << "\nThe average is: ";                // display average
    average.showdist();
    }
```

Chapter 9

Answers to Questions

1. a, c
2. x3.subtract(x2, x1);
3. x3 = x2 - x1;
4. true
5. void operator -- ()   { counter--; }
6. none
7. b, d
8. ```
   void Distance::operator ++ ()
       {
       ++feet;
       }
   ```
9. ```
   Distance Distance::operator ++ ()
       {
       int f = ++feet;
   ```

```
        float i = inches;
        return Distance(f, i);
    }
```

10. There is no difference (at least in current versions of Turbo C++ and Borland C++)

11. c, e, b, a, d

12. twice, same

13. b

14.
```
String String::operator ++ ()
    {
    int len = strlen(str);
    for(int j=0; j<len; j++)
        str[j] = toupper( str[j] )
    return String(str);
    }
```

15. d

16. false if there is a conversion routine; true otherwise

17. b

18. true

19. constructor

20. true, but it will be hard for humans to understand

Solutions to Exercises

1.
```
// ex9_1.cpp
// overloaded '-' operator subtracts two Distances
#include <iostream.h>

class Distance                       // English Distance class
    {
    private:
        int feet;
        float inches;
    public:
        Distance()                   // constructor (no args)
            { feet = 0; inches = 0.0; }
        Distance(int ft, float in)  // constructor (two args)
            { feet = ft; inches = in; }

        void getdist()               // get length from user
            {
            cout << "\nEnter feet: ";  cin >> feet;
            cout << "Enter inches: ";  cin >> inches;
            }

        void showdist()              // display distance
            { cout << feet << "\'-" << inches << '\"'; }
```

```
        Distance operator + ( Distance );   // add two distances
        Distance operator - ( Distance );   // subtract two distances
    };                                      // add d2 to this distance
Distance Distance::operator + (Distance d2)   // return the sum
    {
    int f = feet + d2.feet;         // add the feet
    float i = inches + d2.inches;   // add the inches
    if(i >= 12.0)                   // if total exceeds 12.0,
        {                           // then decrease inches
        i -= 12.0;                  // by 12.0 and
        f++;                        // increase feet by 1
        }                           // return a temporary Distance
    return Distance(f,i);           // initialized to sum
    }
                                    // subtract d2 from this dist
Distance Distance::operator - (Distance d2)   // return the diff
    {
    int f = feet - d2.feet;         // subtract the feet
    float i = inches - d2.inches;   // subtract the inches
    if(i < 0)                       // if inches less than 0,
        {                           // then increase inches
        i += 12.0;                  // by 12.0 and
        f--;                        // decrease feet by 1
        }                           // return a temporary Distance
    return Distance(f,i);           // initialized to difference
    }

void main()
    {
    Distance dist1, dist3;          // define distances
    dist1.getdist();                // get dist1 from user

    Distance dist2(3, 6.25);        // define, initialize dist2

    dist3 = dist1 - dist2;          // subtract

                                    // display all lengths
    cout << "\ndist1 = ";  dist1.showdist();
    cout << "\ndist2 = ";  dist2.showdist();
    cout << "\ndist3 = ";  dist3.showdist();
    }
```

2. ```
   // ex9_2.cpp
   // overloaded '+=' operator concatenates strings
   #include <iostream.h>
   #include <string.h>              // for strcpy(), strcat()

   const int SZ = 80;               // size of all String objects

   class String                     // user-defined string type
       {
   ```
   ```

```
        private:
            char str[SZ];                       // holds a string
        public:
            String()                            // constructor, no args
                { strcpy(str, ""); }
            String( char s[] )                  // constructor, one arg
                { strcpy(str, s); }
            void display()                      // display the String
                { cout << str; }
            String operator += (String ss)      // add a String to this one
                {                               // result stays in this one
                if( strlen(str) + strlen(ss.str) < SZ )
                    {
                    strcat(str, ss.str);        // add the argument string
                    return String(str);         // return temp String
                    }
                else
                    cout << "\nString overflow";
                }
        };

    void main()
        {
        String s1 = "\nMerry Christmas!  ";     // uses constructor 2
        String s2 = "Happy new year!";          // uses constructor 2
        String s3;                              // uses constructor 1

        s3 = s1 += s2;          // add s2 to s1, assign to s3

        cout << "\ns1="; s1.display();          // display s1
        cout << "\ns2="; s2.display();          // display s2
        cout << "\ns3="; s3.display();          // display s3
        }
```

3. `// ex9_3.cpp`
```
    // overloaded '+' operator adds two times
    #include <iostream.h>

    class time
        {
        private:
            int hrs, mins, secs;
        public:
            time()                              // no-arg constructor
                { hrs = mins = secs = 0; }

            time(int h, int m, int s)           // 3-arg constructor
                { hrs=h; mins=m; secs=s; }

            void display()                      // format 11:59:59
                { cout << hrs << ":" << mins << ":" << secs; }
```

```
    time operator + (time t2)          // add two times
       {
       secs += t2.secs;                // add seconds
       if( secs > 59 )                 // if overflow,
          { secs -= 60; mins++; }      //    carry a minute
       mins += t2.mins;                // add minutes
       if( mins > 59 )                 // if overflow,
          { mins -= 60; hrs++; }       //    carry an hour
       hrs += t2.hrs;                  // add hours
       return time(hrs, mins, secs);   // return this value
       }
    };

void main()
   {
   time time1(5, 59, 59);                  // create and initialze
   time time2(4, 30, 30);                  //    two times
   time time3;                             // create another time

   time3 = time1 + time2;                  // add two times
   cout << "\ntime3 = "; time3.display();  // display result
   }
```

4. `// ex9_4.cpp`

```
// overloaded arithmetic operators work with type Int
#include <iostream.h>
#include <process.h>        // for exit()

class Int
   {
   private:
      int i;
   public:
      Int()                            // no-arg constructor
         { i = 0; }
      Int(int ii)                      // 1-arg constructor
         { i = ii; }                   //    (int to Int)
      void putInt()                    // display Int
         { cout << i; }
      void getInt()                    // read Int from kbd
         { cin >> i; }
      operator int()                   // conversion function
         { return i; }                 //    (Int to int)
      Int operator + (Int i2)          // addition
         { return checkit( long(int(i))+long(int(i2)) ); }
      Int operator - (Int i2)          // subtraction
         { return checkit( long(int(i))-long(int(i2)) ); }
      Int operator * (Int i2)          // multiplication
         { return checkit( long(int(i))*long(int(i2)) ); }
```

```
        Int operator / (Int i2)            // division
           { return checkit( long(int(i))/long(int(i2)) ); }
        Int operator % (Int i2)            // remainder
           { return checkit( long(int(i))%long(int(i2)) ); }

        Int checkit(long answer)           // check results
           {
           if( answer > 32767 || answer < -32768 )
              { cout << "\nError: overflow"; exit(1); }
           else
              return Int(int(answer));
           }
     };

  void main()
     {
     Int alpha = 20;
     Int beta = 7;
     Int gamma;

     gamma = alpha + beta;
     cout << "\ngamma="; gamma.putInt();
     gamma = alpha - beta;
     cout << "\ngamma="; gamma.putInt();
     gamma = alpha * beta;
     cout << "\ngamma="; gamma.putInt();
     gamma = alpha / beta;
     cout << "\ngamma="; gamma.putInt();
     gamma = alpha % beta;
     cout << "\ngamma="; gamma.putInt();
     }
```

Chapter 10

Answers to Questions

1. a, c
2. derived
3. b, c, d
4. class Bosworth : public Alphonso
5. false
6. `protected`
7. yes
8. `BosworthObj.alfunc();`
9. true
10. the one in the derived class
11. `Bosworth() : Alphonso()  { }`
12. c, d

13. true

14. `Derv(int arg) : Base(arg)`

15. d

16. true

17. c

18. `class Tire : public Wheel, public Rubber`

19. `Base::func();`

20. false

Solutions to Exercises

1.
```cpp
// ex10_1.cpp
// publication class and derived classes
#include <iostream.h>

const int LEN = 80;

class publication                        // base class
    {
    private:
        char title[LEN];
        float price;
    public:
        void getdata()
            {
            cout << "\nEnter title: "; cin >> title;
            cout << "Enter price: "; cin >> price;
            }
        void putdata()
            {
            cout << "\nTitle: " << title;
            cout << "\nPrice: " << price;
            }
    };

class book : private publication         // derived class
    {
    private:
        int pages;
    public:
        void getdata()
            {
            publication::getdata();
            cout << "Enter number of pages: "; cin >> pages;
            }
        void putdata()
            {
            publication::putdata();
```

```
                cout << "\nPages: " << pages;
                }
        };

    class tape : private publication           // derived class
        {
        private:
            float time;
        public:
            void getdata()
                {
                publication::getdata();
                cout << "Enter playing time: "; cin >> time;
                }
            void putdata()
                {
                publication::putdata();
                cout << "\nPlaying time: " << time;
                }
        };

    void main()
        {
        book book1;                            // define publications
        tape tape1;

        book1.getdata();                       // get data for them
        tape1.getdata();

        book1.putdata();                       // display their data
        tape1.putdata();
        }
```

2. ```
// ex10_2.cpp
// inheritance from String class
#include <iostream.h>
#include <string.h>   // for strcpy(), etc.

const int SZ = 80;   // size of all String objects

class String   // base class
    {
    protected: // Note: can't be private
        char str[SZ];   // holds a string
    public:
        String()   // constructor 0, no args
            { str[0] = '\0'; }
        String(char s[])   // constructor 1, one arg
            { strcpy(str, s); }   //   convert string to String
        void display()   // display the String
            { cout << str; }
```
```

```
        operator char*()              // conversion function
            { return str; }           //    convert String to string
    };

    class Pstring : public String     // derived class
        {
        public:
            Pstring( char s[] );       // constructor
        };

    Pstring::Pstring( char s[] )       // constructor for Pstring
        {
        int len = strlen(s);           // check length of argument
        if(len > SZ-1)                 // if too long,
            {
            for(int j=0; j<SZ-1; j++)  // copy the first SZ-1
                str[j] = s[j];         // characters "by hand"
            str[j] = '\0';             // add the null character
            }
        else                           // not too long,
            strcpy(str, s);            // so copy entire string
        }

    void main()
        {                                       // define String
        Pstring s1 = "This is a very long string which is probably--\
    no, certainly--going to exceed the limit set in SZ.";
        cout << "\ns1="; s1.display();          // display String

        Pstring s2 = "This is a short string.";  // define String
        cout << "\ns2="; s2.display();           // display String
        }

3. // ex10_3.cpp
    // multiple inheritance with publication class
    #include <iostream.h>

    const int LEN = 80;
    const int MONTHS = 3;

    class publication
        {
        private:
            char title[LEN];
            float price;
        public:
            void getdata()
                {
                cout << "\nEnter title: "; cin >> title;
                cout << "   Enter price: "; cin >> price;
                }
```

897

```cpp
    void putdata()
        {
        cout << "\nTitle: " << title;
        cout << "\n   Price: " << price;
        }
    };

class sales
    {
    private:
        float sales[MONTHS];
    public:
        void getdata();
        void putdata();
    };

void sales::getdata()
    {
    cout << "   Enter sales for 3 months\n";
    for(int j=0; j<MONTHS; j++)
        {
        cout << "      Month " << j+1 << ": ";
        cin >> sales[j];
        }
    }
void sales::putdata()
    {
    for(int j=0; j<MONTHS; j++)
        {
        cout << "\n   Sales for month " << j+1 << ": ";
        cout << sales[j];
        }
    }

class book : private publication, private sales
    {
    private:
        int pages;
    public:
        void getdata()
            {
            publication::getdata();
            cout << "   Enter number of pages: "; cin >> pages;
            sales::getdata();
            }
        void putdata()
            {
            publication::putdata();
            cout << "\n   Pages: " << pages;
            sales::putdata();
```

```
            }
        };

    class tape : private publication, private sales
        {
        private:
            float time;
        public:
            void getdata()
                {
                publication::getdata();
                cout << "    Enter playing time: "; cin >> time;
                sales::getdata();
                }
            void putdata()
                {
                publication::putdata();
                cout << "\n    Playing time: " << time;
                sales::putdata();
                }
        };

    void main()
        {
        book book1;            // define publications
        tape tape1;

        book1.getdata();       // get data for publications
        tape1.getdata();

        book1.putdata();       // display data for publications
        tape1.putdata();
        }
```

Chapter 11

Answers to Questions

1. a, b, c, d
2. window()
3. false
4. ```
   int driver=VGA, mode=VGAHI;
   initgraph(&driver, &mode, "\\tc\\bgi");
   ```
   (Use borlandc in place of tc for Borland C++.)
5. 16
6. true
7. b, d
8. circle(99, 44, 13);
   ```

9. true

10. `line(2, 7, 5, 11),`

11. b, c

12. `setlinestyle(CENTER_LINE, 0, NORM_WIDTH);`

13. b

14. `int arrayname[] = { 0, 10, 5, 0, 10, 10 };`
    `fillpoly(3, arrayname);`

15. b, d

16. `sound(1000); delay(2000); nosound();`

17. produce the same sequence of random numbers

18. erase

19. c

20. current position

Solutions to Exercises

```
1. // ex11_1.cpp
   // adds size to ball
   #include <graphics.h>        // for graphics functions
   #include <conio.h>           // for getch()

   class ball                   // ball class
      {
      private:
         int xCo, yCo;          // coordinates of center
         int rad;
      public:
         ball()                 // no-argument constructor
            { xCo=0; yCo=0; rad=0; }
         void set(int x, int y, int r)  // set position
            { xCo=x; yCo=y; rad=r; }
         void draw()            // draw the ball
            { circle(xCo, yCo, rad); }
      };

   void main()
      {
      int driver, mode;
      driver = DETECT;          // set to best graphics mode
      initgraph(&driver, &mode, "\\tc\\bgi");

      ball b1;                  // create three balls
      ball b2;
      ball b3;

      b1.set(250, 150, 50);     // position and size them
```

```
        b2.set(300, 150, 75);
        b3.set(350, 150, 100);

        b1.draw();                    // draw them
        b2.draw();
        b3.draw();

        getch();                // wait for keypress
        closegraph();           // close graphics system
        }
2. // ex11_2.cpp
   // adds size data to shap class
   #include <graphics.h>         // for graphics functions
   #include <conio.h>            // for getch()

   class shape                   // base class
      {
   protected:
      int xCo, yCo;              // coordinates of center
      int width, height;         // width and height
      int linecolor;             // color of outline
      int fillcolor;             // color of interior
   public:
      shape()                    // no-arg constructor
         {
         xCo=0; yCo=0; width=0; height=0;
         linecolor=WHITE; fillcolor=WHITE;
         }                                // set data
      void set(int x, int y, int w, int h, int lc, int fc)
         {
         xCo=x; yCo=y; width=w; height=h;
         linecolor=lc; fillcolor=fc;
         }
      void draw()
         {
         setcolor(linecolor);             // line color
         setlinestyle(SOLID_LINE, 0, THICK_WIDTH); // line width
         setfillstyle(SOLID_FILL, fillcolor);  // set fill color
         }
      };

   class ball : public shape
      {
   public:
      ball() : shape()           // no-arg constr
         { }
      void set(int x, int y, int r, int lc, int fc) // set data
         { shape::set(x, y, r, r, lc, fc); }
      void draw()                // draw the ball
```

```
            {
            shape::draw();                          // set colors
            circle(xCo, yCo, width/2);              // draw circle
            floodfill(xCo, yCo, linecolor);         // fill circle
            }
      };

   class rect : public shape
      {
      public:
         rect() : shape()          // no-arg constr
            { }                                      // set data
         void set(int x, int y, int w, int h, int lc, int fc)
            { shape::set(x, y, w, h, lc, fc); }
         void draw()               // draw the rectangle
            {
            shape::draw();                           // set colors
            rectangle( xCo-width/2, yCo-height/2,    // draw rectangle
                       xCo+width/2, yCo+height/2 );
            floodfill(xCo, yCo, linecolor);          // fill rectangle
            }
      };

   void main()
      {
      int driver, mode;
      driver = DETECT;                    // set to best graphics mode
      initgraph(&driver, &mode, "\\tc\\bgi");

      rect windowbox;                     // create top part of car
      rect bodybox;                       // create bottom part of car
      ball wheel1, wheel2;                // create wheels

      windowbox.set(300, 75, 40, 20, YELLOW, BLUE);  // set size,
      bodybox.set(320, 100, 100, 30, YELLOW, BLUE);  // position,
      wheel1.set(290, 117, 27, YELLOW, BROWN);       // and colors
      wheel2.set(350, 117, 27, YELLOW, BROWN);

      windowbox.draw();                   // draw the car parts
      bodybox.draw();
      wheel1.draw();
      wheel2.draw();

      getch();                            // wait for keypress
      closegraph();                       // close graphics system
      }

3. // ex11_3.cpp
   // makes a car class out of various shapes
   #include <graphics.h>          // for graphics functions
   #include <conio.h>             // for getch()
```

```
class shape
    {
    protected:
        int xCo, yCo;           // coordinates of center
        int width, height;      // width and height
        int linecolor;          // color of outline
        int fillcolor;          // color of interior
    public:
        shape()                 // no-arg constructor
            {
            xCo=0; yCo=0; width=0; height=0;
            linecolor=WHITE; fillcolor=WHITE;
            }                                       // set data
        void set(int x, int y, int w, int h, int lc, int fc)
            {
            xCo=x; yCo=y; width=w; height=h;
            linecolor=lc; fillcolor=fc;
            }
        void draw()
            {
            setcolor(linecolor);                        // line color
            setlinestyle(SOLID_LINE, 0, THICK_WIDTH); // line width
            setfillstyle(SOLID_FILL, fillcolor);  // set fill color
            }
    };

class ball : public shape
    {
    public:
        ball() : shape()        // no-arg constr
            { }
        void set(int x, int y, int r, int lc, int fc)  // set data
            { shape::set(x, y, r, r, lc, fc); }
        void draw()             // draw the ball
            {
            shape::draw();                          // set colors
            circle(xCo, yCo, width/2);              // draw circle
            floodfill(xCo, yCo, linecolor);         // fill circle
            }
    };

class rect : public shape
    {
    public:
        rect() : shape()        // no-arg constr
            { }                                      // set data
        void set(int x, int y, int w, int h, int lc, int fc)
            { shape::set(x, y, w, h, lc, fc); }
        void draw()             // draw the rectangle
            {
```

```
            shape::draw();                          // set colors
            rectangle( xCo-width/2, yCo-height/2,   // draw rectangle
                       xCo+width/2, yCo+height/2 );
            floodfill(xCo, yCo, linecolor);         // fill rectangle
            }
    };

class car
    {
    private:
        rect windowbox;      // create top part of car
        rect bodybox;        // create bottom part of car
        ball wheel1, wheel2; // create wheels
    public:
        void set(int x, int y)
            {                // set size, position, and colors
            windowbox.set(x+10, y, 40, 20, YELLOW, BLUE);
            bodybox.set(x+30, y+25, 100, 30, YELLOW, BLUE);
            wheel1.set(x, y+42, 27, YELLOW, BROWN);
            wheel2.set(x+60, y+42, 27, YELLOW, BROWN);
            }
        void draw()
            {
            windowbox.draw();    // draw the car parts
            bodybox.draw();
            wheel1.draw();
            wheel2.draw();
            }
    };

void main()
    {
    int driver, mode;
    driver = DETECT;                    // set to best graphics mode
    initgraph(&driver, &mode, "\\tc\\bgi");

    car car1, car2, car3;               // create three cars
    car1.set(100, 100);                 // position them
    car2.set(200, 200);
    car3.set(300, 300);
    car1.draw();                        // draw them
    car2.draw();
    car3.draw();

    getch();                            // wait for keypress
    closegraph();                       // close graphics system
    }
```

Chapter 12

Answers to Questions

1. `cout << &testvar;`

2. four bytes

3. c

4. `&var, *var, var&, char*`

5. constant; variable

6. `float* ptrtofloat;`

7. name

8. `*testptr`

9. pointer to; contents of the variable pointed to by

10. b, c, d

11. No. The address `&intvar` must be placed in the pointer `intptr` before it can be accessed.

12. any data type

13. They both do the same thing.

14. `for(int j=0; j<77; j++)`
    `cout << endl << *(intarr+j);`

15. Because array names represent the address of the array, which is a constant and can't be changed.

16. reference; pointer

17. a, d

18. `void func(char*);`

19. `for(int j=0; j<77; j++)`
    `*s2++ = *s1++;`

20. b

21. `char* revstr(char*);`

22. `char* numptrs[] = { "One", "Two", "Three" };`

23. a, c

24. wasted

25. memory that is no longer needed

26. `p->exclu();`

27. `objarr[7].exclu();`

28. a, c

29. `float* p[8];`

30. b

Solutions to Exercises

1.
```cpp
// ex12_1.cpp
// finds average of numbers typed by user
#include <iostream.h>

void main()
    {
    float flarr[100];                   // array for numbers
    char ch;                            // user decision
    int num = 0;                        // counts numbers input
    do
       {
       cout << "Enter number: ";        // get numbers from user
       cin >> *(flarr+num++);           // until user answers 'n'
       cout << "   Enter another (y/n)? ";
       cin >> ch;
       }
    while(ch != 'n');

    float total = 0.0;                  // total starts at 0
    for(int k=0; k<num; k++)            // add numbers to total
       total += *(flarr+k);
    float average = total / num;        // find and display average
    cout << "Average is " << average;
    }
```

2.
```cpp
// ex12_2.cpp
// member function converts String objects to upper case
#include <iostream.h>
#include <string.h>          // for strcpy(), etc
#include <ctype.h>           // for toupper()

class String               // user-defined string type
    {
    private:
       char* str;                       // pointer to string
    public:
       String(char* s)                  // constructor, one arg
          {
          int length = strlen(s);       // length of string argument
          str = new char[length+1];     // get memory
          strcpy(str, s);               // copy argument to it
          }
       ~String()                        // destructor
          { delete str; }
       void display()                   // display the String
          { cout << str; }
       void upit();                     // uppercase the String
    };
```

```
void String::upit()                    // uppercase each character
   {
   char* ptrch = str;                  // pointer to this string
   while( *ptrch )                     // until null,
      {
      *ptrch = toupper(*ptrch);        // uppercase each character
      ptrch++;                         // move to next character
      }
   }

void main()
   {
   String s1 = "He who laughs last laughs best.";

   cout << "\ns1=";        // display string
   s1.display();
   s1.upit();              // uppercase string
   cout << "\ns1=";        // display string
   s1.display();
   }
```

3.
```
// ex12_3.cpp
// sort an array of pointers to strings
#include <iostream.h>
#include <string.h>                  // for strcmp(), etc.
const int DAYS = 7;                  // number of pointers in array

void main()
   {
   void bsort(char**, int);    // prototype
                               // array of pointers to char
   char* arrptrs[DAYS] = { "Sunday", "Monday", "Tuesday",
                           "Wednesday", "Thursday",
                           "Friday", "Saturday"  };

   cout << "\nUnsorted:\n";
   for(int j=0; j<DAYS; j++)     // display unsorted strings
      cout << *(arrptrs+j) << endl;

   bsort(arrptrs, DAYS);         // sort the strings

   cout << "\nSorted:\n";
   for(j=0; j<DAYS; j++)         // display sorted strings
      cout << *(arrptrs+j) << endl;
   }

void bsort(char** pp, int n)     // sort pointers to strings
   {
   void order(char**, char**);   // prototype
   int j, k;                     // indexes to array

   for(j=0; j<n-1; j++)          // outer loop
      for(k=j+1; k<n; k++)       // inner loop starts at outer
```

```
        order(pp+j, pp+k);       // order the pointer contents
   }

void order(char** pp1, char** pp2)  // orders two pointers
   {                            // if string in 1st is
   if( strcmp(*pp1, *pp2) > 0)  // larger than in 2nd,
      {
      char* tempptr = *pp1;     // swap the pointers
      *pp1 = *pp2;
      *pp2 = tempptr;
      }
   }
```

4. `// ex12_4.cpp`

```
// linked list includes destructor
#include <iostream.h>

struct link                          // one element of list
   {
   int data;                         // data item
   link* next;                       // pointer to next link
   };

class linklist                       // a list of links
   {
   private:
      link* first;                   // pointer to first link
   public:
      linklist()                     // no-argument constructor
         { first = NULL; }           // no first link
      ~linklist();                   // destructor
      void additem(int d);           // add data item (one link)
      void display();                // display all links
   };

void linklist::additem(int d)        // add data item
   {
   link* newlink = new link;         // make a new link
   newlink->data = d;                // give it data
   newlink->next = first;            // it points to next link
   first = newlink;                  // now first points to this
   }

void linklist::display()             // display all links
   {
   link* current = first;            // set ptr to first link
   while( current != NULL )          // quit on last link
      {
      cout << endl << current->data; // print data
      current = current->next;       // move to next link
      }
   }
```

```
linklist::~linklist()                // destructor
   {
   link* current = first;            // set ptr to first link
   while( current != NULL )          // quit on last link
      {
      link* temp = current;          // save ptr to this link
      current = current->next;       // get ptr to next link
      delete temp;                   // delete this link
      }
   }

void main()
   {
   linklist li;          // make linked list

   li.additem(25);       // add four items to list
   li.additem(36);
   li.additem(49);
   li.additem(64);

   li.display();         // display entire list
   }
```

Chapter 13

Answers to Questions

1. d
2. true
3. base
4. `virtual void dang(int);` or `void virtual dang(int);`
5. late binding or dynamic binding
6. derived
7. `virtual void aragorn()=0;` or `void virtual aragorn()=0;`
8. a, c
9. `dong* parr[10];`
10. c
11. true
12. c, d
13. `friend void harry(george);`
14. a, c, d
15. `friend class harry;` or `friend harry;`
16. c
17. It performs a member-by-member copy.
18. `zeta& operator = (zeta&);`

19. a, b, d
20. false; the compiler provides a default copy constructor
21. a, d
22. `Bertha(Bertha&);`
23. true, if there was a reason to do so
24. a, c
25. true; trouble occurs it it's returned by reference
26. They operate identically.
27. a, b
28. the object of which the function using it is a member
29. no; since `this` is a pointer, use `this->da=37;`
30. `return *this;`

Solutions to Exercises

1.
```cpp
// ex13_1.cpp
// publication class and derived classes
#include <iostream.h>

const int LEN = 80;

class publication
    {
    private:
        char title[LEN];
        float price;
    public:
        void getdata()
            {
            cout << "\nEnter title: "; cin >> title;
            cout << "Enter price: "; cin >> price;
            }
        virtual void putdata()
            {
            cout << "\nTitle: " << title;
            cout << "\nPrice: " << price;
            }
    };

class book : public publication
    {
    private:
        int pages;
    public:
        void getdata()
            {
            publication::getdata();
```

```cpp
            cout << "Enter number of pages: "; cin >> pages;
            }
      void putdata()
            {
            publication::putdata();
            cout << ."\nPages: " << pages;
            }
      };

class tape : public publication
      {
      private:
         float time;
      public:
         void getdata()
            {
            publication::getdata();
            cout << "Enter playing time: "; cin >> time;
            }
         void putdata()
            {
            publication::putdata();
            cout << "\rPlaying time: " << time;
            }
      };

void main()
      {
      publication* pubarr[100];        // array of ptrs to pubs
      book* bookptr;                   // pointer to books
      tape* tapeptr;                   // pointer to tapes
      int n = 0;                       // number of pubs in array
      char choice;                     // user's choice

      do
         {
         cout << "\nEnter data for book or tape (b/t)? ";
         cin >> choice;
         if( choice=='b' )             // if it's a book
            {
            bookptr = new book;        // make a new book
            bookptr->getdata();        // get book's basic data
            pubarr[n++] = bookptr;     // put pointer in array
            }
         else                          // it's a tape
            {
            tapeptr = new tape;        // make a new tape
            tapeptr->getdata();        // get tape's basic data
            pubarr[n++] = tapeptr;     // put pointer in array
            }
```

711

```
            cout << "   Enter another (y/n)? ";  // another pub?
            cin >> choice;
            }
         while( choice =='y');                   // cycle until not 'y'

         for(int j=0; j<n; j++)                   // cycle thru all pubs
            pubarr[j]->putdata();                 // print data for pub
         }
2. // ex13_2.cpp
   // friend square() function for Distance
   #include <iostream.h>

   class Distance                      // English Distance class
      {
      private:
         int feet;
         float inches;
      public:
         Distance()                    // constructor (no args)
            { feet = 0; inches = 0.0; }
         Distance(float fltfeet)       // constructor (one arg)
            {
            feet = int(fltfeet);       // feet is integer part
            inches = 12*(fltfeet-feet);  // inches is what's left
            }
         Distance(int ft, float in)    // constructor (two args)
            { feet = ft; inches = in; }
         void showdist()               // display distance
            { cout << feet << "\'-" << inches << '\"'; }

         friend Distance operator * (Distance, Distance); // friend
      };
                                       // multiply d1 by d2
   Distance operator * (Distance d1, Distance d2)
      {                                // argument
      float fltfeet1 = d1.feet + d1.inches/12;  // convert to float
      float fltfeet2 = d2.feet + d2.inches/12;
      float multfeet = fltfeet1 * fltfeet2;     // find the product
      return Distance(multfeet);       // return temp Distance
      }

   void main()
      {
      Distance dist1(3, 6.0);          // make some distances
      Distance dist2(2, 3.0);
      Distance dist3;

      dist3 = dist1 * dist2;           // multiplication

      dist3 = 10.0 * dist3;            // mult and conversion
                                       // display all distances
```

```
        cout << "\ndist1 = "; dist1.showdist();
        cout << "\ndist2 = "; dist2.showdist();
        cout << "\ndist3 = "; dist3.showdist();
        }
3. // ex13_3.cpp
   // creates array class
   // overloads assignment operator and copy constructor
   #include <iostream.h>

   class Array
      {
      private:
         int* ptr;                    // pointer to "array" contents
         int size;                    // size of array
      public:
         Array()                      // no-argument constructor
            { }
         Array(int s)                 // one-argument constructor
            {
            size = s;
            ptr = new int[s];
            }
         Array(Array&);               // copy constructor
         ~Array()                     // destructor
            { delete ptr; }
         int& operator [] (int j)     // overloaded subscript op
            { return *(ptr+j); }
         Array& operator = (Array&);  // overloaded = operator
      };

   Array::Array(Array& a)            // copy constructor
      {
      size = a.size;                 // new one is same size
      ptr = new int[size];           // get space for contents
      for(int j=0; j<size; j++)      // copy contents to new one
         *(ptr+j) = *(a.ptr+j);
      }

   Array& Array::operator = (Array& a)  // overloaded = operator
      {
      size = a.size;                 // new one is same size
      ptr = new int[size];
      for(int j=0; j<size; j++)      // copy contents to new one
         *(ptr+j) = *(a.ptr+j);
      return *this;                  // return this object
      }

   void main()
      {
      const int ASIZE = 10;          // size of array
      Array arr1(ASIZE);             // make an array
```

```
      for(int j=0; j<ASIZE; j++)    // fill it with squares
         arr1[j] = j*j;

      Array arr2(arr1);             // use the copy constructor
      cout << endl;
      for(j=0; j<ASIZE; j++)        // check that it worked
         cout << arr2[j] << "   ";

      Array arr3;                   // make an empty Array
      arr3 = arr1;                  // use the assignment operator
      cout << endl;
      for(j=0; j<ASIZE; j++)        // check that it worked
         cout << arr3[j] << "   ";
      }
```

Chapter 14

Answers to Questions

1. b, c

2. `ios`

3. `ifstream`, `ofstream`, and `Fstream`

4. `ofstream salefile ("SALES.JUN");`

5. true

6. `if(foobar)`

7. d

8. `fileOut.put(ch);`

9. c

10. `ifile.read( (char*)buff, sizeof(buff) );`

11. a, b, d

12. the byte location at which the next read or write operation will take place

13. false; *file pointer* can be a synonym for *current position*

14. `f1.seekg(-13, ios:cur);`

15. b

16. a

17. `skipws` causes white space characters to be ignored on input so that `cin` will not assume the input has terminated.

18. `void main( argc, *argv[] )`

19. PRN, LPT1, etc.

20. `istream& operator >> (istream&, Sample& )`

Solutions to Exercises

```
1. // ex14_1.cpp
   // write array
   #include <iostream.h>
   #include <fstream.h>                    // for file streams

   class Distance                          // English Distance class
      {
      private:
         int feet;
         float inches;
      public:
         Distance()                        // constructor (no args)
            { feet = 0; inches = 0.0; }
         Distance(int ft, float in)        // constructor (two args)
            { feet = ft; inches = in; }
         void getdist()                    // get length from user
            {
            cout << "\n   Enter feet: ";   cin >> feet;
            cout << "   Enter inches: ";   cin >> inches;
            }
         void showdist()                   // display distance
            { cout << feet << "\'-" << inches << '\"'; }
      };

   void main()
      {
      char ch;
      Distance dist;                       // create a Distance object
      fstream file;                        // create input/output file
                                           // open it for append
      file.open("DIST.DAT", ios::app | ios::out | ios::in );

      do                                   // data from user to file
         {
         cout << "\nDistance";
         dist.getdist();                   // get a distance
                                           // write to file
         file.write( (char*)&dist, sizeof(dist) );
         cout << "Enter another distance (y/n)? ";
         cin >> ch;
         }
      while(ch=='y');                      // quit on 'n'

      file.seekg(0);                       // reset to start of file
                                           // read first distance
      file.read( (char*)&dist, sizeof(dist) );
      int count = 0;
```

```
   while( !file.eof() )                    // quit on EOF
      {
      cout << "\nDistance " << ++count << ": "; // display dist
      dist.showdist();
      file.read( (char*)&dist, sizeof(dist) );  // read another
      }                                          // distance
   }
```

2.
```
// ex14_2.cpp
// imitates COPY command
#include <fstream.h>              // for file functions
#include <process.h>             // for exit()

void main(int argc, char* argv[] )
   {
   if( argc != 3 )
      { cerr << "\nFormat: ocopy srcfile destfile"; exit(-1); }
   char ch;                      // character to read

   ifstream infile;             // create file for input
   infile.open( argv[1] );      // open file
   if( !infile )                // check for errors
      { cerr << "\nCan't open " << argv[1]; exit(-1); }

   ofstream outfile;            // create file for output
   outfile.open( argv[2], ios::noreplace );  // open file
   if( !outfile )               // check for errors
      { cerr << "\nCan't open " << argv[2]; exit(-1); }

   while( infile )              // until EOF
      {
      infile.get(ch);           // read a character
      outfile.put(ch);          // write the character
      }
   }
```

3.
```
// ex14_3.cpp
// displays size of file
#include <fstream.h>              // for file functions
#include <process.h>             // for exit()

void main(int argc, char* argv[] )
   {
   if( argc != 2 )
      { cerr << "\nFormat: filesize filename"; exit(-1); }
   ifstream infile;             // create file for input
   infile.open( argv[1] );      // open file
   if( !infile )                // check for errors
      { cerr << "\nCan't open " << argv[1]; exit(-1); }
   infile.seekg(0, ios::end);   // go to end of file
                                // report byte number
   cout << "Size of " << argv[1] << " is " << infile.tellg();
   }
```

Chapter 15

Answers to Questions

1. a, b, c, d
2. `#include` directive
3. the project feature to compile the .CPP file and link the resulting .OBJ files
4. b, c
5. class library
6. true
7. c, d
8. true
9. b, d
10. a, c

Chapter 16

Answers to Questions

1. b, c
2. \TC\CLASSLIB\LIB or \BORLANDC\CLASSLIB\LIB
3. true
4. MYPROG.CPP and TCLASSS.LIB (or equivalent for other memory models)
5. b, c
6. `st.printOn(cout);`
7. a, b, c
8. `stack1.push(obj1);`
   `stack1.pop(obj1);`
9. `while( !stack1.isEmpty() )`
   `    { }`
10. true
11. c
12. `array1.addAt(obj1, 3);`
13. false
14. 8
15. a, d
16. Objects are created from an instance class but not from an abstract class.
17. `list1.getItemsInContainer()`
18. `firstThat()` or `lastThat()`
19. a, d
20. true

Solutions to Exercises

```
1. // ex16_1.cpp
   // Array of Times
   #include <array.h>                              // for Array class
   #include <ltime.h>                              // for Time class
   void main()
      {
      Array arr(3);                                // create an Array,
                                                   //    index from 0 to 3

      Time* ptrt1 = new Time(1, 0, 0, 0);          // create four Times
      Time* ptrt2 = new Time(11, 35, 30, 1);
      Time* ptrt3 = new Time(12, 59, 59, 50);
      Time* ptrt4 = new Time(23, 59, 59, 99);

      arr.add(*ptrt1);                             // put Times
      arr.add(*ptrt2);                             // in Array
      arr.add(*ptrt3);
      arr.add(*ptrt4);

      cout << "\nEntire array:\n";
      arr.printContentsOn(cout);                   // display Array

      cout << "\nIndividual elements:";            // display elements
      for(int j=0; j<arr.arraySize(); j++)
         {
         cout << "\nElement number " << j << " is ";
         arr[j].printOn(cout);
         }
      }
2. // ex16_2.cpp
   // Deque and String classes
   #include <iostream.h>
   #include <strng.h>                              // for String class
   #include <deque.h>                              // for Deque class

   int main()
      {
      void actionFunc(Object&, void*);             // prototypes
      int testFunc(const Object& obj, void*);

      Deque deq;                                   // create a Deque

      String s1("Emerson");                        // make some Strings
      String s2("Hawthorne");
      String s3("Melville");
      String s4("Poe");
      String s5("Stevenson");

      deq.putLeft(s1);                             // put Strings
      deq.putLeft(s2);                             // in deque
```

```
            deq.putLeft(s3);
            deq.putRight(s4);
            deq.putRight(s5);

            cout << "\n\nIterate through deque:";
            deq.forEach(actionFunc, 0);              // iterate through deque

                                                     // find first String
                                                     // that's "Poe"
            String& temp = (String&)deq.firstThat(testFunc, 0);
            if( temp != NOOBJECT )                   // check if match
                {
                cout << "\n\nMatch with: ";
                temp.printOn(cout);
                }
            else
                cout << "\n\nNo match. ,

            cout << "\n\nDisplay and remove items from deque:";
            while( !deq.isEmpty() )                   // until deque empty
                {                                     // get String from left,
                String& temp = (String&)deq.getLeft();  // put in temp
                cout << endl;
                temp.printOn(cout);                   // print temp
                }
            cout << "\nContents of empty deque: ";
            deq.printOn(cout);
            }

        // function to perform action on each item in deque
        void actionFunc(Object& obj, void*)
            {
            cout << endl;
            obj.printOn(cout);                        // display argument
            }

        // function to test item in deque
        int testFunc(const Object& obj, void*)
            {
            String& temp = (String&)obj;              // make String from arg
            String test("Poe");                       // make String from "Poe"
            if( temp.isEqual(test) )                  // return 1 if string is
                return 1;                             // "Poe"
            else
                return 0;
            }

    3. // ex16_3.cpp
       // List and user-defined Person class
       #include <list.h>                              // for List class
       #include <string.h>                            // for strlen(), strcpy()
       #define personClass __firstUserClass           // (see CLSTYPES.H)
```

```
class Person : public Object           // user-defined class
    {
    private:
        char* name;
        int age;
    public:
        Person()                                    // constructor
            {
            name = new char;
            name[0] = '\0';
            age = 0;
            }
        Person(const char* str, const int a) // constructor
            {
            name = new char[ strlen(str)+1 ];
            strcpy(name, str);
            age = a;
            }
        Person(const Person& sourcePerson)    // copy constructor
            {
            name = new char[ strlen(sourcePerson.name)+1 ];
            strcpy(name, sourcePerson.name);
            age = sourcePerson.age;
            }
        ~Person()                                     // destructor
            { delete name; }
        classType isA() const                              // isA()
            { return personClass; }
        char* nameOf() const                           // nameOf()
            { return "Person"; }
        void printOn( ostream& outputStream ) const  // printOn()
            {
            outputStream << "(Name=" << name;
            outputStream << ", Age=" << age << ")";
            }
        hashValueType hashValue() const          // hashValue()
            {
            hashValueType hvalue = name[0] + age;
            return hvalue;
            }
        int isEqual( const Object& testPers ) const  // isEqual()
            {
            return age == ((Person &)testPers).age &&
                   !strcmp(name, ((Person &)testPers).name);
            }
    };

void main()
    {
    void actionFunc(Object&, void*);  // prototype
    List lst;                         // create default-size List
```

```
Person* ptrp1 = new Person("Bart", 23);  // create three
Person* ptrp2 = new Person("Casey", 25); // Persons
Person* ptrp3 = new Person("Slade", 27);

lst.add(*ptrp1);    // put Persons on List
lst.add(*ptrp2);
lst.add(*ptrp3);

cout << "\nContents using printOn(): ";  // display contents
lst.printOn(cout);

cout << "\nContents using actionFunc(): "; // display conts
lst.forEach(actionFunc, 0);  // perform action on each item

cout << "\n\nRemove and display: ";        // display contents
while( !lst.isEmpty() )        // while list not empty
    {
    Person& temp = (Person&)lst.peekHead(); // get a String,
    cout << endl;
    temp.printOn(cout);                      // display it,
    lst.detach(temp);                        // remove it
    }                                        // from list
cout << "\nSize of empty list: " << lst.getItemsInContainer();
}

// function to perform action on each object in list
void actionFunc(Object& obj, void*)
    {
    cout << endl << obj;    // display object
    }
```

BIBLIOGRAPHY

Here are some books that might prove interesting to students of object-oriented programming who are using Turbo C++ or Borland C++.

The ultimate reference to the C++ language is *The Annotated C++ Reference Manual*, by Margaret Ellis and Bjarne Strousstrup (Addison Wesley, Reading, MA, 1990). This is not a book for beginners, but as you become more proficient in C++ you will find yourself turning to it to resolve subtle points that other books don't mention. Eventually you will find it indispensable.

If you want to learn more about the C language, try *The Waite Group's C Programming Using Turbo C++*, by Robert Lafore (Howard W. Sams & Co., Carmel, IN, 1990). This book explains many details of how to program in the MS-DOS environment, including details of keyboard use and the process of speeding up the screen display with direct memory access. It also describes hardware-oriented language features that are common to both C and C++ but do not appear in the present book, such as bitwise operators and bitfields.

The Waite Group's Turbo C++ Bible, by Nabajyoti Barkakati (Howard W. Sams & Co., Carmel, IN, 1990) provides a complete list and descriptions, with examples, of Turbo C++ (and Borland C++) library functions.

No one book, including the present one, can cover every detail of C++. Here are several tutorial books that approach C++ from slightly different angles: *C++ for C Programmers*, by Ira Pohl (Benjamin/Cummings, Redwood City, CA, 1989) and *Teach Yourself C++*, by Al Stevens (MIS Press, Portland, OR, 1990). Both of these books assume you already know C, but the present book also gives you all the background you need to understand them.

For more on data structures such as linked lists, queues, and hash tables, not to mention all sorts of other topics such as searching and sorting, read *Algorithms*, by Robert Sedgewick (Addison Wesley, Reading, MA, 1988).

Computers, Pattern, Chaos and Beauty, by Clifford A. Pickover (St. Martin's Press, New York, 1990) is filled with fascinating material, not only on fractals, but on using computer graphics to show chaos, the Mandelbrot set, and other mathematical ideas. The illustrations make it fun to read, and program listings make it easy to reproduce the results on your computer.

If you're interested in fractals, try *The Waite Group's Fractal Creations*, by Tim Wegner and Mark Peterson (Waite Group Press, Mill Valley, CA, 1991). This is an addicting software product that demonstrates fractals and the Mandelbrot set. It's accompanied by a sizable book that explores many byways of the fractal world, while also explaining the operation of the program.

You can read about Conway's game of Life, among other topics (many of which are related in some way to computer programming), in *Wheels, Life, and Other Mathematical Amusements*, by Martin Gardner (W. H. Freeman Co., New York, 1983).

OPERATOR PRECEDENCE

operator	associativity
()	left to right
[]	
.	
->	
!	right to left
~	
- (unary minus)	
& (address)	
* (indirection)	
(type) cast operator	
sizeof	
* (multiply)	left to right
/	
% (modulus)	
+	left to right
-	
<<	left to right
>>	

operator	associativity
  <= > >=	left to right
== !=	left to right
& (bitwise and)	left to right
^	left to right
|	left to right
&&	left to right
|	left to right
?:	right to left
= *= /= %= += -= <<== >>== %= ^= |=	right to left
, comma	**left to right**

STANDARD HEADER FILES

A list of the functions declared in each of the header files is given below

► ALLOC.H ►

brk	calloc	coreleft
farcalloc	farcoreleft	farfree
farheapcheck	farheapcheckfree	farheapchecknode
farheapfillfree	farheapwalk	farmalloc
farrealloc	free	heapcheck
heapcheckfree	heapchecknode	heapwalk
malloc	realloc	sbrk

► ASSERT.H ►

assert
NDEBUG

► BIOS.H ►

bioscom	biosdisk	biosequip	bioskey
biosmemory	biosprint	biostime	

► CONIO.H ►

cgets	clreol	clrscr	cprintf
cputs	cscanf	delline	getch
getche	getpass	gettext	gettextinfo
gotoxy	highvideo	insline	kbhit
lowvideo	movetext	normvide	putch
puttext	_setcursortype	textattr	textbackground
textcolor	textmode	ungetch	wherex
wherey	window		

► CTYPE.H ►

isalnum	isalpha	isascii	iscntrl
isdigit	isgraph	islower	isprint
ispunct	isspace	isupper	isxdigit
toascii	tolower	_tolower	toupper
_toupper			

► DIR.H ►

chdir	findfirst	findnext	fnmerge
fnsplit	getcurdir	getcwd	getdisk
mkdir	mktemp	rmdir	searchpath
setdisk			

► DOS.H ►

absread	abswrite	allocmem	bdos
bdosptr	country	ctrlbrk	delay
disable	dosexterr	dostounix	_emit_
enable	FP_OFF	FP_SEG	freemem
geninterrupt	getcbrk	getdate	getdfree
getdta	getfat	getfatd	getftime
getpsp	gettime	getvect	getverify
harderr	hardresume	hardretn	inp
inport	inportb	int86	int86x
intdos	intdosx	intr	keep
MK_FP	nosound	outp	outport
outportb	parsfnm	peek	peekb
poke	pokeb	randbrd	randbwr
segread	setblock	setcbrk	setdate
setdta	settime	setvect	setverify
sleep	sound	unixtodos	unlink

► FLOAT.H ►

_clear87	_fpreset	_control87	_status87

► IO.H ►

access	chmod	_chmod	chsize
close	_close	creat	_creat
creatnew	creattemp	dup	dup2
eof	filelength	getftime	ioctl
satty	lock	lseek	open
_open	read	_read	setftime

setmode	sopen	tell unlink
unlock	write	_write

► LOCALE.H ►

localeconv	setlocale

► MATH.H ►

abs	acos	asin	atan
atan2	atof	cabs	ceil
cos cosh exp fabs			
floor	fmod	frexp	hypot
labs	ldexp	log	log10
matherr	modf	poly	pow
pow10	sin	sinh	sqrt
tan	tanh		

► MEM.H ►

memccpy	memchr	memcmp	memcpy
memicmp	memmove	memset	movedata
movmem	setmem		

► PROCESS.H ►

abort	exit	execv	spawnv
execl	spawnl	execve	spawnve
execle	spawnle	execvp	spawnvp
execlp	spawnlp	execvpe	spawnvpe
execlpe	spawnlpe	_exit	system

► SETJMP.H ►

longjmp	setjmp

► SIGNAL.H ►

raise	signal

► STDARG.H ►

va_arg	va_end	va_start

► STDIO.H ►

clearerr	fclose	fcloseall	fdopen
feof	ferror	fflush	fgetc

fgetchar	fgetpos	fgets	fileno
flushall	fopen	fprintf	fputc
fputchar	fputs	fread	freopen
fscanf	fseek	fsetpos	ftell
fwrite	getc	getchar	gets
getw	perror	printf	putc
putchar	puts	putw	remove
rename	rewind	scanf	setbuf
setvbuf	sprintf	sscanf	strerror
strerror	tmpfile	tmpnam	ungetc
unlink	vfprintf	vfscanf	vprintf
vscanf	vsprintf	vsscanf	

► STDLIB.H ►

abort	abs	atexit	atof
atoi	atol	bsearch	calloc
div	ecvt	exit	_exit
fcvt	free	gcvt	getenv
itoa	labs	ldiv	lfind
_lrotl	_lrotr	lsearch	ltoa
malloc	max	min	putenv
qsort	rand	random	randomize
realloc	_rotl	_rotr	srand
strtod	strtol	strtoul	swab
system	ultoa		

► STRING.H ►

memccpy	memchr	memcmp	memcpy
memicmp	memmove	memset	movedata
movmem	setmem	stpcpy	strcat
strchr	strcmp	strcmpi	strcpy
strcspn	strdup	_strerror	strerror
stricmp	strlen	strlwr	strncat
strncmp	strncmpi	strncpy	strnicmp
strnset	strpbrk	strrchr	strrev
strset	strspn	strstr	strtok
strupr			

► STAT.H ►

fstat	stat

► TIMEB.H ►

ftime

? TIME.H ?

asctime	CLK_TCK	clock	ctime
difftime	gmtime	localtime	stime
time	tzset		

GLOSSARY

abstraction	Ignoring the underlying details of a problem and concentrating strictly upon the solution of the problem. High-level languages are more abstract than assembly language.
a.out	The executable file created by the assembler and link editor.
address	A value that points to a location in memory. A pointer contains the address or location of a value, as opposed to the value itself.
aggregate	Combines related items into logical groups. In C, arrays and structures are aggregates.
algorithm	A method of solving to a function.
argc	A collection of homogeneous values. Homogeneous values are values of the same type (int, char, and so on).
ASCII	American Standard Code for Information Interchange. The Standard representation of characters within the computer and on disk.
assembler	A program that converts assembled code into machine code.
assembly language	A method of programming that uses symbols to represent machine code. Assembly language lacks the portability and modifiability of high-order languages. Prior to C, most operating systems were developed in assembly language.

attribute	Characteristic of an object. World read access in an example of a file attribute.
automatic variable	A variable local to a function, which is created automatically each time a function is invoked and destroyed when the function is completed.
binary	Base 2 numbering system. Numbers are represented as a series of ones and zeros that are understood and easily manipulated by the computer.
bit	Binary digit.
buffer	Storage location. In C, buffers are used for temporary storage of data transferred from disk.
bug	An undocumented program attribute. An error in a program.
byte	Eight binary digits. A character represented in ASCII requires a byte of storage.
cast	A type conversion mechanism employed by C. A cast will convert a value contained in a variable of one type (**int, char, float, or double**) to another type.
command	A directive to the operating system to provide a specific function.
command line	The entire command issued to the operating system.
comment	An explanatory message placed within a source file to aid others in understanding the program and the algorithm employed. In C, comments are enclosed by /* */.
compilation	The process of converting a high level language into machine language.
compiler	The program that examines another program for proper syntax and semantics and converts its code to an executable format. In UNIX, the executable image is placed into a file called a.out.
concatenate	Appending a string or substring to another string or substring. If the string "system" is concatenated to the string "operating", the result is the string "operating system".

contiguous	A storage characteristic that specifies that the values are stored in consecutive locations either in memory or on disk.
cpu	Central processing unit.
crt	Cathode ray tube. The screen or monitor used for display.
debugging	Process of removing errors from program.
decimal	Base 10 numbering system.
declaration	Specifies the type of internal representation of a variable.
directory	A file that contains information about each of our files such as name, size, accessibility and date of the creation.
DOS	Disk Operating System.
double	The C data type for double precision floating point number.
dumb	Printout of the contents of memory or a file.
EOF	End Of File.
EOL	End of Line.
escape sequence	A special sequence of characters that direct the computer to perform unique function.
executable	A program in machine language that can be executed by the computer.
extern	Specifies that the variable is a global variable.
file	A storage unit that contains data. A file can be stored either on tape or disk.
file descriptor	Used in low level file manipulation to reference the file to be used as opposed to continually referencing a name or file pointer.
file pointer	Pointer to structure that contains information about a file.

float	The C data type for single precision floating point number.
free form language	A programming language that does not require line numbers or restrict instructions to specific locations on the file.
function	A series of instructions to perform a specified task, which can be combined with other functions to create a program.
hexadecimal	Base 16 number system.
initialize	To provide a starting value to a variable.
I/O	Input/Output.
int	The C data type for integer value.
integer	A number without decimal point.
keyword	A word that has a specific meaning in certain contexts.
library	A collection of programs or functions that can be utilised by several programmers.
local variable	A variable declared within a function whose value and existence are constrained or localized to that function.
logical operator	The operators NOT, AND, OR, XOR, which are used to test two or more Boolean (true or false) expressions.
macro	A statement or series of statements inserted in line within a program in the place of a symbol.
parameter	A value or a variable passed into a function.
pointer	Contains the address or memory location of a value, as opposed to the value itself.
portability	The ease of converting a program written to run on one machine to run on a different type of machine.
precedence	Determines the order in which operations are performed.
precision	Specifies the number of meaningful digits in value that must be represented by a fixed number of binary digits.

program	A series of instructions provided to the computer that directs the computer in executing a task. A program is normally comprised of several functions.
recursion	Solving a program by allowing a function that performs a specified task to repeatedly call itself.
register variable	A variable declared in a C program that the programmer wants to be stored within a register as often as possible to increase execution efficiency.
reserved words	Words that have specific meaning within C programs and cannot be used as variable or function name.
string	An array capable of storing zero or more characters. In C, a string is declared as a character array with the NULL (\0) character appended to specify the end of the string.
structure	An aggregate type or structure in C that allows the programmer to group logically related variables within a single structure or record.
syntax	The rules that govern the order of words and relationships in a language.
type	Specifies a set of operations that can be performed upon a variable along with a set of values it can contain. The types supported by C include : **int, float, double** and **char.**
variable	A name associated with a location in memory whose value can change during program execution.

INDEX

WAITE GROUP® PRESS

The Waite Group's C++ Primer Plus

Stephen Prata

Computer mavens expect the new programming language C++ to eventually displace C from its position of near-universal preference. An extension of C, C++ treats data and functions as objects (hence the term object-oriented programming or OOP), making it possible to clone, modify, and build upon them. Unlike existing books on the subject, *C++ Primer Plus* is addressed to those without an extensive programming background. It provides a simple introduction to the standard 2.0 AT&T implementations of C++ while also covering the essential concepts of C. It teaches the basics of OOP and shows how to build programs that are flexible and readily modified.

In the friendly, easy-to-follow style of *C Primer Plus* (the author's best-selling work), *C++ Primer Plus* illustrates the language's fundamentals with short sample programs that are easy to key in and experiment with. A companion disk (available through the order card included with the book) contains all the sample programs and projects. The book is compatible with any AT&T Version 2.0 compliant compiler and works under Unix, Borland, Turbo, Zortec, and Sun C++.

744 Pages, 7 × 9, Softbound   Rs. 195/-

The Waite Group's Object-Oriented Programming in Turbo C++

Robert Lafore

Object-oriented programming (OOP) is the most dramatic—and potentially confusing—innovation in software development since the dawn of the computer age. Based on the idea of treating functions and data as objects, OOP results in programs that are more flexible, more easily maintained, and on the whole, more powerful. *Object-Oriented Programming in Turbo C++* focuses on C as a separate language, distinct from C, and assumes no prior experience with C. Step by step lessons teach Turbo C++, Borland C++, and the basics of OOP at the same time. Suitable for students, hackers, and enthusiasts, *Object-Oriented Programming in Turbo C++* is written by Robert Lafore, author of the best-selling *The Waite Group's Turbo C Programming for the IBM* (over 200,000 copies in print). You'll find details on Turbo C++ graphics and the DOS file system, project chapters enhance your understanding of object-oriented design with a game of life, a program that simulates a town's water distribution system, and a fractal generator, and more. No experience required for this hands-on book.

776 Pages, 7 × 9, Softbound   Rs. 230/-

The Waite Group's Turbo Pascal How-To
Gary Syck

Turbo Pascal How-To is a working programmer's dream: hundreds of typical programming problems, with creative ways to solve them, in an easy-to-use reference format. The solutions provided are designed to work with the latest Object-oriented Version 6.0 of Turbo Pascal, as well as earlier versions and Turbo Pascal for Windows. Experienced programmers will appreciate the ease of incorporating these solutions, which will allow them to concentrate on their program's unique characteristics and not waste time solving problems. At the same time, novice programmers will find they can quickly begin creating functional programs just by building on the modular examples provided here. Borland's new Turbo Vision interface system is covered, too.

The Waite Group's *Turbo Pascal How-To* answers the most practical questions any programmer has, such as: "How do I put information in a window? How do I build a fancy pull-down menu system? How do I scroll the screen? Create a directory? Save memory?" And more. In short, this book has everything readers need to know to write professional Turbo Pascal programs.

496 Pages, 7 × 9, Softbound   Rs. 126/-

Comment Form

Your opinions count

If you have any comments, criticisms, or suggestions for us, I'm eager to get them. Your opinions today will affect our products of tommorrow. And if you find any errors in this book, typographical or otherwise, please point them out so we can correct them in the next printing.

Thanks for your help.

GALGOTIA PUBLICATIONS (P) LTD.
EDITOR

Book title : Object-Oriented Programming in Turbo C++

Dear Galgotia : _____
_____
_____
_____
_____
_____
_____
_____
_____
_____
_____
_____
_____
_____
_____
_____
_____
_____

Name_____

Company (if company address)_____

Address_____

City, State_____